God and Creatures

John Duns Scotus

GOD AND CREATURES
The Quodlibetal Questions

*Translated with an Introduction, Notes,
and Glossary by*

Felix Alluntis, O.F.M.
and
Allan B. Wolter, O.F.M.

PRINCETON UNIVERSITY PRESS
1975

Copyright © 1975 by Princeton University Press
Published by Princeton University Press,
Princeton and London
All Rights Reserved
Library of Congress Cataloging in Publication data will
be found on the last printed page of this book
This book has been composed in Linotype Baskerville
Printed in the United States of America
by Princeton University Press,
Princeton, New Jersey

Contents

Abbreviations	xiv
Acknowledgments	xv
Introduction	xvii
Prologue	3

Question One: IN DIVINE THINGS, IS IT THE ESSENTIAL OR THE NOTIONAL THAT IS MORE IMMEDIATE TO THE DIVINE ESSENCE?

Arguments Pro and Con	5
Body of the Question	6
Article I Preliminary Remarks	6
1. The Meaning of "Essence"	6
2. The Meaning of "Essential" and "Notional"	9
3. The Meaning of "More Immediate"	19
Article II Solution of the Question	20
Article III Reply to various Objections	23
Reply to the Initial Argument	29

Question Two: COULD THERE BE SEVERAL PRODUCTIONS OF THE SAME TYPE IN GOD?

Arguments Pro and Con	31
Body of the Question	32
Article I An Evaluation of the Reasons for the Negative Conclusion	32
Article II Solution of the Question	44
1. Indirect Argument or the *Reductio ad impossibile*	44
2. The Positive Proof	46
3. Confirmation from the Philosopher	48
Article III Objections and their Solutions	50

Question Three: ARE THESE TWO COMPATIBLE: A RELATION RELATED TO ITS OPPOSITE IS A REAL THING; AND, AS RELATED TO THE ESSENCE, IT IS ONLY AN ASPECT?

Arguments Pro and Con	60

CONTENTS

Body of the Question ... 60
  Article I Is the Relation of Origin a Thing and, if so, What Kind of Thing? ... 61
  Article II As Related to the Essence, is the Relation a Thing and What Kind of Thing? ... 64
    1. The Relation as Related to the Essence is a Thing ... 64
    2. Logical Consideration of the Statement "The relation as related to the essence is a thing." ... 66
    3. Solution of the Principal Question ... 68
  Article III Resolution of various Doubts ... 69
Reply to the Initial Argument ... 78

Question Four: COULD THE FIRST DIVINE PERSON REMAIN CONSTITUTED AS A PERSON, DISTINCT FROM THE OTHER PERSONS, APART FROM THE RELATIONSHIP OF ORIGIN?

Arguments Pro and Con ... 80
Body of the Question ... 80
  Article I Is it Repugnant that the First Person be Constituted by a Relation? ... 81
  Article II By What Relation could the First Person be Constituted? ... 83
  Article III What is the Interrelation of those Relations Admittedly Present in the First Person? ... 98
    1. Is there some Distinction of Properties in the First Person? ... 99
    2. From What Considerations could One Prescind and still have the First Person? ... 103
Reply to the Initial Argument ... 105

Question Five: IS THE RELATION OF ORIGIN FORMALLY INFINITE?

Arguments Pro and Con ... 108
Body of the Question ... 108
  Article I The Meaning of the Question ... 108
  Article II Solution of the Question: Paternity is not Infinite ... 114
    1. The First Principal Reason ... 114
    2. The Second Principal Reason ... 118
    3. The Third Principal Reason ... 120
  Article III Objections and Answers ... 123
Reply to the Initial Argument ... 128

CONTENTS

Question Six: IS "EQUALITY" IN THE DIVINE A REAL RELATION?

Arguments Pro and Con ... 130
Body of the Question ... 130
  Article I Is there a Real Foundation for Equality in the Divine? ... 130
    1. The Foundation for Equality in General ... 131
    2. The Foundation of Equality in God ... 132
    3. Is Each of these Foundations for Equality Real? ... 133
      1) First question: Is magnitude in God something extramental? ... 133
      2) Second question: Is eternity a real or extramental basis for equality? ... 141
      3) Third question: Is power a real basis for equality? ... 143
  Article II Are the Terms Related really Distinct? ... 145
  Article III Is Equality in the Persons according to an Extramental Foundation? ... 154
Reply to the Initial Arguments ... 157

Question Seven: CAN IT BE DEMONSTRATED BY NATURAL AND NECESSARY REASON THAT GOD IS OMNIPOTENT?

Arguments Pro and Con ... 159
Body of the Question ... 160
  Article I The Necessary Distinctions ... 160
    1. Demonstration of Simple Fact and of the Reasoned Fact ... 160
    2. Two Meanings of Omnipotence ... 161
  Article II Solution of the Question ... 162
    1. Concerning the First Conclusion ... 164
    2. Concerning the Second Conclusion ... 165
    3. Concerning the Third Conclusion ... 169
    4. Concerning the Fourth Conclusion ... 172
    5. Concerning the Fifth Conclusion ... 181
Reply to the Initial Arguments ... 182
  1. Reply to the Argument about Infinite Power ... 182
  2. Reply to the Argument about the Generation of the Son ... 185
  3. Reply to the Argument about the Creation of the Angels ... 188

CONTENTS

Question Eight: DOES THE DIVINE WORD HAVE SOME CAUSALITY OF HIS OWN AS REGARDS CREATURES?

Arguments Pro and Con	198
Body of the Question	199
Article I Is there some Formal Aspect of Causation Proper to the Word?	199
1. Negative Answer: Three Proofs	199
2. Objection to these Proofs	203
3. Answer to the Objection	204
Article II Is some Mode or Order in Causing Proper to the Word?	210
Article III Is some Relationship of Causality or any Relationship of His to a Creature Included *per se* in the Word's Constitutive Property?	212
Reply to the Initial Argument	216

Question Nine: CAN GOD BRING IT ABOUT THAT AN ANGEL INFORM MATTER?

Arguments Pro and Con	218
Body of the Question	219
Article I The Meaning of the Question	219
Article II Answer to the Question	219
Article III Some Objections and their Solutions	228
Reply to the Initial Argument	235

Question Ten: CAN GOD CONVERT THE EUCHARISTIC SPECIES INTO SOMETHING PREVIOUSLY EXISTING?

Arguments Pro and Con	236
Body of the Question	237
Article I The *terminus a quo* or the Separated Quantity	237
Article II The *terminus ad quem* or What Preexists	242
Article III About the Conversion Itself	251
Reply to the Initial Arguments	255

Question Eleven: IF BOTH BODY AND PLACE REMAIN, CAN GOD CAUSE THE BODY NOT TO HAVE UBIETY?

Arguments Pro and Con	257
Body of the Question	258
Article I Given Place in General, is it Repugnant for a Body in General to Lack Ubiety?	258

CONTENTS

Article II Given Body in General, is it Repugnant to Place in General that no Ubiety Exist?	260
Article III Given this Body, this Place, but this Body not Present in this Place, is it Possible that this Body should Lack this Ubiety?	263
Article IV If this Body and Place Exist and this Body is Present in this Place, can it still Lack this Ubiety?	265
Reply to the Initial Argument	270

Question Twelve: IS THE RELATION OF A CREATURE TO GOD AS CREATOR THE SAME AS THE RELATION TO GOD AS CONSERVER?

Arguments Pro and Con	271
Body of the Question	272
Article I Is the Real Relation of the Creature to God as Creator and as Conserver the Same?	272
Article II Can a Thing be Said to be at once Created and Conserved?	275
Article III Can Something be Created without being Conserved after the Instant of Creation?	277
Reply to the Initial Arguments	282

Question Thirteen: ARE THE ACTS OF KNOWING AND APPETITION ESSENTIALLY ABSOLUTE OR ESSENTIALLY RELATIVE?

Arguments Pro and Con	284
Body of the Question	284
Article I There is some Absolute Entity Involved in Every Operation including Intellection	285
Article II How this Absolute Entity is Related to the Object Connected with It	288
1. The Operation, Some Claim, must Involve a Real Relationship to the Object	288
2. How are We to Understand the Claim that the Operation Implies a Relation?	290
3. Analysis of the Arguments in the First Section	296
Article III Is a Relationship to the Object Essential to the Act of Knowing or Appetition?	302
Article IV The Question Understood as Referring to the Subject	312
Reply to the Initial Argument	312

CONTENTS

Question Fourteen: CAN THE SOUL LEFT TO ITS NATURAL PERFECTION KNOW THE TRINITY OF PERSONS IN GOD?

Arguments Pro and Con	315
Body of the Question	316
Article I Imperfect Knowledge	317
1. Knowledge of the Terms "God" and "Trinity"	317
2. Knowledge of the Proposition "God is a Trinity"	319
Article II Perfect Immediate Knowledge	324
Article III Mediate Knowledge	336

Question Fifteen: IS THE POSSIBLE INTELLECT ACTIVE OR PASSIVE AS REGARDS THE CONCEPT OF A CREATURE?

Arguments Pro and Con	344
Body of the Question	345
Article I Formation of the Word according to the Manner in Which We Understand in the Present Life	345
1. In the Intellective Part of the Soul there is an Active Principle of Intellection	345
2. Which Factor is Active in Intellection?	350
3. Is it the Agent or the Possible Intellect That is Active in Intellection?	355
Article II How the Notion or Word is Formed in the Intellect of the Blessed in Heaven	363
Reply to the Initial Arguments	366

Question Sixteen: ARE FREEDOM OF WILL AND NATURAL NECESSITY COMPATIBLE AS REGARDS THE SAME ACT AND OBJECT?

Arguments Pro and Con	369
Body of the Question	370
Article I Is there Necessity in any Act of the Will?	370
Article II Can Freedom and Necessity Coexist in the Will?	377
Article III Can Natural Necessity ever Coexist with Freedom?	380
Reply to the Initial Argument	385

Question Seventeen: ARE ACTS OF NATURAL LOVE AND MERITORIOUS LOVE SPECIFICALLY THE SAME?

Arguments Pro and Con	388
Body of the Question	388
Article I The Meaning of Natural Dilection or Love	388
Article II The Meaning of Meritorious Love or Dilection	389
Article III Solution of the Question	391
Reply to the Initial Argument	397

Question Eighteen: DOES THE EXTERIOR ACT ADD SOME GOODNESS OR BADNESS TO THE INTERIOR ACT?

Arguments Pro and Con	399
Body of the Question	399
Article I The Source of Moral Goodness or Badness	400
Article II The Source of Laudability and Culpability	406
Article III Is the Goodness or Laudability of the External Action Distinct from That of the Interior Act?	408
1. The Exterior Act has Its Own Moral Goodness	408
2. The External Act is Imputable	416
Reply to the Initial Argument	416

Question Nineteen: IS THE UNITY IN CHRIST OF THE HUMAN NATURE WITH THE WORD MERELY THE ASSUMED NATURE'S DEPENDENCE UPON THE WORD?

Arguments Pro and Con	418
Body of the Question	418
Article I The Type of Unity to be Posited Here	418
Article II The Possibility of Such a Union on the Part of the Assuming Person	421
1. First Proof	421
2. Second Proof	427
3. Proofs Proposed by Others	430
4. Objection to the Conclusion of this Article	431
Article III The Possibility of Such a Union on the Part of the Assumed Nature	432
1. What Constitutes Created Personality?	432
2. Can a Human Nature Depend upon an Extrinsic Person?	436
Reply to the Initial Argument	442

Question Twenty: DOES A PRIEST WHO IS OBLIGED TO SAY A MASS FOR EACH OF TWO DIFFERENT PEOPLE SATISFY HIS OBLIGATION BY SAYING ONE MASS FOR BOTH?

Arguments Pro and Con	443
Body of the Question	443
Article I The Value of the Mass in virtue of the Celebrant's Personal Merit	444
Article II The Value of the Mass by reason of the Merit of the Universal Church	453
1. Can the Priest Apply the Merit due in virtue of the Sacrifice?	453
2. Can the Priest Apply Such a Good at Will?	455
3. One Mass does not Benefit Each of Several as Much as it Would if Offered for One Alone	458
Article III Does the Priest Satisfy his Obligation to Both by One Offering?	461
Reply to the Initial Argument	468

Question Twenty-One: CAN ONE WHO ADMITS THAT THE WORLD IS ETERNAL DEFEND THE POSITION THAT ANYONE COULD ALWAYS BE FORTUNATE?

Arguments Pro and Con	469
Body of the Question	470
Article I The View that Someone is Fortunate	470
1. The Existence and Nature of Good Fortune	470
The Reportatio Version: Can Those Who Admit the World is Eternal also Admit that a Man is Fortunate	473
Body of the Question	474
1. The View that Someone can be Fortunate	475
2. About Aristotle's View that the World is Eternal	482

Appendix

Addition 1.11	485
Addition 1.38	485
Addition 7.38	486
Addition 9.53	487
Addition 11.15	488
Addition 12.28	488
Addition 13.56	488

CONTENTS

Addition 14.25	489
Addition 15.79	489
Addition 18.23	490
Addition 20.49	491
Glossary	493
Index of Authors	541
Index of Subjects	544

Abbreviations

BFS *Bibliotheca franciscana scholastica medii aevi,* cura Patrum Collegii S. Bonaventurae. Ad Claras Aquas, Florentiae, 1903ff.

CCAA *Corpus commentariorum Averrois in Aristotelem.* Ed. H. A. Wolfson, D. Baneth, F. H. Fobes. The Medieval Academy of America, Cambridge, Mass., 1953.

CCSL *Corpus christianorum, series latina.* Turnholti: Typographi Brepols editores Pontificii.

CSEL *Corpus scriptorum ecclesiasticorum latinorum.* Vindeboniae: Academia Vindebonensis, 1866ff.

PG *Patrologiae cursus completus, series graeca,* accurante J. P. Migne, Parisiis, 1857ff.

PhB *Les Philosophes Belges: Textes et études.* Collection publiée par l'Institut Supérieur de Philosophie de l'Université de Louvain. Louvain, 1901ff.

PL *Patrologiae cursus completus, series latina,* accurante J. P. Migne, Parisiis, 1844ff.

Acknowledgments

We are grateful to both the American Philosophical Society for grants No. 5533 and 5968 from the Penrose Fund and to the Catholic University of America for supplementary research grants that made our collaboration possible. Most of Wolter's work on the glossary was done as part of a larger research project on Duns Scotus' thought during his tenure as Senior Fellow of the National Endowment for the Humanities. We also wish to thank the Catholic University of America Press for permission to reprint the translation of question seven, which appeared in Volume 4 of *Studies in Philosophy and the History of Philosophy* edited by J. K. Ryan.

F.A.
A.B.W.

Introduction

John Duns Scotus, known as the Subtle Doctor, was a scholastic theologian and philosopher who for four centuries or more after his death had a profound influence on Western philosophical thought. The American scientist and philosopher Charles Sanders Peirce considered him the greatest speculative mind of the Middle Ages and one of the "profoundest metaphysicians that ever lived."[1] Though Scotus' Latin has neither the simplicity of St. Thomas' nor the beauty of St. Bonaventure's, one seventeenth-century theologian writing about his moral philosophy declares the Scotist school to be more numerous than that of all the others combined.[2] Two international congresses devoted to his thought within the last decade bear witness to the continuing interest in his ideas.[3] Yet as his sobriquet suggests, he is a deep and difficult thinker. Almost invariably his thought develops through an involved dialogue with unnamed contemporaries that taxes the patience of most readers. As one philosopher puts it, his way of writing is "exploratory rather than finished, intended to record Duns Scotus' thought for himself, rather than communicate it to less thorough and critical minds."[4] Yet de-

---

[1] *Collected Papers of Charles Sanders Peirce*, ed. C. Hartshorne and P. Weiss (Cambridge, Mass., 1960), Vol. I, p. 10, par. 1.29: "Duns Scotus and William Ockham are decidedly the greatest speculative minds of the Middle Ages as well as two of the profoundest metaphysicians that ever lived." Of the two, it is clear Peirce regarded Scotus as the superior. See, e.g., pars. 1.6, 1.16, 1.19f.

[2] See the testimony, for instance, of the seventeenth-century Cistercian theologian, John Caramuel y Lobkowicz. In this connection see F. Bak, "Scoti Schola Numerosior Est Omnibus Aliis Simul Sumptis," *Franciscan Studies* XVI (1956), 144-65.

[3] The proceedings are published in the first five volumes of a new series entitled *Studia scholastica-scotistica*. Those of the Second International Scotistic Congress held at Oxford and Edinburgh, Sept. 11-17, 1966, appear in first four volumes under the title *De doctrina Ioannis Duns Scoti* (Romae, 1968); those of the Third International Scotistic Congress held at Vienna, Sept. 28-Oct. 2, 1970, are in a single volume entitled *Deus et Homo ad mentem I. Duns Scoti* (Romae, 1972).

[4] A. Hyman and J. J. Walsh, *Philosophy in the Middle Ages* (New York, 1967), p. 556.

spite this forbidding style that repelled the humanists of the Renaissance and won for him the dubious honor of being dubbed the original "dunce," poets like Gerard Manley Hopkins or Thomas Merton found his writings inspiring and his insights unrivaled "be rival Italy or Greece."[5]

The questions Scotus discusses in this last of his major works were not of his own choosing. They were originally proposed to him in the course of a public debate and reflect some of the interests and concerns of the theological faculty and student body at the University of Paris at the beginning of the fourteenth century. Nevertheless in revising them for publication he wove in so much of his basic philosophy and theology as to make this work one of the mainstays on which his reputation as a thinker depends. It contains the "marrow of his teaching," as Luke Wadding put it, presented "with greater clarity, with a method more facile and with arguments more solid."[6] It is of paramount importance in assessing Scotus' final position on a wide range of topics.

I Life and Works

Only after the fourteenth century, when his name had become a legend in theological and philosophical circles, did writers attempt to reconstruct something of Scotus' early life. Especially among those who venerated him as a saint, fact was mingled with fable, and by the seventeenth century, when his following was at its greatest, critical historians found it practically impossible to sift truth from fiction. Luke Wadding, the great historian of the Franciscan order, confessed that the place and date of his birth as well as his age and the date of his death are particularly uncertain.[7] Writing in the second half of the last century, Ernest Renan remarks it would be difficult to find a famous man of the Middle Ages whose life is less known than that of Duns Scotus.[8]

---

[5] "Duns Scotus's Oxford." Sonnet 44, *Poems of Gerard Manley Hopkins*, 3rd edn., ed. W. H. Gardner (London, 1948), p. 84. See also Thomas Merton, "Duns Scotus," *Figures for an Apocalypse* (New York, 1947), pp. 48-49, and "Hymn for the Feast of Duns Scotus," *The Tears of the Blind Lions* (New York, 1949), pp. 6-7.

[6] L. Wadding's "Praefatio ad lectorem," to Tome XII of *Joannis Duns Scoti opera omnia* (Lugduni, 1639), no pagination.

[7] "Patria, aetas, mors haec plus ceteris incerta," L. Wadding, *Annales Minorum* VI (Romae, 1733), p. 41.

[8] E. Renan, "Jean Duns Scot," *Histoire littéraire de la France* XXV (Paris, 1869), 404.

A half-century of patient research, however, has disclosed a number of facts. The early fourteenth-century manuscript tradition, for instance, provides statements to the effect that John Duns is a Scot, from Duns, who belonged to the English province of Friars Minor[9] (the religious order founded by St. Francis of Assisi) and that he "flourished at Cambridge, Oxford, and Paris and died in Cologne."[10] Having rejected Wadding's earlier suggestion that John might even have been born in Ireland, scholars agree today that Scotland is his native land. But even as late as a decade ago, they had not settled on the exact place of his birth. The fact that in the manuscripts he is called both "John Duns" and "John of Duns" suggested that Duns might be either the name of his family or of the place of his birth or both. In choosing 1966 for the International Congress to commemorate the seventh centenary of his birth, however, and in raising a cairn near the Pavilion Lodge of the Duns castle in Berwickshire, scholars honored a long tradition not only as to the site where he was born but also as to approximately when. The details of his parentage, his early schooling at Haddington, and the story of his entry into the Franciscan order as found in the so-called Tweedy transcription of the Chronicle of Scottish Franciscans cannot be trusted.[11] The earliest reliable date we have of Scotus is that of his ordination at St. Andrew's Church in Northampton on March 17, 1291, by Oliver Sutton, Bishop of Lincoln.[12] In view of the minimum age requirements for the priesthood, Scotus could hardly have been born later than March, 1266, and certainly not in 1274 as earlier historians claimed.

The Scots belonged jurisdictionally to the English Franciscan province. Their principal house of studies was at Oxford. Bramp-

---

[9] See C. Balić, "Life and Works of John Duns Scotus," *John Duns Scotus, 1265-1965*, ed. J. K. Ryan and B. Bonansea, in *Studies in Philosophy and the History of Philosophy* 3 (Washington, D.C., 1965), 2ff.

[10] The colophon of the early fourteenth-century MS. 66 of Merton College reads: "Haec de ordinatione ven. fratris J. Duns de ordine fratrum Minorum, qui floruit Cant., Oxon. et Parisiis et obiit in Colonia."

[11] H. Docherty, "The Brockie Forgeries," *The Innes Review* XVI (1965), 79-127; idem, "The Brockie MSS. and Duns Scotus," *De doctrina Ioannis Duns Scoti* (Acta Congressus Scotistici Internationalis Oxonii et Edimburgi 11-17 sept. 1966 celebrati), I (Romae, 1968), 329-60.

[12] E. Longpré, "L'ordination sacerdotale du bx. Jean Duns Scot. Document 17 mars 1291," *Archivum Franciscanum Historicum* XXII (1929), 54-62.

ton[13] has given the most plausible account of Scotus' studies there, based on the statutes of Oxford University. The theological program leading to the mastership in theology would have lasted some thirteen years. The last four of these would have been spent as a bachelor of theology. Of these four, the first year was usually devoted to preparing lectures on Peter Lombard's *Sentences* and the second year in delivering them.

The bachelor's role at this stage was not to give a running commentary on this theological textbook but rather to raise and answer questions of his own on topics that roughly paralleled the subject "distinctions" in Lombard. Consequently the topics John discusses in his *Lectura oxoniensis* range over the whole field of theology. When the bachelor had finished his year of lectures, he began to revise and enlarge them with a view to publication. Such a revised version was called an *ordinatio*, in contrast to his original notes (*lectura*) or a student's report (*reportatio*) of the actual lecture. If the lecturer himself corrected such a report, it was called a *reportatio examinata*. From a date mentioned in the second question of the prologue, it is clear that Scotus was already at work in 1300 on what would become his major work, the commentary on the *Sentences* known as the *Ordinatio* or *Opus oxoniense*.[14]

University statutes demanded that the third year be devoted to lectures on the Bible; during his final year, the bachelor *formatus*, as he was called, was required to take part in public disputations under different masters including his own. This last year can be dated rather precisely in Scotus' case. He is named among the twenty-two Franciscans, including two masters of theology, Adam of Howden and Philip of Bridlington, presented to Bishop Dalderby on July 26, 1300, for faculties to hear confessions in the friars' church at Oxford.[15] Since the Franciscans had only one chair of theology at the university and there was a long list of trained bachelors waiting to incept or present their inaugural lectures, regent masters (i.e., those who occupied the official chair) were replaced annually. Adam was the twenty-eighth and Philip the twenty-ninth Oxford master, so that Philip's year of regency was just beginning. This must have coincided with Scotus' final and thirteenth year, since he

---

[13] C. K. Brampton, "Duns Scotus at Oxford, 1288-1301," *Franciscan Studies* XXIV (1964), 5-20.

[14] *Ordinatio*, Prol. n.112 (I, 77).

[15] A. G. Little, *The Grey Friars in Oxford* (Oxford, 1892), pp. 63-64.

was the bachelor respondent under Master Bridlington.[16] This would mean, Brampton argues, that by June of 1301, Scotus had completed all requirements for the mastership in theology, yet in view of the long line ahead of him, there was little hope of incepting as an Oxford master for perhaps a decade to come.

When the English province's turn came to provide a talented candidate for the Franciscan chair of theology at the more prestigious University of Paris, Scotus was selected. One *reportatio* of his Parisian lectures indicates that he began his commentary in the autumn of 1302 and continued to June of the following year.[17] But before the term came to an end the long-festering feud between King Philip the Fair and Pope Boniface VIII came to a head. Philip had taxed Church property to support his wars with England and the Pope excommunicated him. The monarch retaliated by calling for a general council of the Church to depose Boniface. He won the support of the university and French clergy generally. On June 24, 1303, a great anti-papal demonstration occurred. Mendicant friars marched through the streets of Paris. Berthold of St. Denis, Bishop of Orléans and ex-chancellor of the university, together with two Franciscans and two Dominicans addressed the demonstrators. The next day royal commissioners examined each member of the Franciscan friary to determine whose side he was on. Some seventy friars, mostly French, favored Philip whereas the rest (over eighty) sided with the Pope. Among the latter were John Scotus and Master

---

[16] The evidence, discovered by Longpré, is contained in quarternus VI, q.20, of MS. Worcester Cath. 99; cf. A. G. Little and F. Pelster, *Oxford Theology and Theologians c. A.D. 1282-1302* (Oxford, 1934), p. 310. Cf. F. Longpré, "Philippe de Bridlington O.F.M. et le bx. Duns Scot," *Archivum Franciscanum Historicum* XXII (1929), 587-88. On the role of the bachelor as respondent see Little and Pelster, *op. cit.*, pp. 31-36.

[17] MS. F. 69 in Worcester Cathedral Library is one of the earliest manuscripts of the *Reportata parisiensia*. The colophon at the end of the list of questions in the first book (fol. 158va) reads: "Expliciunt quaestiones super primum Sententiarum datae a fratre [J. Dons Scoto *written over erasure*] ordinis fratrum minorum Parisius anno domini M⁰ trecentesimo secundo intrante tertio." And at the end of the list of questions in the fourth book (fol. 160va) we read: "Expliciunt quaestiones Sententiarum datae a fratre J[ohanne Duns] antedicto in studio Parisius anno domini M⁰CCC⁰III." See A. G. Little, "Chronological Notes on the Life of Duns Scotus," *English Historical Review* XLVII (1932), 575; C. K. Brampton, *op. cit.*, 11ff.

Gonsalvus of Spain.[18] The royal penalty was exile from France within three days. Boniface responded with a bull of August 15, 1303, suspending the university's right to grant degrees in theology and civil or canon law. As a result of his harassment and imprisonment by the King's mercenaries, however, Boniface died in October. He was succeeded by Pope Benedict XI, who in the interests of peace lifted the ban against the university in April, 1304, and not long after the King did everything to facilitate the return of the exiled students.

Just where Scotus and Master Gonsalvus spent their exile is not clear. It could be that Scotus' Cambridge lectures stem from this period, though he may have given them before coming to Paris. Be that as it may, before the summer of 1304 Scotus was back in Paris, for he functioned as bachelor respondent in the disputation *in aula* (in the hall of the bishop) when his predecessor, Giles of Ligny, was promoted to master. Meanwhile Gonsalvus had become Minister General, or head, of the Franciscan order during the Pentecost General Chapter of 1304. On November 18 of that year he wrote to the Franciscan superior at the Paris friary that the next bachelor to be licensed as regent master was "Friar John Scotus, of whose laudable life, excellent knowledge and most subtle ability as well as his other remarkable qualities I am fully informed, partly from long experience, partly from report which has spread everywhere."[19]

Presumably Scotus became master sometime in 1305. The period following his inception seems to have been one of great literary activity. Aided by associates and secretaries, he set out to finish the *Ordinatio* begun at Oxford, using not only the Oxford and Cambridge lectures but his Parisian ones as well. There is manuscript

---

[18] Longpré discovered the early fourteenth-century document containing the names of the friars who sided for or against the king in the Archives Nationales in Paris and published its contents in *France franciscaine* XI (1928), 137-62, under the title "Le b. Jean Duns Scot O.F.M. pour le Saint Siège contre le Gallicanisme, Paris 25-8 juin 1303." A separate edition with practically the same title was published at Quaracchi (Florence) in 1930. For an identification of the friars of the English province listed there, see A. G. Little, *Chron. Notes*, p. 576.

[19] Gonsalvus' letter dated at Ascoli in the March of Ancona, Nov. 18, 1304, and addressed to William, guardian at Paris (or his vicar), and the masters, has been frequently printed: see, e.g., H. Denifle and A. Chatelain, *Chartularium Universitatis Parisiensis* II (Paris, 1889), 117; and Little, *Grey Friars in Oxford*, p. 220. A complete English translation can be found in Little, *Chron. Notes*, pp. 577-78.

evidence of a magisterial dispute he conducted with Guillaume Pierre Godin, O.P., against the thesis that matter is the principle of individuation,[20] but to date no questions publicly disputed *ordinaire*, that is to say, in regular turn with other regent masters, have been found. Some questions of this sort undoubtedly existed but they may have been incorporated in the *Ordinatio*.[21] Scotus did engage in one solemn quodlibetal disputation during his regency, which is the work translated here. Though not as extensive in scope as the *Ordinatio*, these *Quaestiones quodlibetales* are hardly less important as they represent some of his most mature thinking. Indeed one could say that his fame as a philosopher and theologian rests largely on these two major works.

Of the minor works the most important and extensive are the *Quaestiones subtilissimae super libros Metaphysicae Aristotelis*. These may represent questions discussed privately for the benefit of the Franciscan student philosophers and theologians. The same is true of the series of logical questions occasioned by Porphyry's *Isagoge* and Aristotle's *De praedicamentis, De interpretatione*, and *De sophisticis elenchis*. The relatively short but important *De Primo Principio*, a compendium of what reason can prove about God, draws heavily on the *Ordinatio* and may have been completed by a confrere only after Scotus left Paris to lecture as professor of theology at the Franciscan study house in Cologne for the fall term of 1307.

November 8, 1308 is the traditional date of Scotus' death. His remains lie in the nave of the Franciscan church near the Cologne cathedral, where he is venerated as a saint.

Apparently most of his works were still in an unfinished state at the time of his death. This is true not only of the *Quodlibet*, the last question of which is only partially revised, but also the *Ordinatio*

---

[20] Cf. F. Pelster, "Handschriftliches zu Skotus mit neuen Angaben über sein Leben," *Franziskanische Studien* x (1923), 16. The question is found in Cod. Amplonianus Fol. 369 of the Stadtbibliothek, Erfurt (fols. 71vb-75rb).

[21] We have found several references to a *quaestio ordinaria* in manuscripts of Scotus' quodlibet, and in each instance an appropriate referent on the same topic can be found in the *Ordinatio*. More important, there is at least one clear reference in Codex 137, bibliotheca communalis Assisi, the early fourteenth-century attempt of a critical edition of the *Ordinatio*, to a *quaestio ordinaria* as the source of the section copied by the scribe; cf. fol. 78vb.

of the questions on the *Sentences* of Peter Lombard. Eager pupils completed the works by substituting materials from *reportationes* and possibly from ordinary disputations for the questions Scotus left undictated. Despite their imperfect form, however, these works were widely circulated. Even today they are found in hundreds of manuscripts, and from 1472 onwards went through more than thirty different editions.

II The Quodlibetal Disputation

The *quodlibet* represents a type of scholastic exercise generally practiced in the thirteenth and fourteenth centuries. Its golden age lasted from 1250 to 1320.[22] Introduced in the faculty of theology at Paris, this form of disputation soon spread to Oxford (probably at John Peckham's suggestion), Bologna, Toulouse, and Cologne.[23] It was also adopted by the faculties of arts, medicine, and law.[24] Disputations of this sort took place twice a year: before Christmas (in the second or third week of Advent) and before Easter (around the fourth week of Lent).[25] The origin of this disputation goes back as far as 1230 to 1235 and may have been introduced by the masters of the new religious orders of Dominicans and Franciscans.[26]

Although it involved a number of bachelors as opponents and respondents, the quodlibetal disputation was essentially a magisterial function or exercise in the sense that it had to be conducted under the direction, authority, and control of a regent master, that is, one who held one of the professorial chairs in his respective faculty at the university.[27] The initial respondent to the objections raised was a bachelor.[28] University statutes ordained that no bachelor could be

[22] P. Glorieux, "Où en est la question du Quodlibet?" *Revue du Moyen Age Latin* II (1946), 412; idem, "Quodlibeti" in *Enciclopedia Cattolica* x (Città del Vaticano, 1953), col. 437.

[23] Glorieux, "Quodlibeti," col. 438.

[24] The regulations for the faculties of arts and medicine are well known. We know less about those in the faculty of law. The quodlibetal disputation was adopted as well in the *Studia generalia* of the religious orders of Franciscans, Dominicans, and Hermits of St. Augustine with certain variations and adaptations.

[25] Glorieux, "Quodlibeti," col. 436.

[26] Glorieux, "Le Quodlibet et ses procédés rédactionnels," *Divus Thomas* (Series tertia) XVI (1939), 61.

[27] Glorieux, "Où en est la question du Quodlibet?" 413.

[28] Glorieux, "Quodlibeti," col. 436.

licensed as a master unless he had participated at least once in a quodlibetal dispute, since this was particularly suited to test the candidate's presence of mind, the extent of his knowledge, and the depth of his philosophical and theological preparation. After this initial dialectical encounter, however, it was the master himself who discussed these questions in depth and then "determined" them, that is, gave the definitive solution.[29]

In contrast to the ordinary disputations of a master which the bachelors attended, the solemn quodlibetal dispute drew a larger audience. Anyone present, whether a master, a bachelor, a student, or simply one who came to listen, could pose a question or raise an objection. All courses were suspended so that everyone, including the masters, could attend.[30] The disputation could center on any problem whatsoever (*de quolibet*) proposed by any listener whatsoever (*a quolibet*). Only if the question was trivial, irrelevant, or uninteresting could the master refuse to entertain it. The ordinary disputations (*quaestiones disputatae*) also contained many questions, but they were all interrelated by reason of their subject matter or in virtue of some common text of Holy Scripture. A quodlibetal dispute, on the other hand, not only included many questions but covered a wide variety of topics.[31]

The fact that the questions came from the audience gave the quodlibetal disputation an element of surprise as well as a vital character. The problems posed reflected the interests and preoccupations of the day and the currents of ideas prevalent in university circles.

The unforeseen character or unexpected nature of the questions that might be raised, which could be subtle, difficult or delicate, required the authority and scientific talent of a true master. Apparently not all masters dared engage in such a dispute or had the self-confidence required to undertake such a task. Since it was not obligatory, some never put themselves to this challenging exercise, yet we know of a hundred or more masters who did, some of them many times.[32]

Quodlibetal questions are important for gauging the philosophi-

[29] Ibid.

[30] Ibid. In one quodlibetal discussion Roger Marston conducted, no less than twenty-five masters participated.

[31] Glorieux, *La littérature quodlibétique* II; Bibliothèque Thomiste XXI (Paris, 1935), 45ff.

[32] Glorieux, "Quodlibeti," cols. 436-37.

cal-theological thought of the period, of a particular author, and of the general history of the times. The very nature of the dispute prevented it from being limited in scope and left it open to an infinity of problems. Any vital topic, any novel or challenging view on a contemporary subject, be it economic, social, or political, could be brought up, and the regent master could be expected to give his opinion about it. Quodlibets, in a word, contain valuable insights into the personal opinions of a master and often expressed his mind on a score of topics never touched on in any other work.[33]

During the first day of regular classes following the solemn disputation, the master would discuss with his students the questions debated in the public session after freely arranging them in some orderly fashion. There can be no doubt about the existence of this review session in which the master analyzed the questions with his disciples, corrected possible errors or inaccuracies in their reports, made his terminology and ideas more precise, distinguished the essential from the incidental, classified the questions and gave them a definitive answer.[34]

A few extant quodlibets are in the form of *reportationes* (i.e., first reports taken down at the public dispute), whereas others obviously represent a later redaction or corrected version. Reports of the public disputation reflect the lack of order in which the questions were presented, for anyone could raise any problem he wished at any time; as a result there is no semblance of order in the sequence of the questions. Occasionally, of course, one problem might suggest a second, or a particular solution might give rise to a further question. Generally those in attendance prepared their questions ahead of time but presented them when they had the chance to do so. In contrast to *reportationes* of this sort, the redaction or revision prepared by the master exhibits a coherent pattern or logical order. It reflects the second session or the later work of the master in the tranquility of his study as he edited the text for transcription by copyists and for public dissemination.[35]

A master of theology in the thirteenth century had certain set categories he might use to group the questions in some orderly fashion. God and creatures, visible and invisible creation, creation and redemption, faith and mores, realities and symbols were favorite

---

[33] Glorieux, *La littérature quodl.* II, 45ff.; "Où en est la question du Quodlibet?" 411.

[34] Glorieux, "Le Quodlibet et ses procédés rédactionnels," 62f.

[35] Ibid., 65.

headings.³⁶ Once the master had selected his major division, it was easy for him to set up further subdivisions.

Some authors designate at the outset the division headings they have adopted, whereas others simply present the questions according to some specific order but without mentioning it expressly. Still others not only indicate their classificatory scheme but try to justify their choice and at times may even mention the circumstance of the dispute that accounts for the questions raised. Some begin with a list or summary of all the questions to be treated, whereas others start with a prologue in which some scriptural or patristic citation introduces the general theme of the quodlibet and leads more or less rapidly to a presentation of its major divisions.³⁷

Knowledge of the various editorial techniques is often helpful in identifying a quodlibet, dating it, or determining how complete the manuscripts are that contain it. Thus we can show, for instance, as Glorieux notes, that *Quodlibet* XI of St. Thomas is incomplete, a point to be considered in evaluating the manuscripts that present it in an apparently completed form.³⁸

III *Scotus' Quodlibet*

As the manuscripts indicate, Scotus disputed and determined this quodlibet at Paris. Since he could not have incepted as master before 1305 and since he was teaching at Cologne before the end of 1307, it is one of his very latest works. While its authenticity has never been in doubt, there were some who believed the set of questions represented two quodlibetal disputes, the first of which included the first seven or eleven questions whereas the second comprised those that remained. Wadding, on the contrary, maintained that Scotus held but one such dispute. Contemporary writers have generally accepted his viewpoint,³⁹ and suggest Advent of 1306 or Lent of 1307 as its most probable date.⁴⁰ The number of questions it contains is no counterargument since the average quodlibet included between twenty and twenty-five questions and there are some that have as many as forty or fifty distinct questions.⁴¹

With the exception of the last question, which in the Wadding-

---

³⁶ Ibid.
³⁷ Ibid., 77-81.
³⁸ Ibid., 83ff.; "Où en est la question du Quodlibet?" 410.
³⁹ L. Wadding, "Praefatio ad lectorem."
⁴⁰ Glorieux, *La littérature quodl.* II, 153.
⁴¹ Ibid., 11f.

Vivès edition is in part the *reportatio* version, it is clear that Scotus' *quodlibet* is cast in the form of an *ordinatio*. In the tradition of the Franciscan masters,[42] it opens with a prologue introduced by a line from Scripture: " 'All things are difficult,' says Solomon, 'because man's language is inadequate to explain them.' "[43] Scotus then goes on to interpret these words of Ecclesiastes ascribed to "David's Son" in such a way as to suit his purposes. The distinction of things or beings, he explains, can help us classify the difficult questions that were presented to him. Like the metaphysician that he is, Scotus proceeds to divide being in terms of four classic disjunctions: created or uncreated, self-existent or not self-existent, necessary or possible, finite or infinite. The uncreated, self-existent, necessary, infinite being we call God, whereas the finite, possible, dependent being goes by the common name of creature. Questions, he tells us, were raised as regards both categories.

According to John Damascene's description, the divine perfections or attributes merge to form a simple infinite sea of substance. Nevertheless, Scotus, with his penchant for logical analysis, attempts to separate conceptually the various divine features within the Trinity and arrange them in some kind of ontological order. The logical tool he uses for this purpose is that of non-mutual implication or entailment. If the notion of B implies A, but that of A does not entail B, then A is in some sense prior to B. On this basis, he argues that questions about God in himself (*ad intra*) are prior to those which involve a relationship of the divine nature to creatures (*ad extra*). By the same token, within God, essential features (common to all three persons because of the divine essence they share) are prior to the notional features characteristic of only one or two persons. The first question as to whether the notional or essential is more immediate to the divine essence deals with these various priorities and sets the stage for the sequence in which the remaining questions are to be treated.

Since no questions were raised about essential features *ad intra*, however, Scotus begins with the five questions raised about the Trinity of persons. The first of these (Could there be several productions of the same type in God?)[44] is basically concerned with explaining why there is a trinity and only a trinity of persons in God. The second (Are these two compatible: a relation related to its op-

---

[42] Glorieux, "Le Quodlibet et ses procédés rédactionnels," 81.
[43] Cf. o.1.   [44] *Quodl.* Q. 2.

posite is a real thing; and, as related to the essence, it is only an aspect?)⁴⁵ is concerned with showing that three really distinct persons in God does not entail that there are also three gods. What is commonly said to constitute each person is the unique way in which the persons are related to each other in terms of their eternal origin. Consequently, Scotus' next two questions throw light on how this relationship of origin was conceived: Could the first divine person remain constituted as a person, distinct from the other persons, apart from the relationship of origin?⁴⁶ Is the relation of origin formally infinite?⁴⁷ Underlying these two theological questions is the more fundamental philosophical problem as to whether absolutes or relations are most basic to distinction, and whether it is meaningful to call what constitutes the uniqueness of a person or subsistent individual a perfection. A final question under this subheading is whether the "equality" characteristic of the three divine persons represents a real relation.

After investigating what pertains to God internally, in particular the relationships of person to person, says Scotus, "it remains to study what pertains to God externally, i.e., properties that imply a relationship of God to creatures. Here two sorts of questions could arise, one about the subject of the relation, the other about the term or object to which it relates. Two questions were raised about the subject, one general, the other particular. The first question is this: Can it be demonstrated by natural and necessary reason that God in general, and not just one particular person, is omnipotent? The second question pertains to one person in particular: Has the Son or Word of God some causality of his own as regards the creature?"⁴⁸

The last questions raised about God, says Scotus, "concern omnipotence in relation to its object. There are three questions, the first of which is about omnipotence in relation to an immaterial substance and it is this: Can God bring it about that an angel inform matter? The second question has to do with omnipotence's relation to an accidental form to which it gives existence in a supernatural way and it is this: Can God convert the Eucharistic species into something preexisting? The third question concerns omnipotence in relation to an accidental form existing in a natural fashion and it is this: Can God bring it about that while both body and place exist, the body has no ubiety or local presence?"⁴⁹

⁴⁵ *Quodl.* Q. 3. ⁴⁶ *Quodl.* Q. 4. ⁴⁷ *Quodl.* Q. 5.
⁴⁸ Cf. 7.1f. ⁴⁹ Cf. 9.1.

INTRODUCTION

"Once the questions raised about God have been answered, some questions about creatures follow: first about all creatures in general, then about certain creatures in particular. One question about creatures in general was asked and it is this: Is the created thing's relation to God as creator the same as its relation to him as conserver? . . .[50] As for creatures in particular the only questions raised concerned those endowed either with sensation or intellective life. One question common to either form of life was this: Are the acts of knowing and appetition essentially absolute or essentially relative? . . .[51] The next questions have to do with what pertains particularly to creatures possessing intellectual life. The first of these concern things common to men and angels; the next have to do with what is proper to man. Common to men and angels are intellect and will. Concerning the intellect two questions were raised: one, about the object of the intellect; the other, about the active cause of intellection. The first question was whether the soul, left to its natural perfection, can know the Trinity of persons in God. The same question can be asked as regards the angel. . . .[52] The next question concerns the cause of intellection, or how the intellect passes from [potency] to act. The question is this: Granted that the blessed in heaven have some concept or 'word' of the creature as seen in the divine essence, is the possible intellect purely passive as regards such knowledge? . . .[53] The next questions deal with the will, first, with its action in general; second, in particular with the distinction between two intrinsic acts of the will; and third, with the distinction between an intrinsic and extrinsic act. The first question is this: Are freedom of will and natural necessity compatible in the same subject as regards the same act and object? . . .[54] The next question raised is this: Are acts of natural love and meritorious love specifically the same? . . .[55] The next question concerns the interrelation of the extrinsic and intrinsic acts and asks whether the extrinsic adds some goodness or badness to the intrinsic."[56]

Though these questions are developed more with an eye to man, the general principles used to discuss them are applicable to any rational creature endowed with intellect and will. Though Scotus does not spell this out explicitly, the last three questions involve man or human nature. The first has to do with how the human nature of Christ was united to the Word or second person of the Trin-

[50] Cf. 12.1f.   [51] Cf. 13.1f.   [52] Cf. 14.1f.
[53] Cf. 15.1f.   [54] Cf. 16.1f.   [55] Cf. 17.1.
[56] Cf. 18.1.

ity: "Is the unity of human nature with the Word in Christ merely the human nature's dependence upon the Word?"[57] And in this question he develops his theory of what it means to be a created person. The penultimate question concerns the role of the priest as a person and as an official of the pilgrim Church in offering the sacrifice of the mass. It asks whether a priest who is obliged to say a mass for each of two different people can satisfy his obligation by saying one mass for both.[58] The final question, only partially revised, apparently concerns the possibility of reconciling divine providence in man's regard with the Aristotelian conception of the eternity of the world. The question, however, is developed within a more narrow philosophical context by using the doctrine in the short treatise, *De bona fortuna*, attributed in Scotus' day to Aristotle, with his teaching on the eternity of the world: "Can one who admits that the world is eternal defend the position that anyone could always be fortunate?"[59]

Each question, however it may fit into this general plan, still represents a distinct treatise in itself and touches on a far wider variety of theological and philosophical problems than one might suspect from the wording of the question itself. Scotus uses the customary tripartite scholastic format: the question is introduced with short initial arguments pro and con, next follows the body or corpus, and finally the question ends with answers to the initial counter-arguments. Not only had the corpus become the most important portion of the question by the close of the thirteenth century, but in Scotus' day it had become exceedingly complex because the most important objections and counter-arguments were discussed, often in dialogue fashion, within the confines of the corpus itself. However, in the *Quodlibetal Questions* there is less of this internal dialogue, perhaps, than in his other writings.

IV Some Observations about the Present Translation

The 1968 Spanish translation of Scotus' *Quodlibetal Questions* by F. Alluntis[60] is accompanied by what virtually amounts to a new version of the Latin text found in the Luke Wadding[61] edition re-

---

[57] Cf. 19.1.   [58] Cf. 20.1.   [59] Cf. 21.1.

[60] *Cuestiones Cuodlibetales* (*Obras del Doctor Sutil Juan Duns Escoto*), Latin text and Spanish translation with an introduction, summaries, and notes by Felix Alluntis, O.F.M. (Madrid, 1968).

[61] *Joannis Duns Scoti opera omnia*, 12 vols. (Lugduni, 1639).

printed by L. Vivès.⁶² Alluntis has divided the text into appropriate articles, divisions, and subdivisions so that it is possible to follow the involved dialogue of argument and counter-argument that made the use of this important source of Scotistic thought so difficult in the older editions. He has also introduced a new numbering system for the paragraphs to facilitate cross references. With the exception of the first question where we have restored a portion of the text relegated to a footnote in the Spanish edition, we have followed this numbering system, but to make it an even more effective and convenient reference device, we put before each paragraph number the number of the question followed by a decimal point. Thus 7.44, for example, would refer to question seven, paragraph number 44 in the Alluntis edition. For completeness, the traditional numbers of the Wadding edition (with all the mistakes of omission and duplication) are added in brackets in the margin. As in the Spanish version, the translators have introduced the divisions and sub-divisions they have added to the text without benefit of brackets.

Since the Wadding-Vivès edition has some obviously erroneous readings, fortunately most of them minor, the translators consulted Dr. Carl Balić, O.F.M., director, and other members of the Scotistic Commission in Rome engaged in preparing the critical Vatican edition of Scotus' *Opera omnia*. Of the more than eighty manuscripts available to the Commission, three, all of the early fourteenth century, were recommended as necessary and sufficient for revising the Latin text. Two are from the Bayerische Staatsbibliothek in Munich,⁶³ Clm 8717 and Clm 26309, which we have designated respectively as M_1 and M_2. Marginalia in the first suggest that the scribe who corrected it had access, if not to Scotus' own notebooks, at least to the information these contained; it may even represent the earliest form of *Quodlibetal Questions* still extant. The second, which contains substantially the same version, has a colophon giving the name of the scribe and a completion date of 1311. The third manuscript (F. 60 of the Cathedral Library of Worcester) contains

---

⁶² *Joannis Duns Scoti opera omnia*, 26 vols. (Parisiis, 1891-95).

⁶³ A description of the contents of these two MSS. can be found in F. Pelster, *Handschriftliches*, pp. 17-21. For additional material on Clm. 8717 confer Pelster's second article "Eine Münchener Handschrift des beginnenden vierzehnten Jahrhunderts mit einem Verzeichnis von Questionen des Duns Scotus und Herveus Natalis," *Franziskanische Studien* XVII (1930), 253-72; V. Doucet, "A propos du Cod. lat. Monacensis 8717," *Archivum Franciscanum Historicum* XXVI (1933), 246-47.

additions suggesting a partial revision of the earlier text. Though M_1 and M_2 seem to belong to the same family, omissions in one not made by the other and vice versa suggest they stem from a common source rather than that either is directly dependent on the other. The third, which we designate as W, seems to some extent closer to the Wadding-Vivès version.

As M_1 clearly indicates, the revision or *ordinatio* of the *Quodlibet* was left unfinished. Question 21 ends abruptly with the words: "Tertium membrum" (Cf. 21.16) with the marginal note: "Finis. Quodlibet repertum in suis quaternis. Quod sequitur est de Reportatione."[64] M_2 and W, on the other hand, simply append the original report of the question in its entirety, whereas the Wadding-Vivès text tries somewhat unsuccessfully to avoid overlap by eliminating the first part of the *reportatio* covered in the main by the material in the revised version. A simple comparison of the first part of the *reportatio* version (which we have translated in its entirety) indicates how extensive was the additional material Scotus wove into the framework of the question as originally "determined." This might explain also how it would have been possible to discuss, at least briefly, in a single session the set of questions that make up this *Quodlibet*. Another interesting aspect revealed by the manuscripts is that in several places Scotus refers to a *quaestio ordinaria* where he has treated objections raised, but not answered, in the expanded revision of the present work.

Judging from the three MSS as well as internal evidence, we are of the opinion that most of the Additions found in the Wadding-Vivès texts were added by hands other than Scotus. Since they are useful, however, in providing references, usually to the *ordinatio*, where solutions to objections left unanswered can be found, we have added them in the Appendix. On the other hand, additions found in all or some of the MSS we have used, if relevant to a better understanding of the text, have been put into footnotes. Some of these seem to be simply earlier versions of parallel passages and probably would have been eventually eliminated had Scotus lived to see the revision of the *Quodlibet* completed.

A glossary of technical terms has been included to reduce the number of explanatory footnotes. Since each question represents an integral treatise in its own right and may be read independently of

[64] Clm. 8717, fol. 85vb: "The end! The Quodlibet as found in his notebooks. What follows is from the 'reportatio.'"

INTRODUCTION

the others, we have usually marked with an asterisk the first occurrence of such terms in each question or where one of them recurs after a long interval.

Scotus usually formulates his main arguments in syllogistic form with major and minor premises, possibly to facilitate identification of the principle to which the intricate network of supporting proofs, objections, and counter-objections refers. To enable the reader to see at a glance to what Scotus is referring, we have included in brackets the appropriate paragraph number directly in the text except where the statement he is challenging or proving is immediately obvious from the context.

F.A.
A.B.W.

God and Creatures

Prologue

0.1 "All things are difficult," says Solomon, and immediately adds the reason why he thinks they are difficult: "Because man's language is inadequate to explain them."[1] The distinction of things or beings can serve as the basis for classifying or distinguishing the difficult questions that have been raised. Now a thing* [*res*] is primarily classified (1) as created or uncreated, (2) as having being of itself or having it from another, (3) as necessary or possible, (4) as finite or infinite. The uncreated, self-existent, infinite, and necessary thing or being we call God. The created, the "from another," the possible [i.e., contingent], the finite goes by the common name of "creature." Some questions were raised regarding both types of things.

0.2 What is more, in the divine, according to Augustine,[2] "thing" [or being] is taken either essentially or notionally* [i.e., personally]: "The things to be enjoyed are the Father, the Son and the Holy Spirit, the Trinity itself, the one supreme thing, common to all who enjoy it." In the first part of the text cited, "thing" is taken personally, in the second "essentially." As regards the divine, some of the questions raised concerned the essential, some the notional or personal. But only one question was asked about how the essentials are ordered to the notional elements. It is this question that will be discussed first because its solution will indicate in what order the remaining questions should be treated.

[1] Eccl. 1:8.
[2] Augustine, *De doctrina christiana* I, c.5, n.5; PL 34, 21; CCSL 30, 9.

Question One

IN DIVINE THINGS, IS IT THE ESSENTIAL OR THE NOTIONAL THAT IS MORE IMMEDIATE TO THE DIVINE ESSENCE?

[1]   1.1 The question is raised whether it is the essential or the notional* that is more immediate to the divine essence?¹

Arguments Pro and Con

Proof that the notional is more immediate: That which constitutes the persons of a nature is more immediate to that nature than its properties are. Now the notional characteristics constitute the persons of the divine nature; they are not constituted by the essentials which are like properties of the nature. Therefore, [the notional is more immediate to the divine nature than are the essentials].

Proof of the major: A nature is immediate as regards its own person, for it is predicated of the person according to the first mode of *per se* predication,* whereas nature is predicated of the property, and vice versa, only according to the second mode of *per se* predication.* Therefore, that by which the person is formally constituted is more closely connected with the nature than any of its properties are.

Proof of the minor: The essentials are common to all three persons, consequently a person is not constituted by anything that is essential; therefore, he is constituted by a notional element. Damascene² too claims that the essentials are properties of the nature. "If you should say 'good,' 'just,' 'wise,' or anything else," he says, "you are not saying what the nature of God is, but something about

---

¹ Cf. Duns Scotus, *Ordinatio* I, d.8, nn.167-73 (ed. Vaticana IV, 239-43); II, d.1, q.1 (ed. Vivès XI, 6-45).

For the references to the prologue and the distinctions of the first book of the *Ordinatio* and the *Lectura* we use the critical Vatican edition (I. Duns Scotus, *Opera omnia*, Civitas Vaticana 1950-); for the rest we use the Vivès edition (I. Duns Scotus, *Opera omnia*, Parisiis, 1891-95).

² Damascene, *De fide orthodoxa* I, c.4; PG 94, 799; Versions of Burgundio and Cerbanus, edited by Eligius M. Buytaert, O.F.M. (The Franciscan Institute, St. Bonaventure, N.Y., 1955), c.4, 21.

the nature." And Augustine says[3]: "If I say he is eternal, immortal, . . . just, good, blessed and spirit, only the last of these designations [i.e., spirit] seems to signify substance but the rest signify qualities of the substance."

1.2 On the contrary: That which is a pure perfection* is more immediate to the essence than that which is not a pure perfection. The essentials are pure perfections, the notional [features] are not. Therefore, [the essentials are more immediate].

Proof of the major: That which is a pure perfection is more immediate to the first [or basic] perfection than that which is not. The divine essence is the first [or basic] perfection, and that which is a pure perfection has more in the way of perfection than that which is not a pure perfection.

Proof of the minor: Of the essential in anything, says Anselm,[4] "better it than not it." But such is what is called a pure perfection. The notional is not such, for this reason. Every one of the persons lacks some notional element [viz., that which is proper to the other persons]. Therefore a person would lack something which it would be better for anything to be than not to be. And thus each of the persons would not be simply perfect, which is implausible.

Body of the Question

[2] 1.3 In answer to the question, I say: In the first place, certain preliminary remarks are necessary if the question is to be understood. Second, the question itself needs to be solved. Third, doubts raised against the solution have to be answered.

ARTICLE I
Preliminary Remarks

1.4 [Clarification of terms] Since the question is concerned with the order of immediacy of the notional and essential with respect to the divine essence, what should first be explained is the meaning of the four terms in the question, viz., "essence," "essential," "notional," and "more immediate."

1. The Meaning of "Essence"

[3] 1.5 As for the first term, in the divine there must needs be some real entity, which is there by the very nature of things and is ac-

---

[3] Augustine, *De Trinitate* xv, c.5, n.8: PL 42, 1062; CCSL 50a, 470.
[4] Anselm, *Monologion* c.15: PL 158, 162-63; *S. Anselmi Opera omnia*, vol. 1 (ed. F. S. Schmitt, apud Nelson et filios, Edinburgi, 1946), pp. 28-29.

tually existing. Otherwise, nothing there would be real actually. Either this real entity is assumed to be absolutely unique or to contain some real[5] or conceptual distinction. In either case, however, it will always be necessary to assume the existence of some entity which is real, first, unique, and requires no prior entity. For if everything present there would require some prior entity, none would be first and, therefore, none would be posterior.[6] Also this primary entity must needs be absolute or *ad se*, for as Augustine says[7]: "Every essence which is spoken of relatively, is also something apart from the relationship." And he also adds in the same place: "If the Father is not something absolute, then he can by no means be spoken of in relation to something else." We are faced then with this conclusion: In the divine it is necessary to assume some real entity, actually existing, which is unique, first, and absolute.

1.6 This real entity in God, since it is the primary reason for his being in an unqualified sense, is justifiably called "essence" by the Fathers. That is why Augustine says[8]: "What 'to be wise' is to 'wisdom,' what 'to be able' is to 'power,' 'to be eternal' to 'eternity,' 'to be just' to 'justice,' that 'to be' itself is to 'essence.' " And later on he adds[9]: "The name 'essence' is derived from 'to be.' " Hence, God is most truly called "essence" to whom "to be" belongs most properly, and truly. The same Augustine is the first to write[10]: "It is clear that it is an improper form of speech when we use the more familiar name 'substance' to express essence—which is what God really is and is properly called, so that perhaps God alone should be called essence. For he is truly unique, because incommunicable, and he revealed this as his name to Moses his servant when he said: 'I am who am.' But whether one uses 'essence,' speaking properly or 'substance,' speaking improperly, both are affirmed of what he is in himself and not of what he is in relation to something."

1.7 Of this essence, or less properly substance, Augustine[11] says that among all the other entities in the divine, this alone is being in

---

[5] "Real" seems to refer to the formal distinction *a parte rei*. Cf. Glossary: *"Formal distinction."*

[6] Cf. Duns Scotus, *Ord.* I, d.2, nn.39-156.

[7] Augustine, *De Trin.* VII, c.1, n.2: PL 42, 934-35; CCSL 50, 247.

[8] Ibid., PL 42, 935; CCSL 50, 249.

[9] Ibid., c.4, n.9: PL 42, 942; CCSL 50, 260.

[10] Ibid., c.5, n.10: PL 42, 942; CCSL 50, 261.

[11] Ibid., c.6, n.11: PL 943; CCSL 50, 262.

an unqualified sense. "The substance of the Father is the Father himself, not insofar as he is *Father*, but insofar as he *is*." What he wants to say here is that the essence is not the formal reason of his being Father but of his being, period. Damascene[12] agrees with this, when he says: "Of all the names given to God, the main one is that of 'He who is.'" And he proves it by those words of Exodus[13]: "He who is has sent me." And he adds[14]: "For like some infinite and limitless sea of substance, he contains all being in himself." Rightly, therefore, every attempt to arrange anything in the divine according to some order, will begin by taking the essence as simply first and absolute.[15]

[4] 1.8 [Objections] Two objections can be raised against what has just been said about the term "essence."

First, according to the text cited from Damascene[16]: "... like some infinite and limitless sea of substance, he contains all being in himself," the essence includes all divine perfection. But divine perfection as a whole includes anything that is pure perfection. For if any pure perfection were excluded, we would not have divine perfection *in toto*. Therefore, essence is not just that first entity which is somehow distinct from the essentials, but is one complete entity which unitively contains all the essentials. The very term "sea" seems to imply this, because of the immensity of what the sea contains unitively.

1.9 What Anselm[17] says confirms this: "God is that greater than which nothing can be conceived." But one can conceive of something greater than any individual pure perfection that does not include all that is pure perfection, viz., he can conceive of an entity which does contain unitively all such perfection. Therefore, the divine essence is that which includes all that is pure perfection.

1.10 [Second Objection] In every creature essence, insofar as it is distinct from existence, it seems, is prior to the latter, just as the potential and receptive is prior to the act received. Therefore, something similar, it seems, happens in God. But according to aforemen-

---

[12] Damascene, *De fide orthodoxa* I, c.9: PG 94, 835; Buytaert ed., c.9, 48-49.

[13] Exodus 5, 14.

[14] Damascene, *loc. cit.*

[15] Cf. Duns Scotus, *Ord.* I, d.1, n.148 (II, 98-99); d.2, nn.388-91 (II, 349-51); d.13, nn.88-89, 94-95 (V, 113-14, 117-18).

[16] Cf. *supra*, note 12.

[17] Anselm, *Proslogion* c.2: PL 158, 227; ed. Schmitt I, 101.

tioned citations from Augustine[18] and Damascene,[19] essence is equated with actual existence, as is clear from the quotation from Exodus which both employ: "He who is. . . ." According to these texts, existence, not essence, is the primary entity, or at least these citations do not show that essence is the first.

1.11 [Answer to the Objections] Look for the answer to the first objection elsewhere.[20]

1.12 One can also give another reply to the first objection [in 1.8]. If the argument had any value, it would run counter to what our question assumes, namely that there is some degree of immediacy of the essential to the essence, for our question asks: How much? In favor of this assumption, it is argued that every pure perfection is simply simple.* Proof: If it could somehow be analyzed into two (call them A and B), then neither A nor B can be a pure perfection, because then neither would form a *per se* unity with the other, for nothing that is one *per se* is constituted by distinct elements unless they are related as act and potency.[21]

2. The Meaning of "Essential" and "Notional"

1.13 [Twofold distinction of "essential"] As regards the second term "essential" a twofold distinction seems in order.

[First distinction] Usually philosophers use this term in one sense, theologians in another, especially when dealing with the divine. In philosophy, "essential" is commonly opposed to accidental, where accidental includes both the common accident, or *accidens per accidens*,* as well as property, that is *accidens per se* or *proprium*.* Essential, therefore, signifies in philosophy that which is included *per se* in the essence. For instance, matter and form are said to be the essentials of a real composite, and in the case of a conceptual composition [i.e., a definition] or of something defined, genus and difference are called the essential parts.

1.14 On the other hand, the theologians apply the term essential to the divine in a different sense. The essence, being the absolutely first, as has been said [in 1.5], is common with real community to all three persons alike, for it is affirmed singularly of each person as well as of all three together. For this reason, then, anything else

---

[18] Augustine, *De Trin.* VII, c.5, n.10: PL 42, 942.
[19] Damascene, *De fide orth.* I, c.9: PG 94, 835.
[20] See Appendix, Addition 1.11.
[21] He does not answer the second objection. Cf. Duns Scotus, *Ord.* I, d.2, nn.35ff. (II, 137ff.).

predicated similarly in the divine is called essential, because it is similar to the essence in the mode of predication or in community.

[6] On the contrary, what is neither predicated in this fashion nor has such community but pertains to what is known of the distinction of persons is called "notional." In this way the theologian contrasts the essential to the notional.

1.15 On this point Augustine writes,[22] "In created and changeable things, whatever is not a substantial predicate is an accidental predicate.... But in God nothing is predicated accidentally, and yet not everything said of him refers to his substance, for some relational terms are predicated of him like 'Father' which has reference to a son, or 'Son' which has reference to a father." To Augustine's mind, then, in creatures "essential" is opposed to "accidental," whereas in the divine it is not opposed to "accidental" but to what is relative internally or *ad intra* (i.e., what expresses the relation of one person to another and hence pertains to the notion of one person as distinct from another). For this reason, it is commonly called "notional," in accord with the rule in the text cited above[23] about what is said of God substantially as opposed to what is said relatively. Augustine, however, did not use the term "notional" but "relative" or *ad aliquid*.

[7] 1.16 From what has been said [in 1.14-15], the meaning of the third term, "notional," is clear. For everything notional is something relative internally and vice versa. The essential, however, is not relative internally, otherwise it would be both common [if relative externally] and not common [because proper to a person].

1.17 [Second distinction] A second distinction that can be made in regard to the term "essential" as applied in particular to the divine is this. On the one hand, there is something essential that implies a relation to what is external, and on the other hand, something essential that does not. Let me begin by explaining the first before going on to prove the second, which some perhaps may be inclined to deny.

1.18 [Explanation of the first member] That the first [viz., there is something essential that implies an extrinsic relation] is certain; if one speaks of God in relation to something external, there has to be some proper basis why the relation pertains to him. God is only compared to something outside by reason of something intrinsic to himself, and this can be called the basis for the relation. But by

[22] Augustine, *De Trin.* v, c.5, n.6: PL 42, 913-14; CCSL 50, 210.
[23] Ibid., PL 42, 913; CCSL 50, 208-209.

combining this intrinsic foundation (which is something real) and the external relation (which is conceptual), you do not come up with a concept that is *per se* or essentially one. If you have a name, then, which implies both this relation to the external and at the same time the intrinsic basis for it, then that name either does not signify a concept that is *per se* or essentially one or else it does not signify both components, but only signifies one and connotes the other. As applied to the divine, *essential*, to the extent that it involves a concept that is essentially one, therefore, does not include necessarily and simultaneously both the absolute and the external relation. Hence, if it includes the external relation at all, it does not include it necessarily. What it does include primarily and principally and necessarily is the absolute which is its basis whereas the relation is included by connotation. In this fashion the first member of the distinction should be understood.

[8]   1.19 [Proof of the second member] As for the second member of this distinction you may be inclined to say there is nothing essential which does not include some relation to what is external, since to be without such is the prerogative of the essence alone whereas whatever else is common to the three persons represents an external relation or includes such.[24] Now the solution of our question is dependent on the aforesaid distinction between essential as something absolute within and essential as something which relates to what lies outside. Since some might think this distinction ought to be denied, proof is provided for this second member, viz., for the presence of something essential which does not include any relation to what is external. The first is an argument from authority as to what constitutes a pure perfection. The second stems from what is meant by the divine essence; a third, from the notion of the divine intellect; a fourth, from what is meant by its act or the divine intellection.

1.20 [First proof][25] The first reason is this. No pure perfection as such includes a reference or relation to a creature. But in the divine something essential is a pure perfection. Therefore, [it does not include as such any reference to the external].

1.21 [Proof of the major] Pure perfection does not include as

---

[24] Henry of Ghent, *Quodlibet* v, q.1 (Parisiis, 1518, photoreprint Louvain: Bibliothèque S.J. 1961), fol. 150B-C; *Summa quaestionum ordinariarum* a.66, q.5 in corp. (Parisiis, 1520, photoreprint St. Bonaventure, N.Y.: Franciscan Institute, 1953), II, fol. 215B.

[25] This first reason is missing in M_2.

such anything repugnant to the very notion of such a perfection. Otherwise it would be better in anything, since it is a pure perfection, and it would not be better in anything, since it would include something to which the very notion of pure perfection is opposed.[26] Relation to a creature cannot be a pure perfection, because it involves a term that is imperfect and potential. What necessarily requires something potential in the way that a relation requires a term (i.e., as something simultaneous or naturally prior) is neither simply necessary nor, as a result, simply perfect.

1.22 The minor is evident from the mind of Anselm[27] where he introduces this distinction: "Except for the relative, whatever there is either is such that to be it is better absolutely than not to be it or it is such that not to be it is better for some subject than to be it." Having explained and clarified this distinction, he concludes: "Just as it is impious to suppose that anything that is not the substance of the supreme nature is in any way better than it, so it must needs be whatever, absolutely speaking, it is better to be than not to be." He goes on to infer in particular what it is not. "It is not a body then," he says, "nor any of those things which bodily senses perceive." And after this he explains in particular the kind of thing it is. As he puts it: "It must be living, wise, omnipotent, true, just, eternal, and anything, absolutely speaking, that it is better to be than not to be." Obviously many of these things are essentials for the divine. We have this minor premise then, that something essential to the divine is a pure perfection because in anything it is better than what is not it.

1.23 Anselm's view, it seems, can be found in Augustine[28]: "We recognize that living are to be preferred to non-living things, intelligent to non-intelligent things, just to unjust things, blessed to wretched things. And, therefore, since we doubtless prefer the creator to created things, we must confess that he lives in the supreme sense of the word, that he understands all things, that he is just, most benign, and most blessed." This inference holds, however, in virtue of the following proposition: "The creator must of necessity be everything that it is preferable for anything to be rather than not to be," or as Anselm says: "Better it than not it!"

---

[26] Cf. Duns Scotus, *Ord.* I, d.2, nn.382-84 (II, 346-47); d.8, nn.22-23, 167-68 (IV, 162-63, 239-41).
[27] Anselm, *Monolog.* c.15: PL 158, 162-63; ed. Schmitt I, 28-29.
[28] Augustine, *De Trin.* xv, c.4, n.6: PL 42, 1061; CCSL 50a, 457-68.

[9]²⁹ 1.24 The authority of Hilary³⁰ can also be adduced in favor of this view. Speaking of the Father he says: "There is the complete generation of the perfect God who is your Word,* Wisdom, and Power, so that he is always inseparable from you whose birth from you is revealed through these names of your eternal attributes." Now the Son of God [or Word] did not receive anything by birth which implies a relation that is extrinsic or *ad extra*.

1.25 Second, we could construct another argument with the same middle term [i.e., pure perfection] but making the major term "conceptual relation." The major premise would then be "Pure perfection does not include *per se* a conceptual relation." The minor would be the same as before [viz., something essential in the divine is a pure perfection]. The conclusion would be that there is something essential in the divine that does not include *per se* a conceptual relation. Now every extrinsic relationship of God to creatures is only conceptual, as is clear from what I have said in the second ordinary question.³¹ Therefore, something essential does not include an extrinsic relation.

This major [i.e., pure perfection does not include a conceptual relation] I prove as I did the first major based on the extrinsic relation. Pure perfection is incompatible with a conceptual relation, for such a relation, which has being only in the intellect, is "diminutive being."* It possesses less entity than any real being.

1.26 Third, by the same middle term [of pure perfection], we can formulate another argument using as major term "relation" in general. Pure perfection is not a relation at all nor does it include *per se* any extrinsic relation. [The minor premise would be as before.]

Proof of the major: The relationship of origin is not a pure perfection, as will be shown in Question Five. Now if any relation were a pure perfection, the relationship of origin would be such.

---

²⁹ Lychetus says that from 1.24 to 1.31 is not from Scotus; however, it is found in M₁ and W.

³⁰ Hilary, *De Trinitate* XII, n.52: PL 10, 467.

³¹ While there is some evidence that Scotus' "ordinary questions" were eventually incorporated in the *Ordinatio*, as we noted in the Introduction, this does not seem to be the case here, at least if the reference in 1.25 to the "second" ordinary question is correct, for the corresponding passage here seems to be *Ord.* I, d.30, VI, 169-202, whereas this contains nothing relevant to the problem discussed in 3.16 which seems to refer to matter treated in *Ord.* I, d.2 (II, 245-377).

1.27 [Objections] These reasons which use the same middle term can be refuted as follows. It is one thing to say something is a pure perfection and quite another to say that something pertains to pure perfection. The first implies that the thing in question is essentially or quidditatively a pure perfection; the second does not imply that it is essentially perfection but only that it pertains denominatively to pure perfection.

Something pertains to pure perfection (1) if it requires such perfection in the subject of which it is predicated denominatively, or (2) if it reveals that such perfection does exist in such a subject, or (3) if it is a universal consequence of such perfection. Thus something pertains to pure perfection in three ways: as a prior condition for it, or as revealing its presence, or as a consequence of it.

1.28 A similar explanation can be given to the dictum of Anselm [in 1.22]: "Better it than not it." This is true if we understand this of denominative predication insofar as it prerequires, reveals, or follows from such perfection. "In anything it is better to be such than not to be such," to the extent that to be such, denominatively presupposes there is being that is simply perfect, not in the way that "being white" presupposes "being colored," but in the sense that "being colored" presupposes "being extended." Hence it follows that if in something "being extended" is not better, then "being white" will not be better either.

1.29 The text of Augustine [in 1.23] concerning what is preferable should be explained in a similar way. As for what Anselm had in mind, you should read what he says in chapter seventeen [of the *Monologion*][32] about this divine substance being whatever it is essentially in one way and by virtue of one consideration, and that all these names given to it signify the same thing, namely, the names he used before like "good," "just," and so on.

1.30 Likewise, the argument [in 1.20] is objected to, because it infers that everything essential is something absolute, because everything essential is a pure perfection. But this entailment is invalid as is evident from the examples given by Anselm and Augustine, for Augustine speaks of him being "most powerful" and "most just" while Anselm calls him "omnipotent," "just," and so on. These terms however imply an external relation.

[10]   1.31 [Second proof of 1.19][33] A second proof [that there is some-

[32] Anselm, *Monolog.* c.17: PL 158, 166; ed. Schmitt I, p.31.

[33] The MSS. formulate this second proof differently, but the meaning is essentially the same as that of the Wadding-Vivès edition which we follow here.

QUESTION ONE

thing essential which does not include a relation to what is external] is the following: In God the essence is fully actualized and it is so by the very nature of things, that is to say, it is not just through the consideration of some intellect that the essence and anything necessarily included in it or in its actuality is present there. Understood in this way, the proposition is sufficiently evident from what was said at the beginning of this article [in 1.5-7] when explaining the meaning of the term "essence."

1.32 From this proposition follows the major premise of the proof, viz., if something is essentially the same as the essence, it exists in God as something actualized and extramental. This holds whether the essential sameness is one of adequate identity (as is the case in creatures when what the definition means is identical with what is meant by the defined) or whether it is the identity that comes from being one of its essential components (in the sense that what one part of the definition means is said to be identical with what is meant by the defined).[34] For it seems to be a contradiction that something should be actualized in reality, and yet that something essentially the same as it in either of these two ways should not also be actualized in reality. Intellectuality or the intellective life, however, is essentially identified with the divine essence. The meaning is this. Not only is it really the same as the essence and that by simple identity, as perhaps every attribute is considered to be the same thing as the essence itself, but if the divine essence were to be defined, intellectuality or the intellective life would be included in the definition in a way that "wise" and "good" are not.

[11] 1.33 The major premise is evident. For according to what was said at the outset of this article [in 1.5], essence is present in God by the very nature of things. Consequently everything included in that essence is also there by the very nature of the thing.

1.34 The minor is understood in this way. Intellectuality represents in truth a perfection that is absolutely intrinsic to the essence and not just some attribute that is ascribed to the essence only secondarily as it were. Just as life is not something only attributed or

---

[34] M_1 (fol. 61rb) has the following addition in the margin with the indication it is to be inserted here:

For even though something could exist in the thing extramentally whereas a definition or part thereof would not actually be in the thing but only in the considering intellect, nevertheless what is understood through the definition or part thereof, as the signified through the sign itself, must actually be in the thing just as what is understood through the term defined must actually be in the thing.

ascribed to God but is rather an absolutely essential feature, actually identified with and intrinsic to the essence, so too that perfect intellectual life which pertains to God alone is essentially the same thing as the first essence itself.

1.35 This minor, so understood, is established by both authority and reason. The authority is Augustine,[35] who says: "The life ascribed to God is his essence, his nature itself. This life, however, is not like that of a tree, or of a beast which has senses but no intellect. But the life which God is perceives and understands all things and it perceives them mentally, not corporally, because God is spirit." What he wants to say, then, is that the life which is the divine essence is necessarily intellectual. Augustine[36] also says, speaking of God, "Where the first and highest life is concerned, *to live* is not something other than *to be*, but *to be* and *to live* are one and the same thing." And explaining what kind of life it is, because it is intellectual, he adds: "[He is] the first and supreme intellect, where *to live* is not one thing and *to understand* another."

1.36 The minor premise is also proved by reason. What can be essentially one and the same as the substance does not belong to it most truly unless it belongs to it essentially. But intellectuality can be essentially identical with the being to which it belongs. This is clear from the case of creatures, for intellectuality is part of the essential definition of every intellectual substance. This is particularly obvious in the case of man in whose definition "rational" is included. Consequently, this intellectuality (which is what "rational" means) is essentially identical with man. What is more, rationality is what is most distinctive and adds the final touch to his essence. Therefore, since God is most truly intellectual, his intellectuality will be essentially identical with his essence.

[12] 1.37 [Third proof of 1.19] The third reason is based upon the divine intellect. No intellect possesses that being which is primary, proper, and distinctive of it by virtue of some act of thought appropriate to it or to a person. This is obvious. For every act of understanding naturally requires as a prior or concomitant condition that the intellect to which it belongs possesses that distinctive being proper to it as an intellect so that neither this, nor any thing essentially included therein, is something it has in virtue of being understood. For every act [of understanding] is posterior to what it presupposes. It is not precisely through the act of divine intellection,

---

[35] Augustine, *De Trin.* xv, c.5, n.7: PL 42, 1061; CCSL 50a, 468.
[36] Ibid., vi, c.10, n.11: PL 42, 931; CCSL 50, 241.

then, that God's intellect possesses that primary, distinctive being it has as intellect. The same holds true of anything necessarily included therein. On the other hand, however, the reference of the divine essence to anything extrinsic to itself is something that owes what primary and actual being it has to the divine understanding. Therefore, the intellect in God, insofar as it is actually intellect, includes no reference to something extrinsic to itself.

1.38 Proof of the minor: Since the reference of anything intrinsic to something extrinsic to God represents a conceptual relation, it gets its proper and primary being from the act of the intellect making the reference. But anything intrinsic to God that can be related to something extrinsic by any act of a created intellect can also be related to it by an act of the divine intellect. For the divine intellect is able to understand an object to the degree to which it is intelligible, since it is fully equal to grasping and comprehending it. Whatever the divine mind can refer to anything intellectually, however, it actually does refer to it intellectually, for no potency in God remains unactualized where anything intrinsic to him is concerned. Consequently, anything intrinsic that can be intellectually related to anything else is actually related to it by an act of the divine intellect. Hence the reference of any such thing to any other such gets the actual being proper to itself from the act of the divine intellect making the reference. I do not claim this is true of every reference of the one term with the other, but only of some, since this situation does not hold formally of references made by a created intellect.

1.39 What is additionally evident from this is the second part of the minor, viz., that the relating of something intrinsic to something extrinsic owes what primary and proper actual being it has to this divine understanding, since the latter is the first understanding had of this object. *First* here represents not only an essential primacy or one of perfection, but also a primacy of duration, since it is eternal. For were it either simultaneous with, or posterior to, the created understanding in perfection, it would be limited and measured. Were it either simultaneous with, or posterior to, any created understanding in duration, it would follow that in God understanding as understanding would be something new.[37]

[13] 1.40 [Fourth proof of 1.19] The fourth argument is derived from the operation or act of understanding itself and it runs this way. The act whereby God grasps his essence as a beatific object is pres-

---

[37] See Appendix, Addition 1.39.

ent in God extramentally as just that sort of act. But it is by understanding precisely as understanding that he grasps his essence as a beatific object. Therefore, [it exists there extramentally].

1.41 Proof of the major: Intensive infinity* is a characteristic of a real being and not of a being of the mind. My reason is this. Every being of the mind represents a conceptual relation. Now infinity never characterizes any relation, even one that is real, as will become clear later [in 5.16] in Question Five. Since what is simply infinite in perfection, then, does not include necessarily something to which infinity is intrinsically repugnant, it follows that what is simply infinite is not a thing of the mind. Neither does it include essentially a being of this sort.

1.42 [A combination of these proofs] Taking those propositions we have explained and proved [in 1.20, 1.31, 1.37, and 1.40] as the major and minor of a syllogism, the following arguments can be constructed. What is essentially the same as the divine essence is something extramentally actualized in God. But intellectuality or the intellectual life is that sort of thing. Therefore, it exists in God extramentally.

[14]   1.43 From this it follows further: Whatever is intellectual or lives an intellectual life has or can have in actuality intellect as intellect and understanding as understanding. But that God is intellectual or is living an intellectual life in actuality is an extramental fact (the conclusion established by the first syllogism). Consequently, God has or can have in actuality intellect as intellect and understanding as understanding.

But he cannot have in actuality anything that is real or is there extramentally which he does not already have extramentally, for this would militate against his simplicity. Therefore, God has in actuality intellect as intellect and understanding as understanding, and this as an extramental fact.

But no relation of God to anything extrinsic nor anything which necessarily includes such a relation is actualized in God extramentally, because his relation to anything extrinsic is merely conceptual. Therefore, something essential, such as understanding, is such an absolute that it neither is an extrinsic relation nor includes such necessarily.

1.44 The major of the second syllogism [in 1.43] is proved in this fashion. A nature that is truly living in reality either has or can have a vital operation that is a real being, which means it is neither a thing of the mind nor does it necessarily include such. For an operation of this sort is the proper perfection of an intellectual nature; that is why the ultimate happiness of such a nature is supposed to consist in this operation. But the proper perfection (especially if beatific) of a nature which is living in reality cannot be a thing of the mind nor can it necessarily include such. For so attenuated is this being of the mind that it cannot constitute the essential perfection of a real being. But thinking as thinking is the operation proper to a nature alive with intellectual life.

1.45 To one insolent enough to deny such life to God, it could be pointed out that the Philosopher[38] concedes it to be the case here. Where he treats the question of the divine intellect and its thinking, he speaks in this fashion: "If it (that is to say, the 'divine mind') thinks of nothing, what is there here of dignity? It is just like one who sleeps," he says. "And if it thinks, but this depends on something else (since that which is its substance is not its act of thinking, but a potency) it cannot be the best substance, for it is through thinking that value belongs to it." Hence he says[39]: "Perfect happiness appears to be a contemplative activity. The following consideration will also make this clear. For we assume the gods above all to be blessed and happy. But what sort of actions ought we to attribute to them?" After ruling out any actions stemming from moral virtues, he adds: "Still, everyone supposes them to be living and active, for they ought not to be asleep." And a little later he concludes: "Therefore the activity of God, which surpasses all others in blessedness, must be contemplative. And of human activities, then, the happiest must be what is most akin to this."

3. The Meaning of "More Immediate"

[15] 1.46 A dual distinction needs to be made in regard to the fourth term [of 1.4], "more immediate." Either it refers to a mean between the first and last, and then it is more immediate *positively*; or it implies that between the first and itself there are no intermediaries or else they are fewer than between the first and the third, in which case it is more immediate *negatively*. For instance, surface is more immediate to the substance than is color, so that it represents a positive mean between them. "Able to laugh," on the other hand, is more immediate to man in a negative sense, for it does not function as a positive intermediary between extremes. Rather it excludes any intermediary between itself and man and that even more so

---

[38] Aristotle, *Metaphysica* XII, c.9 (1074b18-22).
[39] Aristotle, *Ethica ad Nicomachum* x, c.8 (1178b8-11).

than between man and color. In brief, one could say the positively more immediate is that which is included as a mean between two extremes and the negatively more immediate is rather that which excludes something as a means.

1.47 Since "more immediate" and "less immediate" (or "more mediate") implies an order, and there is no order without some distinction, one could also distinguish between what is more immediate in reality and what is so according to mind. But since we are not asking how essential and notional are distinguished or how both differ from the essence, we are not concerned at present with this distinction of immediacy. Still, howsoever essential be distinguished from notional and both from essence, so may one of them, namely essential or notional, be said to be more immediate to the essence.

1.48 [Summary of the First Article] To sum up what has been said in the first article, it is the essence to which the elements whose order is under investigation are being compared. Essential and notional are the elements whose order to essence is under comparison. The question at issue is that of their immediacy to the essence. Of prime importance for solving the question are the two distinctions of "essential" and "more immediate" presented in this article. The first of these is the distinction [in 1.17] of essential into that whose whole actuality or ground is internal [*ad intra*] and that which has reference to some thing external [*ad extra*]. The second distinction [in 1.46] is between (a) what is more immediate positively in the sense that it is itself a mean and (b) what is more immediate privatively in the sense that it requires no intermediary between itself and the first as between two extremes.

ARTICLE II
Solution of the Question

[16] 1.49 [Three conclusions] In this second article there are three conclusions: two are brief, the third is the principal one.

1.50 [First conclusion] The first is this. Taking immediacy in the first sense, nothing notional is more immediate to the divine essence than anything essential.

Proof: What is more immediate to the first is not exceeded by the third, for it is an intermediary between the former and the latter. But anything notional is exceeded by something essential for the essential is common to all three persons whereas the notional is not. Therefore, [nothing notional is more immediate than something essential].

1.51 [Second conclusion] The second conclusion is this. Taking immediacy in the second sense, something notional is more immediate to the essence than anything essential which includes a relation to something extrinsic.

Proof: An essential of this sort pertains to God only through the operation of the intellect comparing him to something external. The notional, on the contrary, pertains to the essence by the very nature of things, independently of any extrinsic comparison. A medium is required even less between the essence and the notional than between the essence and an essential requiring the intervention of an act of the intellect.

1.52 [Third conclusion] Our third conclusion is this. Something essential is more immediate to the essence (in either sense of immediacy) than anything notional.

This is proved in two ways.

[First Proof] The same order that would hold for entities were they really distinct would hold for them were they distinct in some other way, except that their intrinsic order in the first case would be real, whereas in the second it would correspond to the type of distinction that obtains between them. For instance, the order would be one of reason, if they were distinguished by reason. were it a reason on the part of the thing or one that resulted from an act of the intellect. Now if there were a real distinction between the essence, the perfect memory* and the perfect speaking* [of the Word], then it would be in virtue of a real order that memory is intrinsically closer to essence than is the utterance [of the Word]. Therefore, the same sequence obtains except that the order of immediacy corresponds to the type of distinction between them.

1.53 The major is proved *a posteriori* in this way. Where there is a distinction of reason (taking "reason" in either of its two senses), we deduce the order of the entities so distinguished from the order they would have were they really distinct. Second, the major is proved *a priori*. By their intrinsic order, I understand that which stems from the *per se* or intrinsic meaning of the terms. And by this I understand the essential or quidditative meaning intrinsic to them, without determining whether the referents exist in reality or in the mind. For whatever exists in either of these two ways would seem to possess an intelligible essential meaning that is independent of which way it exists. From this the major is evident, for where the intrinsic reason for the order is similar, the order itself will be similar. But in things having distinct being in reality or in the mind (call them A and B), there does remain a similar intrinsic reason for their order, namely their respective essential meanings. For it is not its being in the intellect that gives A its essential or quidditative meaning. Therefore, [a similar order obtains between them].

1.54 The minor is evident. For were the essence, the memory, and the speaking of the Word really distinct, this sequence would represent a real order. Since the essence would be a perfect intellectual nature, it would possess a perfect intellect. Furthermore, it would or could have actually present an intelligible object proportionate to itself. What is more, it could or would be a perfect memory, for what "perfect memory" means is "an intellect having actually present an intelligible object proportionate to itself." From this it follows further that if the memory were, or could be, a principle of expression for the person perfectly possessing it, it would or could express the declarative knowledge* which corresponds to that memory. Now the first notional element (at least that which includes the first positive relation to a person) is that of speaking [the Word]. Therefore, something essential, in both senses, is more immediate to the essence than is the first notional element, and hence is more immediate than any notional element whatsoever. The same argument that holds for "memory" and "speaking" can be applied to "will," the "object" present to it, and the act of "spirating"* [the Holy Spirit].

1.55 [Second Proof] A second proof of the same is this. The potency or ability to produce is more immediate to the essence than is the actual productive action. Everything notional, however, is either a productive action of some divine potency or it presupposes such, for it is either the production of a person or presupposes such a production. And action of this sort, however, proceeds from a potency that is essential, for it is an action either of the intellect or of the will. Therefore, [something essential is more immediate to the essence than anything notional].

1.56 [Summary of the Second Article] Regarding this article, then, it is clear that the notional is more immediate to the essence than an essential attribute that refers to something extrinsic in the second sense of immediacy. Nothing notional, however, is more immediate in both ways than anything essential. On the other hand something essential intrinsically (*ad intra*) is more immediate in both ways than anything notional, for the intellect at least is more immediate than "speaking" which is the first of the notionals, and

QUESTION ONE

hence it is more immediate than anything notional. The will too is more immediate than "breathing" [the Holy Spirit] or than anything, consequently, pertaining to the procession of the Holy Spirit.

ARTICLE III
Reply to various Objections

[18] 1.57 In this third article, objections are raised against the two reasons given [in 1.52-55] of the second article for the third conclusion.[40]

[To the First] The argument against the first reason [in 1.52ff.] is put in this way. Where the basis for the order does not remain the same, there is no need to assume the order is the same or similar. But in the divine, where the distinction of essence, memory, and speaking is merely mental, there is not the same basis for the order as there would be were they really distinct. Therefore, [there is no need to assume the order is the same or similar].

1.58 Proof of the minor: In a rational creature, memory precedes speaking, because it is the principle of speaking. But this is not true of God if we are speaking of memory as such, or as distinct from the essence. Furthermore, the principle of the emanation of a person is just the divine essence as an essence to which a real relation is united.

1.59 This is proved in two ways. *First*, the Word is expressive of everything involved as it were in the divine essence. Therefore, in the divine Word, God understands everything he understands distinctly. In the divine intellect, then, between essence and memory, no actual distinction can be admitted that would somehow precede the production of the Word. The first [premise] is proved from Augustine[41] who says that "the Word is the Father's art, replete with all living reasons."*

1.60 *Second*, a conceptual distinction can only exist by an act of thought. But in God the first act of thought, which presupposes the presence of the personal property, is the source of the emanation of the Word, since the Word is produced naturally, i.e., by a nat-

---

[40] Henry of Ghent, *Summa* a.54, q.9 in corp. (II, fol. 104B-D); q.10, ad 2 (fol. 105K-L); a.58, q.1 in corp. (fol. 123G-125V); q.2, ad 3 (fol. 128Y-132R); q.5, ad 1 (fol. 136R); a.59, q.2, ad 1 (fol. 137H); a.60, q.4, ad 1 (fol. 167M-O). Cf. Duns Scotus, *Ord.* I, d.6 (IV, 87-105); d.12 (V, 25-64); II, d.1, q.1 (ed. Vivès XI, 6-45); I, d.32 (VI, 223-41).

[41] Augustine, *De Trin.* VI, c.10, n.11: PL 42, 931; CCSL 50, 241.

ural* [or nonfree] act of the intellect. Therefore, no distinction is possible within or without by reason of any act which would precede, as it were, the production of the Word.

1.61 If you ask them how are intellect and will distinct in God if their distinction is not presupposed by the production of the persons, they answer: Assuming such productions, viz., the speaking and spiration, by the essence as the sole formal principle of both, the intellect can compare them to something similar in the creatures. The production of the [mental words* by the] intellect in creatures is similar to one of the [divine] productions, viz., to speaking [the Word], because it does not presuppose any other production. The production of the will is similar to the other [i.e., to breathing the Holy Spirit], once the "speaking" is presupposed. Thus by comparing them to something extrinsic, the intellect conceives one of these productions as a kind of production of the intellect, the other as a kind of production of the will, because of their resemblance to acts of the created intellect and will. For this reason the intellect conceives the [single] principle of these productions under two aspects, that of intellect and of will.

1.62 [To the Second] What was just said also militates against the second reason. For it is the essence itself and not memory as memory, or as intellect, that is the principle of the "speaking." For it is correctly conceded that the essence is prior to the notional. But from this it does not follow that something essential, which is somehow distinct from the essence, is more immediately related to that essence than anything notional is.

1.63 [Reply to the Objections in 1.57-62] There are many ways of refuting this first objection. It does not seem that two different kinds of productions, particularly where one presupposes the other, can be reasonably assumed to stem from one and the same formal principle. Also, if there is but one formal principle of this kind, and its productions are [not voluntary but] necessary, there seems no reason why they should be limited to any definite number. But I postpone going into this until the following question. Here, I merely reconfirm my first reason [in 1.52ff., against which this first objection is directed].

1.64 The claim was made [in 1.57] against the first reason for the major, that where the grounds are not the same, the same order does not prevail. I grant this to be true where it is a case of the first and necessary cause or reason for the order. Admittedly this holds good of the first and necessary reason for the order of anything. Accordingly, and arguing to the contrary, I assume this major: Where the first, necessary grounds for the order remain the same, the same necessary order prevails. But the first necessary grounds for the order in question (namely, of "memory" and its "speaking") stem from what they necessarily mean, viz., that memory is memory and speaking is speaking. Howsoever they be conceived, be it as having really distinct or only conceptually distinct existence, it appears at once from their very meaning that memory is more immediately related to essence than is speaking. Therefore, whether they have real or conceptual being, so long as these necessary reasons present themselves to the mind, the necessary basis for the order will always remain the same or similar.

1.65 Another point: in the minor [at 1.58] the claim is made that the meaning of "memory" and "speaking" does not remain the same for the divine as for creatures, since there is nothing in the divine corresponding to (1) a source or principle and (2) what proceeds therefrom. Let us grant that the essence is the basis for the order. That is to say, let it be the formal grounds of the acting or action principle. For my purposes this suffices, since, as Augustine[42] says "just as our 'word' is born of our knowledge, so was that Word born of the Father's knowledge." What he wants to say is that to be born of knowledge that exists in the memory is what it means to be the Word. Throughout the text the Word is said to be born of the memory. Now the Son, whose "being produced" consists in his "being spoken," is the Word, according to him. In question 63 of his treatise *Eighty-Three Questions*,[43] Augustine considers the expression "in the beginning was the Word" to be an excellent translation of the name "Second Person." Memory then is the productive principle for the second person. Consequently the basis for an order between "memory" and "speaking" remains.

1.66 Of this I add a confirmation. If the second person proceeded not from the memory as memory but from the memory as essence, what greater need is there for ascribing the production to an act of memory rather than to an act of the will? Essence as essence is not more memory than will. What its production is in reality then is not more a "speaking" than a "breathing" or spiration, nor is what is realized through such a production more a Son or Word than a Holy Spirit, all of which is clearly contrary to the mind of Augustine.

[42] Ibid., xv, c.14, n.24: PL 42, 1077; CCSL 50a, 497.
[43] Augustine, *De diversis quaestionibus 83*, q.63: PL 40, 54.

1.67 [Reply to the proofs for the minor in 1.59f.] We turn now to the reasons given for saying that the formal principle for the production of the Son is the essence under the aspect of essence, to which however a real relation is conjoined.

[20] [To the first in 1.59] Whatever God understands by a distinct intellection, it is claimed, he understands in the Word, once the latter has been produced. Now it is true the Word is produced from all eternity, but we are not inquiring here about the order of duration but about the order of origin. And if the meaning of the statement above is that the Father, as prior in origin to the Word, does not understand things distinctly in themselves, then it is false. It runs counter both to reason and to Augustine,[44] who declares that each person on his own remembers, understands, and loves, and thus he infers that "if it were by the Son alone that the Father understood, he would not be wise of himself, but only through the Son."

1.68 This allows us to formulate our first counter-argument [to 1.59]. Whatever perfection the Father can have, he has as prior in origin to the Son, for he possesses it in himself. For he can possess no perfection except in virtue of himself. If the Father then can comprehend actually and distinctly everything that can be understood, he must know it as prior in origin to the Son. Consequently his distinct knowledge of anything understandable is not, precisely speaking, derived from the Son.

1.69 Augustine also makes this clear[45]: "Though he knows this also in the Son, God the Father knows everything in himself. He knows this in himself as he knows himself." From this a second counter-argument [to 1.59] can be formed. The Father, insofar as he is prior in origin to the Son, knows himself not only through his memory (or *in actu primo*)* but also through his understanding (or *in actu secundo*).* Proof: the order of origin of Father to Son holds alike for their having perfect understanding and their possessing perfect memory, since it is universally true that one who has perfect memory has perfect understanding also. If it is not precisely through the Son but in virtue of himself as prior in origin to the Son that the Father knows himself through memory, as it were, then the same holds true of the actual knowledge that comes from understanding. It follows further that what the Father as prior in origin to the Son has in virtue of his unbegotten understanding is not only

---

[44] Augustine, *De Trin.* xv, c.7, n.12: PL 42, 1066; CCSL 50a, 475-76.

[45] Ibid., xv, c.14, n.23: PL 42, 1077; CCSL 50a, 496.

QUESTION ONE

an actual knowledge or intellection of himself but also actual knowledge of every distinct thing.

1.70 I concede the claim made in the proof [1.59] that the Word is expressive of everything involved as it were in the divine essence. But it is not just the Word that is such. These things are not revealed only in the Word; they shine forth with equal distinctness in the understanding of the Father *qua* Father. As for the text they cite from Augustine[46] to prove this is revealed solely in the Word, their interpretation is refuted by Augustine[47] himself when he speaks of the Word as the art of the Father even as he is the wisdom of the Father. Explaining how he is the wisdom of the Father, he says: "The Son is called the wisdom of the Father in the same sense as he is called the light of the Father. That is to say, just as he is light of light and both are one light, so He is understood to be the wisdom of wisdom and both are one wisdom."

1.71 If one asks why it is the Word rather than the Father himself who is called the Father's Art, I reply: To be declarative knowledge pertains to the second person because of the way this person is produced, namely by an act of the "memory" which expresses knowledge of this sort. Those things which pertain to the perfection of actual knowledge, consequently, are "appropriated"* to the Son. But he is called *Wisdom*, to use the Apostle's[48] designation, more properly than he is called *Art*, as Augustine is wont to do, for his production represents a declarative knowledge of things eternal rather than of things able to be made.

1.72 [To the second proof] The second argument [in 1.60 for the minor of the objection] is based on this proposition: "The first act of understanding in the divine is the proper principle for producing the Word." This proposition is false on two counts. First, the productive principle for the Word is not, properly speaking, an act of understanding. Second, it is not the understanding's first act as the objector interprets this.

1.73 Proof of the first point: What is usually meant by an act of understanding is the operation itself that is called intellection. Therefore, if the first act of understanding, as the objector [in 1.60] interprets it, were the principle of emanation, it would have to be understood in one of these two ways: either (a) it is the formal principle of the production of the Word in the way the heat in a heater

---

[46] Ibid., VI, c.10, n.11: PL 42, 931; CCSL 50, 241; cf. *supra* 1.52.
[47] Ibid., VII, c.1, n.1-2: PL 42, 933-36; CCSL 50, 244-49.
[48] I Cor. 1:24.

is the principle of heating, or (b) it is the principle of emanation, as for instance, an act which produces heating is called the productive principle of the heat produced. Neither of these ways makes sense, however. For understanding is the work of intelligence itself. As Augustine[49] says: "I call intelligence that by which we understand when we are actually thinking." To produce the Word, or to possess the formal principle for doing so, is something that pertains to [his mind] only to the extent that it is also "memory."

[22]   1.74 Proof of the second point [1.72, viz., that the Word is not produced by the first act of the understanding in the sense that the objector interprets first act]: This seems clear from what has just been said [in 1.70]. The distinct intellection that pertains to the Father in virtue of his own unbegotten intelligence is prior in origin to the production of the Word. The Word, then, is not produced by the first act of understanding as he interprets it [in 1.60], viz., as first in origin.

1.75 When he infers this on the grounds that the Word is produced naturally [i.e., not voluntarily or freely], his argument is invalid, for if the intellect is the source or principle of any act at all, it exercises this function by way of nature [i.e., not as a free agent].

1.76 Or, in brief, one can say to the second proof: If one is speaking of the first productive act, then the Word would be produced by the first act of the intellect. This act, although it is one of the intellect, is not precisely an act of understanding. But the Word is not produced by the intellect's first operative act which properly speaking is an act of understanding. The act of understanding insofar as it is an act of paternal intelligence is prior in origin [to the productive act]. In such an anterior act, the Father understands distinctly his own essence. He does not understand it in the produced Word. This distinction between the productive and operative act will appear clear later in Question Thirteen. The operative act has no product [i.e., it does not produce anything] but the act or operation itself is the ultimate term, as is evident from Books I and X of the *Ethics*.[50] On the other hand, the productive act is always productive of some term as such, a term which derives its being from the productive act.

1.77 [Answer to the objection to the second reason in 1.62] What

---

[49] Augustine, *De Trin.* XIV, c.7, n.10: PL 42, 1044; CCSL 50a, 435.

[50] Aristotle, *Ethica ad Nic.* I, c.1 (1094a-18); I, c.9 (1099a24-31); X, c.7 (1177a12-b5).

QUESTION ONE

we have already proved [in 1.64ff.] refutes the objection raised against our second reason. Essence as such is not the immediate principle of producing [the Word] if memory as memory is excluded from what is meant by the total principle.

Reply to the Initial Argument

[23] 1.78 Answer to the argument at the beginning [in 1.1]: It assumes the divine person is constituted by something notional. For the time being let us grant this. Then I reply to the major with a distinction. Sometimes the person is constituted by something that falls into the same genus [or category] as the nature itself does. In this case, the major apparently could be conceded, for not only is the nature more immediate in some sense to the person, but also to that formal element that makes it a person. But if the person were constituted by something generically different and more remote from the nature than is the genus of a property of the nature, the major would be false. If it were a relation that formally constituted the personality of Socrates, then this would not be more immediate to his humanity than quantity or quality, since a relation is more removed from the genus [or category] of substance than either quality or quantity.

1.79 Now suppose a divine person or suppositum* is constituted by a relation. Then one must admit that the person is not constituted by something in the same genus as the nature (in the sense that one can speak of class or categorical distinctions in God). It is constituted by something relative, whereas the nature is something absolute.[51] In some sense, then, this constitutive element is more distant from the nature than a property of that nature would be, for if there were strict generic distinctions in God, wisdom would belong to the genus "quality" and paternity to the genus "relation." Therefore, in God a property in its own way can be more immediate to the nature than the element which is constitutive of the person.

[24] 1.80 Suppose one asks why this person cannot be constituted by something pertaining to the same genus as the nature. This question has to do with something already presupposed by our question, namely, what constitutes a person, and hence is not to the point. For the present, however, I grant what it presupposes. Then one could say that where there is something that is [a "this"] of itself, but which is not incommunicable, no further determination, save to

---

[51] Cf. Duns Scotus, *Ord.* I, d.26 (VI, 1-61); d.30 (VI, 169-202).

what is incommunicable, makes sense. But the divine essence is just this [i.e., something singular] of itself and yet is communicable. If some further determination with respect to person should be considered, it must needs be something which is basically incommunicable, since person is incommunicable. It cannot be something absolute, because—on this hypothesis—everything absolute in God is pure perfection and therefore communicable. What constitutes the person, then, must needs be generically different from nature; not with just any kind of distinction, but with that which obtains between an absolute thing and a relative thing.

The proof cited for the major premise of the initial argument [in 1.1] is invalid except in the case where the element that is constitutive of the person is in the same genus [or category] as the nature.

Question Two

COULD THERE BE SEVERAL PRODUCTIONS OF THE SAME TYPE IN GOD?

2.1 Once we see what, in the divine, is the order of essential and notional* features, the sequence to be followed in the questions about God is clear. If any questions had been raised about the essence or the intrinsic essential characteristics they would have been treated before the questions bearing on the persons or notional. But there was no problem about the essential except that it implies a relation to something external and everything notional is in its own way prior to any essential of this sort. Therefore, questions about the notional should be treated first. Notional features, however, are either relationships or productions.* Whether these be the same thing or not, I do not care.

[1] 2.2 The first of the questions about the notionals or productions is this: Can there be more than one production of the same type in God?¹

Arguments Pro and Con

I argue for the affirmative:

The production of a suppositum* so far as the being of its substantial nature is concerned is called generation.* In the divine, however, there is a twofold production of this sort. Therefore, there is a twofold "generation" and hence a twofold production of the same type.

The minor is obvious since in the divine nature every production of a person terminates in his substantial being.

Proof of the major: Generation, according to the Philosopher,² is distinguished from other kinds of changes precisely because it has as its term a substance or substantial being. Therefore, [the production of a person in substantial being is generation].

2.3 Arguments for the negative:

If there can be many productions of the same type, there can be

¹ Cf. Duns Scotus, *Ord.* I, d.2, nn.197-200, 212-19, 270, 375 (II, 250-51, 255-58, 287-344).
² Aristotle, *Physica* v, 1 (225a10-20).

many "generations"* and many "spirations"* and consequently, many "Sons" and many "Holy Spirits." But the consequence is false, for otherwise there would be more than three persons. Therefore, [there cannot be many productions of the same type].

Body of the Question

[2] 2.4 All theologians accept the negative conclusion. It is necessary, however, to ascertain whether their position is based on reason or faith alone. Different authors give different reasons. In the first place, therefore, we shall treat of the reasons which some cite for this conclusion; secondly, we shall see what it is preferable to hold on this subject; and thirdly, certain doubts which occur will be dispelled.

ARTICLE I
An Evaluation of the Reasons for the Negative Conclusion

2.5 [Reasons] Four reasons are adduced in this connection[3]:

First, a form of the same species or, speaking more properly in the case of the divine, forms of the same type are multiplied only by reason of matter. In the divine there is no matter. In the divine, therefore, there is but one subsistent sonship, just as there could be but one subsistent whiteness.

2.6 Second, with one simple act God understands and wills all things. Hence, in him there can be but one person who proceeds by way of "word"* and one who proceeds by way of love.

2.7 Third, the persons proceed by a natural process. But nature is determined to one [effect or mode of action]. Therefore, [there is but one person for each type of production].

2.8 Fourth, the Son is perfect because he contains the totality of the divine sonship. Consequently, there cannot be any other.

[3] 2.9 [Evaluation of These Reasons: The First Reason] The first [in 2.5], it seems, proves too much and assumes a proposition which many consider dubious or false. The major, viz., "a form of the same species is multiplied only by reason of matter," which they claim holds for the angel as well as for God, can be interpreted in two ways: (i) Every immaterial form is a "this" [or singular] of itself or

---

[3] Thomas, *Summa theologica* I, q.41, a.6 in corp. (Taurini-Romae, 1948) I, pp. 210-11; Henry of Ghent, *Quodl.* VI, q.1 in corp. (fol. 216X-Y and 217H-I); Id., *Summa* a.54, q.2 in corp. (II, fol. 78K); William of Ware, *Sententiarum* I, d.7, q.4 in corp.

QUESTION TWO

by reason of what it is, even as God is a "this" in virtue of his deity so that, were one to think of deity alone, it would be a formal contradiction if God were not a "this." (ii) Some immaterial form is not formally a "this" by reason of its quiddity, yet it still cannot be realized in multiple instances because such a unique singular and individual form would contain in itself intensively and extensively the total entity of that form, as is clear from the case of the sun.

2.10 [Consider the first of these interpretations] If the major is understood in the first sense, it follows that to be multiplied in reality is opposed to, and even contradicts, the specific form of the angels. Even as "being nonrational" conflicts with the concept of man, or "being several" is inconsistent with the concept of God, so "able to be in several individuals" would not be compatible with the concept of this species. Hence whoever would postulate that angelic species could be multiplied would have in his mind notions that are formally repugnant, namely the concept of the angelic species and the idea that it could exist in multiple instances. The same could be said for those who conceive of the angelic species as having the character of a universal in an unqualified sense, viz., as being predicable of many. Indeed, by conceiving the nature as universal in this way, the intellect would contain what is formally repugnant, i.e., the object understood and the manner in which it is conceived.

2.11 This consequent hardly seems plausible, since many theologians, Catholics and others, actually think of the angelic species in this fashion. Without any opposition in concepts, they admit its universality and ability to be multiplied in diverse individuals. The Fathers too seem to favor this view. As Damascene says[4]: "The unique is both incommunicable and communicable; to him pertains the communication of one species and the same divine nature is present in three persons." And he adds afterwards: "In each order of angels and virtues he created different persons; not only that, he created them in each species also so that by the mutual communication of their nature they rejoice in one another, and joined to one another by natural happiness they felt secure and amicably disposed to one another."

[4] 2.12 Besides a condemnation of this consequent seems to be implied, *prima facie*, in the condemnation of three articles.[5]

---

[4] Damascene, *De institutione elementari* c.1: PG 95, 99.

[5] Cf. Denifle, H.-Chatelain, A., *Chartularium universitatis parisiensis* 1 (Parisiis, 1889), p. 548, n.81; p. 549, n.96; p. 554, n.191.

The first was condemned by Lord [Bishop] Stephen [Tempier], who lists as an "error" this proposition: "Intelligences* have no matter and God could not create several of the same species."

The second condemned article cites as an "error": "God cannot multiply individuals under one species without matter."

The third condemned article is this: "Forms are only divided by reason of matter. This is an error unless it be understood of forms educed from the potency of matter." Therefore, to say this of forms not educed from the potency of matter is an error.

2.13 [To the second interpretation in 2.9] If one accepts the second meaning of the major proposition, it follows that the specific nature of Michael [the Archangel] is not of itself an individual or a "this." Therefore, it is not contradictory to such a nature not to be just "this" or not to be in this subject [rather than "that"]. Hence, this nature can be made to exist and not be in this subject by a power able to accomplish anything that does not imply a contradiction.

2.14 Perhaps it will be objected that a situation of this sort cannot occur as long as Michael actually exists. Even so this does not rule out what we wish to prove. Nevertheless, it is false. The first point [i.e., that it does not rule out our contention] is clear enough. Let Michael be destroyed and let his nature be realized in another individual. Hence, it is not absolutely necessary that Michael be this unique subject. Evidence for the second point, [i.e., that the statement is false]: What are simultaneously within an agent's power and are not mutually repugnant can be simultaneously realized. Such would be "this Michael" and "that Michael," if Michael's nature is not of itself just "this."

2.15 Let us suppose the second interpretation were correct. For the purpose of our argument it would at least be true to say that "A form of the same species can only be multiplied by reason of matter" does not rule out absolutely the possibility of more than one divine sonship. And yet such multiplication is simply impossible, since it implies a contradiction. Only if taken in the first sense, therefore, does this proposition entail the conclusion which all concede to be true. But many with good reason regard the proposition in this sense to be false, as we have said. Now it is hardly suitable to hold a most certain and necessary conclusion for a reason that would prove more than is necessary and seems objectionable on several counts.

[5] 2.16 [Objections based on the intellective soul] There are additional objections based on the intellectual soul. For prior by nature

to its infusion into a body, it represents the end product of a creative act. Now what is primarily the term of a creative act as such is formally an individual or a "this." Therefore, in the order of nature the soul is an individual in virtue of its own singularity before its union with something material. For a similar reason, another soul is "that individual" prior to its union with matter. In virtue of its own singularity, then, this soul is just "this" and hence it is "this" rather than "that." Consequently, by this primary distinction of singularity it is differentiated from other individual souls distinct from itself. Therefore, these souls are distinct by nature before being united to matter. Consequently, they are not distinct primarily and *per se* by their matter.[6]

2.17 Proof of the first proposition, namely "That which can exist without contradiction apart from another, but not vice versa, is naturally prior in nature to the second." This is taken from the *Metaphysics*.[7] In Bk. V, chapter 11, we read: "Some beings are prior, it is said, according to nature and substance, namely such as could exist without other things, while the others could not exist without them." And at the end of the chapter, he [Aristotle] reduces all types of priority to this. In the same *Metaphysics*,[8] Bk. II, he says: "The 'being' of substance is the first of all." He gives as proof of this that "None of the others is separable from substance," i.e., none can exist without substance whereas of itself substance and only substance can exist without the others. According to the Philosopher, then, this separability implies priority* of nature. Now the soul can be without matter not only according to substance and essence, but also according to existence and as the end product of a divine creation. Therefore, it can exist without being united to matter. But if it is not singular or a "this" by its own singularity, it cannot be in matter either by creation or in any other way. Therefore, our first proposition to be proved follows.

[6] 2.18 But suppose one objects: Admittedly it is not a "this" by reason of matter, i.e., by its actual union with matter or by its actually being in matter, but it is singular or a "this" by reason of the aptitude it has to exist in matter; now the soul is not prior [by nature] to this aptitude. This evasion still does not invalidate the argument, for the absolute nature itself is naturally prior to the aptitude, and

---

[6] Cf. Duns Scotus, *Ord.* II, d.3, qq.6-7 (ed. Vivès XII, 127-70); III, d.8, q.un., n.6 (ed. Vivès XIV, 364-65).

[7] Aristotle, *Metaph.* V, c.11 (1019a1-5).

[8] Ibid., VII, c.1 (1028a13-15).

this soul has this aptitude to be in this body, and this aptitude for just this body is repugnant to another soul which has the aptitude to be in another body.

2.19 On this basis I argue as follows: What pertains to this, and is repugnant to another individual of the same species, does not pertain to this individual *per se* by virtue of something common to both of them. At least some distinction between this and that is a necessary prerequisite for this aptitude to pertain to this subject and to be repugnant to that. What is needed as a prerequisite, therefore, is some distinction between this and that. Neither the first distinction, then, nor the first singularity of this and of that stems from some aptitude they have.

2.20 Confirmation: An aptitude is not formally speaking something absolute; neither does it have the character of an actual being. Proof of the first point: If it were conceived as an absolute, one could think of it without reference to any other term. The second point appears clear from this that an aptitude can refer to a nonexistent term. What necessarily demands something nonexistent is itself not something existing as actualized. Now this soul is something singular and absolute and it is so by a singularity that is both absolute and actualized. Therefore, its aptitude is not the formal reason for its singularity.

2.21 What we gather from this case of the soul is the following: "A form of the same species cannot be multiplied without matter" is not an absolutely necessary proposition in the sense that its negation is self-contradictory. And even though a form does have an aptitude for matter, its ability to be multiplied is something that is prior by nature to this aptitude. Therefore, the primary reason why it can be multiplied cannot be, in all cases, materiality.

2.22 [The primary reason why something can be multiplied is not materiality] Proof that immateriality is not the primary reason why a form of a given species is an individual or a "this" and that materiality is not the primary reason why a form of the same species can be in more than one individual. That by which something exists in actuality (and not just in the mind or in its cause) is also that by which it is primarily an individual or a "this," because this sort of existence pertains only to individuals. Universality or not being a "this," on the other hand, can only pertain to something in the mind. But for any given entity, particularly one that is something absolute or nonrelative, what has actual existence is the entity itself, for this is what passes primarily from nonbeing to being. Though many concurrent factors may be there if it is to exist, such as matter if the form is to exist or form if the matter is to exist, still none of these concomitants is the primary reason why the entity itself exists. Therefore, it is the entity itself that is primarily a "this" and hence we must seek the primary reason why the divine sonship is uniquely individual in what such sonship is in itself and not in the immateriality which only posits or excludes something peripheral to singularity proper.

[7] 2.23 Authority confirms this. According to Avicenna,[9] even though matter be the matter of the form, it is not *per se* the cause of the form. Now nothing seems to be "this" or individual by something that is not its *per se* cause. This is also the mind of Aristotle[10] in his claim that the material cause as well as the formal and efficient causes all have unity and distinction that is specific and numerical in proportion to products caused by them. "Those things," he says, "in the same species are different, not in species, but in the sense that the causes of different individuals are different, your matter and form and moving cause being different from mine, while in their universal definition they are the same."

2.24 For it is necessary that the essential components of the composite be indifferent or indeterminate where the composite is indeterminate and be determinate where the composite is determinate, for the indeterminate is not made up of determinate components nor is the determinate composed of indeterminates where the indifference or indeterminacy in question is that which is characteristic of universality. It is useless, therefore, to seek the reason for singularity (i.e., the primary reason for this determinate singularity)[11] in something extrinsic as if it were its formal principle, since anything extrinsic would be at best a kind of concomitant cause. It is always necessary that the primary formal reason for just this singularity stem from something intrinsic *per se* to the singular in question.

[8] 2.25 [Evaluation of the Second Reason in 2.6] The argument for the second reason is in the form of an enthymeme, where the suppressed proposition seems to be this: "Where there can be but one unique act of understanding, there can be but one unique word* or 'speaking the word.'" This proposition happens to be true in virtue of its matter in the case of a created intellect, but it is true not

---

[9] Avicenna, *Metaph.* II, c.4 (*Opera latina* II; Venetiis 1508, 75v).
[10] Aristotle, *Metaph.* XII, c.5 (1071a25-30).
[11] See Glossary: *"Haecceity."*

because a "word" is produced by the act of understanding itself, for, as we shall show later [in question 15], a word is produced by an act of speaking* which is not an act of understanding. No, the reason is this. In us all understanding gets expressed in an act of speech and in all speech some understanding is expressed. Therefore, if the understanding is unique or one, so too is the speech.

2.26 But this proposition does not hold good for God, because not every instance of divine understanding occurs by speaking. Indeed, the Father's understanding of all objects is not by way of an act of speech. Hence, so far as the present issue is concerned, the Father might well have one unique understanding of all objects and yet speak them singly if each single object has a word of its own.

2.27 Or, to put it briefly, this proposition does not seem to be necessary in virtue of its form. For even though one subject possess but one absolute form of the same kind, its active production of multiple terms could itself be multiple. For example, the sun, though it is luminous by a single light [form], can still have multiple acts of illuminating. Now to understand is the perfection of an intelligent being and perhaps it represents an absolute form. At least it is a perfection which exists in the subject thinking or functioning, and does not consist in the production of some term. Speaking, on the contrary, is said to be an action productive of a term. Therefore, this does not follow by reason of its form: "If the understanding is not multiplied, neither is speaking."

[9] 2.28 But you may object that speaking is not a transient act like illuminating. The term of the act remains within the same intellect. If understanding in the divine intellect is unique because it is immanent, by the same token speaking will be unique.

It is true that in the divine intellect there is but one act of speaking even as there is but one act of understanding. But one who asks for the reason ought to be shown why this is so. For anyone assuming that in the divine the Son also speaks would claim there are two instances of speaking, one by the Father, the other by the Son. For it is not by the same act of speaking that the Son is produced and also produces. And still such a one would admit but one act of understanding, for understanding is communicable like everything essential in the divine. For this reason, by whatever notional acts it was communicated, the understanding would always remain undifferentiated even though the notional acts were distinct. After all, the essence remains absolutely the same even though it is communicated by different types of productions, and these are even more distinct than two instances of speaking would be, for they differ in their formal constitution.

2.29 On the other hand, by reason of its matter, the proposition "An intellect that has but one act of understanding has but one act of speaking" is true of a created intellect, because here the intellection is the formal term of an act of speaking. And thus by reason of the limitation of the term itself, it is true that in the created intellect a different act of expressing would have a different formal term. But this reason does not hold in the divine, for there the formal term of the act of expressing is unlimited and hence there is no need to introduce distinctions in the term on the basis of the acts of expressing, which are the personal acts. As regards the objects, however, there seems to be some plausibility for the proposition "Where there is one understanding there is one speaking." For an intellect that can comprehend many objects with a single act of understanding can with equal reason express declaratively* knowledge of many things with a single act of expressing. From this, however, it would only follow that by reason of the objects there are not different acts of speaking even as there are not different acts of understanding.

2.30 Furthermore, to justify completely what we intend to prove, it is necessary to show that in the divine there is no other act of speaking as regards the same object whether this be the act of another person speaking (e.g., if the Son were to speak his Word) or of the same person (e.g., if the Father spoke another word).

[10] 2.31 [Evaluation of the third reason in 2.7] In the third reason the proposition: "Nature is determined to one [effect or mode of action]" does not imply that only one person could be produced naturally or by way of nature. For not only the same specific nature, but also a unique nature found in but one singular being, can be a productive principle that is natural as regards many effects. This appears clear from the case of fire which naturally produces many fires. Consequently the meaning of the proposition "Nature is determined to one" is this: It is determined not to one producible, i.e., one in number or to one singular effect, but to one definite manner of producing, for here there is no principle like the will which remains indeterminate with respect to opposite effects.

2.32 But suppose one claims the following: The reason a nature can be the principle or source of many products by way of a natural or nonfree production is that it makes use of many materials and hence needs many things other than itself as a prerequisite condition. This producer [viz., God], however, makes use of nothing other than himself. Neither could there be many distinct materials from which more than one production could occur. An objection of this sort, however, is of no value. If a natural agent can still produce many effects when its effect is only partially within the scope of its active powers (viz., as regards form), then *a fortiori* an agent requiring no previous matter and having its effect completely within the scope of its active power [viz., as regards both form and matter] can produce as many or an equal number of effects. For the perfection of such power does not limit the agent as regards what can be produced. Now a natural agent whose active power extends to its effect only partially (i.e., to its form) can produce many effects of the same kind while remaining the same. Therefore, the same would be possible for an agent whose effect is wholly within the scope of its active power and who requires no previous matter.

2.33 This is obvious. As one species of agent can produce many effects simultaneously, so also can God create many at once. Therefore the reason the same producer can produce many effects does not depend solely on the fact that it does or can produce them from many passive principles. It depends rather on the active power of the agent and whether the product in question is capable of being multiplied. Hence to show that the term of a production is unique or of one kind only, it is necessary to prove it cannot be turned out by several productions of the same kind, whether these be productions out of something or out of nothing or whether the production be a natural process or [one that depends on the will].

[11] 2.34 [Evaluation of the fourth reason] As for the fourth reason [in 2.8, note the following]: The Son is perfect God and yet he does not possess divinity in every way in which it could be had. For another person can possess this same divinity, not another, and do so in a different way. From the fact that the Son is intensively* perfect, therefore, even as he is perfect God, it does not follow that he possesses all possible filiation extensively or at least that he has it in the only way it can be had. However, since filiation is not the sort of thing that can be communicated to several, there is no need to distinguish between different filiations and different ways of possessing it [so far as what we want to prove is concerned]. Indeed, just as the divinity can exist perfectly in one [person] and still exist in a different way in another, so too might filiation exist perfectly in one person and yet be possessed in a different way by another.

[12] 2.35 [Two Other Reasons Given for the Negative Conclusion:

QUESTION TWO

First Reason] Some[12] give this reason for the negative conclusion: If the total fecundity destined for generating the Son is exhausted in producing one son, it would be impossible for a second son to be produced together with him, for the second would have to be produced without that fecundity destined to produce a son. But in God the fecundity for generating a son is completely exhausted in producing the Son, for the Son, the unique act by which he is generated, and the way the two are interrelated all remain the same forever. No fecundity would remain, therefore, for generating a second son unless two complete productions of the same type and from the same source would coexist. But this is just as impossible as it is for the same matter to be moved simultaneously by several movements (either of becoming or alteration) so that the end result is something identical in species but multiple in number. The Philosopher[13] affirms as much when he points out that the same thing cannot be moved simultaneously by several movements of the same kind. Hence we have the minor, viz., that God's fecundity is completely exhausted in producing the Son, for this act continues in existence forever and always proceeds from the same source in the same way.

2.36 An example confirms this. If a man had but one sperm cell and this was all that was available to him for generating a man, and if from this seed this one son would be always begotten, it would be impossible for him to generate another son.

2.37 [Second reason] In brief this argument can be put as follows: If an act is adequate, that is, commensurate with its source or principle, and always remains uniform, it is not compatible with another act of the same kind proceeding from the same active principle. But in the divine the unique act of generation is commensurate with its principle and remains always. Therefore [it is not compatible with another act of the same kind proceeding from the same active principle].

[13] 2.38 [The first reason is invalid] As for the first reason [in 2.35] the word "exhausted," if properly understood of corporeal things, denotes that nothing of what was there before remains in what is exhausted, as is clear from the example of water in the well. But it

[12] Henry of Ghent, *Quodl.* VI, q.1 in corp. (fol. 216X-Y and 217H-I); *Summa* a.58, q.1 in corp. (II, fol. 123G-125V); a.59, q.2, ad 1 (II, fol. 137H); William of Ware, *Sent.* I, d.7, q.4 in corp.

[13] Aristotle, *Physic.* V, c.4 (228a3-6).

cannot be understood here in this way, for in producing the Son the fecundity of the Father is not exhausted, but in its entirety it remains in him forever. Hence another analogy is needed such that "exhausted" would mean that in the Father nothing remains available for a further production or for generating another son, just as we could speak somehow of a spring being exhausted by a continuous act of drinking if no additional water remained for another act of drinking.

2.39 Therefore, the major is conceded, for once the fecundity ordained to generate a son has been exhausted in this way, no other son could be generated. But the minor needs proof, namely, that in the Son's generation, all the fecundity available in the divine for begetting a son is exhausted. Now the proof suggested is that this generation goes on forever and stems from the same source, as it were, and makes use of the same "matter" or passive principle, as it were. Hence many productions cannot exist simultaneously even as several movements cannot [occur at the same time in the same matter].

[14] 2.40 This reason is not enough to prove the point in question. It can be refuted in this way. Every power which could have an additional act if its first did not remain forever is able simply to have another act. But the only reason you give why the generative power in God is unable to have another act is that the first goes on forever. Therefore, speaking absolutely, that power is able to have another act in the sense that no contradiction is involved. If this power can have another act, however, it must have it, for there is nothing possible or noncontradictory in the divine that is not actualized. Therefore, there are many actual generations there. The conclusion is false; therefore one of the premises is also false. It is not the major, therefore it must be the minor, which was accepted, it seems, on the grounds of your argument.

2.41 The major of our counter-argument is proved by reason and example.

The proof from reason is this: Potency is naturally prior to act. Now what is repugnant to the naturally prior only because of something naturally posterior is simply not repugnant to it. For no contradiction arises between something and the naturally prior simply because there is a contradiction between it and the naturally posterior. Therefore, if another act is repugnant to a power only because it is always eliciting the first act, it is not absolutely repugnant to it, and thus can pertain to it simply without contradiction.

2.42 The example is this: Suppose the sun were to light up the universe with an illumination that was adequate both intensively (i.e., it would illuminate as perfectly as it could) and extensively (i.e., the light would extend to everything capable of being illumined by the sun). Suppose further that this action continued forever so that the sun could not light up anything else. The reason for this would not be that it is simply repugnant to the sun as a source of light to be the principle of further illumination, but rather that everything that can be lighted up actually is lighted. On its part the sun, absolutely speaking, is able to illuminate more. Hence, if the sun necessarily produced all the illumination it was capable of, it would actually produce this light. The necessity of this single production, consequently, is never an unqualified necessity nor does it stem from the fact that the one production continues forever.

[15] 2.43 Confirmation of this argument: If a potency or power, of its nature, is not necessarily limited to this act, but merely elicits it at all times, then absolutely speaking such a potency, as prior [by nature] to the act, could have another act. There seems to be no reason, therefore, why the potency elicits this act rather than the other and, consequently, since neither is less necessary than the other, either neither act or both acts would be elicited by the power simultaneously.

2.44 So far as this argument [in 2.35] goes, then, this seems in brief to be the case. Because the act always remains or because the potency cannot be actuated simultaneously by diverse acts are not sufficient grounds to establish the conclusion of the argument to the extent that it is true. What needs proof is that the necessity that there be but one production of the same species is of such a nature that even if, to assume the impossible, this production did not always continue or even if it never existed, no other production of the same type could exist in God. If this Father did not exist, it would be wholly contradictory to speak of a Father in the divine. Similarly if this Father did not beget by this act of generation, or, to assume the impossible, he generated by an act that was momentary rather than permanent, he could have no other generation. For not to admit that the unique production is absolutely and in every way necessary is equivalent to admitting that another production is possible and hence necessary, for whatever is possible there is necessary.

2.45 [Invalidity of the second reason] What we have said also shows the inconclusiveness of the second reason [in 2.37], the one presenting the argument in brief form, based on the act's adequacy. The major takes adequacy either intensively or both extensively and intensively. If taken in the first sense, adequacy does not imply only one production is possible. Another might be possible although not at the same time. All that follows is that at one time only one production is possible. If the only reason one production alone is possible is that another cannot exist at the same time, then, speaking simply, another production is possible, and consequently, in this case, it would be simply necessary. If adequacy is taken in the second sense, then the minor is not proved, unless perhaps it is based on the assumption that this unique production goes on forever, which we discussed earlier [in 2.40].

ARTICLE II
Solution of the Question

[16] 2.46 [Reason can prove that several productions of the same species are impossible in God] As regards the second article, I maintain that the conclusion "In the divine more than one production of the same species is not possible" is not just taken on faith but can be established by necessary reason. The argument can be formulated first in the form of a reduction *ad impossibile*; second, as a positive proof; and third, the thesis can be confirmed from the mind of the Philosopher.

1. Indirect Argument or the *Reductio ad impossibile*

2.47 The argument may be formulated as follows:

If more than one production of the same type can exist, then productions *ad infinitum* can exist. If this be so, then it is necessary that there be an infinity of productions, for nothing can be in God that is not there necessarily. The last consequent is clearly impossible; therefore the first antecedent is also impossible.

2.48 Proof of the first inference from authority and reason:

The authority is that of Augustine:[14] "Far be it from anyone to say that the Father is more powerful than the Son, as you claim, simply because the Father generated the creator and the Son did not. For it was not that he was unable, but it was not becoming." And he explains why it was not becoming: "Divine generation would be unbridled if the generated Son would beget a grandson to the Father. For unless the grandson in turn produced a great-grandson to the grandfather, he would be impotent, according to your amazing

[14] Augustine, *Contra Maximinum* II, c.12, n.2: PL 42, 768.

wisdom. And this last would produce another, and he in turn another, and so on." And he adds: "The series of generations would never be completed if from every one another were generated. Neither would any one finish the series if one omnipotent is not sufficient." According to the mind of Augustine it would follow that if the one person produced by such a production did not suffice to complete the entire production, then no other, nor any number of persons, would suffice. And so whether it would be the Son that generated another son in the direct line, or whether the same Father would generate this son and that son, whatever the reason given for postulating a plurality, the same reason would always justify an infinity of such productions.

2.49 This same inference is proved from reason. Any kind of thing that can be multiplied or exist in more than one individual of the same type is not of itself limited to any certain number. This proposition is evident if you consider the relationship of something common or universal to its singular instances, or of a cause to what it causes, or of a principle to what proceeds therefrom. If instances of the same common thing can be multiplied, such a thing of itself is not limited to a certain number of such instances. Neither is a cause limited of itself to a certain number of results.

2.50 From this proposition just proved it follows that any given type of thing that can be multiplied, so far as itself is concerned, can be multiplied *ad infinitum* unless it is limited on some other grounds. Such limitation cannot come from a source or principle specifically the same as itself. Therefore, if some productive principle in the divine could have more than one production of the same kind, neither of itself nor by virtue of the formal principle from which it stems would such a production be limited to any definite plurality. On neither score is any given number repugnant to it. Therefore, either such productions could be, and hence would be, infinite (which is the conclusion we draw), or else their limitation to a certain plurality would be on grounds other than what they are in themselves or what their productive source is. But in God there is nothing that could account for such a limitation. It could not come from anything posterior [in nature] to the production, for nothing gets its entity, and hence its unity or plurality, from the posterior. Neither can it stem from something simultaneous in nature with the production, for the same reason why one type of production is not of itself limited numerically applies with equal force to what is simultaneous in nature. Neither can the limitation arise from something prior, whether this be the subject or person who does the producing or the formal principle by means of which the production is accomplished. The formal principle cannot account for the limitation, as is clear from the proof of the major, for a productive principle of the same type is not limited of itself to a certain plurality of productions of the same kind. Neither can the limitation come from the person who produces, for the person is able to have as many productions as the productive principle he possesses is capable of. If there is no limitation on the part of the productive principle, therefore, then there is none on the part of the producer. Thus the absurd consequence of denying the thesis we wish to prove seems clear. If in God there could be more than one production of the same type, then an infinity of such would exist.

2. The Positive Proof

[18]   2.51 The second or positive proof is this:

In the divine what cannot be restricted in some way to a certain plurality cannot be multiplied at all. But a production of the same type in the divine cannot be restricted to a certain plurality. Therefore, it cannot be multiplied at all, which is the thesis we set out to prove.

2.52 First I shall explain the major and then I shall prove it.

I speak of a "certain plurality," for instance, two, or three, or four, or some other definite given number. That it be restricted to a certain plurality by something that is posterior or simultaneous [in nature] I claim is impossible and includes a manifest contradiction.

2.53 Understanding it in this way, I prove the major as follows: If something, so far as itself is concerned, cannot be restricted to a certain plurality, then so far as it itself goes there is a possibility of any number of instances of it, for there is nothing contradictory about any given plurality being exceeded and this *ad infinitum*. But in the divine nothing can be multiplied beyond any given plurality, because then it would be necessarily multiplied in this way and thus an infinite multiplicity would exist there.

2.54 Proof of the minor: What does not presuppose several different types of principles that restrict it to a certain plurality cannot be limited at all to a smaller number of the same. A production of the same type in the divine does not presuppose several different types of principles which might restrict it to a certain plurality. Therefore it cannot be limited at all to a certain plurality.

QUESTION TWO

[19] 2.55 I prove the major and minor of this argument.

For the major the proof runs as follows: If the same sort of thing can be multiplied then it is not of itself limited to a certain plurality. This was proved [in 2.50] by the indirect argument *ad impossibile*. For the same reason, individual instances of the same kind are not of themselves restricted to being just so many. As fire of itself is not restricted to any specific number of fires, so neither are the individual fires of themselves limited to any specific number so that there must be just so many. If what can be multiplied is necessarily limited to a certain plurality, this restriction comes from something other than itself. This is not some factor that is either posterior or simultaneous by nature, as we said in the *ad impossibile* argument. Hence the restriction must stem from one or more factors prior by nature. And this prior factor cannot be the same kind of thing, for such would not impose a certain plurality on things that are the same in kind, as we said earlier in the *reductio ad impossibile*. The restriction, then, must stem from some prior factors no two of which are of the same type. Otherwise the same question would arise in regard to them. Neither could they account for the limitation if they were the same in kind. Hence we have this proposition: What cannot be restricted by some prior plurality of factors, each different in kind, cannot be limited to a certain plurality at all.

Proof of the minor: Those different productions which are assumed to be of the same type only presuppose two principles, namely the producer and that formal principle by which the production is accomplished. Neither presupposes as a necessary prerequisite a plurality of factors, each different in kind, which might limit these productions to a certain plurality. Obviously the formal principle does not, since the productions are assumed to be of the same kind. Neither is such a plurality required in the person who does the producing, at least not the sort of plurality that would restrict the production to a certain plurality. This follows from the fact that the person can have as many productions as his productive principle is capable of.

2.56 Summary: The positive argument just established can be summarized briefly.

Every necessarily finite plurality is either of different kinds of things or, if not, it necessarily presupposes some such plurality as its limiting factor. Every plurality in the divine is necessarily finite. Therefore, it is either of the first or the second sort. But neither allows a plurality of productions of the same kind. Therefore, as regards the productions, a plurality of the same type is not possible.

The major of this argument was clearly established in both the *reductio ad impossibile* [in 2.50] and in the positive argument [in 2.55].

The minor of the first syllogism is evident enough. In the divine, possibility entails necessity, and therefore necessary infinity is entailed by possible infinity or even by the lack of necessity for any specific finite number.

The minor of the second syllogism, namely that neither alternative allows a plurality of productions of the same kind, is evident, for they are neither of different kinds, being productions of the same kind, nor do they necessarily presuppose a plurality of different types that might limit their number.

3. Confirmation from the Philosopher

[20] 2.57 Third, the conclusion is established from the mind of the Philosopher[15] in the *Metaphysics* where he argues that "many heavens cannot exist because there cannot be many first movers." He proves this as follows: "Those which are many in number but one in species have matter; the first mover has no matter since it is pure act; therefore, the first mover and immobile being is one in kind and number." From this he infers: "There is but one heaven."

2.58 This position of the Philosopher seems to confirm the first reason of article one [in 2.5], namely that every immaterial form of the same type has a natural unity. But if we examine what Aristotle says in various places, we see he takes "matter" here in a different sense, one that seems to confirm our thesis without lending any strength to the first reason.

2.59 Sometimes he calls matter the receptive principle which with act or form makes up a composite being, as when, in the *Physics* and many other places,[16] he says matter and form are two principles. And by contrast he calls form that other principle which has the character of act and with matter constitutes the composite. In other places, however, the quiddity or essence is called form;

---

[15] Aristotle, *Metaph.* XII, c.8 (1074a32-1074b). Cf. Duns Scotus, *Ord.* II, d.3, q.7 (ed. Vivès XII, 159-70); I, d.2, nn.270-81, 300-303 (II, 287-94, 305-309); d.7 (IV, 107-51).

[16] Aristotle, *Physic.* I, c.7 (190b19-21, 191a8-23); II, c.3 (194b24-30); *Metaph.* V, c.6 (1016b32-33); VII, c.9 (1037b5); XII, c.8 (32-38); *De coelo* I, c.9 (277b27-278b8).

and matter, by contrast, is whatever serves to restrict or delimit that quiddity. Thus in relation to a specific essence the individual difference, whatever it may be, is called matter. Therefore, sometimes he calls matter that which receives an informing form; sometimes, that which contracts or determines an indifferent quiddity.

But such a contracting or determining factor can be understood in two ways: one, as intrinsic to the inferior or determinate member falling into such a common class; the other, as something presupposed, as it were, in the determined. For example, the individual difference of Socrates contracts man in the first way, for it is intrinsic to Socrates. But this body contracts whiteness or color in the second way, for in another body there is another whiteness, and according to this if there could be but three bodies, only three whitenesses could exist. The contracting element in the second sense, however, can be reduced to matter in the first sense or at least it includes a quasi-matter.

Therefore, wherever there is a plurality of the same kind, it is necessary to postulate matter, not in the sense of a recipient, but as a contracting factor in one sense or the other. For there is no way the same kind of nature could be multiplied if there were nothing to contract it in one way or the other. Conversely, where there is no "matter" in this sense, a plurality of the same kind is impossible.

But even this sort of "matter" is not possible in the divine productions, for there could only be such contracting or determining factors if the determination is to a certain plurality and hence presupposes a plurality of different kinds. But no plurality of different kinds prior to the divine productions can be postulated. And in this sense what the Philosopher wants to say is relevant to the conclusion we wish to prove.

[21]   2.60 But if we ask how and where, according to the Philosopher, would it be generally true, it seems that he would say that in the divine, or in anything immaterial, matter even in the second sense cannot be admitted. Hence he writes[17]: "The essence and the thing itself are in some cases the same; i.e., in the case of primary substances.... By 'primary' substance I mean one which does not imply the presence of something in something else, i.e., in something that underlies it which acts as matter. But things which have matter are not identical with their essence."

2.61 Here he does not want to say that in material things the essence and the subject which has it are not the same, though some

---

[17] Aristotle, *Metaph.* VII, c.9 (1037a34-1037b5).

interpret him in this way, contrary to his own mind as we could show by expounding chapter seven (which I will forego doing here). No, his point is that in nothing "material," i.e., which can be multiplied in any way, is the essence and the thing itself absolutely identical, for the thing itself includes "matter," i.e., something which contracts the essence but is not included in its formal notion. We agree with the Philosopher, therefore, in this that a form without matter in the second sense cannot be multiplied, and this suffices for our thesis, viz., that there cannot be multiple productions of the same type. But this does not entail that what has no matter in the sense of a real part in a composite cannot be multiplied. Hence the Philosopher's statement, "The first mover has no matter since it is pure act," [in 2.57] must be understood of matter in the second sense. For it has no "matter" to contract its essence so that it is "this," for it is a "this" or singular in virtue of what it is.

2.62 The question whether that which lacks matter in the first sense may have matter in the second sense would probably be answered differently by the Philosopher and by theologians. At present I am not concerned with this except to say that in the argument from the *Metaphysics*[18] the middle term substantially is not "has no matter in the first sense"—which is how the proponents of the first reason in [2.5 of] Article One understand it—but "has no matter in the second sense." In this sense both philosophers and theologians would admit the major and the minor premise are true. And therefore, since the divine nature cannot be multiplied in diverse subjects, so far as our purpose is concerned, both premises are true of a production of the same type, and hence the conclusion is true.

ARTICLE III
Objections and their Solutions

[22] 2.63 In this third article, objections are raised to what has been said, first to the conclusion and then to the premises.

2.64 [Two objections to the conclusion] Of the twofold objection to the conclusion the *first* is this:

Where the principle is of the same type and where the formal term is of the same type, there the production will be of the same type. But a divine essence of the same type is both the productive principle and the formal term of every production in God. Therefore, every production there is of the same type.

[18] Ibid., XII, c.8 (1074a33-35).

2.65 Proof for the major, it seems, is found in the *Physics*,[19] for productions seem to be distinguished solely in terms of their formal principle or their term.

2.66 Proof of the second part of the minor, that which concerns the formal term. Everything produced gets its essence from the production. Just as the Son has nothing, says Hilary,[20] unless he is born, i.e., he has only what he receives by being born, so the Holy Spirit has nothing but what he receives by proceeding [from Father and Son]. He receives the essence, however, only as a formal term. Augustine[21] confirms this: "As the generation from the Father bestows essence on the Son, so his procession from both bestows essence on the Holy Spirit." What is bestowed or communicated can only refer to the formal term of the production. And since the essence is the source or principle of everything, it is as the first formal term and not as the consequent of another formal term that we must understand its communication through a production.

2.67 From this the second part of the minor is proved, namely that the essence is the formal principle of both productions. The formal term cannot be in any way prior to the formal principle of the producing. If then the essence is the formal term of the production, as we have just proved [in 2.66], and if it is the first being in the divine, as we have established in [1.5 of] the first question, then it follows that the essence as such is the formal productive principle in any production.

2.68 Another proof of both parts of the minor is this: That in which producer and produced are alike, especially when the production is univocal,* is the formal principle and formal term. But in the divine, the essence as such constitutes the first likeness between the producer and the produced. Therefore, it is the formal term of the production and the formal principle of the producing.

[23] 2.69 The *second* objection to the conclusion is this: What has a perfect formal principle for producing can produce with it. But the Son possesses perfectly the formal principle for generating or "speaking." Therefore [he can produce with it].

2.70 Proof of the major: The reason a person can act is that he possesses a principle of acting and one that is most perfect.

Proof of the minor: Perfect memory is the first principle for gen-

---

[19] Aristotle, *Physic.* v, c.1 (224b5-8).
[20] Hilary, *De Trin.* vii, n.26: PL 10, 222.
[21] Augustine, *De Trin.* xv, c.26, n.47: PL 42, 1094-95; CCSL 50a, 528.

erating or "speaking." But it is obvious the Son has memory like the Father ("Every person remembers himself"),[22] and his memory is perfect.

2.71 [Objections to the premise] Third, the proposition that the first finite distinction has to do with things of different kinds is challenged on two counts.

First, a lesser distinction is closer to unity than is a greater distinction. But a distinction between things of the same kind is a lesser distinction than one between things that differ in kind. Therefore, [it is closer to unity.]

Second, more than one thing of the same species can be immediately created by God. Therefore it is possible that a plurality of the same kind [of productions] would be absolutely first and immediate to unity. What holds for cause and caused applies equally to a principle and what issues therefrom.

[24] 2.72 [Answer to the first objection to the conclusion] There are three ways of answering the first objection [in 2.64].

First, against the major.[23] Even if the essence were the eliciting principle, so far as each production goes it would be a distinct principle with distinct determinants, such as this or that relation. And then the major would be false, namely where there is the same kind of elicitive principle, there is the same kind of production, unless the determinative principle is also of the same kind, which is not the case here.

2.73 [This answer is not cogent] Against this reply it can be said that if the elicitive principle without the determinative principle does not suffice, the same question will arise here as before. By what is the essence, which is the indeterminate elicitive principle, determined to this or that determinant? For if the same sort of principle cannot be the *per se* principle of different sorts of things, then neither can the essence, which is the root or basic elicitive principle, be the immediate source of several determinative principles of different kinds. For the same reason why different kinds of things stem from the same source must be given for these differences as for the others. And if these further differences are preceded by others, there will be an infinite regress. Or if this is impossible, then differentiation by relations as the determinative principles is insufficient.

[22] Ibid., xv, c.7, n.12: PL 42, 1066; CCSL 50a, 476.
[23] Henry of Ghent, *Quodl.* III, q.3 (fol. 50I-M); *Summa* a.54, q.3, ad 7 (II, fol. 133C-D); Thomas, *Summa theol.* I, q.41, a.5 in corp. (I, 210).

QUESTION TWO

2.74 Besides, these relations are themselves productions. Now the same thing does not determine itself to itself. To say the essence is determined to active generation by a relation which is nothing other than the active generation itself, as will be shown later [in Question Four], is to claim it is determined to generation by generation, and thus the same thing is a determinative principle of itself.

[25] 2.75 [Another answer to the first objection in 2.64] The second solution also denies the major. Even though the essence is the sole productive principle, the productions themselves can be of different types, for some plurality can be first, but none can be actually, or even potentially, infinite. Now only a plurality of different types, or one which presupposes such, can be necessarily finite. Therefore, given a first, some plurality in the divine must be absolutely first and immediate to the unity. And so one could just as well assume it concerns the productions as anything else. Therefore, the major (viz., where the principle is the same and the term is the same, there the production will be of the same kind) is false in the divine. It holds for creatures, however, of which the Philosopher speaks. For there the formal productive principle is either limited to one type of production, if it is a principle of the same kind [i.e., univocal*], or if it is an equivocal* principle and thus productive of several things different in kind, the formal term of its productions is limited, so that the same thing cannot be both the principle and the term of several different kinds of things. But in God neither can be the case, for here both the principle and the formal term are unlimited.

2.76 [This answer is not valid] Against this is the argument adduced in the first question [in 1.65ff.]. In such a case there is no more reason why the first person produced should be in reality a word rather than a Holy Spirit or why the Holy Spirit should be a Holy Spirit rather than a word.

2.77 Also for a person having the same formal principle for several productions there would be no priority in what he could do through it. Thus the first person could produce the Holy Spirit in the same order as he does the Son, and thus the Holy Spirit would not proceed necessarily from the Son.

2.78 [A valid answer to the first objection] The third solution [to 2.64] concedes the minor, namely that the essence is formal principle and formal term of both productions, but not so completely that nothing else is included *per se* in each. Indeed the essence is included in the formal principle, which is perfect memory and perfect will. The essence is also included in the formal term, which is the perfect Word and the perfect Holy Spirit. And perhaps in each case, the essence functions as a principle, and this with respect to what concurs with it, viz., intellect or knowledge and will or love. Because of the identity of essence, that by which the producer produces and the formal term are the same. But because of the distinction between intellect and will which concur with the essence as productive principle, this and that [total] principle suffice for productions of different types and for terms that somehow differ in kind. Thus we have in the principle essence and intellect, essence and will; in the term, on the other hand, we have essence and knowledge, essence and love. What is identical in the formal term communicated is accounted for by what is identical in the formal communicative principle. What is distinct in the principle is the formal reason for a distinct production and explains why that which concurs in the term is formally distinct.[24]

[26] 2.79 But of these two concurrent components, you may ask, is not one the formal principle and the other only a concomitant factor, so that the principle could be said to be either formally identical or wholly different? I reply: The two elements that concur in the principle, namely, in the perfect memory, essence and intellect, in the perfect will, a will and a lovable object, are related neither incidentally nor *per accidens*, nor as remote and proximate principle. But this whole, viz., an infinite intellect with an infinite intelligible object, constitutes one *per se* principle, so that neither factor without the other is producing principle. Hence there is simply one unique productive principle, not two distinct ones. The same holds for will and object as regards spiration. The situation is similar as regards the terms of the productions.

2.80 Why, you may ask, cannot the essence alone, as distinct from will and intellect, be the source for the communication of itself? I reply: An essence that is merely intellectual is not a principle of any production unless it coincides with memory and will.

[27] 2.81 [Answer to the second objection] A reply to the second objection [in 2.69], first to its content, then to its form.

2.82 To its content, a twofold reply can be given.

First: A form that is a producing principle in one person of a production commensurate with that form, cannot be a principle of producing in another person. Now memory is the producing prin-

[24] Cf. Duns Scotus, *Ord.* 1, d.2, nn.270-81, 300-303 (II, 287-94, 305-309); d.7, q.1, nn.1-91 (IV, 107-48).

ciple in the Father of a production commensurate with that principle. Therefore, [it cannot be a producing principle for another person].

2.83 The major is proved by an example in this way. If the heat in fire were the source or principle for warming wood with a heat production commensurate to itself, and if that same heat were then communicated to the wood, it could not be for the wood a principle of heating. Proof: It would not be heating up itself, for then in the same subject the heat would be [both the effect and] the [cause or] principle producing it. Neither would it be heating another, for by hypothesis its present heat production is all it is equal to producing. And this proof is based on what complete commensurability means, namely the impossibility that the action be [less or] greater than the formal principle of acting. And under this interpretation, the minor is manifest. For just as the Father's memory has such an adequate "speech act" [*dictio*] in the person of the Father that it is impossible for the "speech principle" [*principium dictivum*] to speak more, so is it impossible that in God there be more than just this one "speech act," for it is of itself singular. This is clear from the solution of the question. For everything in the divine that does not of necessity presuppose a plurality of different kinds is of itself just this or singular. But the "speech act" in the divine does not necessarily presuppose such. Therefore it is of itself just this one, and hence its source or principle has this "speech act" that is in every respect commensurate with it. Therefore, memory cannot be a principle [of production] in the Son.[25]

2.84 [Second] The same point can be proved by the following proposition which has roughly the same meaning as the other [in 2.82]. A person or subject receiving a form by a production equal to that form cannot in turn produce by that form. The Son receives memory by a production equal to that memory. Therefore, [he cannot produce by means of it]. The minor is explained as in the previous argument.

2.85 Proof of the major: If the person or subject would produce by it, he would either produce himself or another. Not himself, for this is impossible according to Augustine.[26] Nor would another be produced, for the production is, by assumption, equal or commensurate with the productive principle. Thus there is no need to look for some concomitant determinant factor that would limit the elicit-

---

[25] Cf. Duns Scotus, *Ord.* I, d.3, nn.401-553 (III, 245-330); d.7, nn. 191 (IV, 107-48).

[26] Augustine, *De Trin.* I, c.1, n.1: PL 42, 820; CCSL 50, 28.

ing principle to just one "speech act." Nor, as a formal principle of this sort, can there be anything negative about it. Now granted that the essence or any other positive entity that has been received is, in the Father, the formal reason for "speaking" or generating [the Word], it still cannot be such in the Son. For it functions as an adequate principle of production already in the Father (as the first reason puts it) and is communicated to the Son by that production (as the second reason says).[27]

[28] 2.86 As for the form of the argument [in 2.69], some objection could be made to both the major and the minor. For *have* or *possess* can be given many meanings according to the postpredicaments,* even though it is not proper to speak of something having a form in the abstract, if the form is not possessed in the manner it was meant to be by nature. Thus it would not be proper to say "someone has whiteness" because he has it enclosed in his purse, for whiteness is meant to be by nature a [quality or] form inhering [in a subject].

2.87 Furthermore, when an abstract noun signifying a principle of action is constructed with a gerund signifying some action, it indicates that the principle of action is apt by nature to be possessed in such a way by its subject that the latter can use it to perform the action. I have a power for seeing for example. This power is apt by nature to be possessed by me not just as a form, but as a principle for performing the action that goes with that form. This is what such an abstract term [as "a power" or "a formal principle"] with a gerund [like "for seeing" or "for producing"] means.

2.88 Linguistic usage, also, sanctions this grammatical interpretation. Although "The Son of God knows of the Father's generating" is a true proposition, "The Son has the knowledge for generating" is not. The only reason for this is that the grammatical construction indicates that the subject has the abstract entity [i.e., the knowledge] not only as a form, but also as a principle for performing such an operation himself. Similarly, the proposition "Michael knows God created the world and that the world is created" does not mean he knows how to create the world.

2.89 If in the major "What has a perfect principle for speaking can speak with it," then, "has" is understood properly in the sense that when we speak of having something abstract, it means it is had as the form of the subject, and that when we put the word signifying the principle for the acting with a gerund signifying the action, we mean that in this subject it is a principle for acting in this

[27] Cf. Duns Scotus, *Ord.* I, d.7, nn. 1-91 (IV, 107-48).

way, then I concede the major, since the subject includes all that is required for affirming the predicate of it. For when one has a form as his own form and as his own principle for acting, then he can be a principle of acting by means of it. But then the minor is false, for although the Son has perfect memory in some sense of "has," he does not have it as form, or if he does have it as form, he does not have it as a principle for acting, for reasons given [in 2.82].

[29] 2.90 As for the proof of the minor [in 2.70], one could say that "Perfect memory is the perfect principle for speaking" is an elliptical statement. Something in the dative case should be added to indicate for whom it is a principle for speaking.

2.91 Or, because the statement as it stands is indifferent and not specific, one could admit the memory is a principle of uttering a word, absolutely speaking; the minor says no more about the memory. That the Son has perfect memory [in this unspecified sense] is manifest.

2.92 To conclude, then, the statement "The Son has a perfect principle for speaking," which was the minor of the first syllogism [of the objection in 2.69], is a fallacy of amphiboly, or figure of speech, or of the consequent.

Amphiboly, because the major leaves unspecified the subject from whom the act signified by the gerund proceeds, since nothing definite is set down there as subject of the sentence. That the act is proceeding from some formal principle is all that is indicated, for that is what is set down as subject of the sentence. In the conclusion, however, both the definite subject and the form are designated, and therefore by virtue of its grammatical construction the conclusion indicates that the act is not only referred to its formal principle but also to the subject, as proceeding from someone.

Figure of speech, because of verbal similarities between the act signified by the gerund in the premise and in the conclusion the relation of the act to a formal principle is changed to a relation of act to the person or subject acting. Thus an essential quality or form is changed into this something, a subject.

A fallacy of the consequent, because the act signified by the gerund universally is not compared to any person or subject whereas in the conclusion it is related to a definite person or subject. Now this does not follow: "The act is by this principle, therefore it is by this subject."

[30] 2.93 [Answer to the first objection in 2.71 to the premise] As for the third objection: The proposition "The first plurality necessarily

finite is of different types" is true, for every plurality that is necessarily finite, if it is not of different kinds of things, of necessity presupposes a plurality of this sort by which it is necessarily determined, as is clear from the second article [in 2.55]. Now the first plurality in the divine is both first and necessarily finite. That it is first is obvious. That it is necessarily finite is also clear, for in the divine only that which is actual is possible. Therefore the conclusion follows, namely that the first plurality in the divine is necessarily one of different types, and hence this is closest to unity.

2.94 As for what the major assumes [in 2.71], namely that a lesser plurality is closer to unity than a greater one, I have this to say. "Greater" or "lesser" can be understood intensively or extensively. "Lesser intensively" would mean that there is less reason or ground for the distinction. Thus the middle is distinct from the end to a lesser degree than one contrary from another. "Lesser extensively," whether it refer to a distinction or to a plurality, would mean fewer members. Thus triplets would be less of a plurality than quadruplets. And in this sense, the major is true, for a binary is closer to unity than a ternary or quaternary. But intensively the binary is not a "lesser plurality" than a ternary, for its two members are no less distinct from each other than are the three members in a ternary. Extensively, however, it is, for pluralities or distinctions proceed in an orderly fashion from unity. For the smaller number extensively or numerically is closer to unity or the unit which is the principle or starting point for numbers. And thus I concede that the distinction or plurality in God, although it be a distinction of types, is the least, for there are only two productions and there is no lesser plurality than duality.

[31] 2.95 But if we speak of a distinction or plurality that is intensively lesser or greater, this can also be understood in two ways. Either it is understood *per se*, i.e., with reference to the formal reason or ground for the distinction, or else *per accidens*, i.e., it expresses that the things to be distinguished have a greater or lesser entity or are more or less incompatible. For instance, in terms of reality and incompatibility, Socrates and Plato are more distinct from each other than are the meanings of genus and species, for the latter can concur in the same thing, e.g., color. And the entity of the two factors distinguished is less in the case of "genus" and "species" than in the case of Socrates and Plato. But if the major premise is understood of a distinction that is materially less, perhaps in some case it is true. A conceptual distinction comes closer to something that is primarily

QUESTION TWO

one than does the real distinction. It is also less than the real distinction in terms of the entity and incompatibility of components distinguished. In the case at hand, however, there is no need to be concerned about this kind of majority or minority, for we are not claiming a conceptual distinction as closest or immediate to that from which all multitude proceeds, viz., to the essence itself.

2.96 If we interpret "greater" in a second way, however, namely intensively but *per se* or in terms of the formal reason for the distinction, then the major [of 2.71] is simply false. A distinction of different types has to be closest to the first one from which any distinction whether real or conceptual proceeds, for some distinction must be finite and what is primarily finite is a distinction of different types, as it was argued. This is clear, for according to the common opinion, when a conceptual distinction follows immediately a real unity, those facets that are mentally distinct are presented as distinct in kind, not as the same sort of thing but numerically distinct. And this distinction [closest to unity] is greater in terms of the formal reason for the distinction, although it is lesser in two other ways, namely in number and in terms of the reality and incompatibility of the *distinguenda*.

2.97 [Answer to the second objection in 2.71 against the premise] From what has been said the answer to the objection based on a plurality that comes immediately from God is clear. In creatures where specific natures are multiplied in different subjects none is necessarily determined. There are this many or that many solely by the will of the agent, so that there is no repugnance that the natures be in more than one individual. If therefore several such things of the same type come from God immediately, they are finite in actuality because the divine will impose finitude upon them. But they are not necessarily finite, because there is nothing intrinsic to creatures to which a greater or lesser plurality is contradictorily opposed.[28]

---

[28] He does not answer the initial argument. Cf. Duns Scotus, *Ord.* I, d.10, nn.1-62 (IV, 339-66); d.13, nn.1-103 (V, 65-124).

Question Three

ARE THESE TWO COMPATIBLE: A RELATION RELATED TO ITS OPPOSITE IS A REAL THING; AND, AS RELATED TO THE ESSENCE, IT IS ONLY AN ASPECT?

[1] 3.1 Questions about the relations follow the discussion of the productions.* The first concern relations of origin* [viz., QQ. 3-5] the second, common relations* [viz., Q. 6].

3.2 The first question on the relations of origin concerns their tie in with the essence; the second, how they are bound up with the person; third, their own measure of perfection.

3.3 The first question then is this: Are these two compatible: a relation as related to its opposite is a real thing [*res*]; and, as related to the essence, it is only an aspect [*ratio*]?[1]

Arguments Pro and Con

It is argued they are not:

If it is only an aspect as related to the essence, this is because it merges with the essence. But as related to its opposite, it remains the same thing it was, for as an aspect it is the same thing as the essence and the divine simplicity rules out the possibility of its being in any way not the same. Therefore, if it is only an aspect as related to the essence, then it has to be such as related to its opposite.

3.4 The argument for the opposite is this:

As related to the essence it is an aspect; the divine simplicity proves this much. But as related to its opposite it is not an aspect, but a thing; otherwise it would not constitute a really distinct subject. Therefore, both situations coexist.

Body of the Question

3.5 Here there are three points to be investigated: (1) In itself is the relation of origin a thing, and if so, what kind of thing? (2) As related to the essence, is it a thing and of what kind? (3) How certain doubts raised by the solution to the question are to be resolved.

---

[1] Cf. Duns Scotus, *Ord.* 1, dd.4-5 (IV, 1-86).

QUESTION THREE

ARTICLE I

Is the Relation of Origin a Thing and, if so,
What Kind of Thing?

[2] 3.6 ["Thing" is an equivocal term] As for the first, one should not give a simple answer to an equivocal question and it is clear from those who speak with authority that the term "thing" is equivocal.[2] Hence its various meanings must be distinguished at the outset. From the remarks of the authors one gathers that the term "thing" can be understood (1) very broadly, or (2) generally, or (3) very strictly.

3.7 ["Thing" in the broadest sense] Understood very broadly, it covers anything that is not nothing, and this can be given two interpretations.

Nothing, in its truest sense, is what includes a contradiction and only that, for such excludes any form of existence, either within or without the intellect. Just as what includes a contradiction cannot exist outside the soul, so neither can it be an intelligible something as a being in the soul [i.e., a concept]. Two contradictory notions cannot constitute one intelligible thing, either as a union of two objects or of an object and its mode.

In another sense, nothing refers to what neither is nor can be some being outside the soul [i.e., extramental].

3.8 Being [*ens*] or thing [*res*] in the first of its very broad meanings, therefore, covers anything that does not include a contradiction whether it be a conceptual being [*ens rationis*], i.e., having being or existence only in the thinking intellect, or a real being [*ens reale*], i.e., having some entity outside the consideration of the intellect.

3.9 Though the first of these two meanings (which together constitute the first member of the tripartite distinction) seems to extend the name "thing" exceedingly, it is sufficiently justified by linguistic usage, for we commonly speak of logical intentions and mental relations as "things of the mind" and still these cannot exist outside the intellect. Therefore the word "thing" is not restricted by linguistic usage to a thing outside the soul.

In the broadest sense, where "being" or "thing" means anything conceivable that includes no contradiction (whether its commonness be one of analogy or univocity, I am not concerned at present), one

[2] Aristotle, *De sophisticis elenchis*, c.1 (165a7-22); c.7 (169a23-b18); *Topic.* v, passim (128b10ff.).

could admit that being is the first object of the intellect.[3] For nothing can be intelligible which does not include the notion of being in this sense, since what includes a contradiction, as we said above, is not intelligible. And in this sense, any science, not only that called real, but also a rational science, is about things or beings.

3.10 In the second sense of this first member, however, we say a "thing" is what can have entity outside the soul. Avicenna[4] seems to have this sense in mind when he says that "thing" and "being" are common to all genera. And that this does not refer to the words in one language, for in every language there is one undifferentiated concept that applies to everything that exists outside the soul. For concepts [according to Aristotle][5] are the same in all. In every language generally there is one name imposed on such a common concept, whether its commonness be one of analogy or univocity.

[3] 3.11 The first member, namely the very broad sense, therefore, we have subdivided into (a) that which includes no contradiction, whatever kind of "existence" it has, and (b) that which has or can have proper existence outside the intellect. And Avicenna takes "being" and "thing" either in both senses or at least in the second sense, as has been said.

3.12 ["Thing" taken generally] Boethius takes "thing" in its second meaning, i.e., generally [*communiter*], when he distinguishes between a thing and its mode[6]: "Have I now made clear the difference between the categories? Some indeed reveal the thing as it were, others, however, denote a kind of circumstance of the thing. The former are predicated in such a way as to show something to be a thing, whereas the latter say nothing about its being anything but ascribe something extrinsic to it." He wants to distinguish a thing, then, from the circumstances that surround it. And so for him only three categories, substance, quality, and quantity, are indicative of things; the rest are circumstances of a thing. "Thing" taken in this second or general sense, therefore, means something absolute in contrast to a circumstance or mode which expresses a way in which one thing is related to another.

3.13 ["Thing" taken very strictly] The Philosopher gives us a

---

[3] Cf. Duns Scotus, *Ord.* I, d.3, nn.108-201 (III, 68-123); cf. *infra*, Q. 14.

[4] Avicenna, *Metaph.* I, c.6 (II, fol. 72r).

[5] Aristotle, *De interpretatione* I (16a5-10).

[6] Boethius, *De Trin.* I, c.4: PL 64, 1253; *The Theological Tractates* with an English translation by H. F. Stewart and E. K. Rand (The Loeb Classical Library, Cambridge, Mass., and London, 1946), p. 22.

third meaning in Book VII of the *Metaphysics*[7]: "Accidents are called beings, because they belong to a being." And he adds: "Just as in the case of nonbeing, some say, emphasizing the linguistic form, there *is* nonbeing—not *is* simply—but *is* nonbeing; so too with quality." And farther on[8]: "And in the way in which the unknown may be said to be known and the word 'medical' is applied by virtue of a *reference* to one and the same thing, not *meaning* one and the same thing . . . ," so do we speak of being. And he seems to express the same idea at the beginning of Book IV.[9] As medical and healthy are used in many senses, so too is being. In these places the Philosopher takes "being," when stated simply and in its strongest sense, be it analogous or univocal, to mean that being to which existence pertains primarily and *per se*, namely, substance alone.

3.14 Therefore, the first or broadest meaning includes conceptual being and any kind of real being. The second signifies real and absolute being. The third, [or strictest sense], indicates a real, absolute, and *per se* being.

3.15 [Solution to the question] As this distinction shows, there is no difficulty about the question "Is a relation a thing?" if "thing" be taken in the second and third sense, for a relation is neither a substance nor an absolute. Only the first sense presents difficulty, though not as regards conceptual being, for it is clear that a relation can be thought of without contradiction. Here then the question is whether it has existence or is a thing having a real entity of its own outside the soul [or thinking mind].

3.16 [A relation is a thing] To this I answer, it is a thing. Second, I say what kind of thing it is. I prove that a relation is a thing [in God]. A relationship is real if, given real terms that are really distinct, it is there by the very nature of things. For its entity, whatever it be, is not just in the soul and consequently it is a thing in its own way and in accord with its own entity. But the relationship of Father to Son is this sort of thing, as is evident from the second ordinary question.[10]

3.17 [It is relative being] From what has been said it is clear what kind of thing this relationship is. For if it is a singular thing then it is either absolute or relative. Formally it is relative or "being to another." Neither does this determination "to another" militate

---

[7] Aristotle, *Metaph.* VII, c.4 (1030a23-27).
[8] Ibid. (1030a31-1030b4).
[9] Ibid., IV, c.2 (1003a32-1003b6).
[10] See *supra*, Q. 1, note 31.

against this meaning of "thing" [i.e., as extramental], for in this sense "thing" is not contrasted with a mode or relationship or a circumstance of a thing, but it covers them all.

ARTICLE II

As Related to the Essence, is the Relation a Thing and What Kind of Thing?

[4]   3.18 [Answer to the question] As for the second article, the first point will be that the relation is real; the second will be a logical consideration of this statement: "The relation, as related to the essence, is a thing"; the third point will be to clear up the issue of the compatibility or incompatibility of the two propositions in question.

1. The Relation as Related to the Essence is a Thing

3.19 To the first point, I say that the relation as related to the essence is a thing [res]. This is proved as follows:

First proof: When components that are somehow distinct make up a third, they do so only insofar as they are interrelated and united in some way. This is clear from the case of extrinsic causes which never function as such unless they concur some way in causation. It is even clearer in regard to intrinsic causes which never constitute a subject unless they are united in their own fashion. Now all agree a [divine] person is constituted by the essence and a relation, whatever their function as principles may be. Therefore, they do so to the extent they come together or concur, which could only happen if the relation is in the essence. From this I gather that the two constitute a person only insofar as the relation is in the essence. But for a relation to be in the essence is for it to be related to the essence independently of the mind's consideration in the truest sense of the word. Therefore a relation does not constitute a person except as related to or joined with the essence. But it does not constitute a person except as a thing. Otherwise a person, as formally constituted, would not be a thing. Therefore, the relation as related to the essence is a thing.

[5]   3.20 [Second proof] Another proof is this. Either this relationship to the essence is the whole of the relation or it is something in addition to it—whether this be a thing or an aspect is irrelevant for my present purpose. If it is the whole of the relation, then it is also a thing, from the first article [3.16ff.], and since the relation is its relationship to the essence, then as related to the essence it is a thing. Suppose the second is the case. No additional reference or relation,

QUESTION THREE

be it to something relative or absolute, be it real or rational, destroys that to which it comes. Rather it presupposes such. This is true of second intentions* [i.e., concepts of concepts], which do not destroy the first intentions* [i.e., concepts of things] to which they are added. Therefore the reality of a relation is not destroyed because it is related. Hence our thesis is evident.

3.21 [It is a relative thing] From this it is clear what kind of thing it is. For when anything is related to something, it is still itself, for according to the Philosopher,[11] "What it truly is, is never accidental to it." And even though the substance of an ox, when related to man, does not become the substance of a man, it is still a thing. And what kind? A substance. And what kind of substance? The substance of an ox. For it is what it is. And so this relation, which is essentially "to another" [*essentialiter ad alterum*], is never a non-thing, neither is it ever anything but a relational thing [*res ad alterum*]. For the relating, as we said, never destroys, but rather presupposes, the proper reality of what is related.

[6] 3.22 [Another opinion] Others[12] have a different way of speaking about the divine relations, which is this. The relation implies a relationship both with its opposite and with its foundation. One of these, its relationship with the essence, explains why it is simply real; the other, its relationship with its opposite, explains why one relation is distinct from another.

3.23 [This view is unacceptable] What accounts for any being's entity is the immediate foundation for a unity corresponding to that entity and, hence, for the distinction from anything that lacks unity. What accounts for a relation's being a thing that is actual, not just virtual or *in causa*, therefore, is also the immediate basis for its being distinct from any relation that is not it.

3.24 This is confirmed in particular for the divine relations. Every personal relation, at least, is of itself formally incommunicable.* But what is of itself formally incommunicable is also formally

---

[11] Aristotle, *Physic.* I, c.3 (186b4-5).

[12] Cf. Thomas, *Summa theol.* I, q.28, aa.2-3 in corp. (I, 152-54); q.36, a.2 in corp. (I, 193-94); Giles of Rome, *Sent.* I, d.11, princ. 1, qq.2-3 in corp. (ed. Augustinus Montifalconius, Venetiis, 1521; photoreprint Frankfurt-am-Main, 1968), fol. 64v-65r; d.29, princ. 1, q.2 in corp. (fol. 154r); *Quodl.* I, q.6 in corp. (ed. Simon de Hungaria, Bononiae, 1481), fol. 4r; Henry of Ghent, *Quodl.* v, q.1 in corp. (fol. 150A-154C); vi, q.1 in corp. (fol. 218Q-R); *Summa* a.53, q.9 in corp. (II, fol. 122B-H); a.54, q.4 in corp. (II, fol. 137B-C); a.60, q.1 in corp. (II, 153N-157F).

distinct of itself from anything communicable.* Therefore, the relation is distinct from everything communicable in virtue of that by which it gets the reality that makes it formally incommunicable.

3.25 Besides, if the essence, as they say, is the reality of all the relations and hence as related to the essence they do not differ in reality, then it follows that since this relationship is also in the essence, the relations do not differ really insofar as they are in the essence. Hence insofar as they are there, they do not differ at all, which is absolutely absurd, or else they differ only conceptually. But if this be the case, then the persons constituted by these relations, insofar as these are in the essence, differ only conceptually. But the persons are constituted by these relations, insofar as they are in the essence, as was pointed out in the first proof [3.19]. Therefore, [the persons differ only conceptually].[13]

3.26 Conclusion: Therefore, on this point, it seems more reasonable to hold that the relation's reality and its distinction from the other relations stem from the same source, whatever one understands this to be. For it is nonsense to speak of a relation being real unless its relationship to its opposite is real and as such it is really distinct from its opposite. Neither can it be really distinct from its opposite except as a real relation. And in this way it is a thing, insofar as to be a thing pertains to it. Therefore, of itself it is formally a thing, and of itself it is formally distinct from its opposite. But fundamentally and radically the relation gets both these characteristics from its foundation.

2. Logical Consideration of the Statement
"The relation as related to the essence is a thing."

[7] 3.27 Logically it seems necessary to clarify the statement "The relation as related to the essence is a thing." For terms like "as," "insofar," "*qua*" and the like can have two meanings. Sometimes they indicate the aspect under which the subject they modify is being considered. At other times, however, they imply in addition causality or the reason why the predicate inheres in the subject.

Example: In the definition "movement is the act of a being in potency insofar as it is in potency,"[14] the word "insofar" implies the aspect according to which movement is an act of the mobile. There are two aspects to the mobile; in one sense it is in act; in another, it is in potency to being something else. Motion is the act of the mobile

[13] Cf. Duns Scotus, *Ord.* I, d.11, nn.24-53 (v, 9-24).
[14] Aristotle, *Physic.* III, c.1 (201a10-11).

insofar as it is in potency. "Insofar as it is in potency," however, is not indicative of the cause or reason for the inherence of the predicate, for when such words as "insofar" and the like do introduce the cause, they express what is universal, according to the Philosopher.[15] To say "Justice is good *qua* good," according to him, means "Justice is every good." This is still clearer when it is the subject that is qualified. For from "Man as rational understands" it follows that "Every rational being understands." The same is true when the identical term is repeated as its own modifier preceded by *qua*.

[8] 3.28 In the first sense, then, it is the precise aspect of what is modified that is considered. In the other sense, repetition of the notion indicates the reason why the predicate inheres in the subject. In the first sense we say: "Man considered *qua* man is considered more precisely." In the second sense we say: "Man *qua* man is rational," for what follows *qua* is the reason for the predicate's inherence. The same could be said of "Man *qua* man is risible," for here we have the cause of the inherence of something predicated in the second mode of *per se* predication.*

3.29 Applying this to the issue at hand, I say that "The relation as related to the divine essence, is a thing" can be given two meanings. First, that the predicate "thing" pertains to the relation considered under this aspect, namely, as related to the essence. Or it can be taken in the second sense to mean that this relationship with the essence is the reason why the predicate, viz., that it is a thing, belongs to the subject. In the second sense, the proposition is false, for this relationship with the essence is conceptual since the two terms, i.e., the relation and the essence, are not really distinct. But the mind can connect or join them so that there is a relation between them.

3.30 Hence we do not speak of this second sense but of the first. And then the meaning of the statement is that the paternity, not only when taken precisely as paternity, but insofar as it is considered as related to the essence or insofar as it is in the essence, is a thing. For to relate it does not destroy the fact that paternity is a thing but rather presupposes this, as the second proof for the conclusion [in 3.20] of the second article shows. For example, "Man as risible understands," is not true in the sense that the ability to laugh is the reason why the predicate inheres. It is true, however, in the sense that to man, considered under the aspect of his ability to laugh, the predicate "understands" is not repugnant but suited to

---

[15] Aristotle, *Anal. priora* I, c.38 (49a12-22); *Metaph.* v, c.18 (1022a14-25).

him. In this sense, no qualification under which a subject is considered that does not exclude the predicate falsifies a statement in which the predicate is affirmed of the subject.[16]

3. Solution of the Principal Question

[9] 3.31 [Meaning of "The relation is an aspect"] All this helps us clarify the main issue. But first we should determine what it means to say "The relation is an aspect [*ratio*]." There are two relevant senses in which something can be called an aspect: (1) if it is a mode or modification of that to which it is related and lacks the reality of something absolute, it is not a "thing." In this sense Boethius [in 3.12] calls relations "circumstances" and not "things," because they lack the sort of reality found in the things of which they are the circumstances, and to the extent something departs from perfect reality it approaches the rational. (2) In another sense, something formally mind-dependent [*sub ratione*] can be called a "thing of the mind" or an aspect, just as the universal "man" is said to be such when considered under the aspect of universality which is an aspect *per se*.

In these two ways one can admit that the relation "as related to the essence" is an aspect, for as regards the essence, it is a mode, a kind of "circumstance," since it does not have the kind of entity that the essence has. And also when I say "as related to the essence," this relationship implies a mental referral as I have said before [in 3.27ff.], and paternity is considered under this aspect. Hence, paternity as related to the essence is a mental entity, because viewed as mind-dependent.

3.32 But if in either sense paternity, as related to the essence, is called an aspect, this is not to deny that paternity is a thing. In the first sense, it is its own sort of thing, namely a relational thing [*res ad alterum*] even though it is called an aspect [*ratio*] in comparison to an absolute thing. In the second sense, it is called an aspect as related to the essence, because that aspect under which it is considered does not have entity of itself. Nevertheless, paternity is still a thing, for the aspect under which it is considered does not destroy, but presupposes, its reality. For a relationship of something to another presupposes its entity.

[10] 3.33 [Conclusion] From all this it is clear that these two conceptions are compatible, viz., that the relation itself, as related to the

---

[16] Cf. Duns Scotus, *Ord.* III, d.11, q.2, nn.3-4 (ed. Vivès XIV, 427-28); d.6, q.2, nn.3-4 (ibid., 315-16).

essence, is a *ratio* or aspect in the two senses given above, and nevertheless this relation, as related to the essence, is a thing, as we have just said [in 3.29-30]. This is also consistent with the statement that the relation, as related to its opposite, is a thing, for the relation itself is this relationship with its opposite, and this relation is the thing itself which is this relationship. "Thing" is the more common designation when it is related to its opposite; and *"ratio,"* when related to the essence. For as related to its opposite, it is its equal and has a similar entity. Neither is it a mode of the other, nor the other a mode of it. Also the relation is its relationship with its opposite and therefore when it is said to be so related, it is not being considered under any other aspect which could properly be called *ratio*. For paternity, insofar as it is being compared to sonship, is nothing else than paternity in relation to sonship, and this is specifically paternity *qua* paternity. Therefore these two situations coexist: (1) paternity as related to its opposite is a thing, but not in the way it is a thing as related to the essence, for in relation to its opposite it is a thing in these two ways: (a) in contrast to a mode, it has a distinct entity like its opposite, and (b) it is a thing that is not viewed or considered formally as mind-dependent; and (2) paternity as related to the essence is an aspect for the two opposite reasons: (a) because it is a mode of the essence, and (b) it is viewed as mind-dependent for the "relationship" itself is a "thing of the mind." But for all that, whether it be related to its opposite or to the essence, in both cases it is a thing, and the same thing, for paternity itself is a real relationship, as has been proved [in 3.19-20].

ARTICLE III
Resolution of various Doubts

[11] 3.34 [First objection] In this third article, objections are raised to this solution.

The first is this: If the relation as related to the essence is a thing, this thing is either absolute or relative. But it seems contradictory that a relation should be in any way an absolute thing. Therefore, as related to the essence it is a relative thing. But as related to the essence, it is the same as the essence. Therefore, the relation, as identified with the essence, or as essence, is a relational thing. And to carry the argument a step farther, therefore the essence itself is a relational thing.

The validity of this inference is proved by a simile. If man as rational understands, the rational understands. It is also proved from reason. A predicate which pertains to a subject by virtue of some characteristic it has first pertains to that characteristic.

3.35 [Second objection] Again, if the relation, in relation to anything, is a thing with its own reality, then for like reasons the relation in a creature, in relation to its foundation, is a thing with its own reality which is not precisely the reality of the foundation. Hence there is an accident here with its own accidentality, for there is no substance here. And then it follows that the accidentality of the relation in the creature is one thing and the accidentality of the absolute in which it is founded is another. Thus an infinite regress seems to follow, for that accidentality of the relation has its own proper reality, and this can only be something accidental. Therefore, this too has its own accidentality. And the same thing can be said in turn of the latter, and so on *ad infinitum*.

3.36 [Third objection] Similarly in the divine, if the relation, as related to the essence, has its own reality, this is either substantial or accidental. It is not the latter, for nothing is accidental in God. Recall Book V, chapter five of *The Trinity*.[17] Therefore, the relation has its own proper substantiality. And then the Father, by virtue of his paternity, would have *per se* or substantial being, which is incongruous, for then there would be three substances in the divine for there are three relations. But there is only one unique substance in God, as Augustine points out when he says[18]: "The substance is that whereby the Father is, and whereby the Son similarly is, although it is not that by which the Father is Father."

[12] 3.37 [Reply to the first objection] I reply to the first [in 3.34]: The answer is evident from the distinction [in 3.27-30] made in the second article concerning the proposition: "The relation, as related to the essence, is a thing." This is true if "as" indicates a restriction, specification, or a consideration of paternity under this aspect which is its relationship with the essence, whereas it is not true if the cause of the predicate's inherence in the subject is what it indicates. If one asks then what sort of thing is it on the first interpretation, one could say it is a "relational thing," because to relate paternity to the essence does not make its own reality, which is a relational reality, inconsistent with paternity. But the statement must not be taken to mean that paternity as related to divinity is a relational thing or a "being to another," where the "other" refers to divinity, so that the sense would be "Paternity is a thing that relates

[17] Augustine, *De Trin.* v, c.5, n.6: PL 42, 914; CCSL 50, 210.
[18] Ibid., vii, c.6, n.11: PL 42, 943; CCSL 50, 262.

[the Father] to divinity." The sense is rather "Paternity, as related to the essence, is an aspect, and paternity in itself is a relational thing," namely, it is a "being related to the Son." For one who relates paternity to divinity by excluding or not including the Son, does not relate paternity unless he has two contradictories in his intellect, for paternity, by virtue of what it is, is essentially "being related to the Son." And though paternity is not of itself related to divinity, but to the Son as its correlative, nevertheless paternity as including "being related to the Son" can be related by an intellect to divinity, for the intellect by its act can relate something to that which is not its extramental correlative *per se*. In this sense one can say that paternity, as related to the essence, is a relational thing.

3.38 And when one infers [in 3.34] "Therefore, the relation, as identified with the essence, or as essence, is a relational thing," this may be admitted on a similar interpretation. And when you say further, "Therefore, the essence itself is a relational thing," this can be understood in two ways: (1) by identity or (2) formally.[19] In the first sense, it could be admitted and the meaning would be "Divinity is a relational thing because it is a paternity." But one must not admit formally that divinity according to its form is relational. There was a formal predication in the antecedent, however, in saying "Paternity as related to the essence is a relational thing." But if one infers from this that there is a similar predication in the consequent, "Divinity is formally relational," the validity of the inference must be denied. For if the specification does not indicate the reason for the predicate's inherence in the subject, then the predicate need not pertain to the specification in the same way that it pertains to the subject it specifies, which is the case here.

3.39 From this it is clear how to answer the proof given [in 3.31] for the validity of the inference, viz., "If man as rational understands, the rational understands." Here the inference is valid because the word "as" introduces the cause of the predicate's inherence in the subject, which is not true of the phrase "as related to the essence." The same for the proof that follows. If you have a case where the predicate can be affirmed even more truly of the ground for its inherence in the subject than it can of the subject itself, this is so only because the words "as," "insofar as" or the like are properly reduplicative. But they are not taken that way here, as we said in the logical analysis given in article two [3.27-30].

3.40 You may object: If something is formally in a thing, it can

---

[19] See Glossary: *"Formal distinction."*

denominate or name that thing. If the relation, as related to the essence, is in the essence, the essence can be named after the rela-
[14] tion. Hence the essence formally refers to something else. To this I answer: Some denominative or concrete terms are predicated of their subjects in the first mode of *per se* or essential predication;* others are predicated in the second mode of essential predication or they are predicated accidentally. A concrete or denominative term derived from the form, for instance, is predicated in the first mode of essential predication of the composite of form and whatever receives that form, particularly if the subject term is a concept that is *per se* one. It is in this way that man is said to be rational or living. But the body, which is the other part of the composite, is said to be living denominatively, but in the proper sense of denominative (which is either *per se* predication in the second mode or is *per accidens* predication), for the body is not a whole which includes this form, but the subject which receives it. Wherever there is a form, then, there must be a formal predication of the whole which is in the first *per se* mode. Also in creatures there should commonly be a predication that is properly denominative where the recipient of the form is given a name derived from the form. In the divine the first type of predication is not denied, for the Father begets or the begettor begets. The Father is a kind of composite which includes essentially that form which is predicated of him. But there does not have to be a denominative predication in which a name derived from the quasi form [i.e., the relation of paternity] must be applied to the quasi recipient of that form [i.e., the essence].

3.41 Both reason and authority make this clear. Reason in this way: What is understood as the quasi recipient of the form in God is unlimited as regards the opposite forms or relations, but it is not distinguished by them. What is denominated or named after some form, however, is thereby singled out as distinct from its opposite. Since in this case the form has no proper recipient but one which is common to it and its opposite, and since such a form could only denominate a proper recipient, for only such can be distinct from its opposite, it follows therefore that the relations are not predicated denominatively of the essence.

3.42 Damascene[20] confirms this where he says that the relations distinguish the persons, not the nature. Therefore they are noted for singling out that of which they are predicated concretely, because they relate it to, and distinguish it from, its opposite.

[20] Damascene, *De fide orth.* I, c.10: PG 94, 838; ed. Buytaert c.10, p. 51.

3.43 As for the form of the counterargument [in 3.34], the inference "The relation is in the essence, therefore the essence can be named after the relation" is invalid. The reason has been stated [in 3.40]. When it is claimed that every form can denominate that in which it is, using "denominate" in an extended sense to cover both essential denominative predication of a concrete term (e.g., "Man is living") and denomination proper (e.g., "Man is risible" or "The wood is white" or "A man is thinking"), one can admit that every form denominates that in which it is in one of these two ways, because at least it is predicated of the composite as a concrete term, although this is broadening the meaning of "to name" or "to denominate." But if you take it to mean that the predicate is predicated denominatively in the proper sense of the term of a subject which receives or supports the form, it must be denied, unless this sustaining factor is limited, or the denominative predication implies that it is a proper subject and distinct from its opposite.

[15] 3.44 [Reply to the second objection in 3.35] To the second: Though it would pose a serious difficulty as regards what is *per se*, I will let it pass because it is not relevant to this issue. I concede, however, that a relation, which in creatures is an accident, has its own accidentality, for it is a thing in itself and yet it is not the thing on which the relation is based nor is it a thing that is being *per se*, as substance is. Therefore, one should admit that in itself a relation is a thing with its own accidentality which is not the accidentality of an absolute being but that of a relational being. For just as the absolute and relative entity is not the same, so neither is the accidentality of an absolute accident the same as that of a relative accident.

3.45 And when it is argued [in 3.35] that this entails an infinite regress, I reply that one must stop with the relation itself and not go farther. For example, if whiteness is the foundation for a relationship of similarity, this similarity has some accidentality of its own distinct from the accidentality of the whiteness, even as "relation" is a category distinct from "quality."

3.46 But if you ask: Is the accidentality of similarity something distinct from similarity itself? I say: No. For the similarity is its accidentality towards the foundation, and it is the similarity itself that "befalls" [*accidit*] the foundation just as it is the similarity itself that relates to the opposite [i.e., the object to which it is similar]. For it is always the case that whatever pertains to something in such a way that it would be a complete contradiction for former to exist without the latter, then the latter is really identical with the former. And by contrast, where there is no such contradiction, there is no need for it to exist at all. Now there is a contradiction, however, that there be similarity which is unrelated either to its foundation or to its term. Therefore, its accidentality with reference to the foundation is identical with itself just as its similarity or relationship to its opposite.

[16]   3.47 Hence the regress stops, for the accidentality of the similarity is not a thing distinct from the similarity itself, but similarity is one thing and the whiteness another, for the relation as well as the accidentality of the whiteness can be asserted to be a certain kind of thing distinct from the whiteness, since whiteness is a kind of absolute thing and an absolute accident can exist apart from a subject without contradiction. Therefore, whiteness is not the same as its relation to a subject, nor does it befall the subject itself. This proposition then is false: "The same reason why the accidental similarity of whiteness has an accidentality other than whiteness, also guarantees that the similarity's accidentality will have an accidentality that is other than the similarity itself." This is also false: "The same reason why the accidentality of the similarity is the same as the similarity, also guarantees that the accidentality of the whiteness is identical with the whiteness," for whiteness is an absolute being, whereas similarity is a relation.

3.48 From this it follows that for whiteness to exist with no relation to a bodily surface is not a contradiction, although it is a contradiction for similarity to exist with no relation to its foundation. Hence its relationship to the surface is not the same as the whiteness, whereas the relationship to its foundation is the same thing as the similarity. For similarity to exist means nothing else than that this relationship to the foundation exists. I do not claim, however, that whenever a relation is related to anything, it has this relationship of itself, for it can be related by a mental relationship which is not the same as itself. Perhaps it can also be related by a relationship that is not itself and yet is really distinct from it, as proportionality based on proportion. But this much I do say: If the relation is related to something without which it would be a contradiction to exist, then it refers to this of itself and not by means of another relationship.[21]

[17]   3.49 [Reply to the third objection in 3.36] When it is claimed

[21] Cf. Duns Scotus, *Ord.* IV, d.12, q.1, n.5 (ed. Vivès XVII, 534); q.2, n.18 (573-74); II, d.1, q.4, nn.3-16 (XI, 96-112); III, d.8, q.un., n.17 (XIV, 377).

further that the relation in the divine is substantial, my reply is this: Although the Philosopher distinguishes first substance from second substance in the *Categories*[22] nevertheless in the case at hand the essence functions in both ways insofar as it is related to anything. To the extent that it is common it has the aspect of secondary substance. Not, however, in the sense that it is a universal, i.e., divisible or able to be multiplied, for it is common by a community that is real, says Damascene[23]: "There is a community of substance, which is not merely one of reason" [i.e., created by the mind], as is the case with a created nature. It has the characteristic of primary substance, however, to the extent that it is just this being or singular, for the divine essence is singular of itself.[24] I do not say that it is incommunicable being, for this would imply imperfection. But apart from the essence in God there is no other feature of substance in any sense of the term unless it would be incommunicability. In the divine, however, incommunicability cannot have the meaning of substance *per se*, according to the common opinion which we generally follow in these questions. But we do not raise this issue here, because whatever is there, not only substance, but also what is absolute, is communicable. It is clear then that a relation in God does not have the characteristic of substantiality, but only that of incommunicability, which is neither the meaning of secondary substance, nor that of primary substance—so far as its perfection is concerned, which is to be a "this" or individual. For this the essence has of itself.

[18] 3.50 [Counterarguments to this reply] It may be argued against this that whatever pertains to the first substance has some *per se* characteristic of substantiality. Incommunicability, which is there solely in virtue of a relation, is such. Therefore, [it has some *per se* characteristic of substantiality].

I answer: Understanding incommunicability in the sense that it pertains to the first substance, viz., the incommunicability characteristic of singularity, we can say the minor is true only of creatures, not of God. The reason is that in creatures that which ultimately contracts the nature to singularity or incommunicability is the same sort of thing as the contracted nature, and hence taken in its formal meaning it pertains to the genus or category of substance. In God

---

[22] Aristotle, *Praedicamenta* c.5 (2a12-19).
[23] Damascene, *De fide orth.* I, c.8: PG 94, 827; ed. Buytaert c.8, p. 43.
[24] Cf. Duns Scotus, *Ord.* II, d.3, q.1, n.9 (ed. Vivès XII, 54-55); q.6, n.5 (ibid., 130).

this is not so, as has been pointed out earlier [in 3.49]. Nothing that belongs to the genus or quasi-genus of substance, as we said before, can contract the divine nature to incommunicability, since everything substantial in God is communicable [or capable of being shared by all three persons].

3.51 But someone may still say: Whatever you call it in God that does the contracting or restricting required for incommunicability or the incommunicable, considered formally, it is either substance or accident, since there is nothing in between. Obviously it is not an accident. Therefore, it is a substance and hence has its own substantiality.

I reply with Augustine[25] that not everything in God is predicated by way of substance or accident. For there are things said of him, especially relational assertions, that express something that is neither substantial nor yet accidental.

3.52 But you might still reply: What makes a divine person incommunicable formally is the sort of thing to which "to inhere" either (1) does or can pertain formally, or (2) is formally repugnant. If the first, it is an accident; if the second, then, since that to which "to inhere in another" is repugnant is substance as contrasted with accident, it follows that what makes a person incommunicable is essentially substance, and hence has its own substantiality, which is the thesis proposed.

[19] I answer: According to Avicenna,[26] "not to inhere" and "unable to inhere" is not the essential meaning of substance insofar as substance is a genus or category. Neither is "to inhere" the essential meaning of accident nor any genus thereof, for "to inhere" means to have being or actuality in a qualified sense and implies something which is already a being in an unqualified sense. But substance is that substrate to which "not to inhere" is appropriate or "to inhere" is repugnant, whereas accident, be it quantity or quality, is a nature to which "to inhere" is appropriate. Therefore, let the second alternative hold for God, i.e., "What makes a divine person incommunicable formally is the sort of thing to which 'to inhere' is formally repugnant." For it cannot give qualified being to something that is simply being already. This does not imply it has its own substantiality by definition, because "not to inhere" does not express the complete meaning of substance as contrasted with the other categories.

3.53 A fourth counterreply might be: There is one common rea-

[25] Augustine, *De Trin.* v, c.6, n.6: PL 42, 913-14; CCSL 50, 913-14.
[26] Avicenna, *Metaph.* II, c.1 (II, 74v).

son why "to inhere" is repugnant to anything. But such repugnance is the mark of substance or anything in that category, and according to you, it is also characteristic of an incommunicable property in the divine, and therefore they have some reason in common why this is so. This is not the note of being, for "to inhere" is not repugnant to a being; neither is it anything that comes under the heading of being except substance. This is evident if you run through the possibilities. Therefore an incommunicable property to which "to inhere" is repugnant as such has the mark of what is essential to substance and so has its own substantiality, which is the point at issue.

[20] I answer: An imperfection can be repugnant to something either because the latter includes only pure perfection or because it includes some other imperfection incompatible with the first. For there are many imperfections that are mutually incompatible, e.g., it is repugnant for God to be white and it is repugnant for black to be white; to God, because of his pure perfection, which is repugnant to any kind of color, or for that matter to the entire category of quality and to the whole class of things that are caused; to black, on the other hand, white is repugnant because of its limited perfection within the genus of color, which limited perfection necessarily has imperfection conjoined with it. But this imperfection is distinct from and of a different degree from the imperfection associated with the perfection of white. Therefore we must deny this idea expressed in the major, namely, that the reason why the same imperfection, such as "to inhere" or "to be dependent on substance," is repugnant to anything is that there is something which is the same in each. On the contrary, their repugnance to the same thing may stem from what is proper to each of them.

Applying this to the case at hand, "to inhere" or "to depend on substance" is an imperfection. To substance it is repugnant, then, because substance is the sort of entity to which any diminished or lesser form of entity is repugnant. Substance gives being or existence in an unqualified sense, which is the opposite of the qualified "being" implied by "to inhere." "To inhere" can also be repugnant to the divine relation. For though the relation does not give *per se* being or existence in an unqualified sense, nevertheless it is the sort of entity to which it is repugnant to be a diminished form of being or something that is actual only in a qualified sense. On the other hand, "to inhere" is repugnant to the divine essence because it is pure perfection. And even though the divine relation is not pure perfection, nevertheless by reason of what it is, it cannot be an imperfect entity either, and "to inhere" can only pertain to what is dependent and consequently imperfect.

Reply to the Initial Argument

[21] 3.54 To the argument at the beginning [in 3.3]:

The claim that the relation as related to the essence is an aspect, because it merges with the essence, can have an interpretation, as to both its parts, that is either true or false.

For an "aspect" [*ratio*] can mean something opposed to a thing or being outside the soul, and then the claim is false. For regardless of to what a divine relation is related, it is always a thing outside the soul, with its own reality, which is that of a relation. On the other hand, an aspect can be taken to mean what Boethius [in 3.54] calls a "mode" or "circumstance of a thing," and then one must admit that the relation with reference to the essence is this sort of thing.

3.55 Similarly, one can understand "it merges with the essence" to mean that it does not have an entity of its own which is relational, and in this sense it is false. In another sense, to "merge with the essence" may mean it does not remain really distinct from the essence. And although the question here is not about the identity or distinction between the relation and essence (which is more difficult than the question under discussion), it can still be admitted that the relation, as related to the essence, is an aspect in the second sense, that is, it is a mode or modification of the essence and merges with it, not in the first but the second sense. And in this way, it does not remain really distinct. But for all that, it is a thing outside the soul with its own reality that is relational. Thus "it remains," to the extent that "remains" excludes any merging that is destructive of its proper reality.

[22] 3.56 Similarly, if in the conclusion, it is inferred that the relation, as related to the essence, is an aspect (Add: "with respect to the essence," for it is taken in this sense in the premise), this is conceded, for it cannot be related to anything which would deprive it of its status as a mode of the essence. Nevertheless, this does not follow: "Therefore, as related to its opposite, it is not a thing," for to be an aspect in the sense of "mode" or "circumstance" is not opposed to its being a thing.

3.57 If it is argued: "With respect to the essence it is a thing, therefore it is another thing," I answer: The question about the reality of a relation is not a question about its otherness. The first pertains to "the problem of genus or accident," the second to the "definitory problem of the same or different," as is clear from Bk. I of the *Topics*.[27] It is also clear from this example. Man, with reference to Socrates, is a thing. Indeed, even Socrates, with reference to Socrates, is a thing. Proof of both lies in the fact that real identity is the identity of a thing with respect to a thing, and it is obvious that "a man" [referring to Socrates] is really the same thing as Socrates, and Socrates is the same thing as Socrates (it is understood that the same Socrates is being compared to himself). And still neither man nor Socrates, with reference to Socrates, is another thing than Socrates. In the question at hand, therefore, these are compatible, viz., that the relation, as related to the essence, is a thing, and yet it is not another thing.

3.58 If it be asked whether it is the same thing as the essence or is it something other than it, let us concede that it is really the same. But it is not necessary to discuss this for the question raised here. It suffices to say that it is a thing which relates to another. Therefore, no matter what it be related to, it merges with the essence and remains a relational thing.

[27] Aristotle, *Topica* I, c.4 (101b17-25); ibid., c.5 (102a30-102b27).

Question Four

COULD THE FIRST DIVINE PERSON REMAIN CONSTITUTED AS A PERSON, DISTINCT FROM THE OTHER PERSONS, APART FROM THE RELATIONSHIP OF ORIGIN?

[1] 4.1 The next question concerns the connection between the relationship of origin* and the persons, especially the first person, namely: Could the first divine person remain constituted as a person, distinct from the other persons, apart or prescinding from the relationship of origin?[1]

Arguments Pro and Con

Argument for the affirmative:

What adds to a person already constituted neither constitutes nor distinguishes him primarily. But such is the relationship of origin as regards the first person. Therefore, [the relationship of origin neither constitutes nor distinguishes the first person primarily].

Proof of the minor: A relation of origin results from acting or being acted upon, according to the *Metaphysics*.[2] What pertains to the first person can come only from acting, since he does not proceed from anyone. But acting requires an existing suppositum* inasmuch as the notion of acting presupposes the notion of a suppositum. Therefore, the first person is a person or suppositum by virtue of something antecedent to the relation itself.

4.2 To the contrary:

Apart from the relations, there is nothing but the essence or common substance. Now this cannot be what formally constitutes a person, since it is neither incommunicable* nor proper to any one of them. Therefore, [apart from a relation, there is nothing to constitute a person].

Body of the Question

[2] 4.3 The question itself presupposes the common view that a divine person is constituted by a relation.[3] This is not discussed here

---

[1] Cf. Duns Scotus, *Ord.* I, d.28, nn.1-51 (VI, 107-37); d.26 (VI, 1-61).
[2] Aristotle, *Metaph.* V, c.15 (1020b30, 1021a16-19).
[3] Cf. Duns Scotus, *Ord.* I, d.26, q.un. (VI, 4ff.).

since it is more difficult than the issue raised, but in these questions it has been presupposed as commonly conceded, for there is no need to call everything into doubt when the question at issue can be settled on the basis of what is commonly admitted.

This is not a general question of whether it is possible for some person to be constituted by a relation, but it concerns the first person specifically. For there appears to be a special difficulty in his regard, since his priority to the other persons seems to clash with the nature of correlatives.

Assuming the common opinion, therefore, we have four points to investigate in this special question about the first person: (1) Granted that some divine person is constituted by a relation, as the question seems to assume, would this be something specifically repugnant to the first person? (2) If not, by what relation could the first person be constituted? (3) How are the various relations commonly admitted to be present in the first person interrelated? (4) Finally, by way of corollary, it will become clear what kind of abstracting or prescinding might be compatible with the notion of what constitutes the first person.

ARTICLE I
Is it Repugnant that the First Person be Constituted by a Relation?

[3]   4.4 [It is not repugnant that persons of the same nature have personal properties which are by nature simultaneous] On the first question, I accept this proposition: "To persons of the same nature, it is not repugnant to have personal properties which are simultaneous in nature."

4.5 Proof of this proposition. There is no priority of nature or essence among persons of the same nature. This is confirmed by the Philosopher,[4] who on this point agrees with Plato: "In those things which are of the same species there is no prior and posterior." But, by hypothesis, the second person can be constituted by a relation of origin [viz., begotten]; therefore it is not repugnant to the first person to be constituted by some property which is simultaneous in nature with it, such as another relation of origin [viz., begetting].

4.6 Besides, if it were specifically repugnant to the first person to be constituted by a relationship of origin, it would not be because of something common to him and the other persons, for by stipulation it is not repugnant to another [to be so constituted]. Therefore, it would be by something peculiar to the first person. But this is not

[4] Aristotle, *Metaph.* III, c.3 (999a5-6).

the case, for the first person has nothing special except this priority of origin in virtue of which every other person proceeds from him, whereas he proceeds from none. This priority, however, does not militate against his being constituted by a relationship to the second person. Any repugnance, if there were such, would come from the fact that the simultaneity between the two terms required by the relationship seems to conflict with this person's priority.

But there is no true conflict here. Proof: When there are several orders of different kinds, one of which does not include or presuppose the other as a necessary prerequisite or concomitant condition, the first can be without the other: it can even co-exist with a simultaneity that excludes the other order. This is clear enough from this example. The order of duration and of nature are such that the latter does not include the former, nor does it require it as a prior or concomitant condition. Therefore, there can be an order or priority of nature* without a temporal priority. This is also clear from reason. Separation is never impossible unless one includes the other or has to have it as a prior or concomitant condition. Now the order of nature or essential order,* on the one hand, and the order of origin, on the other, are not so related that the latter always includes the essential order or presupposes it as a necessary or concomitant condition. Therefore, simultaneity opposed to an essential priority* or order is compatible with an order or priority of origin.* But simultaneity opposed to an essential order is enough to account for the simultaneity required for correlatives. Therefore, some things can be simultaneous with the simultaneity characteristic of correlatives (i.e., an essential simultaneity) and nevertheless an order of origin may exist between them.

4.7 Proof of the minor, which has two parts, viz., that the order of origin neither (a) includes the other order, nor (b) has it as a prerequisite. An essential order or order of nature necessarily includes imperfection in one of the extremes, viz., in the posterior.[5] An order of origin, on the other hand, only requires that one come from the other, but the fact that this is so does not necessarily include imperfection in the second, for it does not necessarily imply that the sub-

---

[5] He speaks of the essential order, which exists between an equivocal cause* and its effect. Outside such an order what is posterior in nature is not thereby more imperfect. Cf. Duns Scotus, *Ord.* I, d.8, n.178 (IV, 246-47); IV, d.49, q.4, n.5 (ed. Vivés XXI, 98); *Ord.* prol., nn.265-66 (I, 179-80): cf. *infra, Quodl.* Q. 13; *Ord.* I, d.5, nn.46-157 (IV, 39-86); d.7, nn.1-91 (IV, 107-48); d.12, nn. 54-68 (V, 57-64); d.28, nn.6-51 (VI, 107-37); II, d.1, q.1 (ed. Vivés XI, 6-45).

ject which proceeds is less perfect by nature than that from which it proceeds, for the procession as such does not have to be equivocal* so that the form would be less perfect in the product than in the producer.

ARTICLE II
By What Relation could the First Person be Constituted?

[4] 4.8 a) [Proof it is by a relation opposed to that which constitutes the second person] According to what is assumed [in 4.3, viz., that a person is constituted by a relation], I say about this article that the second person is constituted by one distinct relation and that by another relation opposed to this the first person is constituted.

4.9 It is proved in this way: The first positive incommunicable property is that which constitutes the first person. Such is the property which corresponds correlatively to the first relation in the person produced. Therefore, [this constitutes the first person].

4.10 The major is evident. Since the person includes the essence and an incommunicable entity (which are presupposed in this question) according to Richard,[6] it is not necessary that the property of the first person imply of itself something other than the first incommunicable entity.

4.11 The minor is evident. According to the common view presupposed in this question, only a property that has to do with origin can be incommunicable in the divine. Hence, in the first person only the property pertaining to the first in origin is incommunicable, for what pertains to the second in origin is communicable, because it is shared by two productive persons. What pertains to the first active production, however, is opposed to what pertains to the first passive. As the Son has the first property of being generated or spoken, so the Father has the first incommunicable property of speaking or begetting, for this pertains to the Father insofar as he has a fecund intellect which is the first productive factor in the Father.

[5] 4.12 b) [Objection to the major premise and its solution] Objections are raised to both premises of this argument.[7] First, against the major:

[6] Richard of St. Victor, *De Trinitate* IV, cc.21-24: PL 196, 944-47; ed. J. Ribaillier (Paris, 1958), 186-90.
[7] Bonaventure, *Sententiarum* I, d.27, p.1, a.un., q.2 (*Opera*, ed. PP. Collegii S. Bonaventurae, Ad Claras Aquas, 1883-1902, I, 469ff.); Roger Marston, *De emanatione aeterna* q.2 in corp. (BFS VII, 28-33, 41, 55-56).

[Objection] It seems that the primary factor constituting the first person is his being unbegotten, and then the major is false, viz., that the first positive property is the personal property.

4.13 Authority and reason both substantiate this. The authority is that of Damascene[8]: "The Son has all things whatsoever that the Father has, except the Father's being unbegotten, which does not imply any difference in substance . . . but rather a manner of existence."

4.14 The reason is this: An incommunicable principle is the primary constitutive factor in the first person. This is proved because the essence is not only the reason for a person's being in a simple or unqualified sense, but also for his being this; hence only incommunicability is required to complete the notion of a person, so that the person is the result of what is had first [i.e., the essence] plus incommunicability. But "unbegotten" seems to imply an incommunicable principle. Therefore, [unbegotten constitutes the first person].

4.15 Proof of this minor: What proceeds from one, but has another proceed from it, is related to the first before the second. Proof: It has its first being from its source and any order to what proceeds from it presupposes this being. From this proposition about a positive order to both the prior and the posterior, this consequent is inferred. To a being which has no order to the anterior but only to the posterior which stems from it, the negation of an order to the anterior pertains to it before its order to the posterior. Now the first person is not ordered to anything anterior, but he does have an order to his posterior. Therefore, the negation of any order to an anterior is his first characteristic; such is unbegotten.

4.16 Proof that the negation of any order to an anterior is a characteristic prior to his order to any posterior: Contradictories are referred not only to the same moment of duration or time, but also, one could say, to the same "now" or "sign of nature."* This appears clear inductively. Because "Man is rational" is true in the first mode of *per se* predication,* and "Man is risible" in the second *per se* mode, and "Man is white" in the *per accidens* mode, one could assign instants or signs of nature on the basis of the order among these predications. And then it would not be contradictory to affirm "Man is rational *per se* in the first mode or first sign of nature" and to deny "Man is rational in the second mode or second sign of nature," even as it would not be contradictory to say "Man is white in the third sign" and "Man is not white in the second or first sign." It is

---

[8] Damascene, *De fide orth.* 1, c.8: PG 94, 818; ed. Buytaert c.8, 35.

clear then there would be no contradiction unless it is a matter of the same sign of nature. And similarly as regards "signs of origin,"* it is clearly contradictory "to be from another" and "not to be from another." It would be in the same sign, therefore, that "to be from another" would be ascribed to one who had this characteristic, and that "not to be from another" would be ascribed to another who had that characteristic. And just as his relation to his source is prior in terms of origin to his relation to his product for one who comes from another, so too for one who is not from anyone, the negation of any order to a prior is anterior to his positive order to his posterior.

4.17 If one objects that a negation lacks what is needed to constitute a person, they[9] reply that this personal element, which one thinks of as added to the essence, suffices to give the first grounds for incommunicability. For the essence gives the person his being, his singularity, and whatever positive characteristics he has. If then a further affirmation or negation could be the grounds for incommunicability, this would suffice to constitute the person. But the negation in question does have this property, viz., of being the first grounds for incommunicability, as has been proved [in 4.15ff.]. Therefore, [it suffices to constitute the first person].

[7] 4.18 [Answer to the objection against the major] Against this type of reasoning, it is argued: The property constitutive of a person is in every way formally and primarily incommunicable.[10] No negation of itself is formally and primarily incommunicable. But "unbegotten," insofar as it is distinguished formally from both the essence and the positive relation to the person produced, includes nothing more than a negation formally, for, as many authorities, including Augustine,[11] make clear: "To call the Father unbegotten is not to say what he is, but what he is not." Therefore, [unbegotten is not his constitutive property].

4.19 The first proposition is patent. Since a person is formally incommunicable, that by which he is primarily a person must be formally incommunicable.

The second proposition is clear, for no negation, considered absolutely, is proper to anything. Put another way, if it does pertain of

---

[9] Roger Marston, *De emanat. aeterna* q.2, ad 5 and 13 (BFS VII 35, 37).
[10] Cf. Duns Scotus, *Ord.* I, d.28, nn.12-20, 27-28 (VI, 111-17, 120-21); d.36, nn.58-59 (VI, 294-95); d.23, nn.21-23 (V, 360-63). According to Scotus the divine person is constituted by something positive.
[11] Augustine, *De Trin.* v, c.6, n.7: PL 42, 915; CCSL 50, 212.

necessity to one subject alone, this is because the affirmation opposed to such a negation is repugnant to that subject. Only in virtue of something positive, however, is an affirmation repugnant to anything. If it were repugnant because of some negation, we would have to ask if that negation presupposes something positive to which some other affirmation is opposed. And then either our thesis holds good or something positive is not presupposed (and then a negation is simply first as regards the unity, the distinction, and, therefore, the entity characteristic of a person, which is incongruous), or it must be maintained that the negation presupposes something which, though positive, is not proper (and then it follows that the negation is not proper either, because that in virtue of which it pertains to the person, is not proper to him).

[8] 4.20 [Two counter-arguments to our answer] Against the minor [in 4.18], it is argued[12] that "unbegotten" does not mean simply a negation, but a measure of perfection, since it implies having being or existence of itself or *a se*.

Another challenge to the minor is this:[13] "Unbegotten" implies a fontal plenitude* which is simply perfection in the first person, according to Augustine.[14]

4.21 [Reply to the counter-arguments] Against the first: In [4.20] the phrase "having existence of itself," "of" is either indicative of a cause or positive principle, and then the contradiction is immediately evident, for no mind can grasp the idea of something begetting itself, as Augustine[15] points out, or else it is taken in a purely negative sense, i.e., there is nothing that functions as a cause or source, and then you have what the minor proposed.

Against the second: "Fontal plenitude" [in 4.20] asserts either something negative (the point we wished to make) or something positive. If positive, this is either the essence (and then if "unbegotten" is a personal property, so too is the essence) or a positive rela-

---

[12] Roger Marston, *De emanat. aeterna* q.2 in corp., ad 5, 13, 25 (BFS VII, 28-29, 35, 37, 41).

[13] Walter of Bruges, *Sententiarum* I, d.28, p.1, q.2 in corp.: Cod. Vat. Chigi (B.VI, 94, fol. 53r); q.5 in corp. (fol. 53v); Alexander of Hales, *Summa theologica* I, n.481 (ed. PP. Collegii S. Bonaventurae, Ad Claras Aquas, 1924-48, I, 683-84); Bonaventure, *Sent.* I, d.27, a.un., q.2, ad 3 (I, 470-71); Roger Marston, *De emanat. aeterna*, q.2 in corp., ad 8 (BFS VII, 30-36) Thomas, *Summa theol.* I, q.33, a.4 in corp., ad. 1 (I, 175-76).

[14] Augustine, *De Trin.* v, cc.6-7: PL 42, 914-16; CCSL 50, 211-14.

[15] Ibid., I, c.1, n.1: PL 42, 820; CCSL 50, 28.

tion. Since this is obviously a relationship to a person, it is either to one person or to several. Since it is not a relation to anyone producing, it must be to a person or persons produced. If the relation be to several, it will not be one formal principle, constitutive of a person. If it is a relation to one individual person, this is either the first or the second person produced. In either case, the original assumption is abandoned, viz., that "unbegotten," as distinct from either paternity or spiration,* constitutes the person. If the relation be one which is abstracted from both of these, viz., paternity and spiration, then if some common relationship of this sort can be abstracted from these two, it follows that the first person is not marked out in existence as a person by some one, i.e., singular, relation, but rather by a relation that is somehow one, even though abstracted from two different kinds of relations, for—as we proved [in 2.46ff.] of a previous question—there cannot be two active productions of the same kind in God. Hence, the first person would not be formally constituted by some constitutive factor with at least a kind of specific unity, but by one abstracted from two different kinds of things as it were. There is no need to waste more time here, since many masters admit our thesis about the major, viz., that the first person, with which we are dealing here, is constituted by some positive incommunicable factor.

[9]   4.22 As for the appeal [in 4.13] to Damascene in support of the objection, namely that "unbegotten" is the constitutive factor, we can answer with his own words in that same chapter: "It is only in paternity, filiation, and procession, that we recognize their difference." Therefore, when he says earlier, "The Son has all things whatsoever that the Father has, except the Father's being unbegotten," we must understand "unbegotten" to include paternity. To put it briefly, he uses now one property, now another to designate the first person, as you can see from the different chapters, and hence by any one of them he understands some property peculiar [to the Father].

4.23 As for the proof [in 4.15], I concede a subject's order or relation to what is prior precedes its order to what is posterior, especially if the subject is something absolute. I also admit [regarding 4.16] that the negation of an order to anything prior precedes a positive relationship to what is posterior if the subject is an absolute, but not if it is formally constituted by its relationship to the posterior, for no order in such a subject can be prior to the order by which it is constituted, and the same holds for a negation of order.

If the person were an absolute, one could admit that "unbegotten" was in some sense prior to paternity, but when the proposition "Two contradictories refer to the same *now*, not only in the order of duration but also in the order of nature and origin" [cited in 4.16] is applied generally to any subject which has an order to a posterior but no order to any anterior, the proposition is true if understood of *per se* contradictories, like an affirmation in relation to its negation. It is not true, however, if understood of an affirmation and a negation in relation to some third thing of which they are predicated.

4.24 For example, white in A and non-white in B do not contradict each other as such; neither do they do so when related to anything else. This is so whether we understand A and B to be signs of duration or signs of nature or origin. But if white and non-white are related to something to which they pertain or can pertain, then if white pertains to C at moment A, there is no need that non-white pertain to C at that same moment, for what is absolutely first about anything is that it be itself. Man is first of all man. If he were a stone, he would be first of all a stone, just as stone is first stone. Man is not first of all non-stone, for no negation can be as identical with anything as the affirmation that it is itself. Hence I admit that in order to be contradictory, "to be from someone" and "not to be from someone" must be referred to the same instant or "now" in any order, so that to deny what is affirmed, one would have to say at that same instant it is both "from another" and "not from another." But "not to be from another" need not pertain to its subject with the same perfection and priority as "to be from another" does, if such be the case. Consequently, if a suppositum is not ordered to something prior with a priority of origin, this negation does not pertain to it with the same priority that the affirmation of such an order would, if it were so ordered.[16]

[11]   4.25 c) [Objections to the minor premise and their solutions[17]:

[16] Cf. Duns Scotus, *Ord.* I, d.28, nn.12-20, 27-28 (VI, 111-17, 120-21); d.36, nn.58-59 (VI, 294-95); d.23, nn.21-23 (V, 360-63).

[17] M₁ and W have the following long addition which seems to be an earlier version of 4.25ff.; M₂ gives only the first two objections:

Other objections are raised against the minor of our main argument:
  (1) The first incommunicable property in the first person is not an actual but an aptitudinal relation, since it is not concerned with paternity or generation as such but the ability to generate. Proof: Anything

First objection] The following point is raised against the minor premise of our argument [in 4.9].[18] Although the relationship of the first person as the origin of the second is one in reality, nevertheless the mind makes a distinction as regards the way this relationship to the second person is present in the first. One can understand it (a)

---

else presupposes this ability to generate; hence what we propose follows, viz., what constitutes the first person is not the actual but the aptitudinal relationship to the Son.

(2) What is in the first person as a kind of relationship to the second can be considered in two ways: one, as a property; the other, as a relation. In the second case, because of the nature of correlatives, it is simultaneous with the opposite, i.e., that which constitutes the second person. In the first way, however, it can constitute the first person and the simultaneity characteristic of correlatives is not involved.

Two sorts of replies can be given to these objections, the first of which is a common rejoinder to both objections, the other attacks each separately.

The first common rejoinder is this. In the first divine person there is but one unique entity that is formally and primarily incommunicable and has actual or real existence. This is self-evident, for it is impossible that there should be several primary incommunicable actual entities in one and the same person. Nothing can be a personal property in a person unless it be formally, primarily, and *per se* incommunicable and has actual or extramental existence; for a divine person cannot be primarily this person in virtue of something potential or in some way not real or in virtue of something communicable or something not primarily incommunicable. Therefore, no matter how different the conceptions the intellect may form by abstraction, such as those mentioned above, when it considers what the real and *per se* constitutive feature of the first person is, there is no need to introduce any distinction here, because, as the major understands it, this real constitutive can only be something that is in every way one. And no matter how one thinks of it, this one real entity must be something that in itself is an act and not just a potency or aptitude, for there is nothing [in God] that is not there as fully actualized. In itself, then, this entity is either absolute or relative. And thus no matter how the mind distinguishes generativity or generation in the Father, in reality this first incommunicable entity, which represents the actual relationship of the first person to the second, must needs be the first incommunicable entity in the first person and thus is that which first formally constitutes this person.

Furthermore, one can argue against the two objections in two ways. For the distinctions were introduced in both to avoid this common diffi-

as an aptitude to generate (expressed by "generative") or (b) as an ability of the suppositum (expressed by "one able to generate") or (c) as an act (expressed by "generating") or (d) as having his offspring coexisting (expressed by "Father"). What makes this relationship, which is really one, constitutive of the first person is that aspect of it that gives him his personal being. But this is the first of

> culty, viz., how can the first person be prior to the second and still be simultaneous in nature with him? For this reason some constitutive factor is sought that is to some degree not simultaneous with the second person. This seems to be why the first argument assumes the generative power as quasi simultaneous with, and not prior to, the second person, and the second argument seeks something that is at once a property and a relation. And although it is simultaneous with the Son as a relation, under its other aspect as property it could enjoy somehow a priority. Both ways then, it seems, make some distinction to escape this difficulty, namely, that what is constitutive of the first person is in every way simultaneous with the second as one correlative is with another. But this is really no difficulty, nor is what they want to avoid an incongruity; rather it is something that has to be. Proof: If one order neither includes another *per se* nor requires it as a prior condition, then there is nothing inconsistent about having one order without the other. This clearly holds not only for order but for other things as well. Now an order of origin neither includes *per se* nor prerequires an essential order, at least one where the prior could exist without the posterior. An order of origin, therefore, can be present without an essential order; it is compatible with a simultaneity that excludes any order of the second kind. It is clear, then, that an order of origin can obtain between two *relata* neither of which can exist without the other and are thus simultaneous in nature with a simultaneity, namely, that is opposed to any order of nature. The minor was proved above, because an order of origin implies no more than that this one come from that one; this is compatible with a simultaneity of nature for no aspect of essence or of a principle is included in that order.
>
> (This could be shown by means of an example, although the example is somehow dubious.)
>
> A personal property is in every way proper primarily to the person possessing it. It is impossible that it be in every way first and proper to any other being. Unbegotten as distinguished from the essence and from the positive relationship in the first person implies a negation *per se*. Therefore, etc.

[18] Henry of Ghent, *Quodl.* IX, q.1 in corp. (fol. 341I); q.3 in corp. (fol. 348Q); *Summa* a.54, q.3 in corp. (II, fol. 129O-Q); a.58, q.4 in corp. (II, fol. 134K-135N); cf. nn.4.9 and 4.11.

all these (i.e., the generative aspect), for all of the others seem to characterize a person already constituted. Therefore [it is the first of these that is constitutive of the first person].

[12] 4.26 Clarification of the minor [in 4.25]: The more immediate or basic aspect in virtue of which the first person is ordered to his opposite would be prior, for this distinction of aspects is in view of the way one person is ordered to its opposite. "Generative" is more basic or immediate to the first person than is "Father," for all the other aspects include "generative," but the converse is not true. Not every generative is able to generate, but everything able to generate is generative. Not everything able to generate actually generates, but the converse is true. Not everyone who generates is a father. He may die before the foetus is formed in the womb. Yet every father whose foetus coexists, begets or has generated. Therefore, since "generative" is included in or presupposed by the other notions, it seems to be the first. Therefore, when to beget or generate is cited [in 4.11] as the first incommunicable property of the first person in the minor of our main reason, this is true of the real relation referred to by "generating" or "begetting," but it does not state the correct aspect which is not "generating" but "generative," for this is prior. And if one goes on to say that the second person is constituted by being generated precisely under the aspect of being generated, then this proposition would be false: "The first person is constituted by that relation which is the opposite of that which constitutes the second person," where this is understood not of the relation as it exists in reality but of the formal aspect under which that same relation is constitutive.

4.27 [Second objection] Another point raised against the same minor [in 4.9] is this[19]: What is constitutive of the first person can be considered in two ways; one, as a property; the other, as a relation. Now it constitutes as a property, and therefore not as the relation corresponding to the relation in the second person.

[13] 4.28 Two sorts of replies are given to the objections [in 4.25 and 4.27], the first of which is directed against both conjointly, the second type deals with each singly.

The [first] common rejoinder is this: A relation only constitutes a person to the extent that it is real and extramental [*ex natura rei*]; otherwise it would not constitute a real person, for the real can be constituted only by what is there in reality or extramentally. This relationship of the first person is real or extramental, however, only

---

[19] Thomas, *Summa theol.* I, q.40, a.4 (I, 205); cf. *supra* nn.4.9 and 4.11.

insofar as it is most fully actualized. Now even though the mind could consider this relation either as an aptitude or as actual, since it only constitutes a divine person insofar as it is real or extramental, it follows it is constitutive only under the aspect of fullest actualization.

4.29 The same holds good of the second objection [in 4.27]. Even though the mind could consider paternity either as a property or as a relation, there is only one way that it exists in reality. Only under this real aspect is it constitutive, and this is not as something absolute, but as a relation. Now this relation is none other than that which corresponds to the second person. Thus the thesis we proposed follows.

4.30 The second common rejoinder [to 4.25 and 4.27] goes like this: The common reason for introducing a distinction to begin with (between ways of viewing the generative principle in the first argument; and between property and relation in the second) was to avoid making the constitutive element of the first person completely simultaneous with that of the second, for the former seems to be somehow prior to the latter. But there is no need to avoid this as though it were incongruous. For, as we argued in the first article [4.6], given distinct types of order, if one does not include or presuppose the other as a necessary prerequisite, then order of this type is compatible with a simultaneity that excludes order of the second type. Such is the order of origin (where one comes from another) with reference to the order of nature (where the prior can exist without the posterior). Here the order of origin neither includes nor necessarily presupposes the order of nature. Therefore order of origin is quite consistent with the simultaneity of nature that marks terms that entail each other. Such simultaneity is proper to correlatives. Therefore order of origin between the first and second persons or their respective constitutives is fully compatible with simultaneity of correlation. No ploy for preventing simultaneity is needed like that of the first argument [in 4.25], which makes generativity or some property other than paternity constitutive, or that of the second [in 4.27], which makes paternity as a property rather than as a relation constitutive. It is only in its one real aspect that paternity is constitutive, and as such it is related to the second person and hence simultaneous in nature with him.

[14] 4.31 Confirmation: What gives necessarily perfect being to another is of necessity prior to it in origin but simultaneous in nature inasmuch as it cannot exist without the other. To be prior in origin

but simultaneous in nature then is not inconsistent; indeed the two must go hand in hand where origin is perfect and complete.

4.32 An example provides a further confirmation, although there may be some doubt about this. If Socrates is the father of Plato, not only is Socrates prior to Plato in origin, but Socrates as father is prior in origin to Plato as son. I prove this because paternity is the *per se* cause of priority of origin. Now by including everything that is the *per se* cause of some priority, you do not eliminate this priority. Therefore, Socrates as father (insofar as this includes paternity, the basis for the priority) will still be anterior in origin to Plato as son (where son includes the ground for posteriority of origin). Nevertheless, Socrates as father is simultaneous in nature with Plato as son in the way one correlative is with another.

4.33 [Joint confirmation] The main argument [in 4.9] could also be firmed up against the two objections to the minor in this way: In the case of the second person's constitutive entity no distinction between aptitude and actuality or between property and relation is postulated. Yet there is as much need of a positive and relative entity to constitute the first as to constitute the second person, for both are equally actual and incommunicable and according to the common interpretation only a relation of origin can be the primary incommunicable element.

[15]   4.34 [To the first objection in particular] Against the first objection [in 4.25] specifically it is argued, to begin with, that an aptitude never seems to be incommunicable in a primary sense, for it is incommunicable only in virtue either of its foundation or of that towards which it tends [*terminus ad quem*]*. If an aptitude as such is not primary but pertains to some being which has the aptitude, then neither its unity nor incommunicability will be first in any absolute sense, but they will be reducible to that of some other entity. Now if this were communicable, then the resulting aptitude would also be communicable. In fact, generally speaking, answers in terms of aptitudes have little efficacy unless something is cited to account for the aptitude. Otherwise it would be easy to solve all problems by saying: "This is so because such and such exists." But this will not do. If questioned why a stone falls, it is not enough to say: "Because by nature it has an aptitude to fall." One must give a reason for the aptitude, namely that the stone is heavy and this because earth, the heavy element, predominates in its composition. And earth itself is heavy either by its specific essence or in virtue of some [logically] prior quality. When it is argued then that a relation un-

der the aspect of "generativity" rather than that of actually generating is constitutive, since it is under that aspect that it first imparts incommunicable being, one must reply that this minor is false on two counts: first, generativity as such does not contribute that fully actualized being which alone can exist in the divine. Second, generativity as such does not impart primarily that incommunicable being required *per se* for personal being.

4.35 Also the proof of what is more basic or immediate [given in 4.26] in clarifying the minor actually supports our contention. For the relation of origin the first person bears to the second is most fully actual and simply incommunicable only under that aspect under which he relates immediately to the second. Indeed, if that were eliminated, there would be nothing else there that is most actual or incommunicable. (The suggestion [in 4.25] that all aspects other than "generative" seem to characterize a person already constituted, we shall take up later in our answer to the main argument [in 4.67].) But there is yet another way in which the argument about what is more immediate can be turned in favor of our conclusion. The second person is formally constituted by a relation that refers immediately to the first person. No one assumes he is constituted by his ability to be generated. A similar argument could be made for our thesis.

[16]   4.36 As for the point [in 4.26] that "generative" is included in all the other aspects but not vice versa, note that this does not imply any priority as to personal constitution, for there is no priority as regards incommunicable actuality but only as regards what this implies and here the prior is the more common and the less incommunicable.

4.37 [To the second objection in particular in 4.27] Against the second, we can argue that no individual entity can exist extramentally unless it is formally either relative or absolute. Even though, according to some, it is perhaps possible to have a concept that is indifferent to either the absolute or the relative, no extramental thing could be so indifferent that it would be a *per se* individual entity that is neither absolute nor relative. Let us then call A that property which is said to constitute the person. Now I ask: Is A's entity in reality formally absolute or formally relative? If absolute, then what it constitutes will also be formally absolute, which they deny; if relative, then A is a relation insofar as it formally constitutes the person, which is our thesis.

4.38 Besides, when you say "paternity as property" what do you

QUESTION FOUR

mean? The qualification "as property" expresses either (1) the formal constitutive element or (2) something subsequent to it in reality or in the mind. If you mean the second, then you must concede that the formal constitutive it presupposes and qualifies is "paternity as paternity," for this is the only formal reality subsequently qualified. Hence, the constitutive element is an entity that is relative *per se*. If you mean the first, since what property implies precisely is a conceptual relation, the absurd consequent follows that the first person is constituted by a relation of the mind.[20] The proof that property implies no more than a conceptual relation lies in this, that it asserts the relationship of paternity to the father. Now this is a purely mental relation, for there is no distinction between paternity and the Father.

[17] 4.39 This last point can be clarified in this way. Although [paternity] represents a real relation with reference to a really distinct opposite [viz., the Son], the mind can relate it to its foundation or subject, and if no real distinction is to be found there, then this "relating" is a matter of the mind or reason alone. But now the intellect can consider this subject as rooting this relationship of reason. Reflection of this sort does not change anything in the relation itself which was first considered. For example, man's capacity to laugh can be considered as his property, or "rational" as his specific difference, or "humanity" as his nature or quiddity.* None of these considerations alters *per se* the essence of what is considered. If in answer to the questions "Under what aspect is risibility demonstrable of man?" or "Is risible as risible his proper attribute?" it would be true to say: "Risible as a property is demonstrated of man," what is denoted by "*as*" is not something apart from, but constitutive of, the notion of risible, even though it appears as something appended to it. Consequently, if risible is a quality as such, then even as a proper attribute demonstrated of man, risible is a quality, not a relation, although what is called its mode, namely "property," does assert a relation.

[18] 4.40 Similarly, if rational as such is, in its own fashion, substance, then rational as man's specific difference is substance in the same way, even though the fact that it is a specific difference implies a certain conceptual relation, since it involves a second intention. And so it is in general with any real entity said to belong to something that can be considered either in itself or according to some concep-

[20] Cf. Duns Scotus, *Ord.* I, d.28, nn.89-92 (VI, 152-54); d.26, nn.56-72 (VI, 22-29).

tual relation. If the entity is said to pertain to it "as such," viz., as a property or [specific] difference, the essential meaning of what is qualified by such a relationship is not destroyed. Neither is such a relationship the formal ground for some really inherent predicate. It is merely the aspect under which the predicate pertains to the subject. What this reduplicative phrase "as such" asserts is clear from what was said in article two of the previous question [3.27-30].

4.41 As for the case at hand, since paternity *as property* represents only a certain conceptual relation, the formal meaning of that of which such a relation is asserted will always remain the same, and it will be just this that is the reason why any predicate is asserted of the subject. Thus if paternity as paternity is a relation, then paternity as property will also be a relation. For if the word "as" were understood as expressing the proper causal reason for the inherence of a real predicate in its subject, then just as this proposition, "Paternity as property is a relation to the Son," is false, so too is this other, "Paternity as property is a real relation." As property, it is a relation of reason, for the fact it is a property is not grounds for the inherence of any real predicate, since this formally asserts a mental relation. In particular where real or extramental constitution is involved, an "as" of this sort helps not one whit, for what formally constitutes something real must itself be real and must constitute it as real.

[19] 4.42 [An additional objection to our main argument] There is still another way of countering the minor of our proof [in 4.9] along the lines of the second objection [about paternity] as property [in 4.27]. It claims the divine essence constitutes the person, not considered absolutely as essence, but insofar as it is only mentally distinct from the relation.

Proof of the first point [viz., that essence constitutes the person]: To subsist *per se* is characteristic of the persons, but only the essence gives grounds for subsisting, for as Augustine[21] says: "The substance is that by which the Father is or subsists." And he makes the same point earlier[22]: "Everything subsists in respect to itself; how much more God?" [Proof of the second point]: It is only through the relation, however, that one person is coupled with his opposite.

4.43 [To the objection in 4.42] On the contrary, when the essence

---

[21] Augustine, *De Trin.* VII, c.6, n.11: PL 42, 943; CCSL 50, 262.
[22] Ibid., c.4, n.9: PL 42, 942; CCSL 50, 260.

is said to constitute the first person insofar as it differs only mentally from the relation, "insofar" either gives the formal reason of what is principiated* or it gives what follows that formal reason. If it is the first, since what differs only mentally from the relation is at best a relation of reason, it follows that a conceptual relation is the formal grounds for constituting a person. If it is the second, I ask just what is that [prior subject] as regards which "insofar as" gives some consequent reason. It can only be the essence in itself. For you claim the divine essence [constitutes the person, not considered absolutely but as mentally distinct, etc.]. But then the essence in itself will be the extramental grounds for constituting the person, which is what you deny.

4.44 Besides, the essence as merely conceptually distinct from the relation is either communicable or not. If communicable, then something communicable formally constitutes the incommunicable. If it is incommunicable and the essence *qua* essence differs in every way only mentally from the relation, it will be exclusively an absolute entity and thus will not formally refer to another as does the relation. Nevertheless it will not be really distinct from the relation. Therefore, the essence in every way as essence is only conceptually distinct from the relation and in that case, as before [in 4.37ff.], the essence as essence will constitute the persons.

[20] In similar fashion one could argue that if the essence constitutes solely as conceptually distinct from the relation, then the essence is either absolute or relative. If absolute, what is formally constituted [i.e., the person] will also be absolute; if relative, then the essence as such will be relative, since the essence *qua* essence differs only conceptually from the relation, as was proved.

4.45 Furthermore, it is always the case that what constitutes also provides the reason why one person differs or agrees with another. But the constitutive entity always constitutes of itself and not insofar as it agrees or differs from another. For instance rational is of itself constitutive of man and not insofar as it agrees or differs, although the man so constituted does agree or differ from others formally by reason of what is rational. Distinction or agreement then belong to what is constituted by virtue of its formal constitutive ground, but this is not something included in the constitutive reason itself. Here then you must give some constitutive reason which provides the grounds why the one constituted agrees or differs yet is present there in such a way that precisely as constitutive reason it does not include *per se* and primarily the agreement or difference.

4.46 As for the supporting argument for the objection [in 4.42] based on the notion of "subsisting," I say that "to subsist" is equivocal. In one sense it means "*per se* being or existence" insofar as this excludes inherence or being in another as a part is in the whole. In this sense there is but one subsistence in God even as there is but one *per se* being or existence. It is to this that the texts from Augustine refer. In another sense, however, "to subsist" means to possess being incommunicably. In this sense there are three "subsistents," since there are three persons or personalities, for there are three incommunicable subsistents, even though there is but one *per se* being. If then one understands the major to mean that what constitutes the person gives subsistent being or is the grounds for its subsisting, this must be taken in the second sense, since it is the ground for subsisting incommunicably.

ARTICLE III
What is the Interrelation of those Relations Admittedly Present in the First Person?

[21] 4.47 [Two points for investigation] As for the third article, if something is constitutive in virtue of some [logically] prior aspect, it seems that what is constituted would still remain even if one mentally prescinded from a [logically] posterior aspect. Hence anyone who would claim that the first person is constituted by the relation of origin to the second person under the aspect of generative (which is an aspect of generation that is prior to that of actual generation), would seem to be saying that, even apart or prescinding from actual generation, the first person could exist apart from the second either in reality or at least conceptually; whereas extramentally no separation is possible because they are really the same.

Similarly, if "to generate" were prior to paternity, and to generate under the aspect of to generate constituted the first person, the first person could conceivably remain apart from paternity as paternity.

In this article then two points need investigation. The first concerns reality and it is this: In the first person is there some distinction of properties—not any properties whatsoever (for we are not talking about "unbegotten" or "active spiration"), but of those which assert a relation of origin between the first and second person? The second derives from the first, viz., [assuming some conceptual distinctions are possible,] what considerations could one abstract or prescind from and still have the first person?

QUESTION FOUR

1. Is there some Distinction of Properties
in the First Person?

4.48 On the first point I have two conclusions:

The first is this: Between the first and second person there is one and only one, absolutely unique, relationship of origin so that prior to the consideration of the intellect there is no distinction of any kind in reality.

[22] Second, I say: This relationship, which in reality is absolutely one, can be distinguished conceptually or considered in diverse ways.

4.49 [First conclusion: There is no real distinction in the relationship of origin] There are two proofs for the first conclusion:

One is this: There is but one unique perfect origin of one thing from another, and this holds whether we mean the unique active origin on the part of the originating source or the unique passive origin on the part of product originated, although the former and the latter are somehow two. But the relationship of origin between the first and second person does express the perfect origin of the second person from the first. Therefore, there is but one unique relationship of origin, and this whether one considers it actively from the side of the Father (and then it is unique and active in the Father), or quasi-passively from the side of the Son (where it will be the passive origin, also unique).

Proof of the major: That origination of one from another is not perfect if apart from it, the other would originate from the first no less perfectly than before. But if there were two relationships of origin which were distinct on the part of the thing, call them A and B, then if one were removed, the second person would still originate from the first, because the other, e.g., A is not only a relation of origin but of perfect origin; therefore B is not the perfect origination or the relationship of perfect origin between them. Now if it were distinct from A, B would be a perfect and distinct relationship of origin, and one could argue in a similar way about B apart from A. Thus if either of the two was eliminated, the second person would still be from the first, for his origination would still be from the other, and yet he would not proceed from the first because his perfect origination would be removed.

[23] If you say it is not possible for A to go and B remain, nor vice versa, this will not help. One and the same suppositum cannot orig-

inate from the same other suppositum by means of two origins both of which are perfect, for from either it would receive the fullness of being that could be obtained from its producer, and therefore it is impossible that it would receive any being from the other no matter how it was present or remained there.

4.50 A more logical proof for the same conclusion is this. Relations that are in some way distinct in reality so that formally they are not completely one are not predicated of themselves in the abstract, even when they are in the suppositum. For this is false: "Paternity or active generation is active spiration or innascibility." As Augustine[23] puts it: "To say he is unbegotten is not the same as to say he is the Father, for even if he had not begotten the Son, nothing would prevent him from being called unbegotten." This text has to be understood correctly because in the second article [4.23] it was remarked that the relation to the second person is presupposed by unbegotten. But we can say this much: this predication is not true in the abstract: "Paternity is innascibility," whereas these are true: "Active generation is paternity, and vice versa," and "Generativity is active generation, like paternity, and vice versa."

[24] 4.51 [Objection] According to Book V of the *Metaphysics*,[24] relations of the second type* are based on action and passion, and, what is relevant to our case, he seems to say there that a father is called "father" because he has begotten, whereas a son is called "son" because he has been begotten. Therefore, just as the foundation is not the same as the relation, nor the relation the same as the foundation, so neither are generation and paternity the same. Hilary[25] confirms this: "This procession from God is the perfect birth to which the confession of the Father's name has been joined." What he wants to say is that paternity follows after generation or nativity. This is explained by the fact that a father is not a father just because he generates, but rather because his offspring coexists with him. Now having his offspring coexisting seems to be different from his generating, because in animals the act of generation insofar as it is an act consists in depositing the semen. But at that time the offspring does not yet coexist with him; consequently he is not a father then but later.

[25] 4.52 [Reply to the objection] I say, however, that in God generativity, generating, and paternity are absolutely one and the same

---

[23] Ibid., v, c.6, n.7: PL 42, 914; CCSL 50, 211.
[24] Aristotle, *Metaph.* v, c.15 (1020b30).
[25] Hilary, *De Trin.* ix, n.30: PL 10, 304.

real reason, for as Augustine[26] puts it: "What is proper to the Father alone is such not because a [Son] is born, but because he has generated a Son," and according to Hilary[27]: It is proper to the Father that he is always Father and it is proper to the Son that he is always Son." And the Master of the Sentences[28] quotes several texts to support this. Now there is only one personal property for each person; therefore, this and that are identical.

4.53 [Second conclusion: One real property can be considered differently] This one property, however, can be considered differently and thus acquire different aspects. This is the second conclusion proposed [in 4.48], and it will help in solving objections. There are two ways in which one could make mental or conceptual distinctions in considering this one relation. The one would be in regard to the difference or indetermination or [degree of] abstraction involved in our consideration. The other would be concerned with [the degree of] possibility or actuality (determination, completeness).

4.54 In the first way one could consider the following aspects. First would be one who produces naturally [i.e., non-voluntarily]; second, one who produces something similar in nature; third, one who exists incommunicably [or as a person] and under this aspect produces. It is clear that the third is more indeterminate than the second and the second more so than the first.

4.55 In the second way I can conceive this first person's begetting under the aspect of generative, or able to generate, or generating, or having generated or having his offspring coexisting.

4.56 In creatures, the first difference is that of universality such that it extends itself to many. The second difference which here [in God] is conceptual, in creatures is real and the various aspects are found at times in separation, because of the imperfection characteristic of creatures that is absent in God.

4.57 Although one could somehow save the first conceptual distinction insofar as one could have the less determinate conception apart from the more determinate one, this does not help so far as reality is concerned for what corresponds to this and that concept is absolutely identical extramentally.

---

[26] Ps. Augustine, Fulgentius of Ruspe, *De fide ad Petrum* c.2, n.7: PL 40, 675; CCSL 91a, 716.

[27] Hilary, *De Trin.* XII, n.23: PL 10, 447.

[28] Lombard, *Sent.* I, d.26, c.2: PL 192, 591-92; ed. Collegii S. Bonaventurae, Ad Claras Aquas, Grottaferrata (Romae) I, 197-98.

[26] The second difference preserves in the divine a diversity of concepts or ways of conceiving the same thing, nevertheless when applied to what exists extramentally in each case what is of perfection must be retained whereas what is of imperfection must be discarded. For to be separated from its actualization represents imperfection in an aptitude or potency; and in acting [such as generating] it is something of an imperfection not to have the term of the action coexisting, or for the act to pass away and not continue. And as regards that which results as it were from the action, e.g., paternity, it is a matter of imperfection that it is not always actually communicating its nature, whereas it is a matter of perfection to have its correlative in continual coexistence with it. Therefore, if the perfection is retained and the imperfection suppressed, generation will never be something merely dispositional, but completely productive as regards its offspring. It will be in short perfect generation, complete generation, and one that is not passing but always going on, one that has all that is required [to be perfect]. Also paternity will not follow an act of generation that was previous, transient and, as it were, dispositional. Paternity will be present in its full actuality, it will be communication of the nature that never ceases; it will include all that is required [to be all perfect]. This complete and eternal generation, and this complete and never-ending paternity, and this complete and eternal actuality all express one and the same thing extramentally. But the name "generation" expresses more of one aspect of perfection found in creatures than does paternity, whereas paternity expresses more of another aspect of creatural perfection than does "generation."

[27] 4.58 [Reply to the objection in 4.51] From this we see how to answer the objection raised in this article which seemed to support some sort of extramental distinction between generation and paternity.

Paternity, it was argued first, is based on active generation, according to the *Metaphysics*.[29] The answer to this would require a more extended treatment [than we can give it now]. Besides, we said enough about it earlier [in 4.52]. Nevertheless, I will say this much now. If in creatures generation is somehow prior to paternity, the foundation of generation is not paternity, but the generative power or nature which generates. As dispositional, it is prior; in other words, if this power is non-existent, then paternity will not

---

[29] Aristotle, *Metaph.* v, c.2 (1013a31).

exist. The distinction is one between a previous disposition and what has come to full term. It is evident that this ground for distinction is not present in the divine, because there, generation is present only as complete and with the Son coexisting. Neither does paternity follow [temporally] the communication [of the nature].

4.59 As for Hilary [in 4.51], one could say that the name "paternity" is consequent on generation in God by analogy with creatures; for in God there is indeed a certain conceptual sequence where in creatures there is a real sequence. As we said elsewhere [in 1.45], mentally distinct features have an order of reason similar to the order such features would have in reality were they really distinct.

4.60 But should one quibble about this interpretation of Hilary's text, he could be easily answered in this way. Acknowledgement of the paternal name, and perhaps the paternal name itself, came after the creation of the world, and we are speaking here of the naming and acknowledgement by any created intellect. But it is only in the conceptual order, as was said, that paternity followed either the nativity of the Son (which Hilary had in mind) or the generation of the Son. This also provides the answer to the other point made about paternity [in 4.51], namely that it is a relationship in one whose offspring exists and that therefore in creatures it is really distinct from generation, whereas in God the distinction is only conceptual.

2. From What Considerations could One Prescind and still have the First Person?

[28] 4.61 Given the two conclusions [of 4.48], viz., that the first person's relationship of origin to the second is only one thing in reality but is conceptually distinguished, we can make clear to what extent the first person is separable apart from this relationship of origin to the second. If this means separable in reality, this is clearly false. Neither is there any need to distinguish this or that aspect of the relationship, for in reality it is but one single thing. If this were really removed, what is constituted by it would not remain either. If one means separable conceptually without contradiction, however, in the sense that the notion of the first person in the mind is separable from the notion of the relationship of origin between the first and second person, we must, it seems, make use of the distinction cited [in 4.53ff.] between the diverse ways of considering that one relationship. Of course if one abstracts or prescinds from all the ways at once, the mind will have no conception whatsoever of a supposi-

tum related by such a relationship of origin. It is contradictory that an intellect should conceive the complete absence of any relationship of origin in a suppositum and still conceive of a suppositum related by such a relationship. There is no contradiction, however, that the suppositum considered according to a prior reason should be conceivable apart from the relationship considered under some posterior reason or aspect. Now these diverse aspects in our mind would have that order of prior or posterior conceivability they would be apt to have in those objects suited to move our intellect.

[29] 4.62 Now perhaps one could without contradiction think of someone subsisting incommunicably apart from a relationship of origin to the second person if he were viewed under some special aspect involving a degree of indeterminateness or indifference, or involving only aptitude or degree of actuality or something [e.g., the act of generation] that could conceivably have passed away before [paternity] occurred.

4.63 But if you ask: Under what formal aspect would the first person be thought of as incommunicably existing? I reply: Perhaps one could abstract from the very relative incommunicable concept itself or from that absolute incommunicable form, some less specific concept, namely, "this form" or "this incommunicable entity." And then perhaps one could conceive of this, in its proper singularity, to be that by which this person is incommunicable without conceiving anything more specific about his individuality. I do this sort of thing when I conceive not just "being" but "this being" or "this substance" without thinking of this individual in any more specific way, as I do when I view some distant object, seeing it as a body before perceiving it to be an animal or just one animal. And perhaps it is this indifferent concept of an incommunicable form that he had in mind who thought of a divine suppositum without yet determining in his intellect whether the suppositum is absolute or relative. How else could one explain what philosophers thought of God's activity in the world without assuming their every notion false? For it is clear they did not think of this relative suppositum as moving the heavens, yet they did assume some suppositum did so, because every action is ascribed to some suppositum. If they did not think of the notion of an incommunicable suppositum as indifferent to both absolute and relative, then they necessarily thought that this suppositum moving the heavens was absolute, which is false. What we say here about some concept indifferent to both absolute and relative or about that of an incommunicable suppositum unspecified as either absolute or relative is not in any way at odds with our prior statement [in 4.37] that every entity invested with reality is either formally absolute or formally relative. For one can readily abstract from several things an indifferent concept, neither relative nor absolute. Nevertheless everything when specified to be existing extramentally has to be determinately either one or the other. Hence indifference of the concept that can be abstracted from several individuals does not imply a like indifference in the existing individual.[30]

Reply to the Initial Argument

[30] 4.64 As for the initial argument [in 4.1], it is obvious from the solution of the question that the minor must be denied. As for its proof, we admit the relation constituting the first person is one of origin; it is in fact active origination.*

4.65 To the assumption that action presupposes a suppositum, I reply: The first incommunicable entity presupposes no incommunicable being [ens]. Hence it does not presuppose a suppositum, for a suppositum is an incommunicable being. Now the first productive activity, production, or active origination is the first incommunicable entity to be found in God, for it is preceded only by perfect memory and essence, both of which are communicable. But this first productive act cannot be communicated; otherwise its product would produce itself—an impossible situation which Augustine[31] claims no mind could grasp. Our conclusion then is this: If the proposition "action requires an existing suppositum" refers to hypostatic* being, it could be interpreted to mean either (a) the suppositum exists by reason of some entity prior in nature to the action itself or (b) the person's hypostatic existence is formally constituted by the action itself. Now the first interpretation is false, for prior to the action there is nothing incommunicable here and hence no hypostatic entity. The second, however, is true, for by the very action there is an hypostatic being, because the action is there incommunicably.

4.66 But against this it is objected that since every "acting" [agere] presupposes "being" [esse], the agent's activity cannot be the first ground for its being.

I answer: In the divine, "being" can refer either to "incommunica-

---

[30] Cf. Duns Scotus, *Ord.* I, d.25 (v, 371-76); d.8, nn.137-50 (IV, 221-27).
[31] Augustine, *De Trin.* I, c.1, n.1: PL 42, 820; CCSL 50, 28.

ble being" or to "being" in an unqualified sense. In the latter sense, there is but one being, the essence, as Augustine states repeatedly. But incommunicable or hypostatic being is distinctive for each person there. If your thesis is that acting presupposes being in an unqualified sense, i.e., being as absolute, I concede this. But if you mean that acting presupposes hypostatic being, which in this case means "being in relation to another," your thesis is false, for this acting is itself the first "being in relation to another," even as the productive action itself is the first relationship to another.

4.67 But you may insist that "to act" presupposes not just any sort of being, but a being able to act, for if there is nothing able to act, there will be no action. In God it is only the suppositum that is able to act; therefore "to act" presupposes the suppositum.

[31] I answer: Extramentally to act does not presuppose to be able to act; indeed the agent is potent primarily by reason of the very acting as such. What is presupposed is a formal principle in virtue of which something is able to act. This and everything else said in reply to the initial argument can be made clear if one keeps in mind that in the real order there is but one unique relationship between the first and second person, for there is but one active production and it is a relationship of the producing to his product. But since we commonly speak of production as a relationship or relation, we think of it as having some foundation, just as, when we speak of it as an action, we think of it as having a formal productive principle. Consequently, if one finds no difficulty in the idea that the relation does not presuppose a suppositum but only the essence as a kind of foundation (which the common view generally concedes), then he will also have no difficulty with the idea that the action presupposes no suppositum either as agent or as able to act, but it only presupposes the essence, which is a kind of formal reason for the acting.

[32] 4.68 If you object to this on the grounds that action in the divine is something absolute and not merely a relation, I have this to say. Some would deny this to be true of creatures, at least as regards productive action, for it does not seem that active production could be thought of as absolute rather than relative. Be that as it may,[32] however, in God the productive action is merely a relationship, for according to Augustine,[33] everything in the divine is predicated ac-

---

[32] In *Ordinatio* IV, d.13, q.1, nn.9-11 (ed. Vivès XVII, 668-69) Scotus proves extensively that the six last Aristotelian categories* are extrinsically advenient* relations.

[33] Augustine, *De Trin.* v, c.5, n.6: PL 42, 914; CCSL 50, 210-11.

cording to either substance or relation, and what is predicated according to substance is common [to all three persons]. Therefore, origin, be it active or passive, is formally a relation.

4.69 You may argue, finally, on the basis of logic: Every action denominates or names some agent, in this case, the suppositum; but what names or denominates presupposes what is named or denominated; therefore [action presupposes the suppositum]. But the answer to this is clear from the reply to the first argument in the third article of the previous question [3.40-43]. As we said, in God nothing personal is properly predicated denominatively of any incommunicable subject (which is what we are speaking of now), although one could perhaps speak of it being predicated denominatively of something which concretely signifies the common essence, as "God is generating." But there is no need to speak of this sort of denomination here, because such denominative predication is verified for something [e.g., the essence] contained under the subject [i.e., God]. The reason why in God there is no proper denomination or denominative predication about a non-transcendent subject is that denominative predication proper applies to a subject in the concrete and to what is receptive of the property, not one that includes it [as a formal constitutive element]. In the divine, however, the only concrete non-transcendental subject of which a personal property is predicated is the person himself who is constituted by the property and hence includes it. Hence the personal property is not predicated denominatively of the person. Now the only quasi subject receptive of such a property present in God is the essence, but the property is not predicated of this in the concrete for reasons to be treated at the end of the first article of the following question [5.13-15].

Question Five

IS THE RELATION OF ORIGIN FORMALLY INFINITE?

5.1 The next question raised is about the intrinsic perfection of origin in the divine. It is whether the relation of origin* is formally infinite.[1]

Arguments Pro and Con

[1] Argument for the negative:
Everything formally infinite is a pure perfection,* for nothing can be more perfect than what is formally infinite. The relation of origin is not a pure perfection; therefore [it is not formally infinite].

5.2 Proof of the minor: One person has a relation of origin that another lacks. Therefore, were the relation of origin a pure perfection, one person would possess some pure perfection lacking in another, which is incongruous.

5.3 [For the affirmative] The opposing view is argued for in this fashion. Being is divided into finite and infinite before being divided into the ten categories.* Therefore any being, even if it does not come under some category, will be finite or infinite. The relation of origin is not finite; otherwise it would not be really identical with the divine essence, for the finite cannot be really the same as the infinite. Therefore, it is formally infinite.

Body of the Question

5.4 Three points need investigation here. First, the sense of the question; second, what is to be held; third, the solution of some doubts that occur.

ARTICLE I
The Meaning of the Question

[2] 5.5 [Notion of the infinite] As for the first point, for the Philosopher, "The infinite is that whose quantity is such that no matter how much one removes from it, there is always more for the taking." The

---

[1] Cf. Duns Scotus, *Ord.* 1, d.13, n.39 (v, 84-85); d.3, nn.1-107 (III, 1-68).

QUESTION FIVE

reason is that the infinite in quantity, of which the Philosopher[2] speaks, can have being only potentially, if we take one after another. For this reason, no matter how much is removed, what one takes will still be finite and will represent only a certain part of the infinite potential whole. More of it will always remain for the taking. From this he infers that since the infinite in quantity has only being in the making or potentially, it does not fulfil the notion of a whole, for a whole has nothing outside itself. But there is always something outside this sort of infinite, that is, outside that which of itself has being in potency. It is never perfect, for the perfect lacks no perfection whereas this always lacks something.

5.6 For our purposes, let us change the notion of the potentially infinite in quantity, if possible, to that of quantitatively infinite in act. For just as it is necessary now that the quantity of the infinite should always grow by receiving one part after another, so we might imagine that all the parts that could be taken were taken at once or that they remained in existence simultaneously. If this could be done we would have in actuality an infinite quantity, because it would be as great in actuality as it was potentially. And all those parts which in infinite succession would be actualized and would have being one after the other would be conceived as actualized all at once. Such an infinite in act would indeed be a whole and in truth a perfect whole, since there would be nothing outside it, and it would be perfect, since it lacks nothing. What is more, nothing in the way of quantity could be added to it, for then it could be exceeded.

[3]   5.7 From this, we argue further: If we think of something among beings that is actually infinite in entity, we must think of it along the lines of the actual infinite quantity we imagined, namely as an infinite being that cannot be exceeded in entity by any other being. It will truly have the character of something whole and perfect. It will indeed be whole or complete. While something actually infinite in quantity would not be missing any of its parts or lacking any part of quantity, still each of its parts would lie outside the other and consequently the whole would be made up of imperfect elements. A being infinite in entity, however, would not have any entity outside itself in this way. Neither would its totality depend upon elements which are themselves imperfect in entity, for it is in such a way that it has no extrinsic part; otherwise it would not be entirely

---

[2] Aristotle, *Physic.* III, c.6 (207a7-9).

whole. As for its being perfect, the situation is similar. Although something actually infinite in quantity would be perfect as to quantity, because as a whole it would lack no quantity, nevertheless each part of it would lack the quantity of the other parts. That is to say, an infinite of this sort would not be quantitatively perfect [as a whole] unless each of its parts were not imperfect. An infinite being, however, is perfect in such a way that neither it nor any of its parts is missing anything.

5.8 From the notion of the infinite in the *Physics*,[3] then, applied imaginatively to something actually infinite in quantity, were that possible, and applied further to something actually infinite in entity, where it is possible, we can form some sort of idea of how to conceive of a being intensively infinite* in perfection or power.

[4] 5.9 This enables us to describe a being infinite in entity as a being which lacks no entity in the way that one single being is able to possess it. The qualification "in the way, etc." is added because a single being cannot possess every entity whatsoever formally* and by a real identity. It can also be described in terms of how it exceeds any other finite being in this fashion. An infinite being is that which exceeds any finite being whatsoever not in some limited degree but in a measure beyond what is either defined or can be defined. Consider whiteness, for instance. It is exceeded triply by another entity, knowledge, or ten times by the intellective soul, or a hundredfold by the most perfect angel.[4] No matter how high you go among be-

---

[3] Ibid., c.6 (207a7-9).

[4] Scotus distinguishes between two radically different senses in which "quantity" (or number) can be used to "measure" differences between things. One is the strictly proper sense used by the mathematician or physicist (natural philosopher) which exists between what contemporary philosophers would call *extensive* or *additive* properties like weight, length, time intervals, electric current, etc. The other is analogous to that which holds between *intensive* or *non-additive* differences where these can be arranged serially. We can grade students, for instance, according to intelligence, mastery of a given subject matter, alertness, etc. Numbers can then be assigned to various groups. Thus two in the same percentile may be said to be equal, whereas those in different percentiles are said to be either better or worse than the others. Yet the "degree of difference" is not an exact mathematical one. As Scotus puts it, it is not constituted by some lesser entity to which something has been added, i.e., in the way the mathematician may add lengths, or angles, etc., according to fixed ratios. For a modern analysis of this difference, see M. R. Cohen and E. Nagel, *An Introduction to Logic and Scientific Method* (New York, 1934), pp.

ings, there will always be some finite measure according to which the highest exceeds the lowest. Not that there is any proportion or relative measure, properly speaking, as mathematicians use it, because the angel, being simpler, is not constituted by some lesser entity to which something has been added. It must rather be understood of the relative measure of perfection or power in the way that one species is superior to another. In this fashion, by contrast, the infinite exceeds the finite in entity beyond any relative measure or proportion that could be assigned.

5.10 [Infinity is not a property but an intrinsic mode of being] From this it follows that intensive infinity is not related to the being said to be infinite as a kind of attribute that accrues to it extrinsically. Neither should it be thought of as an attribute or property of being in the way "good" and "true" are. Indeed, intensive infinity expresses an intrinsic mode of that entity. It is so intrinsic that if we abstract from all its properties or quasi-properties, we have still not excluded infinity, but it remains integrally included in that one single entity itself.[5] Hence if we consider that entity most precisely, namely without any property, it will be true to say it has a measure of intrinsic excellence all its own which is not finite, since any limitation of degree is repugnant to it. Therefore it is infinite. That which is infinite, considered most precisely, and not under the aspect of some attributable property such as wisdom or goodness, can also be aligned according to an essential order* with something it excels, but its superiority will not be measurable in any definite degree for then it would be finite. Therefore, the intrinsic mode of

---

293-97. What the threefold, tenfold, or hundredfold indicates in the example given is the relative position the thing in question holds in a scale or ladder of qualities. A classical example of such a scale is Friedrich Mohs' "scale of hardness" used by mineralogists. It has ten degrees which range from talc, the softest, to diamond, the hardest. But the fact that topaz is eighth on the scale does not mean that properly speaking it is twice as hard as fluorite, which is fourth on the scale. What governs the relationship logically is that there is an objective transitive asymmetrical relationship that holds between the various members of the scale. Scotus, following Aristotle's claim that "forms (or essences) are like numbers," believed that things could be classified in the sense that the higher in the scale has all the perfection of something lower in the scale, if not formally,* then virtually* or eminently.*

[5] Cf. Duns Scotus, *Ord.* I, d.8, nn.108-109 (IV, 202-203); IV, d.3, q.1, nn.30-33 (ed. Vivès XVII, 687-89).

anything intensively infinite is infinity itself, which intrinsically expresses a being or essence which lacks nothing and which exceeds everything finite beyond any determinable degree.

5.11 Damascene[6] confirms this corollary when he says that the essence is an infinite and limitless sea of substance. Substance then, insofar as it represents what is absolutely first in the divine, he calls a sea, and as such it is infinite and boundless. But substance in this sense does not include [formally] either truth, goodness, or any other attributable property. Therefore, infinity as such is a mode of essence more intrinsic than any attribute it has.

[5]   5.12 [A relation cannot be infinite] Having examined the notion of infinite, let us turn to the question at issue, viz., Can a relation be formally infinite? Here the question is not whether the relation is really the same as something infinite. Common opinion is agreed that it is, for it is really the same as the essence.[7] Neither are we asking if the relation by identity* is that infinite [essence]. No, the question is this: Considered formally, that is, according to its own relational entity, is the relationship [of origin] intensively infinite and that in virtue of the relational entity's own infinity? In other words, is intensive infinity an intrinsic *per se* mode of the entity proper to this paternity—so intrinsic *per se* that the paternity is not just infinite by reason of something else with which it is really identical? Would this relational entity still be intensively infinite in itself even if one included no other identity than its own, indeed if one excluded anything other than the relational entity itself?

5.13 From this it is clear that the reply commonly given to the question is not to the point, namely, when they answer that the relation of origin is formally infinite, because the essence is infinite and this relation is the essence. For the question is not whether the relation is by identity some thing which is formally infinite, but whether the relation itself, according to the first mode of *per se* predication, is that thing whose *per se* intrinsic mode is infinity. Hence the argument: "Divinity is infinite; paternity is divinity; therefore, etc." is not conclusive. The major is true according to formal predication,* whereas the minor is only true according to predication by identity.* Paternity is deity according to everyone, therefore no conclusion according to formal predication can be inferred. For terms in the conclusion can have no greater identity than that

---

[6] Damascene, *De fide orth.* I, c.9: PG 94, 835; ed. Buytaert c.9, p. 49.
[7] Cf. Duns Scotus, *Ord.* I, d.2, nn.411ff. (II, 362ff.); d.8, nn.218-22 (IV, 274-77); II, d.1, q.4, nn.5ff. (ed. Vivès XII, 98ff.).

which they have with the middle term in the premises.[8] That is why from one necessary and one contingent premise, only a contingent conclusion or contingent union of terms follows. But unless "Paternity is infinite" is true according to formal predication, their thesis is not proved, as is obvious from what was explained above [in 5.6], for it would only follow that paternity through identity is a certain thing that is infinite.

[6] 5.14 But if you intended to infer something according to formal predication, and not merely that of identity, you would be switching from one form of predication to another, thus committing the fallacy of figure of speech. For you go from an essential qualification [*quale quid*] to "this something" [*hoc aliquid*], that is to say, the middle term which is an essential qualification is interpreted as being "this something." For like one who from a middle term that expresses an essential qualification infers a middle term that expresses "this something," so here, by force of an inference according to formal predication, one intends to imply that "this something," which would not follow otherwise, actually does follow by virtue of the argument. The other premise [in 5.13], however, was only true in virtue of identity. The one switching from identity to formal predication, therefore, would seem to be interpreting both premises as instances of formal predication, whereas such is not the case because the minor can only be verified in terms of predication through identity.

5.15 One could say, in short, that this conclusion: "Paternity is infinite" [rather than "Paternity is the infinite"] is, properly speaking, untrue because the formal mode of expression is adjectival and signifies the form to be the form of that of which is asserted. Because of this characteristic, an adjective can only be predicated according to the mode of formal predication. Inferring this conclusion from the premises, then, would be a fallacy of figure of speech, for the reasons given above [in 5.14]. Therefore, if infinite is not simply asserted of paternity according to formal predication, the conclusion is false. If, therefore, the conclusion is interpreted to mean that there is a real identity of something infinite with paternity, then one ought to formulate the conclusion as "Paternity is something which is infinite." But our question poses a special difficulty if we understand [the conclusion] in the other way, namely as if infinity were an intrinsic formal mode of paternity *qua* paternity.

[8] Cf. *supra*, note 7, and *Ord.* I, d.5, nn.17-24 (IV, 17-23).

ARTICLE II
Solution of the Question: Paternity is not Infinite

[7] 5.16 [Triple proof of the conclusion] As for the second article, I hold "Paternity is not formally infinite," in the sense explained [in 5.12-15]. There are three reasons for this conclusion, the first is based on the unity of an infinite being; the second, on its communicability; the third, on its simplicity and incompossibility. For an intensively infinite being is something unique, incapable of being multiplied or replicated; it is not restricted but communicable; and it cannot be a component of something else.

1. The First Principal Reason

5.17 The first reason is formulated in this way: Several beings really distinct and formally infinite cannot exist. But there are several really distinct relations of origin. Therefore, they are not formally infinite intensively; neither is any single one of them infinite, because any reason for one being infinite would hold for the others as well.

5.18 [Three ways of proving the major] The major is proved first by seeing how several infinite things would have to be interrelated; second, by comparing the intensively infinite with the finite generally; third, by seeing how the intensively infinite is related to intellect and will in particular.

5.19 [The first way] The first [of two proofs] is this: The infinite possesses all entity that can be had by any one thing. But it is possible for one supremely perfect being to have every pure perfection really and as identified with itself. Therefore the infinite has in itself really and by identity every pure perfection; but it does not have what is really distinct from it in this way; therefore, no pure perfection or something perfect can be really distinct from it. If there were another really distinct infinite, however, there would be pure [8] perfection really distinct from it. Therefore, we have our major that there cannot be several really distinct infinites.

5.20 But it seems in this proof of the major, that the second proposition, viz., that a supremely perfect being can have every pure perfection by way of identity, needs corroboration. The evidence is this: Nothing is supremely perfect if it lacks some pure perfection, for no pure perfection is incompatible with any other pure perfection. If all pure perfections could not be possessed by the supremely perfect, this would be due to some mutual incompatibility

QUESTION FIVE

among them.[9] The underlying assumption here, that no pure perfection is incompatible with any other, is established from the very meaning of pure perfection. For according to Anselm, a pure perfection is something it is better for anything to have than to have what is not it, i.e., to have anything incompatible with it. (This will be explained in [5.31 of] article II in connection with the second principal argument.) Therefore, if two pure perfections, call them A and B, were incompatible, A would be better in anything than non-A, namely anything incompatible with A, and hence it would be better than B which, by stipulation, is incompatible with A. By the same token, however, B would be better than A. Such circularity is impossible; otherwise one and the same thing would be less perfect than itself.

5.21 A *second* argument for the major using an intercomparison of several [infinites] could be this: When several things are equally good, the goodness of several exceeds that of one alone. Now if there are several infinite beings, each is equally good. Therefore those several good things exceed in goodness any one of them singly, and thus none of them would be infinite.

5.22 If you object that one could use this sort of argument to show God plus a creature exceeds the goodness of God alone, the objection is invalid. The goodness of one [the creature] does not equal or measure up to the goodness of the other [i.e., God] and thus is contained eminently* in that of the other. Hence, to take the two together does not augment or exceed the goodness [of God] in himself. But in our hypothetical case it is just the opposite, since one good is not completely contained in the other eminently, for this would run counter to the idea of the infinite.

[9] 5.23 [Second way] Comparing the infinite with the finite generally, however one can argue [*first*] in this way: One infinite being suffices to ground the dependency of all finite beings, particularly if it be the first being on which they depend. But it is impossible that several should each be the sufficient ground supporting the same dependent being in the same order of dependence. Therefore, there cannot be more than one infinite.[10]

Proof of the major: Just as any form of dependency implies a note of imperfection, so it is a matter of perfection that something be the

[9] Cf. Duns Scotus, *Ord.* I, d.2, nn.377-87 (II, 344-49).
[10] Ibid., III, d.1, q.2, nn.3-5 (ed. Vivès XIV, 59-66); II, d.3, q.4, n.3 (XII, 93); IV, d.6, q.2, nn.2-3 (XVI, 543-44); I, d.2, nn. 70-73 (II, 169-73).

supporting term or ground on which something depends, not indeed in just any way, but first and foremost. But supreme perfection, which cannot be exceeded, exists in one intensively infinite being.

The major is also apparent from the fact that one unique essence actually supports sufficiently the full measure of the dependency of any dependent thing because it represents the first efficient cause as well as the exemplar and ultimate final cause of the dependent's being.

Proof of the minor, viz., There cannot be more than one primary sufficient ground that actually is supporting the same dependency. For no term is actually supporting the dependence sufficiently if it can be eliminated and still leave the dependent being sufficiently supported, for otherwise something would depend on a support, which if written off, the dependent thing would lose nothing in the way of support and could continue to exist. But if two things were each supporting sufficiently the dependency in the same order, then if one were eliminated, the complete dependency on the other would continue. Thus the one eliminated actually gave no support. The same argument would hold for the other, so that neither is supporting the dependent completely or else only one of them is.

Just as the first proof of the major then is based on the fact that the infinite contains really and unitively all pure perfection, since all pure perfection can be possessed in this way by a single subject, so the present proof is grounded on the fact that the infinite contains the content of all limited perfection in an eminent fashion, and this suffices for it to support the full measure of any limited being's dependency. Thus these two proofs are based on what was said about the infinite in the first article [5.9], namely that it has all entity or every aspect thereof in the manner that a single subject can possess it, which for pure perfections is by identity and for limited perfection is by way of eminence.

[10] 5.24 A [second] proof based on the general comparison of finite and infinite can be put briefly as follows: The ascent in an essential order* or hierarchy always leads to unity and hence terminates with some single or unique thing.[11] But the intensively infinite is absolutely the highest in the essential order. Therefore, it is a single unique thing.

5.25 [Third way] Third, the major is proved from the way the infinite is ordered to intellect and will in particular. It goes as follows:

[11] Cf. ibid., I, d.2, nn.64-73, 165-81 (II, 167-73, 226-36).

QUESTION FIVE

An infinite being is the primary object of an infinite intellect and also its beatific object. But the same infinite intellect cannot have more than one object that is both primary and beatific.

A similar argument could be made for the first or adequate beatific object of the will.[12]

5.26 The first proposition can mean primary object in any of three senses and is true for all of them. Accordingly it contains three parts.

One of the primacies an object may have is called "primacy of adequation," namely when the power does not extend beyond this object. The colored or luminous is called the first object of sight in this sense.

Another meaning is "primacy of virtue." Such would be that in virtue of which such an intellect knows or understands everything else. In this way light is the first object of sight.

[11] The third can be called "primacy of perfection." It obtains when the object as supreme contains in itself the perfection of all objects and has the power to perfect the intellect. Now the beatific object is that which quiets, satisfies, and perfects the intellect.

5.27 On this basis three major premises can be formulated.

The same intellect does not have several distinct adequate objects. It cannot know another object that lies outside the extension of its adequate object. Otherwise this adequate object would not really be adequate, since the intellective power in knowing equally well another distinct object would be going beyond it.

A power cannot have several first objects by a primacy of the second type, that of virtue, either. It is not possible for it to understand everything it understands, including B, by virtue of A, and at the same time to understand everything, including A, by virtue of B. That A be the ground for understanding B, and B the ground for understanding A involves circularity, and such circularity is impossible.

Neither can the intellect find its supreme satisfaction in two equally distinct objects, for it does not come to rest and find complete happiness in any object which, if eliminated, it would be no less happy and at rest. But if one of the two were written off, the intellect would still be supremely satisfied, at rest and happy with the other. Therefore, it could not be perfected by the object eliminated, and by the same token neither could it be so by the second.

The three majors then are evident. The same intellect could not

---

[12] Cf. ibid., I, d.3, nn.171-74 (III, 105-107).

have several equally distinct first objects, be the primacy that of adequation, of virtue, or of perfection in the way a beatific object is primary.

5.28 The minor, namely what is intensively and formally infinite is first object of the divine intellect in each of these three ways, is proved first in regard to the second type [that of virtue].

What is ground for being is also ground for knowing. Therefore, the infinite, which in itself contains the entity of everything eminently, also contains in itself all knowability eminently. But if anything contains virtually some object in this way, it is also that which moves the intellect to the knowledge of that object. Therefore, anything intensively infinite in this way will function as first object in regard to the divine intellect, and this by a primacy of virtue.

[12] From this it follows that the intensively infinite is the first object by a primacy of adequation, for as we have shown elsewhere[13] in dealing with the divine intellect, this intellect does not have an adequate object common by way of abstraction from all the objects it knows, but rather one that is common to all *per se* objects by a community of virtue. Otherwise the divine intellect would be demeaned because it could be altered by a finite object. Therefore, that which is its first object virtually is also its first adequate object.

From this the third primacy also follows, viz., that of perfection which is characteristic of the beatific object. For in the most perfect of all objects, which contains in the highest all the perfection of every object, this intellective power is to the highest degree perfected, satisfied, and quieted, and so beatified.

5.29 Confirmation of the major and minor premises of this reason: Suppose there were two distinct infinites A and B. The divine intellect will be able to understand them both; if not, that will be because one is not a being. Neither can be understood, however, except by a comprehensive act, since both are formally infinite. Now two distinct objects, each with its own infinity, cannot be grasped in just one comprehensive act, because a single object intensively infinite is what one infinite intellect is equal to. Therefore, since both A and B are infinite intensively, either both will never be understood, or, if they are, it will not be simultaneously, and thus there will be succession or mutation in the divine intellect.

2. The Second Principal Reason

[13] 5.30 The second main argument based on communicability is formulated in this way. Every pure perfection is communicable;*

---

[13] Cf. ibid., prol., nn.197-201 (I, 133-36).

everything intensively infinite is a pure perfection. Therefore, [it is communicable]. No personal property, however, is communicable, since it is the formal ground for existing incommunicably [or as a person]. Therefore, no personal property is intensively infinite.[14] The [first] minor is evident, because nothing can be more perfect than what is intensively infinite.

5.31 Proof of the first major: From what one gathers of the mind of Anselm in the *Monologion*,[15] a pure perfection is that which, in anything having it, it is better to have it than to have what is not it. This rule needs two explanatory notes.

It does not mean "Better it than [not-it,] its contradictorily opposed negation," for in this sense everything positive would be a pure perfection, since anything positive is simply better than its contradictorily opposed negation. Here "what is not it" means rather "anything whatsoever incompatible, also positively," so that the meaning is: a pure perfection is in anything better than whatever is incompatible with it.

Second, "in anything" does not refer to any nature but to any suppositum,* understood not insofar as it is the suppositum of such and such a nature, but taking it absolutely insofar as it is such a suppositum prescinding from any notion of the nature of which it is the suppositum. This is obvious, since for the gold considered as having the nature of gold or for a gold suppositum not-gold is not something it is better to be than gold. For there are some things for which the incompatible *qua* incompatible is not better, because it destroys a thing's entity. In fact, from this standpoint it is better for gold to be gold than to be anything incompatible with the nature of gold. The meaning then is this: Pure perfection is such that in any suppositum, considered absolutely according to its essential meaning as a suppositum [i.e., as an individual independently existing substance], without specifying of what nature it is or what sort of suppositum it is, it is better to be this sort of thing than to be anything that is not this kind of thing.

5.32 From this the thesis follows that no pure perfection is formally incommunicable.

The implication holds, because what is formally incommunicable is also formally incompatible with any other subject, considering the latter as a suppositum, but not including its nature. Proof of this: What is repugnant to anything is not simply better for it than what is not such, for being repugnant, it would destroy the other.

[14] Cf. ibid., I, d.2, nn.382-84 and the *textus cancellatus* (II, 346-48).
[15] Anselm, *Monolog.* 15: PL 158, 162-63; ed. Schmitt I, 28-29.

But what is of itself incommunicable is repugnant to everything that also has the characteristic of being a suppositum, and hence is not better for it *qua* suppositum than what is not it. We have then this major: No pure perfection is formally incommunicable.

3. The Third Principal Reason

[15] 5.33 The third argument from incompossibility [cf. 5.16] goes this way: Pure perfection must be really identical with whatever is compatible with it in the same suppositum, in the sense that if we take this and that abstractly, it is true to say in the abstract that this is that. But a relation of origin is not identical in this way with everything compatible with it in the same suppositum. Therefore [it is not a pure perfection]. The minor is manifest for this proposition is not true: Active generation is active spiration.

5.34 The major is proved inductively and by argument.

It is established inductively in this way: There is nothing in the divine that is not the same thing as the divine essence and also the same as anything essential, so that considering such in the abstract, one can say simply "This is this." As regards the essence and essentials then, which are generally admitted to be formally infinite, the major is obvious. Each is identical with anything compatible or consistent with it in the same suppositum.

5.35 The major is also proved by this argument. Not only is the infinite not a composite but it is completely incapable of being a component of anything else, because a potential component is a potential part and hence can be exceeded, for the whole is greater than its part. The infinite, however, cannot be exceeded in any way. Therefore, it is completely simple, uncomposed and unable to be a component of anything else. But if something compatible with it in the same suppositum were not the same thing as it, then the infinite would not be completely incapable of being a component, for then there would be in the suppositum some sort of composition, at least that of act and potency. Therefore, we have the first part of the major, viz., that the infinite must be really identical with whatever is compatible with it in the same suppositum.

5.36 Proof of the second part of the major, namely that it is so identical that predication in the abstract, such as "This is this," is true. Since affirmative predication is true by reason of identity, every case of predicating the abstract of the abstract will be true if the ground of the identity is not destroyed by the abstraction. Where abstraction eliminates the reason for the identity, however, the predication is not true.

[16] Example: "Whiteness is color" is true, for though the terms are abstract, still the abstraction is only from a subject of a different nature, and that subject was not the precise ground for the identity of the terms. Even with the subject excluded, therefore, the basis for the identity of nature [of whiteness] with that [of color] remains. Whiteness and music, however, have only an accidental identity by reason of their subject; therefore, even though "The white individual is a musician" is true to the extent that the same subject is characterized by both accidents, nevertheless if you abstract from the subject which was the ground for the identity of the two descriptive terms, it is not true that "Whiteness is music."

It is clear then that predication in the abstract is true when the identity of the terms is such that the abstraction does not remove the reason for their identity. Now when one term is infinite, predication that abstracts from the suppositum does not destroy the ground for its identity with any perfection compatible with it in the same suppositum, and, therefore, because of the infinity, as was argued above [in 5.19-20], compatibility in the same suppositum is possible only where there is a true and perfect real identity. Therefore, whenever the term, in abstraction from the suppositum, retains the formal reason for its infinity, the basis for its identity with the other term is always present and consequently abstract predication, such as "This is this," remains true.

[17] 5.37 [Corollary about predication in the divine] This argument shows in general that in the divine, if it is not a case of predicating one opposite notional* term of another, certain predications are true not only in the concrete but also in the abstract, whereas certain others are true in the concrete but not in the abstract. We are not speaking of those predications not true in either way, namely those where the terms are opposed, for the Father is not the Son, nor is paternity sonship. Where the terms are not opposed, however, but are compatible in the same suppositum, at least in the concrete there is true predication, such as "The Father is the one who spirates [the Holy Spirit]" or "The Father is unbegotten," even though it is not true in the abstract that "Paternity is spiration." Nevertheless the following predications are true: "Deity is paternity" or "Deity is spiration," but this is true only because divinity is formally infinite, not because paternity and spiration are. Because deity, in abstraction from the suppositum, still retains the note of infinity, the reason for its identity, understood simply [not formally], with paternity and with spiration, always remains, and therefore also the basis for true affirmative predication in the abstract.

121

But when one abstracts "paternity," which is not formally infinite, from the suppositum, the reason for its identity with active spiration, which is not infinite either, is no longer there, since neither term, according to its proper notion, possesses infinity. Therefore, even though this is true: "The Father spirates," because both descriptive terms pertain to the same suppositum, nevertheless when one abstracts from this suppositum, since neither of these descriptive notions formally includes "infinite," the abstract predication "Paternity is spiration" is not true.[16]

5.38 A converse argument of the same type is this: Whenever some essential feature is predicated of something essential, or something personal of something essential, or something essential of something personal, e.g., "Wisdom is paternity" or "Wisdom is spiration," the proposition is true and vice versa. For one term (in this case "wisdom") is still infinite, abstracting from the suppositum; hence the ground for its identity with the other is retained despite the abstraction, and consequently also the truth of the affirmative predication.

5.39 This major, then, is evident, namely that the only predication by identity of one abstract of another that must be denied is that in which neither term is formally infinite, such as "Paternity is spiration."

[18] 5.40 As regards this major, however, some[17] give a twofold explanation why in the divine certain predications in the abstract are denied. Although paternity and spiration are really identical, they differ conceptually, and this suffices to invalidate such predications. But when one objects that such a distinction does not allow for the falsity of the proposition "Wisdom is goodness," they reply that just as the attribute "power" is not the attribute "wisdom," so also in the case at hand.

5.41 But this does not seem plausible. An attribute *qua* attribute expresses a second intention or asserts some conceptual relationship of the subject of which it is predicated. Hence one numbers attributes, and it is true to say that "goodness" and "wisdom" are two attributes. In the sense then that they are subject to enumeration, which is in the conceptual order, it is not true to say "This is this." But this does not require one to deny the proposition: "Wisdom is

---

[16] Cf. Duns Scotus, *Ord.* I, d.13 (v, 65-124); III, d.22, q.un., n.21 (ed. Vivès XIV, 777-78).

[17] Thomas, *Summa theol.* I, q.3, a.3, ad 1 (I, 16); q.28, a.3, ad 1-2 (I, 154); q.40, a.1, ad 1 (I, 202); Henry of Ghent, *Quodl.* v, q.1 (fol. 152P); *Summa* a.60, q.10 (II, fol. 172B-173H).

goodness," where the conceptual aspect that allows them to be numbered is suppressed. By analogy, then, if we include only what is of the real order, "Paternity is spiration" would be true if paternity and spiration were absolutely identical in reality, even though "The notion or property of paternity is the notion or property of spiration" would not. For whatever those features be that are simply the same thing in God, they are predicated of each other, also in the abstract and in names of first imposition, but not when they are expressed by names of second imposition or those which designate some second intentional aspect. This is clear from the case of creatures. Although "Socrates is man" is true, this is not true: "That aspect of *Socrates* which is singularity is the aspect of *man* which is universality."

5.42 Another author[18] says, and seemingly with more reason, that the properties in the same person have some extramental difference that goes beyond a consideration of the intellect. This is enough for them to be disparate without being opposed [as paternity and sonship are]. That is why predicating one of the other in the abstract is not correct. The reason why such abstract predication is not true is that this extramental distinction stems from the fact that neither property is infinite. If this or that were infinite, such a distinction would not exist, and there would be nothing to impede predication in the abstract.

ARTICLE III
Objections and Answers

[19] 5.43 [Four objections] As for the third article, four counterarguments are leveled at what has been said, the first of which is this.

[First objection] What is comprehensible only to an infinite intellect is formally infinite. This generation as generation is formally incomprehensible except to the divine intellect. Therefore [it is formally infinite]. The minor is proved from Isaiah[19]: "Who can describe his generation?" Commenting on this text in relation to the eternal generation of the Son, Jerome[20] states: "The Prophet says it is impossible to speak of it, etc." What it is impossible to speak of is incomprehensible to a finite intellect. Ambrose[21] also confirms this: "How, I ask you, do you think the Son is begotten?" And he goes on

[18] William of Ware, *Sent.* I, d.2, q.1.
[19] Isaiah 53:8.
[20] Jerome, *Comment. in Evang. Math.* I, c.1: PL 26, 21; CCSL 77, 7.
[21] Ambrose, *De fide ad Grat.* I, c.10, n.64: PL 16, 543; CSEL 78, 28.

to say: "It is impossible for me to know the secret of his generation. The mind fails, the voice is silent, not only mine but that of the angels. It is beyond the Cherubim and Seraphim and transcends all understanding." He proves this from Paul to the Philippians[22]: "The peace of Christ which surpasses all understanding," arguing "Since the peace of Christ surpasses all understanding, would not such a generation as his surpass all understanding?"

5.44 [Second objection] A second argument is this. Every action equal to its infinite principle and its infinite term is formally infinite. In the divine, however, generation is an action equal to its infinite formal principle and its infinite term, for its source is the essence or infinite memory and it terminates first in the Son, who is infinite; also its formal term is the essence communicated or spoken knowledge, both of which are infinite. It is obvious the action is equal to its source and adequate for its term, because there can be but one action which stems from this principle and ends with this term. Therefore [it is infinite].

5.45 [Third objection] The third argument is that the reason for subsisting is also the basis for having being in the most perfect way. But the first person's relationship of origin is his basis for subsisting. Therefore, it is also the reason for his having being most perfectly, and hence the relationship of origin is infinite.

5.46 [Fourth objection] Furthermore, the divine intellect is formally infinite; otherwise it would not comprehend the infinite divine essence, yet it does so as intellect, a point proved in the first question [1.30-38]. But the divine intellect is only infinite because it is the same thing as the divine essence, which is infinite primarily. But paternity is also the same thing as the intellect. Therefore, for the same reason, paternity is formally infinite.

[20] 5.47 [Reply to the objections] Answer *to the first* [in 5.43]: When an intellect has an object that is first by virtual primacy, then it understands every other object in its hierarchical relationship to that first object. (This is evident from the reason given [in 5.25-28] when treating of intellect and will in article two of this question. For example, when an intellect's first object is one of virtual primacy, then by means of that object it understands more immediately what is identical *per se* with that object than what is identified with it only incidentally or *per accidens*.) But the divine intellect has as its first object, by a primacy both of virtue and of adequation, the same, absolutely identical, thing, namely, the divine essence *qua* essence, as we said [in 5.47]. Therefore, there is nothing personal

[22] Philippians 4:7.

that is this intellect's primary object in this way. (Of course the personal relation is more proximate in this way to the intellect's first object than anything created. To the extent it is really identical with that object, the relation is closer to it in entity and hence also in knowability.)

5.48 As for the form of the argument, the major is true if understood in the sense that if the object is incomprehensible with its own incomprehensibility, it is also infinite with its own infinity. But then the minor is false, viz., that this generation as generation is incomprehensible, even though it could be given a true meaning *per accidens* either by reason of something concomitant with generation or, what is more to the point, by reason of the basis for understanding it. For generation is apt by nature to be understood primarily by means of the essence as first object both by the divine intellect and by that of the blessed, since the divine essence is the first object of both intellects. Now this basis for understanding the generation is indeed incomprehensible, and so the generation itself could be called incomprehensible causally or by virtue of its source [*principiative*]. One could also say that it was incomprehensible concomitantly, i.e., as regards what it includes, for generation includes communication of the essence to a person, and this takes place by means of the essence itself or the person's nature. Now this communication includes the essence's infinity as a presupposition, for if the essence were not infinite, it could not be communicated in this fashion to several persons. Therefore, generation is incomprehensible as regards its presupposition, namely, communication of an essence that has to be infinite.

5.49 [Objection to this answer and its solution] These answers are challenged on the grounds that they ignore the force of what generation *qua* generation means. No matter what the principle be by which generation is understood or what its understanding or communication presupposes, the authorities cited [in 5.43] always seem to be saying that generation itself in its own right is incomprehensible and any intelligible whose intelligibility exceeds comprehension is infinite.

[22] 5.50 To this one could say that what is comprehensible to the finite intellect must be finite, whereas what is incomprehensible to it is non-finite. But from this it does not follow it is infinite. We shall say more about this [in 5.57] in answer to the initial argument. According to this negative interpretation of incomprehensible as something that cannot be comprehended, the major of the argument must be denied. For it to be true, "incomprehensible" would need

to be interpreted quasi-contrarily, namely, as that whose virtual quantity extends beyond or exceeds everything comprehensible, which is not the way it is used here.

5.51 Reply *to the second* objection [in 5.44]: Equality, properly speaking, means that two things are equal in quantity, and in this sense no equality is involved here. In another sense, however, equality refers not to quantity but to proportion. In this sense, one thing is said to be equal to another if it is not disproportionate but supremely adequate. Equality in this sense is that which obtains between effect and cause where the effect is supremely adequate as an effect, even though it is not simply equal to the cause in quantity. Also illumination, if it could be no greater, would be said to be what the sun is "equal to," even though illumination, as an equivocal effect,* could never equal the sun in quantity.

[23] 5.52 As for the form of the argument, the major would only be true of equality taken in the first sense, if such were there; but in that case the minor is false. It would be true of "equality" in the second sense provided this referred not to intension but extension, namely, insofar as this one principle of generation could not extend to any generation other than this. Consequently, there is no quantitative equality involved here or, properly speaking, even equality of intension, but only that of extension, and thus infinity in no way is included in what it is "equal to" [i.e., principle and term].

5.53 Reply *to the third* objection [in 5.45]: As we said at the end of the second article of the previous question [4.46], "to subsist" is an equivocal term. In one sense it refers to being *per se*, and Augustine[23] uses it in this way when he says: "Everything subsists in respect to itself; how much more God?" In another sense, it refers to "being incommunicably *per se*," insofar as communicable means not subsisting, as it were, but what is inhering, as it were, in a subsisting subject and has a quasi-mode of inherence. In the first sense, I concede "to subsist" formally implies most perfect being, and is only affirmed of the essence according to Augustine. In the second sense, "to subsist" presupposes, but does not formally include, perfect being. It only adds incommunicability to being *per se* in the first sense, and is thus a ground for subsisting in the sense of being incommunicably *per se*. The relation is this sort of thing. But the ground for having being incommunicably is not the ground for being most perfectly.

[24] 5.54 Reply *to the last* objection [in 5.46]: I admit the intellect is

---

[23] Augustine, *De Trin.* VII, c.4, n.9: PL 42, 942; CCSL 50, 260.

formally infinite by an infinity all its own which is an intrinsic mode of its proper entity, namely intellectuality *qua* intellectuality. Paternity, however, is not infinite in this way, even though it is in some way really identical with the essence, as is the intellect.

[25] 5.55 To what is added about its infinity being due to identity with the essence, I answer: As we said in the first question [1.5-6], what is absolutely first in the divine is essence *qua* essence, which Damascene [in 5.11] says is a sea because it contains all divine perfections. The essence is infinite in itself, not only intensively but also virtually, as containing primarily and of itself everything intrinsic to the divine. Now everything else contains other features by identity, but not all of them primarily, since it does not contain them in virtue of what it is but by reason of the divine essence, from which its infinity also derives. Therefore, the essence has infinity formally, properly, and primarily, because it contains it of itself. It is called a sea, since it contains every intrinsic entity insofar as it is possible to contain it formally in one single thing. Now from this first entity, and it is licit to speak in this way, emanate all other features in an orderly fashion. First, indeed, are the intrinsic essential features, expressing no relation to anything extrinsic or *ad extra*. Second, come the notional [or personal properties]. Third and last, created or extrinsic things. Now everything emanating receives such perfection as it is consistently able to receive, and the quasi-efficient and primary source of what it gets is the infinity of the essence, although the formal cause or reason is the proper entity itself of what emanates. Therefore, essentials derive from the essence formal infinity, because the essence in its function as principle or foundation suffices to give them such quantity, or virtual quantity, or communicability as is not repugnant to them. To relate to another belongs to the personal relations, but not intensive infinity proper, for the relation is incapable of such quantity even as it is unable to be communicated. In the genre of formal principles there is also something basic. This one receives infinity and that not, because the first receives communicability whereas the second gets incommunicability, the reason being that this is this and that is that. For formal repugnance (like non-repugnance) is formally reduced in the first place to that basic feature said to have it. Finally, creatures receive finite entity from the essence, because only such entity pertains to them.

5.56 As for the form of the argument, therefore, I say that identity with the essence is not the only ground for possessing infinity formally, but it is the sufficient reason for possessing infinity in anything to which infinity is not repugnant formally. As was proved [in 4.17], infinity is formally repugnant to a personal relation, but not to anything essential. And if you ask why infinity is compatible with the latter and not with the former, one can reply by asking: Why—as all admit—is incommunicability repugnant to one and not to the other? The answer is the same for both. It depends on the nature of the formal principle, namely on the fact that this is formally this and that is formally that. Because the essence, then, as the fundamental principle is one unlimited source from which many features emanate or proceed in orderly fashion, everything, in the first instant of its quasi-emanation or derivation, possesses its own proper entity. This has this sort and that has that sort. The ultimate reason why something is repugnant to one but not to another is to be found in the respective entity of each.

Reply to the Initial Argument

[26] 5.57 To the argument [in 5.3] at the beginning I say: As was pointed out in the first article [5.9], infinity in entity expresses totality of entity, whereas finitude in its way expresses only partial entity, for every finite being as such is less than the infinite as such. As Euclid says[24]: "Every lesser number represents a part or parts of a greater number." This should not be taken to mean that this binary is a part of that ternary (for nothing like this occurs in the divine), but according to all the proportions observed to hold between quantities this binary number is related to that ternary number as a part or parts of a whole. For this binary is exceeded by another ternary of which it is a part. And that, I say, is what occurs here. As God is most simple, nothing created can be a part of him, but everything finite, since it is less than infinite entity, can be called a part, although not according to some definite measure, for it is exceeded infinitely. In this way every other being distinct from the infinite being is called "a being" by participation because it captures a part of that entity present there perfectly and totally.

Therefore, the point I wish to make is this: Everything finite, since it is less than the infinite, represents a part. Hence, to whatever it is repugnant to be a part or exceeded in reality by anything, it is also repugnant to be finite. Now to be a part of divinity in this special sense, or to be exceeded by divinity, is repugnant to pater-

---

[24] Euclid, *Elementa* VII, def.4 (ed. Heiberg, in Bibliotheca Teubneriana, II, Lipsiae, 1883, p. 199).

nity, for paternity, because of the infinity of divinity with which it is compatible in the same suppositum, is, simply speaking, identical with it, and consequently in reality it can neither be exceeded, nor be a part, nor have any ground for being a part. Therefore it is neither finite nor infinite, as was proved [in 5.50], for as finite has the characteristic of a part in the manner just explained, so infinite has the character of a whole in this sense, namely, from the plenitude of its "virtual quantity" the infinite is measuring everything else as greater or lesser to the degree it approaches the whole or recedes from it. But neither does paternity have this mark of totality, for measurement according to certain degrees of perfections ends with something first in the order of measurement, which is the absolute essence. Therefore, I say briefly that paternity is neither formally infinite nor formally finite.

5.58 And when you insist that being divides immediately into finite and infinite, even before it splits up into the ten categories, I readily grant that finite and infinite are not further differentiations within some category. Indeed, any genus and being itself just prior to its differentiation into categories is specifically finite being. But finite and infinite are immediate divisions not of being but of "quantified being." For just as finite and infinite, according to the Philosopher,[25] correspond to quantity (which is true of "finite," "infinite," and "quantity" proper), so also, in an extended sense, finite and infinite as proper attributes [in disjunction] of being pertain precisely to a "quantified" being in the sense of having in itself some amount of perfection. But this sort of "quantity" pertains only to entity that can be "total" or "partial" in the hierarchy of essences. For one "quantity" compared with another must immediately excel or be excelled and must have partial or total being, as we speak of "partial" and "total" here. Paternity as paternity, however, can be neither a total nor a partial entity in this sense.

5.59 One could also say that virtual quantity, and therefore finitude and infinity, are characteristic only of a quidditative entity, namely, insofar as it is distinguished from a hypostatic entity. But this entity [i.e., paternity], though somehow quidditative in itself, nevertheless as such is purely hypostatic.

5.60 A third possible answer given is that virtual quantity pertains only to an absolute [or non-relative] entity. But these two last answers admit a dubious point about hypostatic entity and relative entity, namely that they have no virtual quantity.

[25] Aristotle, *Physic.* I, c.2 (185a33-b5).

Question Six
IS "EQUALITY" IN THE DIVINE A REAL RELATION?

6.1 Once the relation of origin* in the divine was discussed, the issue of the common relations* arose. Here there was but one question: Is equality in the divine a real relation?*[1]

Arguments Pro and Con

[1] It is argued that it is: Any relation that has a real foundation and extremes that are really distinct is real. The relation in question is such. Therefore [it is real]. Proof of the minor: In the divine there is real magnitude, namely, that of the essence; also the persons, said to be equal to one another, are really distinct.

6.2 To the contrary: Every real relation is based on either action and passion* or quantity.[2] In God no real relation is based on quantity, for "God is great without quantity," as Augustine[3] puts it. Therefore, no relation there is real unless based on action and passion; but the only relationship of this sort is that of origin, and equality is not a relationship of origin since it has the same basis in both terms of the relation.

6.3 Besides, magnitude,* like essence, is the same in all three persons. Therefore the terms or extremes related are not really distinct, and consequently the relation itself is not real.

Body of the Question

6.4 Three points must be considered here. First, is there any real foundation for the equality of the divine persons? Second, is there a real distinction of extremes? Third, is this equality of the extremes something in them extramentally in virtue of its foundation?

ARTICLE I
Is there a Real Foundation for Equality in the Divine?

[2] 6.5 The first article contains *three* points. First of all, the common basis or foundation for equality needs to be investigated. Second,

---

[1] Cf. Duns Scotus, *Ord.* I, d.19, nn.1-28 (v, 265-79); d.31 (VI, 203-22).
[2] Aristotle, *Metaph.* v, c.15 (1020b25-33).
[3] Augustine, *De Trin.* v, c.1, n.2: PL 42, 912; CCSL 50, 207.

what could be assigned as foundation for equality in the divine, and if there are various possibilities, what are they and how many are there? Third, is each one of these real?

1. The Foundation for Equality in General

6.6 As for the first point, it seems that for the Philosopher, the foundation for equality is quantity. As he says in the *Categories*[4]: "The most distinctive mark of quantity is that equal and unequal can be predicated with reference to it." The words "with reference to it" indicate the foundation of this relation, just as they do in the chapter on quality[5]: "What is distinctive is this, that we predicate likeness and unlikeness with reference to quality only." These statements about the basis for equality or similarity are further explained, it seems, in the chapter on relation in the *Metaphysics*[6]: "The equal, the similar, and the identical are all predicated with reference to unity. Those things are equal whose quantity is one, those are similar whose quality is one, and those things are identical whose substance is one." Here he seems to suggest that the foundation for equality is not just quantity alone, but a unity of quantity is needed.

But then two questions more general than the first come to mind. The first is whether unity is the formal element in the foundation of equality and, if so, whether it is more basic than the quantity itself of which it is the unity, or is quantity more fundamental? The second question is whether unity, insofar as it pertains *per se* to the foundation of equality, implies *per se* something positive or only some privation or negation? If it turns out that it only implies negation, and that it pertains *per se* to the foundation for equality, whether it be as proximate or remote ground, it would follow that equality in general would not be a real relation.

There is no need here to discuss this general conclusion and the two premises from which it follows, for they take us beyond what we have to discuss here. Those who admit that equality is a real relation in other things still deny it to be such in God. Consequently even if equality in general were admitted to be a real relation, whether necessarily positive or not, there would still be the question of whether the necessary conditions for a real relation could be preserved in divine equality as well as in the case of created equality.

[4] Aristotle, *Praedicam.* c.6 (6a27-35).
[5] Ibid., c.8 (11a18-19).
[6] Aristotle, *Metaph.* v, c.15 (1021a10-15).

2. The Foundation of Equality in God

[3] 6.7 As for the second part of this article, namely what the foundation for equality in the divine in particular would be, Augustine,[7] it seems, provides an answer when he says of the three divine persons: "No one precedes any other as regards eternity, nor exceeds another in magnitude, nor surpasses another in power, for the Father is not anterior to the Son nor greater than he." And we could add: Neither is he more powerful. What the Philosopher said provides proof of Augustine's assertion, for if equality has reference to quantity, since quantity* is divided primarily into continuous and discrete, there can be no equality according to discrete quantity. There is only a trinity there, which is not number, or, if it is a plurality, the lesser part is somehow part of the greater and thus is unequal to it. Continuous quantity, however, is divided into permanent and successive. In God there is no successive quantity, although there is something corresponding to it, namely the quantity of duration which is properly called "eternity." Permanent quantity in creatures is commonly called magnitude or mass, and everything corresponding to it in the divine is called magnitude. Therefore, from what the Philosopher says Augustine's position follows, namely, that in the divine what is equal refers either to magnitude or to eternity.

[4] 6.8 Second, we explain Augustine's remark, for it seems from what we have just said that his addition "nor in power" is superfluous. The answer, however, is that the equality of some things is regarded properly as based upon something absolute and intrinsic to them. Thus from the fact that some beings have some form to an equal degree it follows as a consequence that they can act upon extrinsic things to an equal degree. Equality of power, therefore, is not, properly speaking, distinct from the equality of magnitude, but it represents, as it were, an explication of the kind of equality in magnitude, namely, that characteristic of an active form. Thus creatures which possess heat in equal magnitudes have equal power to heat. Consequently, counting the equality which stems from the comparison to extrinsic beings together with that based on what is intrinsic, there are three forms of equality. Properly speaking, however, there are only two, those based on what is absolute and intrinsic, namely equality with reference to magnitude and with ref-

---

[7] Ps. Augustine, Fulgentius of Ruspe, *De fide ad Petrum.* c.1, n.4: PL 40, 674; CCSL 91a, 714.

erence to eternity. Perhaps that is why Augustine in his reply only mentions these two, and omits power, since he says merely that "The Father is not anterior to the Son nor greater than he." He does not add: "Nor more powerful."

6.9 There is another query in regard to Augustine's remark: Why not consider equality in other matters? For the Father and Son are equal as regards wisdom, goodness, justice, and other such attributes.

6.10 I reply: They are equal in wisdom only insofar as there is one magnitude. If they are equal as regards some essential perfection, the proximate reason for the equality is always the magnitude of that perfection. Consequently, through magnitude alone Augustine understands every essential perfection to be the basis for equality, for no perfection serves as a foundation for it except under the aspect of its magnitude.[8]

3. Is Each of these Foundations for Equality Real?

[5] 6.11 [Three questions] To answer the third question in this article, we must clear up three points: First, is magnitude in God something extramental? Second, is eternity there in that way? Third, is power also?

1) First question: Is magnitude in God something extramental?

6.12 [Three subquestions] Three further questions need to be answered before we can reply to the first. First, in what sense can magnitude be said to exist in the divine? Second, since magnitude is always the amount of something, if it is to be extramental, we first need something extramental of which it is the magnitude. Third, is the magnitude of this something also there extramentally? Thus the complete solution of the first question about the reality of magnitude depends on how we answer these three.

6.13 [First subquestion] Of the first, the Philosopher[9] says: "Great and small and greater and smaller, both in themselves and when taken relatively to each other, are by their own nature attributes of what is quantitative; but these names are transferred to other things also." He wants to say that great and small, taken either in themselves or absolutely or taken relatively, pertain of themselves to quantity proper, but in a transferred sense they are applied to

---

[8] Cf. Duns Scotus, *Ord.* 1, d.19, nn.8 and 12 (v, 267-68, 270); d.31, nn.8-11 (vi, 205-208).

[9] Aristotle, *Metaph.* v, c.13 (1020a23-26).

other things as well. This is sufficiently clear from reason, for the Philosopher would not deny that equality pertains to individuals of the same species in any genus and inequality pertains to the species in any genus. Consequently, since he claims equal and unequal are predicated only with reference to quantity, then quantity somehow pertains to every single being of any genus. Hence if great and small according to him are proper attributes of quantity, in their transferred sense, at least, they are transcendentals and proper attributes of the whole realm of being. Now Augustine[10] calls this "great" in the Philosopher's transferred sense, not greatness of mass, but magnitude of goodness and perfection: "In those things which are not great in mass, to be greater is the same as to be better." It is clear then that "great" in the first sense (i.e., in Aristotle's proper sense or what Augustine calls "great in mass") is not applicable either to God or to any spiritual being. Nevertheless, we can assume they are "great" in the Philosopher's transferred meaning of the term, or in what Augustine calls "great in goodness, virtue, or perfection," for magnitude of this sort is transcendental and belongs to everything in its fashion.

[6] 6.14 [Second subquestion] As for the second, let us avoid what is dubious and say for certain that the essence is there extramentally, something we also pointed out in article one, Question One [1.5].

6.15 [Third subquestion] From this we infer immediately the answer to the third question. The divine essence *qua* essence has its own real or extramental magnitude. This is proved from authority and from two rational arguments.

[Proof from authority] Damascene[11] is our authority, when he calls the essence a kind of "infinite and limitless sea of substance." As we have said repeatedly, he calls the essence a "sea" because it enjoys a kind of priority and contains primarily all the divine perfections, and precisely under this aspect, he calls it "infinite and limitless." The divine essence *qua* essence, then, is infinite. From this we argue further that the essence is infinite extramentally, for as a "sea" it is infinite, and as that which is absolutely first, this sea is real or extramental. But the magnitude proper to the essence is called "infinity." Therefore, it has this extramentally. The minor, as regards some sense of magnitude at least, is sufficiently obvious, for just as quantitative infinity refers to magnitude in the proper sense,

---

[10] Augustine, *De Trin.* VI, c.8, n.9: PL 42, 929; CCSL 50, 238.

[11] Damascene, *De fide orth.* I, c.9: PG 94, 835; ed. Buytaert c.9, p.49.

QUESTION SIX

expressing as it does extensively the highest degree of quantity proper, so intensive infinity in perfection expresses the highest magnitude of perfection.

6.16 [First proof from reason] Reason provides this argument: Intensive infinity pertains to the divine essence really or extramentally. But such infinity is the magnitude proper to the essence. Therefore [magnitude pertains to the essence really or extramentally].

Proof of the major: As was pointed out in the preceding question [5.10], intensive infinity* does not refer to a property of the being to which it belongs, but rather represents an intrinsic mode* which would still be present apart from all other properties. Therefore, infinity can only belong to its subject intrinsically in the real or extramental order.

Proof of the minor: It is the characteristic of the entity of any absolute quiddity that is apt by nature to measure or be measured, that it be either finite or infinite, and hence, if it is repugnant to it to be finite, it will be infinite. But the divine essence is this sort of quiddity.

One might also want to argue in proof of the major that intensive infinity could not pertain to a conceptual relation, for then such a relation of the mind would be a pure perfection.* Therefore, neither can infinity pertain to someone only in virtue of a conceptual relation, but it must pertain to it extramentally. But the inference is not valid, for the first causality cannot pertain to someone by reason of a conceptual relation either, and yet it does not follow that the first causality pertains to it really or extramentally.

[7] 6.17 [Second proof from reason] A second argument from reason is this: The mode characteristic of the beatific object *qua* beatific object exists in reality and extramentally. But intensive infinity is this kind of mode in the divine essence. Therefore, it exists there extramentally and consequently magnitude does also.

6.18 [Proof of the major based on the distinction between intuitive and abstract cognition] Proof of the major is found in the perfection of the beatific act. To understand better what is involved, it is helpful to distinguish two acts of the intellect at the level of simple apprehension or intellection of a simple object. One is indifferent as to whether the object is existing or not, and also whether it is present in reality or not. We often experience this act in ourselves, for universals and the essences of things we grasp equally well whether they exist extramentally in some subject or not, or whether

135

we have an instance of them actually present or not. We also have [an empirical or] *a posteriori** proof of this, for scientific knowledge* of a conclusion or understanding of a principle can be equally present to the intellect whether what they are about is existing or not, or is present or absent. In either case, then, one can have an equal understanding of that term on which an understanding of the principle or conclusion depends. This act of understanding, which can be called "scientific," because it is a prerequisite condition for knowing the conclusion and understanding the principle, can very appropriately be called "abstractive" because it "abstracts" the object from existence or non-existence, from presence or absence.

[8]   6.19 But there is another act of understanding, though we do not experience it in ourselves as certainly, but it is possible. It is knowledge precisely of a present object as present and of an existing object as existing. Proof of this: Every perfection which is a perfection of cognition absolutely and which can be present in a faculty of sense knowledge can pertain eminently to an intellective cognitional faculty. But it is a matter of perfection in the act of knowing *qua* knowledge that what is first known be attained perfectly, and this is so when it is attained in itself and not just in some diminished or derivative likeness of itself.[12] On the other hand, a sense power has such perfection in its knowledge, because it can attain an object in itself as existing and present in its real existence, and not just diminutively in a kind of imperfect likeness of itself. Therefore this perfection also pertains to an intellective power in the act of knowing. It could not pertain to it however unless it could know an existing thing and know it as present either in its own existence or in some intelligible object that contains the thing in question in an eminent* way, which we are not concerned with at present.

Such knowledge of the existent *qua* existent and present is something an angel has about himself. For Michael does not know himself in the way he would know Gabriel if Gabriel were annihilated, viz., by abstractive cognition, but he knows himself as existing and as existing in a way that is identical with himself. He also is aware of his intellection in this way if he reflects upon it, considering it not just as any object in which one has abstracted from existence or non-existence in the way he would think of another angel's knowledge, if such did not actually exist; rather he knows himself to be knowing, that is to say, he knows his knowledge as something exist-

[12] See Glossary: *"intelligible species."*

QUESTION SIX

ing in himself. This knowledge possible for an angel, therefore, is also simply possible for our intellective power, because we have the promise that we shall be like the angels. Now this sort of intellection can properly be called "intuitive," because it is an intuition of a thing as existing and present.[13]

6.20 Applying this to the case at hand, we can say that the beatific act of the intellect cannot be one of abstractive cognition; it must be intuitive. Since abstractive cognition concerns equally the existent and the nonexistent, if the beatific act were of this sort one could be beatifically happy with a nonexistent object, which is impossible. Also, abstractive knowledge is possible where the object is not attained in itself but only in some likeness. Beatitude, on the contrary, can never be found unless the beatific object is reached immediately and in itself. And this intuitive intellection is what some call, and rightly so, face-to-face vision, basing themselves on the words of the Apostle[14]: "We see now through a mirror in an obscure manner, but then face to face."

[9] 6.21 From this the major [in 6.17] is manifest. If the beatific act is necessarily an intuition of its object, then it is knowledge of that object as existing and as present in its own existence. Therefore, every condition that is required *per se* of a beatific object must pertain to it *per se* in its real existence, and indeed in its real existence as something present. Hence we have our major.

6.22 [Proof of the minor] We prove the minor [of 6.17], viz., that infinity is an intrinsic *per se* condition of the beatific object. No intellect, or will for that matter, is perfectly satisfied by any object unless it contains the full plenitude of its first object, that is to say, unless its primary object finds its highest possible expression in that object. Such plenitude in the first object of the intellect or will can only be infinity. Therefore, no power capable of beatification can be content with anything unless it is infinite. Infinity then is a *per se* condition of any object that is fully satisfying and therefore beatific.

Proof of the major: Since a power is naturally inclined to its first object, it is not satisfied with anything short of the fullest expression of that object and will indeed push on farther to where that realization can be found.

Proof of the minor: Anything compatible with infinity does not

---

[13] Cf. Duns Scotus, *Ord.* II, d.3, q.9, nn.6-7 (ed. Vivès XII, 212-14); q.11, nn.11-12 (ibid., 278-79); III, d.14, q.3, nn.4ff. (XIV, 524ff.); IV, d.10, q.8, nn.5ff. (XVII, 285ff.); d.49, n.12 (XXI, 17-18).

[14] 1 Corinthians 13:12.

find its fullest expression in anything that is not infinite. This is obvious. Infinity alone represents the full measure of anything consistent with it. Now infinity is not incompatible with the first object of either intellect or will, for whether this object be "being" or "the true" or something similar characteristic of all things, or whether it be the "First Being" or "First Truth," which virtually contains the others, it is clear that infinity is not inconsistent with it. Therefore, it does not find its fullest expression in anything short of the infinite.

6.23 As for this first question on magnitude, then, we have concluded that in the divine there is something extramental possessing magnitude, namely the essence, and that its magnitude is something real and extramental. We also know what sort of magnitude it is. According to the Philosopher, it is magnitude not in a proper but in a transferred sense. In Augustine's terminology, it is not magnitude of mass but of perfection.[15]

[10] 6.24 [Objections and answers] In objection to what has been said, there is Augustine's statement[16]: "In him 'to be' and 'to be great' are identical." For him, then, magnitude is fused with the essence and hence no longer exists there in any proper sense of the word. But magnitude is a foundation for equality only as magnitude, not indeed of mass, but of virtue.

6.25 I reply: The divine essence would still retain its own magnitude or proper infinity, even though—to assume the possible or impossible—it were stripped of all its properties. For it has its own intrinsic degree just as something finite has its own finitude. Man, for instance, even if one abstracts from all his properties, still retains his essential finitude in the hierarchic classification of beings. In this sense, then, I concede that "to be" and "to be great" are identical in God. And there is a sense also in which it is correct to say "to be great" is even more intrinsic to God than is "to be just" or "to be wise," for "great" does not express a property or attribute as "just" and "wise" do. Greatness, therefore, is indeed "fused with him" because of the supreme identity of magnitude and essence. But when you infer from this that magnitude no longer exists there in any proper sense of the word, the implication must be denied. Even in creatures magnitude is so fused with its perfection that it does not represent something really other than that of which it is the degree, yet it retains its own character as magnitude insofar as this is proper

---

[15] Cf. Duns Scotus, *Ord.* III, d.14, q.1, n.1 (ed. Vivès XIV, 490); I, d.31, n.8 (VI, 205-206).

[16] Augustine, *De Trin.* v, c.10, n.11: PL 42, 918; CCSL 50, 218.

QUESTION SIX

ground for equality or inequality. No matter how immaterial they may be, one species of being is equal or unequal to another immaterial species. Therefore, the magnitude of their perfection remains in them as the basis for this equality, and still it is fused into an identity with the essence. As Augustine[17] says of this magnitude: "To be greater is the same as to be better," for the essential goodness that makes one species better than another is not a thing [*res*] added to the essence.

6.26 Neither in God nor even in creatures is there any diametrical opposition between "to be fused with" and "to remain," so long as one correctly understands the *fusion* as implying a real identity and the *remaining* to mean it retains its own quiddity. "It remains" does not entail "it remains really distinct." It only implies here that its proper quiddity has not been destroyed either by its form perishing or by being reduced to potentiality or by fusion into a [chemical] compound. In the first way fire becomes water. An instance of the second would be if God reduced fire to prime matter alone without form. The third would be if fire combined with water to form a composite substance in which neither retained its actuality. In none of these ways does anything "fuse with the divine" and only if it did pass away in some such fashion would it no longer remain. And "it remains, i.e., in its proper, perfect, and full actuality" does not entail "it remains really distinct." If this question were concerned with the real distinction, we could go into this.[18] But this suffices for our purpose, because not only in God but also in creatures the magnitude of perfection remains insofar as it is the proper basis for real equality and nevertheless without any real distinction from it, viz., the essence.

[11] 6.27 But these remarks give rise to another doubt. As magnitude is related to essence, so equality seems to be related to identity. But if magnitude is fused with the essence, then equality dissolves into identity, and thus there will not be the three common relations of equality, similarity, and identity in God.

6.28 One could admit here that equality is not distinct from identity and similarity to the same degree that these two are differentiated from each other, but that what equality asserts is a modality proper to both identity and similarity if they are to be perfect. For, to assume the impossible, if the Father's divinity were greater than

---

[17] Ibid., VI, c.8, n.9: PL 42, 929; CCSL 50, 238.
[18] Cf. Duns Scotus, *Ord.* I, d.8, nn.185, 209, 215-17, 220, 222 (IV, 252-53, 269, 272-74, 276-77); d.26, nn.80-82 (VI, 36-37).

the Son's divinity, there would still be some measure of identity between them but it would not be perfect because of the lack of equality. In like manner, if one person has greater knowledge and another less knowledge, they have a certain similarity, but it is not perfect because their knowledge, on which their similarity is based, is unequal. The same magnitude in the foundation, be it the basis for identity or for similarity, therefore, results in the identity or similarity being perfect. Equality, then, expresses the mode of similarity and the mode of identity, namely, that it is perfect. In the same way, identical magnitude means that the basis for the relationship is perfect.

[12] 6.29 [The unity needed in the foundation of equality] The final point we must examine in this section on magnitude concerns the unity which we said [in 6.6] appears to be required either *per se* or in some other way in the foundation for equality. Now we must recognize that if any unity of magnitude is real or really exists anywhere, it certainly is to be found in the divine. For here the unity is numerical and the two said to be equal share the same individual magnitude, whereas with other things of the same magnitude, there is no numerical unity though, according to some, there is perhaps some universal or conceptual unity, which I am not concerned about here. What is certain, however, is that no unity is more real than numerical unity, and that this is to be found properly in God as something common to all three persons. As Damascene[19] says: "In all created persons, what is diverse is considered to be real, whereas what they have in common, their interconnection and unity, is regarded as the work of the mind. But the converse is true of the holy and incomprehensible Trinity, for here what is common and one is considered to be real, since each is no less one with the others than he is with himself, whereas diversity is due to the consideration of the mind."

6.30 There is also a rational argument for this. According to the *Metaphysics*[20] "one" and "many" are the immediate subdivisions of being. If the magnitude of the essence shared by Father and Son is something real and extramental, as was proved, then such magnitude will be either one or many. Now it is clear there are not several magnitudes of different kinds, nor are there several of the same kind, for the same essence numerically is not great by virtue of several magnitudes of the same sort.

[19] Damascene, *De fide orth.* I, c.8: PG 94, 827; ed. Buytaert c. 8, pp. 42-43.
[20] Aristotle, *Metaph.* x, c.6 (1056b3).

QUESTION SIX

6.31 [Conclusion] Our first conclusion then in this initial article in brief is this: The grounds for being equally great in God are real and extramental as regards everything needed as a basis for equality. The grounds there are equal or even greater than we find elsewhere in any foundation for equality.

2) Second question: Is eternity a real or extramental basis for equality?

[13] 6.32 Now we must consider eternity. It is clear that eternity characterizes something that is really there extramentally, for it characterizes existence *qua* existence, and existence is there extramentally; otherwise nothing would be existing there extramentally. Therefore, we have something extramental to which eternity belongs, but it is necessary to inquire whether eternity *qua* eternity pertains to it extramentally.

6.33 [For the affirmative view] It seems that it does: Just as intensive infinity expresses an intrinsic mode of essence *qua* essence, so eternity *qua* eternity expresses an intrinsic mode of existence *qua* existence. Therefore, since existence, like being, is there extramentally, so for like reasons their respective intrinsic modes are also there extramentally.

In support of this are the words of Dionysius[21]: "God is existing, not in just any way, but simply and in an unlimited way he has the whole of existence in himself beforehand, which is why he is called the 'King of ages.'" And he goes on to say: "He gives existence to all existing things and, as their cause, he is their very existence and he is before ages, for he is 'age of ages' who exists before ages." And he seems to attribute "age of ages"—which means eternity—to God in the same sense that he is existing, namely, simply and without limitation.

[14] 6.34 [Arguments for the negative view] Against this interpretation are the words of Boethius[22]: "Eternity is endless life, possessed perfectly and all at once," and the similar statement of Anselm in the *Monologion*.[23] Richard's remark[24] that "Eternal being results from the absence of a beginning, an end and all mutability" must be

---

[21] Ps. Dionysius, *De div. nom.* c.5, 4: PG 3, 838-39; *Dionysiaca* I (Desclée de Brouwer and Cie, 1937), 333-35.

[22] Boethius, *De consolatione philosophiae* v, prossa 6: PL 63, 858; CCSL 94, 101.

[23] Anselm, *Monol.* c.18 (17): PL 158, 167; ed. Schmitt I, 32.

[24] Richard of St. Victor, *De Trin.* II, c.9: PL 196, 906; ed. Ribaillier, 116.

corrected and interpreted in the light of the preceding where "life" means existence as actual and perfect, just as it does in this text from John[25]: "Just as the Father possesses life in himself, so has he granted it to the Son to have life in himself."

Eternity then includes "life" as part of its connotation, because life is the quasi subject or foundation for eternity. Now it is certain that life, like perfect existence, is in God extramentally. But the other three components of the Boethian definition, namely, "endless" (which excludes cessation), "all at once" (which excludes succession), and "possessed perfectly" (which excludes dependence and participation), only add to "life" a positive or negative relation, it seems. The negative relation would be the denial of termination, succession, and dependence, whereas the positive, potential, or aptitudinal relation would be expressed by "endless" (which seems to express that it can coexist *per se* with any duration or existence whatsoever), by "all at once" (which says that it can coexist with anything whatsoever without variation or succession), and by "possessed perfectly" (which implies it exists of itself with full independence). Now this is the most proper description we find of eternity, and only one element, viz., "life," expresses something extramental whereas the other three, it seems, do not, because they either imply *per se* the negation of some extrinsic imperfection or assert some aptitudinal or potential relationship to something extrinsic, and in neither case would there be anything there extramentally. If this be so, then it follows that eternity *qua* eternity will not be there extramentally either.[26]

[15] 6.35 If you concede this conclusion, then you have a counter-reply to the view previously proposed [in 6.33], namely, that eternity is the proper mode of divine existence even as infinity is for the divine essence. For the parity must be denied, since, to assume the impossible, if the divine essence were suddenly to pass away, both essence and existence would have had their intrinsic mode of intensive infinity, but the existence would not have had eternity, which means durational infinity. This adds to intensive infinity only a denial of cessation or a conceptual relation of potentiality, namely, of coexisting with any possible being, a relationship which is mind-dependent.

This appears clear from the following: If an angel were annihilated tomorrow, he would not have any different intrinsic mode in

---

[25] John 5:26.
[26] Cf. Duns Scotus, *Ord.* II, d.2, q.2, nn.2-3 (ed. Vivès XI, 247-49).

QUESTION SIX

his nature than if he remained forever, as he actually will, and—according to some—without succession, for they deny this is present in aeviternity.* Therefore, it is impossible to think of perpetual duration as some extramental quantity in God that is other than the intensive infinity of either essence or existence and which is called the magnitude of one or the other. Any additional factor is at most a conceptual relation or a negation. And while it is true that existence, like essence, has a mode intrinsic to it, that mode is nothing but intrinsic infinity. It is not eternity *qua* eternity, or endless duration *qua* endless duration.

[16] 6.36 As for Dionysius [in 6.33], I grant that God's existence is extramentally without limit, that is to say, it is intensively infinite, so that its magnitude is infinity and it would still be such even if, to assume the impossible, God should suddenly cease to exist. What they add about him being "age of ages," i.e., eternal or eternity, is certainly true, for it is repugnant to the sort of existence he has that he should ever cease to be, and the basis for this repugnance, viz., the existence, is there extramentally. But the formal ground for repugnance to ceasing to be, whether it be the negation of any termination or the necessity of coexisting with any possible, adds to what is extramental only the negation of imperfection or some extrinsic conceptual relation. Neither does Dionysius say that "age of ages" is there extramentally in the way his existing is, or in the way, following Augustine, we say that God is great, is wisdom, is good, etc. However, it is not necessary, because of this, that this or that attribute pertain to him without any negation or conceptual relation.[27]

6.37 [Conclusion] As for this section of the first article, then, we know to what eternity pertains, namely, to existence. As for whether eternity represents something that is in God extramentally, one can choose whatever opinion seems more probable to him.[28] As for the unity required of eternity if it is to serve as a basis for equality, we need not add anything here to what was said before [6.29-30] about the unity of magnitude.

3) Third Question: Is power a real basis for equality?

[17] 6.38 As for the third point [in 6.11] about power, we can say that power implies in the main a relationship to the possible, and hence

---

[27] Ibid., I, d.8, nn.177ff. (IV, 246ff.). In this and other places Scotus affirms that the attributes are formally distinct from each other and from the essence. See Glossary: *"formal distinction."*

[28] Cf. Duns Scotus, *Ord.* II, d.2, q.2 (ed. Vivès XI, 246-67).

a conceptual relation, for God cannot have a real relation to anything distinct from himself, as we have proved elsewhere.[29] Therefore, if power as power is taken to be its foundation, so far as this foundation goes, equality will not be there extramentally.

6.39 But power may also be taken to mean something in God, perhaps the will, which allows one to assert this relation to the possible, for the principle behind all possibles is something absolute. And if the will *qua* will is assumed to be there extramentally (a point alluded to in [1.47 of] Question One), it follows that this foundation, which is real, is there extramentally. However, the foundation for equality in power is not the will taken absolutely, but taken under the aspect of a power over extrinsic objects. According to the will, taken absolutely, Father and Son are equal only in virtue of the intrinsic magnitude of their will, but this is the first, not a third, basis for equality.

6.40 Therefore, insofar as the will serves as a third basis for equality of Father and Son, it is as principle or source of the possibles, so that equality of power is always the equality of a principle *qua* principle. In the sense that Augustine [in 6.7] intends to give three grounds for equality, therefore, power *qua* power or active causality is always part of the foundation, and since this represents a conceptual relation, the foundation assigned as a third basis of equality is not something that is there extramentally.

6.41 [Objections and solutions] The objection is made, however, that a relation cannot have a relation as its basis; hence equality cannot be based on power. Proof of the first: If this were not so, there would be an infinite regress. Also there is that principle of Augustine[30]: "Everything which is spoken of relatively is also something apart from the relationship." It is necessary to trace it back to something absolute, and the relation must have its foundation in something absolute.

Perhaps one could claim the antecedent is not true, for Euclid[31] gives this definition of proportionality: "Proportionality is a similarity between two proportions." Now this similarity expresses what is formally a relation and it holds between a proportion and a proportion, which represent two similar foundations. But a proportion obviously implies a relationship.

---

[29] Ibid., I, d.30 (VI, 169-202).
[30] Augustine, *De Trin.* VII, c.1, n.2: PL 42, 934-35; CCSL 50, 247.
[31] Euclid, *Elementa* v, d.6 (II, 3).

6.42 Be that as it may,³² however, so far as our case is concerned, we can say that one conceptual relation may well have another conceptual relationship as its basis. Speaking of second intentions* [or concepts of concepts] it is true to say: " 'Genus' is a species." This intention "genus" is conceived as falling under a more universal intention, namely "universal," and it is conceived as differing specifically from the intention "species" and the intention "difference," and what comes under "genus" in this sense are only numerically distinct members, for the intention "genus" as found in "color" and in "animal" is only numerically different. Therefore, this intention "species" has its foundation in the intention "genus." The reason this is possible in conceptual relations is that any relation of this sort can become the basis for a further conceptual relation in which the first notion is related to another. I can understand a conceptual relationship and compare it with another such relationship. Therefore, this second relation [i.e., the comparison] is based upon the first relation. A relationship of equality based on power, however, is only a conceptual relation, just as that aspect of the foundation that gives rise to it is also only a conceptual relation.

ARTICLE II
Are the Terms Related really Distinct?

[19] 6.43 [Three theses] As for the second principal article, I assert three points: First, that the terms related by equality in the divine are really distinct. Second, that this equality also requires a real distinction between them. Third, that this necessary requirement is not of just any sort, for instance, that of a concomitant condition, but this distinction is a prerequisite condition for the equality.³³

6.44 [The terms are really distinct] This first point is clearly the case, because it is one person who is said to be equal to another in virtue of this equality; the essence by contrast is never said to equal itself or to be equal to a person or vice versa. Now one person is really distinct from another.

6.45 [Equality requires a real distinction] The second point is proved by the authority of Hilary³⁴: "Similarity does not obtain be-

---

³² Cf. Duns Scotus, *Ord.* II, d.1, q.4, nn.3ff. (ed. Vivès XI, 96ff.); I, d.19, nn.15-17 and *textus interpolatus* (V, 271-79); d.31, nn.11-18 (VI, 207-11); IV, d.6, q.10, n.5 (ed. Vivès XVI, 620-21).
³³ Ibid., I, d.19, nn.1-28 (V, 265-79); d.31 (VI, 203-22).
³⁴ Hilary, *De Trin.* III, n.23: PL 10, 92.

tween a thing and itself." Now if similarity did not require a distinction between the related terms, a thing could be similar to itself in the same way a thing can be identical with itself. For identity is self-reflexive and requires no distinction of terms. Augustine[35] proves the same point when he declares that the first instance of equality is to be found in the Son. If equality did not require distinction, the Father could be equal to himself and, being prior to the Son in origin, he would represent the first instantiation of equality. But Augustine's statement is true, for equality in God only obtains between distinct persons and therefore it is present only when the Son is generated. Consequently the first equality is to be found in the Son as a term, viz., the equality by which the Father is equal to him, and also the first equality quasi-denominatively or relatively to a term that is somehow subsequent.

[20] 6.46 [Equality demands real distinction as a prior condition] The third point, viz., that the real distinction of terms is a prerequisite for equality, is proved from John[36] who says: "He called his father God, making himself equal to God." This text supports the following demonstration. Christ said most truly that his Father was God; therefore, he made himself (i.e., he affirmed himself) to be God's equal. Now there is no perfect communication of nature unless that nature is given in full, and therefore it will not be imparted without equality being given as well. Proof that the communication or generation implied in the fact that the Son called his Father God is a prerequisite condition for equality. The order that obtains between two things conceptually distinct is the same as that which would hold if they were really distinct. We have frequently alluded to this principle [e.g., 1.59; 1.66; 4.59]. Now if the magnitude of the essence would be really distinct from the essence, the essence would be prior to magnitude, and hence its communication would be prior to that of the magnitude. Therefore, no matter what kind of distinction would exist between the essence and magnitude, essence would be communicated prior to magnitude and hence prior to equality, for this is present in the second extreme only because of the magnitude.

[21] 6.47 A second argument for the same is this: Plurality of the same type that is necessarily finite presupposes necessarily a plurality of a different kind by which it is limited to a certain number. This was explained in the solution to the second question [in 2.50].

[35] Augustine, *De Trin.* VI, c.8, n.9: PL 42, 930; CCSL 50, 238.
[36] John 5:18.

QUESTION SIX

Now the plurality of equalities in the divine persons is of the same kind and is necessarily finite. Therefore, it presupposes a plurality of another kind by which it is determined to a definite number. This plurality of a different kind, which is a necessary prerequisite, can only reside in a personal property.

6.48 Proof of the first part of the minor, viz., that there is some plurality of equality in the divine persons. What are relatively opposed are necessarily distinct and consequently several. Since the relations in the persons provide the basis of their opposition, with equal or greater reason will these relations be opposed and distinct. If the same thing cannot be similar to itself, as Hilary pointed out above [in 6.45], then all the more reason for the equality of one equal being distinct from the equality in another.

6.49 The other portion of the minor, viz., that the equality is of the same kind, is sufficiently evident, because this is so in every instance of equality.

6.50 The third part of the minor, viz., that it is necessarily finite, is clear, for otherwise the equalities in the divine could be infinite and hence would be infinite in number.

6.51 If one objects that the major proposition is true only of real plurality and not of any other kind, and that there is a begging of the question if one understands plurality of equality in the minor to be real, I answer: The major is true of every kind of plurality be it real or conceptual. The minor is also proved, howsoever it be understood, viz., that plurality is necessarily present, for the impossibility of having the same relation in both extremes holds not only for real relations but for others as well. It is true indeed for conceptual relations, for though compared to real relations they are of diminished entity,* nevertheless they have in their entity that opposition and distinction corresponding to such entity, just as real relations have that which corresponds to their entity. This appears clear in the following appropriate example. In God the relationship of being a cause is only conceptual, and yet this cause in its way is as much opposed to and unidentifiable with its effect as paternity is to the Son. There is no begging of the question consequently in the minor by assuming the plurality to be real. It only states in general that there is a distinction between the equality in one correlative and that in the other, and this holds good whether the relation be real or conceptual. The plurality is necessarily finite and is of the same type. Therefore, the conclusion follows, viz., that such plurality presupposes a distinction of another kind which limits the number, and there is no such distinction, be it real or conceptual, to be found outside the plurality of personal properties.

6.52 [Corollary] From what has been said, the following corollary is evident, viz., that it is by a demonstration of the reasoned fact* that the common relations are proved to be present in the persons in virtue of their relationships of origin, just as we said in [1.42-49 of] the second article of the first question, that it is through their essential properties that the personal properties of the persons are inferred by an argument of the reasoned fact. Thus by means of "perfect memory"* it is inferred that the person who has such a memory of himself is the one to whom "speaking* the perfect Word" pertains. Similarly we conclude by means of "perfect will" that "to spirate"* pertains to the person who has such a will of himself. The conclusion in this case is of the same sort as would be the case if memory were distinct from speaking or will from spirating. The situation is similar here with the way personal and common relations are interrelated, for if "to have this identical nature by generation" and "to be the same," or "to have the same magnitude by generation" and "to be equal," were really different, then from the fact that A produces B perfectly with perfect magnitude, one could demonstrate the equality of A and B. And it would be the same whatever the sort of conceptual distinction that obtains, for there would be the same order of concepts in terms of their knowability and hence also in terms of their demonstrability.

[23] 6.53 [Objections] Two aspects of what was said in this article are challenged. The first is the conclusion; the second is the proof for the third point about the prerequisite condition.[37]

6.54 [Against the conclusion in 6.43: First objection] Against the conclusion this argument is raised. The equality that exists among several things is nothing more than the relationship of their respective magnitudes being commensurate with one another. Therefore, unless there is more than one magnitude to be compared there will be no equality. Since the equality of the persons is due to the magnitude of their essence in which there is not real plurality but at most a conceptual one, the same magnitude has to be considered twice to be the basis for equality, once in this person and once in the other. Therefore, the prerequisite distinction in the foundation is due to the mind and hence is purely conceptual.

[37] Thomas, *Summa theol.* 1, q.28, a.4, ad 4 (I, 155); q.42, a.1 in corp., and ad 4 (I, 212).

6.55 [Second objection] Besides, a form of the same kind, according to the *Metaphysics*,[38] is distinguished only by matter. Equality is only a form and, as the argument admits, it is the same kind of form in both, and there is no matter present. Therefore, one equality is not distinguished from the other. Not only is there no distinction in the foundation (as the first argument points out) but there is no distinction of opposed relations (according to this argument).

6.56 [Third objection] Third, the terms *qua* terms are proved to lack the prerequisite distinction, for they are terms only insofar as they are terms of the relation and they are such only insofar as they have a foundation for equality. Insofar as they have this foundation, however, they are not distinct.

6.57 [Fourth objection] Fourth and finally, what pertains to the divine persons according to substance is not distinguished in them. As Augustine says[39]: "In what respect is the Son equal to the Father? Certainly not in what is said relatively with reference to the Father; therefore, it remains the Son is equal in what is said with reference to himself." And he infers that equality is there according to substance. Therefore, we have the minor we want.

6.58 Of these four reasons, the third confirms the first and the fourth confirms the second. Still they can be treated as distinct arguments.

[24] 6.59 [Answer to the first objection] The first argument [in 6.54] seems to be the basis for the opinion of one [Doctor][40]; therefore, we begin by challenging what he takes as the foundation of the argument, viz., that real equality requires distinct and commensurate magnitudes.

First of all, relations based on some foundation *qua* one require no greater distinction in it than relations based on something but not *qua* one, and we are referring in both cases to real relations. Now the relationships of origin are not based on the divine essence *qua* one, so that unity is not the proximate reason for founding such relationships. The common relations, on the other hand, are based on this foundation *qua* one. To be real, then, the common relations need no greater distinction in the foundation than do the relations of origin. But all admit the latter require no distinction [in the essence]; therefore, neither do the common relations.

---

[38] Aristotle, *Metaph.* XII, c.8 (1074a32-36).

[39] Augustine, *De Trin.* v, c.6, n.7: PL 42, 915; CCSL 50, 212.

[40] Henry of Ghent, *Quodl.* I, q.1 (fol. 1A-B); *Summa* a.63, q.2 in corp. (II, fol. 196B-197E).

6.60 Furthermore, the essence in itself, and not as considered twice by the mind, constitutes the basis for the different relationships of origin. And the reason seems to be that both as a fecund communicative principle and as the communicable term it is formally infinite. But the essence, in terms of the degree of greatness virtually present, is formally infinite, indeed, it is infinite quantity. By the same token, then, insofar as it has this degree of greatness in itself, and not only because the mind considers it twice, the essence can be the basis for common relations between opposite persons that are also real.

[25]   6.61 Furthermore, there is the point added [in 6.54] about distinct commensurate quantities. Now I ask: How are we to understand his claim that real equality can exist only between magnitudes that are commensurate in this way? Does their being commensurate refer to the formal reason for the equality or does it indicate some prior fundamental aspect? If it means the first, there is an obvious begging to argue there is no real commensuration, therefore there is no real equality. If it means the second, it does not seem probable that the commensuration in the foundation is presupposed by equality. Indeed, actual commensuration seems subsequent to equality, for it seems to imply bringing two equals together and coextending them, and presupposes they have some mode of extension or quantity that they can be coextended and brought together for purposes of measurement.

6.62 That is why the body of Christ in the Eucharist is not measured by anything having quantity; neither is it in proximate potency to be measured by anything its equal so long as it exists in the way it does in the Eucharist. Therefore, there is no argument that allows one to infer from "There is no real commensuration," as somehow prior, to "There is no real equality."

[26]   6.63 Consequently, to the argument [in 6.54] I make this reply: If there were two magnitudes neither of which exceeded the other, even apart from the notion of quantity that serves as the basis for their equality they would have some unity (but in a diminished and qualified sense). But when two supposita* have the same magnitude numerically, then along with the distinction of terms there is unity in a simple or unqualified sense. There is simply a distinction of terms, then, and simply a unity of form according to which they are interrelated. Therefore, we have what is required for a common relation even more truly than would be the case if the unity of form in the terms were one only in a qualified sense. For what a common

relation has in general with other relations is a distinction of the related terms, but its special requisite is the unity of its foundation. Consequently, we must deny this proposition: "Equality is only real where there are several magnitudes." Indeed, equality in such a case is only real in a qualified sense, for it is based on a qualified unity of magnitude. But where the magnitude is simply one, there is no need to take this one magnitude twice to have real equality in an unqualified sense. The repeated consideration adds nothing to the foundation, but rather detracts from the whole. Indeed all that is required is that there really be one thing present in really distinct terms.

6.64 [Answer to the second objection] To the second argument [in 6.55], I say that the way to understand the major proposition [viz., a form of the same kind is distinguished only by matter] was explained in Question Two [2.5, 2.59] in expounding the mind of the Philosopher.[41] Matter there does not refer to matter as the recipient of form, but it refers to anything that is a prerequisite for a form such that its plurality determines how many forms there will be. And in this sense, equality has "matter," for the plurality of equality necessarily presupposes plurality of another sort which determines its number. This is clear from the third conclusion of this article [cf. 6.46], which was that equality prerequires the relationships of origin.

6.65 [Answer to the third objection] To the third argument [in 6.56], one can understand the claim that "the terms *qua* terms are the terms" in different ways. Either the relative, which is called the opposite or correlative, is reduplicated*; or it is the ultimate formal reason by which it is in the last analysis formally a correlative or relative that is reduplicated, or it might be some other formal reason that is reduplicated which is not ultimate but is still fundamental or a prerequisite. In the first and second sense, the major is true, namely, that a term insofar as it is a term must be really distinguished from the other term. In the third sense, however, the major is false, but it is only in this third sense that the minor is true. Hence the proof, which accepts the principle that the term *qua* term acts as the term of the relation, would require that "*qua* term" be distinguished as before, and only in the third sense does it function as term, for it does so insofar as it has the foundation for the relation in itself.

[41] Aristotle, *Metaph.* XII, c.8 (1074a34-36).

6.66 [Answer to the fourth objection] To the fourth argument [in 6.57], I say that the prepositional phrase "according to" viewed in relationship to the predicate does not always indicate that the term dependent on the preposition expresses the ultimate formal reason for the inherence of the predicate in the subject; more frequently or, at least, commonly, it indicates only that it is a fundamental reason. I say, for example, that Socrates is similar to Plato according to whiteness, even though it is not whiteness, but his similarity, that is the formal proximate reason why he is similar to Plato, just as whiteness is the ultimate formal reason he is white. To the extent that whiteness is still a fundamental reason for similarity, I say that Augustine, in the text cited, had in mind that the Son is equal to the Father according to substance, because paternity and filiation are not properly speaking fundamental reasons for equality, but that this must be something absolute and common to both. Therefore, when the major is taken as saying that whatever is predicated of the persons according to substance is not numbered [or distinguished] in them, this is true insofar as "according to" designates the proximate formal reason, but then the minor is false and does not express the mind of Augustine, for when he understands equality to be there "according to substance," what follows the preposition gives at most a fundamental reason for equality being there.

6.67 You may object: Why then is the Father not called Father according to substance, since substance is a fundamental reason for paternity and is so more immediately than it is a fundamental reason for equality, according to you?

One could say that when equality is said to be there "according to substance," substance or essence is taken insofar as it is one. There is indeed one existing essence that is the foundation for both relationships [viz., of equality and origin], but it is not the foundation for both *as one*. It is *as one* that it is the foundation for equality in all three persons. However, this essence, which is one, is also the foundation for paternity or filiation, but not as one thing found in all three. It is rather as a fecund principle and as a communicable term that the essence represents a quasi-proximate foundation for both paternity and filiation.

6.68 Another possible answer would be to say that, logically speaking, nothing is truly said to pertain to anything "according to A" if A is a transcendent [i.e., an inadequate] reason, and this whether a formal or fundamental reason. Hence "Socrates according to color is white" would be false, whereas "Socrates according to whiteness is white" would be true. Now the essence is a fundamental reason for paternity, but it is a transcendent reason, whereas it is a non-transcendent and adequate fundamental reason as regards equality. Therefore, according to logic, Augustine said properly that this is true: "In some way the Father according to essence is equal" in a way that "According to essence he is Father" is not true. On the contrary, "According to memory he is Father" is the truth of the matter, because memory is a fundamental reason that is adequate to this relationship.

[29] 6.69 [Objection to the proof for the third conclusion in 6.46ff.] A second aspect challenged concerns what was said in article two about the prerequisite condition.

For equality, it is said,[42] is not some real relationship distinct from the personal relations, but its concept includes these relations as well as the unity of the essence. This is inferred as follows: In the divine there is nothing to be considered except the essence and the real relations, which introduce distinction. Now the same thing is not referred to itself nor is one relation referred to a second relation by means of a third relation, for when paternity is said to be in relative opposition to filiation, this opposition is not some intermediate relation between paternity and filiation, for in this way relations would be multiplied *ad infinitum*. Therefore, equality implies both the distinction of persons and the unity of essence, because what makes the persons equal is their having the same one magnitude. The concept of equality, therefore, includes both the distinguishing relationships and the unity of the essence.

6.70 [Answer to the objection] If "includes" in the above argument is taken to mean "includes *per se*," and not just "includes quasi-materially" or "includes as a prerequisite condition," then the argument seems to be false, for the following reasons.

First, essence and relation do not constitute a concept that is one *per se*, for no single concept is both *per se* absolute and *per se* relative. Equality, however, seems to be a concept that is one *per se*.

6.71 Furthermore, what includes *per se* elements of different kinds does not retain the same *per se* meaning. But equality seems to have one *per se* meaning for both Father and Son; therefore, it does not include *per se* the relationships of origin these persons possess, because they are of different kinds.[43]

[30] 6.72 Therefore, I say that equality fundamentally implies the es-

[42] Thomas, *Summa theol.* I, q.42, a.1, ad 4 (I, 212).
[43] Cf. Duns Scotus, *Ord.* I, d.13, nn.77ff. (v, 105ff.).

sence, but requires the personal relations as presuppositions. But equality *per se* implies neither the essence nor the relations, but a relationship and one that is different in kind from the relations of origin. A remote foundation for the relationship of equality is the proximate foundation for the other relation. The persons constituted by the relationships of origin are interrelated by this common relationship.

6.73 On this basis then I reply to the argument. I readily grant that the essence is not referred to itself or paternity put in relative opposition to filiation by means of equality. But it does not follow from this that paternity is not another relation than equality. In point of fact, it is the Father having both paternity and the divine essence who is related to the Son by equality. Neither is there any probability in this implication: "Equality is a relation other than those of origin, therefore, according to equality, either the same thing is referred to itself or a relation is referred to an opposing relation." What is more, not even through paternity is the same thing referred to itself, nor is one relation referred to its opposite. What is referred is one relative to its opposed correlative. And so it is in the instance at hand, except that in the case of origin the relative is constituted primarily by the relationship relating it to its correlative, whereas in the case of equality the relative is only denominated [or called "equal"] by virtue of the relationship which relates it [to the other persons] as it were extrinsically [to what constitutes it].

ARTICLE III
Is Equality in the Persons according to an Extramental Foundation?

[31] 6.74 [The answer is affirmative] As for the third article, I say that the relation of equality present in these extremes is there according to a foundation that is in them extramentally. I prove this by two texts from the Gospels, two texts from Augustine, and two arguments from reason.[44]

6.75 The first text is the one from John cited earlier [in 6.46]: "He called his father God, making himself equal to God."[45] For with the same necessity and reality that the Father generated a Son, he also generated someone equal to himself. As Augustine[46] puts it: "If we should want to say that the Father is greater than the Son because

---

[44] Ibid., d.19, n.13 (v, 270); d.31, n.11 (vi, 207-208).
[45] John 5:18.
[46] Augustine, *Contra Maxim.* I, c.5: PL 42, 748; II, c.18, n.3 (col. 786).

QUESTION SIX

he begot whereas the Son did not, I will immediately counter. Indeed the Father is not greater than the Son because he begot a Son that is his equal." Even the Jews, blind though they were, understood this, as Chrysostom[47] explains, because when Christ called himself the Son of the Father, they understood him to be saying by this that he was the equal of God.

6.76 A second text from the Gospel and another from Augustine proves the same. "What my Father has given me is greater than all."[48] Commenting on these words of John, Augustine says[49]: "The Father begot the Word, equal in all things to himself, for he would not have uttered himself completely and perfectly, if there were anything less or more in his Word than in himself." This leads to the following argument. The most perfect communication must involve the most perfect term communicable and with the highest possible magnitude, so that the produced is the complete equal of the producer. Therefore, if the communication in the divine generation is of necessity most perfect in reality or extramentally, since a most perfect term is communicated in its fullest magnitude, by which—as Christ says—something greater than all things is given to the Son, then he has been given in reality and extramentally equality with the Father, who has the same essence and in the same measure.

[32] 6.77 A third text from Scripture supports this interpretation[50]: "He thought it not robbery to be equal to God." Augustine[51] agrees with this in his comment on this "making himself equal to God": "He did not make himself equal to God, but the Father had begotten him equal." What Augustine wishes to say is that the Son did not make himself equal to God by stealing or usurping equality, but made himself, i.e., asserted himself to be, equal because he was born of God. That is why Augustine adds in the same work: "Christ was born equal to the Father; hence the Apostle exalts him by saying: 'Who being in the form of God, thought it not robbery to be equal to God.' What does 'he thought it not robbery' mean but that he did not consider being equal to God a usurpation, but rather that with which he was born." Hence he had prefaced these words with the remark: "Notice that the Jews understood what the Arians, who

[47] Chrysostom, *In Iohannem homilia* 39, n.3: PG 59, 223ff.
[48] John 10:29.
[49] Augustine, *De Trin.* xv, c.14, n.23: PL 42, 1076; CCSL 50a, 496.
[50] Philippians 2:6.
[51] Augustine, *In Iohannis Evangelium tractatus* XVII, n.16: PL 35, 1535; CCSL 36, 178.

claim the Son is unequal to the Father, have not grasped. Not that the Jews thought the Father to be equal to the Son, but they did understand that by such words the Son had declared himself the equal of the Father."

6.78 From all these citations from Scripture and Augustine we seem left with this conclusion: Just as by natural generation the same nature and magnitude of substance has been communicated to the Son, so too has equality been imparted to him.

6.79 [Two proofs from reason] The first reason in proof of this conclusion is the following. If the magnitude of the Father were other than that of the Son, as the Arians claim, then the Son would be less than the Father by a real relationship of inferiority and not just a conceptual one, for relations of the first type based on different degrees of greatness are real. By the same or even greater right will the equality be real if the same degree of greatness is communicated.

[33] 6.80 A second reason, which is a kind of confirmation of the first, is this: It hardly seems probable that, of two opposites, the imperfect would be present in things extramentally whereas the perfect could not be there extramentally. Now equality is the perfect opposite and inequality its imperfect opposite, according to Augustine[52]: "You value equality above inequality as I believe everyone with human sensitivity would," he says to his disciple. Now the inequalities among things are perfect in the sense that the superiority or inferiority is something real and extramental; therefore, it would seem unreasonable that perfect equality as something real and extramental should not also exist in things. But it is only perfect in the divine persons for in no other place is the magnitude perfect.

6.81 One could argue the same way about identity and diversity, because identity is the more perfect of these terms or opposites. According to many, however, some diversity among things is perfect in the sense of being a real relation; therefore some identity is perfect in the sense of being a real relation. Never is it so perfect, however, as found in the divine persons. For a person's identity with himself is not a real relation, nor is the identity of one creature with another perfect, since they can only be "one" in a qualified sense.

6.82 [General conclusion] From what is said in these three articles, the solution to our question follows. If, according to the common opinion, a real relation requires only these three conditions: (1) that the foundation be real, viz., something extramental in a

[52] Augustine, *De quantitate animae*, c.9, n.15: PL 32, 1044.

QUESTION SIX

thing; (2) that the terms be real and really distinct; (3) that the relation inhere in things extramentally, i.e., independently of any intellectual consideration or the operation of an extrinsic power, then these three conditions are realized in the divine equality to an equal or greater degree than they are in the case of any other equality among beings, as is clear from the preceding articles. It follows therefore that this equality will be a real relation, and just as real or more real than any other.

Reply to the Initial Arguments

[34] 6.83 To the first counter-argument at the beginning [in 6.2]:

The answer is evident from the first point made in the first article about magnitude [in 6.13], for the magnitude in this case is not that of mass but of perfection. And thus God, according to Augustine, is great, not without magnitude of any sort, for that would be a contradiction, nor is he great without some sort of "quantity," but he is great in one way, without quantity, and in another way not.

6.84 To the second argument [in 6.3]:

Magnitude is not numbered, as is obvious from our solution [at 6.63] to the first objection to what was said in the second article.

6.85 A third argument [for the opposing view that might have been cited at the beginning] is this: A relation does not exist extramentally, if, prescinding from real existence, it would still be present to the same extent in virtue of the consideration of the intellect. But even if we prescind from the real existence of the divine persons, to assume the impossible, and retain only their consideration in the mind, we could still think of their equality as we think of equality among conceptual entities that do not exceed one another in entity. Equality of the persons, therefore, does not necessarily require their real existence in the sense that we could not think of them as equal apart from such existence.

6.86 I answer: What is a necessary consequence of something as existing or according to existence follows it *qua* existing, just as what is a consequence of its being understood follows it *qua* understood. Just as his existing ability to laugh is a consequence of the really existing man, so if one understands what man is, whether he exists or does not exist, the concept of risible is a necessary consequence of what man is understood to be. But this does not say "risible" is not a real attribute of man. The situation is similar here, for equality is a necessary consequence of distinct supposita in the divine nature, and if they are existing, then the equality follows them as existing, whereas if they are thought of by prescinding or abstracting from existence, the equality is a consequence of what they are in concept.

As for the form of the argument I say: The major, which takes a relation not to be real if it pertains to extremes having only conceptual being, can be admitted if it means the relation would pertain to them only if they had conceptual existence. But then the minor is false, for equality pertains to the persons not only insofar as they have conceptual existence, but also insofar as they have real being, and therefore equality is there in reality.

Question Seven

CAN IT BE DEMONSTRATED BY NATURAL AND NECESSARY REASON THAT GOD IS OMNIPOTENT?

[1] 7.1 So far we have investigated what pertains to God internally and in particular the relationships of person to person [QQ. 1-6]. Now it remains to study what pertains to God considered externally, i.e., properties that imply a relationship of God to creatures. Here two sorts of questions could arise, one about the subject of the relation [QQ. 7-8], the other about the term or object to which it relates [QQ. 9-11].

7.2 Two questions were raised about the subject, one general, the other particular. The first question is this: Can it be demonstrated by natural and necessary reason that God in general, and not just one particular person, is omnipotent?[1] The second question pertains to one person in particular: Has the Son or Word of God some causality of his own as regards the creature? Consider the first of these.

Arguments Pro and Con

7.3 First, the argument for the affirmative.

"God is omnipotent" seems demonstrable by natural reason, since natural reason can demonstrate that God has infinite power and, therefore, is omnipotent. Proof of the antecedent: The Philosopher[2] proves that God has infinite power from the fact that he produces motion over an infinite span of time. Proof of the implication: No power could be greater than the infinite. One could not even think of anything greater. If a power could be surpassed, it would not be infinite. But every power which is not omnipotence could be thought of as surpassed by a power which is omnipotence.

[2] 7.4 Arguments to the contrary:

If it can be demonstrated that God is omnipotent, it can also be demonstrated that God can generate the Son. The consequent is

---

[1] Cf. Duns Scotus, *Ord.* I, d.42 (VI, 341-49); d.2, nn.111ff. (II, 189ff.).
[2] Aristotle, *Physic.* VIII, c.5 (256a12-256b2); *Metaph.* XII, c.6 (1071-22).

false because this is a matter of pure belief and hence cannot be demonstrated by natural reason. The implication is proved from Augustine[3]: "If the Father did not generate a son equal to himself it was because he was either unable or unwilling to do so." And he argues further: "If you say he was unwilling, you accuse him of envy; if you say he was unable, where is the omnipotence of God the Father?" His point is: if the Father could not beget a son equal to himself he would not be omnipotent. Conversely, then, if he is omnipotent, he can generate a son equal to himself, and thus if the antecedent is demonstrable, so also is the consequent.

7.5 Furthermore, if God's omnipotence could be demonstrated, it could also be demonstrated that he could create anything that could be created. The consequent is false, for an angel can be created and still it seems impossible to demonstrate by natural reason that an angel can be created by him. The Philosopher following natural reason did not assume that the Intelligences* were created by God; rather he assumed them to be necessary of themselves, that is, they were not effects produced by anything else. In the *Metaphysics*[4] he shows that a separate substance* has no magnitude on the following grounds. It has infinite power and infinite power cannot have magnitude. Then he asks whether there are one or many separate substances, and concludes there are many. According to him, then, not only the first, but any immaterial substance, is infinite, and by the same token it is necessary of itself.

Body of the Question

[3] 7.6 We must first make two necessary distinctions and then solve the question accordingly.

ARTICLE I
The Necessary Distinctions

1. Demonstration of Simple Fact and of the Reasoned Fact

7.7 The first distinction is taken from the *Posterior Analytics*,[5] namely, there is a difference between (1) a demonstration of the reasoned fact* [*propter quid*; διότι], i.e., by way of the cause and (2) a demonstration of simple fact* [*quia*; ὅτι], i.e., by way of the effect.

This distinction is proved by argument. Every necessary truth that is not evident from its terms, but is connected necessarily and

---

[3] Augustine, *Contra Maxim.* II, c.7: PL 42, 762.
[4] Aristotle, *Metaph.* XII, c.7 (1073a3-12); c.8 (1073a14).
[5] Aristotle, *Anal. post.* I, cc.13-14 (78a22-79a33).

evidently with another necessary truth that is evident from its terms, can be demonstrated by means of this other evident truth. Sometimes this truth is derived from the cause, sometimes from the effect, for not only can truths about causes entail certain truths about effects, but truths about effects can also entail truths about causes. Therefore, some true propositions can be demonstrated either (1) by means of another evident truth derived from the cause and in this case the demonstration is of the reasoned fact, or (2) by means of a truth derived from the effect and then the demonstration is one of simple fact.

From this a corollary seems to follow. Principles that are immediate or evident from their terms cannot be demonstrated by a demonstration of the simple fact. If this be true, there are some truths intermediate between the first truths and the last conclusions, and they alone are demonstrable by simple fact through such ultimate truths as are themselves evident. How a truth based on an effect can be evident, whereas the truth taken from the cause is not evident, becomes clear if one considers the way of acquiring scientific or epistemic knowledge by experience which Aristotle describes in the *Metaphysics*[6] and *Posterior Analytics*.[7] Through the experience of many individual instances perceptible to the senses, we know that an effect occurs, and yet we do not know the reason why it does so, because the cause is not given through sense perception but requires further investigation.

2. Two Meanings of Omnipotence

[4]   7.8 The second distinction refers to omnipotence and presupposes the following general meaning of the term. Omnipotence is not passive but active, and not just any type of active power, but a causal one. This implies that omnipotence refers to something causable in essence that is distinct from the cause. For there is no causality except as regards something simply distinct. Hence it is a power or potency related to the possible. "Possible" is not understood as opposed to "impossible" nor as equated with "producible" insofar as this is opposed to "absolutely necessary of itself."[8] Rather, "possi-

---

[6] Aristotle, *Metaph.* I, c.1 (980b28).

[7] Aristotle, *Anal. post.* II, c.19 (100a3-12).

[8] Scotus' point here is to distinguish a divine person like the Son or the Holy Spirit from the divine essence on the one hand, and from something causable, like a creature, on the other. The deity or divine nature is shared perfectly and hence is possessed perfectly by all three persons. It is said to be "absolutely necessary of itself." The process whereby it is shared or

ble" as the correlative of "omnipotence" is equated with "causable" because it represents the term of a causal power.

[As the component *omni*, i.e., "all" or "every," in the word indicates], omnipotence also asserts some sort of universality. This does not refer to potency, considered simply in itself (for omnipotence is not formally all or every instance of power, for it is not a power of the creature). The power's universality is not taken simply but with reference to the causable (i.e., the possible or what can be created), so that the meaning is this: "Omnipotence is that active power or potency whose scope extends to anything whatsoever that can be created." But this can still be understood in two ways. In the first sense it is taken disjunctively to mean the power can produce either mediately or immediately "everything that can be created." In the other sense, it means the power can produce "everything that can be created," and can do so immediately, at least so far as causes are concerned. In other words, no other active cause need intervene.[9]

ARTICLE II
Solution of the Question

7.9 In the second article we must see whether omnipotence can be demonstrated (1) by a demonstration of the reasoned fact or (2) by a demonstration of the simple fact.

---

communicated is called a "divine procession" or "production" and is twofold. The Father, or first person of the Trinity, communicates or shares his divine essence with the second person, called the Son, or the Word, or *Logos*. The Father and Son, as a single principle, communicate their essence to the Holy Spirit. Because it is one and the same numerical essence that is shared or communicated in the Trinity, medieval theologians felt justified in distinguishing such divine productions or eternal processions from a causal production where not only is the cause really distinct from the effect, but the effect has a nature or essence that is numerically distinct from that of the cause. According to this technical usage, for example, the Father can be called a "producer" (*producens*) or a "principle or source" (*principium*), but not a "cause" (*causa*). The Son and the Holy Spirit, conversely, cannot be called "effects" or said to be "caused" but they can be called "producibles" or "possibles" (in the sense of not being something "impossible") or *principiata* (singular *principiatum*) in the sense that they represent something "which proceeds from a principle."

[9] Cf. Duns Scotus, *Ord.* I, d.8, nn.302-306 (IV, 326-28); d.20, nn.24-34 (V, 313-18); d.42, nn.8-9 (VI, 342-44).

QUESTION SEVEN

7.10 There are three conclusions about its demonstrability as a reasoned fact.

The first is this: "God is omnipotent" (in either sense of omnipotence) is a truth that, in itself, is demonstrable as a reasoned fact.

Second conclusion: This truth can be demonstrated to a person in the present life under certain conditions.[10]

Third conclusion: This truth cannot be demonstrated to one in the present life in terms of what he knows naturally and according to the present dispensation.[11]

7.11 As for the demonstrability of omnipotence as a simple fact, there are two conclusions:

The first is this: The proposition "God is omnipotent in the sense that the scope of his power extends immediately to every possible"

---

[10] The Latin text reads "istud verum est demonstrabile viatori stante simpliciter statu viae." As Scotus subsequently explains (cf. 7.19), this means that without destroying his status as a pilgrim in this life, a man could have, or be given, such a perfect concept of God that he would be able to use it as the middle term of a syllogism to demonstrate that God is omnipotent. Scotus considers only the beatific vision itself, or some such ecstatic or mystical experience in this life in which God is seen face to face, to be inconsistent with man's status as a pilgrim. This leaves open the question as to how such knowledge could be communicated to him. Presumably it would have to be given somehow directly by God. According to Scotus, if one had at some time intuitive knowledge* of God, this would suffice for him to form an abstractive concept of God (so-called because it "abstracts" from the fact of whether the subject still exists or does not exist). Since God can cause immediately whatever he can cause through secondary or created causes, he could infuse such a concept directly into the human mind. Scotus' point is that given the existence of such a concept in the mind, whether it be acquired, infused, or what have you, man in virtue of his native ability or natural power to reason and to draw conclusions could use such a concept to demonstrate this truth as a reasoned fact.

[11] We have translated *de lege communi* (literally, "according to the common law") as "according to the present dispensation." This refers not only to man's natural endowments, but to such supernatural gifts as are available to the generality of mankind. What is excluded is such special supernatural or mystical experiences as those had by the patriarchs, prophets, or apostles to whom God imparted his original revelation. Such chosen individuals presumably possessed a direct experiential knowledge not given to the ordinary believer to whom they communicated what God revealed to them.

is true, but we cannot demonstrate it by a demonstration of simple fact.

The second conclusion: "God is omnipotent in the sense that his power extends mediately or immediately to every possible" is a proposition that can be demonstrated as a simple fact by a person in the present life.

7.12 We have five conclusions, then, which, taken together, give a complete answer to the question.

1. Concerning the First Conclusion

[5] 7.13 Proof of the first conclusion [in 7.10]

If a truth can be demonstrated as a reasoned fact from another prior truth, it possesses this property in virtue of its terms.[12] "God is omnipotent" (in either sense of omnipotence) is a truth of this sort. Therefore, [it is demonstrable as a reasoned fact].

7.14 The major is clear: A truth of this sort is the kind of truth it is in virtue of what its terms mean. Consequently, a truth that is self-evident is one that is known to be such from the meaning of its terms, and from this it follows that the truth is self-evident to any intellect which conceives the meaning of these terms.

7.15 The minor is proved. A truth that in virtue of its terms is necessary, but not immediately known, also has the property of being demonstrable as a reasoned fact in virtue of its terms. "God is omnipotent" (in either sense of omnipotence) is a truth of this sort. Proof: That we are dealing with a truth that is both true and necessary is clear, but we do not prove it here because it is not in question. Our problem refers only to the way in which this truth can be known or proved.

7.16 There are two arguments to prove that this necessary truth is known mediately.

First, the sequence or order in which things can be known is the same as it would be were they really distinct. It makes no difference how the mental existence of one is to be distinguished from that of the other. But if nature, intellect, will, and external power were really distinct from one another, their real order or sequence would be this: (1) the nature, because it has (2) such an intellect and (3) such a will, would be (4) externally potent in the way that it is. Therefore, no matter what kind of distinction exists between these

[12] Cf. Duns Scotus, *Ord.* I, d.2, nn.14-24 (II, 131-37).

QUESTION SEVEN

things their order of knowability is always the following: (1) the divine nature, because it has (2) such an intellect and (3) such a will, has (4) the sort of potency that is omnipotence. It is obvious then not only that some medium for this necessary truth exists, but also what that medium is, namely, that the divine nature has intellect or will or both.

[6] 7.17 A second proof that this is a mediate truth would be this: Every necessary truth is either mediate or immediate, but this truth is not immediate, therefore, [it is mediate]. Proof of the minor: One of the conclusions we arrived at in solving the First Question [in 1.44] was that the personal or notional properties pertain more immediately to the essence than properties implying relationship to the external. But the notional does not pertain to the divine essence as immediately as does something essential, as the proof in the solution of the same question shows, for the property of perfect memory is the medium in virtue of which "speaking"* pertains to the divine essence. *A fortiori*, therefore, omnipotence, which asserts a relationship to external things, does not pertain to God or to any divine person with an immediacy that is absolute.

7.18 To the first of these two proofs a further clarification could have been added as to just which power is formally omnipotence or, to be more exact, which is the immediate foundation of omnipotence. Is it the divine intellect or the divine will? For our purpose, however, it is not necessary to determine which of these it is, since what we are trying to prove follows just as well from either alternative.

2. Concerning the Second Conclusion

[7] 7.19 [Exposition and proof] The second conclusion [in 7.10] should be understood in this way. A demonstration of God's omnipotence as a reasoned fact (taking omnipotence in either sense) is possible for a person in this life who possesses nothing repugnant to his status as a pilgrim, whether this be something passing, like St. Paul's ecstasy, or something permanent [like the beatific vision].

Proof of this conclusion: Any intellect that can have a simple concept that includes virtually an immediate truth together with another mediate truth can also know the mediate truth through a demonstration of the reasoned fact. But the human intellect in the present life, apart from any permanent or transient knowledge inconsistent with its pilgrim status, can possess a simple concept which virtually includes both the truth "God is omnipotent" as well as another truth from which it follows immediately. Therefore, ["God is omnipotent" can be known through a demonstration of the reasoned fact].

7.20 This minor seems obvious at least as regards the assertion that some simple concept virtually includes the truth ["God is omnipotent"] by means of another immediate truth. For this would follow from what was established [in 7.16f.] in proving the first conclusion, namely, that God's omnipotence is a mediate truth.

What still remains to be proved is that such a concept can exist in the intellect of a person in this life who has the status of a simple pilgrim, in other words, one who neither is in a state of rapture nor possesses the beatific knowledge. This is proved first by an example, second by an argument.

The example is this: Something can be understood only incidentally. For example, man is understood only in terms of something accidental to him when we think of him as "the white one" or "the one able to laugh." Further knowledge of man would be in terms of something essential to him but still general. For example, to think of animal is also to think of man. Third, something can be understood in terms of what is both essential and specific, and yet the knowledge in a technical sense is confused. Such would be the case if I understood what a man is [in the sense of being able to apply the name correctly] but did not know how to define him or even what the more generic elements were that would enter into such a definition. Of course, one could distinguish between the absolute and the relative as the first step in that direction. However, the final step in knowing some object with scientific knowledge or, more precisely, with knowledge immediately preceding scientific knowledge, is the knowledge of its definition. For this knowledge is the most distinctive and the most specific essential knowledge one can have of it. It goes far beyond that vague knowledge of which the Philosopher speaks in the *Physics*[13] in expressing how names are related to definition. In such knowledge by definition at least we have a concept which includes evidently and virtually all the necessary truths about such an object.

[8]   7.21 This example provides the following argument. Apart from the immediate vision or intuitive knowledge, it is possible to have a most distinctive conception of an object which precedes scientific knowledge, and such a concept, which would include in the most evident way truths about principles and about conclusions, would

---

[13] Aristotle, *Physic.* I, c.1 (184b10).

suffice for having scientific knowledge of such an object. But for a person in the present life, any knowledge of God, except immediate vision or intuitive knowledge, is simply compatible with his pilgrim status. Therefore, it is possible for him to have such a concept of God that is both consistent with his pilgrim state and sufficient to know propositional truths [including that of God's omnipotence].[14]

7.22 The major of this syllogism [in 7.21] is evident from the example cited above as well as from the distinction between abstractive and intuitive knowledge explained in the first article of the sixth question [6.18f.]. I repeat it here briefly. Although abstractive knowledge can be either of the non-existent or the existent, intuitive knowledge is only of the existent as existing. Abstractive and definitional knowledge of man, however, can be of the non-existent as well as the existent. This appears clear from what was said there [in Question Six]. It is also obvious in itself, because the same knowledge is there whether the thing exists or does not exist. Therefore, this definitional knowledge which is non-intuitive is of the universal defined object.

7.23 The minor [in 7.21] also appears clear from what was said [in 6.20]. For only intuitive knowledge of the divine essence puts man beyond the status of the pilgrim, either permanently if he possesses such knowledge permanently or for the time being if he has it only for a time. The example [in 7.20] provides proof of this.

It is also proved by argument in this way: Where any object of science is concerned, apart from intuitive knowledge, it is possible to have abstractive knowledge that is most distinct. Now God as such is an object of some science. Therefore, besides intuitive knowledge of him it is possible to have a most distinct knowledge of this sort, which was what we set out to prove. For such knowledge does not put one outside the pilgrim state, and yet it would include virtually and evidently all necessary truths about God.

7.24 Proof of the major: Every science is concerned with the thing but not precisely as existing. I understand this to mean that although the existence itself is seen to be something in the object or associated with the object, it is not necessarily required that existence actually pertains to the object insofar as the object is knowable by way of demonstration.

[14] Cf. Duns Scotus, *Ord.*, prol., nn.61-65, 141ff. (I, 37-40, 95ff.); 1, d.3, nn.25-26, 56, 58, 61 (III, 16-17, 18, 38-39, 40, 42); ibid., nn.158-61 (III, 95-100).

[9] This is evident from the mind of the Philosopher[15]: "Demonstration concerns necessary truths, and definition is a scientific process. Now just as scientific knowledge cannot be sometimes knowledge and sometimes ignorance, so neither can demonstration nor definition be sometimes the sort of things they are and at other times not the sort of things they are." From this he concludes[16]: "Therefore, neither definition nor demonstration is possible in relation to perishable individuals, for perishing things are not revealed to those who have scientific knowledge when they have passed from our perception. Though their meaning remains in the soul unchanged, there will no longer be a definition or demonstration." I understand the meaning of the Philosopher to be this: If there were definitions or demonstrations of the contingent or the perishable as such, these would exist at one time and not at another. For even though the concept of the perishable object remained in the soul, it would still follow that one would know it at one time and not know it another time, and there would be a demonstration of it at one time and not at another. But this is impossible.

7.25 From the foregoing, then, I obtain this proposition: Since the notion can remain in the soul even if the actual existence of the object does not remain, it follows that such existence is not essential to the object insofar as it can be known scientifically. For the scientific definition or notion cannot remain the same in the soul if what is essential to such knowledge does not remain. But whether an object that can be known scientifically is able or not able to exist in reality, at least its notion as an object of scientific knowledge can remain the same in the soul even if its existence does not continue. Scientific knowledge, therefore, abstracts from existence in the sense that actual existence is not included in its definition as an object that can be known scientifically [i.e., by way of demonstration].

[10] 7.26 In accord with this conclusion one could draw this following corollary. It is clear how theology can exist as a science in the intellect of a person in this life who retains his pilgrim status. For the intellect that can possess a concept which virtually includes all necessary truths about that object, both those that are immediate and those which are known by means of the others, can have a complete science of that object. The intellect of the pilgrim can have such a

[15] Aristotle, *Metaph.* VII, c.15 (1039b30-1040a7); *Anal. post.* (71b15-16); (75b24-25).
[16] Aristotle, *Metaph.* VII, c.15 (1040a-10).

QUESTION SEVEN

concept of God. Therefore, [it can have a theology or scientific knowledge of God].

7.27 The minor is manifest. A most distinctive concept of the subject of theology (which is God) is possible apart from intuitive knowledge, and such a concept contains virtually and evidently all necessary truths about that subject. However, it cannot contain contingent truths, for these are not apt by nature to be included in the notion of any subject, for only such truths as are necessary are included sufficiently in any simple concept.

However, there are some necessary truths about contingent things, not indeed about their actuality but about their possibility. Such truths can also be known scientifically in the aforesaid way. Truths of this type, for instance, are "God has the power to create, the power to raise from the dead, the power to beatify," and so on, with all the other articles of faith that concern the contingent. Beyond these necessary truths about what God can do, however, nothing can be known about him in a properly scientific way so far as this property [of omnipotence] is concerned.

Therefore, a pilgrim in this present life would be a theologian in a perfectly scientific way if, in virtue of the most distinct concept of divinity obtainable apart from intuitive knowledge, he knew all necessary truths in an orderly fashion, both those which refer to intrinsic properties which are there necessarily and those which concern what is possible externally.

7.28 [The view of Henry of Ghent][17] From this it follows that if theology is assumed to be properly science in some light other than the light of glory but more than the light of faith, and that such light would be the knowledge or the concept of the object, then such an opinion would be true. But the one who defended this opinion concerning the light [namely, Henry] apparently did not understand it in this way, for according to him the light would be that in which the object would be known and not be, it seems, the formal meaning or the formal knowledge of the object itself, as is claimed here.

3. Concerning the Third Conclusion

[11]   7.29 [Exposition of Proof] Our third conclusion [in 7.10] is this. By his purely natural endowments, man in the present life cannot demonstrate as a reasoned fact that God is omnipotent. Proof of this conclusion: A mediate proposition cannot be known as a reasoned

---
[17] Henry of Ghent, *Quodl.* XII, q.1 (fol. 483Y-Z); q.22 (fol. 498D); *Summa*, a.13, q.2 (I, fol. 91T-Y).

fact except by means of the appropriate immediate proposition. This can be known simply from its terms, especially from the meaning of the subject term, namely, from the fact that the subject includes the predicate and therefore includes the truth or knowledge of the proposition immediately. Therefore, the coordinate knowledge of the reasoned fact is only possible to an intellect possessing a concept of the subject that virtually and evidently includes the whole coordination. But such a concept of God is not possible to a person in this life by purely natural means so long as he remains in the pilgrim state.

7.30 Proof of this: The only concepts such a person can have naturally are those caused by the agent intellect working with sense images, for by God's common dispensation no other factor moves the mind of the pilgrim naturally. But agent intellect and sense images cannot give rise in us to a concept so distinctive of God that it contains virtually and evidently the whole orderly sequence of demonstrable truths including that of his omnipotence in either sense.[18] The proof for this last statement depends on [my] solution to the question: "In what manner is God knowable to one in this life?"[19]

7.31 This brief sketch of the salient points, however, can be given here. The most perfect simple concept a pilgrim can attain of God by natural means does not transcend the most perfect idea of God possible to the metaphysician, for the knowledge of faith does not yield a simple concept of God. It only inclines us to assent to propositions which are not evident from the meaning of the simple terms they contain. Faith produces no simple concept, then, that goes beyond all simple concepts of the metaphysician. Added evidence is this: A believing and an infidel metaphysician have the same concept, for when the believer affirms something of God that is denied by the infidel, they do not contradict each other in words alone but in what they mean.

[12] 7.32 Now the most perfect simple concept a metaphysician gets of God, however, does not evidently include an orderly sequence of truths extending all the way to this proposition: "God is omnipotent," where omnipotent is understood in either sense. For many philosophers have presumably had concepts of God that are the most perfect it is possible for one in this life to reach by natural

---

[18] Cf. Duns Scotus, *Ord.*, prol., n.41 (I, 23-24); I, d.2, n.39 (II, 148-49); d.3, nn.230ff. (III, 138ff.).

[19] Cf. ibid., I, d.3, nn.1-5, 10-68 (III, 1-3, 4-48).

means. And still they were unable to arrive at a knowledge of this truth. But it would have been possible to do so had they had such a simple concept. Indeed, it would have been almost necessary for them to do so, for by means of such a concept they would have perceived the immediate truth of the proposition from which omnipotence follows, and by making the necessary deduction they would have reached this mediate truth.

7.33 There is another way to prove this point. The first principle proper to God reached by the metaphysician is known to him only as a simple fact. But it would have been known to him as a reasoned fact if he could have a concept of God that included virtually and evidently the orderly sequence of truths about God. Therefore, [he had no such concept].

7.34 Proof of the first proposition, namely, the first principle proper to God reached by the metaphysician is known to him at best as a simple fact. The premise which provides the means for inferring anything proper to God is always some particular proposition in which a predicate pertaining to a created being is asserted of some being. From such a premise the metaphysician draws a conclusion in which a predicate proper to God is affirmed of some being. He argues, for instance, in this way: "Some being is caused, therefore something is an uncaused cause," or "Some being is finite, therefore some being is infinite," or "Some being is possible, therefore some being is necessary."[20] Proof that all these conclusions follow is found in the fact that the less perfect condition cannot be true of anything unless the more perfect condition also is true of something, for the imperfect depends upon the perfect. All these inferences, it is clear, are only proofs of the simple fact.

[13] 7.35 [Objections] To the foregoing these objections are raised:

According to the first proof of the first conclusion [in 7.16], the will provides a means for inferring omnipotence of God by a demonstration of the reasoned fact. And the intellect of one in this life can know there is in God a will, in fact the first and most perfect will. Therefore, the intellect can also know God is omnipotent through a demonstration of the reasoned fact.

7.36 Also, every true and necessary proposition whose terms are primitive or irreducibly simple concepts is self-evident. But a proposition asserting any attribute of God is this sort of proposition. Therefore, [it is self-evident].

[20] Cf. ibid., d.2, nn.41-47 (II, 149-215).

7.37 Furthermore, the known properties of a natural being imply that God has certain perfections. Imperfection in what is mobile implies perfection in the first mover. From natural effects, therefore, the philosopher of nature can know God by demonstration of the simple fact. If the metaphysician could only know of God through proofs of simple fact, his knowledge would not transcend physics or natural philosophy.

[14] 7.38 [Answer to the Objections] Look for the answers elsewhere.[21]

4. Concerning the Fourth Conclusion

[15] 7.39 Next we must consider the conclusions involving a demonstration of the simple fact [in 7.11], the first of which is about immediate omnipotence with respect to every possible. Here we shall first explain what immediacy means; second, what the philosophers held; third, what our position should be.

7.40 The mediacy of a cause to an effect can be understood in two ways: (1) a cause that causes by means of some intervening cause, or (2) a cause that causes by means of some effect. For not every effect that is intermediate with respect to a further effect is also a cause of the latter. Consequently, the immediacy of an active cause to its effect can be understood either as excluding every intermediary active cause or as excluding every prior intervening effect.

7.41 If "immediacy" means both types of mediacy are ruled out, then I say that not only philosophers but also theologians would deny God is immediately omnipotent, for they admit that God cannot cause a relation without first (either in time or in the order of nature) causing its foundation. And so he is not able to cause immediately every effect whatsoever, i.e., without causing previously, by a priority of nature, some intermediate effect as it were.

7.42 Hence the problem is limited to immediacy in the sense of excluding an intervening efficient cause. The effective intervention is understood quite generally to cover the case where the causation of the intermediate cause extends either (a) to the main effect or (b) only to some effect that is prior or dispositional with respect to the main effect.

[16] 7.43 What the philosophers held was our second point [in 7.39]. It seems they felt that not only was God's immediate omnipotence undemonstrable, but that it was simply impossible that he could be

[21] Cf. ibid., n.29 (II, 140-41); d.3, n.65 (III, 46-47). See Appendix, two additions to 7.38.

QUESTION SEVEN

omnipotent in this way. The basis for their view seems to be this proposition: "A source or principle that is necessary and absolutely perfect is not related immediately to anything in a contingent fashion." The proof is this: No novelty or contingency could be ascribed to what immediately emanates from such a source. To begin with, this principle, since it is simply necessary, can behave in but one way. And given this uniform behavior there is nothing else needed for it to act nor is there anything to impede its action. It is not an imperfect principle and therefore it cannot be impeded or be insufficient or require anything else.[22]

7.44 If the aforesaid proposition (viz., that a necessary and sufficient principle could not produce anything immediately and at the same time contingently) were true, it would follow at once that it could not cause every possible thing immediately. This implication is proved, first, generally. Then it is proved specifically of motion, for it follows that God cannot cause movement immediately, whether this be locomotion in particular or, more specifically, the circular movement of the heavens.

[17]   7.45 This implication can be proved, it seems, according to the mind of the Philosopher.

First, generally, if God could cause every effect immediately without any secondary cause, he could deprive secondary causes of their proper action. But from the exegesis of the Commentator[23] on a text of the *Metaphysics*, "When beings have no action of their own, they have no essence of their own," it is clear the Philosopher considers it incongruous that God should be able to destroy the essences of all other things, since he holds that some things other than God are formally necessary.

7.46 Confirmation: If God could cause any effect independently of the ordered sequence of causes in the universe, the causal order that exists between the causes would not be simply necessary. Consequently, it would not be essential either—something the philosopers would consider incongruous.

7.47 Second, the implication is shown to hold particularly of movement. According to the Philosopher, in the *Physics*,[24] an infinite power cannot immediately move a body in time. If it could,

---

[22] Aristotle, *Physic.* VIII, c.6 (259b32-260a19); *Metaph.* XII, c.7 (1072a20-25).

[23] Averroes, *Metaph.* IX, com. 7 (*Aristotelis opera cum commentariis Averroes*; Venetiis: Apud Juntas, 1562-74; Minerva G.m.b.H., Frankfurt-am-Main; Unveränderter Nachdruck, 1962, VIII, fol. 231H).

[24] Aristotle, *Physic.* VIII, c.10 (266a24-266b6).

some finite power could move the body in equal time. For, as he argues there, if the motive power were increased, the time it takes to move would be shortened. Therefore, according to Aristotle's mind, it follows that God could not immediately cause motion properly so-called. For, since motion involves succession, it necessarily will take time.

7.48 Suppose this objection is raised. By an instantaneous change without any succession, God can cause the thing moved to pass to that stage to which it is moved in time by a finite cause. Answer: This does not solve the difficulty for God cannot cause immediately the circular movement of the heavens. He cannot cause it in time as is admitted, nor in an instant, for in that instant the heavens as a whole and each of its parts would be in the same place as they were before. Therefore, in that instant the heavens would not be moved.

[18] 7.49 Third, it seems that the same point can be established as regards every material effect, for it seems that such effects are produced by a transmutation of matter. In the *Metaphysics*[25] Aristotle proves, apparently against Plato, that what is separated from matter cannot transmute matter immediately. The Commentator says in the same place[26]: "It is impossible that a form separated from matter transforms matter. Nothing transmutes matter except what is in matter, and this is relevant to those who say the world is generated and that the one who transmutes it is an individual thing or something individual like a particular body."

7.50 Finally, it seems that these proofs can be confirmed from the mind of the Philosopher in the *Physics*.[27] What he wants to say there, apparently, is that everything God can cause immediately and as total cause, he causes necessarily. For it seems that when the effect depends totally and exclusively on the agent, the only grounds for introducing contingency as regards causing or not causing is some mutability in the agent. If God could cause immediately everything causable, every one of these things would depend totally and exclusively on him, and, consequently, God would cause everything causable necessarily. From this many incongruities would follow, namely, that secondary causes would be deprived of their activity, which the first reason [in 7.45] touched on; that God would cause immediately every movement, which the second proof [in 7.47] mentioned; and that God would cause immediately every material effect, which the third reason [in 7.49] brought up.

[25] Aristotle, *Metaph.* VII, c.8 (1033b25-1034a8).
[26] Averroes, *Metaph.* VII, com. 28 (VIII, fol. 178C).
[27] Aristotle, *Physic.* VIII, c.6 (259b32-260a19).

QUESTION SEVEN

[19]   7.51 As regards the third point, it should be maintained: (a) according to the common opinion of the theologians, God is so omnipotent that without any other agent, he can cause everything causable, and still (b) this fact cannot be demonstrated even by a demonstration of the simple fact.

7.52 The first point is proved by authority: "In the beginning God created the heavens and the earth."[28]

7.53 A reason is also adduced to prove this. The active power of any secondary cause exists in the first cause in a more eminent way than in the second cause. Now what possesses the active power more eminently can cause the effect, it seems, without the intervention of what possesses it only in a lesser degree. To produce an effect no imperfection is required in the active power. For imperfection is not essential to acting, it is rather an impediment.[29]

Confirmation: We see equivocal causes* producing effects as perfect as those of univocal causes.* This would not happen unless they possessed active power sufficient for perfect causation. But they do not possess univocal power, only eminent power. Therefore, [this eminent power suffices].

7.54 This reasoning [in 7.53], although it seems probable, would not be a demonstration for the Philosopher. For he would deny this proposition: "Everything that possesses in itself eminently or virtually the active power of the proximate cause can produce the effect of this proximate cause immediately." For he would say a cause with such eminent power can indeed produce the effect of such a power, but only in its own orderly way, which means it functions precisely as a higher and more remote cause.

[20]   7.55 To the claim [in 7.53] that no imperfection is required for causing he would give this reply: When I say "cause immediately" I assert two things: (1) causation—which requires perfection, and (2) immediacy or the way it takes place—which requires some measure of imperfection. Consequently, imperfection is needed in the agent, not indeed as the basis for causing but as a necessary condition for causing immediately.

For where an essential order* exists, nothing can be adjacent to the least perfect unless it is in some measure imperfect. If it were right next to the most imperfect, the perfect would be equally immediate to every other member distinct from itself. And then an essential order would not obtain among these things, even as there

---

[28] Gen. 1:1.
[29] Cf. Duns Scotus, *Ord.* I, d.8, nn.223-306 (IV, 279-328).

would be no such order or sequence among the natural numbers if each proceeded from unity with equal immediacy.

7.56 From this it appears that the Philosopher would deny "The more perfect a cause, the more immediately it causes," if by "more immediately" we mean the exclusion of intervening causal agents. Furthermore, he would say, "The more perfect the superior cause, the more the intermediary causes through which it acts." These intermediary agents are not required to contribute causal perfection. This exists already in all its fulness and perfection in the first cause alone. They are needed to tone down the perfection gradually until the least perfect effect is achieved. Such a tempering occurs only where there is a diminution of perfection and some measure of imperfection is introduced.

[21] 7.57 Proofs for the second point [in 7.51], namely, that this truth is not demonstrable by a demonstration of the simple fact.[30]

The first proof is from authority. Philosophers could have arrived at a knowledge of such truths as are demonstrable as simple facts. Now they were unable to reach a knowledge of this truth. Indeed they held the opposite view. This hardly seems probable if the truth in question were demonstrable as a simple fact.

7.58 The second proof is from reason. Nothing about the way causes are ordered or interrelated implies the superior cause can produce the same effects with or without the inferior cause. The sun alone, for instance, cannot generate a man without a father's intervention though it can do so with the father. By the same token, then, nothing about the way causes are interrelated implies that a first cause can produce the same effect without the secondary cause that it can produce together with it.

7.59 For other kinds of causes this is even more obvious. Suppose it were true, as some claim, that an essential order exists among materials or material causes. Suppose, for instance, that the matter immediately informed by the intellectual soul is the body with its organs, and that this in turn is composed of other materials, and ultimately of matter that is primary in an unqualified sense and is the matter proper to the first substantial form. It is not necessary that this primary matter be able to be the immediate matter of every form that can inform a secondary or higher form of matter.

7.60 It is clear the same holds good of forms. There is no need that everything that can be immediately informed by a secondary form can also be immediately informed by the first form. This is

[30] Cf. ibid., d.2, nn.118-20, 178-81 (II, 193-97, 234, 236); d.42 (VI, 341-49).

true whether the forms be first and second in the order of generation or that of perfection.[31]

[22] What was said of the material and formal causes would be more convincing if the theory of a plurality of forms, which is not at issue here, were true. For our purposes, however, it suffices that if there were such an order among material and formal causes, the first cause would not have to be the immediate cause of everything causable. Still less, then, among efficient causes where such an order does in fact exist, must the first cause be able to be the immediate cause of everything.

7.61 This also appears clear in the case of the efficient causes of knowledge. As the *Physics*[32] puts it, principles are the causes for knowing conclusions. The first principle has truth most evidently. It also contains eminently and virtually the truth of all the propositions that follow from it. Its ability to be the immediate cause of knowing each of these propositions, however, is not required. Indeed, to acquire knowledge of a remote conclusion it is necessary to use intermediary steps in an orderly way.

7.62 Lastly, it appears clear in the case of final causes. It is not necessary that the last in a chain of final causes be the immediate end of each of the links. An end close at hand is only linked to the ultimate end by some intervening cause. For example, the exterior organs for eating and drinking are aimed at health only by means of their own ends or purposes, namely, eating and drinking.

[23] 7.63 Although the theologians' view is not demonstrable, since it is in fact true, its opposite is not demonstrable either. For this reason the arguments adduced for the philosophers' view should be answered.

[To the first in 7.45] The theologian might well concede the first cause can deprive these caused causes not only of their activity but also of their entity, for it can annihilate them. In calling the eviternal* perpetual, however, he does not agree with the Philosopher's statement that all perpetual things are formally necessary. For it is simply possible for the eviternal not to exist even though this is not by reason of some intrinsic passive potency like that found in perishable things.

7.64 Another answer is this: God could deprive secondary beings of their activity simply by anticipating their causality and producing the effects they might have caused. He would not need to de-

---

[31] Cf. ibid., IV, d.11, q.3, nn.22-57 (ed. Vivès XVII, 388-438).
[32] Aristotle, *Physic.* II, c.9 (200a15-16).

prive them of their entity. They could remain in existence and yet not produce their effects because these were caused immediately by another cause. Still they could have caused those effects. This particular fire, for instance, might remain in existence without producing fire in this wood because this was anticipated by a stronger agent which set it afire. Yet it could have caused this effect for it has the form of fire which is the source for setting things on fire.

7.65 As for the Commentator's dictum [in 7.45]: "If beings have no action of their own, they have no essences of their own," how is the antecedent to be understood? Actually or dispositionally? Not just actually! For in such a case his argument would be: "If the less fundamental is removed, so too is the more fundamental." But this would be a fallacy of the consequent, for the absence of action could be due to other factors. A stronger agent might anticipate the action or a counter-agent might prevent it. Hence his meaning must be: "Dispositionally or virtually they have no action of their own." In such a case, it would indeed follow that they have no essence of their own, for every agent by its own form and power possesses its action virtually even when it is not actually producing it.

[24] That the antecedent should be so interpreted can be gathered from the preceding remarks of the Commentator: "These agree that no being has any natural action of its own." And he adds: "If beings have no action of their own"—i.e., naturally or dispositionally in accord with their proper nature—"they have no essences of their own." The "moderns," against whom he argues here, assume one agent produces all beings without benefit of any intermediary. But this is not what Christians claim. As Augustine[33] says: "God administers the things he has created in such a way that he lets them exercise their proper functions." God could have done everything. By so doing he would not have destroyed the entities of things, although he would have left them idle and barren. Still, he preferred to endow them with active powers and actions of their own even as he gave to each its entity. For he did not deprive them entirely of the perfection of which they were capable.

7.66 Answer to the *third* reason [in 7.49][34]: The Philosopher does not deny the material form is induced in matter immediately by God. Later on, in the question [21] on good fortune, we shall dis-

---

[33] Augustine, *De civit. Dei* vii, c.30: PL 41, 220; CCSL 47, 212.

[34] Scotus apparently forgot the original sequence in which these objections occurred. He calls this "the second reason," and calls the second objection, which he answers in 7.70, "the third reason."

QUESTION SEVEN

cuss what Aristotle thought about the intellectual soul. But what about that text of the *Metaphysics*[35] where the Commentator is cited to the effect that nothing immaterial can transmute matter immediately? The theologian would deny this, particularly if this is understood of God, as seems to be the case from the Commentator's allusion to those "who say the world is generated."[36] He repeats the same opinion later on in the third comment[37]: "What moves matter has to be a body with an active quality." And he ascribes this view to Aristotle.

[25] 7.67 If the text of Aristotle can be given a sound interpretation, whereas that of the Commentator cannot, it seems better to make sense of Aristotle and argue that Averroes misunderstood him. This can be done here, it seems. For the present I will only touch the problem briefly, but it appears Aristotle here is arguing against Plato to prove the Ideas are not necessary for generation, since this individual suffices to beget that individual. What is more, the Ideas cannot beget an individual [since they are universals]. If the one generating is not an individual, what is generated will not be individual either.

7.68 Both inferences suffice to show a Platonic Idea begets nothing, but they must not be applied to the present case, namely where God is concerned.

For if an Idea would generate, it would function as a univocal cause, for [a prototype and its effect must be] of the same species. No univocal cause is necessary, however, unless it be composite and material like the thing generated. This is the proof of the first part of the argument, viz., that the ideas are unnecessary.

7.69 The second part, namely that the ideas cannot generate, makes this point. If the univocal generator is not an individual material composite, what it generates will not be individual.

Now God can be a cause of generation and he is required for generation, not as a univocal cause but as an equivocal cause. And in this role he acts as the supreme equivocal cause in virtue of which every other cause, be it univocal or equivocal, exercises its function.

7.70 Answer to the *second* reason [in 7.47]: We have to concede absolutely that both Aristotle and Averroes[38] denied that God could

---

[35] Aristotle, *Metaph.* VII, c.8 (1033a25-1033b11).
[36] Averroes, *Metaph.* VII, com. 28 (VIII, fol. 178C).
[37] Ibid., com. 31 (fol. 181G-H).
[38] Ibid., XII, com. 41 (VIII, fol. 323v-325v).

immediately move a body. And on this point the theologian must contradict them both. They did hold, however, that God could move the heavens mediately, that is to say, by means of an Intelligence which is the proper mover of the heavens. Of this we will say more in answering the third of the arguments at the beginning of the question.

[26] 7.71 Answer to the *fourth* argument [in 7.50] used to confirm the first three proofs: One can say it was not the mind of Aristotle that God is an absolutely necessary cause of whatever he causes immediately, i.e., without some intervening agent. This will be discussed later in speaking of the intellectual soul in [21.45 of] the question on good fortune. Only if every medium whatsoever be excluded, be this (1) an agent productive of the effect itself or of some prior disposition towards the effect, or (2) some medium caused or prior to the effect, did Aristotle believe that God does necessarily whatever he can do immediately. Whatever can act without benefit of any intervening prior effect or previous agent, acts necessarily. And he gives this reason: Since the effect *in toto* depends immediately on God alone, he would say, any novelty in being or contingency it might have would be traceable in the last analysis to some novelty in God. He makes this point in Bk. VIII of the *Physics*.[39] For if no prior effect, no other agent, no dispositional cause is involved or intervenes, this novelty in the pattern of change or in the absolutely first effect, whatever this may be, would come immediately from God.[40]

7.72 But consider something God can cause immediately in the sense that he effects it directly and not just through some vicarious agent, and yet he makes use of some dispositional cause or at least some prerequisite effect. Now Aristotle would not claim it was with simple necessity that God causes such an effect. It is the necessity of inevitability* only, and presupposes the dispositional causes and prerequisite effects are given.

7.73 On neither of these points, of course, would the theologian agree with Aristotle, since he claims God by his will relates contingently and freely to every external thing that can be caused. Not only is necessity of immutability* excluded but that of inevitability as well.

7.74 Hence I admit Aristotle would in principle claim there are

[39] Aristotle, *Physic.* VIII, c.6 (259b32-260a19).
[40] Cf. Duns Scotus, *Ord.* I, d.8, nn.223-306 (IV, 279-328).

QUESTION SEVEN

many things God is unable to cause immediately, for example, everything whose production is simply contingent and neither immutably nor inevitably necessary. But the theologian would contradict him here, as was said.

7.75 [Conclusion] Consequently, our fourth main conclusion about demonstration is this: It is true that God is omnipotent immediately as regards everything causable, but we cannot demonstrate this by a demonstration of simple fact.

5. Concerning the Fifth Conclusion

[27] 7.76 [Exposition and Proof] The fifth main conclusion [in 7.11] is this: It can be demonstrated as a simple fact to a person in this life that God is omnipotent mediately or immediately. That is to say, he can cause everything causable either immediately or by means of something subject to his causality.

7.77 The proof of the conclusion is this: There must be an end to efficient causes, as Bk. II of the *Metaphysics*[41] proves. Put briefly, Aristotle's argument is this: The totality of effects itself has a cause which is not part of the whole, for then the same thing would be cause of itself. Hence it is something outside the totality as a whole. Consequently, if causes cannot ascend indefinitely, not only will each effect be caused, but the whole multitude will be caused, and hence by something outside the whole multitude. And here it will end with a cause that is simply first.[42]

7.78 But another proof of this conclusion can be given. It is this: The higher the efficient cause, the more perfect its causality. Therefore, if above a given cause there is another infinitely superior in causing, this will be infinitely more perfect in causality, and hence will possess an infinitely perfect causality. But no causality that is caused or dependent in causing is infinitely perfect, because it is imperfect with reference to that on which it depends. Therefore, if the causes ascended *ad infinitum*, some cause will be uncaused in an absolute sense and independent in the exercise of its causation. Hence, with this sequence of causes will end, so that this will be an efficient cause that is not itself caused or dependent in causing. And from it a lesser cause will get all its causality or at least will cause in virtue of it.

7.79 From this our thesis follows. Everything causable mediately

[41] Aristotle, *Metaph.* II, c.2 (994a20).
[42] Cf. Duns Scotus, *Ord.* I, d.2, nn.41ff. (II, 149ff.).

or immediately by a lesser cause can be caused by a higher cause, at least by means of the proximate cause. Consequently, the first cause is omnipotent in the sense we understand it in this conclusion.

[28] 7.80 [Objections to this argument] This argument [in 7.78], it seems, could be challenged on two counts:

First, one could say the order of efficient causes indeed ends with one efficient principle; yet this is not God but some Intelligence which moves the first heaven. All that natural reason deduces is that, beyond such a motor, God "moves" immediately, but only as final cause. The Philosopher, it seems, attributed this manner of moving to God in Bk. XII of the *Metaphysics*[43] where he says God moves as loved and desired.

7.81 Second, one could say there is no proof that the first efficient cause, whatever it may be, has power to cause everything in some way, namely immediately or mediately. Its only power is over those effects related to it through a chain of causes. What needs proof is that there are no other possible effects outside this concatenation.

7.82 Answer to the objections: The fact that there is but one being that exists of itself and does not come from another rules out both of these assumptions. From this it follows that there is but one unique agent, independent in its acting. For what is dependent in its being, is dependent in its acting, if it acts.

Reply to the Initial Arguments

1. Reply to the Argument about Infinite Power

[29] 7.83 As for the first of the initial arguments [in 7.3], two aspects must be investigated, first the antecedent and afterwards the implication itself.

[To the Antecedent] As for the antecedent, some say Aristotle thought the First Being did not have infinite power intensively. In other words, his power was not infinite in depth. It was just that what power he has is exercised over an infinite time span.[44]

7.84 For the reason he gives entails only that the First Being moves with a movement that is infinite. But this movement is only infinite in duration and for this a power infinite in duration suffices.

7.85 This is challenged on two counts: first, that it misrepresents the mind of Aristotle; second, that the proof given is no good.[45]

---

[43] Aristotle, *Metaph.* XII, c.7 (1072a25-1072b15).
[44] Cf. Duns Scotus, *Ord.* I, d.2, nn.111ff. (II, 189ff.).
[45] Cf. ibid., d.2, nn.74ff. (II, 174ff.).

QUESTION SEVEN

Consider the first [in 7.83]. From the antecedent "God is of infinite power," Aristotle concluded "Therefore, this power cannot be in magnitude or have magnitude, be this infinite or finite." For there is no such thing as infinite magnitude, he argued, and for any power of finite magnitude, there can be some power which is greater. What Aristotle understood by infinite power in the antecedent, then, was something that to his mind was not consistent with the opposite of the consequent, viz., to be in magnitude or to have magnitude. To say that he thought the opposite of the consequent was compatible with the antecedent would be to claim he drew an inference which to his mind was invalid. Now a power of infinite duration is compatible with having magnitude, which is the opposite of the consequent. For it is clear the heavens have magnitude, and yet —according to him—they have a power of infinite duration. Indeed, according to his statements in Bk. IX of *Metaphysics*[46] and Bk. I of *On the Heavens and Earth*,[47] and in many other places, he claims: "Everything perpetual is formally necessary and thus if it is active, it has an active power of infinite duration." Hence, in the antecedent, according to his mind, Aristotle did not understand infinite power to be one of duration, but rather some other kind, one that was incompatible with magnitude. But this could only be intensive infinity. I agree, therefore, with this conclusion that Aristotle— whether or not he proved his point sufficiently—was thinking of intensive infinity of power.

[30]   7.86 The second point about the proof [in 7.84] remains to be discussed, namely whether it is any good. About this I say: One can infer as much about the perfection of a power from what it is able to do as from what it actually does. Now Aristotle's [proof of the] antecedent, namely, "God moves with a movement that is infinite," is false according to the theologians. Nevertheless many of them concede that he could have moved with a movement that was infinite. They admit this also as regards the past, even as all concede he can continue future movement *ad infinitum*. Where they part company with the Philosopher, however, is in his assumption that this power is necessarily actualized. For between two related extremes each of which is immutable in itself, the relationship that holds is absolutely necessary. Such are God and the heavens. They are necessarily related with a necessity of immutability. From this it follows further that the movement caused in the heavens by God

[46] Aristotle, *Metaph.* IX, c.8 (1050b6-8, 20-22); c.7 (1072b10-15).
[47] Aristotle, *De caelo* I, c.12 (283b6).

is also necessary, though not with the necessity of immutability but with that of inevitability; therefore, it cannot cease. The theologian not only disagrees with Aristotle's first proposition that a necessary and absolute relation holds between God and the heavens. He also rejects the second proposition [about the necessary motion of the heavens], for the theologian does not assume that God moves the heavens necessarily. He only claims that God could produce movement for an infinite period of time. Now one could conclude that his power is infinite from the fact not only that he does move in this way but that he can move in this way.

[31] 7.87 But does this imply the power is also intensively infinite? I say it does. For no power can move for an infinite time unless it does so of itself or in virtue of another power. Even if we assume the latter, we must eventually end up with some first power which moves of itself. Therefore, Aristotle argues that the power of the first mover is such that it moves of itself and not in virtue of another. From this it can be inferred that such a power is intensively infinite. Something that has active power of itself also has entity of itself. What possesses something of itself possesses it in all the fulness it is possible to have. For nothing possesses a limited amount of anything unless it gets it from some agent which limits it to that specific degree. Suppose one being possessed of itself the plentitude of entity, whereas another of itself had only a limited entity. There would be absolutely no more reason why one rather than the other had the plentitude of being. On the contrary, it would seem to be pure chance that this is so, and there can be no chance in things which exist of themselves. From this, then, it follows that the first mover moves by itself and hence exists of itself. Since the fulness of active power and of entity is not possible without intensive infinity, it follows that the first mover possesses infinite power intensively.

7.88 An objection is raised to assuming in proof of the antecedent [in 7.3], that the first mover moves with infinite motion. According to you, the intended conclusion would follow just as well if the first mover moved with infinite motion but did so of itself.

I grant that the main strength of the argument comes from the fact that it moves of itself. However, the argument based on infinite movement has some evidence in its favor for, according to Aristotle, the first movement is primarily infinite, and that is why it is more appropriate to the first mover. Now it is the primacy of movement that provides the means for inferring the intended conclusion, so that in the assumed proof of the antecedent the proposition "it moves with an infinite movement" must be understood of the first infinity, namely, that which is not derived from the infinite movement of another but exclusively from the mover's own power.

[32] 7.89 [To the implication] Let us consider the implication in the first main argument. Although an infinite active power is truly omnipotence, this inference does not follow: "Natural reason can prove God has infinite power, therefore natural reason can prove God is omnipotent." For it is not known by natural reason that infinite power is the same thing as omnipotence in the sense that the scope of God's power extends immediately to everything that is possible.

7.90 Consider the proof for the implication [in 7.3] that infinite power is omnipotence, namely "No power can be greater than the infinite; one cannot even think of anything greater. But every power which is not omnipotence could be thought of as surpassed by a power which is omnipotence." The Philosopher's answer would be this: The power that is supreme is not omnipotence as we understand omnipotence. Nevertheless it is infinite power. Because it is intensively infinite, we cannot even think that it is surpassed in intensity. Even though one could somehow think of it as being exceeded extensively (for it is not omnipotence as we understand it), one could not really think this in the technical sense of "to think" or "to understand," since we cannot do so without contradiction. For the Philosopher would claim that the very idea of one and the same subject being omnipotent immediately as regards every possible is self-contradictory, since it would do away with the essential order of causes.

7.91 While it is true that the supreme or infinite active power is omnipotence, it is not known by natural reason that the highest power possible, even if it be intensively infinite, is omnipotence properly so-called, namely, the power of causing immediately everything possible.

2. Reply to the Argument about the Generation of the Son

[33] 7.92 [Causal vs. Productive Powers] As for the first negative argument [in 7.4], namely, the one referring to the generation of the Son, I have this to say: Active power can mean two things: (1) a causative power whose correlative is the possible, i.e., the causable —and this is the proper sense of the term—or it can be understood in a wider sense as (2) a productive power whose correlative is the possible, i.e., the object producible. Therefore, omnipotence can be understood in two ways: (1) As a causative power of everything causable and (2) as a productive power of everything producible.

185

If it is understood in the second sense, only the Father is omnipotent. He is the fruitful source for producing anything producible. The Fathers of the Church, however, do not speak of omnipotence in this sense. They speak of it only insofar as it implies causative power in regard to everything causable, i.e., possible.[48] In this sense, neither the Son nor the Holy Spirit is a "possible," although they are producible, for they are not able to be caused or produced with a distinct nature of their own. If we take omnipotence as the Fathers of the Church understand it, i.e., as a causative power of everything causable common to all three persons, it must be admitted absolutely that omnipotence does not refer to an intrinsic notional act [productive of a divine person]. Therefore, even if it could be demonstrated that God is omnipotent, it could not be demonstrated that he is potent as regards such notional acts.

7.93 [To the authorities cited] It does seem, however, that the texts cited from Augustine [in 7.4] and Richard [in 7.94] conflict
[34] with what has just been said. To the citation from Augustine used against us, it can be replied, "If the Father cannot generate the Son, or cannot generate a son equal to himself, he is not omnipotent," is not a formal consequence or implication in the same way that an argument from the destruction of a quantitative part to the destruction of the whole would be a formal consequence.[49] But it is [a material consequence] from the destruction of something posterior which follows necessarily, to the destruction of what is prior. If the Father could not generate the Son or an equal son, it would be because this ability is neither a part of his essential perfection nor a personal property of his. The second possibility is excluded because that person [i.e., the Father] exists of himself, and therefore it is not repugnant to what is peculiarly his own to produce something actively. If the first alternative is the case, he would not have the perfect nature which in some person is able to produce everything producible. Therefore, even though the denial of the notional act does not formally entail the denial of omnipotence, by reason of its matter the consequence is valid for this person for whom such a notional act is compatible by reason of what is proper to him as a person.

7.94 Against this it is objected that, according to Richard,[50] the

---

[48] Cf. Duns Scotus, *Ord.* 1, d.20, nn.24-34 (v, 313-18).

[49] For the distinction between material and formal consequences see E. A. Moody, *Truth and Consequences in Medieval Logic* (Amsterdam, 1953), pp. 70-80.

[50] Richard of St. Victor, *De Trin.* 1, c.25: PL 196, 902; ed. Ribaillier, 106.

QUESTION SEVEN

proper object of omnipotence seems to be God or a divine person. He says that if there were two omnipotent beings, one would make the other completely impotent. This would not follow unless the object of one's omnipotence was the other omnipotent.

[35] 7.95 This can be answered as the argument from Augustine was [in 7.93]. The inference "He is omnipotent, therefore he is powerful as regards another God or omnipotent" does not hold like the consequence about the whole in quantity. For, if another God were assumed to exist, he would not be the object of omnipotence properly so-called, but would exist of himself necessarily. However, the consequence holds for extrinsic objects. With his will one omnipotent agent could produce all possibles, and everything that could coexist with them. The other omnipotent agent, however, could by his will impede the production of the same set of possible objects. Therefore, the second would render the first totally impotent, not by acting or doing something to him but to the objects of his power.

7.96 If you say the two could always agree with each other about the objects to be willed, I answer: Although this seems to be pure fiction as regards objects to which both wills relate contingently and with an equal degree of independence, it would still follow that one omnipotent could make the other completely impotent, because there cannot be two total causes for one and the same effect. Either the effect would receive existence twice, or else each cause as distinct in itself would not be the complete cause. But this omnipotent, who, according to your assumption, would agree with the other about the objects to be willed, could by his own will be their complete and total cause. Therefore, the other could not be a distinct total cause of the same set of objects. And what holds for two objects, holds for all. Just from the standpoint of the objects, then, the will of one omnipotent agent could reduce the other to impotence in the sense that the second would be unable to actualize anything since the will of the first as a distinct and total cause of the same would prevent the second from doing anything.

[36] 7.97 To these answers [7.93f.] to the authorities of Augustine and Richard this objection is raised: The following are all formal consequences: "If the Son is omniscient, he knows of the generation of the Father," "If he wills all things, he wills this generation." Similarly, then, "He is omnipotent, therefore he can generate the Son" is a true and formal consequence and not just one that holds by reason of its matter.[51]

7.98 In answer one could say that the distribution in all these

---

[51] Giles of Rome, *Sent.* I, d.20, princ. 1, qq.1-2 in corp. (fol 114-15).

terms "omnipotent," "omniscient," and "willing all" is not over acts but over objects of the same act. That is why one can infer formally that they hold for this object, for that object, and hence for any object whatsoever of such an act. Now the notional act is a simple object of the divine knowledge and will of any divine person; but the notional act is not an object of omnipotence. That is why "omniscient" and "willing all" formally entail the knowledge and volition of the notional act whereas "omnipotent" does not entail the power of producing that act. The reason for this difference is that the notional act is something that can be known and willed, but it is not simply a possible insofar as "possible" means "causable." For although the notional act has the characteristic of being good and true, it does not have that of being causable or caused.

3. Reply to the Argument about the Creation of the Angels

[37] 7.99 As for the second argument [in 7.5] about the creation of the angels,[52] I concede that just as the proposition "God can cause everything causable mediately or immediately" is demonstrable, so too one can demonstrate specifically that God can cause a particular causable, but only when the minor by which the conclusion is to be inferred is evident and demonstrated; not otherwise. As the Philosopher says[53]: "It happens that every mule is known to be sterile. But it is not known to hold for this mule, unless the minor 'This is a mule' is known to be true." Now the minor that allows one to conclude "God can cause an angel" is the proposition "The angel is causable."

7.100 [Two Questions: Is it demonstrable that the angel can be caused? What did Aristotle think about this?] Some say this minor [in 7.96] is merely believed but is not demonstrable. Hence the conclusion is merely believed even though the major be demonstrable.

7.101 Second, it is claimed that, according to the Philosopher, one must deny the minor and hence the conclusion also. For they say it is clear from the *Metaphysics*[54] that the Philosopher held that since every Intelligence is necessary, each exists of itself. What is caused by another, however, is of itself nonbeing and in itself is only possible. On the other hand, the simply necessary is in no sense just a possible. Aristotle consequently did not hold both of these two con-

---

[52] Thomas, *Summa theol.* 1, q.46, a.2 in corp. (1, 237-38).
[53] Aristotle, *Anal. post.* 1, c.1 (67a33-36).
[54] Aristotle, *Metaph.* XII, c.7 (1072b10-15).

QUESTION SEVEN

tradictory propositions, viz., "An Intelligence is necessary" (a point he clearly held) and "Nevertheless it is caused by another."

7.102 Some[55] also say Aristotle held that an Intelligence is infinite, and from this it follows that it exists of itself, for finite is only what exists by means of another. Proof of the antecedent: In the *Metaphysics*, Bk. XII, chapter [7],[56] Aristotle states again that it was proved that the first mover cannot have magnitude because he has infinite power and no finite being has infinite power. And immediately afterwards, at the beginning of chapter [8],[57] he asks whether it is necessary to postulate one or several substances of this sort and decides that there are several depending on the distinct number of celestial movements. Therefore, his intention, to put the two conclusions together, is to show there are many substances without magnitude because many have infinite power. And farther on in the same chapter he says[58]: "It is clear then that there must be many substances which are of the same number [as the movements of the stars] and in their nature eternal and in themselves unmovable and without magnitude, for the reason mentioned above," in the previous chapter, namely, that they have infinite power, which cannot exist in finite magnitude; neither can it exist in infinite magnitude since there is no such thing.

[38] 7.103 We ought not to attribute to any author a false or absurd opinion, however, unless he states such expressly or unless it follows evidently from what he does say. Now the proposition "An angel is a being which exists of itself" is not only false (as is obvious) but is absurd as well (since its opposite can be demonstrated, as we shall see). Since no text of Aristotle expressly states such a proposition, it seems unreasonable to attribute it to him.

7.104 [Answer to the First Question: It is demonstrable that the angel is causable] In opposition to what has been said, therefore, I make two observations regarding this minor "The angel is causable." First, it is demonstrable; second, Aristotle admitted it.

Proof of the first: Two intellectual natures that are simply infinite cannot coexist. But an intellectual nature that exists of itself or is uncaused is simply infinite. Therefore, there cannot be several intel-

---

[55] Henry of Ghent, *Quodl.* VI, q.14 in corp. (fol. 253); *Summa* a.25, q.3 in corp. (I, fol. 154H).
[56] Aristotle, *Metaph.* XII, c.7 (1073a4-12).
[57] Ibid., c.8 (1073a15).
[58] Ibid., c.8 (1073a37-b2).

lectual natures that are simply uncaused. Now the first intellectual nature is uncaused, otherwise it would not be first. Therefore, every other nature is caused.

[39] 7.105 The first proposition of this deduction [i.e., that two infinite intellectual natures are impossible] is proved at length in the question on the unicity of God.[59] Here I will touch on only one proof.

Each of these natures would understand the other most perfectly, that is to say, in all its intelligibility and comprehensibility. Similarly, each would love the other insofar as it is capable of being loved. Each would also comprehend and love himself in the same way. Thus each would be beatified in intellect and will not only by himself but by the other as well. And yet it is impossible that one and the same potency should simultaneously comprehend two objects each of which is infinitely adequate, for each would be fully equal to the total strength of that potency. Furthermore, one and the same power or potency cannot have two objects that are first to the same degree. But the essence of one would be the first object of his intellect; the essence of the other consequently could not be its first object, but neither could it be its secondary object. For since it is just as infinitely perfect as the first, it could not be posterior to it in entity. Consequently, it could not be posterior to it in intelligibility either. It is also impossible for one power to comprehend the essence of the other nature as perfectly as its own, particularly if its own nature does not include the other nature eminently, or if the other is not essentially dependent upon it, or if the two natures are not the same sort of thing. Yet all of these situations would be true on the assumption that God and an Intelligence were both infinite.

7.106 The second proposition of this deduction [in 7.104], i.e., nature which exists of itself is infinite, appears clear from what was said above [in 7.87] about how the Philosopher proved the prime mover to be infinite because it has its power of itself and hence has the plentitude of power.

[40] 7.107 [Answer to the Second Question: According to Aristotle, the angel is causable. Proof from the *Metaphysics*] Proof of the second point, namely that Aristotle admitted this minor [in 7.104, i.e., that the angel is causable].

First proof from his mind in Bk. XII of the *Metaphysics*.[60]

He admits all things have an essential order to one another and even more so to one First Being. Now the intensively infinite cannot

[59] Cf. Duns Scotus, *Ord.* I, d.2, nn.157-90 (II, 222-43).
[60] Aristotle, *Metaph.* XII, c.10 (1075a18-19).

QUESTION SEVEN

be subordinate to another as its end, for an infinite good does not exist for the sake of some other good. The good of the whole universe, however, is subordinated in two ways, namely, (1) in the way one being is ordered to another and (2) in the way they are all ordered to something best which exists apart. Neither can the infinite be subordinated to some higher source for its active power is infinite. And also, according to him at the end of Bk. XII, "Things refuse to be governed badly, therefore, one ruler let there be."[61]

7.108 It may be objected that Aristotle admitted an order among beings that have no matter because the second cause, although it is not produced by the first, still depends upon the first cause, as happens in the case of species of numbers and figures.[62]

7.109 Answer: Nothing depends for its being on anything that is not some kind of cause. The same holds true of its continuing to exist. What is said of number does not contradict this, for a lesser number taken potentially or materially is a part of a greater number. But a part functions as a material cause, as one gathers from Bk. V of the *Metaphysics*[63]: "Parts are causes of the whole in the sense that they are that out of which the whole is made." And Aristotle adds in the same place: "The parts are causes in the sense of being the substrate." If the smaller number be taken actually and formally, however, it is not a part of the larger number nor does the latter depend upon it for its being.

7.110 Furthermore, in the same Bk. XII of the *Metaphysics*[64] Aristotle declares that the first mover moves as the object of thought and desire. What can be known and loved, however, moves without being moved. It is in this way that God moves the Intelligence closest to him. Therefore, he is the cause of this Intelligence's intellection and they say this intellection, according to Aristotle, is identical with the substance of the Intelligence.

7.111 It may be objected that "to move" in this case is understood metaphorically and that properly speaking it does not mean "to cause something." Answer: Every intellection not identical with its object is caused by that object, and according to the Commentator,[65] it appears this means it is caused efficiently, for he says there: "The bath insofar as it is in the mind moves as an efficient cause, and insofar as it exists outside the mind it moves as a final cause."

7.112 [Proof from the *Physics*] The same point [in 7.104] can be

[61] Ibid. (1076a-5).
[62] Ibid., v, c.2 (1013b18-25).
[63] Ibid.; cf. *Iliad* 11, 204.
[64] Ibid., XII, c.7 (1072a27-28).
[65] Averroes, *Metaph.* XII, com. 36 (VIII, fol. 318I-K).

proved from Aristotle's mind in Bk. VIII of the *Physics*.⁶⁶ Here he shows that an infinitely powerful mover cannot move immediately. Now the heavens are moved; therefore they are moved immediately by someone with finite power. Such a proper mover is an Intelligence. Therefore, Aristotle wants to say the Intelligence is finite and hence does not exist of itself. The validity of this implication was established earlier [in 7.86ff.].

7.113 Another argument from the same Bk. VIII is this: There the Philosopher wants to show that a mover of infinite power moves the heavens with an infinite movement. But, as we said [in 7.47], he does not do so immediately; therefore, he does so mediately, i.e., by means of an Intelligence. And the Commentator⁶⁷ affirms it to be the mind of Aristotle that a finite mover moves the heavens immediately and the infinite mover moves it mediately. So far as the heavens go, therefore, there are two ordered movers.

From this I argue that wherever several agents are essentially ordered, what the second receives from the first is either (a) its existence (e.g., the heavens and the sphere of fire) or (b) some influence, if not its existence (e.g., to put a ball in motion a bat must be given movement by the hand), or (c) both produce the same effect immediately, but according to a certain order, namely one is the major, the other the minor agent, but both achieve the same effect (e.g., the father and mother in the generation of offspring according to the opinion that maintains the mother plays an active role).

In which of these three ways, I ask, are these two agents related to each other in moving the heavens? Certainly not in the third way, for it would follow immediately that the finite and the infinite power would move for an equal time, indeed for the same time period, since both cause the movement immediately as their proper effect. If it be the second way, we have what we intend to prove, since nothing receives from an Intelligence anything other than its essence, according to Aristotle. If they are related in the first way, this is clearly our proposal. Obviously then Aristotle conceived these agents to be so ordered that the second came from the first. The first, in such a case, would move mediately and would give being and power to the immediate mover. And because it would give these perpetually, the first agent would be the cause of the perpetuity of the motion whereas the finitude of power which is not distinct from the angel's nature would be the cause of the succession

⁶⁶ Aristotle, *Physic.* VIII, c.6 (259b32).
⁶⁷ Averroes, *Metaph.* XII, com. 41 (VIII, fol. 323v-325v).

in the movement, for the mobile could offer some resistance to a finite power, something it could not do to an infinite power.

[42] 7.114 [Confirmation from Averroes and Avicenna] A third proof for our claim [in 7.104] is to be found in what Averroes thought of the matter. Speaking of Aristotle's mind in *De substantia orbis*,[68] he writes: "The heavenly body not only needs the power of locomotion but also a power which gives it being, substance and eternal permanence," etc. Then he adds: "Some have said that he, viz., Aristotle, did not say that the sky had an efficient cause, but only a moving cause, and this was most absurd." Aristotle, then, maintained that the heavens, like the Intelligences, were formally necessary. For he held as a universal principle that every perpetual substance is formally necessary. This is obvious from Bk. IX of the *Metaphysics*[69]: "Nothing perpetual is potential," etc. What his mind was on this subject appears obvious enough from Bk. XII of the *Metaphysics*.[70] That God be the cause of the being and substance of the Intelligence, then, is just as consistent with the mind of Aristotle as is the view that he caused the being and substance of the heavens, which Averroes interpreted him to mean.

7.115 Furthermore, it is the express view of Avicenna[71] that every Intelligence is caused by the First Being. And perhaps he not only did not contradict Aristotle here but explained the manner and order of their production, which Aristotle did not go into. If it be maintained that Aristotle thought that every Intelligence was produced immediately by the First Being, then Avicenna would indeed contradict him as to the order of their production, but not as regards the conclusion we set out to establish, namely, that the Intelligence is produced. On this they would agree. As for the way it was caused, we know well enough that Avicenna did not think of it as involving change or novelty. According to him, the complete being of the Intelligence would be always emanating from the First but its essence would be distinct and separate. It would be similar to the way we believe the Son to be always proceeding from the Father except that Father and Son have the same essence. Or, according to Aristotle, it would be like the perpetual light in transparent bodies that never fall into the shade of any body that could cause shadows in the universe. And still the sun would effectively cause this continual

---

[68] Averroes, *De substantia orbis* c.2 (IX, fol. 6I; 7A).
[69] Aristotle, *Metaph.* IX, c.8 (1050b7-10, 15-30).
[70] Ibid., XII, c.7 (1072b10-15).
[71] Avicenna, *Metaph.* IX, c.4 (104v-105r).

light in the luminous bodies, for such light is not said to exist of itself. If it did, it would not be the same kind of light as that in a part of a transparent body which is not always illuminated. For when it is illuminated anew, this is certainly caused by the sun. What is caused, however, is not the same in kind as what exists of itself.[72]

[43]   7.116 As for the proof that Aristotle thought the angel was not caused, because he held it to be formally necessary, I say that Aristotle did not consider "caused" and "formally necessary" to be mutually repugnant, since he says in the *Metaphysics*[73]: "The principles of perpetual things must be always most true, for they are the cause of truth in other things." Hence he admitted that perpetual things, which are formally necessary, have principles. Again he says in the chapter "On the necessary" in the *Metaphysics*[74]: "There is nothing to prevent some necessary things from having other causes." This also appears clear from the case of principles and conclusion, namely where the principle is the cause of the conclusion being true.

7.117 As for the argument [in 7.101] that the caused is of itself nonbeing and properly speaking is only possible being, we must reply that this means it is not being of itself or, better, it is not being which exists in and through itself. Thus what is required is that it does not have the mode of being characteristic of the self-existent, not that some kind of nonentity pertain to it. A negation of this first sort, however, is compatible with the necessary whereas negation of entity is not.

7.118 As for the dictum "The caused is of itself only possible" [in 7.101], if "possible" means that subdivision of being that is opposed to "actual," then this is not necessarily found in everything caused, but only in such cases where the caused is something new. Causation and novelty were not necessarily connected for Aristotle, nor are they for those theologians who claim God could have produced something from eternity. Yet everything caused is a possible in the sense of being an object of a causative power, but this "possibility," although it is incompatible with "necessity of itself," was not repugnant to "formal necessity" according to Aristotle.

7.119 The opinion attributed to Aristotle [in 7.102] about an Intelligence being infinite, however, must be rejected. The opposite

---

[72] Cf. Duns Scotus, *Ord.* I, d.8, nn.232-62 (IV, 282-302).
[73] Aristotle, *Metaph.* II, c.1 (993b26-30).
[74] Ibid., V, c.5 (1015b9-15).

is not only true but it is demonstrable in itself and, as we have shown above [in 7.104-116], it represents the mind of Aristotle.

7.120 [Reply to citations to the contrary] Therefore I answer those texts adduced by those who would ascribe this opinion to him.

Reply to the first [in 7.102]:[75] The final conclusion [of chapter 7] is not that the first mover is without magnitude because it is of infinite power, but rather another conclusion which he says has been proved earlier, viz., "It is impassive and unalterable, for all other changes are posterior to change of place."[76] Now this substance is not capable of local motion, as can be proved from what he had said before. Then he concludes, therefore, it cannot be moved by any movement that presupposes local motion, and thus it is unalterable. Next follows his question at the beginning of the subsequent chapter: "Is there one substance of this sort or more than one, etc.?"[77] Hence this refers to the unalterable being of which he was just speaking and not to a being of infinite power mentioned earlier. For what continuity would his words have if they did not refer to what he had just been talking about, but to something he has said previous to that?

Or if he was referring to the earlier remark, one could say it must be the conclusion he meant, namely that it has no magnitude. And I concede that there are many things without magnitude just as there are many that are unalterable and impassive.

7.121 To the other text,[78] I have this to say. By demonstration of the reasoned fact, a negation can be inferred of some subject using as many media as there are causes why the opposite affirmation is repugnant to that subject. Now if some single thing were the adequate cause of such repugnance, it would be an adequate means of establishing such a negation. Intensive infinity is one cause why it is impossible to have magnitude but it is not an adequate cause. To have intellectuality without matter, however, is adequate. For the middle term to be sufficient, however, it is necessary to have both intellectuality and immateriality conjoined, since intellectuality

---

[75] Cf. ibid., XII, c.7 (1073a2-12), where he says that the first mover cannot have magnitude because he has infinite power. Cf. *supra*, 7.102.

[76] Ibid., XII, c.7 (1073a10).

[77] Cf. ibid., c.8 (1073a15).

[78] Cf. ibid., c.8 (1073a37), where Aristotle says such substances are "in their nature eternal and in themselves unmovable and without magnitude, for the reason mentioned above." Cf. *supra*, 7.102.

alone does not suffice according to Aristotle (as is clear from the case of man); neither is immateriality alone sufficient (as is clear from the case of the heavens).

[45] 7.122 Consequently, my answer to the text in question would be this. Absence of magnitude can be inferred from infinite power. It is in fact so inferred in the penultimate conclusion [of chapter seven][79] and also in Bk. VIII of the *Physics*.[80] But it can also be inferred from immateriality together with intellectuality. Something purely intellectual [i.e., without matter] cannot have magnitude. The intellectual form itself cannot be extended, but if something intellectual is also something quantitative, it is because it has matter perfected by an intellectual form. It receives quantity, not because of its intellectuality, but because of its materiality which is perfected by an intellectual form as is the case with man. "A nature with infinite power has no magnitude" is a true proposition, but this proposition is also true: "An intellectual nature that has no matter has no magnitude." In the passage cited toward the end of the [seventh] chapter,[81] it is proved that the first mover has no magnitude because he has infinite power. But this means is not adequate so far as this predicate goes. In the previous chapter,[82] near the beginning, it is stated that immovable substances must be without matter because they must be perpetual and if something is perpetual in actuality, it is without matter in actuality. Later on, at the beginning of the [seventh] chapter[83] it is explained how these moving substances are intellectual natures.

7.123 From these two we have a second means for eliminating magnitude, namely intellectuality without matter. And so far as this predicate is concerned, this middle term is adequate. Therefore, when it is said [in chapter 8][84] that there must be many substances without magnitude "for the reason mentioned above," this must be taken to refer to the adequate cause (i.e., intellectuality without matter, which was mentioned at the beginning of both chapters six[85] and seven)[86] and not to the proposition about infinity of power at the end of the [seventh] chapter.[87] This interpretation does not do violence, it seems, to the words of the text, for intellectuality with-

---

[79] Ibid., c.7 (1073a2-12).
[80] Aristotle, *Physic*. VIII, c.10 (266b7-8).
[81] Aristotle, *Metaph*. XII, c.7 (1073a2-12).
[82] Ibid., c.6 (1071b21).
[83] Ibid. (1072b16-25).
[84] Ibid., c.8 (1073a30).
[85] Ibid., c.6 (1071b21).
[86] Ibid., c.7 (1072a20-25).
[87] Ibid., c.7 (1073a2-12).

out matter is the proper cause, indeed the adequate cause, as regards this predicate [i.e., "to be without magnitude"]. "To have infinite power," however, is not its proper or adequate cause, because this predicate pertains to every intelligence whereas the middle term [viz., "to have infinite power"] pertains to God alone, to whom be honor and glory into ages of ages.

Question Eight

DOES THE DIVINE WORD HAVE SOME CAUSALITY OF HIS OWN AS REGARDS CREATURES?

[1]   8.1 The next question concerns omnipotence or active causality insofar as it pertains in particular to the Son in the divine and the question is this: Has the Son or the Divine Word* some causality of his own as regards the creature?[1]

Arguments Pro and Con

It is argued that he has:

An art implies a relation of causality to the artefact and of the idea to its ideatum* or concrete realization. But to be art and to contain in himself the ideas of all that can be made is something that pertains properly to the Divine Word. Therefore [he has a relation of causality to the artefact and ideatum].

The minor appears clear from Augustine[2]: "The perfect Word, to which nothing is lacking, is the art of the omnipotent and wise God." This proves the first part of the minor. And he continues: "Full of all living and immutable reasons," which proves the second part of the minor, because by those "reasons," he understands the Ideas,* as appears clear from his mind in *Eighty-Three Questions*,[3] question 46. And in the same place [in *The Trinity*] he adds: "In him God knows all things which he has made through him." These words prove both parts of the minor and must be understood in this fashion. God knows everything in him as in an art wherein the essences of the artefacts are relucent.

[2]   8.2 It is argued for the negative:

Augustine[4] speaking of the Incarnate Son says: "He could not be sent by the Father without the Holy Spirit." And after some lines,

---

[1] Cf. Duns Scotus, *Ord.* II, d.1, q.1 (ed. Vivès XI, 6-45); I, d.27 (VI, 63-106); d.10 (IV, 339-66); d.12 (V, 25-64).

[2] Augustine, *De Trin.* VI, c.10, n.11: PL 42, 931; CCSL 50, 241.

[3] Augustine, *De diversis quaestionibus 83*, q.46, n.2: PL 40, 30.

[4] Augustine, *De Trin.* II, c.5, nn.8-9: PL 42, 849-50; CCSL 50, 89-90.

he adds: "Perhaps someone thinks we should say that the Son has also been sent by himself, because that conception and birth from Mary is the work of the Trinity by whose causation all things are caused." He concedes implicitly this conclusion in his answer to an objection: "How has the Father sent him, if he has sent himself? First of all, I answer him, etc."

8.3 In the same place he understands the incarnation to be the work of one and the same identical operation of Father and Son and Holy Spirit inseparably.

8.4 Again Augustine writes[5]: "I assert with absolute confidence that the Father, Son, and Holy Spirit, being of one and the same substance, God and Creator, the omnipotent Trinity, work together inseparably."

Body of the Question

[3] 8.5 This question stated generally could be understood of any form of causality which God has with respect to creatures, but the arguments refer in particular to efficient causality.

Therefore, it is first necessary to inquire about efficient causality, and here there are three points requiring investigation. First, is there some formal ground of causation that is proper to the Word? Second, is some mode or order in causality or in causing proper to him? Third, is some relationship of causality or any relationship of his to a creature included *per se* in his constitutive property?

ARTICLE I
Is there some Formal Aspect of Causation Proper to the Word?

1. Negative Answer: Three Proofs

8.6 [Proof from authority] As regards the first point, we can say that no formal ground of acting *ad extra** is proper to him. This can be shown in three ways: first by authority, second by reason of [an empirical] or *a posteriori** proof, and third by an *a priori** proof.

The authority is that of Augustine,[6] who says: "In relation to the creature, the Father, the Son, and the Holy Spirit are one principle even as they are one creator and one Lord." This indicates that just as there is in them a formal deity by which they are called God, so there is also one formal reason by which they function as cause and

---
[5] Ibid., IV, c.21, n.30: PL 42, 909; CCSL 50, 202.
[6] Ibid., V, c.14, n.15: PL 42, 921; CCSL 50, 223.

principle in virtue of which they are all referred to as one creator and one principle. Dionysius[7] says much the same: "All causable things are common to the divinity as a whole."

[4] 8.7 [Proof *a posteriori*] The *a posteriori* proof is taken from the evaluation of an act of causing, of which the Savior says[8]: "Whatever the Father does, the Son does likewise." The word "whatever" indicates clearly that Father and Son are not related to each other in their action as a universal and a particular cause, in the way, for example, the sun* and the father are in begetting an animal. The word also indicates that they are causes not of different effects but of the same effect. The verb "does" shows that they are not related to each other as agent and formal ground for acting, for the "reason for acting" does not act, properly speaking. The word "likewise" reveals clearly that in their action, they are not related as a higher cause in respect to a lower one which does not act of its own power, but only in virtue of another and in comparison to which it acts only dependently and imperfectly. Neither do they act as two partial causes of the same type (like two men pulling a boat), or as two causes of different types (as some say the agent intellect and phantasm cooperate in moving the possible intellect) in such a fashion that together they constitute one complete cause, for in situations of this sort neither cause can be complete. Only together do they form the complete or total cause, whereas each in itself is at best a partial or diminished cause. For that reason it is more correct to say that each cooperates with the other rather than that each causes the effect. Also two causes of this sort do not cause the effect in exactly the same way.

Having excluded these various imperfect ways of causing Christ means to say that the Father and Son, and by the same token the whole Trinity, simultaneously cause whatever they cause and they do so completely and with equal perfection. From this it follows that the Word has no formal ground of action that is his alone.

8.8 Proof of the consequence: No suppositum formally acts unless it be in act through something that functions as a formal ground for acting, which I understand in this way. Either this ground is the informing form, as in the case of creatures (for which reason Aristotle[9] concludes that the soul is the act and form of the body be-

---

[7] Ps.Dionysius, *De divinis nom.* c.2, n.1: PG 3, 638; *Dionysiaca* I, pp. 66-67.

[8] John 5:19.

[9] Aristotle, *De anima* II, c.1 (412a20).

cause it is the source [*principium quo*]* of an animated body's operations); or else that which is the principle of acting is wholly identical with the acting suppositum,* as in the case of a simple subsisting form which, according to the *Metaphysics*,[10] is at once the whole of what it is and therefore acts as a whole. Now what is proper to one person cannot be the act of another person in either of these two ways, which is what Augustine[11] means when he writes: "The Father cannot be wise with begotten wisdom." Therefore, it follows that if the formal ground for acting with some action is proper to one person, then another person will not be formally acting by that action.

[5] 8.9 [Objection and its solution] You may object, following one Doctor's opinion,[12] that the three divine persons in their common, essential intellect have one Word (which represents a quasi-proximate principle of causing even as the essence is the quasi-remote principle), but that the Father has this Word *a se* by speaking* it, as it were, whereas the Son and Holy Spirit have it only from the Father, who, acting for all the persons, speaks the single Word to perfect the essential intellect. And he says something similar of the Holy Spirit as regards the will.

I answer: The Father certainly does not have the Word as his formal act in either of the ways mentioned [in 8.8]. Therefore he could only have the Word as something either correlative or consubstantial, but in a suppositum distinct from himself. Yet neither alternative would suffice for the claim that one who has the Word in this way is acting by an action whose formal principle is possessed as a form or as the act of the one having it. But this is a minimum condition for claiming that the one having it acts by such an action. This is clear from the case of creatures not only as regards correlatives but also as regards persons, howsoever distinct, in regard to the same action.

[6] 8.10 [Proof *a priori**] A third way to prove the thesis is *a priori*:

First, by a proper middle term in this way. In God the proximate formal ground for causation is intellect or will, or some act of theirs. But the three persons share the same intellect and the same single will, and consequently all have the same act of understanding and of volition and the same object, be it primary or secondary. There-

---

[10] Aristotle, *Metaph.* VIII, c.6 (1045b23-24).
[11] Augustine, *De Trin.* VII, c.1, n.2: PL 42, 936; CCSL 50, 249.
[12] Henry of Ghent, *Quodl.* VI, q.2 (fol. 219A-B); *Summa* a.60, q.4, ad 1 (II, fol. 172B-173H).

fore, the same proximate formal ground for causation is common to all three persons.

8.11 Augustine[13] touches on this when he writes: "How has the Father sanctified him, if he has sanctified himself? For the same Lord mentions both." And he proves this, and then adds: "How did the Father deliver him, if he has delivered himself, for the Apostle Paul says both?" And he gives this reply: "He will answer, I believe, if he grasps the words correctly, 'Because the will of the Father and Son is one, and their operation inseparable.'" And this is confirmed from another remark[14]: "The will of God is the first and supreme cause of all things," that is to say, it is the formal ground for causation.

[7] 8.12 [An objection and its solution] One[15] might object to this that even though the will or intellect is the formal ground for causing, it is not such in every person, but only one person has the power properly insofar as it is the formal or proximate principle of causation.

Answer: If it is the same power with the same act and same object, then no matter what person it be in, it will always provide him with the same basis for causation as regards object that can be caused by such a power, for the suppositum does not provide the formal ground for acting with some new form of causality, but rather the suppositum takes on the formal character of an agent precisely because it has a formal ground for acting. Therefore every person with the same power will have the same relationship to a causable object.

8.13 [An invalid argument] Another proper middle term used to prove the thesis is the divine being, which is used as follows. The divine being is common to all three persons, because of the divine essence they have in common. But the divine being is the proper principle of causing, the proof of which is this: the being of things is properly a being that is caused and it must be caused by something similar to it; therefore it is caused *per se* by the divine being.[16]

On the contrary, essence *qua* essence as a principle of acting acts only after the manner of nature* [i.e., necessarily]. Now God causes nothing extrinsic to himself in this fashion.[17]

---

[13] Augustine, *De Trin.* II, c.5, n.9: PL 42, 850; CCSL 50, 90.
[14] Ibid., III, c.4, n.9: PL 42, 873; CCSL 50, 136.
[15] Cf. *supra*, note 12.
[16] Thomas, *Summa theol.* I, q.45, a.6 in corp. (I, 232).
[17] Cf. Duns Scotus, *Ord.* II, d.1, q.2, n.5 (ed. Vivès XI, 54); *Lectura*, d.39, nn.42-61 (XVII, 492-500); cf. *infra*, q.16.

QUESTION EIGHT

8.14 [Another *a priori* proof] Finally, the thesis is established by an *a priori* common middle term in this fashion. Everything caused depends *per se* upon a first cause as the imperfect and possible depend on the perfect and simply necessary. Therefore, whatever is the formal ground for causing will also be the formal ground for supporting this causal dependence, and hence it will be the formal reason for being perfect and necessary. But the three persons share in common the same necessity and perfection. Therefore the informal ground for acting will be common also.

2. Objection to these Proofs

[8] 8.15 Against these proofs [in 8.6ff.] one could argue:[18] Knowledge and love, insofar as they are divine processions,* are "reasons" according to which creatures are produced and fall into the category of formal causality in the sense that without them the essential intellect and will would not be sufficiently disposed to produce these creatures. Now the Word is the knowledge proceeding [from the Father] just as the Holy Spirit is the love proceeding [from Father and Son]. Therefore, the Word has some aspect of formal causality peculiar to himself and the same is true of the Holy Spirit.

8.16 The major premise is proved in four ways, the first of which is this: Wisdom *qua* essential is only speculative, whereas wisdom *qua* personal is practical with reference to what is to be accomplished, containing in itself the ideas which are the principles of operating. But no knowledge suffices as the proximate basis for operating if it is not practical. Therefore [wisdom *qua* essential is not sufficient].

8.17 The second proof is by way of an example, that of a created artist. An artisan wise in his art has a twofold knowledge of an artefact: (a) one is the simple knowledge of his art in general, by which he views everything that can be produced in a purely speculative way; (b) the other is dispositional knowledge as regards a specific work. By this knowledge of a particular art, which stems conceptually from the universal art, the artist sees the order he will follow in producing the work. This knowledge is practical, and without it he cannot execute the work. In a similar way, God knows the singular simply and he knows it absolutely as a particular manifestation [of himself] through his essential knowledge, but by his produced knowledge [or the Word] he knows the same intrinsic and extrinsic things as a kind of expression of himself. And in particular, he knows in the Word all the things that can be made and knows just

---

[18] Cf. *supra*, note 12.

how to make them. Therefore, just as the knowledge of the universal art without that of the particular art does not suffice, so in God the essential knowledge without the productive knowledge is not sufficient.

[9] 8.18 The third proof of the major is by way of an analogy taken from natural things. As the natural form is not a principle of action insofar as it represents a perfection of the subject in which it exists, but only insofar as it expresses a relation to an effect, so wisdom and love are only principles of operation insofar as they imply a relationship to an effect. Now dispositional wisdom and affective love, which imply a relationship to an effect, are none other than the wisdom proceeding [from the Father] and the love proceeding [from Father and Son].

8.19 A fourth proof of the major based on how the intrinsic order of production is related to the extrinsic is this. Where the conceptual order among the essentials in God ends, there the order of origin* among the persons begins. By the same token, then, where the order of origin among the persons ends, there the order of origin as regards creatures begins. Therefore, the Father cannot produce a creature if the Word and Holy Spirit have not been first produced. But if the Father formally possessed in himself all that was needed to produce the creature, so that no causal aspect supplied exclusively by the Word would be required, then the Father, it seems, could cause even without first producing the Son.

Augustine's words confirm this:[19] "Our word can exist and yet no work may follow it, but there can be no work unless the Word precedes, just as the Word of God could be, even though no creature existed, but no creature could be, except through that Word through whom all things were made."

3. Answer to the Objection

[10] 8.20 The major in the argument [in 8.15] must be denied, for as we said [in 8.10-11], knowledge and love, insofar as they figure in God as the cause of creatures, are common formally to all three persons.

8.21 [To the first proof] The answer to the first proof for the major [in 8.16] is this. In us knowledge in the memory and in the word are not speculative and practical respectively. They only differ as habitual and actual knowledge and are always of the same type, being either both speculative or both practical. Therefore, if

[19] Augustine, *De Trin.* xv, c.11, n.20: PL 42, 1073; CCSL 50a, 489.

QUESTION EIGHT

the essential knowledge in the Father is related in analogous fashion to his knowledge in the Word, then the former will not be speculative and the latter practical knowledge, but both will be practical or both will be speculative. What is added about the ideas being contained in his wisdom will be resolved in the answer to the initial argument [at 8.56].

8.22 [To the second proof] As for the second proof [in 8.17], I deny that the knowledge of the creature in the Father is related to knowledge in the Word as knowledge of an art in general would be. This is clear from what we have just said, for the relationship between the two is that of knowledge in the memory and an act of understanding, and though knowledge in the Father is as it were habitual and the other quasi-actual, both would be equally universal or equally particular.

[11]   8.23 The assertion [in 8.17] that universal art is speculative whereas particular art is practical does not seem to be true either. As the *Ethics*[20] defines it: "Art is a state of knowledge concerned with making which involves a true course of reasoning." Therefore, it is clear that all art is practical, since all knowledge of this sort is practical.

The admission that the particular art has its conceptual origins in the universal art also suggests this counterargument. Practical conclusions must be traced back to practical principles, at least proximately. What is more, there seems no way in which they could be derived from speculative principles unless the practical is the logical subalternate of the speculative, for in every discipline the conclusions proper to it are traced back to principles also proper to it, unless the lower science is logically subalternated* to the higher, the conclusions of which it uses as its principles.

Consequently, if some author claims that a universal art is speculative whereas the particular art is practical, this needs further exegesis and one could explain it in this way. The more an intermediate term recedes from one extreme, the more it approaches the other and may even be said to take on the character of the other, as is clear from the *Physics*[21] where red in relation to white is called black. Now purely speculative knowledge is in no way directed to the production of a work, whereas purely practical knowledge is immediately directed to its production. Any intermediary knowledge, therefore, to the extent that it recedes from the one ex-

[20] Aristotle, *Ethica ad Nic.* VI, c.5 (1140a20-21).
[21] Aristotle, *Physic.* V, c.5 (229b15-21).

treme, can be said to fall under the other. Now general knowledge of an art is not immediately directed to producing a particular work, since every actual production involves an individual object, as the *Metaphysics*[22] makes clear. Knowledge of a particular art, however, is immediately directive. To the extent, therefore, that general knowledge of an art is not immediately directive in the way the specific knowledge is, one could call it "speculative," even though it is not speculative in an unqualified sense, but is rather directive, although mediately, since the particular knowledge is, by virtue of it, immediately directive.

[12]   8.24 As for the added remark [in 8.17] that God knows in the Word all the things that can be made and how to make them, I ask: What is this knowledge in God supposed to be? In our own case, I find there is at first knowledge about what can be done and this determines what has to be done. This knowledge is followed by an act of my will, by which I choose to act correctly in conformity with the dictates of reason. This volition is followed by the knowledge that I have chosen to act in this way, and if I knew my will would never change or could not be impeded, I would know that in time I would accomplish what I set out to do.

In God, however, there are no really distinct acts, but there is at most a conceptual distinction. By this dispositional knowledge, therefore, either you refer to that knowledge that precedes as it were every act of his will or else you refer to the act by which he wills to produce in this way. And then it follows that if such dispositional knowledge is present in one person, it is also in the others, for all God's knowledge which is prior as it were to every act of the will is present in the divine intellect in virtue of the object which first moves it [i.e., the essence]. But such an object moves the divine intellect necessarily to all knowledge that precedes any act of the will, because in the whole process the only motive principle is one which acts the way nature does, which is necessarily. Or if by dispositional knowledge you mean that which is subsequent to some voluntary determination, then it follows that every person knows this determination of the will to be in every other person just as much as it is in himself, so that every person has equal knowledge about what can be done and how it can be accomplished.

Neither is it correct to say that one person knows that another, and not himself, has made this sort of decision as regards this possible work, for as we argued [in 8.10-11] for our main conclusion of

[22] Aristotle, *Metaph.* I, c.1 (981a15-24).

this article, if there is but one will then what it decides is also one, and so if one person decides about a specific work in this particular way, it follows the other person who has the same will-act does so in the same way, and when he reflects in his mind upon this will-act, he will know that he is disposed to this particular work in the same way as the other persons are, and so this dispositional knowledge in their mind is something common to all three persons.

[13]   8.25 [To the third proof] As for the third proof [in 8.18] about a natural, active form, my answer is this: Although a natural, active form does have a certain relationship to its product which is indicated by the word "principle" or "potency," it still remains a fact that the subject of this relationship, which we call a principle and a potency, is a form that is not relative but absolute.

Proof: What an action or movement formally begins with is certainly no less something absolute than what it terminates with, particularly if this proposition is true: "The formal principle of acting is that which is alike in the agent and its product." As the *Physics*[23] makes clear, the formal term of the action or movement not only can be something absolute, but it must be an absolute form which does not include some relation. Therefore, it is necessary, or at least possible, that the formal principle of acting be an absolute term and an absolute form.

An example illustrates this. Although heat has the power to warm and what I call a power or potency implies a relation concretely, nevertheless this relationship is not included *per se* in the definition of that active principle insofar as we take the active principle to be the subject said to have this power.

A somewhat more abstract example illustrates the same point. To be an object implies a relationship, as the very words indicate, yet [14] if one is asked what the first object of vision is, it is no answer to cite something relative, for then it would be a simple matter to list all the objects of the various powers, for instance, that the object of vision is the visible, the object of hearing is the audible and so on. One must assign as first object something absolute which is the substrate of the relationship implied in its being an object, and the form of that absolute is what moves such a power *per se*, such as light or color as regards vision, or sound as regards hearing, and so on. Aristotle says as much in the *De anima*[24]: "The object of sight is the visible." And he continues: "What is visible is color and color is what

[23] Aristotle, *Physic.* v, c.2 (225b10-15).
[24] Aristotle, *De anima* II, c.7 (418a26-30).

lies upon what is in its own nature visible; 'in its own nature' here means not that visibility is involved in the definition of what thus underlies color, but that this substratum contains in itself the cause of visibility. For every color has in it the power to set in movement," etc. He wants to say that if color is the first object of sight, it is visible of itself, not according to the first mode of *per se* predication* (indicated by the words "not involved in the definition," that is to say, the predicate "visible" does not fall under the definition of the subject), but according to the second mode of *per se* predication,* because the subject contains the cause of the predicate, and this is what he wants to express when he adds: "but that this substrate contains in itself the cause of visibility."

8.26 It is the same in many other instances and, in particular, in our case. When we ask for the active principle behind some action, we do not have in mind the concrete relationship implied by the fact that it is an active principle (otherwise it would be easy to state the principle behind every action, for the source of the heating would be the heating principle, the source of illumination, the illuminating principle, etc.). What we are looking for is the proximate basis for this relationship. Now this basis is an absolute form and it does not include the relation, for this could not be present in something which is prior by nature to the term of the relation, yet the active form is prior in nature to the term produced by the action, at least in equivocal* actions. Applying this to our case, we could say that if there is no more reason for the knowledge, as the formal basis for producing the creature, including the notion of the relationship to this creature, than there is for a natural, active form including the relationship to its effect (and here the form does not include the relation, but the relation follows from the form), then it would seem to follow that this relationship to creatures is not included in the definition of God's knowledge insofar as it is the formal principle for producing a creature.

8.27 To put it another way, briefly, we could say that in the knowledge produced [in the Word] there is no relation to what can be created that is not already present in the knowledge common to all three persons, a point we proved earlier [in 8.10-11].

[15] 8.28 [To the fourth proof] As regards the fourth proof of the major [in 8.19], although one could show many places where the proposed parallel between the two sets of priorities breaks down, still the conclusion that the Father could not produce creatures without first producing the Son and Holy Spirit is true enough.

8.29 The reason for this is that whenever the same principle produces one thing with simple necessity and another contingently, he cannot produce that to which he is contingently related unless what he produces necessarily has already been produced, particularly when the necessity of producer and produced is one and the same. Now the extrinsic product is produced contingently, whereas the intrinsic one is produced necessarily and in such a way that the latter is necessary by the same necessity as that which characterizes the producer. Therefore, the order of external products cannot begin unless the order of internal processions have taken place.[25]

8.30 Another reason is this: Causality over what is posterior is communicated to the prior product if such causality is not repugnant to what it properly is, for being the first to be produced, there is no inconsistency stemming from the order in which they are produced. Therefore, since the person produced is produced prior to any creatures, as the previous argument indicated, and since causality with respect to creatures is not repugnant to him by reason of his production, it follows that he is prior to the creatures not only because he is produced before them but also insofar as he is productive as regards creatures.

[16] 8.31 This twofold basis for priority can be inferred from Augustine's words [in 8.19]. The first is expressed when he says: "The Word of God could be, even though no creature existed, but not vice versa," whereas he mentions the second when he states that it is the Word "through whom all things were made."

8.32 But it does not follow either from these two grounds for priority or from this authority that the Word has some formal basis for causation that is peculiarly his own, for even without such he could still be prior as a person to a creature either as one product to another or as a productive principle to what is produced.

For there is no need that the product more immediate to the producer, even if this product be productive of some third thing, have some ground for producing that is exclusively its own. It is sufficient that it share the same common basis had by the first producer so long as this is communicated to him before the final product is produced, and so it is here. From this it is clear why the Father cannot create if Son and Holy Spirit are not produced, because if that is not produced to which the producer is necessarily related, then he cannot produce the other to which he is contingently related. Also if that person is not produced who was born to have the same causal

---

[25] Cf. Duns Scotus, *Ord.* II, d.1, q.1, nn.12 and 14 (ed. Vivès XI, 22-26).

relationship to some third being as the first producer has, then this third being cannot be produced. Hence the assumption made [in 8.19] that if no causal aspect exclusive to the Word were required, the Father could create even if he did not produce the Word, is clearly false for the two aforesaid reasons.

[17] 8.33 One might object that according to Augustine the creature necessarily presupposes the Word in some causal role, since he says [in 8.19]: "No creature could be, except through that Word through whom all things were made." But he would not be needed necessarily as a cause if the complete and total causality resided in the Father.

To this I answer: That the Word is a necessary causal prerequisite for the creature's production can be understood in two ways. Either he is needed to perfect the causality or he is needed because he shares the same causality possessed by the first producer. Now the Son is not required in the first way, since he does not perfect the Father's causality. The Father possesses perfect causality in and by himself and he communicates this to the Son, who has it because the Father does. But the Son is required in the second way, for before the creature can be produced, the same nature possessed by the Father is communicated to him and consequently he has the selfsame active power as regards anything subsequent by nature. It follows that the Son shares with the Father the same causality that is a necessary prerequisite for the production of a creature.

8.34 Another answer, which says roughly the same thing, is that for an effect to need something as a causal prerequisite can be understood in two ways. One would be if it were needed simply from the viewpoint of the effect itself, namely if such a cause were not there, the effect would be lacking something sufficient to produce it. The other way would be because it is needed as a necessary concomitant in the cause. In the first way, the Son is not a necessary causal prerequisite, but he is in the second way, for the Father would possess the same total causal perfection, if *per impossibile* he alone existed. Nevertheless, because he is unable to act with this causality the Son first concurs with him and shares the same perfection with him, and uses it to perform the same creative act.

ARTICLE II
Is some Mode or Order in Causing Proper to the Word?

[18] 8.35 [The answer is negative] As for the second main question [in 8.5], I say that the Son himself denies he has any primary causal-

ity: "The Son can do nothing of himself."[26] Nevertheless he does attribute to himself a subordinate authority in causing when he adds: "Except what he sees the Father doing." And further on he continues: "The works which the Father has given me to accomplish, these very works I do," etc.[27] "The Father has given me,"—here is his authorization. "I do,"—here is the causality. The Son has a similar authority with respect to the Holy Spirit. The reason for both assertions is the same. The source of a person's principle of action is also the source of his acting and is the one by virtue of whom he acts. This other does not play the role of a superior cause, however, because he does not have a distinct power from the other, but the second person acts in virtue of the first as the principle communicating the causality to him and therefore as having authority over this causality, over which the recipient has a subordinate authority.

8.36 [Objections and their solution] If by his origin the Father causes before the Son, then the Son does not cause that effect, for what is caused before cannot be caused afterwards, unless the same thing could be caused twice, which is impossible.

8.37 One could argue from the order of origin the same as from the order of causality. If the Father makes something by himself, whereas the Son does not, then the Father causes something which is first in origin and, as first, it cannot be caused by the Son, as it were, in the second sign* or instant of origin, because the same thing cannot be caused twice.

[19] 8.38 To these objections I reply that an order in causing can be understood insofar as the action refers either to the producer or to the thing produced. If we take it in the first way, then there is an order of authority and subauthority in the case at hand, for such an order obtains between the agents insofar as one receives the formal principle of acting from the other. Taken in the second way, however, there is no order involved, for the creature is not put into existence first by the Father and only afterwards by the Son, but before the term is produced, the power to cause it is there in both, but it is there according to some order, viz., that of origin. But the order of origin being completed, all three persons possess this same power at the same sign of nature so that the effect is put into existence by all three at once. Therefore, the statement [in 8.36] that what is caused before cannot be caused afterwards is admittedly true if "before" and "afterwards" refer to the very same causing.

[26] John 5:19. [27] Ibid., 36.

and it is in this sense that the proof given for the statement holds. But this does not justify the claim that the one person who has the causal power first in the order of origin and the other who has it afterwards in the order of origin cannot both use that power, which they possess simultaneously by nature, to cause the effect simultaneously.

8.39 One could give a different answer, especially to the second objection [in 8.37]. "To be first in origin to cause" means "to cause by oneself"; "to cause as posterior in origin" means "to cause by another." But just as a principle has the power of causing from another or of itself, so too does it have its causation. And it is not true that what is caused by one first in origin cannot be caused by another that is posterior in origin, for this would mean that something could not be caused by one thing of itself and by another not of itself, which is clearly false where the same active power exists in both the producer and the one produced.

ARTICLE III
Is some Relationship of Causality or any Relationship of His to a Creature Included *per se* in the Word's Constitutive Property?

[20] 8.40 [The answer is negative] As for the third main question [in 8.5], I say that no relationship to a creature could be included *per se* in what is constitutive of the person of the Word.

8.41 [It is proved by three arguments] First, everything included *per se* in the person of the Word is real, where "real" is opposed to conceptual being, for the Word is constituted as real in this sense, and hence whatever is included in him *per se* is also real in this sense. Now in the divine, every relationship to a creature represents a conceptual relation. Therefore [it is not included *per se* in the Word].

8.42 Second, every relationship of God to a creature has as its proximate foundation something that is common to all three persons. Here I do not take "proximate" to mean that the relation would arise from the very nature of the foundation, for then it would be a real relation, but I understand "proximate" in the sense that it is the proximate reason why the act of the intellect conceptually relates the divine persons to the creature. For in using the method touched on [in 8.10] of the first article in regard to intellect and will, we could prove that any perfection of God can be conceptually related to a creature by an act of his intellect. But when the proximate foundation for relating something in this way is common to all three persons, then the relation itself cannot be proper to any one of them. Therefore, no relation to a creature is included *per se* in the property of any person, for whatever is included in that way is something exclusive to that person.[28]

8.43 Third, according to the first way, one could argue that whatever is in a divine person is of itself necessary being, where by "of itself" is excluded any derivation from a cause, but not necessarily from a principle,* for whatever is in a divine person is uncaused although it could be there as "stemming from a principle" [*principiatum*].* No relationship to a creature, however, be it real or conceptual, can be necessary in this sense, because the creatural term of the relation cannot be necessary in this way, for in whatever being it may have, a creature is either possible or at least not necessary of itself. Therefore, no relationship to a creature, whatever be its being, can be included *per se* in a divine person.

8.44 This argument, however, though it proceeds from true premises perhaps, could, it seems, be challenged or refuted on several grounds, and could only be shown to hold evidently by a reasoning so complicated that I have no intention of going into it here.

8.45 [Objections] To what was said [from 8.40 on], however, it is objected that the very term "Word" implies a *per se* property of the second person and that in addition it implies *per se* a relationship to a creature. Therefore [the Word implies a relationship *per se* to a creature].

The first proposition appears clear from the beginning of John's Gospel[29]: "In the beginning was the Word," where the Evangelist intends to refer properly to the second person in the divine, and Augustine says[30]: "By that by which he is the Son, by that he is the Word."

The second proposition is proved also from Augustine[31] where he is explaining John: "In the beginning was the Word, which in Greek is called *logos* and in Latin *Verbum*, and signifies a 'reason.' But here 'Word' or *Verbum* is the better interpretation since it signifies not only a relationship to the Father, but also a relation to those things which have been made through the Word as an operative power." According to Augustine, then "Word" implies a relationship to a creature.

---

[28] Cf. Duns Scotus, *Ord.* I, d.27, nn.91-96.   [29] John 1:1.
[30] Augustine, *De Trin.* VII, c.2, n.3: PL 42, 936; CCSL 50, 250.
[31] Augustine, *De diversis quaestionibus* 83, q.63: PL 40, 54.

8.46 Specifically it is objected to the reason given [in 8.43]: If the claim were true that no creature is necessary of itself, whatever its mode of being may be, and hence no relationship to a creature can be necessary in this way, then it would follow that neither of the following relationships in God would be necessary of itself, viz., as knower to the creature known or as creative to a creature as something able to be created. But there is nothing formally or necessarily in God that is not necessary of itself. Therefore, it would follow that God does not necessarily know the creature nor is he necessarily able to create it, both of which are false.

[22] 8.47 [Solution to the objections] In the first objection [in 8.45], there is a twofold weakness: one concerning the real state of affairs, the other stemming from the meaning of "Word." As for the first of these, I say that in what is proper to the second person there is no [real] relationship *per se* to a creature, for the reasons cited [in 8.41-43].

8.48 As for the second, I insist that a real relation and a conceptual relation do not make for anything that is *per se* one. Hence if the name "Word" implies two relationships of this sort, it follows there is no single *per se* concept bound up with the name "Word," because the relationship to the Father as "speaking the Word" is real whereas the relation to the creature as "spoken" or "caused" is purely conceptual. Therefore, if "Word" *per se* implies but a single concept, then it denotes only one of the two and just connotes the other. And if this is true, then one could probably say that just as "Son" [*Filius*] and "the act or state of being a child" [*filiatio*] signify the same thing although the manner of signifying differs, so "Word" as a kind of concrete term and its corresponding "act or state of being a word" [*verbatio*], if one might be permitted to coin a term, signify the same thing, though the manner in which they do so differs. For "to be a word" is the same as to be spoken or be expressed intellectually. Hence "Word" implies in the concrete that which is intellectually expressed and then it will also connote a relation to that which is spoken through the word insofar as it connotes perfect knowledge and such knowledge has a conceptual relation to the things known through it.

Therefore, according to this interpretation, there would be this order in what is signified by "Word." First and *per se* it signifies the relationship of origin, namely as a passive intellectual expression, but it does so concretely; second, it connotes the knowledge, which is the quasi-formal term communicated through this expression, and this knowledge is common to all three persons although it is appropriated* to the Word; third, however, from the fact that this knowledge has a relationship to what is knowable, the name "Word" connotes this respect. According to this, then, the second proposition assumed in the argument has to be denied.

8.49 And as for its proof from Augustine [in 8.45], one could say that it would be better to translate *logos* as "Word" rather than "reason," because this name "reason" [*ratio*] implies neither his proper relationship of origin nor his appropriated subsequent relationship to the creature in the same way that "Word" does. Hence Word *qua* Word can be related by the mind to anything and hence can have the appropriated conceptual relationship. Augustine's words "as signifying a relationship to the Father" must be taken to mean what is signified first and principally, whereas his added phrase "but also to those things which have been made" must refer to what is connoted.

8.50 As for the second objection [in 8.46], one could say that what is "necessary of itself" without inconsistency on its part could be had where there is no real being of anything that is not necessary of itself, for there is no contradiction on the part of some prior absolute that it exist without the existence of what is posterior, and still such a necessary being might be unable to exist without the "known being" of the other, because it would have a knowledge of the other necessarily and hence would have to have the other in its "known being," and also in its "possible being" for similar reasons. Therefore nothing real can pertain to a divine person unless it is necessary of itself, in the sense of being uncaused. But whatever is included in the property of a person does pertain to that person as something real. But it is possible that "to know something" or "to have power over something" does pertain to a person, even though neither the thing itself nor its "existence" as a thought object or possible represents a thing that is necessary of itself.

8.51 Another possible answer would be to say that so necessarily does God know and have causal power over the creature that each of these can be said to be formally something "necessary of itself" insofar as they are uncaused, but they are not "necessary" so far as their real existence goes but only in their diminutive being* or "existence" [as objects of knowledge or power]. But whatever is included in the person's property has to be necessary (in this sense of uncaused) so far as its real being goes. Now what is necessary of itself does not require as a necessary concomitant the real being of anything else, though it may require something else's "being known" or its "diminutive being."

8.52 A third possible answer would be to distinguish between (a) what is necessarily required (be it as a prior or as a concomitant condition) for something to have being as something necessary, and (b) what is necessary as something which is a consequence of another's necessary being.

8.53 [Exemplar and final causality] From what has been said about efficient causality, the solution to the question about exemplar* and final causality [in 8.5] should be clear. There is some formal ground by which each of these causes functions in its respective way, even as there is such a ground in the case of the efficient cause. It follows then by analogy that none of these "causalities" can be proper to one person unless the formal ground for causing is also proper. Therefore, there can be no more reason for any person to possess an exclusive ground for functioning as an exemplar or final cause than for doing so as an efficient cause.

8.54 This can be proved by the arguments cited in regard to efficient causality, but the last [in 8.14] seems most clearly applicable as a proof of our thesis. For the formal ground supporting any form of causal dependence in any of the causal categories that we are speaking of here has to be some perfection, and if we are speaking of the first cause in any of these categories, it will have to be a pure perfection.* Therefore, if every pure perfection is the same in all three persons, it follows that all of these categories of causality have to be common to all.

Reply to the Initial Argument

[25] 8.55 As for the argument for the opposite opinion [in 8.1], I say to the minor that any person is an artist to the extent he is creative, and since a divine person is simple, "having" and "what is had" do not differ, so that each person is the art and his art is in equal measure particular and actual, as is clear from the answers to the objections in the first article [8.20-22]. Nevertheless, by appropriation* the Word is called "Wisdom" and "Knowledge" insofar as by reason of the way he proceeds from the memory of the Father, it is particularly appropriate to speak of him as the actual knowledge of that memory and as expressing everything contained therein. This appears clear from Augustine[32]: "Thus the Son is called the wisdom of the Father, just as he is called the 'light' of the Father," and he

[32] Augustine, *De Trin.* VII, c.1, n.2: PL 42, 936; CCSL 50, 249.

immediately explains in what sense this is so: "Just as he is the light of light, and both are one light, so he is understood to be wisdom of wisdom, and both are one wisdom." In like manner I say he is art of art and both are one art.

8.56 The answer to what was said in the minor [of 8.1] about the ideas should be clear from our reply to the first objection [in 8.20-21] of the first article. The ideas are common to all persons, although they are appropriated especially to the Word because of the peculiar way in which he emanates or proceeds as the Father's actual knowledge, namely, as the actual expression of every object contained, as it were, habitually in that paternal memory.

Question Nine

CAN GOD BRING IT ABOUT THAT AN ANGEL INFORM MATTER?

[1]   9.1 The next set of questions concern omnipotence in relation to its object. There are three questions, the first of which is about omnipotence in relation to an immaterial substance and it is this: Can God bring it about that an angel inform matter? The second question [10] has to do with omnipotence's relation to an accidental form to which it gives existence in a supernatural way and it is this: Can God convert the Eucharistic species* into something pre-existing? The third question [11] concerns omnipotence in relation to an accidental form existing in a natural fashion and it is this: Can God bring it about that while both body and place exist, the body has no ubiety* or local presence?

Arguments Pro and Con

9.2 To the first question,[1] the argument for the affirmative is that since God can cause a material form to exist without matter, he can also bring it about that an immaterial form be in matter and hence that an angel exist in matter and function there as its form.

The antecedent is proved in this way: God causes a material accident to exist without its subject in the sacrament of the altar.*

Proof of the entailment: There seems to be no greater inconsistency about an immaterial form's being in matter than a material form's existing without matter.

9.3 On the contrary: If an angel would inform matter, it would impart to it actuality in an unqualified sense, i.e., substantially, or give it incidental actuality. Being something that subsists *per se*, the angel cannot give it actuality in the first way, because it cannot combine with it to form something that is one *per se*. A substantial act,* however, does constitute a *per se* unity with what it informs. It does not give actuality in the second way either, because according to

---

[1] Cf. Duns Scotus, *Ord.* II, d.1, q.5 (ed. Vivès XI, 185-94); IV, d.43, q.2 (ed. Vivès XX, 34-59); II, d.8, q.un. (ed. Vivès XII, 417-22).

QUESTION NINE

Aristotle in the *Physics*[2]: "What truly is, is not incidental to anything." But an angel is what truly is, i.e., substance. Therefore [it is not incidental to anything].

Body of the Question

[2]   9.4   Here there are three points to be investigated: First, the meaning of the question must be explained; second, it must be answered so far as possible; third, some doubts have to be solved.

ARTICLE I
The Meaning of the Question

9.5 We explain the meaning briefly. The question is not whether an angel contains matter as a constitutive part, for in such a case it would not be the angel as a whole, but his form, the non-material part, that would inform matter, just as it is not fire, but its form, its other part, that informs matter. Neither are we asking whether the angel can inform matter in the sense of effectively changing the form something has, if not by his own power perhaps, at least by that of God, who would make the angel become the efficient cause of matter's information, as some[3] claim God makes the body act upon the spirit as an efficient cause. The question is rather about formal information, namely whether God could make the angel become an informing form.

ARTICLE II
Answer to the Question

[3]   9.6   [The answer is negative] As for the second point, a negative conclusion must be held. Two reasons can be given for this, the first of which is based on a middle term that would hold commonly for other situations as well, the second uses a middle term more proper to the angel. Finally we shall study some additional arguments to see if they are conclusive.

9.7 [First reason] The first argument is this: What is simply subsistent *per se* cannot be the form of matter. The angel is this sort of being. Therefore [the angel cannot be the form of matter].

Clarification of the major: A *per se* being can mean three things.

---

[2] Aristotle, *Physic.* I, c.3 (186b4-5).

[3] Thomas, *Summa theol.* I, q.51, a.2, ad 2-3 (I, 259); Richard of Middleton, *Sent.* II, d.19, a.1, q.1 in corp. (Brixial, 1591), II, 242-43.

First, it can designate something which exists in isolation or apart from a subject, in the third mode of *per se* referred to in the *Posterior Analytics*.[4] In this sense, an accident can be a *per se* being when it does not inhere in a subject. Second, a *per se* being is contrasted with one that exists in another, and in this sense it is a thing which neither actually inheres in another nor has an aptitude to do so. Every substance, not only one that is composite, but matter and form as well, are all beings *per se* in this sense, for though a substantial form is in the matter it informs, it does not inhere in it like an accident, for "to inhere" says that it does not inform its subject *per se*. What inheres is neither an act simply, but only in a qualified sense, nor does it form one thing *per se* with the subject in which it inheres. What informs *per se* has the opposite characteristics. Third, a *per se* being may refer to one which has its ultimate actuality, so that it is simply unable to be ordered *per se* to some ulterior act beyond that which it has, where the ulterior actualization would belong to it *per se*, either in a primary or in a participated sense.[5] A *per se* being in this sense is called a suppositum,* and if it is of an intellectual nature, it is called a person. Only this third is properly said to be subsisting, in the sense the Philosopher[6] has in mind when he says: "Matter is only potentially 'a this' and the form is that in virtue of which a thing is called 'a this,' but that third being compounded of both matter and form is simply 'a this.'" In other words, something subsisting *per se* has its ultimate actualization so that it is unable to be ordered *per se* to some ulterior act.

[4] 9.8 With this understanding we prove the major. A substantial form is ordered *per se* to the being of the whole composite. This being, however, is simply the act of the composite primarily and that of the form participatively, because a part is only said "to be" incidentally (i.e., *per se* participatively), whereas the whole is said "to be" primarily. Therefore, what subsists and is unable to be ordered *per se* to some being cannot be a form *per se*.

9.9 Proof of the minor: An angel is specifically perfect, indeed it is even more perfect than some species of material substances are. For the hierarchical order of substance is like that of numbers ac-

---

[4] Aristotle, *Anal. post.* I (73b5-9).

[5] The accidents receive their ultimate actualization or suppositality through the substance; "primary sense" refers to substance; "participated sense" refers to accidents.

[6] Aristotle, *De anima* II, c.1 (412a6-10).

cording to the *Metaphysics*.⁷ But some material substance is in ultimate act in such a way that it is unable to be ordered *per se* to some ulterior act; otherwise there would be an infinite regress in material substances such that each could be part of another. Therefore, all the more is an angel subsisting *per se* in the aforesaid sense.

9.10 This argument uses a common middle term, viz., "*per se* subsisting," which would apply just as well to fire as it would to an angel; indeed it would suffice to prove our thesis of anything which is complete in any species of substance.

9.11 Hence it is also clear that "unable to be united" does not represent any difference that would distinguish an angel from a soul, because it is common to the angel and to fire.

9.12 Hence it is obvious also why a soul apart from a body is not a person, since it cannot be a *per se* being in the third sense, even though it is not apt by nature to inhere (and hence is *per se* in the second sense) and could also be one in the first sense, that is, it could exist alone not merely in virtue of some extrinsic cause in the way an accident or material form could, but by reason of the nature it has and because it does not necessarily depend upon matter for its own existence. Only a *per se* being in this third sense is called a suppositum, and where it is found in an intellectual nature, it is called a person. Thus a person is incommunicable, because it is repugnant to him that he be communicated not only as a universal is communicated to its singulars but also as a form is communicable to the matter to be actualized through it.

[5] 9.13 [Second argument] A second reason for our conclusion [in 9.6] is this: Whatever can be a substantial form has the immediate ability through its essence to give actuality in an unqualified sense to matter itself, for it is clear from the *Metaphysics*⁸ that the only reason form can combine with matter in a *per se* unity is that form is *per se* act and matter *per se* potency, and no further reason can be given for either except that this has this nature and that has that. If it is impossible then for anything to be the act of matter, this stems precisely from its proper nature.

Proof of this implication: The impossibility of being the act of matter indicates a greater measure of perfection than does the corresponding possibility. Therefore, if its ability to inform matter stems from the proper nature of the form, all the more so will the

---

⁷ Aristotle, *Metaph.* VIII, c.3 (1043b33-1044a).
⁸ Ibid., c.6 (1045a23-30).

impossibility to inform matter stem from the proper formal nature of the substance. Therefore, if one knew the essential definition of an angel, he could show by a demonstration of the reasoned fact* just why it is impossible for an angel to inform matter.

9.14 While this reasoning proves that if the conclusion were known, the middle term establishing it would be proper to the angel, it still does not show that the conclusion is true, so that anyone who denied it would claim it is not impossible for an angel to inform matter, and there is nothing proper to an angel that rules out such a possibility.

Hence we need this further confirmation. Rooted in the proper nature of anything that is simply act is either an aptitude to inform *per se* or a repugnance to do so. But the essence of the angel contains no basis for the first, therefore it has the second, and then it follows further, as was argued [in 9.13], that the proper grounds for the repugnance is the essence itself.

Proof of the minor: An unactualized aptitude implies imperfection.

[6]   9.15 [Third argument] A third argument that might be brought up is this.

The order of perfection among forms seems to depend on how far removed they are from matter, just as a more perfect act is further removed from potency.[9] But so far is the intellectual soul removed from matter that left to its own nature, it can exist on its own without matter. An angel, therefore, who is more perfect than any intellectual soul, should be still more remote from matter, yet if it were not impossible for it to be in matter, it is hard to see how it could be further removed from matter.

9.16 This argument, it seems, does not prove much, for there are many ways other than this remoteness from matter in which one act could excel another. Furthermore, while the intellectual soul could exist without matter, on the other hand it can be just as perfectly united to matter as an inferior form can. By the same token, then, one could claim that while an angel can certainly exist without matter in an even more perfect way than an intellectual soul, it could still exist in matter, for even though to depend on matter represents an imperfection, it is not clear that an angel's ability to communicate this actuality to matter represents an imperfection, especially

[9] Aristotle, *De anima* II, c.1 (412a-413a10); *De generat.* II, c.1 (731b24-732a10).

when such communication could take place without his being dependent, as would be the case here.

[7]   9.17 [Fourth reason] Some,[10] it seems, would derive a fourth argument from the characteristic way an angel functions, viz., by understanding.

"To understand," after all, is a spiritual or immaterial function. Therefore the intellect is an immaterial potency, and hence the intellectual nature is also an immaterial or spiritual nature.

9.18 Proof of the first entailment: An operation is no more abstracted from matter than is the potency on which it depends, for the operation is in the agent by reason of some faculty of its own that is the proximate ground for the action in question. Consequently, if the faculty is material, its operation will not be immaterial.

9.19 Proof of the second entailment: A potency is no more excellent than the substance which has it, and this seems to be true chiefly of a nature that is purely intellectual, like that of an angel, whereas it is not so obvious for a nature like our soul, which is intellectual in a lesser degree and has sense powers as well. For our soul depends on matter for some of its operations at least, whereas a purely intellectual nature would depend on matter in no way, either for its operation or, consequently, for its being.

9.20 Further confirmation that the first antecedent entails the final consequent [in 9.17], can be found, it seems, in the commentary to the penultimate proposition of the *Liber de Causis*[11]: "It is impossible that there be anything whose substance is temporal, but whose action is eternal, for in that case, its action would be better than its substance."

9.21 The first antecedent [in 9.17] is proved from the object, for every act gets its specification and perfection from its object. But the object of intellect *qua* intellect abstracts from matter, because the forms in matter are all individual but the intellect does not grasp them as individual.

[8]   9.22 One might object that the argument [of 9.18 and 9.19] would allow one to infer that the rational soul is immaterial because of its intellective powers and operations, yet it would be wrong to conclude that it is immaterial, i.e., it is not the perfection of matter,

---

[10] Thomas, *Summa theol.* I, q.50, a.2 in corp. (I, 253); q.89, a.1 in corp. (I, 253); q.89, a.1 in corp. (I, 436).

[11] *Liber de causis* prop. 32 (ed. C. Pera, O.P., *S. Thomae Aquinatis in Librum de causis expositio*, Taurini-Romae, 1955), 146.

though, according to some,[12] it is true that it is not material, i.e., it is not composed of matter and form.

9.23 They would answer that intellective power is indeed immaterial and the soul is also immaterial in this way, since it is not immersed in matter or totally taken over by matter. The explanation lies in the fact that the more noble the form, the more it dominates corporeal matter and the less it is joined to it and the more it excels it in strength. So far as nobility of form is concerned, however, our soul is highest in the hierarchy of forms. Therefore, it excels matter insofar as it possesses some power and some operations that in no way depend on corporeal matter, and this power is called intellect.

9.24 To this it is objected that man is not man just as soul; he is man only insofar as the soul informs matter. Therefore the soul does not act with an operation peculiar to man save insofar as it informs matter. Consequently, either man does not understand insofar as the soul is the form or principle of this operation or else he understands insofar as the soul informs matter.

Proof of the first proposition: A composite only is what it is in virtue of its parts and not insofar as these are separated but *qua* united, as is clear from the example in the *Metaphysics*[13] that the syllable *ba* is not the same as *b* and *a*, and this is in general true of whole and parts. Not only does it hold for the material parts, which the Philosopher calls elements, but also of the essential parts, which are matter and form, for the composite is one precisely because the first is matter and the second act, as the *Metaphysics*[14] puts it, that is to say, it is one because the potential part is informed and the act is informing it.

[9] 9.25 A second objection [to 9.23] is that the soul informs matter according to its highest degree of essential perfection; but "to understand" cannot pertain to the soul according to some degree higher than its highest; therefore, it cannot pertain to it insofar as it exceeds matter, where "exceeds" means it does not inform it. The first proposition is clear, for otherwise man would not be the highest corporeal being, nor, as a consequence, would he be next to the angel in the order of species, for he would not be formally actual-

---

[12] Thomas, *Summa theol.* I, q.75, aa.2 and 6 in corp. (1, 353 and 355); q.50, a.2 in corp. (1, 253).

[13] Aristotle, *Metaph.* VII, c.17 (1041b12-14).

[14] Ibid., VIII, c.6 (1045b17-21); ibid., VII, c.8 (1033b16-20); ibid., VII, c.11 (1036b21-24); ibid., VIII, c.6 (1045a23-25).

QUESTION NINE

ized through what is highest in the intellective soul, which is the form that is next to the angel.

9.26 [An evaluation of the fourth reason] As for this fourth argument, we must first examine the antecedent, namely, that "to understand" is an immaterial function. This can be understood in three ways.[15]

[First way] "Immaterial" in this first sense would contrast it with the sense functions which are called "organic" because they are exercised through a specific organ and are thus material, requiring as they do that a distinct part of the body be structured in a specific way. Intellection, on the contrary, is a nonorganic function, for it is not exercised through some definite bodily part and, in this sense, is the act of no single part of the body, meaning by this that the intellect, unlike the sense powers, does not exercise its operation properly speaking by any specific bodily part.

[10] But from this meaning of the antecedent, it is hard to see how the immateriality of the form is inferred, for even a purely material form like fire is not said to act through an organ, provided it be uniformly in the whole and in each part thereof. The Commentator, in explaining Bk. VII of the *Metaphysics*[16] about the powers present in the seed, says: "These powers are similar to the intellect in that they do not act through an organ." And he adds a little further on: "The powers which are in the bodies of animals act through specific instruments and have a part of the body as their own." But the power that forms and informs the body does not act through a specific member, and the reason is that only that form is called the principle of organic life which is somehow unlimited in its operation so that it can be the principle of different actions which can be exercised only by means of dissimilar parts. That is why whatever is perfectible through such a form must have unlike parts by means of which these organic functions can be exercised, and such a form is only a soul, which because of its superiority in perfection to inferior forms can be the principle of several operations which pertain to it as a whole. Hence it needs, as its adequate perfectible component, a body with a greater diversity of parts corresponding to its own greater potentialities as a principle.[17]

---

[15] Cf. Duns Scotus, *Ord.* IV, d.43, q.2, n.9 (ed. Vivès XX, 39-40).
[16] Averroes, *Metaph.* VII, com. 31 (VIII, fol. 181E).
[17] There is an addition in all three MSS.:

Furthermore, by understanding the antecedent in this sense, one could argue, it seems, that intellection is just as material a function as vision

[11] 9.27 [Second way] Another way in which the antecedent could be interpreted would be to say that "to understand" is immaterial terminatively, i.e., it tends towards an object abstracted from matter. This seems to be the sense in which the antecedent was proved [in 9.21] from the immateriality of its object. But this proof does not establish immateriality in an unqualified sense, not even terminatively. For all admit that the quiddity of a material thing can be the *per se* object of our intellect. But if all that is required is to have immateriality in the object, i.e., abstraction from individual matter, then the operation of our intellect is immaterial terminatively, because it is indifferent to singular material objects. But to get the conclusion we want, one would have to show that this operation which has the universal as its object could not be communicated to matter in some way.

9.28 [Third way] A third interpretation of the antecedent would be this. What is proximately and properly the recipient subject of intellection is the form and not something material, and what is more, it is not the form of the whole (which is the quiddity like humanity) but that which is simple and is the other part of the composite.[18]

---

is. For vision can be exercised by a given part of the body, whereas intellection is primarily an operation of the whole rather than that of a specific part, since it is not the hand, but man who understands.

But suppose the soul could be the principle of understanding or intellection, not insofar as it perfects the whole, but the parts, then it could be such a principle as perfecting any part whatsoever—just as it is the principle of intellection as it perfects the whole—and then one could say that the finger understands as man does, for the finger would be actualized by the form as a principle of intellection. Consequently, if the whole is just as material as any of its parts, or more so, then it follows that this function which only pertains to the form insofar as it is in the whole, is just as material as is a function that pertains to the form insofar as it is in a part.

Now I reply to this: If the operation which pertains to a form insofar as it is somehow an unlimited perfection is communicated to matter or the whole, it is communicated to the whole as actualized by a form unlimited in this way. Now what is actualized by an intellectual soul, which has understanding insofar as it is this sort of unlimited form, is not just a part, but the whole.

[18] Namely, the soul. This distinction between the "form of the whole" and "form of the part" is explained by Giles of Rome (who popularized, though he did not create, the distinction) as follows:

QUESTION NINE

The proximate recipient of any sensitive operation, however, is primarily composed of matter and form, as is clear from the opening passages of *De sensu et sensato*,[19] for what is the subject of vision is not the soul itself, but the organ composed of soul and a definite part of the body. It is not the soul, nor any part thereof, nor the form of the chemical compounds that are in a definite part of the body, but it is the form of the organ as a whole which is the proximate ground for receiving the vision, like humanity is the form of man as a whole.

9.29 Hence it appears clear that if we call an "organ" that part of the whole animal which is the proximate subject of sensation, we must say it is composed of the soul as the principle of the operation and of a part of the body structured in a certain way, and then it will be clear why a blind eye is an "eye" only in a qualified sense, for it is only one part of that composite which is meant to be called an eye and is missing the other part needed for a complete eye.

It will also be clear in the light of this that if a power is what is called the proximate ground for receiving an act, the visual power will not be the soul alone, but will either be the form of the organ as a whole or something that results therefrom.

It is also obvious why the soul separated from the body cannot feel anything, for it lacks the proper subject for sensation which is an organ and the formal ground for receiving the sensation which

---

The essence in relation to the suppositum* has the character of form, hence the whole essence and the whole nature which results from matter and form can be called the form of the whole, i.e., the form which is the whole. It is well said, then, that humanity is the form of man and that man has being or existence [*esse*] through humanity. Now humanity does not mean the form alone (or the soul) nor the matter alone (or the body), but rather the nature composed of and resulting from these two, viz., matter and form (or a rational soul and a body). Hence if man has both a soul and humanity, each of which has the character of form, though in a different way, because soul means a part and is the form of the part whereas humanity means the whole and is the form of the whole, then it is well said that in man there is both a form of the part and a form of the whole. And what is said of man is true of every material thing, because each happens to receive of twofold form, that of the part and that of the whole.

Aegidii Romani Theoremata de esse et essentia, ed. E. Hocédez (Louvain, 1930), 44-45.

[19] Aristotle, *De sensu et sensato*, c.1 (436a11-12, 436b1-10).

is the whole form of the organ. In the case of understanding, however, we have just the opposite, for its proximate subject and formal ground for its reception is the soul or some portion of the soul which has no matter. That is why the soul apart from the body can still understand, because the proximate recipient of intellection remains.

[12] 9.30 According to this third interpretation of the antecedent (which comes closest to the truth), understanding is an immaterial operation because it has as its immediate subject something which has no corporeal matter at least and hence it is possible to have this sort of function without such matter. Now what can function without matter can also exist without matter. Therefore, that nature whose proper function is understanding can also exist without matter.

With the aid of this middle term, viz., an immaterial operation, it is possible to infer that the nature possessing it has this sort of immateriality, namely, that it can be separated from matter, but it does not justify the further inference that the immateriality is of such a type that it is impossible for this nature to inform matter. And it seems reasonable that if you use as a middle term the sort of intellection that is common to the soul and an angel, you can infer the sort of immateriality they have in common.

ARTICLE III
Some Objections and their Solutions

[13] 9.31 [Objections to the first reason in 9.7ff.] In the third main article, we consider some objections raised against our first argument.

[First objection] According to the *Metaphysics*[20]: "Being pertains more to the form than to the composite." Therefore, form is not ordered to the being of the whole as to something more perfect.

9.32 [Second objection] Another objection has to do specifically with the soul, since this seems to be something *per se* subsistent, for it functions *per se*. Any function which is an operation of the composite *per se* does not pertain to the form alone. But to understand does pertain to the soul when separated from the body.

9.33 [Third objection] The being of the soul is the composite's being. Therefore, the being of the soul is not ordered to the being of the composite.

Proof of the antecedent: The human soul retains its being when

[20] Aristotle, *Metaph*. VII, c.3 (1029a6-7).

QUESTION NINE

man as a whole is destroyed, which is not the case with other forms. This is only because the being of the whole man is the being of the soul, which is not so with the other forms.

9.34 [Fourth objection] This drop of water can be part of a larger body of water and thus can be ordered to something more perfect in which it participates. Hence this drop of water is not now something which subsists *per se*.

9.35 [Fifth objection] If it is impossible for an angel to inform matter there must be just one reason why this is so, for when one thing is inconsistent with another there is always one reason why this is so. Hence there are not two reasons for this inability of the angel to inform matter, one common, as the first argument [in 9.7] assumes, and the other proper, as the second argument [in 9.13] claims.

9.36 [Sixth objection] According to the philosophers,[21] the heavens seem animated, yet we cannot assume they have an intelligent soul, because something intelligent that is less than an angel can only perfect a body by reason of the vegetative and sensitive perfection it possesses, or if these be distinct principles, they would have to be perfecting the body at the same time.

9.37 [Seventh objection] There are times when an angel takes on a body and performs vital functions in it. Therefore, since "to act" presupposes "to be," the angel must give the body living being, and therefore must inform it.

[14] 9.38 [Answer to the objections]

[To the first in 9.31] To the first of these objections, I say that "more" like "prior" refers here not to perfection but to superiority and independence, because the being of a superior principle is independent of what proceeds from that principle or what is inferior to it.

9.39 [To the second in 9.32] As for the second objection, although the basis for the conclusion seems to be the intellective soul's subsistence, the soul is not subsistent, it seems, in the third sense mentioned [in 9.7]. Furthermore, when joined to the body, it is not subsistent [in the first way] either, like the accidents [or appearances of bread or wine] in the sacrament of the altar, for then the soul would not inform the body [any more than accidents of bread inform the body of Christ], since what is *per se* in this sense is not informing anything. Consequently, if the soul were a *per se* being like

---

[21] Aristotle, *De caelo* II, c.2 (285a28-286a2); *Metaph.* XII, c.5 (1071a1-4); Avicenna, *Metaph.* IX, cc.2-4 (II, 103r-105r).

them when joined to the body, [so far as intellection goes] it would have the same mode of being whether it was informing or not informing [the body as a vegetative or animated form].

9.40 As for the reason given there [in 9.32], we could argue that intellection as an immanent operation of the agent could be said to belong *per se* to something in two ways. Either that something is a proximate subject or it is a remote subject. For example, a surface is called white in the first way, but not in the second way, whereas we can say man is white in this second fashion. Now the soul is said to understand *per se* insofar as it is the proximate recipient of intellection, but when it is united, the soul is not just a recipient in this first way, since it is then also the reason why understanding pertains to man as a whole in virtue of his form. But man is only said to understand *per se* as a remote subject, for he is the recipient of intellection only because the soul, his form, receives it proximately. Therefore, when it is assumed in the major that what acts *per se*, subsists *per se*, this is true only of a first agent, i.e., one which so acts that it is not that in virtue of which some further subject acts by that operation. Now if something were not subsistent, but was a form functioning as such, then it could not be in operation without being in addition the reason why the whole is said to operate in this way. But in this sense, the minor is false, viz., that the soul understands *per se*, since this is not true except insofar as the operation pertains to a form as its immediate recipient.

[15] 9.41 From this it becomes clear in what sense intellection is immaterial, namely it is not that intellection does not pertain to the soul as informing matter, but because it pertains to the soul alone as immediate recipient, whereas the whole composite is the remote subject of intellection but is so in virtue of its form.

9.42 [To the third in 9.33] To the next objection, I say that what has absolutely the same being as another would not be simply imperfect, it seems, if it were not communicating that being to another. If it is true then that the being of the soul is the same as the composite's being, then why should the soul's mode of being when separated from the body be imperfect since it is deprived of nothing except that it is not communicating its being to another? And why would the soul be imperfect in being whereas the whole is perfect in being, if they both have the same being? Or how does being of the whole remain, if the whole itself does not?

9.43 I claim therefore that the being of the soul remains the same

QUESTION NINE

as long as the soul is a thing with that being, and this is true whether it is joined to or separated from the body. Analogously, the being of the whole only remains the same as long as the whole continues to exist with that being, for the actual being of nothing remains the same unless the subject which has that being continues to exist. It seems, therefore, that we must deny that the being of the soul is the composite's being, since the soul with the being it has seems to be only a part of the whole with its being. Analogously, then, the being of one is but a part of the being of the other.

[16]   9.44 And the proof adduced for the antecedent, namely, that unlike other forms, the soul retains its being when the whole is destroyed, does not prove what it was set up to do, but rather its very opposite. The reason the soul retains its being is that that being is completely incorruptible both *per se* and *per accidens*. Now if its being were the same as that of the composite, then it would be corruptible, it seems, since the composite truly perishes. For just as what comes to be appears to have as its term the being of what is generated, so the being of what perishes seems to be the *terminus a quo** of the corruption and, hence, the term which does not remain. Other immaterial forms, however, do not retain their being once the whole perishes, but not because their being is not distinct from that of the composite which perished, but rather because they are corrupted *per accidens*. This happens either because the corrupting agent, in producing a form contrary to them, affects them incidentally as contraries, or at least this agent affects the composite causing it to perish, and these other forms are unable to exist apart from the composite. Neither of these situations however is true of the intellective soul.

9.45 Those who raise the objection [in 9.33][22] claim the intellective soul is incorruptible, because being *per se* belongs to a form that is act and whatever pertains *per se* to anything is inseparable from it. Therefore just as it is impossible to separate the form from itself, so it is impossible that a subsistent form should cease to be. Now I claim that if this be the reason why the intellective soul is incorruptible, then it is not so because its being and that of whole are identical, for its being, though inseparable from it, is separable from the whole.

---

[22] Those who reason according to the third objection; cf. *supra*, 9.33; Thomas, *Summa theol.* 1, q:75, a.6 in corp. (I, 355); q.50, a.5 in corp. (I, 257).

[17]   9.46 [An answer to both the second and third objections] To understand more clearly the answers to the arguments [in 9.32 and 9.33], we can distinguish two senses of "being" [*esse*]. "Being" can mean that by which anything first departs formally from nonbeing. Now anything departs primarily from nonbeing by whatever makes it something extramental and something more than a mere possibility in its cause. In this sense anything that lies outside the intellect and its cause is properly being. In another sense, "being" means the ultimate act, viz., that to which nothing further is added giving being in an unqualified sense, and that is said to have being simply to which being in this sense primarily pertains. And I say "primarily" to exclude the idea that it is [a form] which gives to something else grounds for being by such being. And in this sense only the composite specifically complete is called being, a part of the composite on the other hand is called being only incidentally [*per accidens*] or, more properly, participatively [*participative*], sharing as it does in the being of the whole. Taking being [*esse*] in this second sense, only the composite is a *per se* being [*ens*]; the intellective soul, however, is not called subsistent except improperly and in a qualified sense, although it is called a being [*ens*] and one that is *per se*, taking being [*esse*] in its first meaning. And this would be the answer to the first argument [in 9.32].

9.47 The same distinction would solve the second [viz., that in 9.33], for in the first meaning of "being," that of the form and of the composite is not entirely identical, whereas it is identical in the second sense of "being," but then it is not the being of both the soul and the composite in the same fashion, for it is primarily of the composite and participatively of the part.

[18]   9.48 From this it is also clear in what sense the separated soul is said to be imperfect in being, since to the extent it is united, it can be called perfect in being, not indeed essentially or primarily, but participatively, for in its own being it is equally perfect whether separated or united, but when it is united it is perfected participatively, though not primarily, by the being of the whole, whereas in separation it is imperfect insofar as it lacks this being of the whole. And one could call this imperfection simply imperfection because it lacks that being which is simply perfection, though this be not proper to itself alone. Indeed this perfection is an even greater one than is the soul's own perfection, because it includes that of the soul. Consequently, the soul is not called an imperfect form solely be-

cause it does not communicate its perfection to another, even as it is not perfected by its communicating, but it is called imperfect in its lack of the perfection of the whole being, which lack is something concomitant, i.e., associated with the fact that it does not communicate its being to the composite.

9.49[23] [To the fourth in 9.34] As for the fourth objection, something [like a drop of water] can become an integral part of a homogeneous whole. And while it participates in the being of the whole when it is in the whole and does not do so when it is outside the whole, it is not called imperfect when it is separated from the whole, for the being it has [e.g., as water] is equally perfect as that being of the whole with which it fuses. Hence it is not properly said to be able to be ordered to the being of the whole, in the way that an essential part is apt by nature to be ordered to the being of the composite that is meant to have it by nature; neither can such an essential part be the same sort of thing as the composite.

9.50 [To the fifth in 9.35] To the next objection, I say that there can be several independent reasons in the same subject why something is repugnant to it. And in this case any one of them can be formal grounds why the subject as a whole cannot contain the thing in question. For example, it is repugnant for man to be whiteness by reason of his substance, even prescinding from everything else; it is also impossible for him to be whiteness, because he is rational. Consequently, we have to deny the principle that when one thing is inconsistent with another, there can only be one reason for this inconsistency. And if one goes on to add, "there can only be one unique reason that is first," one can still make a distinction inasmuch as the ground of the impossibility [insofar as this is a positive entity] will be congruous with only one of the extremes (that which has this reason as something positive) whereas it will be repugnant to the other.[24] Therefore, either (1) the primary refers to this congruence, and then the primary reason for the impossibility will be that which is primarily congruous with one and repugnant to the

---

[23] There is a slight discrepancy in the MSS., none of which follows the Wadding-Vivès text, regarding the order of paragraphs 49-53 inclusive. However, there is no substantial difference of sense. We have altered the sequence of Wadding to a minimal degree consistent with the continuity of meaning.

[24] For example, to be quantity is repugnant to man because he is a substance. The positive reason for the repugnance or the substantiality pertains to man and is repugnant to quantity.

other, or (2) the primacy refers to the incongruity, and then the first reason for the impossibility will be whatever is diametrically opposed to the "reason" in sense (1) and pertains to the second extreme.

With both (1) and (2) one can further distinguish between (a) a primacy of community [i.e., of the several said to have this "reason" one has it primarily] and (b) a primacy of perfection [i.e., one is primary because it has more independent grounds for the impossibility].

9.51 "To be quantity" is first repugnant to substance before it is to animal, if we are speaking of a primacy of community, whereas the opposite is true of a primacy of perfection, for an animal includes more reasons for the impossibility than substance does.

[20] [9.52 Similarly so far as primacy of community is concerned, "to be a substance" pertains to man before "to be rational" does, whereas the reverse is true of the primacy of perfection.][25]

However, if we stay within any one meaning of primacy, it is true that for any two things that are inconsistent or mutually repugnant, there is but one unique reason that is primary. From this it follows that the two arguments we gave [in 9.7 and 9.13] do not each cite a primary reason for the inconsistency, in the same sense of primary, which I readily grant.

9.53 But if you object: The same [positive predicate] pertains to the same [subject] only in virtue of the same reason; therefore, the same holds good for inconsistency or mutual repugnance, I reply that the two cases are not on a par. The same predicate, at least one that is nonessential, does not pertain to several things commonly, unless they all have the same common ground for it. On the other hand, a predicate can be repugnant to several things without all of them having the same common ground for it. For example: "to be an angel" is repugnant both to man and to whiteness. And though both man and whiteness may be, perhaps, "a being" or *ens* in a common univocal sense, this is not the reason for the impossibility, since it pertains to the angel as well. A clearer example is this. It is impossible that a stone, whiteness, or a chimaera be God, but it is obvious it is not because they have something in common.[26]

[25] This paragraph, found in M_1 and W but omitted in M_2, seems to fit in best here; cf. note 23.

[26] The answers to the last two objections are missing; cf. *supra*, 9.36-37. See Appendix, Addition 9.53.

QUESTION NINE

Reply to the Initial Argument

[21] 9.54 As for the argument [in 9.2], I deny the consequent follows from the antecedent on this ground. The reason something is unable to be present in a certain subject may represent a prior aspect of that subject, namely, wherever it would be posterior by nature to that subject, if it could be there. Thus man is incapable of braying and the reason for this is to be found in that which makes man formally a man. Nevertheless, if he has that ability [as a donkey does], it would be posterior to man in the sense that any attribute is posterior to [or presupposes] its subject. There is a priority, then, about the simply necessary cause of the incompatibility (namely, that it would be contradictory for the subject to have this predicate), whereas the reason why some posterior predicate is suited to the subject is not so necessary, namely, that it would be contradictory for the subject not to have what is suited to it, for it is not a contradiction for some prior absolute to be separated from something posterior.

9.55 Applying this to our case, we can say that for matter to be separated from form requires only that form is not an absolutely necessary reason why form be united to matter, and such is actually the case, since form is an absolute entity, and hence prior in nature to its union with matter. But that some immaterial form like the angel be capable of union with matter would imply a combination of different elements, one of which—as was shown in the solution to the question—is the ground for the impossibility of such a union.

Question Ten

CAN GOD CONVERT THE EUCHARISTIC SPECIES INTO SOMETHING PREVIOUSLY EXISTING?

Arguments Pro and Con

[1]   10.1 As regards the second question [in 9.1], namely: Can God convert the Eucharistic species* into something previously existing,[1] it is argued he cannot:

Nothing can be converted into something else unless the two have something in common. These species, however, have nothing in common with what already exists. Therefore [they cannot be converted into something already existing].

Proof of the major: If nothing common would remain, then the species would be annihilated and not transformed.

Proof of the minor: These species do not inhere in a substance nor do they modify matter, which serves as the primary subject in such things as are transformed into one another.

10.2 To the contrary:

If nature can convert these species into something which did not exist before, then God can convert them into something which did exist before.

The antecedent is clear: In the act of nutrition these species are transformed into the substance of the one who benefits from their nourishment, so that by virtue of natural causes they become flesh which did not previously exist. If it is claimed that the flesh did exist before, all the better for our thesis. Similarly, fire could produce fire from them and by the powers of the heavens some form of animal life could be produced from their putrefaction.[2]

Proof of the implication: It seems that the divine power could convert these species more readily into something previously existing than nature's powers could turn them into something which did

---

[1] Cf. Duns Scotus, *Ord.* IV, d.10, q.1 (ed. Vivès XVII, 152-86); d. 11, qq. 1-5 (ibid., 314-471); d.12 (ibid., 518-652).

[2] See Glossary: "*Sun.*"

QUESTION TEN

not exist before, for the divine power infinitely excels that of nature and whether the term preexists or not, will not alter infinitely its nature.

Body of the Question

[2] 10.3 The question is not a general inquiry as to whether one thing can be completely converted into another, but it concerns specifically such terms as are involved here, since they raise a special difficulty of their own. For the solution of the question, then, we must first see whether these terms under investigation possess some special characteristic that would make their complete conversion impossible, and here we shall look first to the *terminus a quo*,* or separated quantity, and second to the *terminus ad quem*,* which refers to what is already existing. A third point will take up the question of the kind of conversion involved, for instance, whether it entails an annihilation.

ARTICLE I
The *terminus a quo* or the Separated Quantity

[3] 10.4 [Proof there is no impossibility on the part of the quantity] As for the first point, I say there is no special reason why it should be impossible for separated quantity* to be converted into something any more than it would be for some other created thing, where complete conversion is assumed to be possible. For the present this brief proof can be given:

An agent whose active power completely dominates both terms alike as to their being or not being, as well as controls whatever is a necessary concomitant of their being, can convert one completely into the other. But any two creatures are equally in God's power in this way. Therefore [he can convert one completely into the other].[3]

10.5 First, we explain the major as follows: "Whole" is sometimes taken categorematically and then it designates the same as that which has all its parts. At other times it is taken syncategorematically[4] and signifies the same as any one of its parts. When a sub-

---

[3] Cf. Duns Scotus, *Ord.* IV, d.11, q.1, n.4 (ed. Vivès XVII, 321); q.2, n.3 (ibid., 388).

[4] What Scotus understands by "categorematic" and "syncategorematic" is clear enough from the context, though it is being used in one of its less familiar senses. Categorematic terms are usually defined as terms which signify something *per se*, whereas syncategorematic terms only signify some-

237

stance is generated, according to the Philosopher,[5] one whole is changed into another whole. Here "whole" is understood in the first sense and it means that both what perished and what came to be were one *per se* and hence each was truly a whole. However, when something comes to be only in a qualified sense as is the case where the form is altered or the quantity augmented, what is generated, according to the Philosopher,[6] is not something that is one *per se*: "The quality does not come to be, but wood of that quality, and the quantity does not come to be, but the wood of that size." And therefore in the case we are discussing what comes to be is not something that is truly one.

In our thesis, then, "complete conversion," or the change of one whole into another, refers to a "whole" taken syncategorematically, namely when one composite is converted into another, as occurs when matter is transmuted into matter and form into form.

10.6 Understood in this way, the major is proved as follows: An agent that has one part of both terms equally under his active power can change one by a partial conversion into the other. Just as a generator that has in his active power the form of what perishes and the form of what comes to be can convert the former into the latter by a partial transformation affecting the form, so also that agent who has equally in his power the form of what is corrupted and the form of what is generated can equally convert the one into the other by corrupting or generating. By the same token, then, that agent who has in his active power alike both the matter and form of this and the matter and form of that, and whose power dominates whatever these two have and whatever is a necessary concomitant of their being, can transmute this term into that term by a complete conversion affecting the matter and form of both. Such an agent, however, is God.

10.7 A second proof is this: One thing can be turned into another in the same fashion that it is possible for the second to succeed the first temporally. Now by divine power, however, any created being in its totality or any part thereof can succeed any other created be-

---

thing as a modification or determination of something else. For a classical interpretation of all that this implies see, for example, *Peter of Spain: Tractatus Syncategorematum and Selected Anonymous Treatises*, trans. J. P. Mullally (Milwaukee, 1964), pp. 17ff.

[5] Aristotle, *De generat.* I, c.4 (319b6-320a).
[6] Aristotle, *Metaph.* VII, c.9 (1034b11-15).

ing. Therefore, [by divine power any created being can be turned completely into another].[7]

[4] 10.8 To this argument, however, objections are raised.

[First objection] The first is that if the argument were valid, God could as easily change a bodily substance into an incorporeal one or convert one spiritual substance into another as he can turn one corporeal substance into another. The implication is clear, for the divine power dominates the terms equally in either case. But the consequent is false.

10.9 Proof of this is Augustine,[8] who says: "There were not lacking those who claimed that any body can be changed into any other, but I do not know of any who thought that a body could be turned into a soul and become a spiritual nature, nor does faith require us to believe this." And in the same book,[9] he repeats this even more explicitly: "It is credible that any body can be changed into any other body, but that a body could be turned into a soul is absurd."

10.10 Besides, Boethius,[10] in his work *On Two Natures and One Person in Christ*, in the section where he argues against Eutyches, declares: "A corporeal substance cannot be changed into an incorporeal one, nor can one incorporeal substance be transformed into another, for only those things that have a common subject matter can be changed into one another."

10.11 [Second objection] A second objection to our argument [in 10.4] is this. Since it is not only substance but every created thing alike that falls equally under the divine power, it would follow that if God could completely convert one created thing into another, then he could do this with any created thing whatsoever, and then many absurdities would follow, for instance, that a substance could be turned into an accident, i.e., into something which exists only in another, and vice versa, or something absolute could become something relative and thus have two terms, and conversely the relative could be made into an absolute.

10.12 [Third objection] A third objection to our argument is that if an agent controls both terms completely by his active power, this only implies that he can destroy one and create the other. But to

---

[7] Cf. Duns Scotus, *Ord.* IV, d.11, q.2, nn.7-8 (ed. Vivès XVII, 340-41); q.13, nn.17ff. (ibid., 377ff.).

[8] Augustine, *Super Gen.* VII, c.12, n.19: PL 34, 362.

[9] Ibid., c.20, n.26: PL 34, 365.

[10] Boethius, *De persona et duabus naturis*, c.6: PL 64, 1349; *The Theological Tractates . . .*, p. 108.

GOD AND CREATURES

create one thing and to annihilate another is not to convert one into the other. Therefore [one cannot infer such an agent can convert one into the other].

[5] 10.13 [Solutions to the objections] To these objections we reply:

[To the first in 10.8ff.] What Augustine had in mind in the text quoted [in 10.9] was to prove that the soul, when first produced, was not made from some body. The manner in which he proceeds reveals as much. First he considers each sort of body in particular and then he sums up the matter in the text cited, viz., "But that a body could be turned into a soul, etc." And he continues: "Now this first production is not something miraculous, but is the sort of thing that is suited to what is produced." Consequently, he has no wish to deny that God could convert body into soul, but only wanted to say this is not what occurred when they were first made, or this could not have happened then, since they were produced in a manner suited to their natures and not miraculously. Such was the mind of Augustine.

10.14 If one insisted, however, that Augustine's words indicate that one body can be turned into another, but not into a soul, and that only divine omnipotence makes the first possible, and even this cannot make the second possible, my answer would be this: If there are several concurrent reasons for something's impossibility, then something else which lacks some of these reasons can be called possible, not in an absolute sense, but in relation to the first. For example: Sight is impossible for a stone, a blind animal, and a kitten not yet nine days old; yet sight is always possible in the second and third cases with reference to what precedes, since they lack the reason for the impossibility found in the preceding.

[6] 10.15 If you examine the following examples, you will see the relevance for our thesis. It is impossible for fire to be transformed into a celestial body for many reasons, such as the lack of active or passive qualities that are formally or virtually opposed, which might serve as principles for the transformation of one into the other. They also lack the recipient subject that would underlie such a transformation. The impossibility of turning a body into a soul stems not only from these grounds but also from the fact that one is extended and the other not, and thus they lack a common element such as that which persists when one body is transformed into another, for one corporeal thing is transmuted into another only by an alteration that is received by the bodily substance as extended, and thus it is only as something extended and as having a corresponding mode of existence that such a product is brought into existence.

10.16 To the citation from Boethius [in 10.10] I say that what he had in mind was that only such things can be converted into one another as have some matter in common, and he claims it is not even possible for all of these, but only for such as can act and be acted upon. Hence he points out there that brass cannot be turned into stone. Consequently, he is not referring to every conversion possible to God, but only to such transformations as require a common matter and in addition such opposite active and passive qualities as would suffice for a purely natural change. For the impossibility of changing brass into stone only refers to a natural process and not just any such but to a direct transmutation.

[7] 10.17 You may object that if we take his words in this way, they would not support what he wants to prove, namely that humanity could not be converted into divinity, because on the interpretation we have given, one could only exclude the possibility of a direct natural conversion of one into the other, which was not what Boethius had against Eutyches.

10.18 I answer: Boethius' argument, given its premises, entails no more than what was said above, namely that human nature cannot be converted into divinity by the sort of transmutation that requires a common subject and mutual principles of acting and being acted upon. To draw the conclusion he wanted, viz., that no power could turn humanity into divinity, one would have to add the proposition: "The degree to which divinity excels the productive capacity of any active causal power is certainly not less than that by which one natural thing exceeds the natural power of any natural agent." This is evident. Since divinity is infinite and cannot be caused, there is no way it can be the result of a causal power; but every created thing can be, and this not only in an absolute sense, but also with reference to some other thing which it succeeds. Then the Boethian argument may be formulated according to the dialectical rule *a maiori*[11] in this way: If all created power cannot transform brass immediately into stone, then for like, or even greater, reason no active power whatsoever can convert humanity to divinity.

[8] 10.19 [To the second objection in 10.11] What is said there about substance and the absolute could be conceded, namely that there

---

[11] Rule *a maiori* is a destructive argument from the superior to the inferior. It can be formulated thus: If the superior cannot effect something, neither can an inferior. Example: If a king cannot take a castle by storm, then neither can a knight. Cf. William of Sherwood's *Introduction to Logic*, trans. N. Kretzmann (Minneapolis, 1966), p. 95.

could be a type of conversion which began with a substance and ended with an accident, or that began with an absolute and terminated with something relative. It does not follow, however, that substance, while remaining a substance, would inhere in another, for both terms of the conversion would have the mode of being proper to their status, so that if substance were the *terminus a quo,** it would have a *per se* mode of existence, and if the *terminus ad quem** were an accident, it would have the sort of existence appropriate to accident, namely existence in another. Therefore the conversion would not result in a substance inhering in another, but rather what would happen is that the *per se* being of a substance as *terminus a quo* would be followed by the *per accidens* being of the *terminus ad quem*. Something similar could be said of the relative and absolute.

10.20 [To the third objection in 10.12] As for the third, one could say that the creation of one substance and the annihilation of another would not prevent quantity from being completely converted, even into something previously existing. If the argument ruled out anything, it would be total conversion in general, but in this question it seems that some sort of total conversion is presupposed, and granted that, the difficulties associated with a specific type of conversion would have to be ironed out.

ARTICLE II
The *terminus ad quem* or What Preexists

[9] 10.21 [The *terminus ad quem* presents no special difficulty] As for the second main point, [in 10.3] it is generally conceded that the prior existence of the *terminus ad quem* introduces no special reason why such a conversion should be impossible, since it is assumed that in the Eucharist the bread is converted into the preexisting body of Christ.

10.22 [One theory] One suggested explanation for this article of faith is this.[12]

Since God, the first agent, acts not as an instrument does, it follows.he could act without movement, and hence could restore to the same matter the numerically identical form that had perished, since the reason a created agent cannot do this is that its action involves movement, which, being successive, can never return to what is

---

[12] Giles of Rome, *Theoremata de corpore Christi*, prop.1 (Romae, 1554), fol. 1r.

numerically the same. Furthermore, God regards matter *qua* quiddity* and as such it is indistinct. Therefore, any form that could be imposed on such matter could be put into any matter whatsoever.

10.23 These two points permit the following argument. It follows (from the first) that God can restore to its matter a form that was destroyed, and consequently (from the second) that he can put this form into any matter. By the same token, he is able to put a form existing in its own matter into any other matter, but because of the numerical identity of the form, it follows that the resulting matter will be the same matter. Consequently, God could make any matter become this matter, even as he could make it come under this form. Hence he could make the form of the body of Christ take over the matter of the bread, if he could make its matter come to exist under this form, and thus this matter of the bread is converted into the matter of his body and its form into his form and the whole into the whole.

10.24 Any explanation of the many assumptions underlying this inference would become prolix and in the interests of brevity can be omitted. Indeed, the force of the argument in short seems to be this: The complete conversion of the composite A into the composite B consists in the potential element of A being informed by B's form; but this is possible; therefore [the complete conversion of A into B is possible].

Proof of the first premise, viz., that the information of A's potential component by B's form, makes it become B's potential component. Identity of form implies identity of matter; thus the conversion of A into B implies not only that the form of A turns into the form of the other, but that the matter of A becomes that of B. The same would hold if the process were reversed.

Proof of the second premise: The potential components of A and B as quiddities are indistinct, and hence the same form can be induced in both by an agent who regards the potential as a quiddity.

In this abbreviated form of the argument, the point made about the possibility of restoring the identical form that had perished seems unnecessary.

[10] 10.25 [This theory must be rejected] What is objectionable about the theory is this:

The claim that all matter is the same *qua* quiddity* (the aspect under which God views it in acting) either means it is the same numerically or at least the same in kind.

10.26 In the first sense, the claim seems to be false and runs counter to what Aristotle says in the *Metaphysics*[13]: "The causes of things in the same species are different, not specifically, but in the sense that the causes of different individuals are different, your matter and form and moving cause being different from mine, while in their universal definition they are the same."

10.27 Again, if the matter of A and of B are identical numerically, since the form of A cannot be educed from the matter of A because the matter of A already has it as actualized, then for the same reason it cannot be educed from the matter of B either. Let A stand here for the body of Christ, and B for the bread. Now if the body of Christ is educed from the matter of bread, the matter of bread will not thereby become or be converted into the matter of the body. For matter has a certain priority here as regards the form according to Augustine[14]: "Certainly some unformed being can be formed; but what is not, cannot be formed." Therefore, matter is somehow prior to that which is made out of it. And in another passage, Augustine[15] says: "Since the matter of heaven is other than the matter of earth, heaven and earth are specifically different, you made matter entirely from nothing and the species of the world from informed matter; however you made both simultaneously."[16]

10.28 There is also this argument from reason: Matter itself is the same under opposite forms, but form cannot remain without matter. Now a variation in what is posterior by nature does not imply variation in what is prior. Therefore if this form is received into some other matter, it does not follow that the matter of the one will become the matter of the other. All we would have is that a form is induced into matter which did not have it before. But the matter passing from privation to form does not thereby become another matter which it was not before.

10.29 But if matter is understood to be the same in the second way [of 10.25], namely, in kind, then it does not follow that the form which is in this matter could be numerically the same as that which is simultaneously in the other matter; all that follows is that the two forms are of the same kind, which does not suffice to prove the theory proposed.

---

[13] Aristotle, *Metaph.* XII, c.5 (1071a25-30).
[14] Augustine, *Confess.* XII, c.6, n.6: PL 32, 827; CSEL 33, 313.
[15] Ibid., XIII, c.33, n.48: PL 32, 866; CSEL 33, 385.
[16] There is a reference to *Metaphysics* I, c.8 (989b65) that is left incomplete in MSS. and text edition.

[11] 10.30 [Three meanings of "conversion into what preexists"] I say further, as regards this article, that we can understand "conversion into what existed before" in two ways, accordingly as "what existed before" refers either to (1) something which once was, but does not exist at present, or to something which not only existed before but retains its same being now. And this latter can have two further meanings depending on whether that which previously existed and continues to do so, as the term of this new conversion, either: (2) has something new added to its being, such as that here this term is now present to something in a way it was not present to it before, or (3) has nothing new about either its essential being or anything it has posterior to that being.

10.31 [About the first meaning] Let us look at these three in turn. The first presents no greater difficulty for a term that preexists than for one that does not, as long as one admits that God could restore the identical thing that was destroyed—something all Catholics concede, and no wonder, since there is nothing self-contradictory about it.

10.32 [As for the second, this is possible] The other way, however, presents more of a difficulty, namely, when what existed before retains its same being now, for none of the changes listed by the Philosopher in the *Physics*[17] seem applicable to the case where the *terminus ad quem* preexisted. The first interpretation of this, however—which is our second main division [in 10.30]—seems possible, because this seems to be what *de facto* must take place in the Eucharist. For the body of Christ, retaining the same being it had before, through this conversion now becomes present in a new way to the species of bread. The same could be said of the quantity to be converted into what preexists, for there is no impossibility on the part of the *terminus ad quem*.

[12] 10.33 [Three objections to 10.32] This claim, however, is contested on the following grounds:

First, it is objected to what was said of the Eucharist. Something is *per se* the *terminus ad quem* of the conversion only insofar as it succeeds the *terminus a quo*. But according to you, what succeeds the bread is not the substantial being of the body, but only the new presence it acquires. Hence it is a *per se* term insofar as it becomes present here or acquires this presence, but this sort of presence is not substance or anything substantial. Therefore, the *per se* term of the conversion in the Eucharist would not be substance, and conse-

---

[17] Aristotle, *Physic.* v, c.1 (225a-35).

quently the conversion itself would not be a transubstantiation,* because transubstantiation is the transition of one substance into another.

10.34 Second, the claim made for quantity is challenged for several reasons, the first of which is this: What comes to be is in the same place in which what perished was before, because the reason for being in place, which is quantity, remains the same in both. So too in the Eucharistic conversion, the reason for the bread's being in a certain place [viz., its quantity] remains behind, and thus the body of Christ, which is the term of the change, can be said to be there or to have such a presence. Conversely, then, it would follow that if the quantity of the *terminus a quo* did not remain behind, then the *terminus ad quem* would lack such presence and would not be there. But if the quantity is converted into something else, it is clear that the reason for being in that place has vanished, for quantity was the basis for being in place.

[13] 10.35 Furthermore, if the conversion of quantity into something, made the latter take presence in this place, then it would have the same sort of presence here that the quantity had when it was here. But quantity was here circumscriptively.* Therefore, the *terminus ad quem* is here circumscriptively.

10.36 From this two absurdities seem to follow:

First, the same thing would be present in two places at once. Proof that this follows: The *terminus ad quem*, which becomes localized here, could remain located in its proper place as well, just as the body of Christ now is located in heaven. This result of being localized in two places at once, however, seems to involve many impossibilities. For instance, the same thing could be moving and at rest simultaneously, because it could be in motion there but not here. Similarly it could be heated and cooled at the same time because here it was near fire and there near water. Likewise, it could be both continuous and discontinuous, if it had a part severed from the whole here but not there. The same thing could also be at once living and dead, for instance, if an animal suffered a fatality in one place, but had all that was necessary and sufficient for health in the other.

10.37 The second main absurdity that would follow from being localized both here and there is that two bodies could coexist in the same place. Proof that this follows: This [quantity] could be converted into two bodies, each of which would be localized here for the same reason. Also it could be converted into a larger body, and

QUESTION TEN

if this had to occupy the same place, one part would have to overlap another. Aristotle, however, in the *Physics*,[18] it seems, has proved the impossibility of two bodies being in the same place at the same time.

[14] 10.38 [Reply to the first objection in 10.33] To the first of these, I say that if the *per se* term of transubstantiation is substance *qua* substantial being, as it is argued, since the body of Christ does not properly follow in the place of the bread according to its substantial being, the proposition "Something is *per se* the *terminus ad quem* of the conversion only insofar as it succeeds the *terminus a quo*" has to be denied. For although the body has being there after the being of the bread, it does not begin to exist only when the bread ceases to be, which seems to be necessary if we are to say that it follows the being of the bread here, speaking properly. Otherwise, we could say the being of the sun follows the decay of the worm because its being succeeds that of the worm. Hence, as I say, we have to deny the proposition, since only insofar as the body of Christ is the same now as before, and therefore not properly as succeeding anything, is it the *terminus ad quem* of the transubstantiation. For since this does not produce the *terminus ad quem*, but only converts something else into it, the body *qua* substantial being does not properly succeed the *terminus a quo*, as we said. But one could admit that there is something new about the *terminus ad quem* and as such it does, properly speaking, follow the *terminus a quo*. And then one could grant that as long as the substance of bread occupied this place, this novel situation would not have occurred, namely that the body of Christ became really and truly present here where it was not present before.

[15] 10.39 [Reply to the second objection in 10.34] I say to the second that the body of Christ is where the bread was, but the formal reason for this is not the quantity which was the formal reason for the bread being there. For this quantity is not formally in the body of Christ and hence nothing pertains to his body formally because of it. Also, quantity can only be formal grounds for locating something circumscriptively, for it is the specific reason something has this type of location. If quantity were the formal ground for anything being here, therefore, it would have a circumscriptive presence in place, and this is not the way the body of Christ is sacramentally present. Consequently, it is clear [that quantity is not the formal ground for Christ's presence here]. Therefore, even if that which

---

[18] Ibid., IV, c.5 (212b26-30).

was the formal reason for bread occupying a place did not remain, God could still have made the term of the conversion present here where bread had been.

Also the first statement [in 10.34], about "what comes to be" having the same place as "what perished" had because the quantity remains, does not prove what it is supposed to, because it is not necessary that the term that results from the conversion be localized in the same way the other term was. Indeed, it will be present there in the mode of existence given it by the agent effecting the change.

[16]   10.40 [Reply to the third objection in 10.35] As for the other, one can deny this proposition: "The resulting term has the same sort of presence here as the initial term had." One could object that the substance of the bread, which was changed, had been present here in one way, namely, the way it can exist anywhere in place because as extended each part occupied a part of the whole place in which it was *in toto*. But the substance of the body of Christ into which it was changed is not present in that fashion. Indeed it exists whole and entire in every part of the place. Consequently, it does not follow that the term into which the quantity is changed is necessarily localized there in the same way as the other term was.

10.41 But if one admitted that God could convert quantity into something which did become localized in that way, perhaps some would not consider the resulting consequences [of 10.36-37] to be simply impossible, in the sense of implying a contradiction. And it is only this sort of thing that we say is impossible to God,[19] "for no word shall be impossible with God," where "word" means any concept possible to the intellect, and that would be any concept in which contradictory elements are not included.

10.42 To the many apparently impossible consequences, therefore, that seem to follow from the first absurdity [mentioned in 10.36], viz., that the same thing could be in two places at once, one could provide a probable solution through the use of two principles.

The first is this: "Forms prior by nature to ubiety* as such do not vary with variation of the ubiety itself, because the prior does not vary because of variation in the posterior." From this proposition it would follow that anything present in two places at once would undergo change neither as to substantial form nor as to anything in the category of quantity or quality, for forms in these categories are simply prior to ubiety itself.

[19] Luke 1:37.

[17] The second proposition is this: "Anything affecting its substantial form or its quality or quantity that a body might suffer from two agents acting on it at one place, it would also suffer from them if one acted on it at one place and the other acted on it at the other place." Example: Putting fire and water near a piece of wood here would have the same effect as putting fire near it in one of its locations and water near it at the other. This would follow from the preceding principle because an absolute form,* being simply prior to ubiety, does not vary because it is in different places.

10.43 A judicious use of these two principles will serve to solve the various instances raised in the objection as well as other similar quandaries.

Take the first case, viz., that the same thing that was moving in one place was at rest in the other. There is no contradiction here any more than there is for it to be both here and there. For local motion and rest are posterior by nature to ubiety itself and hence can be varied according to variation in what is prior.

10.44 The second case about heating and cooling can be solved by the second principle. For the result of heating and cooling something at two locations would be no different than trying to do both at one location. Should one agent prevail over the other, it would produce its effect in the body and prevent the effect of the other. If both were equally strong, they would induce some intermediate state. The same thing would happen if the body were simultaneously in two places.

[18] 10.45 The same principle solves the continuity problem. If a divisive agent should prevail over whatever preserves the continuity of the body, then wherever it be, it will be divided, though not by someone at both places. The reply here is similar to the question as to how Christ's body would exist in the consecrated host when it was separated from his soul on the cross.

10.46 The fourth case about something being both living and dead can be solved even more easily in the same fashion, for if the substantial form is simply separated from matter by an agent acting on the living body at one place, then it will not remain united to that matter at the other place. Thus the body of Christ would not be said to be living in the Eucharist when it was dead on the cross.

10.47 As for the second principal "absurdity" [in 10.37], viz., that two bodies could coexist in the same place, one could say this is neither incongruous nor impossible, for there is no apparent contradition involved. For oneness of place is not formally unity of body. Indeed, the body has its own intrinsic unity to which unity of place is incidental. Therefore, this does not follow: "Every body that is in this same place is the same body." Simultaneity does not alter the oneness of the body or of the place.

10.48 As for the authority [in 10.37] of Aristotle's *Physics*, one could say that his proof only shows that a body by its own power or that of any created nature cannot be in more than one adequate place. It proves nothing about what unlimited divine power can accomplish.

[19] 10.49 [About the third meaning] As for the third interpretation [in 10.30], viz., that something which previously exists and continues to be can become the term of a new conversion without acquiring anything new at all, one could declare this is possible as follows. When God conserves a creature, the term of the conservation is not something new; it is the same thing that is conserved and it has the same being it had before. Conservation, then, be it regarded actively or passively, requires no novelty in its term. Therefore, neither does conversion.

10.50 Explanation of the entailment: As God conserves this thing by willing it to have being, as it were, after having had this being, so by willing that this thing have being after that, God could convert that into this, because he makes the latter exist. And in some sense, at least, what ceases to be is succeeded by the being of what existed before and continues to exist, even if "succeeded" is not taken in its proper sense. To be the term of an action, however, it is not necessary that something follow another in the simple and proper sense of "follow," namely as something new, as is clear from the case of conservation. On this interpretation, one could say that just as God with the same volition creates something, insofar as he wills it to exist after it did not exist, and he conserves it, insofar as he wills it to be, as it were, after it had been, so he could by the same volition turn that into this because he willed this to continue after that.

10.51 You may argue: How can this be the term of a conversion or of any action positively if it does not get some being in the process, since even the term of a divine action receives being through that action?

One could say that all that is required of the term of the action is that the being which positively results from the action is something it gets either simply or with reference to something else. And thus the term of the conversion could be said to receive being with ref-

QUESTION TEN

erence to what was turned into it, insofar as God wanted its being to follow that of the other.

[20] 10.52 Another solution would be to say that a positive action produces its term either simply or equivalently, and that this conversion is of the second type insofar as the productive action, on its part, suffices to give being to the term and if the latter does not receive being, it is only because it already had it.

10.53 One argument against the explanation [in 10.30] is that on this interpretation one could say that whatever God annihilates, he turns into the sun,* because he wants the sun to retain its being after the being of the thing he annihilates, just as he wants this preexisting thing to remain after the being of whatever is turned into it.

10.54 Another way of explaining how a conversion of the sort [in 10.39] is possible might be this: If something can be the term of a conversion when accompanied by something posterior in the sense that *per se* the term itself does not include it, then it can also be the term of a conversion where this accompanying feature is absent. This is clear, because as prior, it is the term of the change, and from the prior *qua* prior, the posterior can be absent. But it is the substance of Christ's body that is the *per se* term of transubstantiation, even though accompanied by a new presence, namely it is now under the species of bread, as we said in explaining the second meaning [in 10.32]. Therefore, Christ's body could also be the term of a conversion without this presence or anything new which would be posterior to the being of the body itself.[20]

ARTICLE III
About the Conversion Itself

[21] 10.55 As for the third point [mentioned in 10.3], it is generally held that this conversion does not involve an annihilation of the *terminus a quo*.

10.56 [An unacceptable theory] One opinion[21] deduced from this is that after the change it is not true that nothing of the bread remains. Proof of the entailment: If there were nothing, one would have to say that the bread was annihilated. And if there is not noth-

---

[20] He is not speaking of the type of conversion that requires the permanence of something common to both terms. Cf. Duns Scotus, *Ord.* IV, d.11, q.3, n.17 (ed. Vivès XVII, 377-78). As was said above in this same question, what is required in this type of conversion is that the terms be under the power of the agent as regards their being and non-being.

[21] Henry of Ghent, *Quodl.* IX, q.9 (fol. 371O; XI, q.4 (fol. 450L).

ing, the argument continues, then there is something, but this is not what was there before, for that was changed. Neither is it something outside the *terminus ad quem*. This is evident if we run through the various alternatives. Therefore, after the change there is that into which it was turned, so that it is true to say: What was bread is now the body of Christ. Or if this be denied, then one has to admit that something of Christ's body is what was formerly bread.

10.57 Against the added comment that after the change what remains of the bread is not nothing, therefore it is something, one can argue first as follows:

What is no different in itself after the change than it was before does not acquire something it did not have before. Now the body of Christ is no different in itself after the conversion than it was before. Now before the bread was changed, his body did not have in itself something of the bread; neither was something of his body something of the bread. Therefore, his body does not have something of the bread in it after the conversion.

10.58 Furthermore, the existence of the *terminus ad quem* of the change requires the nonexistence of the *terminus a quo*. This is clear if the terms are opposed, since the existence of one opposite excludes that of the other. Therefore the *terminus ad quem* of the conversion as such does not contain in itself the entity or any part of the *terminus a quo*.

10.59 [Another unacceptable view] Another explanation[22] is that the bread is not annihilated because it remains potentially in the matter of Christ's body.

10.60 Against this it is argued that then God could not annihilate something material unless at the same time he would annihilate everything material, for if anything material remained it would contain potentially every material thing.

10.61[23] Furthermore, where one whole turns into another whole, the matter of the *terminus a quo* does not remain. In transformations of this sort which require matter, then, any matter remaining would be that which perished.

10.62 [A third inadmissible opinion] Another[24] gives this explanation: According to Aristotle,[25] natural change takes various forms. One is from no subject to a subject and that is generation.* Another

---

[22] Giles of Rome, *Theoremata*, prop.1,32 (fol. IV, 22r-23r).
[23] This paragraph, 10.61, is not found in the MSS.
[24] William of Ware, *Sent.* IV, d.11.
[25] Aristotle, *Physic.* V, c.1 (225a3-6).

QUESTION TEN

is from a subject to no subject and that is corruption.* Still another is from one subject to another, as in the case of alteration and generally in the case of any movement, which is properly movement. The case is similar in regard to supernatural transmutations. One form is from no subject to a subject, as in the case of creation; another is the converse, as in annihilation; still another is from a subject to another subject, as the total conversion of one positive thing into another. Therefore this conversion is not an annihilation, because it has something positive as a *per se* term.

10.63 Against this one can argue that if there are two positive terms, accompanying them are two negative terms. The situation is similar to natural changes where both generation and corruption* are involved. Here the two negative terms are associated with the two positive ones, as when the being of the water that is to perish is linked with the non-being of the fire to be generated, and the being of the fire is accompanied by the non-being of the water.

[22] It is the same in our case. The being of the bread is associated with the non-being of the body of Christ and the being of the body is accompanied by the non-being of the bread.

10.64 And then one can argue. The change can be called creation or annihilation in virtue of its *per se* terms but not in virtue of what accompanies them, even as generation is not *per se* creation, because the *per se terminus a quo* is not nothing but privation, and the same is true of the *per se terminus ad quem* of the corruption. Hence, when one compares the *per se* terms of this conversion, which are the existence and nonexistence of the bread, since this nonexistence is total inasmuch as nothing of the bread remains, it would follow that this destruction considered *per se* would be an annihilation.

10.65 [A more plausible explanation, apparently Scotus' own] One could put forth another explanation that would apply to our case the example [in 10.63] of something perishing or corrupting, where the transmutation ends with something positive that is not only its *per accidens* term (namely that which is the *per se* term of the concomitant generation) but also (since the corruption which affects the form alone is only a partial destruction) with the *per se* other part of the composite, viz., the matter. Hence the resulting corruption is not an annihilation, because something of what was destroyed remains. Similarly, what remains is not the *per se termi-*
[23] *nus ad quem* of the corruption. Therefore this destruction is distinguished even more from annihilation by its *per se* term, because this is not an absolute negation or pure nothingness, but a negation

in something which has an aptitude for form, viz., a privation.[26] Therefore, one could say that the form is not annihilated, because what succeeds it as a term is not nothing, but a privation of this form. And even if both of these grounds were wanting, for example, if God suddenly converted the whole of fire into the whole of water without any common subject remaining, it still would not be an annihilation, because the *terminus ad quem* [the water] of this destruction of fire, although it is not properly a privation of the form of fire [as would be the case if the matter of the fire continued to exist under the form of water], it is still not a negation that rules out every category of being [i.e., it is not pure nothingness that is the term of this conversion but the whole of water], but it is a negation included in the opposite positive form [i.e., it has a kind of potentiality in the other positive thing in that God, by a reverse action, could reconvert the whole of the water back into the whole of the fire]. But a negation that is [a quasi potentiality] in some category of things cannot be the *terminus a quo* of a creation.

10.66 In the case of transubstantiation, though the first two grounds [mentioned in 10.65] are wanting, since nothing of the *terminus a quo* [i.e., the bread] remains and properly speaking its form does not "remain" as a privation, because the same substrate [or matter] that had received it is not carried over, nevertheless the third ground [for denying annihilation] still obtains, for the destruction of the bread ended with a negation that did not rule out eveything but is "included" in the being of the *terminus ad quem* [i.e., the body of Christ].

10.67 But against this, it is objected: That the *terminus ad quem* is something positive is only incidental to the term of the destruction. Therefore, in essence [*quantum ad per se rationem*] this destruction now is precisely the sort of thing it would have been had this positive term not accompanied it.

10.68 To this one could counter that an absolute negation, a negation that does not rule out every kind of thing, and the negation called "privation" are no different formally as negations. Nevertheless they are distinguished in that one and not the other is the *per se* term of a certain type of change, such as decay. So too in the case of transubstantiation, the negation as included in the positive term that results is the *per se* term of the change.[27]

---

[26] Cf. Duns Scotus, *Ord.* I, d.28, nn.12-15 (VI, 111-14).
[27] Ibid., IV, d.11, q.4, nn.6ff. (ed. Vivès XVII, 448ff.).

QUESTION TEN

Reply to the Initial Arguments

[25]   10.69 [To the first argument in 10.1] As for the initial argument, something can be a common term in two ways. Either (1) there is a real commonness such as matter, which is the common substrate of both terms when something perishes. In a complete or total conversion there is no need for this sort of common element, indeed it is inconsistent with the very idea of such a conversion. Or (2) the common term may refer to something conceptual, for instance, that both terms fall under the notion of being. And this suffices to exclude the notion of annihilation and creation. In this way, one may say that these species and the preexistent [body of Christ] have something in common.

10.70 There is another sense in which we could say the terms have something in common though not essentially. It is their common relationship to the same agent, since both terms of the conversion fall under its power in the same way. This would also be enough to rule out annihilation, because pure nothingness does not fall under any agent's power, properly speaking, since it is not something causable.

10.71 [To the argument in 10.2] The counter-argument proves that nature can convert one thing into another by a complete conversion and thus requires no common substance, which is manifestly incongruous so far as any natural transmutation is concerned, according to the Philosopher.[28] Therefore, to this argument we must reply: I concede a natural agent can cause every change in these species that can be caused in a changeable subject. But in the Eucharist there is no substance that could be changed substantially because here there is no substance, neither matter, nor the composite. Hence a natural agent cannot cause a substantial change but only an accidental one in which quantity suffices as subject. Since nature never corrupts anything except by inducing incompatible qualities, in that moment, then, in which the Eucharist first ceases to exist through the action of a natural agent, there would be produced by virtue of nature a certain accidental combination, namely, of a quantity of such quality as would be incompatible with the Eucharist which perishes; and the subject of this composite [i.e., the quantity] preexisted, and the form was induced by a created agent which possesses such a form [virtually] in its active power.[29]

---

[28] Aristotle, *Physic.* I, c.7 (190a32-35, 191a8-13).
[29] Cf. Duns Scotus, *Ord.* IV, d.12, q.4 (ed. Vivès XVII, 614-31).

[26] 10.72 But is any substance produced in such a case? I reply: Not by any action of nature, for there is nothing from which nature could produce a substance. Consequently, if substance is produced, it is by the action of God, who has so ordained that an accident never exists without a subject except as long as the Eucharist remains. Therefore, when it has ceased, God produces the composite substance which is naturally suited to support these accidents caused by the natural agent. This new substance, however, would not be needed for the action of nature. Indeed, in the order of nature, it follows such an action. Neither does it occur necessarily for God could fail to produce this substance. It follows only because God so disposes.

10.73 [The cessation of the Eucharistic presence] There are two opinions as to how the Eucharist ceases to be present.

One, which seems to be that of Innocent,[30] claims [the substance of bread returns]. As he says in *De officio Missae*, although the species that remain could still inhere in the substance of bread or wine were they present, yet if their alteration has progressed to such a stage that if bread and wine appeared such it would not be suitable nourishment, the Eucharist ceases to exist and at that same instant by divine action a new substance will come to be there which is suited to be of this quality. Now this will be the substance of bread, and it will continue to undergo alteration until the moment the new substance is generated, and nature will produce this by corrupting that composite substance which the divine action restored.

10.74 The other opinion[31] is that the Eucharist remains as long as those qualities remain that could characterize the substance that was converted [i.e., bread or wine], even though if bread or wine were there they would not be regarded as suitable for nourishment. The Eucharist then would not cease to exist until the stage at which bread would cease to exist. And according to this view it must be said that in that instant when the species are corrupted or perish, then there is a new substance, but it is not bread, because it would not be apt to support the qualities, inconsistent with bread, that have already been induced. But this substance is the sort that nature would have produced from the bread that perished, if the substance of bread had been there.

---

[30] Innocent III, *De sacro altaris mysterio* IV, c.9: PL 217, 861-62. Cf. Duns Scotus, *Ord.* IV, d.12, q.6, n.3 (ed. Vivès XVII, 640-41).

[31] Thomas, *Summa theol.* III, q.77, aa.4-5 (IV, 518ff.).

Question Eleven

IF BOTH BODY AND PLACE REMAIN, CAN GOD CAUSE THE BODY NOT TO HAVE UBIETY?

Arguments Pro and Con

[1] 11.1 As for the third question [in 9.1], we proceed in this way.[1]

It is argued that God cannot cause a body to lack ubiety,* so long as a body and a place* exist, for the extremes of a relation cannot continue to exist without the relation between them also existing. Two white objects, for instance, cannot exist without their being similar. Body and place seem to be terms for the intervening relationship of ubiety, as it were, according to the description in the *Six Principles*[2]: "Ubiety is the circumscription of the body which comes from its circumscription by the place."

11.2 Against the preceding opinion it is argued that body and place are related to ubiety as agent and patient are related to acting [*actio*] and being acted upon [*passio*].* Given the existence of both, God can prevent one from acting upon the other. Therefore, [God can let a body and a place exist, without the one locating the other and hence without ubiety].

Proof of the major: Ubiety seems to be the relationship between place and a body, just as acting and being acted upon are relationships between agent and patient.

Proof of the minor: As it is said in Daniel 3,[3] the fire did not burn the three young men thrown into the furnace. Yet the fire was active, because the spurting flames killed those who threw them into the furnace, and the bodies of the young men were able to suffer, for it is improbable that they had the gift of impassibility.*

---

[1] Cf. Duns Scotus, *Ord.* II, d.2, qq.5-9 (ed. Vivès XI, 324-518); IV, d.10, qq.2-3 (ed. Vivès XVII, 190-225).

[2] *Liber de sex principiis* (attributed to Gilbert de la Porrée; cf. ed. A. Heysse-D. van den Eynde in *Opuscula et textus*, ser. schol. 7, Monasterii W., 1953) v, n.17, p.20.

[3] Daniel 3:21-25.

Body of the Question

[2] 11.3 This question can be understood in two ways. In one sense, it can refer to body and place in general; in another, to a definite body and a definite place. Both of these can be subdistinguished. Therefore, there are four questions in all to be answered.

First, given place in general, is it repugnant for a body in general to lack ubiety?

Second, given body in general, is it repugnant to place in general not to circumscribe it, so that there will be no ubiety?

Third, given this body, this place, but this body not present in this place, is it possible that this body should lack this ubiety?

Fourth, if this body and this place exist and this body is present in this place, can it still lack this ubiety?

ARTICLE I

Given Place in General, is it Repugnant for a Body in General to Lack Ubiety?

[3] 11.4 [Proof it is not impossible] As for the first subquestion, I claim it is not a contradiction that a body exist without some containing body and, consequently, without ubiety. As a matter of fact, this is the case with the outermost heavenly sphere, which lacks a container.[4] Similarly, given a place, and not just any place, but one capable of circumscribing this body, it would not be contradictory that this body lack ubiety there.

The reason is this: It is not contradictory that the absolute remain without a relationship to what is not prior to it, or at least to that which by nature is neither prior to it nor simultaneous in nature with it. But place is by nature neither simultaneous with, nor prior to, body. Rather, it seems to be subsequent by nature to it. Therefore [it is not contradictory that a body be without ubiety].

From the foregoing, the reason for the second proposition can be formulated.

11.5 [Three objections] To be in a place pertains to body *per se*, so corporeity is the reason for its being in place. But it would be a contradiction to claim that the formal ground for something exists while the thing in question does not exist.

11.6 Besides, the located body depends on the locating body; therefore the relation of the locating to the located is a type of

---
[4] Aristotle, *Physic.* IV, c.5 (212b8-10).

dependence-relation. But if an absolute by nature can have such a dependency, then it cannot be without it.

11.7 Contrary to what was said of the outermost heavenly sphere [in 11.4], it is argued that if this body moves, it has locomotion. But locomotion requires that it have some location, for locomotion means that the body is in a different place than it was before. And if one claims the heavenly body is at rest, it follows that its state of rest is opposed to some motion that it is able by nature to have and so it is at rest in place, which is the intended conclusion.

[4]   11.8 [Answer to these objections] To the first [in 11.5], one could say that the proximate reason fundamentally for being in place is extension. And if the formal reason is understood in this way then it can indeed be separated from that relationship for which it is said to be the reason. "Separation" here refers to actuality, for extension cannot be separated from the aptitude or potency to be in a place. For example, whiteness in this way is the reason for being similar, and nevertheless there is no contradiction for whiteness to exist without there being any actual similarity.

11.9 To the contrary, if extension is the proper fundamental reason for being located, then this proposition, "A body is located, just as color is seen," will be at least *per se* in the second mode, although not in the first mode of *per se* predication.* Since such a proposition is simply necessary, the subject cannot be without the predicate.

11.10 I reply: Corporeity is the fundamental reason why a body can be in place and why it actually is in place, and it is indeed the proper and proximate reason for both, for the subject of the actuality is the subject with the corresponding potentiality. But it is a necessary reason only as regards the potentiality, because the aptitude is intrinsic [to a body] by the strict definition of corporeity, but it will only be actualized by an agent which reduces this potentiality to act. Therefore, one must deny the assumption that "A body is located" represents an instance of *per se* predication in the second mode, although it must be admitted that "A body can be located" does. For example, "Man is risible" is in the second mode of *per se* predication, whereas "Man laughs" is contingent.

[5]   11.11 To the second objection [in 11.6], I say that this dependence of what is located upon its place is not simply necessary on the part of what is said to be dependent, in the way, for instance, that the caused is dependent upon its cause, although there is a kind of dependence on place as upon something that was meant by nature

to satisfy a natural disposition. For the body indeed is apt by its nature to be kept in its natural place. However, absolutely speaking it can exist without its being kept in a place.

11.12 To the third objection [in 11.7], one could say that if the outermost heaven moves, it moves as locating and not as located, because it locates the body contained by it differently now than it did before. But the first heaven itself is not located any differently, for the simple reason that it is not located at all. In this way the dictum of Averroes[5] is to be understood, viz., "Heaven is in place through the center," because its being "in place" consists in its locating the firmament which can be in place.

11.13 And if one asks to what category does this "locating" pertain, so that he might classify the corresponding "movement," the answer is that it does not pertain to the category of ubiety or *ubi*, because ubiety means being surrounded by a place. Neither does it fall under any other category, because then motion would pertain to more categories than enumerated by the Philosopher in the *Physics*,[6] and if you examine the other categories you will not find that it pertains to any of them.

[6] 11.14 Furthermore, if the outermost heavenly sphere could rotate although it is not contained by any body, then it could rotate if it did not contain a body either, for instance, if it were a continuous spherical body. And then this fluid form according to which rotary movement exists *per se*, could also exist *per se* without reference to either a container or content and thus would be [not a fluid form but] one that is purely absolute.[7]

ARTICLE II
Given Body in General, is it Repugnant to Place in General that no Ubiety Exist?

[7] 11.16 [Proof it is not impossible] As for the second question [in 11.3], I say that there does not seem to be any contradiction that a concave spherical surface should exist without any container-relationship to another body, even though there be another body which

---

[5] Averroes, *Physic.* IV, com. 42 (IV, fol. 140E-140M).

[6] Aristotle, *Physic.* V, c.2 (226a20-30).

[7] [11.15] "*Responsionem quaere*" ("Look for the answer") is added in the Wadding-Vivès text. The editors evidently believed the two preceding paragraphs to be objections of some sort to Scotus' position. See the addition 11.15 in Appendix. However, only M_2 has *Responsio* followed by the second article. M_1 and W had added *Responsio* (the former in the margin) but deleted it. In our opinion no answer is required.

was meant by nature to occupy this place, for one can argue here about locating in the same way as we argued before about being located [in 11.11].

11.17 This is confirmed from the fact that the heaven is indestructible,[8] and even though the elements taken in themselves as a whole [i.e., the sublunar world] are imperishable according to the Philosopher,[9] their indestructibility is not like that of the heaven. Since the form of an element is of the same type in the whole [i.e., the atmosphere, the hydrosphere, or fire sphere] as it is in a part [i.e., that portion which combines to form minerals, organic substance, etc.], it follows it can no more be reason for the indestructibility of the whole [sublunar world] than for a part. And even though there is no natural cause that could destroy the element as a whole, like those which transform a part of it, nevertheless to reduce to act this intrinsic possibility of an element's perishing is not as impossible as it would be to make the heaven perish. Or at least, according to the theologians, it is possible for God to annihilate the elements, which are destructible as to their form, without annihilating the heaven, which is indestructible as to its form, since to conserve the prior and more necessary there is no need to preserve something less necessary as a means to that end. Absolutely speaking, then, the elements could be annihilated without causing any change in the heaven, and if this happened, the sides of the heaven would not instantly collapse, because nature cannot cause such a transmutation in an instant. Therefore, the concave surface of the heaven could remain and nevertheless contain no body.

11.18 [Three objections] Against this it is argued that a vacuum is simply impossible, as Aristotle proves in the *Physics*.[10] But if a concave surface existed without a body, there would be a vacuum. Therefore [this is simply impossible].

[8] Proof of the major: One reason the Philosopher[11] gives in the chapter about place against those who argue that place is empty space is this: There would be an infinity of places, he says, and to prove this follows, he adds: "For when water and air change places, all the portions of the two together will play the same part in the whole which was previously played by all the water in the vessel."

---

[8] Aristotle, *De caelo* I, c.3 (270a12-22); II, c.1 (283b27-32).

[9] This seems to be a consequence of the Philosopher's view that matter is eternal.

[10] Aristotle, *Physic.* IV, c.7 (214a15-217b).

[11] Ibid., c.4 (211b20-23).

11.19 Besides, there is nothing between the sides of a vacuum, but according to the Philosopher,[12] these sides that have nothing between them are together. Therefore, if a vacuum existed, the sides would be together and not be together.

11.20 Besides, it is contradictory that there should be two separate moments of time with no interval of time. By the same token, then, it is contradictory that there should be two things locally separated with no body in between.

11.21 [Answer to the objections] As for the first [in 11.18], although the Philosopher's proof of the implication is explained in many ways,[13] whatever the explanation chosen, it only holds on the assumption that a vacuum is empty space with actual dimensions, although lacking any natural qualities. For as long as one assumes that there are actual dimensions, according to the Philosopher there will always remain a reason why this is not compatible with another body unless one causes the other to part. But the vacuum that is assumed in this article to be possible to God is not a space with positive dimensions, but all that is there is the possibility of having such together with a lack of any dimensions in actuality. And in this way one can answer all the arguments given there by the Philosopher. They are valid only against the notion of a vacuum in one sense, viz., an empty space without a body but with actual dimensions, and thus prove nothing about the sort of vacuum that we claim is possible for God.

[9] 11.22 To the second objection [in 11.19], I say that "in between" can refer to something positive and actual or privative and potential, and for the sides to touch and be together, there must be nothing in between in either sense. Though the boundaries of a vacuum have nothing in between in the first sense, they do, however, have something in between in the second sense, because the intervening space could hold a body only as large as that which would be there if that space were actually filled. It follows then that what is in between is a privation, because there is lacking as large a content as could be placed within these boundaries.

11.23 To the third objection [in 11.20], one could say that without motion there could be rest even in the proper sense of the term. For if no body were in motion, there could be some body that has uniform existence, just as after the [last] judgment, the body of the blessed could exist unmoved, even though no body would be any different, since there is no need that some less perfect body be dif-

---

[12] Ibid., v, c.3 (226b21-22).
[13] Averroes, *Physic.* IV, com. 76 (IV, fol. 165L-166I).

ferent for the blessed to remain unchanged; nor does this latter require that some other bodies would have to be in motion. For even to this uniform immobile existence there corresponds a proper measure, which is time. And between any two imagined instants of this duration there could have been an interval of so much movement, and so, if we call time the measure of flow or motion, then this immobile existence would have a time period, although the flow of time would not be actual or positive but only potential and privative. Hence, if a mind aware of actual positive time were to use it to measure this period of uniform duration, it would know how long it was, namely, the positive extent of time that would have elapsed if time had been positive.

[10] 11.24 Now something analogous occurs in the case of positive and privative local distance. As a privative space of time measures the successive parts of something, so privative extension measures its permanent parts. This is so because privation is equal in its way to its corresponding possession. Hence the previous argument can be adapted to confirm our thesis as follows: It is possible to have some interval between moments that is quasi-temporal, although no positive time intervenes, i.e., there is no measure of actual movement. Potential time, or time taken privately, is sufficient to create a quasi-temporal interval which justifies speaking of one moment occurring before or after the other. Hence, one can say the same of place and local distance.

11.25 If one argues against this that there is no distance unless there be something in between in which it exists, which is not the case here, this answer could be given. Formally, distance implies a relationship between two extremes, but the relationship to the other term exists in one extreme. Now in the case we are discussing, although there is no positive medium in between them, the two extremes are positive. Now if this suffices to call the relation positive, I admit there is positive distance here. But if for this a positive medium is further required, then at least our intended thesis can still be saved, for even if actual distance does not exist, its privation does and positive distance is there potentially.

ARTICLE III
Given this Body, this Place, but this Body not Present in this Place, is it Possible that this Body should Lack this Ubiety?

[11] 11.26 [Proof this is possible] As for the third question, it is obvious that if this body is not present to this place, it is not circum-

scribed by this place and hence has no ubiety there, even though this place could exist, since it is the innermost surface of the containing body. This is clear from what was said in [11.16ff. of] the second article.[14]

Also, if the body is not in this place, in the natural course of things it will be somewhere else, but not in two places at once. Hence it will not have ubiety here.

11.27 [Objection] Against this it is argued that "containing" is part of the definition of place, since the container's inner surface alone, apart from the notion of "containing," is not a place. But, since "containing" expresses a relationship, it will not remain, it seems, if the term contained is not the same. Therefore, when this content replaces that, apparently the place is no longer the same. But when this body is no longer present to this place, the content is not the same.

11.28 [Solution] In *Physics*,[15] the Philosopher claims the place remains the same despite the successive replacement of bodies. From this it seems clear that this place does not become another place simply because it contains another body. As for the argument about the relation of "containing to the contained," one could grant that place implies, in addition to the surface, a relationship of containing, as is indicated by the words "the innermost . . . of what contains" (i.e., what proximately and immediately contains) in his definition [viz., "The innermost motionless boundary of what contains is place"]. It follows then that either (a) we must say that a change in the content does not alter the relationship of the container, that is to say, it does not alter the way in which the container is related to what it contains, because the *per se* term of this relationship is not this particular content, but some content in general; or (b) we could say that as the content varies, the corresponding relation also changes, so that "containing this" differs from "containing that," although the term so related does not vary, since the container remains the same, and so we have the same place. An example of this: If, because of its whiteness, a body is similar to many objects, then it has many similarities, because their number corresponds to the number of related terms. But the body remains one similar thing, not many similar bodies, just as it is one knower who knows many things. For concrete subjects are not numbered solely on the basis

---

[14] In 11.26 we follow the order of M_1 and M_2, not that of W or Wadding.
[15] Aristotle, *Physic.* IV, c.4 (212a20).

of the number of their forms [or qualifications] but we must consider along with these how many subjects have them.[16]

ARTICLE IV
If this Body and Place Exist and this Body is Present in this Place, can it still Lack this Ubiety?

[12] 11.29 [Three possible meanings of the question] The fourth question, it seems, can be understood in three ways: first, if this body is quantitatively present in the place without another body being there in the same way; second, if two bodies are both copresent there quantitatively; third, if this body is present to this place but not quantitatively.

11.30 [Proof that the answer to the first meaning of the question is negative] As for the first, it seems clear that presence of this sort could no more exist without ubiety than it could without the body's being circumscribed by the place, for this circumscription apparently adds nothing to the fact that the body is present in this place in a quantitative way, i.e., as coextensive and coincident with the place.

11.31 But then this doubt comes to mind. Formally this circumscription or presence seems to express nothing more than a relation, and hence ubiety itself would be formally just a relationship. But this consequent seems false, for there is no *per se* motion with respect to relation, according to the Philosopher in Bks. V and VII of the *Physics*,[17] yet in Bk. II[18] he tells us there is *per se* motion with respect to the category of place or ubiety.

11.32 And should someone claim that ubiety implies not only a relative but an absolute, and it is the latter that distinguishes it from other categories which simply imply relationships but with distinct foundations, one can counter with this argument. An absolute and a relation do not form one concept *per se*, but the concept of any category is one *per se*; therefore [an absolute and a relation do not constitute the category of ubiety]. Neither does an absolute contract "relation" *per se* to form the genus of "ubiety" or that of any species under that category, and this for the same reason, viz., that an absolute and a relation do not form a concept that is one *per se*.

[16] Cf. Duns Scotus, *Ord.* II, d.2, q.6, nn.7-8 (ed. Vivès XI, 331-33).
[17] Aristotle, *Physic.* V, c.2 (225b10-19); VII, c.3 (246b10-14).
[18] Ibid., II, c.1 (192b13-16).

[13] 11.33 Using this same reason one could argue further that you may take both of these *per se* concepts [viz., one absolute and the other relative], and if each is common, then it is predicable of several things *in quid*,* and therefore upon analysis will yield one ultimate most general concept that is predicable *per se* of everything under it. And thus the analysis of both the absolute and the relative notions will end with the concept of that ultimate category proper to each concept.

11.34 [The distinction between "relation" and the last six categories] One could resolve this doubt along these lines. If, as is commonly claimed, the distinction between the ten categories ought to be preserved, then the last six ought not to be brought under the category "relation." But on the other hand, since they seem neither to be absolute forms nor to imply both an absolute and a relation, for the reason given [in 11.32], one would have to say that they are essentially relationships, yet do not fall under the category "relation." Hence, we need a distinction between relations even at the categorical level. But we can distinguish the relationships implied by the last six categories from those in the fourth category, properly called "relation," if we accept the common statement that relations in the fourth category are intrinsically advenient,* whereas those in the last six are extrinsically advenient. We can interpret this as follows. No relationship advenes* to an absolute so intrinsically that it pertains to it *per se* or *qua* absolute, for then it would not be a relation, since the very notion of a relation is "of one to another." Therefore that relation is said to be intrinsically advenient which is a necessary consequence of its foundation once the terms are given, because a relation cannot be more intrinsic to an absolute than that. By contrast, a relation is extrinsically advenient which is not a necessary consequence of the foundation even if the terms are given.[19]

[14] 11.35 [Interpretation of Aristotle] If this be true, then one can reply to the testimony of the Philosopher in the *Physics*[20] [referred to in 11.31]. He denies motion only with respect to relation proper, viz., that which pertains to the fourth category, but not with respect to every relationship pertaining to the last six; in fact he admits there that change occurs in ubiety, and it is commonly admitted

---

[19] Cf. Duns Scotus, *Ord.* IV, d.13, q.1, nn.9-11 (ed. Vivès XVII, 668-69); d.6, q.10, nn.3-4 (ed. Vivès XVI, 617-18).

[20] Aristotle, *Physic.* V, c.2 (225b11-12).

that this does not involve motion with respect to any absolute form, for ubiety, as we have seen, is not an absolute form but the relationship of the contained body to the place that contains it.

11.36 But the reason why "relation" and the other six relationships are different in regard to motion seems to stem from the fact that a relation proper, since it follows necessarily once the extremes are given, can never be acquired in the other related term. Now the Philosopher[21] denies that motion can terminate *per se* in what is acquired only accidentally, viz., when another entity has been acquired. A relationship, however, that is not a necessary consequence of the extremes can have a novelty of its own apart from any novelty in one or the other terms, and hence can be acquired *per se*. Now this seems to be the case with ubiety, for God can conserve the identical localizable body as well as the place, and still the latter need not circumscribe the former, because the body can be absent from that place, and nature itself can do this by putting another body in its place. Therefore these two extremes of "place" and "localizable" do not necessarily entail ubiety. Consequently, ubiety can be new with its own novelty and can be acquired by the body without anything absolute being added to either the body or the place.

11.37 But one may ask: How can the acquisition of a relation be successive if there is no succession as to anything absolute? The answer is that the body makes its several parts successively present to the same part of the place. Similarly, the same section of the body makes itself successively present to different segments of the place, and thus both the divisibility of the body and that of the place result in the fact that the bodily circumscription by the place is also divisible into parts, and this segmentation is successive when one part is acquired only after another. Hence there is no divisibility in the relationship [of ubiety] without some divisibility in what is absolute, but there is a succession in the relationship of circumscription without any succession in the absolute form of the body or the place.

[15] 11.38 [As for the second meaning of the question, the answer is also negative, but not all accept this] As for the second meaning [given in 11.29] to this article, viz., whether this body can lack ubiety in this place if there is another body copresent quantitatively with it, it might seem that one could claim it would not have it here, because if it could, the other body could also have it here. But two

[21] Ibid., c.1 (225a20-225b13).

ubieties in the same place are impossible because one place has but one circumscription.

11.39 Also, the located body separates the sides of the container. But the second body that comes to this place will not be able to separate these sides, for they have already been separated by the body that came here first.

11.40 Confirmation: If both caused the sides to separate, both would constitute a medium between them. But where there are several *per se* media, there would seem to be several distances, and thus there would be a double distance between the sides.

11.41 [Scotus' own opinion] But one can say that in such a situation, both bodies would have ubiety in this place, for when both would be placed here as coextensive and coincident with the place, then either both will be located there, which is our contention, or neither will, and then the place would be vacuous in which two extended bodies were placed, which no one would maintain. Similarly, if either of the two was removed leaving the other, the remaining body would have ubiety here. But for its part the body would not be here any differently than it was before as regards the way it is extended throughout the container.

11.42 This appears clear if we contrast a body with an angel. For if an angel were together with a body, it would not have ubiety proper in that place, whereas the extended body would have it. The reason is that the angel is not coextensive and coincident with that place nor does it displace anything. Hence if the body were removed and the angel alone remained, the place could properly be called empty. And the opposite would be true if two bodies coexisted in the same place.

11.43 You may ask: How can a place already filled be filled again? I answer by refuting the arguments for the other view.

11.44 [Reply to the counter-arguments] To the first [in 11.38] according to our view which asserts that there can be many relations of the same type to different terms in the same subject and with the same foundation, I would have to admit that the same place could actively circumscribe more than one body, and that corresponding to this there would be in the several bodies distinct passive relationships of being circumscribed.

11.45 To the other objections [in 11.39], one could point out that "separating the sides" could be understood in two ways: either effectively, in the sense that an agent forced the sides apart, or quasi-formally, and thus anything in between them could be said to separate them. In this second sense, it must be admitted that each body existing extensively would separate the walls of the place because each is in between them. In the first sense, however, neither of the two bodies forces the sides of the container apart, but this was done by the agent that first divided one surface of the container from the other. And this also makes clear how each body can fill the place, for they do it formally, not effectively. For it is no more incongruous that a place already filled acquire a new body that fills it formally than that a container with a body commensurate to what it can contain should acquire another similar relationship to a second body.

[16] 11.46 As for the confirmation [in 11.40], one may say that if distance be taken to mean the way in which one distant object stands in respect to another, then there is but one distance between the same terminal points whether the intervening bodies be one or many, and in this sense it is not true that where there is another *per se* medium, there is another distance *per se*, unless one take "another *per se* medium" to mean whatever is required in addition to fill in the intermediate distance, but in the case under discussion the second body does not fulfill this function. If, however, one took "distance" to mean the total size of the contents that have been packed between the sides of the container, then one would have to admit that with two bodies between the walls, the "distance" between them has been doubled.

[17] 11.47 [As for the third meaning of the question the answer is positive] The third sense given [in 11.29] to this article was whether a body can lack ubiety if it is present to this space but not in a quantitative way, i.e., not as coextensive or coincident with the place. To this we can say that the body under these conditions would not have ubiety here properly speaking. For ubiety proper is a form that is divisible as such, because there can be a *per se* motion with reference to it. For this reason ubiety pertains only to something divisible with a corresponding mode of existence there. A body, however, that would not be coextensive with place, but was so present there that the whole of it was in each part of the place, would not have a divisible mode of existence with reference to that place, and consequently it would not have ubiety proper there. However, if we extend the meaning of ubiety to this sort of simple presence according to which an angel is said to be here, then one would have to concede

that a body present in this way could be said to have ubiety improperly, because it is truly in this place but is not circumscribed by it.

Reply to the Initial Argument

11.48 To the argument at the beginning [in 11.1]: If the major is accepted as true, then it holds good only for "relation" properly speaking. The relationship, however, which ubiety implies is not of this sort. This is clear from what was said [in 11.34] when treating the first sense of the question in the fourth main article.

Question Twelve
IS THE RELATION OF A CREATURE TO GOD AS CREATOR THE SAME AS THE RELATION TO GOD AS CONSERVER?

[1]   12.1 Once the questions raised about God have been answered, some questions about creatures follow; first about all creatures in general, then about certain creatures in particular.

12.2 One question about creatures in general was asked and it was this: Is the created thing's relation to God as creator the same as its relation to him as conserver?[1]

Arguments Pro and Con

Argument for the negative:
Something can be created and not conserved. Consequently, it can have a relation to God as its creator only and not as its conserver. Therefore the two relations are not identical. Proof of the first antecedent: A thing is not conserved at the instant of its creation, for conservation is required only when it is able not to be and tends of itself to nonbeing or nonexistence. While it is being created, however, it cannot not be or tend to nonexistence, since it accepts being at that moment. Nothing is conserved, then, unless it continues to exist after the moment of creation. But God can create something that does not remain after the instant of its creation, for there is nothing contradictory about its having existence at but one moment and that it be created in that instant.

12.3 It is argued to the contrary that the relationship of one simple thing to another simple thing is one and the same real relation. Now it is the same volition by which a creating and conserving God formally creates and conserves, and the existence itself of the created subject is identical with that of the conserved subject. Therefore the relation of the created and conserved to the creating and conserving God is one and the same.

[1] Cf. Duns Scotus, *Ord.* II, d.2, q.1, nn.19-20 (ed. Vivès XI, 237-38).

Body of the Question

12.4 There are three points to be investigated in this question. The first is the main question itself, namely: Is the real relation of a creature to God as creating and conserving identical? The second is a point raised by the first argument, namely: Can a thing be said to be simultaneously created and conserved? This is more a linguistic difficulty. Third, there is a connected question also touched on by the first argument, namely: Can something be created that is not conserved after the first instant of creation?

ARTICLE I
Is the Real Relation of the Creature to God as Creator and as Conserver the Same?

[2]   12.5 [Affirmative answer and its proof] As for the first, the relation of a creature to God as creator and conserver can be said to be the same.

Proof: For something that is the same both conceptually and in reality there is but one essential dependence of the same type upon something conceptually and really the same. But the existence [*existentia*] of a permanent* or enduring creature is absolutely the same in creation and conservation, and the supporting term, namely, the divine volition, is absolutely identical both conceptually and in reality; and the relationship not only to the creator but also to the conserver is the same sort of essential dependence. Therefore [there is but one relation of the creature to God as creator and conserver].

12.6 Proof of the major: If there were several absolutely essential dependence-relations between extremes absolutely identical, they would be like the dependence of the creature on God as efficient and as final cause. But these two types of dependence seem to be of different kinds, for if they were of the same nature they would be incompatible in the same subject under the same aspect. If something depends upon another in such a way that the latter's support is adequate, it will not depend upon it with a second dependence-relationship of the same kind. Otherwise it would be completely supported in each of these dependencies without the other and would depend and not depend upon such—and this, when the term provides complete and full support in each case of dependency.

[3]   12.7 The minor has three parts:

Proof of the first part, viz., that the existence of something that is permanent or endures is the same in creation and conservation: The

QUESTION TWELVE

difference between the permanent and the successive* consists in this, that what is successive as long as it continues always has a new or different being [*esse*] for each successive part. The permanent on the contrary always has the same being. Neither does it change partially, for otherwise it would be successive. Neither does it change totally, for otherwise for each different moment it would have a totally different being, which is absurd.

12.8 Proof of the second part of the minor, viz., that it is the same divine volition that supports the dependence-relation of the thing both as created and as conserved: The divine volition remains the same in regard to anything that is able to be willed. Now this volition represents the proximate intrinsic term for anything extrinsic.

12.9 The third part of the minor, viz., that both relations are relationships of essential dependence, is clear as regards creation. As for conservation, the proof is this: A thing depends essentially in existing [*in essendo*] on that from which it has being [*esse*]. Such is the conservation of the conserving cause according to the words of Augustine[2]: "For the power of the creator, omnipotent and supporting all, is the cause by which every creature subsists. If such power should cease to rule what has been created, all would cease to be and nature would vanish. It is not like the case of a builder of houses. When he has completed the construction, he leaves, and after he has ceased working and has gone away, his work still stands. But the world could not stand, not even for a wink of the eye, if God withdrew his ruling hand."

[4] 12.10 [Objections and their solutions] Here one[3] might object that the ground for the creature's relation to God as creator is not its existence taken in an absolute or unqualified sense, but rather the creation itself considered passively. Similarly the ground for the creature's relation to God as conserver is not its existence taken absolutely but rather the conservation itself considered passively. This is proved from the Philosopher,[4] who says that relations of the second type are based upon activity and passivity. Now even though a creature's existence considered absolutely be the same afterwards as it was at the first moment, it is no more obvious that creation and conservation considered passively are the same than are the relationships we are investigating.

[2] Augustine, *Super Gen.* IV, c.12, n.22: PL 34, 304.
[3] Bonaventure, *Sent.* II, pars. 1, a.3, q.2 (II, 33ff.).
[4] Aristotle, *Metaph.* v, c.15 (1020b26-32).

12.11 To this it can be said that the Philosopher does not think that acting [*actio*] and being acted upon [*passio*]* are the proximate foundations for relations of the second type, for a relation does not remain if its foundation is gone. Relations of the second type,* however, do remain even though the action and being acted upon do not. For example, one remains a father even though his begetting is not an ongoing act. What he says about the second-type relations being founded on the active and passive must not be understood to mean that action and passion* are the proximate grounds or foundation proper, but rather that they represent an intervening disposition between the relation and its proper foundation. Now it is the active and passive potencies themselves that can be called the immediate grounds for acting and being acted upon. And although the intervention of action and being acted upon are required, they are not needed to ground the relation, but are a kind of prerequisite, as it were, if the relationship is to be based upon such a ground [as the potencies].[5]

[5] 12.12 In our particular case, however, there seems no need to admit that the fundamental reason for the creature's relationship to God as creating and conserving is that it is being acted upon or affected. For properly speaking, the capacity of being acted upon [*passio*] occurs only when the patient receives some form from the agent, for according to the Philosopher in the *Metaphysics*[6]: "The active potency is the principle of transmuting another *qua* other." Therefore the passive potency is the principle of being changed or transmuted by another. Such a change only occurs when a patient receives something from an agent. But in conservation and creation this does not occur, but the whole is created and the whole conserved completely by the creator and the conserver, and it is not just a part of it as is the case when a patient receives a form from the agent.[7]

12.13 But here there is an objection[8] based on Augustine's words[9]: "Air is not made bright by the sun, but it becomes bright." Otherwise, when the sun sets, the air would remain bright. Now it seems that every creature depends on God for its being in the way

[5] Cf. Duns Scotus, *Ord.* IV, d.13, q.1, nn.3-18 (ed. Vivès XVII, 662-79).
[6] Aristotle, *Metaph.* V, c.12 (1019a15-16).
[7] Cf. Duns Scotus, *Ord.* II, d.1, q.4, n.30 (ed. Vivès XI, 180-81); IV, d.13, q.1, n.29 (ed. Vivès XVII, 686-87).
[8] Bonaventure, *loc. cit.*, d.37, a.1, q.2 (II, 864).
[9] Augustine, *De Gen. ad litteram* VIII, n.26: PL 34, 383; CSEL 28I, 250.

QUESTION TWELVE

the air depends upon the sun for its illumination, which was the point of his analogy of being illumined by the sun. Therefore no creature is made into a being [*facta in esse*], but it continually comes to be [*fit in esse*], and as a consequence the being [*esse*] of a creature is in a continual state of becoming.

[6]　12.14 I reply: The Philosopher[10] says that some things [like the day or a game] are in a state of becoming [*in fieri*] and do not have complete being [like a substance], but are in succession. By contrast, some [like man or a house] are said to be in fact [*in facto esse*], when they have their being complete and do not depend for their being on something extrinsic. Now a creature, however, is at all times equally dependent upon God for its being, for it always has the same being from him through the same divine volition. In this sense one could say that the production of a divine person is always *in fieri*, for such a person could never have being if he were not actually receiving it from his producer, and nevertheless the being of the person is most permanent. In similar fashion, although the being of a creature is permanent, nevertheless as regards God it is always in a quasi state of becoming, that is to say, it is always actually depending on the cause which gives it being and it is never *in facto esse*, i.e., it is never actual [*in actu*] apart from and independent of everything else. However, it is not *in fieri* in the sense that it is different from moment to moment, and in contrast to this, it is *in facto esse*, i.e., it has being complete and needs nothing in addition.[11]

ARTICLE II
Can a Thing be Said to be at once Created and Conserved?

[7]　12.15 [Relations concomitant with creation and conservation] As for the second article [of 12.4], I say that other relations can concur with that which a creature having being has to God as the source of its being [*esse*]. For sometimes this being immediately follows the state of nonbeing opposed to it, as in the case when something first begins to be. At other times, however, this being does not immediately succeed nonbeing, but follows, as it were, the identical being it had before. This must be understood in the sense that, although there is no genuine priority in the very being itself, still we may

---

[10] Aristotle, *Physic.* III, c.6 (206a14-206b6).

[11] Cf. Duns Scotus, *Ord.* II, d.1, q.4, nn.27-28 (ed. Vivès XI, 177-79); d.2, q.1, nn.19-21 (ibid., 237-39).

speak of priority there inasmuch as what was there before is still there at present. The first relation, viz., of the being itself to the previous state of nonbeing, does not represent something real, namely, that of the being to the same being as quasi-preexisting, or better as now existing but having also been before, for in this case the two terms are really identical. But the relationship of the being to its cause is real, and hence is not to be identified with either of the other two relations.

Still it happens that the same word at times implies several distinct things. Now one word can be imposed to signify not only the dependence of this being upon its cause but also its relationship to a prior state of nonbeing, and this is just what the word "create" or "creation" does, since it indicates not only the dependence of the thing upon its cause, but also that it has being for the first time, having been until then nonexistent. In like fashion, one can also impose a word that not only indicates this dependence on its cause but also the second relationship, viz., of this being to itself as something that was there before, and when we want to indicate this situation we make use of the word "conserve."

[8] 12.16 [Solution to the question] Properly speaking, then, it is only true to say that a creature is created at the first moment [of its existence] and only after that moment is it conserved, for only then does its being have this order to itself as something that was, as it were, there before. Because of these different conceptual relationships implied by "create" and "conserve," it follows that one does not apply to a thing when the other does. Nevertheless, the relationship to the cause of the being always remains the same, and if both words signified just this relationship, then they might be truly predicated of the same thing at once, even as "to be from another that gives being" and "to receive being from another" do signify precisely that relation. And here "to give" and "to receive" must not be taken to mean there is something new present, nor do the words themselves imply this, for it is true to say that the Son receives deity from the Father and that the Father gives and communicates deity to him, and yet the two expressions can always be predicated simultaneously of the same situation.

12.17 Here I am not concerned whether "to be created" signifies *per se* the relation to the creator and only connotes the relationship to the prior state of nonbeing, or conversely whether this latter is signified *per se* and the relationship to the cause only connoted, or whether both relations are signified *per se*, in which case the word

QUESTION TWELVE

no longer signifies a concept that is one *per se* but rather two relationships, one real, the other conceptual, the combination of which do not make for a single notion *per se*. For any one of the three preserves this, at least, that both relationships are somehow implied by the expression, and it is precisely because of the conceptual relation that we deny something is at once created and conserved.[12]

ARTICLE III
Can Something be Created without being Conserved after the Instant of Creation?

[9] 12.18 [The answer is affirmative] As for the third main question [in 12.4], I claim there is no contradiction that some being should have being [*esse*] only for an instant, for the instant itself passes suddenly, so that it exists, so to speak, instantaneously. Or if you say an instant according to substance always remains the same, speaking of a substance that is able to change, since that substance is not a *per se* term of a [temporal] continuum in the category of quantity, it follows that what you call an instant according to substance is not a term that involves *per se* a temporal process. But at least an instant according to being [*esse*] does not remain, but quickly passes, and so one would have to speak of a change and, hence, of an instant as the measure of change. But where a permanent [i.e., nonsuccessive] thing is concerned, there does not seem to be any greater contradiction about its having being only for an instant than that an instant or change itself should exist, for while a permanent thing could have the same being or existence continue [through a time period], whereas the instant or change could not, still the permanent entity could have the whole of what it is at one instant, because it is precisely on this score that it differs from what can exist only in succession. Therefore, there is no contradiction if it did not have being for more than an instant.

[10] 12.19 [Three objections] Aristotle[13] apparently is against this, for he says: "Becoming and perishing are opposites; therefore, provided it is impossible for a thing to undergo opposite changes at the same time, the change will not be continuous, but a period of time will intervene between the opposite processes." And at the end of this chapter he declares[14]: "It would seem to be an utterly absurd thing if as soon as anything has come to be, it must necessarily perish and cannot continue to exist for any time."

[12] Ibid., d.2, q.1, n.19 (ed. Vivès XI, 237-38); d.1, q.4, n.27 (ibid., 177-78).
[13] Aristotle, *Physic.* VIII, c.7 (261b5-10). [14] Ibid., c.7 (261b21-24).

12.20 Second objection: Further on in the same chapter[15] he says we should not consider the last moment of being of what will perish but the first in what will come to be together with the first moment of nonbeing of what is to perish: "It is true that the point is common to both times, the earlier as well as the later ... being the finishing point of the one and the starting point of the other; but so far as the thing is concerned it belongs to the later stage of what happens to it." And he adds a little later: "It has become and is [such] at the last moment of the actual time in which it was becoming [such]."

12.21 Third objection: If the created thing only has being in an instant, then it can be truly said of that instant that this thing begins to be because it exists for the first time, and at the same time it is true to say that it ceases to be, for then it exists for the last time. Now it seems impossible that a thing should begin to be and cease to be at the same time.

[11] 12.22 [Reply to the objections] As for the first [in 12.19], I say that what the Philosopher had in mind in the text cited is that local motion alone and no other movement or change can be continuous and perfect, and he proves this from the fact that all other motion and change is from one opposite to another[16]: "Thus for the processes of becoming and perishing the limits are the existent and nonexistent, for alteration the various pairs of contrary affections," etc. Therefore if any of these changes could be perpetual and continuous, it would not be from the same *terminus a quo** to the same *terminus ad quem,** for of movement that is simply one in this way the statement of the *Physics*[17] holds good: "No process of change is infinite." Therefore, if the motion were to continue on it would have to do so by a continuous oscillation from one term to the other. If something changed from hot to cold, the movement would cease so far as these terms are concerned unless it was followed immediately by a change from cold to hot. But the reverse movement cannot be a continuation of the preceding movement since the two changes are opposed to each other and could not form one continuous motion.

[12] 12.23 And the reason is this: The changeable would have to move in opposite directions at the same time. Proof that this follows: Where continuous movement is concerned, it is true to say from the beginning that the subject is being changed to its final state. If this was one of heat, then it would be true to say at the outset of the

---

[15] Ibid., c.8 (263b12-15). [16] Ibid., c.7 (261a30-33).
[17] Ibid., VI, c.10 (241a27).

QUESTION TWELVE

change that the subject is being heated. Now if the heating could continue on as cooling, it would be true to say that the subject was being simultaneously heated and cooled. By a similar argument [Aristotle] proves in the passage cited that perishing cannot continue onward as generation so as to constitute a single movement, for otherwise from the outset something would be undergoing opposite changes, because it would be both perishing and coming to be, since of any single or continuous movement it is true to say from the beginning that the subject is being changed to its ultimate state. But since this is generation, then from the beginning of the change it is being generated, and nevertheless it would be in the process of perishing, if the assumption were correct that the previous corruption continued on as generation. Now this does not militate in any way against our thesis that something could exist for just a moment, namely, at the instant of creation, for I do not admit that annihilation is a continuation of creation so that they constitute a single movement, for then, according to the Philosopher's argument, it would be true to say that when it is created, it is being annihilated. All I claim is that annihilation follows the creation.

[13] 12.24 You may argue that both annihilation and creation take place in an instant, because both are the result of infinite power which cannot act in time, as the Philosopher seems to prove. Therefore, in the proposed case either creation and annihilation will occur at the same instant, which the Philosopher[18] would consider absurd, viz., that the same thing would be subject to opposite changes, or else creation and annihilation would occur at different instants; but then one would have to follow the other immediately, which the Philosopher also considers absurd.

12.25 To this I say that the argument of the Philosopher that was mentioned, viz., that the same thing cannot be simultaneously in motion with opposite movements, proves that perishing cannot continue on as generation. But besides this there is another true conclusion, namely, that perishing cannot immediately follow generation; but there is another reason for this, namely, that each takes place in an instant and not in the same instant, as is obvious; therefore, they occur at different instants, but no two instants are immediate to one another.

12.26 This proof, which is according to the mind of the Philosopher,[19] though he does not cite it here, does not militate against

[18] Ibid., VIII, c.10 (266a24-266b6).
[19] Ibid., c.7 (261b5-15).

our thesis. For if the created thing exists only at the instant of its creation, then its annihilation is not in an instant but at a time when the instant of creation is over. Indeed, after the instant there is not something in time that is indivisibly immediate but divisibly so, namely, with such an immediacy as a continuum that is finished or over is next to its term. In this way movement is immediately adjacent to the last moment of rest, because immediately following rest is movement, as the divisible is after the indivisible which is the beginning.

[14] 12.27 Consequently, when it is argued [in 12.24] that annihilation takes place in an instant, this would have to be denied of annihilation in the case of which we are speaking, understanding always by "instant" an instant of time, whether we speak of creation and annihilation taking place in time or, better, with time.

As for the proof based on the principle "an infinite power does not act in time," the Philosopher would only admit this holds good of an infinite power acting with natural necessity. But if the infinite power is of another kind [e.g., if it acts contingently], there is nothing absurd about the conclusion he draws, viz., that an infinite and a finite power take equal time to act. Theologians, however, will not admit that where creatures are concerned, God acts with natural necessity.

12.28 But even admitting that God acted with natural necessity, could one not grant that something could remain for an instant only, since change, even according to the Philosopher, remains only for an instant? Look for the answer elsewhere.[20]

[15] 12.29 Another interpretation, distinct from the preceding, is needed for the other text of the Philosopher [in 12.19][21] about nature not producing anything to have it destroyed immediately or that as soon as it came to be, it must necessarily perish, as he says. The reason is that the nature producing it also influences its conservation so that the product can exist for a time. Destructive agents are either kept at a distance or are unable to overpower the agent that generates and conserves it. Otherwise the agent would be prevented from generating it. But the only impossibility you can infer from this concerns the interplay of natural causes, and not the divine power.

12.30 [To the second objection in 12.20] As for the other, I say that so far as natural generation and corruption are concerned,

[20] See Appendix, Addition 12.28.
[21] Aristotle, *Physic.* VIII, c.7 (261b21-24).

what perishes has no being [*esse*] at the end[22]; otherwise it would have qualities appropriate to what comes to be, at least to the degree that they could coexist with the form of the latter, and if so, they would not disappear suddenly, nor would what is to perish, perish suddenly. And as what perishes does not have its being at the end, so it has its first instant of nonbeing, since the nonbeing of what perishes concurs with the being of what comes to be. But what came to be has being at the instant of its generation, because then its form is in the matter and then it has its first being because at that moment the form immediately succeeds privation, and just as the thing generated has its first moment of being, so what is destroyed has its first instant of nonbeing. But if by some power a thing were conserved in being at some last instant, then there would not be the first moment of nonbeing. This would be the case with a permanent [i.e., nonsuccessive] creature that existed only for a moment. However, I say in general that with things that succeed one another, whether they be opposed privatively, contradictorily, or contrarily, as it were, since both are something positive, the last of the preceding never coincides with the first of the following. Otherwise opposites would coexist at the same instant or two instants would be immediate. However, there is always either the last of the prior or the first of what follows, for the divisible is immediate only to the indivisible and the mutually successive things are immediate opposites.

[16]   12.31 Some things then which get being after nonbeing pass away instantly, other permanent or enduring things are naturally generated or perish, and there can be still other permanent things that are produced or destroyed by divine power. In the first, namely, those that pass away instantly, there is both a first and last moment in being, because there is that sole instant in which they have existence, and therefore there is neither a first nor a last moment of nonbeing, for during the whole time preceding this instant as well as during the entire time that follows it they have nonbeing. In the second type, however, there is a first moment in being but not a last, and similarly with nonbeing there is a first and not a last, as we explained [in 12.22] when expounding the mind of the Philosopher. In the others, however, which are produced or destroyed by divine power, either of these situations could obtain as well as a third, viz., there can be a last moment in being without a first moment in nonbeing, because that power can cause one thing to succeed another in any way that does not include a contradiction.

[22] Aristotle, *De caelo* I, c.12 (283a4-b22).

12.32 [To the third objection in 12.21] To the other, I say that the expression "begins to be" can have two meanings. One affirms the present and negates the past in the sense that it implies that something exists now but before it did not. The other negates the present and affirms the future inasmuch as it implies that something does not exist now but it will be. "Ceases to be" can likewise have two interpretations.

12.33 I say, then, that on one interpretation, it is true that something starts to be and ceases to be simultaneously, for what passes away instantaneously "begins to be" in the sense that it is now and it did not exist before, and it "ceases to be" in the sense that it is now but it will not be. In both cases, being [*esse*] is affirmed and the negations "was not" and "will not be" are not opposed. "To begin to be" and "to cease to be," however, are not mutually consistent if they are given meanings such that something identical is affirmed by one and denied by the other, or in which opposing features are included.[23]

Reply to the Initial Arguments

12.34 To the first argument at the beginning [viz., in 12.2]:

It is clear from the second main article [in 12.15f.] in what sense the first antecedent is true, viz., that something can be created and not conserved. It holds good only by reason of the different relationships implied by the two terms, namely, in the case of creation, the relation to its opposite, the state of nonbeing that preceded it, and in the case of conservation, the relation to the same being as something it had before. Both relationships are merely conceptual. The first is negative since it regards nonbeing and no relationship of this sort is real. The second refers to the same being as it had before, just as the first relation refers to this being as not having been there before.

12.35 The antecedent, however, is not true of the relation of the being to its cause. Hence the inference that "it can have a relation to God as its creator only and not as its conserver" can be conceded only if the terms be taken in the same sense as before, i.e., if we claim that God never conserves the created in the full meaning of "to conserve." But if we understand this to mean that what was created will never have this relationship to God implied by being conserved by him, then the entailment must be denied, for even though

---

[23] Cf. Duns Scotus, *Ord.* II, d.2, q.1, nn.3ff. (ed. Vivès XI, 214ff.).

what can be created will never have this dependence relationship with a cause together with the other conceptual relationship of quasi-succeeding itself, it will nevertheless have to have that [real] dependence relation. And then the final conclusion [viz., that the two relations are not identical] can only mean that the full meaning of "to be created" is not the same as the full meaning of "to be conserved," viz., that the twofold relationship in the one is not the same as the twofold relationship on the other, which is true enough, because even though the [real] relation implied by both terms is absolutely identical, still the [conceptual] relation implied by creation is not the same as that implied by conservation.

Question Thirteen

ARE THE ACTS OF KNOWING AND APPETITION ESSENTIALLY ABSOLUTE OR ESSENTIALLY RELATIVE?

[1] 13.1 As for creatures in particular the only questions raised concerned those endowed either with sensation or intellective life.

13.2 One question common to either form of life was this: Are the acts of knowing and appetition essentially absolute or essentially relative?[1]

Arguments Pro and Con

It was argued that they are relative because such acts cannot be thought of apart from their terms. But the absolute can be thought of apart from the thought of any term. Therefore [they are not absolute]. Proof of the major: Vision cannot be thought of apart from an object or something visible. The minor is evident.

13.3 To the contrary: Such acts are qualities. Now every quality represents a form that is simply absolute, for the categories are not intermixed [i.e., qualities are not relations]. Therefore [such are something absolute].

Body of the Question

[2] 13.4 This question is not about the act that results in knowledge, viz., that which produces, educes, or induces knowledge, but rather about the act of knowing, viz., the actual knowledge itself. If this be called an action, it does not fall under the category of "action" (for this latter is always directed to some term which somehow gets its being [*esse*] through the action). It is rather understood to mean the action in the sense of that operation by which the agent is ultimately perfected. For brevity's sake throughout this entire question we shall use "action" to mean the category by that name, viz., that

---

[1] Cf. Duns Scotus, *Ord.* 1, d.3, nn.537ff., 600-603 (III, 320ff., 354-56); d.6, nn.11-14 (IV, qq.2-94); d.12, nn.14-18 (V, 32-35); IV, d.12, q.3, nn.40-41 (ed. Vivès XVII, 613-14); d.11, q.2, n.5 (ibid., 339); d.13, q.1 (ibid., 660-95); d.49, qq.1-4 (ed. Vivès XXI, 5-100).

productive action or at least that activity which in some fashion causes its term to exist, whereas "operation" will be taken to mean that intrinsic act by which the operator himself is ultimately perfected.

13.5 While the question could be understood as referring to the relation to either object or subject, the arguments [pro and con] seem to restrict it to the object.

13.6 Hence this meaning of the question must be discussed first. Is actual knowledge essentially a relation to the object known, and, similarly, is actual appetition a relation to the object wanted?

13.7 There are three points to be dealt with here: First, to show that in all intellection and, in general, for any operation we are speaking of here, there is some absolute entity. Second, we must see how this absolute entity is related to the object connected with it. Third, we must find out whether this relationship is essential to the act.

ARTICLE I
There is some Absolute Entity Involved in Every Operation including Intellection

13.8 There are three proofs for the first conclusion.

[First proof from the nature of perfection] The ultimate perfection of a living substance destined by nature for sensitive and intellectual activity is not a mere relation. But its operation is the ultimate perfection of such a substance. Therefore its operation is not a mere relation. Hence [it is something absolute].

13.9 Proof of the major: What is wanted above all else by either the natural or the free appetite of a nature whose desire is most perfect is not just a relation. But the ultimate perfection of the living nature is what such a nature desires above all else by natural desire. Augustine's words can be understood as referring to such desire when he declares[2]: "We all want to be happy." This is always true whether we actually think of beatitude or not, and yet without actual knowledge we can have no actual volition. In the same book he also says: "Whatever else it is that anyone secretly will, he does not withdraw from this common will." This beatitude is also freely desired above all by a will that is well disposed.

13.10 Proof of the minor: There are the Philosopher's statements in the *Ethics*[3] where he wants to say that well-being or happiness,

---

[2] Augustine, *De Trin.* XIII, c.4, n.7: PL 42, 1018-19; CCSL 50a, 389-91.
[3] Aristotle, *Ethica ad Nic.* I, c.9 (1099a24-31); X, c.7 (1177a12-14).

which is the ultimate end of an intellectual nature and consequently something supremely desirable, either is the best operation or it consists in such an activity. And he says the same in the *Metaphysics*,[4] speaking of God's mind: "For if it thinks of nothing, what is there here of dignity?" And he adds immediately: "If its substance is not intelligence, but a potency, it cannot be the best substance." By "intelligence" he means the act of "thinking," for to prove the entailment, he adds: "For it is through thinking that its value belongs to it." And he repeats the same idea elsewhere in the

[4] *Metaphysics*[5] where he says that actuality is prior to potency, not only in time and the order of knowing but also in substance, i.e., perfection. And to prove "act is prior in substance," he uses the example of man as prior to boy and human being to seed. And he also gives this reason for his conclusion, viz., the actuality is the end, and it is for the sake of this that the other things are acquired, which he illustrates with many examples.

13.11 Also there are many citations from authority about happiness as the ultimate and most desirable end, whether they make it consist in knowledge (as in that text from Augustine[6] that "vision is the whole reward") or in love (according to his statement[7] that "The supreme regard is our enjoyment of him"). All these agree at least in this, that the last and most desirable end is an activity or consists in an operation.

13.12 [Second proof from the novelty of the absolute] The main conclusion is proved secondly in this fashion: A relation proper is not new unless there be in either the subject or the term some prior absolute entity that is new. But an operation can be new without any other prior absolute being present in either the operator himself or in the term of the operation. Therefore the operation is not precisely a relation proper. Hence [it is something absolute].

13.13 Proof of the major: First, from what the Philosopher says in *Physics*, where in Bk. V[8] he denies there is motion with respect to relation, and says even more expressly in Bk. VII[9] that acquired states of excellence or defects are not alterations because they represent relations: "Relatives are neither themselves alterations nor

---

[4] Aristotle, *Metaph.* XII, c.9 (1074b18-21).
[5] Ibid., IX, c.8 (1050a3).
[6] Augustine, *De Trin.* I, c.13, n.31: PL 42, 844; CCSL 50, 78.
[7] Augustine, *De doctr. christ.* I, c.32, n.35: PL 34, 32; CCSL 32, 26.
[8] Aristotle, *Physic.* V, c.2 (225b1-12).
[9] Ibid., VII, c.3 (246b10-12).

the subject of alteration or becoming or in fact of any change whatever." Second, from reason: A relation proper follows necessarily once the *relata*, or terms, are given. Hence it cannot be something new without some novelty in one of the related terms.

13.14 Proof of the first part of the minor: A subject which passes from accidental potency to act does not receive a new form prior to the operation itself; otherwise it would have been in essential, not accidental, potency. The second part of the minor is manifest, for it is obvious that something visible does not acquire anything absolute by the fact that it is actually seen; neither then does an intelligible object, and the same is true of other objects.

[5] 13.15 [Third proof from the distinction between the relation and its foundation] Furthermore, every real relation, once the terms are given, necessarily follows or accompanies its proximate foundation or the reason that grounds it. Now the actual relation to the object does not necessarily accompany the operative potency. Consequently, the power or potency itself is not the proximate ground of the relation. Hence if an actual relationship of the operator to the object does obtain, something posterior to the potency itself is needed as its proximate ground which is a kind of intermediary between the power itself and this relationship. It seems the only medium of this sort is the operation itself. Now the proximate foundation for the relationship either is something absolute (according to that dictum of Augustine[10]: "Every essence which is spoken of relatively is also something apart from the relationship") or at least is not precisely the relationship whose foundation it is. Therefore, the operation itself is not precisely the relationship of the operator to the object, and by the same token the operation is not precisely some relation.

13.16 [The operation is not a relation] From this conclusion just established we infer our intended thesis in this way: If this operation were precisely a relationship, then it would be a relation proper, for "relative," insofar as the Philosopher admits this is in someway applicable to an operation [like knowledge or perception] pertains properly to the category of "relation" and falls under the third type of the "relative,"* as is clear from the *Metaphysics*.[11] But since an operation is not precisely a relation, as the [three] reasons given above demonstrate, it follows that it is not precisely a relationship of any sort, and that, hence, some absolute entity exists there, which is our contention in this article.

[10] Augustine, *De Trin.* VII, c.1, n.2: PL 42, 935; CCSL 50, 247.
[11] Aristotle, *Metaph.* v, c.15 (1020b30-33).

ARTICLE II
How this Absolute Entity is Related to the Object Connected with It

[6] 13.17 [Three points to be investigated] In this second main article we must consider three points: First, it is argued that the operation has to involve some real relationship to its object; second, we must say just how this is to be understood; third, we shall analyze the argument cited in the first section.

1. The Operation, Some Claim, must Involve a Real Relationship to the Object

13.18 [Three reasons they adduce] The first point is shown in three ways, and these correspond to the three proofs cited in the first article.

[First proof from the nature of perfection] The first proof is from the notion of perfection which was the middle term for the initial argument [in 13.8] of the first article. The last and highest perfection of an active or functional nature cannot be without a real relationship to the most perfect object it was designed by nature to have. But the highest perfection of such a nature is its operation. Therefore [it cannot be without a real relationship to its most perfect object].

13.19 Proof of the major: If the claim were made that the highest perfection of a living nature is something insofar as it is an absolute thing, then its substance would be its supreme perfection, for according to Aristotle's *Metaphysics*,[12] the substance is more perfect than any of its accidents. If one admits then that the consummate bliss of a creature is an accident of a nature able to be beatified and is nevertheless that nature's supreme perfection, this cannot refer to beatitude insofar as it is something absolute but precisely to the extent that it connects or joins the nature with its ultimate end in an unqualified sense, namely, with the extrinsic object that beatifies. Therefore, it is its relationship to the object that is the formal reason why beatitude is called the highest perfection.

[7] 13.20 This is confirmed from Augustine,[13] who, after rejecting the other definitions of beatitude, gives this as its true notion: "He alone is blessed who has all he wills and wills nothing wrongly." From this it is argued: When there is a concrete predication* in the first mode

---

[12] Ibid., VII, c.1 (1028 a34-1028b5).

[13] Augustine, *De Trin.* XIII, c.5, n.8: PL 42, 1020; CCSL 50a, 393.

per se, then it follows that the abstract can be predicated of the abstract, as is clear from this example: "The white is colored" represents a concrete *per se* predication of the first mode, not by reason of the subject but in virtue of the form, and hence it follows that this abstract predication, "Whiteness is color," is also true. If then it be true *per se* according to the first mode that "The blessed has all he wills well," then it follows that beatitude is, so to say, the possession of everything that is willed correctly. Now this possession or "having" seems to imply *per se* a relation.

13.21 [Second proof from the novelty of the absolute] Furthermore, the other middle term [in 13.12] of the second argument, namely, the novelty of something absolute, is used to construct this argument. In regard to an absolute form *per se* change is possible. In regard to operations like knowing *per se* change is not possible. Therefore [operations of this sort are not absolute forms].

13.22 Proof of the major: A subject can acquire an absolute form not just *per accidens*, viz., when something else is acquired, but *per se*, viz., it can be acquired on its own, because the form can be the first *per se* to follow its own privation.

13.23 The minor is proved from what the Philosopher says in the *Physics*[14]: "The states of the intellectual part of the soul are not alterations. For the knower is above all said to be related to something." Other similar expressions found in the same section in the Philosopher's own words as well as in the commentary[15] seem to show this to be his view.

13.24 [Third proof from the distinction between the relation and its foundation] What is more, from the third middle term [in 13.15], namely, the distinction between the relation and its foundation, this argument is formulated. Nothing whose substance includes a relation can be something absolute. But the substance of one of the terms, viz., the measured, of [Aristotle's] third type of "the relative" includes a relation, for an operation [like knowing or perceiving] refers to its object in this third way. Therefore [the operation is not something absolute].

13.25 Proof of the major: The absolute does not include relative in its essential meaning; otherwise it would be at once relative *per se* because of the respect it includes and not relative *per se* because by stipulation it is absolute.

---

[14] Aristotle, *Physic.* VIII, c.3 (247b2-4).
[15] Averroes, *Physic.* VII, com. 20 (IV, fol. 322E-323K).

13.26 The minor is evident from the Commentator's explanation on Book V of the *Metaphysics*[16] to the effect that with relatives of the third type the relationship is only given in the substance of one of the terms, e.g., in the intellect, but not in the intelligible. He says: "The relation is not in the substance of what is known but in the intellect," etc., and in the same place he explains the Philosopher's remark that "the same would be said twice" as follows: " 'Intellect' does not refer to the one knowing but to what is known; otherwise the intellect would be constituted by the one knowing, whereas it seems to be the other way about. If it worked both ways it would follow that what is constituted by another also constitutes this other." Just as he argues that if intellect referred to the knower, it would constituted by him, so the Commentator understands the intellect to be constituted by the intelligible to which it refers. But if the intellect were something absolute in itself, it would not be constituted by the intelligible.

2. How are We to Understand the Claim that the Operation Implies a Relation?

[8] 13.27 [A distinction between operations] As for the second point [of 13.17] in this article, I make a distinction in regard to operations that is more manifest in regard to the act of knowing, but can be assumed to be present, perhaps, also in the act of appetition.

There is some knowledge of the existent as such, such as that which grasps the object in its actual existence, e.g., the sight of color and in general of any sense perception involving the external senses. There is also knowledge of the object, but not as existing as such, either because the object does not exist or at least the knowledge is not of the object as actually existing. One can imagine color, for example, both when it exists and when it does not.

13.28 A similar distinction can be shown to obtain in intellectual knowledge.[17]

This is proved, first, since it is clear that there can be some intellection of the nonexistent. But there can also be intellectual knowledge of the existent *qua* existent, for the blessed will have such

---

[16] Averroes, *Metaph.* v, com. 20 (VIII, fol. 129G).

[17] Cf. Duns Scotus, *Ord.* I, d.1, n.35 (II, 23-24); d.2, nn.139, 394 (ibid., 210-11, 352); d.3, nn.95-98, 41-44, 61-64 (III, 62-63, 27-29, 42-46); II, d.3, q.3, n.6 (ed. Vivès XII, 212-13); d.9, q.2, n.17 (ibid., 453); III, d.14, q.3, n.4 (ed. Vivès XIV, 524); IV, d.10, q.8, n.5 (ed. Vivès XVII, 285); d.45, q.2, n.12 (ed. Vivès XX, 304-305).

knowledge of the beatific object [God]. Otherwise someone could be beatified by the object even if, to assume the impossible, it did not exist. And yet there is admittedly a clear face-to-face vision of this object, since the act of knowing it tends to this object as present in itself with its own actual existence.

13.29 A second proof of the same is this: Everything that is part of the perfection of knowledge can pertain to intellectual knowledge with greater right than to sense knowledge. Now the possibility of grasping the object in its reality is a part of perfection, whenever this would not be prejudicial to the power of attaining the object because of its imperfection. Therefore, the intellect can have an act whereby the object is grasped in its real existence, at least that object which is more noble or on a par with the intellect. And if one concedes that our intellect can grasp some existing object in this way, then with equal reason we could admit it is possible for any object, since our intellect has the capacity for receiving the knowledge of anything intelligible.

13.30 [Two objections against this distinction] Against this distinction it is argued first that in knowing our intellect abstracts from the here-and-now and by the same token from anything concerned with the existent *qua* existent. Therefore, knowledge of anything as existing does not pertain to it *per se*.

[9]   13.31 Furthermore, if two such intellections were possible for our intellect, then it should be possible, on like grounds, to have both of these as regards the same object. And then, I ask, how would they possibly be distinguished, not only numerically (since two accidents of the same species cannot coexist at once in the same subject) but even specifically (for whether the act is specified in terms of the faculty or the object, since here the potency and object are the same for both types of knowledge, what specific difference could we claim was there)?

13.32 [Reply to these objections] To the first of these [in 13.30] one could say that the common distinction made between intellective and sensitive knowledge, namely, that we understand the universal, but we sense the singular, must not be understood as referring to disparate but equal powers such as obtain between sight in seeing colors and hearing in perceiving sounds. Rather the distinction is one between a higher cognitive faculty and one subordinate to it, and hence the superior power can know some object or aspect thereof that the inferior cannot know, but not vice versa in the sense that the inferior could know some object or aspect of it without the superior faculty being able to know that object even more perfectly or under the same aspect of knowability [e.g., as existing]. And thus one could admit that the intellect does not know the object as here-and-now because it grasps it in its absolute quidditive form, whereas the senses cannot know the object in this fashion because the power of each is limited to knowing it under the aspect of existing. But this does not mean the intellect is so determined that it has to know the object only in some different way than as existing, for it is not limited to knowing it in only one way.

[10] 13.33 To the second objection [in 13.31], one could admit that there are two kinds of knowledge of the same object at once, because the object of one is not distinguished from the other as essence from existence. For even if there were some distinction on the part of the object between essence and existence, it does not suffice for our purpose, because existence itself can be conceived abstractly, for just as we can understand essence so can we conceive of existence even when it is not confronting us extramentally. Hence we may say that the two kinds of knowledge are distinct, and this, specifically, because the formal grounds that move the mind to each type of knowledge are not the same, since in the case of intuitive knowledge it is the thing in its own existence that is the *per se* motive factor objectively, whereas in the case of abstractive knowledge what moves the intellect *per se* is something in which the thing has "knowable being" [*esse cognoscibile*], whether this be the cause that virtually contains the thing as knowable or whether it be an effect such as the [intelligible] species* or likeness that contains the thing of which it is the likeness representationally.

[11] 13.34 [The first type of knowledge involves a twofold real relationship] Given the distinction [in 13.27] between the two acts of knowing, one could say that the first, viz., of the thing as existing, must include in itself a real and actual relation to the object itself. The reason is that there can be no knowledge of this sort unless the knower has to the object an actual relationship that is such that the *relata* actually exist and are really distinct and given the nature of the *relata* the relationship arises necessarily.

13.35 But more specifically there seems to be a double actual relationship to the object in this act. One could be called the relationship of the measured or, more accurately, of the measurable to its measure. The other can be called the relationship of becoming one with the term to which one is united, which has the formal character of being something in between the two. And this relation of the uniting medium can be given the special name of reaching out and coming in contact with the other term [*relatio attingentiae alterius ut termini*] or a stretching out or extending into the other as term [*relatio tendentiae in alterum ut terminum*].

13.36 But this distinction between the two relationships, namely, of the measurable to its measure and of contact with the term, seems to be sufficiently evident, for each can be separated from the other, as is the case with essences where the superior has the character of a measure with respect to the inferior, yet the inferior does not always have this relationship of contact with the superior of which we are speaking. Also, in the case where the intellect or the will is totally causing its object, there seems to be the relationship of extending into the term of the intellection or volition, whether this relationship be real or at least conceptual, and yet intellection or volition of this sort does not have the relationship of being measurable by this object but rather that of being its measure.

[12] 13.37 As for the first relationship, that of the measurable, Aristotle in the *Metaphysics*[18] declares it pertains properly to the third type of the "relative."* Here it should be noted that for "something to be measured" means that it is made certain of the specific quantity by the other [i.e., the measure], so that it implies a relationship both to the intellect that gets the certitude and to the measure which imparts it. The first of these is not real, just as the relationship of the knowable to the knowledge is not real. The second relationship is of the caused, not in being, but being known, to the cause of its being known, and this relationship is real insofar as the dependence of the caused upon the cause is concerned, which dependence arises from the character of the *relata* and not just because of an act of the mind referring one to the other. Nevertheless, because this relationship of dependence (not indeed of the knowledge itself upon the cause of that knowledge, which is quite real, but of the object as known to the object as that by which it is known) is between the *relata* insofar as they have this characteristic of "being known" [*esse cognitum*], it follows that this relationship is not, simply speaking, real. But neither is it a purely conceptual relation, like that of the universal to the singular or of one contradictory to another, for Aristotle does not say that a "relative" of the third type is of the measured to the measure, but of the measurable (i.e., that which is suited by nature to be measured) to the measure (i.e., that which is designed by nature to measure).

[18] Aristotle, *Metaph.* v, c.15 (1020b26-32).

13.38 One could understand this as follows. Just as "to be measured" is to depend for being known actually (as is clear from what has been said), so "to be measurable" implies an aptitudinal or potential dependence for being known, which is to assert a dependence as to knowability. But everything is related to entity as it is to knowability. Consequently, the measurable refers to that underlying being which is the reason why this is measurable, and this entity is caused or "participated," so that when something in the third class of "relatives" is said to be "as the measurable to its measure," this is understood to mean that it is dependent in entity upon that in whose entity it participates, so that there does exist a relationship of the third type on the part of the measurable that is simply real, for it is understood to be a being by participation or imitation in relation to something else.

13.39 One could say further in favor of our proposal that since something could participate in the perfection of another in many ways, so the act of knowing is also related to the object participatively in the way a likeness is to that of which it is the likeness. I am not referring here to the sort of likeness that involves a communication of the same form, as in the case of the likeness between two white objects, but rather the likeness peculiar to imitation which is the likeness of the ideate* to the idea.

[13] 13.40 [Abstractive cognition has only a potentially real relation together with another conceptual relationship] The second act of knowledge, viz., that which does not have to be of the existent *qua* existent, does not require an actual real relationship to the object, since this sort of relation requires real and actual terms. Still, this second act of knowlege can have a relationship to its object as something potentially real, where "real" would refer to the first relation mentioned in the preceding section [13.35], viz., that of the measurable or dependent, but would not refer to the second, viz., that of union or contact. In addition, abstractive knowledge can also have an actual conceptual relationship to the object, but for the knowledge to be of the object itself this is not required.

13.41 [Four points to be clarified] There are, then, four points to be explained here:

First, that abstractive knowledge has a real potential or aptitudinal relation, viz., of the measurable with reference to the object, even if this is not existent. Proof: Whatever has an actual relationship to an existent term and for its part always relates to that term in the same way, will have an aptitudinal relationship to that term when it is not existing. But an operation is this sort of thing because it is something measurable by the object, i.e., it is apt by nature to depend as to its entity upon the object, with that special sort of dependence that characterizes a likeness that imitates or participates in [the perfection of] that of which it is a likeness. But all these conditions would exist as actualized so far as the foundation goes, if the term actually existed.

[14] 13.42 Second, namely, that so far as the relationship of reaching out and contacting the term goes, one can say that neither a real nor an aptitudinal relationship of this sort is characteristic of abstractive knowledge. Proof: Such a relation does not pertain to the foundation on its part, and it would not actually pertain to abstractive knowledge actually even if the term did exist in reality, for the latter is not designed by nature to contact the term in its actual existence.

13.43 Third, namely, that so far as the conceptual relation present in abstractive cognition is concerned, one can understand it in two ways:

One is this: When a term does not exist extramentally but has being only in the intellect, any relationship to it must be one of reason, i.e., conceptual, since a relation can have no truer being than does the term to which it relates. Now the object that is the term of abstractive knowledge needs only to be in the intellect. Therefore [any relationship to it can only be conceptual].

13.44 The other way to understand the conceptual relation is this: The act of knowing an object abstractively can itself be grasped in a reflex act. For since this intellection by reason of the object known is a natural likeness of the object, it can be known by reflection, and the intellect that grasps this intellection in this way can relate it to the object. But this intellection which is related in this fashion through the act of the intellect is being related by means of a conceptual relation.

[15] 13.45 There is a difference between these two conceptual relations, for just as the second can be a relationship to a nonexistent object, so also it can be a relation of a nonexistent cognition, just as long as this cognition remains known through reflection or is related by the intellect. But the first relation can only hold for an existing act, and not just for it as an object known through some reflex act or as the *relatum* in the relating mind.

And from this difference follows the other, viz., that the second relation is one of reason on the part of both extremes, whereas the first conceptual relation is one of reason only on the part of the object, but on the part of the act it is real, because it is seen to follow from the nature of the act, and does not pertain to it only insofar as it is an object of the intellect or is related.

13.46 Against this it is argued that a real being does not require that anything not real follow or accompany its nature. Hence the real act of knowing has no relation of reason that follows from its nature.

I reply: Through the act of knowing the object has "known being" [*esse cognitum*]. Therefore, some relation which refers to the object as having such "being" can follow the nature of the act.

13.47 From this the *fourth* point becomes clear, namely, how the conceptual relation is a necessary concomitant, because this is true of the first relation of reason [mentioned in 13.43], for abstractive knowledge could exist without the second relation [in 13.44], viz., as a direct act without the following reflex act. And *a fortiori* the object could be the term of such an act without having to have the conceptual relation to the act. The second relation is caused contingently after the direct act of intellection. Therefore there was no necessary ground in the object for it having to be the term of this reflex act.

3. Analysis of the Arguments in the First Section

[16] 13.48 Now in this third section of this article, we must reply to the arguments given in the first section [13.18-26] to the extent that they seem to be inadequate.

As for the first [in 13.19-20], I concede that the operation which represents the ultimate perfection of a functional nature must involve a relation. For instance, if we speak of the beatific operation of a man or an angel, this relation must exist, for if this operation refers to cognition, this is intuitive, and if it refers to volition, this is necessarily associated with intuitive knowledge. But when it is said [in 13.19] that the operation is the ultimate perfection precisely insofar as it unites one with the object, I answer that "ultimate perfection" can mean either some supreme perfection that is *per se* one or else a perfection which consists of the supreme perfection together with all that necessarily accompanies it.

13.49 In the first sense, I say that the operation itself is the ultimate perfection and it is simply more perfect than anything accompanying it, including also that relationship which the union formally implies, for if I could have the operation without the relation, I

QUESTION THIRTEEN

would still be beatified. I would not possess consummate bliss, however, if I had the relation without the operation.

13.50 This is clear as regards God's beatitude, which formally consists in an operation, according to those words of the Philosoper[19] where he is speaking of God's mind: "For if it thinks of nothing, what is there here of dignity? It is just like one who sleeps, and if its substance is not its intelligence," i.e., actual thinking, "it is not the best substance." And he proves the entailment: "For it is through thinking that its value belongs to it." His beatitude, however, does not require a conceptual relationship between the operation and its object, for even though his intellect could relate its act with the object, still such a referral or conceptual relation is not included in the operation itself, which in its own right is beatific. For it does not seem reasonable that there are stronger reasons for saying that God is formally happy by an operation that includes a conceptual relation than for saying that an angel's beatitude includes such a relation.

13.51 Created beatitude, however, does necessarily require a relationship to the object, and this is a real relation. The reason for this is that the operation can have no greater unity with the object than the unity of a relationship. But God's operation has a true union or identity with the object, and therefore no relation is required there for the operation alone and as something absolute to be fully beatific.

[17] 13.52 And here we see one way in which divine beatitude excels created happiness, because as something absolute, it is fully God's ultimate good, whereas created happiness is ultimate only where there is a relationship conjoined with it. Consequently, when it is claimed that the perfection is ultimate precisely insofar as it unites one with the object, the added qualification can refer either to the relation or to its foundation. If the first is meant, then the statement must be denied, because the beatitude is not the ultimate perfection precisely insofar as it is formally a relation. If one takes the second sense, then it can be conceded that beatitude insofar as it connects, i.e., insofar as it is the proximate connecting foundation, is the ultimate perfection.

13.53 The same distinction makes it clear how to answer the confirmation [in 13.20] that "He alone is blessed who has all he wills, etc." For if "has" is understood there as implying a relation, then

[19] Ibid., XII, c.9 (1074b17-18).

either something necessarily accompanying the beatific operation is being described, or else the word "beatitude" does not imply precisely something absolute but includes a relationship to the object. But if "has" refers *per se* to the operation by which God is possessed, in the sense Augustine[20] says: "To have God is nothing else than to know," then the beatific possession does not imply *per se* a relation, but this latter only accompanies it.

13.54 [Objections and their solution] Against this it is argued that there is no contradiction that the absolute should be separated from the relation, as prior from the posterior, particularly if the relationship is not one of essential dependence. Therefore, if the operation that beatifies is something absolute, it could be separated from the relationship to the object by the divine power, and then one could be beatified with no connection with the object.

[18] 13.55 Besides, according to the Philosopher,[21] where generation or becoming is concerned, the posterior is more perfect. But a relation, if it be other than the absolute operation, is posterior in becoming. Therefore [it is more perfect].

13.56 Look for the answer to the first objection elsewhere.[22]

13.57 To the second objection, I say that the principle of the Philosopher must be understood to refer to the same order, for if something is posterior in becoming in another order or genus, there is no need that it be more perfect. Otherwise an accident would be more perfect than the substantial form. But it is only in this latter way that a relation is posterior to the absolute for it does not advene* to the absolute as its proper complement in the same order, but only when the absolute with its own complete perfection is given, does the relation arise from this perfection.

[19] 13.58 [To the second proof in 13.21-23] As for the second argument based on the *Physics*,[23] it seems that Aristotle, according to the Commentator,[24] is expressing not his own view but the opinion of Plato, for he says at the end of his comment: "Aristotle does not want to expound his own opinion here but to show the strength of this particular view." And the view seems to be that which Augustine[25] and Aristotle[26] impute to Plato, namely, that "To learn is

---

[20] Augustine, *De diversis quaest. 83*, q.35, n.1: PL 40, 24.
[21] Aristotle, *Metaph.* IX, c.8 (1049b19-22, 1050a3-5, 1051a4-5).
[22] See Appendix, Addition 13.56.
[23] Aristotle, *Physic.* VII, c.3 (247b2-4).
[24] Averroes, *Physic.* VII, com. 20 (VII, fol. 323H).
[25] Augustine, *De Trin.* XII, c.15, nn.24-25: PL 42, 1011-12; CCSL 50, 377.
[26] Aristotle, *Anal. prior.* II, c.21 (67a22); Topic. II, c.4 (111b27-31).

nothing other than to remember." For Aristotle says[27]: "The original acquisition of knowledge is not a becoming or an alteration. . . . For the terms knowing and understanding imply that the intellect has reached a state of rest and has come to a standstill . . . just as when one awakes from sleep." And the Commentator[28] explains (and in the alternate translation the same view is expressed) that the soul is not changed in the first acquisition of knowledge, just as it is not changed when, after the impediment of sleep or drunkenness, one can use the knowledge he could not use before.

13.59 One can put it another way, however. If Aristotle was expressing his own view when he said this, he still did not affirm that movement and change exist *per se* with respect to any form except that which can be acquired on its own. Hence he did not claim there is any change as regards a form that can be acquired only by first getting something else, which is the case with acquiring a relationship. What he wants to say in the text cited is that there is no alteration in qualities that occurs only when other factors are altered, i.e., the alteration takes place in other things: "Though it may be true that every such becoming is necessarily the result of something's being altered, the result, for instance, of the materials being condensed or rarified or heated or cooled, nevertheless it is not the things that are coming into existence that are altered and their becoming is not an alteration."[29] Afterwards he says[30]: "Thus bodily excellences such as health and a good state of body we regard as consisting in a blending of hot and cold elements within the body in due proportion in relation either to one another or to the surrounding atmosphere." And, therefore, health is not properly the term of the alteration, but some other alteration ends with a certain degree of heat or cold, and this is in harmony with the other bodily qualities and thus health results. Now if it were evident that knowledge or the actual consideration of something were a relation only, then it would be sufficiently apparent that, according to the mind of Aristotle, these states would undergo no change or alteration. But we proved in [13.8ff. of] the first article that an operation is not just a relation, and by equal or even greater reason, neither is habitual knowledge a relation.

[20] 13.60 Hence it seems that something further should be added, namely, that Aristotle admits qualitative alteration only as regards

[27] Aristotle, *Physic.* VII, c.3 (247b10-18).
[28] Averroes, *Physic.* VII, com. 20 (IV, fol. 323H).
[29] Aristotle, *Physic.* VII, c.3 (246a2-10).
[30] Ibid.

a quality that can be acquired first, that is to say, a quality which neither follows incidentally some induced form the way a relation does, nor is it induced necessarily given the induction of some prior form. And then this conclusion of his [in 13.23] is not true of any alteration except that which is immediate to the first thing producing the alteration in some order. And so knowledge or the consideration of something does not involve this sort of alteration because the external object is the first thing to produce an alteration in the order [of knowledge], but the knowledge in the intellect itself is not caused immediately by the object but by something inside. For we exercise our knowledge when we wish to, as the *De anima*[31] puts it, whereas sensation does not depend on our wishes. The reason for this is that an internal object is needed for understanding, but sensation requires an external object.

[21]   13.61 That Aristotle had this sort of alteration in mind is shown from the fact that just before he admitted that the senses are changed, declaring that the senses themselves are altered, since they are acted upon, for sensation results from a bodily movement and the sense being acted upon. Here [in the *Physics*],[32] however, he denies that the intellectual part of the soul is altered, and the reason he seems to give is that intellectual knowledge is not received immediately from an external object, which is the first cause of alteration in the order [of knowledge], but it requires the mediation of sense knowledge. Hence, to prove that knowledge is not the result of a movement or change, properly speaking, he says: "It is when it meets with the particular object that the soul knows it in a universal manner." Thus his words there that "the knower is said above all to be related to something," is to be understood in the sense that "related to something" refers to the object inside and not immediately to the external object which is the first cause of the alteration. And this conclusion, understood in particular of the first alteration, suffices for his purpose here, since he intends to prove by enumerative induction for each case of movement the conclusion that the mover and moved are simultaneous. And it is especially in regard to alteration that he seems to have an instance of those qualities not immediately induced by the first cause of the alteration, for although what is altered here exists at the same time as its proximate cause, it does not exist at the same time as that which more obvious-

[31] Aristotle, *De anima* II, c.5 (417b24).
[32] Aristotle, *Physic.* VII, c.3 (247b1ff.).

ly seems to be the first cause of the alteration in this order [of knowledge, viz., the external object].

13.62 The third way to understand Aristotle's dictum [that the states of the intellective soul are not alterations] would be to take "alteration" as referring to motion, or if the alteration is not divisible, then it refers to a change terminative or continuative of motion, or at least to a change that a natural agent can produce in a mobile or mutable subject. None of these situations holds good of the intellective part of the soul, for it is not divisible and hence it is not the recipient of motion which requires a divisible subject. Also, being indivisible, it is not locally present to any natural agent, since it does not occupy a place. A physical agent, however, only acts on a patient locally present to it. By contrast, the sense can be said to be altered, because in this something composite receives something extended and from a natural agent locally present.

13.63 Though this third interpretation is true enough, it is not clear how it can be derived from what Aristotle says here.

[22] 13.64 [To the third proof in 13.24-26] As for the third argument, one could say that just as in the first two types of relatives the relationship is admittedly in the substance of both *relata*, so in the third type we concede it is to be found in the substance of only one of the terms. That is why the Commentator[33] says here that "a relation occurs in two ways; either in the substance of both terms or in the substance of only one of them." However, in the first two types of relatives,* the relationship is not included essentially in either term, for each is something essentially absolute. But the relation in this case is said to be in the substance of both terms in the sense that the proximate basis or reason for grounding the relation is in both, whereas in the third type of "relative"* this is characteristic only of one *relatum*.

13.65 The other translation [of Aristotle][34] makes this even clearer: "Relative terms which imply number or potency,"—i.e., relatives of the first and second type—"are all relative because their essence includes in its nature a reference to something, not because something else involves a reference to it; but that which is measurable or sensible or thinkable is called relative, because something else involves a reference to it." What he wants to say is that, in the first two types, what is related is of itself relative and is not just said to

[33] Averroes, *Metaph.* v, com. 20 (vii, fol. 129G).
[34] Aristotle, *Metaph.* v (1021a27-30).

be related because something else is related to it. In the third type, however, only one term has essentially the basis for the relationship, whereas the other is only said to be related because the first is related to it.

[23] 13.66 To put it briefly, the difference between the two cases is that in the first two types the relationship is mutual, so that in each extreme there is a reason for grounding one relation and being the term of the other. In the third type, the reaction is non-mutual, and the foundation for the relationship is characteristic only of one *relatum*, whereas the other has the aspect of being the term of this same relation.

13.67 What the Commentator[35] adds there about "the same would be said twice," and so on, can be understood in the sense that we can speak of a thing being constituted by that on which it depends essentially, even if that on which it depends is not intrinsic to it, and it is in this way that a thing is constituted by its measure. Therefore, if the intellect referred to the knower as its measure, then it would be constituted by it in this fashion. But the knower is constituted by the intellect as by its form. Hence there would be circularity as regards their constitutions, even though they would not be constituted in the same way. But such circularity is impossible if each depended essentially on the other in this way, because there can be no circularity where essential dependence is concerned. This seems to be the sense of the Commentator's words there: "The same would be stated twice and then the same will be both cause and effect of the same identical thing." The text of Aristotle here, however, is more easily explained according to the other translation. For if "intellect" would refer to the knower as its measure and to the intelligible as its measure, then we would be saying the same thing twice, i.e., we would be saying twice how it is measurable by referring it to each as its measure. Where the latter are disparate, however, it is simply incongruous that each should be the complete measure of the thing.

ARTICLE III
Is a Relationship to the Object Essential to the Act of Knowing or Appetition?

[24] 13.68 [The manner in which relation can be connected with something absolute] As for the third main article [in 13.7], I say

---

[35] Averroes, *Metaph.* v, com. 20 (vii, fol. 129G).

that a relation can be involved with something absolute in three ways: (1) contingently and accidentally, as for instance similarity as regards whiteness; (2) necessarily, as the relationship of a creature to God; (3) according to true identity, as the personal relation in the divine to the essence. It does not seem possible, however, to have any greater identity that could be called, in any proper sense, "essential identity," for neither can the relationship be included essentially in the absolute (otherwise the same thing would be essentially absolute and essentially relative), nor can the absolute and relative be included in anything that is one *per se*, so that it would come under a single genus and there would be a proper concept of it that is one *per se* and would be classified essentially under one category. For just as disparate elements do not combine to form a thing that is one *per se*, unless they are related properly speaking as act and potency in the same genus (as is clear from the Philosopher in the *Metaphysics*)³⁶, so also nothing can have a concept that is one *per se* and still include *per se* distinct conceptual elements unless one of these is *per se* potential and the other is *per se* actual, delimiting the potential. A relation and an absolute, however, cannot have concepts such that one is *per se* determinable and the other *per se* determining. For if some absolute concept were indifferent, then it could be contracted by some absolute concept until it became the most specific of absolutes. Similarly, a relational concept could be made the most specific of relations. Neither concept, then, is *per se* a specification or determinant of the other, for each is apt by nature to have a most determinate concept in its own order.

13.69 [The relation is not essential to the act] Applying this to our case, we claim that in the act of knowledge under investigation there is some absolute entity as the first article proved [in 13.8ff.]. There is also some relationship there, as the second article showed [in 13.17ff.]. Now from what we have just established in the present article, we conclude that the absolute and relative in this case cannot constitute something that is one *per se*; at least they cannot consist of something that pertains to the same category, namely, that has a concept that is one *per se*.

13.70 From this it follows that either the act of knowing is not something *per se* one pertaining to a single genus, or else it does not

---

³⁶ Aristotle, *Metaph.* VII, c.8 (1033b16-19); ibid., c.11 (1036b21-24); VIII, c.6 (1045b20-21); see also VIII, cc.1-6 (1042a-1045b).

include *per se* the two elements which were proved to concur in it. But the first article, especially the first proof [in 13.8-11], seems to establish that the absolute element is included essentially. Consequently, the act does not appear to be essentially relative in the sense of including the relation *per se*. Or if it may be called a kind of whole which includes both, then it is not something that is one *per se*, but is a kind of accidental unity which includes the other part "essentially" only in the loose sense that a white man is essentially white. For this is an improper way of speaking, since properly speaking nothing is predicated essentially of anything that is not in itself essentially one, just as nothing can be true of that which is false in itself. For [according to Aristotle] the false in itself is something whose concept includes incompatible elements, and since it is not possible in itself, nothing possible can be asserted of it or nothing is possible for it. So in the case at hand, nothing can be truly or essentially identical with something that is not essentially [*per se*] one.

[25] 13.71 [Three proofs that cognition and appetition fall under the category of quality] But it may be asked: Supposing that the operation is essentially [*per se*] one, and consequently is generically one, under what category does it fall? It can be said that it pertains *per se* to the category of quality.

You will find proof of this if you run through the different categories. It obviously does not fall under substance, nor under categories other than quality, relation, action, and passion.* Now it is not a relation, as the first article proved [in 13.8ff.]: neither is it action or passion.

My first proof makes use of that common middle term, namely, [the notion of perfection used in 13.8 of] the first article. Just as the ultimate perfection of an agent or functional nature is not a relation, so neither is this perfection anything that falls under the categories of "action" or "passion." But this operation is [the agent's ultimate] perfection. [Therefore it does not pertain to the categories of "action" or "passion."]

13.72 Furthermore, action is the transmutation of another as other, even as an active potency, according to the Philosopher,[37] "is a principle of transmuting another *qua* other." Passion is also the transmutation by another *qua* other. An operation like knowing or appetition, however, is neither a transmutation of another nor one that is by another. Although this seems obvious enough, it can be

---

[37] Ibid., v, c.12 (1019a15-20).

proved in this fashion. Active and passive transmutations both end with a term that receives being by the transmutation, for the patient or the one affected now exists differently than before in virtue of the formal term of the transmutation. The operation, however, bears no relation to a term which receives being through it. Indeed, to the extent that there is a term toward which it tends, the operation does not produce it or educe it from the potency of the patient or induce it into the patient. Rather it presupposes this term. Now every action in the category "action" either produces, educes, or induces its term. Indeed by the very fact that one postulates action of this sort in the divine, such as "generation"* or "spiration,"* one also postulates there is some term that receives being through the action, such as the suppositum* generated or spirated.

13.73 A third proof is this: He who acts with an action falling under the category by that name never becomes simply more perfect through that action. Rather from the fulness of its perfection such an agent acts by communicating perfection to another. Now an operation is simply the perfection of the one operating.

Therefore, it follows, by default, that the absolute entity in the operation belongs to the category of quality.

13.74 [What type of quality is it?] And if one asks: To what species of quality* does it belong? One could say that if you consider the different types, it seems more reasonable to place it in the first species, for it cannot fall under any of the others. It clearly does not belong to the second or the fourth. And if the third includes only sensible qualities, as the *Categories*[38] seems to say and as the *Physics*[39] also seems to imply, then it is also obvious it does not belong here.

All spiritual qualities also seem to fall under this first species whether they represent being at rest, like habits,* or are dynamic [*in fieri*], like operations. Or perhaps one[40] would want to say that operations pertain to the third species and are spiritual affections, or passions, and would go on to explain that while the Philosopher expressly mentions there only the bodily affections as being the more obvious, one ought to understand also the spiritual affections underlying them. It is possible in the soul to distinguish an operation proper from an affection, like delight or sadness in the will (because an operation proper tends as it were to the term of the

[38] Aristotle, *Praedicam.*, c.8 (9a29-10b25).
[39] Aristotle, *Physic.* VII, c.3 (247b7-8).
[40] Cf. Duns Scotus, *Ord.* III, d.15, q.un., nn.8ff. (ed. Vivès XIV, 572ff.).

operation, whereas the affection is, as it were, caused by the term in the subject, as sadness in the will is caused by something able to make it sad). Nevertheless, spiritual operations and affections have this in common that both represent a dynamic state [*in fieri*] of the subject, and as such each could be called an affection pertaining to the third species of quality.

But whatever is to be said about its belonging to the first or the third species, this much at least seems probable, namely, that an operation is in the category of quality.

[26] 13.75 [Six objections to the view that operation is a quality] The words of the Philosopher seem to oppose this interpretation. In the *Metaphysics*[41] he says: "Where there is no product apart from the action, the action is present in the agent, for instance, the act of seeing is in the seeing subject and the act of theorizing in the theorizing subject." His purpose is to distinguish between immanent and transient action.* What he wants to say here, then, is that some action is immanent, and he gives as examples vision and speculative thinking. Both of these, however, are operations. Therefore, according to him an operation is an action.

13.76 In the *De anima*,[42] the Philosopher says: "Thinking is a kind of passive affection," and so on.

13.77 Also in the *Ethics*[43] he says: "If pleasure is not a quality, it does not follow that it is not a good, for the activities of virtue are not qualities either, nor is happiness."

13.78 Also in the *Physics*[44] he speaks of having scientific knowledge and knowing as asserting a relation, where the Commentator[45] adds: "It is better to think of these as belonging to the category of relation than to that of quality."

13.79 There are in addition arguments from reason. An absolute is not specifically distinguished by something extrinsic but by some absolute intrinsic difference of its own. Operations, however, are distinguished specifically by objects that differ in species, for there is a greater distinction between operations that have specifically different objects than between those which have to do with the same species of objects. But the latter differ numerically; therefore, the former differ by more than a numerical distinction. Hence they differ specifically.

[41] Aristotle, *Metaph.* IX, c.8 (1050a33-1050b).
[42] Aristotle, *De anima* III, c.4 (429b13-14, 429b26).
[43] Aristotle, *Ethica ad Nic.* x, c.2 (1173a14-16).
[44] Aristotle, *Physic.* VII, c.3 (247b4-5).
[45] Averroes, *Physic.* VII, com. 20 (IV, fol. 322F).

13.80 Furthermore, an operation derives its peculiar perfection and nobility from the object, as seems sufficiently obvious. It is also proved by this passage from the *Ethics*[46]: "In the case of each sense, the best activity is that of the best-conditioned organ in relation to the finest of its objects."[47]

[27]   13.81 [*Answer to the first objection in* 13.75] To the first of these objections I say that an operation has two conditions it shares with action. The first is that it is always in a state of becoming [*in fieri*], not in the sense of being in a state of succession, because the operation is not [temporally] divisible, but it is *in fieri* in that it is in continual dependence upon the same cause and in the same way that an object conserved depends on the cause that conserves it, which we explained earlier in the question [Twelve] which dealt with this matter. The second condition is that the operation, as it were, passed into the object as its term, although the latter does not receive being from the operation but its being is presupposed.

And because of these two characteristics an operation can be called "action," just as it is because of these that it is expressed grammatically by an active verb and is referred to as a "second act."*[48] Thus this distinction of action in this sense into immanent and transient is not one of a genus into its species, but of a word into its meanings. For a transient action is a true action in the category of "action," whereas an immanent action is a quality and it is called "action" equivocally because of the aforesaid conditions.

Actions of the genus "action" can also be divided in another way into immanent and transient actions, as a superior class into its inferiors.[49] For not only does "action" in the category of that name refer to the form induced by the motion in a patient other than the agent, but it also applies to the form induced by the change into the agent itself. For this absolute form insofar as it is something new is the term of some action proper by which it receives its being. Therefore, when the form that is the term of the action lies outside the agent itself, then this action is transient; when this form is in the agent itself, however, the action is immanent.

13.82 The difference between these two ways of understanding immanent action is clear. What is called an immanent action in the first sense is called "term of an immanent action" in the second sense. And it is an immanent action in the second sense that we have

---

[46] Aristotle, *Ethica ad Nic.* x, c.4 (1174b17-20).
[47] Cf. Duns Scotus, *Ord.* I, d.3, nn.65ff. (II, 49ff.).
[48] Cf. Duns Scotus, *Ord.* I, d.3, nn.600-603 (III, 354-56).
[49] Cf. ibid., nn.524-27 (III, 312-14); IV, d.11, q.2, n.5 (ed. Vivès XVII, 339).

in mind when we use the verb "to elicit" in speaking of a power eliciting its operation, and when we use the verb "to speak" in declaring that the memory,* or the person through the memory, "speaks the Word,*" and when we use "to spirate" in saying that someone spirates love through the will.

[28] 13.83 What the Philosopher meant by the distinction of immanent and transient action, however, was the first, not the second, meaning, even though the latter distinction exists. This is clear from his words in the *Metaphysics*[50]: "There is no product apart from the action." He calls the product the term of the operation [*operatum*]. But in addition to that action by which the operation is induced or educed, there is some product, that is, the operation itself which is the product of the one operating. And he continues: "The action is present in the agents; for instance, the act of seeing is in the seeing subject." Here he makes it clear that he is calling vision the immanent action, and not something else of which vision is the end product.

13.84 [Answer to the second objection in 13.76] To the second, one could say that just as to be white is to have whiteness as a form, so to feel or be sentient is to have sensation as a form. Hence, if the object or God caused the sensation as efficient cause, they would not be said to be sensing, but the sense in which the sensation is subjectively received would be sensing. To *sense*, then, is to receive or have the sensation, and in this way to *think* is to receive thought, for even though the intellect were to cause the thinking in itself by some operation, it would not be said to think or understand insofar as it causes the thinking. However, one could very well indicate this fact in addition by using a word that would signify such an action or causation denominatively, for instance, by coining such a word as "I-am-producing-the-thought" [*intelligifico*]. Therefore, the statement that "Thinking is a kind of passive affection" does not prove that thinking falls essentially into the category of "passion" but only that it is formally designated by a term indicative of the fact that the thinking is received by something as a subject, so that the meaning would be, to think is to receive understanding and to "receive" is a kind of passive affection or passion.[51]

[29] 13.85 [A twofold answer to the third objection in 13.77] As for the third objection based on the *Ethics*,[52] one answer could be that

[50] Aristotle, *Metaph.* IX, c.8 (1050a33-34).
[51] Cf. Duns Scotus, *Ord.* I, d.3, nn.386, 537 (III, 235, 320-21).
[52] Aristotle, *Ethica ad Nic.* X, c.3 (1173a14-16).

the "operations" or activities that stem from a virtue are called the actions which elicit the operation proper, and such actions are good because the production of a good is good. But these actions are not qualities, but belong properly to the category of action. This can be inferred from the words of the Commentator,[53] who to prove that "the activities of virtue are not qualities" says this: "Although an operation is an operative movement, the motion itself is not a quality." Here "operative movement" could be the name of the motion that results in the existence of the operation.

13.86 And if one objects to this on the grounds that [in 13.77] he adds the rider "nor is happiness," one could say that just as "operation" is taken less properly to mean the action which ends with the operation proper, so happiness could be taken more broadly to refer to the action which ends with happiness. It was enough for Aristotle to take the activities or "operations" of virtue and happiness to mean something which would suffice to counter the claim that "every good is a quality," which is what he intended to challenge.

13.87 The citation in question could also be explained away in this fashion: Aristotle only intended to speak here of qualities which do not have their being in flux [*in fieri*], since he says: "Neither are the activities of virtues qualities." This is clear from the fact that he denies that this follows: "Pleasure is not a quality, therefore it is not a good," and proves this from the counter instance that "The activities of virtues are not qualities." For the antecedent of this entailment, "Pleasure is not a quality," is true only if one is referring to a permanent quality, for pleasure is truly a quality but one in a state of flux [*in fieri*]. Therefore, it is enough for his purposes to object that the "activities of virtues" are no more permanent qualities than pleasure is. But that pleasure is truly a quality can be proved from what he says in the same context: "For speed and slowness are thought to be proper to every movement, and if a movement ... has neither speed nor slowness in itself, it has this in relation to something else; but of pleasure neither of these things is true. For while we may *become* pleased quickly, we cannot *be* pleased quickly." What he wants to say is that pleasure is not something one attains quickly but progressively; hence it is not a movement. But if one could be transported or changed quickly into this state, then pleasure could be the end of a rapid transformation and hence could be the term of a change. But according to the Philosopher in the

---

[53] Averroes, *Ethica* x, c.3 (III, 145L-146M).

Physics[54] there is no motion *per se* as regards action or passion; therefore, pleasure is neither acting nor being acted upon. And if you run through the rest of the categories, you will see that it is a quality.

13.88 Hence those who would argue for this entailment, viz., "Pleasure is not a quality, therefore it is not a good," presuppose the following to be true: "Every good is a quality with quiescent being; pleasure is not such; therefore [it is not a good]." And it is to this major of the [first] enthymeme that the Philosopher replies with the counter instance of the operation or activity of virtue. And he proves that not every operation is action proper with these words from chapter 5 of this same book [of the *Ethics*]:[55] "One might think that all men require pleasure," which he supports with the argument "because they all desire to live; but life is a kind of activity." And then he goes on to show how life or living could be called an action in the category "action."

13.89 [Answer to the fourth objection in 13.78] As for the other objection based on the *Physics*,[56] we claim the words of the Philosopher must be interpreted as follows according to what was said [in 13.58-60] of the second article. Scientific knowledge necessarily includes a relation to an internal object and this is not produced immediately by the first cause of the alteration [viz., the external object]. Consequently scientific knowledge does not represent an alteration acquired first. As for the Commentator's explanation[57]: "It is better to think of these as belonging to the category of relation than to that of quality," this can be given another interpretation that we shall take up in answering the initial argument [in 13.101].

13.90 [Answer to the fifth objection in 13.79] As for the first argument from reason, one could say that the acts are distinguished by objects only insofar as these are a more manifest indication of a more fundamental difference in the acts themselves and that we learn of this distinction of acts from the more obvious distinction of their objects.

13.91 This is confirmed from the *De anima*.[58] As the Philosopher there wants to distinguish the acts by their objects, so he also wants to distinguish the powers by their acts. To the extent that the ob-

---

[54] Aristotle, *Physic.* v, c.2 (225b14).
[55] Cf. Aristotle, *Ethica* x, c.4 (1175a10).
[56] Aristotle, *Physic.* vii, c.3 (247b-10).
[57] Averroes, *Physic.* vii, com. 20 (iv, fol. 322F).
[58] Aristotle, *De anima* ii, c.4 (415a17-22, 418a10-17).

QUESTION THIRTEEN

jects are prior to the acts, the more one ought to treat the distinction of objects before that of the acts. But none of this refers to essentials, for the act is essentially posterior to the power, and what is posterior is not the essential basis for distinguishing what is prior. Hence neither should the distinction of acts by their objects be understood here of an essential distinction.

[31] 13.92 Another answer could be this: The unity of anything, and hence its distinction, stems from the same source as its entity. As an effect receives its entity from any *per se* cause, so it receives its unity and its distinction from it. The same is true of anything dependent with respect to that upon which it depends essentially. This is particularly true when it depends upon anything as a proper cause or that which properly supports its dependence, for when there is only a common term upon which both this and something else depend, the unity or distinction in such a common term provide no grounds for unity or distinction in what depends upon it. Now the act does depend upon the object in a proper sense and, therefore, one can admit that acts are distinguished by their objects as through something extrinsic upon which they are properly and essentially dependent. However, they are not distinguished by the objects as their formally distinctive characteristic, nor, which is relevant to our thesis, are they differentiated by them insofar as the objects are the terms of the relations included in the acts. And when it is said that absolute things are distinguished by intrinsic features, this is true so far as the formally distinctive characteristics are concerned. If, however, one were to accept the principle that absolute things are not distinguished by intrinsic features, this is true so far as the formally distinctive characteristics are concerned. If, however, one were to accept the principle that absolute things are not distinguished by extrinsic factors, this would have to be admitted if it is understood to mean that they are distinguished not through their correlatives and by the essential terms of a relation, for no absolute requires anything extrinsic essentially as its correlative or *per se* relational term. Nevertheless, absolutes can be distinguished by extrinsic things as things caused are distinguished by their proper causes or by those things upon which they depend properly for their unity and entity. Now objects bear this relationship to operations [like knowing and appetition].

13.93 [Answer to the sixth objection in 13.80] The answer to the other argument is evident from the foregoing, for even though the act is not essentially relative, nevertheless, to the extent that it is the essential means whereby the potency is united with its object, it could be called more perfect as its object is more perfect. But this perfection does not stem from the object as an intrinsic, but as an extrinsic, principle, or at least it derives from the object as something extrinsic upon which it depends essentially.

ARTICLE IV
The Question Understood as Referring to the Subject

[32] 13.94 As for the fourth main point [viz., the alternate meaning of the question mentioned in 13.5], it can be said that this quality, which is either the operation itself or is included in it, does not have a relationship to its subject that is any more essential than that of other qualities. And, therefore, if one does not assume that the other qualities, not now in question, are essentially related to their subject, then neither will this quality be so related.

13.95 If it is objected that this operation has being in flux [*esse in fieri*] and, therefore, is bound up more essentially with its subject than qualities whose being is not in a state of becoming [*in facto esse*], I answer: This does not change the dependence-status of the quality on its subject; it only alters the sort of being the form has in itself or at least in relation to the cause which gives it being.

Reply to the Initial Argument

13.96 As for the argument at the beginning [in 13.2], it can be answered that if some word were imposed to signify precisely that absolute entity, pertaining to the category of quality, which the operation either is or includes, then the meaning of that word could be understood without thinking of its object-term. But the words imposed by common usage to designate operations do imply relationships either directly or by connotation. The reason for this is that we commonly think of the operation under its [intentional] aspect as tending to an object, and it is this aspect of it that is usually signified.

13.97 For example: The intelligible species* is an absolute quality. At least this much must be admitted by anyone who maintains the species to be the formal reason for understanding, viz., that which essentially initiates the act [*ratio per se principiativa actus*]. Yet it is commonly called a "likeness of the object," not because it is a relation, which this name "likeness" essentially implies, but because by its nature it is a certain imitative and representative form of the object. Therefore, it is called this sort of likeness, viz., one of imitation. Even when it is designated by the term "species," what is

QUESTION THIRTEEN

signified is not just its absolute aspect, but the relationship under which it is commonly thought of is included as well. Hence a "species" is said to be a "species of some object." The situation is similar with words used to signify an operation.

13.98 [Objection] You may object that some operation, for instance, that which is not concerned with the object as existing, has only a potential relationship to the object. However, it is necessary that one understand at the same time the object also as the term of an actual relation, because one who understands the act of knowing must at the same time understand the object not only as knowable but also as something actually known. Therefore, "to know" implies an actual relation.

13.99 [Answer] I reply: A relation, which would be actual so far as its foundation goes, but is only possible because of the term's nonentity, is frequently asserted of the foundation or subject as though it were actually present, so to say. For example, the soul separated [from the body] admittedly is said to be not only potentially but also actually inclined towards the body, and still there is no actual inclination present because its term does not actually exist. But for all that, the soul is spoken of as being actually there because, so far as the soul is concerned, it would be there actually.

Similarly, we say practical knowledge "directs," even though there is no actual direction by it going on: for instance, where no power besides the intellect is operating, this knowledge is not actually directing anything.

In like fashion, we speak of whiteness as the measure of all colors and the first thing in any category as the measure of all that comes after it, even when there is no actual mensuration because no term exists.

One could say analogously here that since the relation of the operation to the object would always be actually there, so far as the operation is concerned, it is actually thought and spoken of as if the relationship were something actually inhering in it, and so the object is understood at the same time as the term of an actual dependence.

13.100 What has been said would be true if the object were always thought of as the measure, because the relationship of measurable is there potentially, as was said above [in 13.35-38]. Now, however, it is necessary in understanding the operation to know at the same time the object as that which is attained through the operation.

To speak more truly, then, one should say, it seems, that object must be thought of simultaneously with the act as the term of an actual union rather than as the term of dependence or measurability. This union or attainment of the object, however, is a conceptual relation in an abstractive act of knowledge, but one usually thinks of this relationship of attainment as one of actual union, even though it is not the actuality of something real but the actuality of a conceptual relationship. Consequently the operation is usually signified as one of an actual relationship of this sort, and the object must be thought of at the same time as the term of this actual relationship.

13.101 [Reply to the authority of Aristotle] From what has been said [in 13.96ff.] it is obvious that Aristotle's statement in the *Categories*[59]: "There is nothing to prevent the same thing being predicated of several genera," does not hold true of anything that is *per se* one, but only of what is one accidentally, which at times is also designated by a single name, as is perhaps the case with the name "knowledge." But this does not make it properly one in the sense that it is one according to its essential formula or definition. As he puts it in the *Metaphysics*[60]: "We have a definition not where we have a word and a formula identical in meaning (for in that case all formulae or sets or words would be definitions)." And he proves that this follows: "For there will be some name for any set of words whatever, so that even the *Iliad* will be a definition [namely, of the word 'Iliad']." And from this one could understand Averroes' statement,[61] "It is better to think of these as belonging to the category of relation than to that of quality" [which we promised in 13.89 to reinterpret]. For this is perhaps true of what is more formal in the meaning of name that signifies both the absolute and its relationship or the accidental combination as a whole.

13.102 And from this one could perhaps also understand that statement in the *Metaphysics*[62] that according to their genus some things are called relative, "as medicine is a relative term, because its genus, science, is thought to be a relative term." While the name "species," perhaps, is imposed precisely to signify the quality without reference to its proper correlative [i.e., the object], the same "genus" here is not imposed precisely to signify the genus or quality, but to signify it as something related.

---

[59] Aristotle, *Praedicam.*, c.3 (1b21-22).
[60] Aristotle, *Metaph.* VII, c.4 (1030a7-10).
[61] Averroes, *Physic.* VII, com. 20 (IV, fol. 322F).
[62] Aristotle, *Metaph.* V, c.15 (1021b3-5).

Question Fourteen

CAN THE SOUL LEFT TO ITS NATURAL PERFECTION KNOW THE TRINITY OF PERSONS IN GOD?

[1] 14.1 The next questions have to do with what pertains particularly to creatures possessing intellectual life. The first of these concern things common to men and angels; the next have to do with what is proper to man. Common to men and angels are intellect and will. Concerning the intellect two questions were raised: one, about the object of the intellect; the other, about the active cause of intellection.

14.2 The first question was whether the soul, left to its natural perfection, can know the Trinity of Persons in God.[1] The same question can be asked as regards the angel.

Arguments Pro and Con

It seems so: He who can know a cognitive act can also know the object of that act. The soul or the angel can know by its natural perfection the beatific act of another soul or angel and the object of such an act is God as a trinity. Therefore, [the soul or the angel can know God as a trinity].

Proof of the major: The act is a natural likeness of the object. Besides, it tends to the object of itself. From these two conditions of the act, it follows that he who knows it, knows the object.

Proof of the minor: A [cognitive] power, if unimpeded and left to its natural perfection, is able to know everything contained under its primary or adequate object; otherwise, that object would not be adequate. But the adequate object common to our intellect and that of the angel is being in general, or at least limited being. And the beatific act of the creature falls under such an object. [Therefore, the cognitive power knows it by its natural perfection.]

14.3 On the contrary: The creature cannot know a supernatural object in virtue of its natural perfection. Otherwise, the object

---

[1] Cf. Duns Scotus, *Ord.*, prol., nn.1-94 (I, 1-58); I, d.3, nn.1-332, 569-604 (III, 1-200, 338-57); III, dd.23-24 (ed. Vivès XV, 5-53).

would not be supernatural. The Trinity is a supernatural object. Moreover, it is the beatific object. Therefore, [the creature cannot know it].

Body of the Question

[2] 14.4 [Preliminary observations] To understand the question, certain preliminary clarifications are necessary. The *first* refers to the natural perfection of the soul or the angel. The human soul in any state, be it that of original, fallen, or restored nature, has the same natural perfection, if this is taken to mean what necessity of nature demands. However, it only attains the supreme natural perfection in the third state, in which it will possess not only the supernatural perfection of glory but also the supreme perfection of its nature.[2] Therefore, the question could be understood of the natural perfection it always has, or of this supreme [natural] perfection. The question raised about the first is whether the soul left [to its natural perfection can know the Trinity of Persons in God]. But in the second sense, it is more proper to inquire whether the soul elevated to its supreme natural perfection could thereby know the Trinity.

14.5 A *second* prefatory remark is this: For the soul to know an object may mean (a) that it can *receive* such knowledge or (b) that it can *attain* such knowledge either on its own or by the cooperation of such causes as are adapted by nature to work with it in producing that effect. The second of these entails the first, but not vice versa. For the bare capacity [to receive such knowledge] suffices for the first. A stone, by contrast, cannot know because it is simply incapable of receiving knowledge. For the second [i.e., the attainment of such knowledge], some naturally active cause corresponding to this capacity is required.

14.6 Since the difficulty lies principally with this second member, we treat the first only in brief. The possible intellect* is the proper receptive potency for any intellection whatsoever, so that, if anything prior to the intellection is required, it is not required by way of a receptive potency or as the grounds for receiving the intellection, in the way a surface, for example, is the ground for receiving the color. If this be so, one can grant that every being endowed by nature with a possible intellect can know naturally everything knowable, i.e., so far as such a thing itself is concerned, it is capable of receiving such knowledge.[3]

[2] Cf. ibid., I, d.3, nn.113-24, 185-88 (III, 70-77, 112-15); II, d.3, q.8, n.13 (ed. Vivès XII, 194-95); d.11, n.4 (ibid., 531-32).
[3] Cf. ibid., prol., nn.7, 73-78 (I, 56, 44-47).

14.7 The *third* prefatory remark is this: Intellectual knowledge (and only such is in question here) is either *imperfect* or *perfect*. By "perfect," I do not understand perfection in an intensive sense [so that the knowledge itself would be infinite], but perfection as to the object. Perfect in this latter sense is a knowledge which captures the object as such; i.e., it is proper and distinct* knowledge of the object as it is in itself. By contrast, knowledge which only captures the object incidentally, or in some common and confused* concept, is imperfect.[4]

14.8 Again, distinct knowledge can be either *mediate* or *immediate*. By immediate, I mean that the object is not understood by means of some other object, in or through which it is known. Therefore, it excludes any medium that is itself known, one which would be merely a means of knowing or understanding [i.e., the medium is not itself an object of knowledge].

14.9 From this it follows that to solve the question three points need to be clarified: first, the nature of imperfect knowledge; second, the nature of perfect immediate knowledge; third, the nature of mediate knowledge. We need to know which of these a soul or angel is able to acquire by its natural perfection, taking natural perfection in either of its two meanings [in 14.4].

ARTICLE I
Imperfect Knowledge
1. Knowledge of the Terms "God" and "Trinity"

[3] 14.10 According to the Philosopher[5] the intellect has a twofold function. It understands simples [i.e., the meanings of conceptual terms] and it understands combinations thereof, that is to say, it joins them [in affirmative propositions] or separates them [in negative propositions]. The first kind of understanding can be had without having the second, but the second is impossible without the first.

14.11 Consequently, the first type of understanding should be our initial consideration.

Now I declare that the soul, even by the natural perfection it possesses in its present state, which is the lowest of the three, is able to know the meaning of the terms "God" and "trinity" imperfectly, even though it does not understand them perfectly.

14.12 From the knowledge of an individual being, the meaning of "being" itself can be known by abstraction. The same is true of

---

[4] Cf. ibid., I, d.3, nn.20, 25, 68 (III, 11, 16-17, 48).
[5] Aristotle, *De anima* III, c.6 (430a26-28).

"good." And this takes place in the way Augustine indicates when he writes[6]: "Consider this good and that good. Take away the *this* and the *that* and view *good* itself, if you can, and then you will see God." And in the same passage he goes on to show how God can be known not only in this quasi-confused concept of good, but also in a concept that is in some sense proper to him, for example, if one thinks of the highest good or of what is good by its essence.[7] "If it were possible," he says, "to put aside those goods which are such by participation, and to see the good itself of which they are a participation ... you would see God."

Similarly, from a particular instance of the true, the true itself can be understood. According to Augustine[8]: "God is truth. When truth is spoken of, keep thinking of truth if you can, and if you understand by it not only truth in general, but truth in its essence, you already have a concept that is somehow proper to God."

14.13 To put it briefly, what I am saying is that any transcendent notion arrived at by abstraction from what is known of a creature can be thought of in its indifference [i.e., as common and unspecified] and in such a case God is conceived confusedly as it were, just as in thinking of animal, man is being thought of. But if such a common transcendent concept is thought of as qualified by some more specific perfection such as supreme, first, or infinite, we obtain a concept which is proper to God in the sense that it is characteristic of no other being.[9]

14.14 In a similar fashion, the notion of a "trinity" can be abstracted from a number in its properly accepted sense, viz., as discrete quantity, by concentrating on the abstract notion of discreteness. Now the nature of the soul is such, even in its present state, that it suffices for awareness of the meaning of these terms "God" and "trinity."

[4] 14.15 [Proofs] First proof: An infidel and a man with faith in contradicting each other as regards the proposition: "God is three and one," not only contradict one another in words but in concepts as well. Unless both have in mind the concepts in question this would not happen.

14.16 Second proof: The faith which distinguishes the faithful from the infidels is not a habit which inclines one to assent because

---

[6] Augustine, *De Trin.* VIII, c.3, n.4: PL 42, 949; CCSL 50, 272.
[7] Ibid., n.5: PL 42, 950; CCSL 50, 273.
[8] Ibid., c.2, n.3: PL 42, 949; CCSL 50, 271.
[9] Cf. Duns Scotus, *Ord.* I, d.3, nn.58-60 (III, 40-42).

the terms are known. Neither then is such faith the basis for knowing [the meaning] of the terms. Rather it presupposes such knowledge.

14.17 Third proof: The abstraction of the notion "being" from this individual being and the abstraction of the notion "highest" from this highest among sensibles is a natural process. Neither is there anything repugnant to joining these two notions. "Highest being," therefore, is not an idea that is false in itself in the sense that the Philosopher defines[10]: "What is false in itself includes contradictory notions and cannot be conceived by a simple act of the intellect." By contrast "highest being" can be so conceived because its elemental notes are not mutually repugnant.

2. Knowledge of the Proposition "God is a Trinity"

14.18 What remains to be seen is how a soul, possessing knowledge of the terms "God" and "trinity," could by its nature know that "God is a trinity" is true. Since propositional knowledge may be either a matter of belief or of epistemic* knowledge, and if epistemic, it may represent knowledge of the simple fact* or knowledge of the reasoned fact,* we must see which of these could occur in the case of this proposition "God is a trinity."

14.19 [Belief by acquired faith is naturally possible] As for belief in the proposition, I say that this is possible even in this life and on natural grounds, at least by *acquired* faith.

Proof: As Augustine puts it[11]: "When things are not present to our senses, we are unable to know them on our own authority, so we seek out and believe witnesses to whose senses, we believe, these things are or were present." And again[12]: "Far be it from us to deny what we have learned from the testimony of others; for otherwise, we would not know that there is an ocean; we would not know that there are lands and cities which the most celebrated fame commends."

[5] 14.20 These and similar texts of Augustine indicate that belief in the testimony of others can be so firm as to warrant its being called "knowing." The more truthful the witness, then, the more we can and ought to believe him. And a community can be trusted even more than an individual. The Catholic Church is a most truthful community, however, for it condemns lying and commends truth in

[10] Aristotle, *Metaph.* v, c.29 (1024b17-20).
[11] Augustine, *De civit. Dei* XI, c.3: PL 41, 318; CCSL 48, 323.
[12] Augustine, *De Trin.* xv, c.12, n.21: PL 42, 1075; CCSL 50a, 493.

the highest measure. Therefore, its testimony can be believed with the greatest of certitude, especially where it damns a lie the most, in matters of faith and morals.[13]

14.21 The pilgrim, then, having heard and understood the Church's common teaching, is able by nature to assent with firm belief to what she teaches about morals and faith. Most important among such teaching is what she has to say about the trinity in the divine. To such acquired faith the Epistle to the Romans[14] seems to refer when it states: "Faith comes from hearing" (i.e., the salvific doctrine of Christ). For it adds: "Hearing depends on the word of Christ." To faith of this sort Augustine's words can be referred when he writes[15]: "I would not believe in the Gospel, did not the authority of the Catholic Church compel me."

14.22 [Belief by infused faith is not naturally possible] In addition to this acquired faith, however, we possess a faith that is infused. And while man can naturally dispose himself to receive this,[16] his intellect is unable to attain it in virtue of its intrinsic nature, even with the cooperation of all the causes that move it naturally. God alone can infuse it, and he does not function as a cause that moves any created intellect in a *natural** fashion.

14.23 [How acquired and infused faith agree and differ] Comparing infused and acquired faith to the act of belief, we see they agree in this: When both are present in the same soul, one and the same act of belief is elicited in accord with both inclinations, for where two forms naturally incline the same agent towards action, they do so necessarily and always so far as they are concerned. Consequently, whenever the act is elicited, it is in accord with the inclination of both. And if "An act of belief is based on faith" is taken to mean that the act is elicited in accordance with faith's inclination, then the act of belief must admittedly be based on both faiths.

[6]   14.24 So far as eliciting the act is concerned, however, one difference between the two is this: An act of belief could be elicited by acquired faith, even if it alone were present, in the same way that we believe certain articles to which no infused faith inclines us simply because testimony of the witness deserves to be believed. A here-

---

[13] Cf. Duns Scotus, *Ord.* III, d.23, n.4 (ed. Vivès XV, 7-8).

[14] Romans 10:17.

[15] Augustine, *Contra epist. Fundamenti*, c.5, n.6: PL 42, 176; CSEL 25, 197.

[16] He speaks of a remote disposition. Cf. Duns Scotus, *Ord.* III, d.23, n.14 (ed. Vivès XV, 22); d.25, q.1 (ed. Vivès XV, 57-158).

tic disagrees with one article while believing in others. He does so not by virtue of infused faith since it cannot coexist with heresy about any article [of faith]. On the other hand, no one can elicit an act of belief by infused faith alone. This refers to God's general dispensation, for he could, of course, assisting infused faith, move the intellect to assent in fact to something to which such faith merely inclines it. But even in this case, perhaps it would be the divine movement and not the mere inclination of infused faith that is responsible for eliciting the act. Still less in God's ordinary dispensation can infused faith alone give rise to an act of belief. The case of the baptized child makes this clear, for should he subsequently be raised by infidels or grow up in a deserted place, receiving no instruction in the articles to be believed, he would never elicit a correct act of faith.

The reason is that infused faith inclines one to believe in propositions in cases where evidence for them does not derive from their terms, or if the meaning of the terms can be ascertained from sense perception, there is no evidence of their connection.

14.25 One could object to this reason that such evidence is not supplied by acquired faith either. Look for the answer to this objection elsewhere.[17]

[7] 14.26 Another difference [between the two faiths] stems from the point of view of the act based upon them. Infused faith is unable to incline one towards something false since it inclines in virtue of the divine light of which it is a participation. Thus it inclines only to what conforms to that light. The act of belief, then, insofar as it is based upon infused faith, cannot tend towards something false. Acquired faith, on the contrary, is generally based on the assertion of some fallible witness. Consequently, there is no guarantee that the act of belief based upon it cannot extend to something false. Still, it is frequently the case that such belief is not false, namely, when the witness upon whose testimony it is based is truthful. I said "generally" advisedly, for one could believe by acquired faith something revealed immediately by God,[18] unless what it means for a truth to be revealed by God is that God immediately causes the act of belief or knowledge in the person to whom the revelation is given.

14.27 When both infused and acquired faith incline towards the same act of belief, acquired faith cannot incline towards what is false. Not that the impossibility stems from the acquired faith as

[17] See Appendix, Addition 14.25.
[18] Cf. Duns Scotus, *Ord.* III, d.23, nn.15, 18 (ed. Vivès xv, 22-23, 26-27).

such. It is due rather to the infused faith which concurs with it. The act of belief then rests on (a) infused faith as upon a rule that is certain and absolutely infallible, one which excludes any possibility of the belief being false; and (b) acquired faith as upon a less certain rule, one which does not exclude all possibility of the act being false or of its being concerned with a false object.

14.28 One might object to this last difference that when the same act rests upon a fallible rule, although an infallible rule concurs with the fallible rule, that act is not infallible. Proof by analogy: No necessary conclusion follows from two premises, one of which is necessary, the other contingent. The reason is this: What depends on more than one is no stronger than its weakest support. Now every act of belief, however, depends for its elicitation upon the motivation of acquired faith. If the latter be fallible, no act elicited from such a source could exclude the possibility of the belief being false.

[8] 14.29 To this I reply: Anything to which the light of infused faith inclines is definitely true. If something else, which if left to itself could incline one to err, inclines one to assent to this same definite truth, the impossibility of deception does not stem from this second factor but from the light of the infused faith.

14.30 A third difference, connected with the first, could be adduced. I do not perceive myself to be inclined to an act [of belief] by reason of infused faith, nor am I aware that I elicit an act in accord with it. All I perceive is that my assent is in accord with my acquired faith or the source from which it stems, namely, the testimony I believe. If I perceived that my act stemmed from infused faith and knew that only belief in what is definitely true is consistent with such faith, I would perceive that my act could not be false. From this it would follow that I would perceive that the object of that act could not be false. Hence I would know it epistemically, i.e., I would recognize it infallibly as being true. But no one, I believe, experiences personally when he possesses both faiths or when he gives his assent in accord with both. It is only in this general principle, then, that we believe, namely, that one could not err about a proposition if he tends to assent to it under the inclination of infused faith. But nobody, neither he who possesses infused faith nor anyone else, knows or experiences with certainty when someone tends to assent to a proposition by reason of infused faith.

14.31 An objection to this: In the *De Trinitate*,[19] it says: "Faith

[19] Augustine, *De Trin.* XIII, c.1, n.3: PL 42, 1014; CCSL 50a, 383.

is not so seen in the heart in which it is, by him whose it is, but we know most certainly that it is there and our conscience proclaims its existence.... We cannot see that which we are commanded to believe; yet when the faith itself is in us, we see it in us."

14.32 I reply: What [Augustine] means is that faith is seen in the same fashion that he admits the soul knows itself at all times. He does not mean that there is at all times an elicited act, but that an object able to be known actually is fully present at all times. Hence he adds[20]: "The faith of things that are absent is present [and the faith of things that are without is within, and the faith of things that are not seen is seen]." In other words, where we would say the soul is in proximate accidental potency* to know something, Augustine would speak of this as something the soul "knows."

14.33 Another way to answer this objection would be to say that Augustine takes "faith" to mean the act of belief, of which he says a little later[21]: "But sometimes our faith," i.e., our act of believing, "is accommodated even to false things."

[9] 14.34 [Epistemic or demonstrative knowledge of the simple fact is not naturally possible] So far as epistemic knowledge of the simple fact* [*scientia quia*] is concerned, I say that no one can acquire such knowledge of the divine trinity in the present life by natural means. For no one can prove by a demonstration of simple fact [*demonstratio quia*] that a cause possesses some characteristic which, if eliminated, would still leave the cause with all it needs to produce that effect. But if being a trinity were eliminated, to assume the impossible, God would still have all that is required to produce a creature. For the formal principle of production, complete and perfect, together with a subject [*suppositum*]* which has it, would remain, as is evident from an earlier discussion of this matter [in Question Eight]. A perfect subject possessing a perfect formal principle seems to be all that is required for causation.[22]

14.35 [Epistemic knowledge of the reasoned fact is not naturally possible] As for epistemic knowledge of the reasoned fact* [*scientia propter quid*], I say that the soul cannot acquire naturally such knowledge as regards "God is a trinity." Knowledge of what is most proper to a subject is virtually contained in a primary and evident way only in a *per se* and proper concept of that subject or in the subject itself which is conceived in this way. But so far as God is concerned, to be a trinity is this sort of thing. Hence it can only be

[20] Ibid.   [21] Ibid.
[22] Cf. Duns Scotus, *Ord.* I, d.4, n.11 (IV, 5-6).

known as a reasoned fact if one has such a concept of God. But such is not had by God's ordinary dispensation in the state we are at present,[23] as is clear from our first conclusion [in 14.13] which had to do with the simple understanding of the meaning of the terms.

Proof of the major: One would know such a proper attribute either as belonging to the subject conceived properly and *per se* (in this case the truth of the major would be evident) or else as belonging to the subject conceived in a universal fashion or indistinctly (and in this case one could have such knowledge by a demonstration of the reasoned fact only if one had as middle term a concept of it that was proper and distinct). For example, one could not prove by a demonstration of the reasoned fact that the predicate "first figure" belongs to the subject "some figure" in general except by a proper middle term, namely, a term which gave the meaning or definition of a circle. Nor is this surprising, for to know syllogistically the reason why a proper attribute [i.e., one which belongs necessarily to this and only to this subject] inheres in its respective subject, what is needed is a middle term that expresses what that subject properly is. It was just such epistemic knowledge of the reasoned fact that we were looking for as regards the first two conclusions in [7.10 of] the question on omnipotence earlier; but these conclusions themselves, though true, are not relevant to our present problem since we are here concerned with what kind of knowledge it is possible for us to have in this life on purely natural grounds.

ARTICLE II
Perfect Immediate Knowledge

[10]   14.36 [The Trinity cannot be known naturally by immediate and perfect knowledge] We come now to the second main point [of 14.9, the possibility of immediate perfect knowledge]. Although knowledge that is *per se*, proper, and immediate could be either intuitive or abstractive (a distinction we dealt with earlier [in 13.27ff.]), the following conclusion seems to apply to both types: The soul by its natural perfection, considering its nature in any state, is unable to attain knowledge of God that is immediate and proper, even with the cooperation of all the causes that naturally move it to know. The same should be said of the angel. The reason is this: Any such intellection, namely, that which is *per se*, proper, and immediate, requires the presence of the object in all its proper

[23] Cf. ibid., d.3, nn.56-57 (III, 38-39); d.2, n.183 (II, 237-38); prol., nn. 167-68 (I, 109-12).

intelligibility as object [*propria ratio objecti*]. If the intellection is intuitive, this means in its own existence it is present as object. If the intellection is abstractive, it is present in something which represents it in all its proper and essential meaning as a knowable object. But only if God wills it, is he present to any created intellect in all the proper and essential meaning of divinity [*sub propria ratione divinitatis*].[24]

That God is not really present to it appears clearly from the commentary of Ambrose on Luke[25]: "Though it is not of his nature to be seen, it is within his power to be seen. If he wants it, he is seen; if he does not want it, he is not seen." He puts it excellently when he says "It is not of his nature to be seen," (i.e., by the creature), because his nature is not a naturally active cause of this vision. Neither can any created nature by its natural activity produce this vision or make this [divine] object perfectly present, since it cannot contain within itself in a perfect way this divine essence, neither in its entity nor as an intelligible object.

[11] 14.37 For the same reason, it is clear that no created being can be the cause of the abstractive presence of God in the intellect, for it cannot cause any representation which of itself and properly presents the divinity in all its essential meaning as a knowable object. Such a representation could only be caused by the knowable object itself or by something containing it perfectly in all its intelligibility. Consequently, even though God could be known through something which represented him, only God himself could produce this, and he would do so by means of his will.

14.38 Against this argument it is objected that a power or potency is able to attain naturally anything which comes under its first natural object; otherwise, the first object would not really be adequate but would rather transcend the capacity of the power in question. But being [*ens*], which is the first natural object of the intellect, applies most truly to God himself. Therefore, [the intellect can attain God naturally].

14.39 In reply one could say that "first natural object" can be understood in two ways. In one sense, it means the object to which the potency is inclined; in another, it means the object which is within the natural reach of the power, namely where only *natural* causes are operative. Now while "being" taken commonly (whether its commonness be one of univocation or analogy, I do not care at pres-

---

[24] Cf. ibid., II, d.3, q.9 (ed. Vivès XII, 201-19); I, d.3, n.57 (III, 39).
[25] Ambrose, *Expositio Evangelii Lucae* I, n.24: PL 15, 1543; CCSL 14, 18.

ent) may be stipulated for any created intellect to be its adequate object in the first sense, it is still not its adequate object in the second sense, no matter in what state it exists. Only "finite being" is adequate in this second sense, since this is all that any created intellect can reach by virtue of causes which naturally move it.

14.40 [What is to be said about the natural object of the human intellect] Some[26] claim that the natural object of the human intellect is not "being" in its generality but is restricted to the essence or quiddity of a material thing. They adduce this argument: A power or potency is proportionate to its object. Cognitive powers are assumed to be threefold: one, completely separated from matter both in its being and in its knowing (e.g., the intellect of a separate substance)*; another, united to matter both in its being and in its functioning (e.g., an organic power like the senses); a third, proper to that form which has its being in matter, but does not use either matter or a material organ to function (our intellect is this sort of thing). Proportionate to this threefold power is a threefold object. Quiddity completely separated from matter corresponds to the first; to the second, the singular that is completely material; to the third, corresponds the quiddity of a material thing which, though it exists in matter, is not thought of as limited to this particular matter.

[12]   14.41 But against this view one[27] can argue that if this means the material quiddity is the proper object of our intellect insofar as it is the power it is, then it follows that the quiddity of material things is also the adequate object of the blessed [in heaven], or if it is not, then their intellect is no longer the same potency or power it was. But both alternatives are false.

14.42 It cannot be countered that the intellect is elevated by the light of glory. No habit which elevates a power can have an object that transcends the primary object of that power. Otherwise it would not be a habit of that potency but it would represent a power or potency in its own right, or else it would transform our early power into another power entirely, for it would have a different primary object.

14.43 The commensurate object naturally within the reach of our intellect in its present state may indeed be the quiddity of material things or, more precisely, the quiddity of a sensible thing, meaning

---

[26] Thomas, *Summa theol.* I, q.12, a.4 in corp. (I, 54); q.84, a.2 in corp. (I, 414); q.85, a.1 in corp. (I, 416).

[27] Cf. Duns Scotus, *Ord.* I, d.3, nn.110-24 (III, 69-77); IV, d.49, q.11, n.3 (ed. Vivès XXI, 389-90).

QUESTION FOURTEEN

by this not just that of the sensible proper but also the quiddity of what is essentially or virtually included in the sensible. Still, I maintain that if we consider the nature of our intellect as a power or potency, its adequate or commensurate object is no more restricted than that of the angel. Whatever can be understood by one can be understood by the other.

14.44 This at least is what would have to be admitted by a theologian who claims our present state is not natural and that our impotence in regard to many intelligible matters represents a penal, not a natural, situation, according to [Augustine] in *De Trinitate*[28]: "Things that are certain are revealed to your interior eyes by that light," namely, that eternal light of which he has spoken. "What is the reason, then, why you are unable to see it with a steady gaze except indeed your infirmity; and what has brought this upon you except sin?" About this he had written earlier[29]: "And you, o my soul, where do you feel yourself to be? Where do you lie down?" And he adds: "You recognize that you are in that inn to which that Samaritan brought him whom he found half dead from the many wounds inflicted by robbers."

14.45 The Philosopher, however, would say this present state is simply natural to man, having experienced no other and having no cogent reason for concluding another state exists. He perhaps would go on to claim that the adequate object of the human intellect, even by its nature as a power, is simply what he perceived to be commensurate to it at present, [i.e., the quiddity of sensible things].[30]

[13] 14.46 [An objection to 14.41-44] Against this, however, it is argued that the object which naturally moves a created intellect is being [*ens*], not merely limited being but also unlimited being. Thus being in its indifference to either is the object that is naturally commensurate to it, in other words, any such object is able to be attained by the action of a cause that is acting naturally.

The first proof cited is this: The way in which the same first object, taken in all its indifference [or broadest extension] moves the potency or power to which it primarily refers, understanding that type of potency in all its indifference [or broadest sense], is the same, i.e., either it always moves naturally or it always moves non-naturally [or voluntarily]. Now the unlimited being naturally moves some intellect, i.e., the divine intellect. Therefore, it moves every

---

[28] Augustine, *De Trin.* xv, c.27, n.50: PL 42, 1097; CCSL 50a, 533.
[29] Ibid., PL 42, 1096-97; CCSL 50a, 531, 532.
[30] Cf. Duns Scotus, *Ord.* I, d.3, nn.115, 123-24 (III, 71-72, 76-77).

intellect in this way. Or this other minor premise could be used: Some being moves the created intellect naturally. Therefore, every being moves it in this way.

Proof of the major: This is proved first inductively, i.e., by considering each type of potency and its object. A second proof from reason is the following: The proper object taken in all its indifference is the object that is adequate or commensurate, and what it refers to properly is the potency or power taken in its broadest or generic sense. Consequently, there is some proper way in which these two terms, namely, object and power, relate to each other in general, a way that would also hold good for any particular instances falling under these general terms. For particular terms include [in their definition] the first or more general terms, and consequently they relate to or confront each other in the same way as do these first terms.

14.47 [Second proof] Every act prior to the will-act is merely natural [and therefore is not free but necessary]. But any action of the divine essence, even when it functions as an object which moves a created intellect, is prior to the will's act. Therefore, [it is a merely natural act, not one that is free or voluntary].

Proof of the minor: The beatific object is the essence as essence, not the essence as will or as willing. To move a created intellect to the beatific act, therefore, is a function of essence as essence and hence as prior to any action on the part of the will.

14.48 Confirmation of this argument: If, to assume the impossible, God were not a voluntary agent, his essence would naturally move the intellect to perceive it. Hence it will also function in this same way at present, since it is not as a voluntary agent that God moves or functions as first object.

14.49 [Third proof] Every object begets actual knowledge of itself. This production or generation is natural, [not voluntary]. That is why Augustine[31] speaks of what is generated as "offspring." It is in a natural fashion, therefore, that the essence produces a vision of itself in the intellect of the blessed.

14.50 [Fourth proof] If the will must cooperate with the essence as motive principle for the beatific act of a created intellect, how—I ask—are essence and will functionally related? The will cannot be called the motive factor and the essence reduced to second place, moving as it were only in virtue of the will. It would have to be the other way around, then, so that the essence would be the prime

---

[31] Augustine, *De Trin.* IX, c.12, n.18: PL 42, 970-72; CCSL 50, 310.

QUESTION FOURTEEN

mover. As such it would have to have its own proper way of moving. For it is not determined by, but determines itself to move, the second mover. Thus we see that what acts naturally so far as it depends on itself, acts necessarily, whereas if its action is subject to the will, it does not act necessarily. Its action can either occur or not occur. But this is not something it has of itself. Rather it stems from the contingency characteristic of the will's action. Conversely, if in acting the will were subject to some other principle, it would naturally be determined by the latter to act in a definite way.

[14]   14.51 [Before answering these arguments, a word on how the various movements are interrelated] Keep in mind that the absolutely first movement in things has to be natural, for every voluntary movement presupposes another. And if there is some movement among things that is not natural, all the more will the movement of the will not be natural.

14.52 It is also conceivable that some movement is directed towards a goal that is simply infinite. On the other hand, there is movement that tends to a finite goal or to an infinite goal. That which tends toward the simply infinite, however, is the prior movement, since the infinite cannot have the finite as a presupposition.

14.53 If we take motion in an improper or extended sense, we can arrange the varied movements of things in some sort of order. If motion be understood in a broad sense, the first thing movable by a natural* movement, absolutely speaking, is the divine intellect. Hence it is the divine essence as primary object of God's intellect which first moves with a movement that is natural.[32] Consequently, the movement that is absolutely first would be the natural movement of the divine intellect by its object, the divine essence. What moves naturally, however, moves the movable as far as this is possible. Hence the object in this case can move the unbegotten intellect of the Person in whom the essence exists primarily, not only to actual knowledge of himself, but also to the actual knowledge which he begets. Though it moves naturally to both types of knowledge, it does so according to a certain order. For if, in a given subject, something is the source of both an immanent activity and an operation that produces a product distinct from himself, the former function is somehow prior.

14.54 Should you object that, in the divine, the production is just as immanent* as is the activity, I reply: The production is not im-

[32] Cf. Duns Scotus, *Ord.* I, d.2, nn.231-34, 311-12 (II, 265-68, 314-15).

manent so far as its term is concerned; the operation, on the contrary, is immanent in every way.

14.55 The essence is also a natural mover for knowing all simple intelligibles, but only after the essence is possessed by all the Persons. This does not mean that [the essence] would be deficient as an active principle apart from this condition. It only means some order is required on the part of the terminus of its action.³³

Hence that action which is purely natural as regards the absolutely first or infinite term is thus complete. The absolutely first movement, in this case, is that of eliciting knowledge, as it were, in the intellect of the Father. Next to this is the movement of begetting the Word.*

[15] 14.56 This is followed by an action which, by nature, has to do with the absolutely first term, namely with the communication of the first essence. Though it is not natural, this action is absolutely necessary. It is a movement of the will and is twofold, as it were: one, to simple loving; the other, to Love proceeding [as the Holy Spirit]. This twofold motion of the will parallels the twofold natural motion said to be in the intellect, the one to simple knowing, the other to "speaking"* [the Word].

14.57 Objection: Given the same subject, natural action precedes that which is not natural. According to you, however, it is by a natural action that the divine intellect knows what can be created. Hence, this action precedes every action of the will and hence that of "spirating"* or breathing the Holy Spirit.

I answer: The major is true where the same order holds for the terminus of the action. In this case, however, the order of the first term is different from that of the second. Hence the natural in one order follows the non-natural in another order. In distinguishing orders, one looks first to the nature of the terms and only second to the way in which the principles function.

14.58 On the contrary, replies my objector, the order based on principles is prior to that based on the terms, even as principle is prior to term, for the term is produced or communicated by the principle.

I answer: The antecedent is true of something that is a term in the fullest sense of the word, namely something which receives existence in an unqualified sense. It is not true, however, of a formal term, which is given being only in a qualified sense [as is the case with possible creatures in the divine mind].

³³ Cf. ibid., II, d.1, q.1, nn.8-11.

14.59 Once the whole process of origin is complete as regards the first term (namely, the divine essence to be communicated), another order follows as regards the second term of the essence (namely, of what is able to be created). In this second order, it is the divine essence itself that first moves the divine intelligence, insofar as this is present in all three persons, to the simple awareness of every intelligible. It does not move the intelligence to a distinct knowledge of the truth of every proposition, however. For if it would move it to know definitely one of the two possible statements about any future contingency, since a natural mover moves necessarily, it would follow that the divine intellect would know in a necessary fashion which of the two contradictory statements will be true. Hence, either it can err or the opposite could not occur, and then what is assumed to be contingent is really not contingent but necessary.[34]

[16] 14.60 Since the way everything intelligible is ordered to the first intelligible seems to be the same, why does not the first intelligible [namely, the divine essence] move [the divine intellect] with equal necessity to whatever it knows? My answer is this: It does move naturally, and hence in a necessary fashion, to whatever it is possible to know naturally and in a necessary way. Such are all simple objects and all necessary truths. A proposition about the existence of something contingent, however, is not this sort of thing. There is nothing in the nature of a contingent event that requires it to be true.

14.61 You might ask, why does the divine essence not move the divine intellect necessarily to have such knowledge as it is possible to have about such a proposition? I reply: either it would move it to a disjunctive type of knowledge so that it knows only that the event will either occur or not occur, but does not know which will be the case, or else, if it did move the intellect to a definitive knowledge of one of the two, it would follow that that alternative was necessarily determined.

14.62 Contingent movement, therefore, is subsequent to the whole order of necessary movements. It is not possible that contingent movement proceeds from a principle of natural motion, since it is characteristic of such to move in a necessary fashion. Hence will must be postulated as the source of such movement. Such contingent movements have their own order. The first is internal, for if the will itself did not decide to will one of the two possibilities,

---

[34] Cf. ibid., I, d.38, nn.5-6 (VI, 304-305); *Lectura* I, d.39, nn.62-65 (XVII, 500-501); *Ord.* I, d.40 (VI, 309-13).

nothing definite would ever take place in the world outside. Hence his will first determines itself to will what will be; second, his intellect, seeing this infallible determination of the will, knows that this will be. Contingent and necessary movements, therefore, are inversely related. In necessary movements nature is the first principle, therefore it is first naturally determined to its own action. In contingent movements, however, the first principle is free. Subsequent to its action in the first order is the natural movement.

14.63 Motion in regard to what is external is subsequent to all contingent movement that is internal. All such external motion consequently is contingent and hence has God's will itself as its immediate principle. No created intellect, consequently, is moved in a natural fashion by the essence as essence. All knowledge of this essence, not caused by anything created, is caused immediately by the divine will.[35]

14.64 [Reply to the arguments in 14.46-50] The answer to the counter-arguments cited earlier now becomes clear. The major of the first argument must be taken to mean that the object moves uniformly any potency that can be moved *immediately* by it. As for the first minor, the divine essence immediately moves the divine intellect, not the created intellect. For the divine intellect is the absolutely first thing that can be moved, and therefore is moved first by the motive form that is first. There is nothing else able to be moved immediately by this first motive form, for it is only able to move immediately according to the first type of movement, and there is nothing else that is suited by its nature to be moved in this fashion. If you wish to conclude, therefore, that the divine essence moves every intellect in the same way, one may grant this holds true of any that it moves immediately. But the only instance of this is the divine intellect, as is obvious from what has been said [in 14.53].

14.65 Now the other minor proposed, namely, that a created object moves in a natural manner, is true only of the intellect it moves immediately. It would be false, however, if it were to move some intellect by means of an act of the will, for it would not move it naturally. Such would be the case if my will could freely cause in you knowledge of my essence. But perhaps this kind of knowledge is not characteristic of any created essence and will, since every such essence is capable of moving immediately a created intellect, and hence would do so by a movement that is natural. On the other hand, no created will moves to perfect knowledge of any essence as

---

[35] Cf. ibid., *Ord.* IV, d.49, q.11, n.9 (ed. Vivès XXI, 417-18).

QUESTION FOURTEEN

such, for it does not contain any essence in an eminent and unitive way. But to whatever extent created objects move intellects naturally, it is clear from what was said above how the principle applies to the divine essence, for it moves immediately the first intellect and no other.

14.66 My answer to the second argument [in 14.47] is this: To move [a created intellect] to the beatific vision is not the act that properly characterizes the divine essence, nor is it prior to the will. Properly speaking, it is an act of that will. Though the essence, as in some sense prior to the will, is the first and immediate object that is seen through that vision, it is not the immediate moving object. Only remotely does it move, to the extent, namely, that it moves the divine intellect to that vision which precedes the volition by which the intellect of Michael is moved to the vision [of God].

14.67 This shows clearly how the confirmatory argument [in 14.48] is to be answered, for if that essence was not formally a voluntary agent as well, it could cause absolutely nothing outside itself, since it could only cause naturally. But since everything extrinsic, formally speaking, is only possible, it could only proceed from something necessary in a contingent fashion.

[18] 14.68 As for the [fourth][36] proof [in 14.50], one could say that, properly speaking, essence and will are not related as higher and lower motor causes in the sense that both act upon what is moved. Only the [divine] will acts on the created intellect. As a presupposition for this action, however, the movement of the divine intellect by the essence is required. The essence functions as a "mover" in regard to the created intellect's vision of itself only to this extent: before the will can move the created intellect, the divine essence must have moved the divine intellect to this vision of itself.

14.69 But suppose one argues against this as follows: Will as will can only move an intellect to envision the will as will. It cannot move to a vision of essence as essence. To see the will as will but not the essence as essence is not to see the beatific object. Proof of the minor: The beatific object of the divine and created intellect are the same. Now the divine intellect is not beatified by a vision of the will as will. The will is not its primary object, and the intellect is only
[19] beatified by obtaining its primary object. Proof of the major: The will, as a property, is posterior to the nature as it were. As such it cannot be the causal principle of a perfect vision of the essence as

[36] Scotus changes the order of the arguments in his answers to them. Cf. *supra*, 14.50.

333

essence. For the latter is somehow prior and more perfect according to the words of Damascene[37]: "Like some infinite and limitless sea of substance, he contains all being in himself."

To this objection I reply: The will is perfectly identical with the essence. Consequently it can be the moving principle of a vision of the essence as essence. Therefore, the major must be denied. The affirmative claim that the will can be the moving principle of a vision of will as will is certainly true, but the negative claim that it cannot be the principle for seeing the essence as essence is false. To the proof of the major, I answer: The priority here is a kind of priority of foundation. But not only is this foundation perfectly identical with what is thought to rest upon it but the latter also possesses the formal perfection of being formally infinite. For this reason it contains the perfection of its foundation in a perfectly identical and unitive way. Hence, the will can be the source that communicates the essence since it possesses in a completely identical fashion the same perfection as does the essence.

14.70 To the remaining [or third proof in 14.49] one could say that Augustine[38] is speaking, in the text referred to, of that knowledge which is the Word.* Hence, after having pointed out that "the offspring that is born is knowledge itself of the Trinity," he adds at the end of the chapter: "There is a certain image of the Trinity the mind itself and its knowledge, which is its offspring and the Word about itself, and love as a third." Consequently not all actual knowledge of the object represents its Word but only that which is born of it as offspring, i.e., that which not only is its natural image but is begotten *naturally** by being born of it.[39] Actual knowledge produced by the will, therefore, is not the Word of that object, for although it be the natural image of the object it is not begotten naturally.

14.71 There is another way one could answer the citation from Augustine[40] where he says: "Everything we know begets in us the knowledge of itself." These words could refer to what we know naturally, namely, by means of causes which naturally move our intellect. Certainly things either in themselves or in their causes "beget." That is to say with natural fecundity and of necessity each causes

---

[37] Damascene, *De fide orth.* I, c.9: PG 94, 835; ed. Buytaert, c.9, 49.

[38] Augustine, *De Trin.* IX, c.12, n.18: PL 42, 970-72; CCSL 50, 309-10.

[39] Cf. Duns Scotus, *Ord.* I, d.3, nn.569-604 (III, 338-57); II, dd.16 and 24 (ed. Vivès XIII, 23-47, 177-84).

[40] Augustine, *De Trin.* IX, c.12, n.18: PL 42, 970; CCSL 50, 309.

in us knowledge of itself as its natural image. The word is generated in this way only by the memory.* There is no need that an object which is made known by an act of the will have prior existence in the memory, or at least it does not act insofar as it has such prior existence. In this way, then, we can preserve the proper meaning of "Word."

[20] On the other hand, if "everything" in an extended sense refers also to the divine essence, then what follows, namely, "begets knowledge of itself" must be understood either (a) formally as referring to an object which moves naturally, or (b) equivalently as referring to the uncreated object since this, either by itself or by something identical with it, causes in us knowledge of itself. This knowledge, so far as its perfecting the intellect is concerned, is equivalent to an offspring that is naturally begotten, because it is a likeness leading naturally to knowledge of the object, just as it would if it were produced naturally by the object.

14.72 From what was said, it seems to follow that before the vision of the essence is caused in Michael the essence is not, by any priority of nature, representative of itself so far as Michael is concerned. All the more, therefore, it is not representative of anything else. Both the essence as well as other things are contingently represented by an act of the will so that its representation does not precede in any way the actual understanding of the object said to be represented.

14.73 But this raises a question. For in God the representation that is in some sense prior to actual understanding is found only in the memory. And strictly speaking, there is nothing in the divine memory besides the object (which, as it were, has given it its first actuality), something that is immediate to the second act (i.e., to actual understanding). But that which actualizes in this way is the presence of the first object in its entirety, namely, the divine essence. If this be the case, how can the blessed see a secondary object in the essence if it is not somehow represented there? It is not represented to him in the will either, even if one grants the will does the revealing, since the will is not a mirror in which it might be seen.

I answer: A stone is seen in the divine essence but not in the way an object present is reflected by a mirror, for prior to the act of understanding the divine essence represents only itself and only to its own intellect. The stone, however, is seen in the divine essence in the way a secondary object is perceived in the first object. The first object [the divine essence], however, does not move [the intellect of the blessed] to a knowledge of the second object in the same way it moves its own intellect or in the way a principle moves our intellect to draw a conclusion. Another factor is involved, namely, the will. This moves the intellect towards two objects of knowledge according to a certain order, so that they terminate the act of the intellect as a primary and a secondary object.

ARTICLE III
Mediate Knowledge

[21] 14.74 [The Trinity cannot be known naturally by mediate knowledge] As regards the third main problem [in 14.9], I affirm that by their natural powers neither the angel nor the soul in any of its states can have mediate knowledge of the divine essence in all its proper meaning, so that the sense or meaning of that essence would be grasped in knowing or by knowing some intermediary object. Nothing can be known in itself distinctly in this intermediate fashion unless it be contained in the medium essentially or virtually, and this, perfectly, i.e., in all its knowability.[41] But nothing else contains the divine essence in this way. Therefore, [it cannot be known in this way by an angel or by the soul]. Proof of the minor: Nothing distinct from divinity contains it perfectly under the aspect of entity; neither then does it contain divinity perfectly under the aspect of knowability. Proof of the major: If an object moves to any knowledge, it moves most effectively to a perfect and proper knowledge of itself. Hence it cannot move to knowledge that is simply more perfect than this. Neither then can it move to proper knowledge of a more perfect object.

14.75 [Objections] To begin with, exception is taken to the argument itself. All that is required of a cause is that it contain virtually that of which it is the cause, not that of which it is not the cause. Whatever moves to distinct and perfect knowledge of the divine essence, however, only needs to be the cause of that knowledge, not the cause of the essence itself. Admittedly, as the proof shows, no cause contains the divine essence itself. Still, it could contain knowledge thereof, if it were more perfect, for instance, than the knowledge, in the way that a substance is more perfect than an accident. This would suffice for moving the intellect to knowledge of this sort. Such knowledge, it seems, could be contained eminently in the angel's or the soul's substance, since this substance is much more

[41] Cf. Duns Scotus, *Ord.* II, d.3, q.9 (ed. Vivès XII, 201-19).

QUESTION FOURTEEN

perfect than is its knowledge, and far closer in the essential order [of perfection] to the [divine] object itself.

14.76 Two further objections are raised to the conclusion. The first is this: An object, it seems, can be known distinctly by means of its own image. Thus the sense of sight knows distinctly the object in the mirror. According to Augustine,[42] however, both the angel and the soul are the image of God. Even by their natural powers, both can know themselves distinctly. He affirms this of the soul where it is not so obvious[43]: "Just as it comprehends that it always knows itself and always wills itself, so it also comprehends that it always remembers itself and understands itself and loves itself, even though it does not always think itself to be different, etc." And he adds, in the same work[44]: "The mind of man, we said, knows itself. For the mind knows nothing so well as that which is present to itself, and nothing is more present to the mind than the mind is to itself." In chapters six and seven he has much the same to say.

14.77 A second objection to the conclusion is that the created intellect of the blessed can know its beatific act naturally. Through it, therefore, the object of this act can be known naturally. Proof that this follows: (1) the act is a natural likeness of the object. Indeed it seems to be a more express likeness than the intelligible species,* if there be one. Hence, the object can be known distinctly through it as through a natural likeness. (2) It hardly seems possible to know the act as envisioning this object, unless one knows this object as envisioned by the act.

[22] 14.78 [Answer to the objections] To the first of these [in 14.75] I say: Nothing contains knowledge virtually in an adequate way unless the knowable object is represented there either properly (i.e., formally) or else virtually. The proper species of an object, even though it be a lesser entity than is the object itself, still contains the latter in the first of these ways, namely, the object is formally represented by it. Even when the medium is not a formal representation of the object, it must still contain such a proper representation virtually. And when it performs this representative function only to the extent that the medium itself is known as object, then it must contain this other object that has to be known through it.[45]

14.79 As for the other two arguments [in 14.76f.], a tempting

[42] Augustine, *De Trin.* XIV, c.8, n.11: PL 42, 1044; CCSL 50a, 436.
[43] Ibid., X, c.12, n.19: PL 42, 984; CCSL 50, 332.
[44] Ibid., XIV, c.4, n.7: PL 42, 1040; CCSL 50a, 429.
[45] Cf. Duns Scotus, *Ord.* II, d.3, q.9, n.5 (ed. Vivès XII, 205-206).

solution would be to deny that a soul or an angel could know itself or even its beatific act by its natural powers. But since both seem to fall within the scope of what is a proper object for both the angelic and human intellect, and indeed a proper object naturally attainable (namely, a limited or finite being), another way to answer the objection might be this: While it may be true that both angel and soul are able to know themselves naturally for the absolute things that they are,[46] they cannot know themselves naturally to the extent they are images of God. In other words, they are not aware that they are the image of God. Augustine[47] seems to favor this solution: "Those who see their mind and behold the trinity in it, viz., memory, intelligence and, will, and still do not believe what they are knowing is the image of God, see indeed the mirror but still do not see through it. That is to say, they do not know the mirror they see is a mirror, i.e., a likeness."

[23] 14.80 This answer can be objected to on two counts, the first of which is this: Either the image-relation is identical with the soul's or the angel's essence, or it is at least a necessary consequence of its nature. Through a knowledge of the nature, then, the relation itself can be known. Proof of the antecedent: A relationship of essential dependence is either the same thing as the dependent nature or a necessary consequence thereof. If it were only contingently connected with the nature, the nature could exist without it, and hence be essentially independent. The image-relation, however, seems to be a dependence relationship of the imitation upon what is imitated.

14.81 The second objection is this: A cognitive power can know naturally anything contained under its first natural object. Now the image-relation is an instance of limited being, which is the first natural object of a created intellect. For this relation is not infinite, since it is rooted in the finite.

14.82 To the first of these objections [in 14.80]: A relation can only be known when both terms are known. If the meaning of the term is not included in that of the foundation, knowledge of the latter is not a sufficient reason for knowing the relation. Such is the case here. From the claim that the relation is a necessary consequence of the foundation, it does not follow that the relation can be known perfectly by means of its foundation. Only an absolute entity could be known perfectly in this way, since this presupposes knowledge of no further term.

14.83 But this is no solution, for what includes another's entity in-

---

[46] Ibid., qq.8-9 (ed. Vivès XII, 179-233); d.9, q.2 (ibid., 427-518).
[47] Augustine, *De Trin.* xv, c.24, n.44: PL 42, 1091; CCSL 50a, 522.

cludes it as something knowable. Now the foundation includes the entity of this relation which is a necessary consequence of it. Hence it also includes it as something knowable.

To this I reply: It includes the relation's entity not as total cause, but only as a proximate cause which presupposes another cause, viz., the term. For the foundation itself requires this other cause. In like fashion, I grant that the foundation includes the relation as something knowable, but only if the other cause of its knowability be given or presupposed. If this be given simply, the relation is simply knowable; if it be given only to some, only for such is the relation knowable. But to the knower in this case, viz., the angel or the soul, the term or object is not given as something naturally knowable, in the sense that the knowing is a natural process or results from causes that move naturally. Consequently, even though the foundation can be known naturally by such a knower, it does not follow that he can know the relation naturally.

[24] 14.84 Answer to the second objection [in 14.81]: A finite being, considered either absolutely or as related to another limited being, is a natural object for the created intellect. But an entity which is essentially a relationship to something unlimited, even though it be limited in itself, is to the created intellect no more intelligible naturally than is the [infinite] term without which the relationship itself is unthinkable.

14.85 [Counter-arguments] The foregoing replies seem, in all probability, to do justice to this fact. The soul might well have natural knowledge of its absolute entity or of its beatific act, and still be unable by nature to understand its relationship to this term, so that God need not be known as the term of the relation. Nevertheless, those arguments about the soul and its beatific act [in 14.76 and 14.77] pose this further common problem. An object may be known by means of its natural image, even if this reveals no knowledge of the image-relationship itself. For example, one sees something white by means of the [sense] species of white in the eye, and still the relation of this species to the white object is not seen. The same is true of the intellect in the case of the intelligible species. For the formal reason for knowing the object is not the *relation* grounded in the sensible or intelligible species but the *form* grounding that relation. In the case at hand, therefore, the soul's or the beatific act's relation to God may be unknown naturally and nevertheless, since the foundation is the sort of thing that is of itself a likeness of the object, it could be the means of knowing that object.

[25] 14.86 The point made about the act [in 14.77] also appears to be

cogent, since the act seems to be a formal likeness of the object and one that is more in a state of actuality than an intelligible species would be, if such existed. If the object could be distinctly grasped or known through the species, then *a fortiori* or *a pari* it could be grasped through the beatific act.

14.87 The other point mentioned there also appears to be well taken, for there does seem to be something contradictory about the act being recognized as envisioning this object and yet the object, as envisioned by the act, remaining unknown. The beatified soul, however, by its natural endowments could recognize what the beatific act is all about, and hence perceive it as envisioning the beatific object. For even though this act is not something the soul has of its own nature, still it can reflect upon it once the act is there and it can do this in virtue of its natural powers.

I prove this first from Augustine[48]: "He who says 'I know that I live' knows one thing. If he were to add 'I know that I know I live,' he knows two things." And the text continues: "And so he can go on to add a third, a fourth, and countless other items, until he has enough." Now if it is up to him to continue with such reflex acts, then—I say—he can do so by reason of his natural endowments.

A second proof for this: If something supernatural were required to reflect upon an act, then for each new act a new supernatural factor would be needed. Now since it is possible to continue such reflex acts *ad infinitum*, supernatural factors *ad infinitum* would be required. Proof: The third act in relation to the second would be like the reflex act in relation to the direct act. If, given the direct act, the soul can only reflect upon it by virtue of some supernaturally elevating factor, by the same token then its third act, a reflection on the second, is made possible only through some additional supernatural factor.

A third proof for this: The intellect by its nature as a faculty can perceive and experience its own act in all its proper perfection, just as, when I see, I perceive that I do so by a natural power. I could do this by the visual power itself if it were reflective the way the intellect is.

[26]   14.88 [Reply to the counter-arguments] In answer to these I point out that a "medium of knowledge" or "means of knowing" can have two meanings: (1) the medium itself is known so that by knowing it something else is known, as is the case when a conclusion is

[48] Ibid., c.12, n.21: PL 42, 1074; CCSL 50a, 441-42.

QUESTION FOURTEEN

known by means of a principle; (2) the medium itself is not known but it merely functions as a means of knowing, in the way, for instance, that the sensible species in the sense faculty is a means of knowing.[49]

[49] There is an addition that is found in M_1 and M_2. M_1 inserts it here; M_2 adds it at the end of 14.91:

An example from sense perception makes this clear. When a ray of light passes through a piece of red glass, it causes red to appear on the opposite wall. Now the red on the wall is not a means for seeing the red of the glass properly, but one sees the red of the glass only in a derivative sense or perhaps not at all, for there is only some similarity between the red on the wall and that of the glass. But when a sensible species is the reason for perceiving an object properly, then that species itself is not seen by the senses, as is clear in the case of direct vision where nothing intervenes between the color and the eye and still the color is transmitted through the intervening space.

An objection to the contrary: While what was just said may be true of direct vision, it is not so in the case of reflected visions, for there the species or likeness itself seems to be seen, for what is seen is obviously seen in the mirror, and yet in such reflex vision the likeness in the mirror is the reason for perceiving the object in itself, for the object is seen under its proper aspect as something visible. Therefore, analogously in the question at hand, God would be seen by means of something in which is mirrored and yet he would be seen under an aspect proper to himself.

Answer: Alhacen in his *Optics,* book four, chapter four, declares explicitly that the species or likeness is not in the mirror as its subject or as terminating the act of vision. This can be shown quickly in one experiment, for that which exists somewhere is seen in itself by an eye in this place and also by another eye at another place, just as long as the medium is illumined and nothing opaque intervenes. But the eye which is at one place will see a white object in the mirror whereas one located at a different place will not see it, for vision only takes place at that point reached by the reflected ray. This reflected ray is always in the same surface as the incident ray and with the latter constitutes an angle equal to that angle formed by the incident ray and the body upon which it falls.

Our point is also proved from the fact that some mirrors like polished steel or polished silver or gold are not formally transparent. Bodies seen in such resemble bodies seen in mirrors, yet the color is not received in the polished metal, for color is only apt to be received by something transparent; therefore, it is received only in the air next to such mirrors. Insofar as it exists in the air, however, it cannot be itself an object of

In the first sense, nothing can be a means of knowing another object unless it contains the other's knowability and, to the extent it does, the second is known through the first. If the object exceeds the medium in knowability, then no matter how perfectly the medium is known it will lack something of the knowability of that object.

In the second way, however, something can be the means of knowing another even though its own knowability is inferior to that of the other, provided it is designed by nature to lead one to know the other.

14.89 This distinction provides an obvious solution to the first counter-argument [in 14.85]. Suppose the soul is an image of God. This does not say it is designed by nature to be a means of knowing God in the second way, but only in the first way, as one could gather from Augustine's words, "Those who see their mind," etc., cited above [in 14.79]. But if medium were taken in the second sense with reference to the medium known [i.e., the soul as known], it would be something which properly and formally represents the soul itself [in other words, it would be the concept of the soul]. And what would be the most perfect object that could be represented by it? It would be the soul itself, not God in the fulness of his intelligibility. In something which merely imitates or participates in his intelligibility, God could only be dimly mirrored.[50]

14.90 The same reasoning applies to the second counter-argument [in 14.86]. The [beatific] act is a likeness that is itself known. It no more suffices to know that of which it is an act than an intelligible species in one person's intellect, if perceived by another intellect, would suffice for the second mind to know perfectly the object it refers to.

14.91 On the contrary, you may say. In the intellect in which it exists, this act is reason for attaining perfectly the object made present through the act. Anyone who perceives the act as present, then, could attain the object by means of the act he knows. For in and through the act the same object is presented to him.

---

vision although, when it is received in a transparent mirror of glass, the vision does not terminate there but in some opaque substratum, such as the lead backing or something similar. Therefore, I claim that in such mirrored reflections the species or likeness itself is not seen, but it is only the means for seeing the object of which it is the species, and that not directly but by a reflected line which converges with the direct line at that point where the visual ray converged with the perpendicular line.

[50] Cf. Duns Scotus, *Ord.* II, d.3, q.9 (ed. Vivès XII, 201-209).

I answer: Only in the intellect in which it exists does the act function as the proximate reason for attaining the object, but it presupposes the object's own presence. One who merely perceives this act [as object] does not possess the act in such a way that it functions as the proper reason for attaining the object. To have an act which functions in this fashion two things are needed: the object's own presence and another act.

14.92 As for the third counter-argument [in 14.87], one could deny the claim that the soul *by nature* could reflect upon the beatific act as beatific. It is certainly true that the soul can reflect upon it, but only by that in virtue of which it possesses the direct act.

The text from Augustine [in 14.87] proves no more than this, since he does not claim the soul could continue to reflect by its nature alone. All he maintains is that once the soul has the act, it can reflect upon it. This might be in virtue of its nature or in virtue of that by which it has that act.

There is no incongruity of an infinite regress here because the supernatural factor suffices for the direct act and all the reflex acts.[51]

How to answer the third proof [in 14.87] based on the sense of sight is also clear. For it is not through the power of sight that I *perceive* that I see. But neither is it through some lesser power. Perhaps it is due to some superior potency whose function it is to know the act of vision.

[51] Ibid., I, d.3, nn.554-604 (III, 330-57).

Question Fifteen

IS THE POSSIBLE INTELLECT ACTIVE OR PASSIVE AS REGARDS THE CONCEPT OF A CREATURE?

[1]   15.1 The next question concerns the cause of intellection, or how the intellect passes from [potency] to act.

15.2 The question is this: Granted that the blessed in heaven have some concept or "word"* of the creature as seen in the divine essence, is the possible intellect* purely passive as regards such knowledge?[1]

Arguments Pro and Con

It is argued that it is:

The possible intellect is the recipient of its intellection. But the same subject is not both active and receptive as regards the same thing, for that which receives is in potency whereas that which acts is in act, and the same entity cannot be at once in potency and in act, since these are primary divisions of being. Therefore, the possible intellect has no activity as regards the "word," and consequently is purely passive.

15.3 For the negative view: If a "word" is formed there, I ask by what is it formed. It cannot be said that it is formed by the object, because intellection is an immanent action* according to the Philosopher,[2] and if there were any action of the object upon the intellect, intellection would be a transient action.* Neither can it be said that the "word" in this case is formed by the agent intellect,* for the agent intellect, according to the Philosopher,[3] makes the potentially intelligible an intelligible actually. All of its action, then, is complete before there is actual intellection and hence before there is a "word." Neither can one claim the memory actively forms the "word," because the "word" is formed through the act of knowing

---

[1] Cf. Duns Scotus, *Ord.* I, d.3, nn.333-553 (III, 201-330); IV, d.10, qq.8-9 (ed. Vivès XVII, 282-304).

[2] Aristotle, *Metaph.* x, c.8 (1050a35-1050b).

[3] Aristotle, *De anima* III, c.5 (430a14-17).

or understanding. The memory does not understand, but every act of understanding pertains to the intelligence itself, according to *The Trinity*.[4] Therefore, there is nothing else left in the soul except the possible intellect* that could form the "word."

Body of the Question

15.4 The question here is not whether it is possible to have a "word" of the beatific object itself, or of the secondary objects seen in the primary object [God], or whether the "word" of the first and second of these is distinct; but it presupposes there is a "word" of the secondary object [i.e., of the creature] and it asks: Just what is the function of the possible intellect in its formation? Therefore, beginning with what is more manifest, we shall inquire first about the formation of a "word" according to the mode of understanding we now possess. And, second, we shall explain how this applies to intellection in heaven.

ARTICLE I
Formation of the Word according to the Manner in Which We Understand in the Present Life

[2] 15.5 [Three points to be investigated] As for the first, I assume that there is perfect intellection, for instance, definitional knowledge of a definable object and whether such intellection be the "word" itself or not, at least it does not exist without the "word" of this object. Consequently, if anything is active with respect to this perfect understanding, then it is somehow active in the formation of the "word." Therefore, there are three points to be investigated as regards the cause of our intellection in the present life. First, that in the intellective part of man there is an active principle of intellection. Second, we must see whether this is something of the intellective soul itself or whether it is only the object, which is said to be in the soul inasmuch as in the soul, as an accident but not as a part of its nature, there is something representative of the object. Third, given that the active principle is something of the soul itself, we shall ask whether it is the agent or possible intellect.

1. In the Intellective Part of the Soul there is an Active Principle of Intellection

15.6 Proof: The first conclusion is established in this way: We all experience some intellection in us as new, and this is an

[4] Augustine, *De Trin.* xv, c.10, n.19: PL 42, 1071; CCSL 50a, 485-86.

absolute form, as we said in [13.8ff.] in the question dealing with this matter. But every absolute form, since it is the term of some action, has an active principle which gives it existence. Therefore, every new intellection in us has an active principle or source. This is intrinsic to the intelligent subject, as is clear from the Philosopher in the *De anima*[5]: "But between the two cases,"—add "of the intellect and the senses"—"there is a difference. The objects that excite the sensory powers to activity, the seen and the heard, etc., are outside." And he continues: "The ground of this difference is that what actual sensation apprehends is individuals, while what knowledge apprehends is universals, and these are in a sense within the soul. That is why man can exercise his intellection when he wishes, but his sensation does not depend on himself—a sensible object must be there." Therefore, we have this certain conclusion that the active principle that suffices for this new intellection is intrinsic to the intelligent subject.

15.7 With this in mind, then, we argue further by the method of division that this principle pertains (1) either to the will, or (2) the sensitive part, or (3) the intellective part insofar as this is distinct from both will and sense. The first alternative is unacceptable, at least if we are dealing with the initial intellection, for this precedes every act of the will.[6] The second alternative, viz., that this principle pertains to the sensitive part as such, cannot be admitted either. Therefore, by default it pertains to the intellective part of the soul.

[3] 15.8 [Three proofs it is not in the sensitive part] The second statement, namely that it does not pertain to the sensitive part, is proved in three ways, the *first* of which is this: An equivocal effect* is always less noble than its total equivocal cause,* as we gather from *Super Genesim*.[7] Intellection, however, is simply more perfect than the phantasm* or any such perfection whatsoever in the sensitive part, for intellection is properly a perfection of the intellectual natura *qua* intellectual and as such is more noble than the entire sensitive soul, and so more perfect than any perfection therein.[8]

15.9 The second proof is this: The angel does not always possess all the intellection it can have. Otherwise, since he can know every intelligible object, either he would have one single intellection

---

[5] Aristotle, *De anima* II, c.5 (417b19-25).

[6] Cf. Duns Scotus, *Ord.* II, d.42, q.4, n.3 (ed. Vivès XIII, 451); I, d.6, nn. 13ff. (IV, 92ff.).

[7] Augustine, *Super Gen.* XII, c.24, n.51: PL 34, 474-75.

[8] Cf. Duns Scotus, *Ord.* IV, d.12, q.3, n.14 (ed. Vivès XVII, 590).

QUESTION FIFTEEN

which embraces all intelligibles at once or else he would have as many distinct intellections as there are distinct objects. But neither of these seems a viable alternative.

The first would ascribe too great a perfection to his intellection. Indeed, it would seem to attribute infinite perfection to it, since even the divine intellect would not surpass it as far as the multitude of objects is concerned. The second hypothesis would seem to ascribe too much perfection to his intellect, for it would know all these objects at once by different acts just as distinctly as it knows one object by one act.

It follows, then, that since the angel could understand every intelligible object, it would be able to have some new intellection. Therefore, it seems that we must attribute to him whatever perfection is present in an intellect able to have some new knowledge.

But it is part of such perfection to have such perfect habitual knowledge as to be only in accidental potency* to understanding,[9] in the sense that the Philosopher speaks of it in the *De anima*.[10] Referring to the possible intellect, he says: "Once the mind has become each set of its possible objects, as a man of science has, when this phrase is used of one who is actually a man of science (this happens when he is now able to exercise the power on his own initiative), its condition is still one of potentiality, but in a different sense from the potentiality which preceded the acquisition of knowledge." What he means is that even though a mind with a habit that enables it to act on its own is in potency, it is not essential potency, that is to say, in potency to the form or the principle of acting, but only in accidental potency to the intellective operation. And this is a more perfect disposition which enables one to go from the potentiality of operating to its actual exercise.

[4]   15.10 It could be objected here[11] that it is purely a matter of belief that an angel could have a new intellection, for the principal philosophers did not see this to be the case.

15.11 Also, one could claim that God immediately moves the angel to whatever intellection he happens to have.

15.12 Answer to these objections: Perhaps the Philosopher, who affirms that the angel's intellection is identical with his substance, would say as a consequence of this view that whatever produced his

[9] Ibid., II, d.3, q.8, n.8 (ed. Vivès XII, 186); q.10, nn.15-16 (ibid., 255-57).
[10] Aristotle, *De anima* III, c.4 (429b5-10).
[11] Godfrey of Fontaines, *Quodl.* VI, q.7 in corp. (ed. Hoffmans in PhB III, Louvain, 1914, p. 168).

substance also caused his intellection. Similarly a Catholic, who claims the intellection by which an angel understands himself is coeval* with him and is a kind of proper perfection which is a necessary consequence of his nature, would probably say that such intellection somehow derives immediately from God according to this probable principle: "An accident that is coeval with or proper to its substance stems from the one generating the substance." It does not seem probable, however, that an accident that is *per accidens* or contingently in the substance was produced by the one generating the substance.[12]

15.13 Confirmation of this: Although God could cause immediately any intellection, if as a matter of fact there would be one, for instance of this object, that he did not cause, but left its causation up to the angel and the natural order of efficient causes, it hardly seems probable that the angel could never know this object, since the soul left to itself and natural causes can attain such knowledge naturally, although through the mediation of the senses. For it does not seem possible that the soul, even with the help of the senses, could apprehend an object which the angel could not grasp without the senses.

[5] 15.14 But what is said of the Philosopher seems to substantiate our thesis. For if the Philosopher had realized that an angel could have a new intellection, he would have maintained that at times the angel is in a state of accidental potency, since this is the most perfect disposition anyone could have who is at any time in potency to intellection. Anyone, then, who defends the position that an angel is capable of a new intellection, whether this be on grounds of faith or reason, would have to admit logically that the angel is in accidental potency to this knowledge, even as the Philosopher would, had he held the same thesis. Now one who, on holding some antecedent, would concede a consequent that the Philosopher would have admitted, had he held that antecedent, would agree more with the Philosopher than someone, who, on holding that same antecedent, would deny that consequent, for Aristotle himself would not have denied it, had he granted the antecedent.

15.15 The third proof [of 15.8] is from authority. Augustine[13] says: "What excels in the soul is called mind." He adds: "A man is not called the image of God according to everything that pertains

---

[12] Cf. Duns Scotus, *Ord.* II, d.3, q.11, nn.11-12 (ed. Vivès XII, 278-79).
[13] Augustine, *De Trin.* xv, c.7, n.11: PL 42, 1065; CCSL 50a, 475.

to his nature, but according to the mind alone." And earlier he had declared:[14] "The image of his nature ought to be sought for and found there in us, where there is also the best thing that our nature has."

[6]   15.16 From this and other like passages, one would conclude that every *image* is in the intellective part, understanding by this the part that transcends the sensitive. But an image, as is obvious from the last chapter of *The Trinity*,[15] and from many other texts from Augustine, includes both "parent and offspring."[16] Hence the "parent," who begets this knowledge which is the "offspring" and hence is the active principle of intellection, is to be found in the intellectual part of man. Therefore, anyone who would claim that the reason for the immediate generation of actual knowledge is the phantasm or some similar form in the sensitive part would not preserve the analogy, it seems, of the mind being the "parent" of its thought in any proper sense.

15.17 Besides, Augustine says in *The Trinity*[17]: "The memory of man, and particularly that which beasts do not have, namely, that in which the intelligible things are so contained that they do not come into it through the senses of the body, has in this image of the Trinity a likeness, unequal of course but a likeness of whatever kind it may be, to the Father." He explains this in another passage as follows[18]: "But that word of ours . . . is so born from our knowledge as that Word was also born from the knowledge of the Father." And in another place he writes[19]: "We attribute to the memory everything that we know."

15.18 According to these texts the memory, which animals lack, viz., that which is properly intellectual, has a likeness to the Father, because our "word" is born from it or from knowledge that is in it, just as the eternal Word is born from the knowledge of the Father. These quotations suffice, it seems, to show that according to Augustine the active principle of intellection is in the intellectual part properly speaking.

[14] Ibid., XIV, c.8, n.11: PL 42, 1044; CCSL 50a, 436.
[15] Ibid., IX, c.12, n.18: PL 42, 970-72; CCSL 50, 309-10.
[16] Cf. Duns Scotus, *Ord.* I, d.1, n.13 (II, 8); d.3, nn.583-88 (III, 344-47); II, d.16, q.un., n.20 (ed. Vivès XIII, 45-46).
[17] Augustine, *De Trin.* XV, c.23, n.43: PL 42, 1090; CCSL 50a, 520.
[18] Ibid., c.14, n.24: PL 42, 1077; CCSL 50a, 497.
[19] Ibid., c.21, n.40: PL 42, 1088; CCSL 50a, 517.

2. Which Factor is Active in Intellection?

[7] 15.19 [What the authorities say] As for the second point in [15.5 of] this first article, this much is certain. To cause intellection the concurrence of some part of the intellective soul and the presence of the object, either in itself or in some representation, is required. But authorities seem to disagree as to which of these factors is active *per se*.

15.20 Augustine says[20]: "No one should think that any body acts on the spirit as if the spirit played the role of matter under the domination of the body. For what makes something is in every way more excellent than what is made, and the body is in no way more excellent than the spirit. On the contrary, the spirit excels the body. Therefore, even though the image begins to exist in the spirit, the body does not produce it there, but the spirit with wonderful rapidity produces it in itself."

15.21 And in *The Trinity*,[21] also, he says: "The soul fastens together and forces into itself the images of bodies."

15.22 As for the activity of the object, however, he says[22]: "The thought, formed from that thing which we know, is the word which we speak in our heart." In the same section he adds: "The word is born from the knowledge itself which is retained in the memory." And in another passage he writes[23]: "The word is a likeness of the thing known from which it is begotten, and it is an image of the thing."

15.23 The Philosopher seems to argue in favor of the object, for that which reduces something from essential to accidental potentiality seems to be an active principle. Now this would seem to pertain to the object, for what makes the object present under the aspect of being actually intelligible is the species* and this is caused by the object.

15.24 The text from *De anima*,[24] quoted [in 15.6] favors his opinion: "And these [universals] are in a sense within the soul. That is why a man can exercise his intellection when he wishes." It is as if he said: The intelligible objects are present to the soul, and there-

---

[20] Augustine, *Super Gen.* XII, c.16, n.33: PL 34, 467.
[21] Augustine, *De Trin.* x, c.5, n.7: PL 42, 977; CCSL 50, 321.
[22] Ibid., xv, c.10, n.19: PL 42, 1071; CCSL 50a, 486.
[23] Ibid., c.12, n.22: PL 42, 1075; CCSL 50a, 493.
[24] Aristotle, *De anima* II, c.5 (417b24).

QUESTION FIFTEEN

fore the soul is in accidental potency to understand when it wants to.

15.25 On the other hand, this text from the *Metaphysics*,[25] according to some, favors the activity of the potency: "Speculative thought is an immanent action." If the intellection were not caused by the intellect, it would not be an immanent but a transient action.*[26]

[8] 15.26 [Scotus' own view is that both factors concur] As for this problem, it could be said that both [the soul and the object] concur as active principles of intellection.

And it seems Augustine agrees with this[27]: "We must obviously hold fast to this principle that everything which we know begets the knowledge of itself within us. For knowledge is born of both, from the one who knows and the object which is known." He also writes[28]: "Vision is produced both by the visible thing and the one who sees." And although he adds there: "The informing of the sense, which is called vision, is imprinted by the body alone that is seen," this does not count against our position, for the term "vision" is used equivocally, first for the act of seeing, and second for the likeness of the thing seen, and only the latter is caused by the body. This equivocal usage can be gleaned from a study of many expressions in that chapter.

There is also an argument from reason for our interpretation. When the intelligible object is actually present to the intellect, an actual intellection of this object is possible. But no intellection can be had without a perfectly active principle. Therefore, either only one of the two factors is the complete active principle, or both together constitute a single complete active principle in such a way that each is partially active.

15.27 [The object alone is not the complete active principle] That neither factor alone is the complete active principle is proved first in regard to the object.

(1) No object, in the form of a sensible accident is more noble than intellection itself. But an active principle, to be complete or perfect, if it is equivocal [or unlike its effect], must be more perfect than the form it causes.

---

[25] Aristotle, *Metaph.* IX, c.8 (1050a21-1050b1).
[26] Cf. Duns Scotus, *Ord.* I, d.3, nn.401-553 (III, 245-330).
[27] Augustine, *De Trin.* IX, c.12, n.18: PL 42, 970; CCSL 50, 309.
[28] Ibid., XI, c.2, n.3: PL 42, 986; CCSL 50, 336.

15.28 (2) A second proof for the same is this: Where the object is present to the same degree, the greater the effort and intent to understand, the more perfect the intellection can be. We see this to be so because the more perfect the intellection, the more lasting the impression it leaves. Hence it is this greater voluntary effort that causes somehow a more perfect understanding. Now this would hardly be the case if the object alone were the active cause of this. For the object is not a free agent essentially, as is clear. Neither is it free somehow by participation, it would seem, for it is not of the same nature as the will. Therefore, it seems it would always act to the utmost of its power.

[9] 15.29 (3) The same point can be shown, third, as follows: The operation whereby an agent elicits something through the help of some incidental perfection it has *per accidens* is not an essential or *per se* perfection of that agent.[29] For example, to heat or even to warm something is not a *per se* perfection of a warm piece of wood. It only pertains to wood because of the warmth which is something accidental to the wood. But that by which an object other than the soul is present to the intellect is a *per accidens* accident, since sometimes it happens to be there and at other times not. If it were the only active principle of intellection, therefore, intellection would not be the proper perfection of the intellect or of man.

15.30 [The intellect alone is not the complete active principle] Second, there is proof that the total activity involved in intellection is not due to the intellect alone, because the act of intellection seems to be a proper likeness of the object.[30]

The object also seems to account for the specific character of a given intellection, not indeed as an intrinsic formal constitutive principle, but as a *per se* extrinsic principle.

Intellection also seems to depend essentially on the object. For that reason the object is referred to the intellection [by Aristotle], a relationship that puts it among the third class of "relatives."* But this would not seem to be correct, if the object were merely an incidental cause [*causa per accidens*] or just a necessary condition [*causa sine qua non*].

15.31 Therefore, I accept the authorities cited [in 15.19-25] in favor of both sides, whether they apply to the intellect or to the object. For it is indeed true that each plays somehow a partial but

[29] Cf. Duns Scotus, *Ord.* I, d.3, nn.427-29, 463-70 (III, 260-61, 279-82).
[30] Ibid., nn.413-14 (III, 250-52).

active role in intellection. Both are integrated, however, in such a way as to constitute one complete active principle.[31]

[10] 15.32 [Solution of some doubts] But here two doubts arise. First of all, how do the two factors make up one complete principle? Second, how are we to interpret in favor of the object certain authorities cited earlier, such as Augustine's statement [in 15.22] that "The word is born from the knowledge itself," or Aristotle's claim that "What knowledge apprehends is universals, and these are in a sense within the soul."[32]

15.33 As for the first problem, I say that at times concurrent causes are of the same type or order, as in the case where we have more than one pulling a boat. At other times, however, they are of different types and orders, and this can occur in two ways. Sometimes the posterior cause derives its power from the prior cause, as is the case of the sun* and the father in the generation of a man. In other cases, however, the posterior cause does not derive its power from the anterior, nor does it depend on it for the possession of that power, but only for the exercise of its own power in such a way that the superior cause acts to a greater extent as the principal cause, and the other to a lesser extent. An example, perhaps, would be the father and mother in begetting a child, according to what seems to be asserted in *De animalibus*[33] about the mother being somehow active in generation. This seems reasonable, since powers specifically the same should be the consequence of having the same specific form, and male and female, according to the Philosopher,[34] do not differ specifically. The mother, however, does not receive her active power from the father, nor does she depend upon his for its possession. She only depends on him for the exercise of her own power and plays a less active role.

15.34 Applying this to the case at hand, we could say that the concurrence of intellect and object is not of the first type because the first sort of cooperation is necessary. And this is not because of the nature of the cooperating agents, but because of a lack of strength in one of them, for if his strength were doubled, one alone could do the job. But such is not the situation here, for no matter how perfect the object or intellect was, neither could cause intellec-

---

[31] Ibid., nn.486-94, 559-62 (III, 289-93, 333-34).
[32] Aristotle, *De anima* III, c.7 (431b10); cf. *supra*, nn.6, 24.
[33] Aristotle, *De animal. generat.* I, cc.17-22 (721a32-730b32).
[34] Aristotle, *Metaph.* x, c.9 (1058a29-35).

tion without the other. On the other hand, they do not cooperate in the second way, since the intellect does not receive its active power from the object, nor vice versa. Therefore, they cooperate in the third way.

15.35 It is not necessary here to discuss which of the two plays the major role.

[11] 15.36 As for the second problem [raised in 15.32], I say that for Augustine these three expressions are equivalent: "The word is generated from the memory," "The word is generated from knowledge in the memory," and "The word is generated from the thing known." For by "knowledge," here, he means the initial act whereby the soul is sufficiently actuated as regards the intellective act. Now the "word" is generated in virtue of this initial act, and since the object shines forth in that act, he says the "word" is generated from the object. The "word," then, is generated by knowledge as its formal principle, and by the object as shining forth in this principle, and by the memory insofar as it contains this principle. All such statements of Augustine then, to his mind, speak in favor of an activity on the part of the object.

15.37 A similar interpretation can be given to those texts of Aristotle cited earlier [in 15.6 and 15.9] about "what knowledge apprehends is universals" and "a man can exercise his intellection when
[12] he wishes" or "a man of science . . . is now able to exercise that power on his own initiative." We must understand Aristotle here to be referring, like Augustine, not to "knowledge" or "science" as the habitual knowledge acquired by repeated acts that gives one the facility to perform similar acts, but rather to whatever it is that makes the object present as something actually intelligible, whether this be an intelligible species or something else. For science is that by which the soul is educed from essential to accidental potency. Now the science acquired by repeated acts that gives a facility as regards other acts does not precede every actual intellection.

15.38 Similarly, according to Augustine, science is the formal reason or ground whereby memory gives birth or generates. But the science acquired by many repeated acts is not the formal reason or ground for generating any intellection. On the contrary, science itself is generated from many prior acts.[35]

15.39 You might object that the text from *Super Genesim*[36] not

---

[35] Cf. Duns Scotus, *Ord.* I, d.3, nn.523-27, 512-14, 504-506 (III, 311-14, 303-305, 298-300).

[36] Augustine, *Super Gen.* XII, c.24, n.51: PL 34, 474-75; cf. *supra*, 15.20.

only affirms that the soul is active in intellection, but also denies that the object acts upon the soul. And as for Aristotle, he not only concedes that the object acts, but he also seems to deny that the intellect acts at all, for he speaks of "thinking as a passive affection."[37]

Answer to the first: It could be said that Augustine denies there that the object acts *immediately* on the soul according to the material being it has in the extramental world.

Answer to the second: Aristotle, it seems, speaks more frequently of the activity of the object and passivity of the potency. The reason for this is that he usually refers to the powers of the soul insofar as they represent that whereby formally we can be operating, for instance, he speaks of the sense as that by which we formally sense, the intellect as that by which we formally understand, just as he says the soul is that whereby we formally live. Now even though the intellect actively causes the intellection, it is not said to understand insofar as it causes this, for if God were to cause this same intellection, we would not say that he understands by virtue of such intellection, but rather that the intellect in which he produces this intellection understands. And, therefore, in the present case we say that the intellect understands not because it causes, but because it receives the intellection. And thus it is true to say that "thinking is a passive affection," because the intellect only understands to the extent that it receives the intellection. But whether the text from the *Metaphysics* [cited in 15.25] favors the activity of the object or not should be clear from what was said [at 13.81-83] in the question about the act of knowing and appetition.

3. Is it the Agent or the Possible Intellect That is Active in Intellection?

[13] 15.40 [Arguments in favor of the agent intellect] Our third main problem in this first article is to determine whether the active principle in the intellective part of the soul is the agent intellect or the possible intellect.[38]

It would seem to be the agent intellect because the possible intellect receives the intellection. If, in addition to receiving the intellection, it should also cause the intellection, with equal reason the possible intellect could be said to be active in regard to the intelligible species it receives, and thus there would be no need of the agent intellect for any intellectual act.

---

[37] Aristotle, *De anima* III, c.4 (429b24-25).
[38] Cf. Duns Scotus, *Ord.* I, d.3, nn.333-568 (III, 201-338).

15.41 The fact that the potencies of the soul are distinguished into active potencies and passive potencies confirms this position.

15.42 A second proof that the agent intellect is the active factor is this: The Philosopher,[39] in distinguishing the agent from the possible intellect, explains that "The intellect as we have described it is what it is by virtue of becoming all things, while there is another intellect that is what it is by virtue of making all things." Hence it seems to follow that the agent intellect is paired with the possible intellect as what is active to what is passive. It is active, then, with respect to everything that the possible intellect can receive and, therefore, also as regards intellection.

15.43 A third proof is found in [Aristotle's] statement that the agent intellect "is a certain habitual state like light."[40] Intellectual light, however, appears to be the active principle for knowing intelligible truths, according to [Augustine's] explanation in *The Trinity*[41]: "The nature of the intellectual mind is so formed as to see those things which, according to the disposition of the Creator, are subjoined to intelligible things in the natural order, in a sort of incorporeal light of its own kind, as the eye of the flesh sees the things that lie about it in this corporeal light."

15.44 A fourth argument based on [Aristotle's further description of the agent intellect][42]: "The active," he goes on to say, "is always more noble than the passive factor, the originating force than the matter which it forms." He wants to say, then, that the agent intellect is either more noble, or at least no less noble, than the possible intellect. Now the "image" [of God in us] consists of what is best in our nature, as was proved from Augustine [in 15.15] in the first part of this article. The agent intellect belongs to the image, and it obviously must be part of the memory. Now memory has two functions, one to conserve the object or likeness [*species*] of the object; the other to express or generate its actual knowledge. Now the first function obviously cannot pertain to the agent intellect, since it is not a receptive or conserving power. Hence, its function must be the second, namely, to express knowledge.

15.45 [Arguments in favor of the possible intellect] In favor of the possible intellect, however, we have the following arguments:

First, there is Aristotle's explanation [in 15.43] that the agent in-

---

[39] Aristotle, *De anima* III, c.5 (430a15).
[40] Ibid. (430a16-18).
[41] Augustine, *De Trin.* XII, c.15, n.24: PL 42, 1011; CCSL 50, 378.
[42] Aristotle, *De anima* III, c.5 (430a18-20).

tellect is "like light," which the Commentator[43] interprets in this way. As light somehow converts potential color into actual color, so the agent intellect transforms the potentially intelligible into what is actually intelligible. Therefore, its action ends with the object as actually able to be known, which is prior to intellection itself.

15.46 This is confirmed by the observation of the Commentator[44] that if things were the way Plato assumed they were, no agent intellect would be needed. Hence the agent intellect is only introduced to make the object actually universal. But this precedes actual intellection.

15.47 A second argument is based on the Commentator's[45] explanation that the agent intellect is postulated in order that it may transfer the object "from one order to another." This transfer can be taken to mean one that moves from the sensible to the intelligible order, and hence from the corporeal to the spiritual order. But why is something needed to effect this transfer? The reason seems to be that a corporeal agent has no basis for acting on anything but a corporeal patient, for such an agent requires that the patient be located next to it. Otherwise it would be as if the patient were not present to such an agent. Therefore, a corporeal agent can never be the immediate cause of something spiritual, and consequently it cannot be the proximate reason why anything is transferred from one order to another. This seems to be Augustine's argument in *Super Genesim*.[46] But when an object that is actually intelligible becomes actually known, there is no transfer of this sort from one order to another. Hence the agent intellect is not required in such a case.

15.48 This is confirmed by the fact that no such transfer from one order to another is postulated for something known to be actually willed, because the actually known is sufficiently commensurate to the will. Hence it follows that since the actually intelligible present in the intellective memory is an equally commensurate intelligible, namely, as regards its being understood actually, no power is needed to transfer such an object from one order to another.

[15]   15.49 A third argument is this: If the agent intellect were *per se* active for actual intellection, then, by the same token, it would be

---

[43] Averroes, *De anima* III, com. 18 (*Averrois Cordovensis Commentarium magnum in Aristotelis de Anima*, ed. F. Stuart Crawford, Medieval Academy of America, Cambridge, Mass., 1953, p. 439).

[44] Ibid., com. 18, p. 440.   [45] Ibid., n.18, p. 440.

[46] Augustine, *Super Gen.* XII, c.16, n.33: PL 34, 467.

necessary to postulate an active and possible potency wherever any power is assumed to be both the cause and the recipient of its own operation. Thus, for instance, an agent and possible will would be required according to the common opinion that the will is both the agent and recipient of its volition. Similarly, if anyone assumed the sense faculty to be active, perhaps because he held the sensation itself to be something more noble than the external sensible object, he would have to distinguish an agent sense and a possible sense. Since the Philosopher himself never assumed any such distinction between "agent" and "possible" except in regard to the intellect, it would follow that the basis for such a distinction is not something the intellect has in common with the other potencies, and hence not because the power is both the agent and recipient of its action.

15.50 A fourth argument can be drawn from [Augustine's][47] statement in *The Trinity* that "Knowledge is born from both the one who knows and from the object that is known." But it is not the agent intellect but the possible intellect that knows. Therefore, intellection is born of the possible intellect, and hence it is active as regards intellection.

[16] 15.51 [Conclusions that follow from the first opinion] In this section, then, if one held to the first view, he could say that the agent intellect has two sequentially related actions. The first is to make the potentially intelligible actually intelligible, or the potentially universal, actually universal. The second is to make the potentially understood actually understood.

The first of these functions would be understood as follows: From the phantasm or sensible image in the imagination there would be produced in the intellect by virtue of the agent intellect an intelligible species, or something in which a thing appears as actually intelligible and which can be called, for brevity's sake, an intelligible species. And this very real production of one representation from another is accompanied by a metaphorical "transformation" of one object into another, namely, of something sensibly imaginable into something intelligible. And this metaphorical description is a reasonable account of what goes on, because the object has a similar sort of existence as object [*esse obiectivum*] in the one representation as it does in the other. Therefore, in the real change whereby a spiritual representation is produced with the help of a corporeal representation, namely, where a universal representation is produced with the help of a singular representation, one can speak or

[47] Augustine, *De Trin.* IX, c.12, n.18: PL 42, 970; CCSL 50, 309.

think of a similar "transformation" of a corporeal object into a spiritual one, or of a singular object into a universal one.

The second function would consist in transforming the potentially known into the actually known. In this case also there is a metaphorical "transformation" of objects corresponding to the real transformation on the part of those things whereby one tends towards the objects, for actual intellection really follows the intelligible species. And just as the first transformation from potency to act is ascribed to the agent intellect, so also is the second, both metaphorically as regards the objects and really as regards those things in which the objects are represented. For to the extent that the intelligible species would be generated by the agent intellect from the phantasm, the actually intelligible would be generated, metaphorically speaking, from the potentially intelligible. And in the second act, as actual intellection is generated from the potentially intelligible, so, metaphorically, objects potentially intelligible become actually intelligible.

[17] 15.52 Similarly, one could postulate a twofold passive aspect in the possible intellect corresponding to the twofold activity of the agent intellect. The first of these would be the reception of the intelligible species from the phantasm through the first action of the agent intellect; the second would be the reception of intellection itself from the intelligible species through the second action of the agent intellect.

And according to this interpretation both agent and possible intellect would pertain to the intellective memory. The agent intellect, however, would not belong to it in virtue of its first function, which is to make the potentially intelligible actually intelligible. Indeed, the memory in act would be the term of such an action, for it would be in virtue of such activity that the intellect would have the object present to it as actually intelligible. It would be in virtue of its second action that the agent intellect would be included in memory, since the function of memory would be to make express the actual knowledge of intellection, and the agent intellect's second action would contribute to this action. The possible intellect, however, would be called memory insofar as its reception of the intelligible species is concerned, whereas it would be called intelligence so far as second receptive role is concerned.

15.53 [How this theory would solve the counter-arguments in 15.45-50] According to this view, one could reply to those arguments that seemed to support the contrary position on the grounds that the first function, that of abstraction, is more proper to the agent intellect than the second, that of causing intellection, for this kind of activity could be something it shares with other powers. But no other power transfers the object from one order to another, i.e., from the corporeal to the spiritual order. Even the will, which some claim, in causing its action, transforms metaphorically its object from the intelligible to the appetible order, needs no "agent will" to effect the transfer. That is to say, no agent is required to prepare its object to become actually "volible" in the way the agent intellect prepares the object to become actually intelligible, because once the object is actually known it can be an object of volition, and hence no action is needed to prepare the object for the will.

Therefore the authorities cited do affirm what is true of the first act of the intellect. And even though at times it is said that it is only for this purpose that an agent intellect is postulated, this is still true of that function that is proper to this intellect, for only here is there a power that prepares an object; for the second act is not something proper to an agent of such virtue, for other powers can be active in operating, once their object is given.

[18] 15.54 [Conclusions that follow from the second opinion] But if one held the other view, viz., that the possible intellect is the active factor in intellection, and that the action of the agent intellect is limited to abstracting the object, then one would have to say that the agent intellect does not pertain to the memory, but that its action (as regards sensibles) ends at the memory, since it ends at that form through which the object as actually intelligible is shown to the intellect, and this is the form that constitutes perfect memory. As for pure intelligibles, however, such as spiritual things, it would have no action whatsoever. This would be true whether such things were understood directly or by means of a species, since they could cause such by their own power. The possible intellect, however, would belong to the memory not only insofar as it retains all the representations of objects actually intelligible, but also insofar as it actively expresses actual knowledge.

15.55 [How this theory would solve the counter-arguments in 15.40-44] One could then answer those arguments adduced against this view.

[19] As for the first [in 15.40], one can say the operative potency is not active as regards its object, even though it is active as regards its act about the object. That it can cause its own intellection, therefore, is

QUESTION FIFTEEN

no reason to claim the possible intellect can cause the intelligible species.

15.56 As for the confirmation [in 15.41], one could say that if we speak of potency insofar as it implies a relationship, then we may well divide potencies into the active and the passive. But if we are referring to what underlies this relation, as we commonly do when we speak of a potency, for example, when we say that heat is a potency for heating, then there is no need to distinguish active from passive potencies. Otherwise the will would have to be two potencies.

15.57 As for the other argument [in 15.42], Aristotle's words that the agent intellect is "what it is in virtue of making all things" must be understood to mean "making all things actually intelligible."

This can be gathered from what follows about "light makes potential colors into actual colors,"[48] since it makes them actually visible. This is understood in the sense that even though the nature of color as an absolute quality remains the same in the dark, nevertheless it is not able to be seen, if we are speaking of proximate potency, for whenever two causes must concur to have an action, one of them—the second—is not in proximate potency unless the other—the first—concurs. Now for color to act upon sight, another cause, namely the light, is required for the action; therefore, color is only proximately visible when it is illuminated. In this way too, the phantasm cannot produce the intelligible species without the concurrent action of the agent intellect.

The agent intellect, therefore, makes all things actually intelligible in the sense of putting them in proximate potency to being known. For in the intelligible species it makes appear what was only in remote potency before, because they appeared there in a material representation which presented them in their singularity. But [Aristotle] nowhere says that the agent intellect is that which makes all things actually known.

Consequently, the conclusion that the agent intellect's action is coextensive with the possible intellect's receptivity must be taken in the same sense as referring to making and receiving something actually intelligible, not something actually understood.

15.58 As for the third argument [in 15.43], it is the truth of a principle that is seen in the meaning of its terms. The meanings of these terms, however, as actually intelligible and universal, appear in the intellect through the action of the light of the agent intellect,

---

[48] Aristotle, *De anima* III, c.5 (430a16-17).

not in the sense that the light is the immediate cause of seeing them. It is only the mediate cause, insofar as, in causing the meaning of the terms to become intelligible, it subsequently causes through those terms the act of seeing the truth of the principles.

15.59 As for the fourth argument [in 15.44], one could say that the agent intellect is more noble than the possible precisely in regard to sensible objects, for it is just in respect to these objects that it acts on the possible intellect.

[20]   15.60 [Scotus' own view] Regarding this third section of this article, then, it seems that we should retain Augustine's distinction in *The Trinity*[49] between memory, intelligence, and will. Comparing Aristotle's distinction of agent and possible intellects with this, we see that only the possible intellect corresponds to intelligence because only this receives the act of intellection. And Aristotle himself generally speaks this way of the intellect, viz., as that by which we understand or that by which we receive intellection. The possible intellect also corresponds to memory insofar as it pertains to memory to store habitual knowledge according to Augustine, who speaks in *The Trinity*[50] of "the science or knowledge we retain in the memory." Thus Aristotle refers at times to the possible intellect as that by which we know or that by which we have knowledge or science, which transforms the intellect from essential to accidental potency.

15.61 As for the other act of the memory which consists in generating actual knowledge, it is clear that this still pertains to the possible intellect *per accidens*, for when an active form exists in some subject, the action resulting from such a form pertains to the subject *per accidens*, just as, for example, the wood warms *per accidens*. Now that by which the object plays an active role in producing intellection [viz., the intelligible species] is a form in the possible intellect. Hence the possible intellect is at least productive *per accidens*.

15.62 But if the further question is asked as to whether the act of generating knowledge pertains *per se* to the same intellective part, one can hold, according to what has been said [in 15.51 or 15.54], that this pertains either to just the agent intellect or to the possible intellect alone, and consequently the one or the other would belong to the memory. Or one could postulate a third alternative, namely, that the act of generating intellection pertains to both, but to the

---

[49] Augustine, *De Trin.* x, c.11, nn.17-18: PL 42, 982-84; CCSL 50, 329-30.
[50] Ibid., xv, c.10, n.19: PL 42, 1071; CCSL 50a, 486.

agent intellect to a greater degree and to the possible intellect to a lesser degree. It does not follow that just because both belong to one nature, one cannot have a greater and the other a lesser causal action as regards the same action. This is clear from the analogy of the intellect and will, one of which, many claim, is the principal agent in certain actions while the other plays a subordinate role, yet they constitute but one nature. According to others, however, the case here is not really similar because both intellect and will do not immediately attain the same causal effect, but one, by means of the operation it causes, moves the other to its operation.

15.63 In brief, if the real distinction of potencies, either in terms of something absolute or in terms of real relations, is not admitted, but it is claimed that one and the same absolute reality, somehow unlimited, is the immediate principle of different acts, but is called now this potency, now that, with reference to different acts, then the first way seems probable.[51]

ARTICLE II
How the Notion or Word is Formed in the Intellect of the Blessed in Heaven

[21] 15.64 [The intellect of the blessed can have a notion of the creature known in its own right] As for the second article, I say that the intellect of the beatified can have a "word" of the creature known in its own right [*in genere proprio*],[52] and that the possible intellect plays the same role in its formation as it now does, for according to the words of Augustine[53]: "God so governs the things he has created, that he lets them perform their own actions." Therefore, in heaven the action which naturally pertains to the perfection of nature will remain.

15.65 But it is doubtful whether the blessed intellect has a "word" proper to a creature as seen in the divine essence. But if it does, one would have to say the role of the possible intellect in its formation is the same whether it is seen in the divine essence or on its own [like anything else of its kind].

15.66 [There is no word of the creature as seen in the divine essence] But one could say in heaven there is no "word" of the object as seen in the divine essence for these reasons:

[51] Cf. Duns Scotus, *Ord.* II, d.16 (ed. Vivès XIII, 23-47).
[52] Ibid., d.3, q.11 (ed. Vivès XII, 270-80); IV, d.45, q.2 (ed. Vivès XX, 279-307).
[53] Augustine, *De civit. Dei* VII, c.30: PL 41, 228; CCSL 47, 212.

One who has a "word" [or notion] of a thing immediately grasps the object of which it is the "word." But a stone, seen in the divine essence, is not attained immediately as the object of the act of vision, for it is only attained this way in itself. But in heaven only the divine essence is attained immediately, for it alone moves [the intellect] in a primary sense, and hence it moves it to grasp the essence itself.

15.67 Also, the proper "word" of anything is begotten of scientific knowledge or of a likeness or species of the object itself. Now the memory of the beatified, however, contains neither the science nor the species of a stone, as seen in a "word," because through a "word" nothing is seen except in its own right.

15.68 Likewise, the divine essence and what is seen therein are perceived by the same act. But the envisioning intellect would not have a "word" of the essence seen because then it would not be seeing the essence immediately. Therefore, it would not have a "word" of the thing seen in that essence.

[22]   15.69 [Objections] These reasons, however, are challenged.

Against the first [in 15.66]: Although a conclusion can be known through a principle [or premise], it can also be known immediately as an object of knowledge, for inferred or discursive knowledge does not have as its terms just the principle on which the inference was based, for then it would be necessary to continue further back and as a consequence the inferential process or discourse would never end. But the conclusion is the inferred term of a demonstrative syllogism. Therefore, once the inference is over, the intellect possesses immediate knowledge of the conclusion. By the same token, then, although the divine intellect moves [the intellect of the beatified] initially to the vision of itself, nevertheless, because it is a mover without limitation, it moves [the created intellect] secondarily to the vision of the creature. Therefore, when this process is over, the intellect can see the creature as an object envisioned immediately.

15.70 The second [in 15.67] is challenged in this fashion: What suffices to generate a "word" of any object is a perfect memory, whether this contains the object in question actually or virtually, even as habitual knowledge of the principle can be enough to generate actual knowledge of the conclusion. There is no need that the memory contain the knowledge of the object formally; that it is contained virtually suffices. And so the intellect of the blessed, having the divine essence actually present as intelligible, also has a proper memory as regards the vision of that essence, and with this, it has a perfect memory that contains virtually the vision of the creature; for as the creature is contained virtually as to its entity, so is it contained as to knowability. Therefore, the one beatified does have a memory or knowledge adequate to produce a "word" [or notion] proper to the stone. And it does not follow in this second argument, any more than it does in the first, that resulting vision will be that of the object functioning "in its own right" [*in proprio genere*] since this sort of vision takes place by means of some "reason for seeing" that is taken from some created thing.

15.71 Against the third reason [in 15.68] it is argued: No act is proper knowledge of any object, if this act can remain in the intellect and still that object is not known in any way. Now the vision of the divine essence can remain in the beatified intellect without this intellect seeing the stone. Therefore [the vision of the divine essence is not proper knowledge of the stone]. Proof of the major: The formal ground in the intellect for knowing this stone as an object is this act itself, inhering in the intellect, of knowing the object. Now it does not seem possible that the proximate formal reason for something [like knowledge of the object] is in anything without there also being there that of which it is the formal reason, just as whiteness cannot be present in anything without its being white.

15.72 Furthermore, if the act of vision of the essence itself were the same as that of everything seen in it, then by the same token one finite act could envision the infinity of possible creatures to be seen in that essence, for the same reason for denying there is any impossibility for two or three objects [being envisioned in such an essence] would hold for all objects whatsoever.

15.73 Also, the validity of the entailment is not evident; if the vision of the divine essence and the stone is the same, then, if there is a "word" of the stone, there is also a "word" of the essence.

15.74 [Reply to the objections] To the first of these [in 15.69], it might be admitted that what is known through another, could be known indeed immediately. But this would be so if it were known precisely in this other in the way the divine intellect knows the creature in its essence alone and not through the creature as an immediate object, because it would demean the divine intellect to know it in any other way. Something analogous could be said of the beatified intellect if it had a "word" of the creature in its vision of the divine essence.

15.75 In answer to the second [in 15.70] it could be said that the divine essence prior to its being in the understanding of the blessed is not present to a created memory, because no form representing that essence has been formed in the beatified intellect. But it is the vision itself that is first caused in the beatified intellect, and this is produced in understanding itself.

15.76 Or another answer would be that this immediate vision is caused by the divine will, as was said in [14.36-37 of] the question immediately preceding. Now the vision of the stone is caused in the same way, and consequently neither of these visions is generated by memory, neither the memory of the one seeing these things, nor by any other memory.

15.77 Against this it is objected that the intellection of the divine essence contains virtually the intellection of the stone. Therefore, the first of these intellections generates the second and then this second represents a "word."

I reply: The intelligence or understanding does not generate "a word." Or it can be said that both visions are caused immediately by the divine will.

15.78 To the third objection [in 15.71], the argument would seem to militate against the divine intellect knowing its essence and secondary objects in one and the same act, and yet all deny these are two different acts. Hence the major of the argument must be denied, unless it is understood exclusively of the first object.

15.79 As for the answer to the other objections, look elsewhere.[54]

Reply to the Initial Arguments

[24] 15.80 [To the first argument in 15.2] As for the first argument, if one holds in the third section of the first article [15.40ff.] that the agent intellect is active and the possible intellect passive, then it is not according to the same aspect that the soul moves and is moved to intellection. On the other hand, neither do agent and possible intellect represent distinct subjects, for this is not the way these two are distinguished.[55]

If, however, one claims that the possible intellect is active in regard to intellection, then it is the same thing that moves and is moved to intellection and this according to the same entity.

15.81 And if one says this is impossible because the same thing according to the same aspect cannot be both in potency and in act,

[54] See Appendix, Addition 15.79.
[55] Cf. Duns Scotus, *Ord.* II, d.25, n.20 (ed. Vivès XIII, 212-14); I, d.3, nn. 512-51 (III, 303-305); II, d.3, q.8, n.16 (ed. Vivès XII, 200); q.11, n.5 (ibid., 272-74); d.2, q.10, n.12 (ed. Vivès XI, 540).

QUESTION FIFTEEN

I answer: Every action that results in a form that is not active is the work of an equivocal,* not a univocal* agent. If it were univocal, the form whereby it acts would be the same in kind as that which it produces, and thus the resulting form would be active. Now an increase in size and many alterations as well as local motion generally are not active forms. Therefore, the mover in these cases, and in general the agent of equivocal effects, is not in the same kind of act as is the term to which the mobile is in potency, but it is rather the sort of act that contains this term virtually or eminently. And thus it would be claimed here that in the soul the ground for containing intellection virtually as an equivocal effect and the ground for receiving it are the same.

15.82 Against this it is argued that whatever has a more noble form is unsuited by nature to receive a less noble form. Therefore, if it possesses the inferior form in a more noble way, namely, virtually, then it is not suited by nature to receive it formally.

15.83 This is confirmed from the fact that on the same grounds one could claim that anything that is formally one sort of thing would also be virtually the same sort of thing, and thus anything could be transformed by itself.

15.84 To this I say that a form of the same kind cannot be had in a greater and lesser degree at the same time; neither can two contrary forms, nor one such contrary and another intermediary form, be present at once in the same subject. But two disparate forms can coexist, even if they fall under the same remote genus, like [the qualities] of heat and color, of which one, however, is more noble than the other.

15.85 As for the confirmation [in 15.83], one could say that here the caution is relevant about transferring oneself from the role of opponent to that of respondent because of a defect in the argument.[56] Neither does it seem to obligate the respondent to any more than proving one manifest necessary truth, for instance, that not everything moves itself.

And as for the proof introduced with the words "on the same grounds," etc., one could say that although the fact that "being in potency to such and such a thing formally" is not inconsistent with "being this sort of thing virtually," and vice versa, so far as the meaning of the terms goes, for otherwise wherever such terms obtained this inconsistency would be present, nevertheless, in certain cases some accompanying factor in one of the terms makes it incon-

---

[56] This seems to refer to one of the classical rules for debate. See some of the medieval logical treatises under the heading *De obligatione*.

sistent with the other. And then, by virtue of the matter in the special case, it is true that what is virtually such cannot be formally such. But this is not *per se* because the subject has this form virtually but for some concomitant reason.

For example, the sun is hot virtually, and nevertheless it cannot receive heat formally. But the reason it cannot be formally hot is not that it is hot virtually, because Saturn which is virtually frigid cannot be hot formally. The reason for this impossibility, however, is common to the sun and Saturn, namely that a celestial body cannot receive an elementary form or the form of any perishable body, nor vice versa. And so in the case at hand, something, which is able to have this form, has at the same time something which makes it impossible to contain this form virtually, just as wood has something which makes it impossible to contain heat virtually, but this is not because it is receptive to heat, but because it has such a form as that characteristic of a [chemical] compound.

15.86 [Answer to the argument to the contrary in 15.3] As for the argument for the opposing view, when it is argued about the object [not causing the word], because the action is immanent, I grant the action, i.e., the operation, is an action that is simply immanent in the power operating; but as for the action which falls into the category "action" which results in this [quality which is the] operation, there is indeed some action which is immanent not only in the sense of being in the same subject, but also in the same intellective part [of the soul], and according to one view explained in the third part of the first article [15.54], it is immanent in the possible intellect. However, for such an intellection there is some action which is not immanent, viz., that which proceeds from the object.

15.87 When it is argued [in 15.3] that "the memory does not understand," this proof fails on two counts. (1) The fact that something is not a matter of memory does not permit one to conclude it does not pertain to the possible intellect. Quite the contrary, for as it was pointed out in the third section [15.60], either the possible intellect itself is the memory or at least it is necessarily included in the memory. (2) The other mistake is this: That the memory does not understand does not imply it is not active in such a way that intellection is the end product of its action. However, the word is not the terminal product of intellection, but results from some productive action that falls under the category "action."

Question Sixteen

ARE FREEDOM OF WILL AND NATURAL NECESSITY COMPATIBLE AS REGARDS THE SAME ACT AND OBJECT?

[1] 16.1 The next questions deal with the will; first, with its action in general, second, in particular with the distinction between two intrinsic acts of the will, and third, with the distinction between an intrinsic and extrinsic act.

16.2 The first question is this: Are freedom of will and natural necessity compatible in the same subject as regards the same act and object?[1]

Arguments Pro and Con

It is argued they are not:

Necessity and freedom, it seems, are mutually repugnant. Augustine writes[2]: "It was shown to our satisfaction that a mind becomes a slave of sinful desire only by its own will." And soon after he adds: "If this movement is looked upon as culpable . . . then it is not determined by nature but is voluntary. It resembles in this respect the movement of the stone in its downward course, since one movement belongs to the soul, just as the other belongs to the stone. But it is unlike it in another respect, namely, that it is not within the power of the stone to check its downward fall"—which is not the case with the soul. Then he continues: "Hence the movement of the stone is fixed by nature, whereas that of the soul is voluntary." And soon after follow these words of the disciple, approved by Augustine: "If the movement by which the will can turn in different directions were not voluntary and subject to our control, a man ought not to be praised, blamed . . . or admonished . . . , but anyone who would think that man should not be admonished, should be banished from the company of men." These words make it clear that the

---

[1] Cf. Duns Scotus, *Ord.* I, d.1, nn.77-158 (II, 59-108); IV, d.49, qq.9-10 (ed. Vivès XXI, 316-83).

[2] Augustine, *De lib. arbitrio* III, c.1, nn.2-3: PL 32, 1271-72; CCSL 29, 272.

same movement towards the same object cannot be both natural and free.

16.3 Against the preceding view it is argued:

Augustine says in *The City of God*[3]: "If by necessity we mean what is beyond our power and has its way even when our will is opposed to it, like the necessity of death, then our decisions to live well or ill obviously are not subject to such necessity." Later he continues: "If we take necessity to mean that in virtue of which something must be so and so or must happen in such and such a way, I do not see why we should be afraid of such necessity taking away our freedom of will. We do not put the life of God and the foreknowledge of God under any necessity when we say that God must live an eternal life and must know all things." And he adds afterwards: "When we say we must choose freely when we choose at all, what we say is true; yet we do not subject free choice to any necessity which destroys our liberty."

Body of the Question

[2] 16.4 Here three points must be investigated: (1) Is there necessity in any act of the will? (2) Is there in addition freedom in the will? (3) Can natural necessity at times coexist with freedom?

ARTICLE I
Is there Necessity in any Act of the Will?

16.5 [The acts by which the divine will loves itself and spirates the Holy Spirit are simply necessary] As for the first problem I reply that there is simple necessity both in the act by which God loves himself and in the act by which he spirates* the Love that proceeds [from Father and Son], i.e., the Holy Spirit.

This is obvious. God is necessarily happy; therefore, he necessarily beholds and loves the beatific object. Similarly, the Holy Spirit is God and consequently is supremely necessary in being. Therefore, since he receives being by proceeding [from Father and Son], the act whereby he proceeds from them is most necessary.

16.6 Both conclusions are proved by a demonstration of the reasoned fact* in the following way:

The infinite will is related to the most perfect object in the most perfect way possible. The divine will is infinite. Therefore, it is related to the supremely lovable object in the most perfect way that

---

[3] Augustine, *De civ. Dei* v, c.10, n.1: PL 41, 152; CCSL 47, 140.

a will can relate to it. But this would not be the case unless the divine will loved this object necessarily and adequately, and unless it spirated a Love adequate to that object. If either of these conditions were absent, it would be conceivable without contradiction that some will could be related to that object in a more perfect way, for a more perfect way is conceivable and it involves no contradiction. It is not self-contradictory that an infinite will have an infinite act, and hence a necessary act elicited necessarily with respect to an infinite object. Were it lacking such, it would not be supremely perfect.

16.7 Also, if a Love adequate to the object can be spirated, as we believe, then it would pertain to the divine will above all to be the principle or source of that spiration.

[3] 16.8 [Proofs given by others] Some[4] adduce proofs for this conclusion which apply to every will as regards that [divine] object, whether this be seen clearly [as in heaven] or apprehended only in a general way, as it is at present.

16.9 The first proof is this: The will necessarily wills that which includes all goodness, for it cannot fail to love an object in which there is no evil or lack of goodness. Now the last end is such an object.

16.10 The second proof is based on the words of the Philosopher in the *Physics*[5]: "The end serves the same function in the practical sciences as principles do in the theoretical sciences." And also in the *Ethics*[6]: "As postulates are to mathematics, so is the end to matters of conduct." Now the intellect in theoretical science assents necessarily to the principles, therefore, the will assents necessarily to the last end in matters of conduct.

16.11 That in which everything else participates that the will loves is itself willed necessarily. Now the last end is such. Therefore [it is willed necessarily].

Proof of the major: Every variable leads back to something invariable. And so the variety of acts concerned with what is ordered to an end presupposes an invariable act, and hence presupposes such an act particularly as regards that in which all other objects of the will participate.

---

[4] Henry of Ghent, *Quodl.* III, q.17, ad arg. princ. (fol. 79H); IV, q.11 in corp. (fol. 102R); XII, q.26 in corp. (fol. 503F); Thomas, *Summa theol.* I-II, q.10, a.2 (II, 57-58).

[5] Aristotle, *Physic.* II, c.9 (200a15-16).

[6] Aristotle, *Ethica ad Nic.* VII, c.9 (1151a16-17).

The minor is proved by that text from *The Trinity*[7]: "Take this good and that good, abstract from it being 'this' or 'that' and see Good itself, if you can; thus you will see God who is good not by another good, but is the good of every good."

16.12 [Counter-arguments] These reasons do not hold necessarily of every will. Neither are they necessary arguments in themselves.

Proof of the first point: Given two absolute and essentially ordered natures, it is not self-contradictory that the first exist without the second.[8] Each of these, viz., (a) the lovable object, (b) the apprehension or vision of this object by a created intellect, and (c) the created will itself, is something absolute and naturally prior to the will's act of loving that object. Therefore, it is not self-contradictory that any one of them, or even all of them, could exist without the act of love. Neither then is its opposite simply necessary in the sense that the opposite of the self-contradictory is necessary.

[4] 16.13 Objection: The major is true only when two of the absolutes are mutually independent and are not both dependent on the third. But in the case at hand both vision and [the love or] fruition depend upon the same third, namely, the object.

Answer: God can cause any absolute immediately and yet without necessity. If he uses an intermediary cause, he can still produce it without necessity, for the intermediary cause does not force him to cause its effect. Therefore, though both [i.e., the intermediary cause and its effect] be caused by a common cause, not only will the ultimate effect be contingent, but even if the intermediary cause be given, the effect will still be caused contingently.

16.14 Besides, if a power or potency acts necessarily as regards its object, it necessarily continues that act as long as it can. But the will, at least that of the pilgrim,* does not necessarily continue its act, as regards the end apprehended only in general, as long as it could. Therefore, it does not act necessarily in regard to that end.[9]

16.15 The example of the sense appetite illustrates the major. But it seems it can also be proved by reason. Whatever be the intrinsic reason a power acts necessarily will also be grounds for its acting necessarily always, so far as this depends on the power itself. Thus

---

[7] Augustine, *De Trin.* VIII, c.3, n.4: PL 42, 949; CCSL 50, 272. Cf. Duns Scotus, *Ord.* I, d.1, nn.83-85 (II, 62-63).

[8] Cf. Duns Scotus, *Ord.* II, d.12, q.2, n.3 (ed. Vivès XII, 576).

[9] Cf. ibid., d.42, q.4, n.5 (ed. Vivès XIII, 454); I, d.1, nn.93ff. (II, 67ff.).

it will be reason for the action continuing as long as the power can do this.

16.16 Proof of the minor: The will of the pilgrim could have continued the intellect's contemplation of the end, when it failed to do so and turned the intellect's consideration to something else or at least did not prevent some other object present from blotting out this consideration of the end. But when the intellect's consideration is discontinued, so too is the will's act as regards that object, whereas if the consideration continues, the will's act continues.

16.17 Proof of the same minor by a text from the *Retractations*[10]: "Nothing is so in the power of the will as the will itself." This should be understood as referring to the will's action rather than to the will itself. It is in the power of the will that by its command another power act or refrain from acting, for example, that the intellect refrain from considering at least that object whose consideration is not required for issuing the command. Hence it is in the power of the will that it does not act regarding that specific object.

I do not understand this in the sense that the will could voluntarily suspend all its activity. It could voluntarily not will that object and still have another volition, viz., one that reflects on its own act, for instance, "I will not elicit an act as regards that object." This can well happen; otherwise the will could not suspend any act after deliberating. Now this holds for will and intellect alike, namely, that while the will cannot suspend such intellection as is necessary for the volition by which it suspends intellection, it can suspend any other intellection. So too it cannot at a given moment suspend all volition, for it cannot suspend the act by which it suspends, but it can suspend any volition that is not necessary for this.

16.18 Furthermore, necessity in acting stems from some *per se* principle of action, for if the latter is not related necessarily to acting, then neither will anything else acting in virtue of it. But the recipient of the action is of itself in potency of contradiction. Therefore, if you claim the object is the reason for the necessity in volition (for you maintain [in 16.9-11] that every will that relates to that object necessarily wills it, although no will necessarily wills every object), then it seems to follow that the object is the principal active

---

[10] Augustine, *Retract.* I, c.9 (8), n.3, and c.22 (21), n.4: PL 32, 596, 620; CSEL 36, 39.

factor in volition, a position not admitted by the one who proposed this argument.[11]

[5] 16.19 [These proofs are not necessary arguments] The second point [in 16.12], namely, that these proofs are not necessary in themselves, becomes clear if you examine them one by one.

As for the first [in 16.9], the major is untrue. Even though in some object there be the fulness of perfection, still, for the act to be necessary, the potency must tend necessarily to that object. Now whatever be the case with the created will of the blessed and the supernatural perfection by which it tends to that perfect object, we must admit the will of the pilgrim tends to it only contingently, even when it is apprehended in general. For such apprehension is not grounds for making the will love that object necessarily. Neither does the will, given such apprehension, determine itself necessarily, even as it does not necessarily continue to will, as was mentioned in the second reason [in 16.16-17].

16.20 It could be conceded, however, that the will cannot recoil from or refuse an object in which there is no evil or lack of goodness, for as good is the object of volition so evil or lack of goodness (which is regarded as evil) is the object of nolition. And it does not follow, further, "The will cannot refuse this perfect object, therefore it necessarily wills this," for as was stated above [in 16.17] about the *Retractations*, it may be neither willing nor unwilling with respect to this object.[12]

16.21 Against this one could argue: If it cannot be unwilling to love this object, it is because this object has in itself something to which such nolition is repugnant. Now the repugnance can only consist in the fact that it actually does love or will the object. Therefore, this love or volition exists in it necessarily. Proof of the major: If one of two incompatible elements is repugnant to it, the other is necessarily there. Proof of the minor: A mere aptitude or habitual inclination to love or will the object would not explain why an act of nolition or positive refusal to love is repugnant to the will, because such an act could coexist with a potentiality or aptitude for the opposite act.

In answer: One could say that what is repugnant to such a nolition or positive refusal to love the end is the will's very power or

---

[11] Cf. Duns Scotus, *Ord.* I, d.1, nn.93-96, 134-37 (II, 67-74, 90-93).

[12] Cf. ibid., nn.149-51 (II, 100-103); IV, d.49, q.10, nn.4-10 (ed. Vivès XXI, 330-33); d.50, q.2, nn.14-16 (ibid., 540-42); II, d.6, q.2, n.13 (ed. Vivès XII, 359); d.43, q.2 (ed. Vivès XIII, 490-94).

potency itself, for it can have volition only for what is lovable and nolition only for what is undesirable; to love or to refuse to love respectively is possible in regard to no other objects. But the end, having no evil or defect of goodness, lacks all grounds of undesirability. Hence, "a nolition of the end" is a self-contradictory or meaningless expression, like "seeing sound." Augustine wants to say as much in the *Enchiridion*[13]: "We so will to be happy that we not only do not want to be miserable, but are quite unable to will this." Hence just as there is something repugnant about misery being an object of volition, so there is something contradictory about beatitude being an object of nolition. The latter perhaps is even more repugnant because misery does not lack all grounds for being wanted in the way that beatitude lacks all undesirability.

[6] 16.22 Reply to the second proof [in 16.10]: The Philosopher's analogy that the end functions like a principle must be interpreted with reference to two orders: (1) that which obtains between the intelligible and lovable objects themselves and (2) that which holds between such objects and the respective potencies or faculties which tend towards them in an orderly fashion.

The first of these I understand in this way: The order of goodness or desirability between the end and what exists for the sake of the end is like the order of truth between a principle and a conclusion, which has derivative or participated truth from the principle, for what serves an end has only derivative or participated goodness in comparison to the end. And from this the second order follows, namely, that as an orderly intellect assents to the truth of the conclusion because of the truth of the principle, so an orderly will tends to what serves an end for the sake of the end.

But this second parallel no longer holds if we consider these potencies according to what they can do absolutely [i.e., not just when acting orderly]. Otherwise a will could only love a means by using it, i.e., loving it for the sake of the end. But Augustine says in the *Eighty-Three Questions*[14]: "Perversion of the will consists in loving the end as means and the means as end." This implies that the will can enjoy as an end an object meant to be used as a means. The intellect, on the contrary, cannot act in this fashion. It cannot see a truth, knowable only as a conclusion, as a principle, i.e., as a proposition evident from its terms.

The reason for this difference is that the intellect is moved nat-

---

[13] Augustine, *Enchirid.*, c.28, n.105: PL 40, 281; CCSL 96, 106.
[14] Augustine, *De diversis quaest.* 83, q.30: PL 40, 19.

urally by its object whereas the will moves itself freely. It is also clear that there is not the same necessity in each case, for the conclusion must needs be known through the principle, whereas that which serves an end need not be desired or sought just because of the goodness of the end.[15]

16.23 As for the third proof [in 16.11], one can simply deny the major. If the will wills nothing necessarily, then it need not will that object in virtue of which it wills other things in any necessary fashion either. To will it contingently suffices for willing other things in the way that the will does.[16]

16.24 Another answer is that the major can have two meanings. One is this: The will wills that object more or first, if it wills other things precisely because they participate in it as willed. The other meaning is this: The will wills that object first, if the other things it wills participate in the entity of that object.

Only in the first sense and not in the second does the major seem to be true. Although the color I see receives entity by participation in the First Being and visibility by participation in what is first visible, the vision of color is possible without first seeing the First Being or what is first visible, for the participation is not in something as *seen* but as a being or as visible. Now the minor [in 16.11] is true only in the second sense, and the argument in support of it only proves that what is willed is able to be willed or is good by participation in what was first able to be willed. It does not prove it was willed precisely because that in which it participates was willed.

[7]   16.25 [Conclusion of the Article] As regards this article, then, I maintain that whatever be the case with the created will of the blessed (i.e., whether or not it is necessitated to will the last end by something supernatural), it seems at least probable that not every created will is necessitated by its nature to will the end. This is so not only of the will considered absolutely [i.e., without previous knowledge]—which is clear—but also when the obscure apprehension of that object is given—as is the case in the present life.

16.26 As for the divine will at least this seems certain: it is simply necessitated to love its own goodness.

16.27 And if you ask: Does the divine will necessarily will any object other than God? The following answer could be given. If we rule out necessity of coercion of which there is no talk, necessity can mean two things: (1) necessity of immutability, which excludes a

---

[15] Cf. Duns Scotus, *Ord.* I, d.1, n.147 (II, 97-98).
[16] Cf. ibid., n.148 (II, 98-99).

change of will in which at some subsequent moment the divine will would will differently than at present; the other is (2) necessity of inevitability or determination, which not only excludes change or succession but rules out that the divine will could have willed other than it has.

16.28 Speaking solely of the first type, we say God wills necessarily whatever he wills. For neither on the part of the act nor on the part of the object could a different state succeed the present one, for this would mean some change in God.[17] That an object be willed does not imply something extrinsic to God and it cannot be willed after being not willed, nor vice versa, without a change occurring in something. Nothing unaltered passes from one contradictory state to the other. Otherwise there would be no reason why one contradictory would be more true now than before or why the other would be false.

16.29 As for the second type of necessity we could say this: Although the divine will necessarily takes complacency in everything intelligible insofar as some participation of God's own goodness is revealed therein, it does not will necessarily any created thing with a volition that is efficacious or that determines it to exist. On the contrary, it wills the creature's existence contingently, just as it causes it contingently. For if it necessarily willed it to be in this second sense of necessity, it would cause it necessarily with a necessity of inevitability, at least at that moment when God wants it to exist.

ARTICLE II
Can Freedom and Necessity Coexist in the Will?

[8] 16.30 [Affirmative View] As for the second article [in 16.4], I claim that both freedom and necessity in willing can coexist in the will.

Proof from authority: The first is that text of Augustine from the *Enchiridion*[18]: "It was fitting that men should be made in the first place with the power to will both good and evil—if good, not without reward; if evil, not with impunity." That is to say, in that first state, man is capable of both merit and demerit. And he continues: "In the afterlife he will not be able to will evil and yet he will not be deprived of his free will. In fact, his will will be much more free in that it will in no way be subject to sin." And he adds a proof, as it were: "For the will is not to be blamed nor should we say that it

---

[17] Cf. ibid., d.8, nn.294-301 (IV, 322-26).
[18] Augustine, *Enchirid.*, c.28, n.105: PL 40, 281; CCSL 96, 106.

was no will or that it was not free, when we so will to be happy that we not only do not want to be miserable, but are quite unable to will this. Just as our soul is at present unwilling to be unhappy, so then it will for ever be unwilling to be wicked."

Also there is that text from Anselm in Chapter I of *Free Choice*[19]: "Whoever has what is appropriate and advantageous in such a way that it cannot be lost is freer than he who has this in such a way that it can be lost." From this he concludes: "The will then which cannot cease to be upright is freer."

16.31 Reason proves the same point. The first is a proof of simple fact. From the preceding article we know the divine will necessarily wills its own goodness, and yet is free in willing this; therefore [necessity and freedom coexist there]. Proof of the minor: A power or potency that acts with respect to an object, not as something absolute but as related to another, acts with respect to both objects. Thus the Philosopher argues in *On the Soul*[20] that the faculty by which we know the difference between one object and another is apt by nature to know both objects in themselves. He illustrates this as regards the common or central sense. Now the divine will relates to the end other objects willed for the sake of the end, therefore, as the same basic power, it acts with respect to both. But it acts freely as regards things other than the end, since it wills them contingently. Contingency in acting stems from a principle that is freely, not naturally, active. Therefore, the will as the same basic power wills its own goodness freely.

16.32 Furthermore, there are proofs of the reasoned fact* to establish our claim. The first is this: Action that has to do with the ultimate end is the most perfect. But freedom pertains to the perfection of such an action. Therefore, the necessity to be found there does not do away with but rather demands what is needed for perfection, namely, freedom.

Furthermore, an intrinsic condition for a power, considered absolutely or in relation to a perfect act, cannot be opposed to perfection in acting. Now liberty is an intrinsic condition of the will, either considered absolutely or as regards a perfect act. Therefore, liberty can coexist with that condition in acting that is the most perfect possible. Such is necessity, particularly where it is possible to have this. But it is always possible where neither of the extremes [i.e., the subject willing and the object willed] demands contingency in the ac-

---

[19] Anselm, *De lib. arbitrio*, c.1: PL 158, 491; ed. F. S. Schmitt I, 208.
[20] Aristotle, *De anima* II, c.4 (415b15-21).

QUESTION SIXTEEN

tion between them [i.e., the willing]. Such is the case here, as the previous article proved.

[9] 16.33 How freedom coexists with necessity: If you ask, how does freedom coexist with necessity, I answer with the Philosopher[21]: "Do not seek a reason for things for which no reason can be given: for there is no demonstration of the starting point of demonstration." And so I say here: As this proposition, "The divine will wills the divine goodness," is immediate and necessary, for which no reason can be given other than that this will and this goodness are the sort of things they are, so also "The divine will contingently wills the goodness or existence of another." Again no reason can be given except that it is this sort of will and that sort of good, unless we add in general one brief remark that an infinite will must necessarily have an act as regards an infinite object, because this pertains to perfection, and by the same token it does not act necessarily as regards a finite object, because this would imply imperfection. For it is a matter of imperfection to be necessarily determined to what is posterior [i.e., less perfect] and a matter of perfection to be so determined to what is prior [or more perfect] and it implies concomitant perfection to be so determined to what is on a par with it.[22]

16.34 Confirmation: The division of agents into those which act naturally and those which act freely is not the same as the division of agents into those acting necessarily and those acting contingently. For some natural agents act contingently, because their action can be impeded. For like reasons, then, it is possible that some free agent act necessarily without detriment to its freedom.[23]

---

[21] Aristotle, *Metaph.* IV, c.6 (1011a12-13)m.
[22] Cf. Duns Scotus, *Ord.* I, d.10 (IV, 339-66), IV, d.49, q.10, nn 2-3 (ed. Vivès XXI, 318-19).
[23] Addition found in all three MSS:

But there is always this doubt: In what precisely does the essence of freedom consist? For neither the view that it consists in [the will's] determination to act nor in its mastery over its acts seems to be applicable here.

[10] One could say in reply [according to Henry of Ghent, in *Summa*, a.47, q.5 (II, fol. 47X-48Y)] that the statement "The will necessarily wills" can have several meanings. Either "necessarily" refers to the fact that it must will some object and in this case the statement is true if the object in question is the divine goodness, the sole proper and *per se* object of that will. (Other things are not such and the will does not will them necessarily.) Or "necessarily" refers to the way the act of willing proceeds from the will, and this can be interpreted in two ways: One, that the

ARTICLE III
Can Natural Necessity ever Coexist with Freedom?

[11]   16.35 [In the production of the Holy Spirit there is both] As for the third main point [in 16.4], it is claimed[24] that in one act of the divine will, namely, the spiration of the Holy Spirit, natural necessity is somehow involved. This should be understood to mean that the will, simply as will, is not the elicitive principle of the notional* act whereby something similar in form to the producer is produced. Otherwise in anything where will existed, it would be the principle of an act by which something similar in form was produced, which is false in the case of creatures. The way to understand this claim,

---

necessity is prior to the will. In other words, the will is coerced by some necessity extrinsic to itself which impels it to act and keeps it acting. In the other interpretation, the necessity is concomitant, or controlled by the will which by the very steadfastness of its freedom imposed upon itself the need to elicit and continue the action.

In the spiration [of the Holy Spirit], however, there is [in addition] a concomitant necessity of nature, for there is a certain "force of nature" whether "nature" be taken in the primary sense of "essence" or in the secondary sense of a productive principle therein whose operation is [not free but] natural. Some such force must assist the will in communicating the divine nature to the Holy Spirit. Hence we have a fourfold order (or degrees) of necessity. The first is that by which God necessarily lives, the second, that by which he necessarily knows or understands; the third is that by which he necessarily communicates the divine nature to the Holy Spirit; the fourth is that by which he necessarily loves himself.

In what then does his freedom in loving himself consist? I answer that it consists in the fact that he elicits this act and perseveres in it as something delightful which he has elected, as it were, to do.

Objections: According to Richard [of Middleton, *Sent.* II, d.38, a.2, q.1 in corp. (Brixiae, 1591), II, p. 465], what is possessed by a necessity of nature is more glorious than what is had in some other way.

I answer: That there be an act of the will is a necessity of nature, but it is not by necessity of nature that God wills, for that would imply a contradiction. Hence, in this proposition, "It is necessary that God loves himself," which is a statement about a statement, the distinction is clear that necessity can be attributed to the act of willing in different ways. This is not so clear in this statement of fact: "God wills necessarily." Nevertheless, the truth common to both is this: The act is there by a necessity of nature, but he does not will the object by a necessity of nature.

[24] Henry of Ghent, *Summa*, a.60, q.1 in corp. (II, fol. 153H-157F).

QUESTION SIXTEEN

then, is that the will, by virtue of the divine nature in which it exists, has a certain "naturality" to produce the notional act, and is thus its elicitive principle.

By the fact that it is rooted in the divine nature or essence, the will has annexed to it a certain natural force. From this "naturality" or natural force working with it, it acquires a certain natural necessity and thus becomes the elicitive principle of the notional act. There is in the essential will-act as ordered to what is supremely loved a necessity of immutability* stemming from free will alone. Nevertheless, insofar as the will's activity is ordered to and terminates with the production of the beloved [i.e., the Holy Spirit], a necessity of immutability accrues to it from this "naturality" which has to do solely with the notional act elicited by the will, or rather by the freedom of the will when conjoined with such "naturality."

In addition the point is made that this "naturality" in the will in no way impedes its freedom, nor is it the elicitive principle of the notional act (for that would militate against the freedom of that act). It is rather something consecutive, annexed to the will, something with the assistance of which the will itself by its power as will and as free is able to elicit its notional act, an act it could not elicit apart from such assistance.

The following propositions, then, are necessary in different ways: (1) "God necessarily lives," for he lives by a necessity of nature; (2) "God necessarily understands,"—the necessity here has a different basis, for it stems from an intelligible object determining the intellect to know it; (3) "God necessarily produces the Holy Spirit," for he does so by a natural necessity which does not precede but accompanies [the will's act]; (4) "God necessarily loves himself,"—here the necessity is a consequence of liberty's infinite [perfection] and there is no necessity of nature involved.[25]

[12]   16.36 [Objections] Counter-arguments: Nothing based upon something, it seems, could have additional grounds for its being necessary than that upon which it is based. Neither could there be two reasons for it being necessary whereas the foundation has only one. Otherwise, if the single basis in the foundation were removed, be this possible or not, the one in what is founded would still be there and hence the foundation would still be necessary and nevertheless no necessity remains there. Now, according to some, notional acts are based upon an essential act, and according to all, essential

---

[25] Cf. Duns Scotus, *Ord.* I, d.2, nn.270-81 (II, 287-94); d.10, nn.10-12, 30-58 (IV, 343-44, 352-63).

acts are somehow prior to notional acts. Hence it is impossible that the essential act whereby God loves himself has but one necessity stemming from the single ground, viz., the infinity of the liberty, whereas in the act of spiration there be conjoined to this another ground, viz., natural necessity.

16.37 Furthermore, as perfect memory* in the appropriate person is the perfect principle for producing a perfect Word,* so a perfect will in the appropriate person or persons would seem to be the perfect principle of producing Perfect Love. Therefore, as memory in the Father is the principle of begetting the Son, so will in Father and Son is the principle of spirating the Holy Spirit. Neither does the co-assistance of something in addition to perfect memory and will seem necessary, in the sense that without such assistance the will could never cause the act of spirating nor the memory the act of speaking [the Word].

16.38 On the other hand, if the assistance be understood as that of object to potency, then memory would require such as much as the will. Perhaps it would be needed even more to communicate the nature by their respective acts than it would be needed to make the act necessary. For of these two principles, viz., object and potency, each is a *per se* reason for the necessity characteristic of the elicitation of these acts. But perhaps each is not *per se* a perfect reason why the resulting term is consubstantial with the producer, and then it would be true that such assistance to the essential act is not required. For although an object is required for the act, it would not be needed as the source of the communication of its own perfection.

[13]   16.39 [Solution] As for this article one could say there is no difficulty here if "nature" be taken broadly insofar as it applies to everything. For in this sense we call "will" nature and we apply the term even to nonbeings when we speak of the nature of negation. In this broad sense, necessity in any being could be called natural. And since the divine will at least has necessarily some volition by virtue of its perfect liberty, this necessity of perfect liberty could be called "natural" in this way.

But a difficulty arises if we take "nature" more strictly, viz., insofar as "nature" and "liberty" are the primary differences of "agent" or "a principle of action." The Philosopher speaks in this fashion in the *Physics*[26] when he divides "cause" into "nature" and "purpose."

[26] Aristotle, *Physic.* II, c.5 (196b17-22).

"Of the former," namely, those things performed for the sake of an end as are all actions of a *per se* cause, "some are in accordance with deliberate intention, others not." And he adds a little later: "Events that are for the sake of something include whatever may be done as the result of thought or of nature." To these two *per se* causes he reduces the two incidental causes of chance* and fortune.* He speaks of this distinction again in the *Metaphysics*[27] when he indicates the way rational and irrational powers perform their acts: "As for potencies of the latter kind,"—i.e., irrational powers—"when the agent and patient meet in the way appropriate to the potency in question, the one must act and the other be acted upon, but with the former kind of potency"—i.e., the rational—"this is not necessary"—i.e., even if agent and patient meet, it is not necessary that one must act and the other be acted upon. Of this distinction Augustine speaks in *The City of God*[28]: "There is a fortuitous cause, a natural cause, and a voluntary cause." And he explains each.

16.40 This division of "active principle" is expressed by different names not only by different authors but by Aristotle himself as is clear from the *Physics*.[29] After having remarked, "Some are in accordance with deliberate intention, others not," he adds: "as the result of thought or of nature." In the *Metaphysics*[30] he speaks of "rational" and "irrational potencies."

By the three expressions: "not by deliberate intention," "by nature," and "irrational potency," Aristotle understands the active principle we commonly call "nature." By the other three expressions [viz., "by deliberate intention," "as the result of thought," and "rational potency"] he understands the active principle in which intellect and will concur with regard to an extrinsic act.

16.41 But each of these two potencies, taken in itself, has its own way of functioning as a principle. The intellect does so by way of nature [*per modum naturae*]. Hence, in relation to its own act it is *nature*. Thus the Son in the divine Trinity is produced by way of nature, although the productive principle be "memory." The will, on the other hand, always functions in its own peculiar way, viz., freely. That is why when it concurs with the intellect, as in the production of artifacts, the whole effect is said to be produced freely and intentionally or with deliberation, since the intention is the su-

[27] Aristotle, *Metaph.* IX, c.5 (1048a5-7).
[28] Augustine, *De civ. Dei* v, c.9, n.4: PL 41, 151; CCSL 47, 139.
[29] Aristotle, *Physic.* II, c.5 (196b17-22).
[30] Aristotle, *Metaph.* IX, c.5 (1048a5-7).

perior and immediate principle of the extrinsic production. If at times some naturally active power concurs with the will as one of the subordinate potencies we use in acting, the action, insofar as it stems from the natural active principle, is properly speaking "natural." But since the act as a whole falls under the will, we employ the subordinate potency freely and we are said to act freely by virtue of the higher power. In this way Aristotle speaks in the *Metaphysics*[31] where he wants to introduce some determining factor besides intellect, such as desire or conscious force. Otherwise the intellect would produce simultaneously contrary effects, for knowledge itself at once reveals contrary effects and insofar as itself is concerned, it would be a principle that acts naturally and would cause necessarily everything to which it is in potency: "The rational potencies produce contrary effects, so that if they produce their effects necessarily, they would produce contrary effects at the same time. But this is impossible. There must be, then, something else that decides,"[32]—i.e., something that determines the potency to one of the contraries. And he adds: "I mean by this 'desire' or 'conscious choice.' "[33]

[15] 16.42 [Conclusion] As for our proposal, I say that even if in the will's action some principle might concur (the object, according to some; the intellect, according to others) and would do so as naturally active, so far as itself is concerned, the will *per se* is never an active principle that acts naturally. To be naturally active and to be freely active represents a primary division of "active principle." The will is a freely active principle, which is precisely why it is called "will." It can no more be naturally active than nature, as other than will, can be freely active.

16.43 But here the question arises: Why is it that the will, although it acts necessarily, does not act naturally, since nature could no more determine it to act than does the fact that it has to act?

Answer: Every natural agent either is first in an absolute sense, or if not, it will be naturally determined to act by some prior agent. Now the will can never be an agent that is first in an absolute sense. But neither can it be naturally determined by a higher agent, for it is active in such a way that it determines itself to action in the sense that if the will wills something necessarily, for example, A, this volition of A would not be caused naturally by that which causes the will even if the will itself were caused naturally, but once the first

[31] Ibid. (1048a10-15).   [32] Ibid., IX, c.5 (1048a5-10).
[33] Ibid., IX, c.5 (1048a10).

act by which the will is caused be given, if the will were left to itself and could have or not have this volition contingently, it would still determine itself to this volition.

16.44 To the claim, then, that a natural principle cannot be more determined than a necessary principle, I say: Although the necessary be most determined in the sense that it excludes any indetermination as regards an alternative, nevertheless one necessary thing may in some way be more determined than another. That fire be hot or the heavens be round is determined by the cause which produced simultaneously the being of the heavens and its shape. A weight, on the other hand, is determined to descend. Still it does not receive from its progenitor the act of descending, but only that principle which naturally causes it to descend. But if the caused will necessarily wills anything, it is not determined by its cause to will such in the way the weight is determined to descend. All it receives from the cause is a principle by which it determines itself to this volition.

16.45 You might object, if the descent is caused by the body's intrinsic heaviness, then the heavy body moves itself. But why then is it not just as free as a will moving itself to a volition which it causes necessarily?

To this I answer: Causation by gravity is natural whereas the will's causation is free, and the reason is the will is a will and the weight is a weight.

16.46 To put it briefly then, like a form and its mode of being, so an action and the mode of acting are inseparable. Just as there is no reason why this being has this mode of being except that it is that sort of thing, so also there is no reason why this agent has this mode of action (i.e., free, though necessary) except that it is that sort of active principle.[34]

Reply to the Initial Argument

[17] 16.47 The argument for the negative view [in 16.2] can be answered in this way: Augustine's intent in the text cited there was to argue against Cicero[35]—who denied God's foreknowledge—that the admission of such knowledge did not commit him to a denial of our

---

[34] Cf. Duns Scotus, *Ord.* I, d.10, nn.6-9, 30-58 (IV, 341-42, 352-63); d.2, nn.327-44 (II, 322-32).

[35] M. T. Cicero, *De natura deorum* III, cc.26ff. (*Opera omnia*, ed. C.F.A. Nobbe, Nova ed. stereotypa IX, Lipsiae, 1849, pp. 144ff.); *De divinatione* II, c.37 (IX, 250-51); *De fato*, c.10 (IX, 290ff.).

freedom. Augustine[36] shows how to reconcile the two by this argument: "If God be certain of the order of all causes—which Cicero himself admitted—the fact remains that all our choices fall within that order, for human choices are the causes of human acts. Hence he who foreknew the causes of all things could not be unaware that our choices were among those causes." And he adds later[37]: "How then does it follow that the order of causes, known for certain though it be in the foreknowing mind of God, brings it about that there is no power in our will, when those very choices have such an important place in that order of causes?" And in the following chapter he says[38]: "It does not follow then that there is no power in our will, because God foreknew what was to be the choice in our will. ... If he who foresaw what was to be in our will foresaw, not nothing, but something, it follows that there is a power in our will, even though he foresaw it."

His answer seeks to show the compatibility of (a) that necessity which foreknowledge requires in the foreknown and (b) the fact that the foreknown is in the power of our will. This would not be true if there were such coercion in the will as he refers to when he says: "It has its way even when our will is opposed to it, like the necessity of death." But if it be the sort of necessity of which we are wont to say: "Something must be so and so or happen in such and such a way," there is no need to fear our liberty will be destroyed if such necessity characterize our act as foreknown. Although the necessity* of the foreknowledge or of the foreknown as foreknown is one of immutability, it is not simply a necessity of inevitability* or absolute determination. It is only inevitable on the assumption that God foreknows that this will take place.

[18]   16.48 To show not every necessity destroys freedom Augustine adds:[39] "We do not put the life of God and the foreknowledge of God under any necessity." Had he restricted himself to God's foreknowledge, it would be easy to see why no necessity repugnant to freedom is imposed upon it, for any item of that knowledge is something God knows freely and contingently; yet assuming he does foreknow it, that foreknowledge cannot change.

16.49 But the phrase "the life of God and the foreknowledge of God" is more difficult to explain. Still two answers are possible. One

---

[36] Augustine, *De civ. Dei* v, c.9, n.3: PL 41, 150-51; CCSL 47, 138.
[37] Ibid., n.4: PL 41, 151; CCSL 47, 139.
[38] Ibid., c.10, n.2: PL 41, 153; CCSL 47, 141.
[39] Augustine, *De civ. Dei* v, c.10, n.1: PL 41, 152; CCSL 47, 140.

takes "life" to mean the beatific act, as in John 17[40]: "This is eternal life, that they know you." As the Philosopher says in the *Metaphysics*[41]: "The activity of the mind is life." By the same token the will's activity is life and even in God this life does not fall under that necessity which excludes freedom.

16.50 But if "life" refers to God's own natural life, it must not be taken to mean that life considered simply in itself but rather as something accepted by the divine will. Something may well be necessary in itself with a necessity repugnant to freedom and still be accepted freely and even contingently. For instance, if one voluntarily dives off a cliff and, while falling, continues to will this, he falls necessarily with the necessity of natural gravity and yet he freely wills that fall. Thus God, though he lives necessarily by a natural life and with a necessity that excludes all freedom, nevertheless freely wants to live such a life. Hence we do not put the life of God under any necessity if we understand "life" as loved by his free will.

[40] John 17:3.
[41] Aristotle, *Metaph.* XII, c.7 (1072b25-30).

Question Seventeen

ARE ACTS OF NATURAL LOVE AND MERITORIOUS LOVE SPECIFICALLY THE SAME?

[1] 17.1 The next question raised is this: Are acts of natural love and meritorious love specifically the same?[1]

Arguments Pro and Con

It is claimed they are not:

Acts elicited by specifically different principles are themselves specifically different. Such are these acts of natural and meritorious love. Therefore [they differ specifically].

Proof of the major: In what issues from a principle, the difference is not less but greater than that of their principles.

Proof of the minor: The will elicits natural love by its own natural action whereas meritorious love is elicited by means of the supernatural habit of charity. Now natural and supernatural are specifically different.

17.2 It is argued against this view that the specific difference among acts is derived mainly from their *per se* objects. But the *per se* object of both natural and meritorious dilection is God loved under the aspect of the supreme good.

Body of the Question

[2] 17.3 In this question we must first see what natural love means, then what meritorious love means, and then determine the truth of the matter.

ARTICLE I
The Meaning of Natural Dilection or Love

17.4 As for the first point, note that here "natural love" does not mean the inclination to good coeval* with nature and perhaps not distinct from it, but rather the elicited act of dilection. This inclina-

---

[1] Cf. Duns Scotus, *Ord.* I, d.17, nn.129-59 (v, 202-15); IV, d.49, qq.9-10 (ed. Vivès XXI, 316-83).

tion is not an elicited act, though it could be called "habitual love," for, like a habit, it precedes the act and remains afterwards.[2]

17.5 The natural love we are asking about could be understood in two ways. It could mean an act elicited in accord with a natural inclination, as when the soul [*mens*] actually loves itself or actually loves what is advantageous. In another sense, it could be contrasted with supernatural and would refer to such natural acts as the will could perform of itself, regardless of whether it be in harmony with a natural inclination or not. Thus the will of itself could have a vicious act, even though Damascene[3] would style such an act unnatural [*contra naturam*] or anatural [*praeter naturam*]. In this question natural love seems to have this latter meaning, for the first argument [in 17.1] proceeds on this assumption. It should be noted, however, that the first sense of natural dilection perhaps falls under the second sense in most cases at least, for our natural powers suffice to elicit most acts to which we are naturally inclined. Not all, however, for we do have a natural inclination to the most perfect act of love for the ultimate end and yet we cannot attain that act by our nature alone.[4]

ARTICLE II
The Meaning of Meritorious Love or Dilection

[3] 17.6 [Relations involved in the meritorious] To the second point [in 17.3], I say that the meritorious act is one acceptable to God in a special way, viz., as worthy of reward. I say "in a special way" because God accepts all acts with a general acceptation. He loves them according to the measure of their goodness and orders them to himself as their last end. A meritorious act, however, he accepts with reference to some good which ought to be justly awarded it. "Meritorious," then, implies two additional relations in the act, one to the accepting will, the other to the award that the will has assigned to the act. This second is analogous to what is involved in using something, for just as to use is to order the willed object to something else as an end, so the will to whom the act is of merit orders this act to something as its reward. Neither of these two relations is real (or non-mental), for neither pertains to the act in virtue of some new reality therein. It arises solely through the act of the will accepting it. Not only can the intellect relate an object by a re-

---

[2] Cf. ibid., IV, d.49, q.10, nn.2-3 (ed. Vivès XXI, 318-19).
[3] Damascene, *De fide orth.* II, c.30: PG 94, 975; ed. Buytaert, c.44, p.162.
[4] Cf. Duns Scotus, *Ord.* prol., nn.12-39, 57 (I, 9-22, 35).

lationship that does not stem from the very nature of the thing, but the will can do the same. Where the intellect relates it by knowing it, the will relates it by accepting it. This ability to relate by a relationship that does not stem from the very nature of the object may be due to what these two powers have in common, their immateriality.

[4] 17.7 You may wonder whether a relation in the object produced by the will should be called a conceptual relation. One could say that if "conceptual relation" be taken strictly to mean a relationship produced in the object by an act of that faculty which is in essence rational (i.e., the intellect), then it should not be called such since it stems immediately from the will eliciting the relational act. Then it would follow that if "conceptual relation" be taken strictly, not every relation is either real or conceptual, for a third type exists, namely, "a relation of will" which arises from the will's relating one thing to another. But "conceptual relation" could also be taken to mean any relation stemming from the relating done by any faculty that is rational either in essence or by participation, and then this third type could be called a "conceptual relation."

17.8 What is more, "meritorious" connotes or demands as a kind of prerequisite that the act issue from a double principle, as it were. One is the will as freely eliciting or commanding the act, for nothing is accepted as meritorious unless it be freely in the power of the agent. Further, what merit and demerit have in common, viz., imputability, demands this relationship to a will as master of its acts. For nothing is imputed to anyone as deserving reward or punishment, and hence as praiseworthy or blameworthy, unless it lies in his power. The other requirement in the act is its relationship to a supernatural form which renders the person or operative power acceptable and is assumed to be grace or charity.[5] No act is accepted as worthy of reward unless the person performing it is acceptable. As *Genesis* puts it[6]: "God looked with favor on Abel and his offering," first on Abel, then on his gifts, for the offering of one unloved is not pleasing. Hence, *Genesis* adds: "But for Cain and his offering he had no regard."

[5] 17.9 It is not clear, however, just what relationship to charity is needed in the act for it to be meritorious. It seems enough that char-

---

[5] Cf. ibid., n.18 (I, 12-13); I, d.17, nn.142ff. (v, 207ff.); III, d.19, q.un., n.7 (ed. Vivès XIV, 718-19); d.18, q.un., n.4 (ibid., 663-64); II, d.7, n.11 (ed. Vivès XII, 386-87); IV, d.6, q.6, n.2 (ed. Vivès XVI, 578-79).

[6] Genesis 4:4.

ity exist in the agent, since his act would be especially acceptable if he is especially loved because of charity. Thus we see one person's prayer accepted whereas another's supplication is not, yet there is no difference between them in anything that functions actively in the act of supplication. It is just that one suppliant is especially loved, the other not.

17.10 Against this view it is argued that a person possessing charity can sin venially. Reply: Such an act is unacceptable since it contains something reprehensible. But if there be nothing offensive about it, the person's acceptability suffices to make the act acceptable.

17.11 What militates against this reply, it seems, is that a person possessing charity can still elicit an indifferent act.[7] There is no apparent inconsistency about such a person eliciting an act without directing it to the ultimate end either actually or virtually (that is, by virtue of some act that is directed immediately to that end). Such an act would not be meritorious, but neither would it be sinful, since no precept exists obliging one to order all his actions to God either actually or virtually in the aforesaid way.

17.12 [Conclusion] One can say, then, that the mere possession of charity does not suffice to make a person's act meritorious. In addition, the act must be elicited in accord with the inclination of that charity. For God, who loves only himself for his own sake, can give to a creature some Godlike form; he who has such is loved in a special way, and the work it inclines him to do is itself especially acceptable to the degree it accords with that inclination.

ARTICLE III
Solution of the Question

[6] 17.13 [Natural and meritorious love are not specifically different] To the third main point [in 17.3], one can say that meritorious and natural love do not differ in species if we are speaking of a *per se* difference in what their essential concepts mean, though not if we are speaking *per accidens* of a difference, namely, some concomitant factor such as a difference of objects or something similar, including even some specific difference in the natural being of the act.

17.14 Proof of the conclusion understood in this way:

One absolute form is not distinguished from another by a relation alone but by some absolute difference within the same genus, ac-

---

[7] Cf. Duns Scotus, *Ord.* II, d.41, q.un. (ed. Vivès XIII, 431-36).

cording to that dictum in the *Categories*[8]: "When genera are coordinate and different, the differentiae will differ specifically." Therefore, the absolute is not distinguished specifically by something relative. Now the act of love is an absolute form (as was shown [in 13.8-16] in the question on this matter), whereas the meritorious, as we said [in 17.6-8], only implies a relation. Therefore, [the act of love is not distinguished specifically by a relation].

17.15 Even if one of the premises of this argument should be denied, these two propositions at least seem to be true: "No specific difference is produced by a conceptual or non-real relation alone," and, as it was said [in 17.6-7], "Meritorious only implies formally a relation or relations that are not real, i.e., to the accepting will and to the reward with reference to which it is accepted."

17.16 [Objections and Answers] It could be said that while these reasons imply that the natural act of love is not distinguished from that of meritorious love in terms of its nature, it can still be distinguished in terms of its moral dimensions. For the latter distinction is based on a relationship, since circumstances indicate relations, and perhaps some, like that of the end or purpose, are not real relations. For that someone wills this act for that end implies no more in the act, it seems, than the relation of having been willed and related to such an end by an act of the will.

[7] Against this it is argued: What is properly potential to a specific form is not specifically distinct from the species itself, for insofar as it is potential, it is not a complete species. Now the natural act of love, as we speak of it here, is properly potential as regards the meritorious act. For the natural act, regarded as being in the power of the will, is capable of the ordering that "meritorious" implies. For instance, if an animal were constituted only by the form of animal and not by a specific form under the genus of animal, it would not be specifically distinct from any species under the genus animal, for it would be properly potential as regards the specific form. The same can be said of the nature of the act when compared to those additional conditions which "meritorious" implies.

17.17 One might object that the moral act could still be said to be specifically distinct from the meritorious act in the moral order, because it belongs to the species of moral virtue whereas the meritorious act belongs to a specifically different virtue, namely, one that is supernatural. Now these two virtues differ specifically; consequently, the corresponding acts also differ specifically in the moral order.

[8] Aristotle, *Praedicam.*, c.3 (1b17-18).

Now the act of a moral virtue is natural in the sense that it is within the native powers of the will, for the act does not exceed the totality of its power [as does the supernatural act].

I answer: The act with all the circumstances required for moral virtue is still potential with reference to that virtue which is meritorious [i.e., the supernatural virtue]. It is even more immediately potential than is the natural act, where "natural," refers to the bare nature which moral virtue presupposes. For it is reasonable that a merely natural act first receive such perfection as that of moral virtue which does not transcend nature's powers, and only then, that it receive further such perfection as is simply supernatural. Hence the reason given above [in 17.16], viz., that the potential is not specifically distinct from that in relation to which it is potential, not only holds for a purely natural act with respect to moral perfection but also for the perfectly moral act, for under the major premise, we could include a minor which would apply not merely to the natural act but also to the moral act.

[8] 17.18 When it is argued: "Moral virtue differs specifically from charity; therefore their respective acts differ specifically in the moral order," the entailment is not valid if we are speaking of subordinate virtues. Although it would seem that the acts of opposed virtues would be specifically distinct, at least in their moral being, nevertheless when one virtue is superior and the other subordinate there is no need that the goodness which the act derives from one be absolutely distinct in species from the goodness derived from the other. It is rather that the higher virtue gives additional goodness which completes, as it were, that given by the subordinate virtue. Thus charity is said to be the form of the other virtues because meritorious goodness—which stems somehow from charity—brings to perfection any other goodness in the act.

17.19 Against this it is argued: Although the act insofar as it is meritorious or stems from charity is not in a disparate species from the species of the act *qua* moral, it will at least be in a higher species that is more complete than that in which it would be if it were merely moral, and a specific difference of this sort suffices for our proposal.

Here one could concede the conclusion, and then we would say that a meritorious act of love possesses a certain specific element lacking in a natural act of love *qua* natural, even though the numerically identical act be natural when regarded as the presupposition for the meritorious aspect. Hence the meritorious factor is what brings the preceding goodness to completion as a species, but it is not a disparate specific difference. Neither do the arguments [in 17.16 and 17.18], based on "what is properly potential" or "the perfection that completes the goodness," prove anything more. If the supreme virtue and form of the other moral virtues were general justice, however, then something similar to what has been said of charity would be true of it.

[9] 17.20 Putting it another way, we could say that the meritorious is not a specifying and completing factor in the moral order, because it does not indicate some intrinsic goodness or rectitude in the agent but it only presupposes such and bespeaks in addition a relationship to the accepting will. However, if "meritorious" does not just presuppose moral goodness in the act but the goodness charity gives, then, since the latter is more complete than moral goodness, it follows that a meritorious act does have some specific goodness beyond that of moral goodness. For while the meritorious does not imply such ulterior goodness, it does presuppose it, and this seems probable, for otherwise an act with only natural goodness could be meritorious.

17.21 Against this it is argued: An act which is morally complete even specifically can exist in the absence of a virtuous habit. In general such is the act of choice by which a moral virtue [or habit] is generated. By the same token, then, all the goodness the act would have when charity is present could be there when it is absent.

Answer: The argument proves that the act could have all that rectitude because the same conformity to a rule or true dictate of reason is there. Hence it would have the same moral goodness, for such rectitude is either moral goodness itself or, at least, cannot exist without it. Besides its rectitude or conformity to directive knowledge, however, the act of charity has a goodness of its own because of the fact that it is in accord with the inclination of charity. Indeed, to be in accord with such is precisely what it means to have charitable [or supernatural] goodness. This is not the case with the other moral virtues.

[10] 17.22 [Other objections] The conclusion [in 17.13] defended in the solution of the question, however, is challenged on this ground.

The natural knowledge of God and that of infused faith are specifically different acts of the intellect. By the same token, then, natural love and the dilection that is charity are specifically distinct acts of affection.

17.23 Proof of the antecedent: The infused act of faith is necessarily veridical, whereas belief acquired from natural sources can be false. Now cognitive acts that are necessarily veridical differ specifically from those which are not. This is clear from Bk. VI of the *Ethics*,[9] where suspicion and opinion, which can be false, are specifically distinguished from those intellectual virtues which must be veridical states of knowledge.

17.24 Another proof of the antecedent is that natural scientific knowledge of God manifestly differs specifically from any kind of belief.

In proof of the entailment there is: (1) an argument from analogy, for there is a similarity between these acts of the intellect and those of the will; (2) an argument from causality, for when the antecedent acts of knowledge differ specifically the subsequent acts of the will do too, for things of the same species do not have specifically different presuppositions.

17.25 [Answer] The antecedent [in 17.22] can be denied of natural and supernatural acts of belief, for supernatural belief is an act elicited in accord with the inclination of infused faith, whereas natural belief is elicited in accord with the certainty derived from some witness. Now we said in [14.23 of] one of the earlier questions that with one and the same act one can believe something on the testimony of a witness and at the same time do so in virtue of infused faith, if it be present. Hence it is the same act in reality. As natural, it is potential as regards the perfection received from infused faith. But the potential is not different in species from its respective actualized or perfected entity, even though the latter has a perfection of its own in addition to that of the potential.

[11]   17.26 As for the proof of the antecedent [in 17.23] one can grant that certain knowledge, which has its own intrinsic grounds for certitude, be they the terms of the proposition or the object which includes the knowledge [virtually] or some *per se* causal factor, is specifically distinct from uncertain knowledge. For instance, knowledge of a premise gets its certitude either from itself or from the object or from some other principle which is in turn either manifest of itself or is at least evident in virtue of the terms which are the *per se* cause of the principle which includes them. A conclusion, on the other hand, is certain in virtue of the premise which is the cause of its certitude. An act of infused faith, however, is certain in neither

---

[9] Aristotle, *Ethica ad Nic.* VI, c.3 (1139b15-24).

of these ways; its certainty stems from some extrinsic factor. For the light of infused faith, because it is a certain participation of the divine light, can incline the intellect only to some definite truth. Hence that certitude in the act is derived from a certain relationship to some infallible extrinsic factor to which it corresponds. It does not stem from any intrinsic perfection of the act, for the latter, were it elicited by acquired faith alone, would be equally perfect as regards anything intrinsic to it.

17.27 Against this it is argued: At least it has this certitude from its *per se* cause and this suffices.

Answer: Whatever be infused faith's causality in an act of belief, at least it does not make the intellect any more certain than if infused faith had not caused it. For certitude is apt to exclude from the act of the intellect in which it exists not only deception but doubt. This occurs only if the intellect perceives why its act is certain, for if it can see no grounds for being certain, it would appear it could still doubt. But in the case of infused faith, the intellect does not perceive the principle which produces the certitude.

[12] 17.28 While the other proof of the antecedent [in 17.24], that which has to do with a scientific act of knowledge, is based upon what is obviously true, the implication there must be rejected. For this is a *non sequitur*: "If the intellections are not specifically distinct, neither are the volitions." What needs to be added in the antecedent is that the intellections, precisely insofar as they are *per se* preconditions, are specifically distinct, that is to say, to have such volitions there must be a specific distinction in the intellections. Such is not the case here, for if two persons elicit an act of love of God, one because he naturally knows God to be good, the other because he believes this to be so, neither the scientific* act of knowledge nor the act of faith regarded individually is required *per se* to have the act of love. Both are needed for what they have in common, namely, both reveal the existence of the object to be loved.

17.29 A similar response could be given to the other proof of the antecedent [in 17.23] based on the difference between infused and acquired faith.* Although such acts differ specifically, they do not do so precisely as preconditions for love. That is to say, they are not preconditions because they are specifically distinct. For example, if one person were shown demonstratively and another dialectically that a given object must be loved, their resulting acts of love would not differ specifically, for the specific difference in the knowledge is not part of its being a precondition for the love.

QUESTION SEVENTEEN

Reply to the Initial Argument

[13] 17.30 [An invalid reply] Some answer the initial or main argument [in 17.1] as follows: A habit is not the cause of the substance of the act but only of its mode, and one could admit that this mode differs specifically in its way from the substance of the act.[10]

17.31 This answer seems to have some plausibility (a) if we are referring to those characteristics conferred by the habit such as that the act is performed delightfully, easily, promptly, and expeditiously (for an acquired habit commonly confers such a mode, if it be one, or such modes of action), or (b) even if we are speaking of that additional mode conferred when the habit is a virtue, which consists in acting righteously or virtuously. None of these, however, is actually proper to charity or to the meritorious act. For, as we said [in 17.6], "meritorious" refers to an act accepted by the divine will in relation to reward. Now that the act be accepted by the divine will, or that the [divine] will accept the act in just this way, are one and the same thing, and nothing caused can be the formal reason for this (where "formal reason" means something which mediates between the possibility of acceptation and its corresponding actuality). Therefore, charity can hardly be called the source or principle of this mode in the act to which it properly corresponds.

17.32 [Valid answer] Consequently, the argument can be answered in another way. The major, viz., that acts elicited by specifically different principles are themselves specifically different, is true only of the principle as a whole, for acts receive their total entity from such and, therefore, also their unity and distinction. It is equally true of partial principles if they are disparate and are required precisely insofar as they are disparate. But if the principles are subordinated one to the other, or if it is not required as such that they be disparate, then the acts need not be specifically distinct. Now charity is neither the total principle of the will's act nor is it a disparate principle. It is rather a subordinate principle, for the will uses charity and not vice versa. Neither is charity required *per se* for the substance of the act nor for the act to be meritorious. It is only a precondition for the act's being accepted.

17.33 But even for this it is not a *necessary* precondition if the necessity referred to be that characteristic of an essential order of causes. It is needed only because of a disposition of a will that con-

---

[10] Godfrey of Fontaines, *Quodl.* II, q.4 in corp. (ed. Pelzer in PhB II, Louvain, 1904, p. 94).

tingently decided not to accept the act unless it be elicited in accord with such an inclination. But to specifically distinguish the act, the principle must be either its *per se* principle (and hence that which gives the act such real being as it possesses in itself) or at least the source of its being specifically distinct, or if it is only a dispositional distinguishing principle, then it must be so *per se*, i.e., it must so dispose *per se* that the effect as something distinct be caused according to an essential order of causes.* But none of these conditions accrues to the act in virtue of the habit of charity.

17.34 In this connection note the order that obtains between (1) the bare act to which blame or praise is imputable, (2) the virtuous act, which stems from moral virtue, (3) the charitable act, and (4) the meritorious act.

The first expresses a relationship to the potency which freely elicits the act; the second adds to this a relationship to the virtue which inclines to such an act, or rather to the rule of virtue, i.e., a dictate of right reason; the third expresses a relationship to charity which inclines the will to such an act; the fourth adds a relationship to the divine will which accepts the act in a special way. The third adds some goodness over and above that conferred by the second and is itself required for the fourth, not indeed by the very nature of things, but rather by a disposition of the accepting will.

Question Eighteen

DOES THE EXTERIOR ACT ADD SOME GOODNESS OR BADNESS TO THE INTERIOR ACT?

[1] 18.1 The next question concerns the interrelation of the extrinsic and intrinsic acts and asks whether the extrinsic adds some goodness or badness to the intrinsic.[1]

Arguments Pro and Con

Argument for the negative:[2]
That which is not voluntary is neither good nor bad. Now the external act insofar as it is distinct from the internal is not voluntary. It derives what "voluntary" character it has from the internal act. Therefore, the external act has no goodness or badness of its own and, having none, it cannot add any to the internal act.

18.2 Against this it is argued that what is forbidden by a distinct negative precept includes its own distinct illicitness. But the external act is forbidden by one precept and the internal act by another. This is clearly the case with the precepts "You shall not commit adultery" and "You shall not covet your neighbor's wife"[3] as well as with the precepts "You shall not steal" and "You shall not covet your neighbor's goods."[4]

Body of the Question

[2] 18.3 It is moral, not natural, goodness that poses the major difficulty, for the answer is clear enough as regards natural goodness, no matter how you understand this term, since internal and external acts are by nature different. Indeed, they are elicited immediately by different powers, the internal by the will and the external by some external power subject to the will's command.

18.4 Neither does the question pose a problem where the external and internal are distinct acts either because they are elicited by dif-

---

[1] Cf. Duns Scotus, *Ord.* II, d.42, q.5 (ed. Vivès XIII, 448-77).
[2] Aristotle, *Ethica ad Nic.* III, c.7 (1113b5-19).
[3] Exodus 20:17. [4] Ibid.

ferent persons (where one has the internal act, for instance, and the other the external) or because they are performed by the same person at different times (for instance, the same subject has only an internal act at one time and an external act at another). Only when the two acts are conjoined does the question become difficult (when, for example, in the same person the internal act is followed by an external act).

18.5 Third, the question must be understood extensionally and not as the addition of intensive goodness or badness. For as regards both good and bad actions, it frequently happens that desire for the absent is a weaker act than an act concerned with something present, which Augustine calls "love." "Wanting what is present," he says, "is love in the one who enjoys it."[5] But whether they be one or distinct, love is more perfect intensively than desire, since it satisfies the will in a way desire cannot do. When there is an exterior act, then, it can happen that the interior act is intensified. But this is not what the question is about. The issue is whether the external act of itself adds additional goodness to that which is proper to the internal act.

18.6 The sense in which the question creates the most difficulty, then, is this: Does the external act, when united with the internal act in one and the same person, have a moral goodness of its own distinct from that of the internal act?

18.7 To solve this question, three points require investigation: (1) Whence comes the moral goodness or badness of an act? (2) Does its laudability or its culpability spring from the same source? (3) Is the goodness or laudability of the external action distinct from that of the interior act?

ARTICLE I
The Source of Moral Goodness or Badness

[3]   18.8 [Description of moral goodness] The moral goodness of an act consists in its having all that the agent's right reason declares must pertain to the act or the agent in acting.

18.9 [Clarification] This description is explained as follows: Just as the primary goodness of a being, called "essential" and consisting in the integrity or perfection of the being itself, implies positively that there is no imperfection so that all lack or diminution of perfection is excluded, so the being's secondary goodness, which is something over and above, or "accidental," consists in its being per-

[5] Augustine, *De Trin.* IX, c.12, n.18: PL 42, 971-72; CCSL 50, 309-10.

fectly suited to or in complete harmony with something else—something which ought to have it or which it ought to have. And this two-way suitability is commonly connected. As an example of the first, health is said to be good for man because it suits him. [As an example of the second,] food is called good because it has an appropriate taste. Augustine gives examples of both.[6] "Health without pain or fatigue is good," he says. This refers to the first type of suitability, since health is good for man because it suits him. Then Augustine adds: "Good is the face of a man with regular features, a cheerful expression, and glowing color." This is an instance of the second, because here the face is called good for having what is appropriate to it.

There is this difference between the two. What suits someone is said to be good for him, that is, for him it is a good or a perfection, but we do not speak of it as being accidentally or denominatively good in itself. That to which something is appropriate, on the other hand, is called good denominatively because it has what is suited to it. In the first case, the form takes its name from the subject in which it is. As the soul is called "human," so something is called "good for man" because it is a human good. In the second case, the subject gets its designation from the form. Thus we say a man is good because of some good he has.

Now an act is by nature apt to be in agreement with its agent as well as to have something suited to itself. On both counts then it can be called "good" with a goodness that is accidental. This is true in general of a natural act as well, so that this goodness, which consists in having what is appropriate to it, is not only an accidental, but also a natural, goodness.[7]

[4]   18.10. Furthermore, some agents without intellect and will neither judge nor can judge what is appropriate to their acts. In such a case, what is suitable is determined by natural causes alone

---

[6] Ibid., VIII, c.3, n.4: PL 42, 949; CCSL 50, 272.

[7] There is an addition found in M₁ at the end of 18.9. In M₂ and W it follows 18.10:

And this suitability stems either from the nature of the terms or if it must generally be traced back to the judgment of some intellect (since the intellect is the measure of suitability), this judgment will be that of the intellect which is the rule of the whole of nature, viz., the divine intellect. Indeed this intellect, just as it knows perfectly every being, so it knows perfectly the harmony or disagreement of one thing with another.

and they incline the agent to act. Or if in addition there be the judgment of some mind and the movement of some will, it would be that of God alone as universal director and mover of the whole of nature. Now the goodness in the act of an agent without intellect and will is merely natural.

18.11 Over and above this general judgment [of God] about the suitability of the action (which concerns agents alike that act with or without knowledge), a general judgment is involved in the case of agents endowed with an intrinsic knowledge of their actions. Those with sense knowledge alone somehow apprehend the suitability of the object of their action. But whether or not they judge the action appropriate, the goodness of the action does not transcend the natural. Others act by virtue of intellectual knowledge, which alone is able to pass judgment, properly speaking, upon the appropriateness of the action. Such agents are suited by nature to have an intrinsic rule of rectitude for their actions. Only they can have an act whose goodness is moral.

18.12 But for this it is not enough that the agent have the ability to adjudicate the appropriateness of his acts. He must actually pass judgment upon the act and carry it out in accord with that judgment. If one is in error and still acts in accord with the correct judgment of another, he is not acting rightly, for by his own knowledge he was meant to regulate his actions and in this case he is not acting in accord with it but against it, and hence he does not act rightly.

[5] Similarly, such an agent elicits the sort of act as lies in his power. Now he has in his power the sort of act he deliberately elicits, for the power of free choice consists either formally or concomitantly in knowledge and election. And so it appears clear how the moral goodness of the act lies in its suitability judged according to the agent's right reason.

18.13 [Explanation of all that right reason demands of the act] We explain the added qualification [in 18.8], "all that must pertain to the act," in this way: Every judgment begins with something certain. Now the first judgment about the appropriateness cannot presuppose some knowledge determined by another intellect; otherwise it would not be first. Hence it presupposes something certain but judged by this intellect, namely: the nature of the agent and the power by which he acts together with the essential notion of the act. If these three notions are given, no other knowledge is needed to judge whether or not this particular act is suited to this agent and this faculty. For instance, if one knows what man is, what his intellectual powers are, and what an act of understanding is, then it is clear to him that it befits man to understand with his intellect. Knowing what it means to attain knowledge, it would also be clear to him what it is not appropriate for his mind to reach. Similarly, it is evident from the notions of the nature, the potency, and the act why understanding does not befit the brute, or rather why it is not compatible with his nature. For this first judgment, based precisely on the nature of the agent, the operative power and the act, reveals not something just ill-matched, i.e., some unbecoming or disorderly connection, but a simple inconsistency, i.e., the absolute impossibility of any such union.

[6] 18.14 What is more, from these three notions one can conclude what object is appropriate to a given act of a certain agent. Take the act of eating, for example. Food capable of restoring what man has lost would be its appropriate object, whereas a stone or something nourishing for animals but not for man would not be.

This delimitation introduced by the object first brings the act under the generic heading of moral. Not that the nature of its object determines its moral species; rather it opens it to further moral determination, for when an act has an appropriate object, it is capable of further moral specification in view of the circumstances in which it is performed. That is why an act is said to receive its generic goodness from its object, for just as genus is potential with respect to differences, so the goodness derived from its object first puts it into the generic class of moral acts. Only goodness of nature is presupposed. And once it has generic goodness, the way is open to all the additional moral specifications.

18.15 The procedure for determining specific goodness, called "goodness from circumstances," is as follows: The first goodness comes, it seems, from the circumstances of the end, for given the nature of the agent, of the action, of the object, one immediately concludes that such an action ought to be performed by this agent for such an end, and that it ought to be chosen and wanted for the sake of such an end. This circumstance is not precisely characteristic of the act as actually performed or not, but rather of the act as willed and related to this end by an act of the will. Indeed, the decision to do something for a worthy purpose is no less good when the external act that ensues fails to achieve that end than when it succeeds.

The next circumstance seems to be the manner in which the action is performed. How it ought to be performed we infer from all or from some of the aforementioned considerations.

Next come our conclusions regarding the appropriate time. For a given action done for such a purpose and in such a manner is not always befitting such an agent; it is appropriate only when the act can be directed to or can attain such an end.

Last of all is the circumstance of place. Indeed there are many acts with complete moral goodness in which place plays no part.[8]

18.16 It is clear then how many conditions right reason sets down, for according to the description given above [in 18.8], to be perfectly good, an act must be faultless on all counts. Hence Dionysius[9] declares: "Good requires that everything about the act be right, whereas evil stems from any single defect." "Everything," he explains, includes all the circumstances.

[7] 18.17 Objection: Circumstances are relations whereas good is a quality, according to the *Ethics*[10]; virtue is also a quality, according to the *Categories*.[11]

I answer: According to the *Physics*[12]: "All virtue and malice are relative." That acts be good or virtuous, therefore, implies one or several relations. But like "healthy" or "beautiful," "good" or "virtuous" are spoken of, and predicated, as qualities, and this commonly happens with the fourth type of quality.*

18.18 [The source of moral badness] In view of the second part of the citation [in 18.16] from Dionysius we ought to look into the source of moral badness in an act.

Badness can be opposed to goodness in an act either privatively or as its contrary. Man is said to be bad in this second sense if he has some vice, for though this implies a privation of a perfection that should be there, a vice is certainly a positive habit. In the other sense, man is said to be bad privatively if he lacks the goodness he ought to have, even if he does not have the contrary vice or vicious habit.[13]

18.19 We find this distinction in Boethius[14] where he explains the

---

[8] Cf. Duns Scotus, *Ord.* II, d.40, q.un. (ed. Vivès XIII, 424-27).
[9] Ps. Dionysius, *De div. nomin.*, c.4, 30: PG 3, 806; *Dionysiaca* I, 298-99.
[10] Aristotle, *Ethica ad Nic.* X, c.2 (1173a13-22).
[11] Aristotle, *Praedicam*, c.8 (8b30).
[12] Aristotle, *Physic.* VII, c.3 (246b2-8).
[13] Cf. Duns Scotus, *Ord.* II, d.7, q.un., n.12 (ed. Vivès XII, 387).
[14] Boethius, *In categorias Aristot.* III: PL 64, 255.

first characteristic of quality: "They say justice is not contrary to injustice, for they think injustice is a privation and not a contrary state." And he adds in refutation: "Many habits are expressed in privative terms such as 'illiberality' and 'imprudence.' These would never be contrasted with virtues, which are habits, if they themselves were not habits."

18.20 Reason also justifies this distinction. For it can happen that an act is performed under circumstances that are not all they should be [to make the act morally good], yet neither are they so improper that they ought not to be there, for instance, when an action is neither directed to an appropriate end nor to an inappropriate one. In such a case the act is bad only privatively, not contrarily as it would be if it were performed for some unlawful purpose. And from many similar acts, a corresponding habit would arise, namely, one whose "badness" is privative rather than a positive contrary. For example, to give alms, not for a good end such as the love of God or to help one's neighbor, but not for a bad end either such as out of vainglory or to hurt someone, is an act of this sort that is privatively, not contrarily, bad.

[8] It is to such privative "badness" that Dionysius refers when he states that the absence of any one of the required circumstances suffices to render the act bad. But for it to be bad contrarily there must be some positive circumstance present that involves some deformity.

18.21 Briefly, then, just as moral goodness is integral suitability, so moral badness is unsuitability. Privative badness is a lack of suitability, i.e., the absence of what ought to be there, whereas badness as the contrary of goodness is unsuitability as a contrary state, i.e., as some condition that is incompatible with suitability.

18.22 [Corollary] From what has been said this corollary follows: The same fundamental act can have a manifold moral goodness. It is not just that it is correct in all its circumstances (something which invests the act not with many goodnesses but with one integral goodness), but it can also have at the same time all that is needed for two distinct virtues, and thus be directed to several ends according to different dictates of perfect prudence. For example, I go to church to fulfill an obligation in justice, because of obedience or some vow. And I also go out of charity or love of God, to pray or to worship him. And I also go out of fraternal charity to edify my neighbor. In short the more morally good motives there are, the better the act is. This is true whether the goodness in question be moral goodness alone or that additional goodness we call meritorious.

18.23 In like fashion, badness multiplies if one and the same act violates several dictates of reason.[15]

ARTICLE II
The Source of Laudability and Culpability

[9] 18.24 [Meaning of the terms, especially "imputable"] In regard to the second main problem [in 18.7] let me say that "praiseworthy" and "blameworthy," and more generally "remunerable" or "punishable," come under the general designation "imputable." What all these have in common is that the acts to which they refer are in the free power of the agent. Now although this power involves both intellect and will, it is only the will, I say, that can completely account for the indifference or indeterminacy as regards the alternative—the indifference, namely, that consists in the fact that the action which occurred might not have occurred, or vice versa ("indifference to the alternative" must be understood here disjunctively, not conjunctively, that is to say, *in sensu diviso*, not *in sensu composito**).

Every other active potency acts naturally,* and of itself is thus determined to one effect, i.e., to one of two contradictories. Even if its activity ranges over disparate effects as is the case of the manifold terrestrial effects produced by the sun, if we consider one particular effect or its contradictory, we see the cause is determined to produce this. Thus the sun* is determined to cause this herb to grow or this worm to be produced, and the same with other effects.

The will alone is indeterminate as regards contradictory effects, and it determines itself to one of the two, as is clear from the *Metaphysics*[16]; otherwise it would cause contrary effects at the same time.

It is because the will has its act in its power indeterminately, presupposing only knowledge, that the act is essentially imputable to the agent. Hence St. Augustine says[17]: "It is clear that if this movement is called culpable, it is not natural but voluntary." And then the disciple's comment follows: "If the movement by which the will

---

[15] See Appendix, Addition 18.23.
[16] Aristotle, *Metaph.* IX, c.5 (1048a5-15).
[17] Augustine, *De libero arbitr.* III, c.1, nn.2-3: PL 32, 1271-72; CCSL 29, 275-76.

QUESTION EIGHTEEN

turns in different directions were not voluntary and under our control, man would not deserve praise or blame," as we said in the question [in 16.47ff.] on the natural necessity in the will.

18.25 "Imputable," then, implies a dual relationship, one to the dominion or power of the agent, the other to something which in justice corresponds to the act or to the agent because of the act. The first relation remains unchanged whether the act be good or bad; whereas the second varies. Not, indeed, that it changes formally from good to bad, but given the difference between good and bad judged in terms of suitability or lack thereof, as explained in the first article [in 16.8ff.], the second relation varies accordingly. For good is imputable for praise or reward, whereas evil is imputable for blame or punishment. A neutral or indifferent act is imputed to the agent in whose power it lies as somehow blameworthy because he could have acted according to the dictates of right reason, or at least it is credited to him as unpraiseworthy and this because of a defect on his part, for he could have acted in a praiseworthy fashion.

[10] 18.26 From all this it is clear that an act is not imputable and formally good in a moral sense for the same reason. It has moral goodness because it conforms to a rule or norm as it should. It is imputable because it lies in the free power of the agent. Praiseworthy and blameworthy presuppose both. For while they formally assert the act is imputable (specifying that for which it is imputable), they connote materially the reason why the act is imputable in one way or the other, namely, the goodness or badness, which are the grounds for its being imputed for praise or punishment.

18.27 [Two types of imputable acts] We can distinguish two senses of "imputable." What is most properly imputable lies immediately in the power of the will, and in this sense only volition itself is imputable since it alone is immediately in the will's power.

In another sense, anything is imputable that falls simply, though not immediately, under the control of the will. If the will by its command can make another power elicit an action or can prevent it from doing so, then that action is also imputable to the will, for the whole causal chain leading up to and including that act lies in the power of the will.

[11] 18.28 There is a difference between what is imputable in the first and second ways. For the first, only the potency of the will and the intellection which the act of the will presupposes are needed, be-

cause volition is an immediate effect of the will. In this sense Augustine's statement should be understood[18]: "Nothing is so in the power of the will as the will itself." By "will" we should understand not its entity but its proper act. For the execution of an act imputable in the second way, however, another potency besides the will is required.

18.29 From this it follows that the contingency or indeterminacy of the act imputable in the first sense is somehow greater, since only the will plus sufficient intellectual light is needed for it. Consequently nothing posterior can impede its execution. An act imputable in the second way requires another faculty whose impotence can impede the will's power over the act. Its contingency does not depend only on the indifference of the will as does the contingency of the first act. And since the contingency of any other cause or power is more removed from the single contingency characteristic of the will's causation, it follows that the contingency of an act imputable in the first way is simply greater than that of an act imputable in the second way. Nevertheless, since an act imputable in the second sense depends on different factors and any one of them or their absence can impede the effect, we could say that such an effect is more contingent or, better, is contingent on more than one count.

ARTICLE III
Is the Goodness or Laudability of the External Action Distinct from That of the Interior Act?

[12]   18.30 [Two points must be studied] As for the third main problem [in 18.7] we can say first of all that the external or commanded act has some moral goodness of its own distinct from that of the interior elicited act. Second, we shall see whether it has its own imputability or not.

1. The Exterior Act has Its Own Moral Goodness

18.31 [Two proofs] The first conclusion is established in two ways.

First by a text from Augustine[19]: "For though everyone is made wretched by the bad will alone, he becomes more wretched by the power whereby the desire of the bad will is satisfied. And though he would be wretched by the bad will alone, yet he would be less

---

[18] Augustine, *Retract.* I, c.9 (8), n.3, and c.22 (21), n.4: PL 32, 596, 620; CSEL 36, 39.

[19] Augustine, *De Trin.* XIII, c.5, n.8: PL 42, 1020; CCSL 50a, 392.

wretched if he could have had nothing of those things which he has wrongfully willed." "Wretchedness" obviously does not refer to pain or suffering, for he who wants something and cannot get what he desires has more pain than he who satisfies his desires. Hence it must be understood of the wretchedness of guilt. Therefore, the evil of the external act adds to the misery of guilt present in the internal act.

18.32 Reason proves the same point. From the first article [18.8ff.], we know that moral goodness consists in an act having all that the agent's right reason declares must pertain to the act. But the demands of right reason are different for the internal and external acts. Therefore, their moral goodness or badness is also different. This holds true whether the badness be privative (because something is missing that should be there) or contrary (because something is present that is incompatible with what should be there).

18.33 Proof of the minor: Right reason does not demand the impossible. Now what suits or can suit the internal act cannot possibly also suit the external act if we consider both acts in their real being and what is appropriate to this. For while the external act as an object willed, but not as an elicited act, does in some sense pertain denominatively (by a kind of extrinsic denomination) to what is appropriate in reality to the internal act, still the same thing does not suit each in the same way. Since the potencies responsible for the internal and external acts are incapable of having the same act, indeed their natures differ, it follows that what suits their respective acts must also differ in nature, or at least—and this suffices for our purpose—what is appropriate to each is different.

With this in mind, the answers to certain objections to our position become clear.

[13] 18.34 [Objections] Against the foregoing it is argued:

First, the truth of the act of understanding and of the object understood is one and the same. For like reasons the goodness of the act of willing and of the object willed should be the same.

The antecedent seems clear from these examples: As the truth of a principle is immediate, so the knowledge of it can be called immediate in contrast to the mediate knowledge of the conclusion. Similarly, the knowledge of a principle is derived from its terms, and the knowledge of a conclusion is derived from principles. In this same way truth pertains to principles and truth pertains to conclusions.

18.35 Confirmation of the same point: Where one thing exists because of another, we have but one thing. Now the external act has goodness only because of the goodness present in the internal act. Therefore, the goodness of one is not distinct from that of the other.

18.36 Besides, according to Anselm,[20] sin is lack of due justice. But there is but one such lack in the internal and external acts, for justice and injustice—according to him—are by their nature able to exist only in the will.

18.37 Besides, where there is but one act of aversion and inordinate desire, there seems to be but one formal reason for sin. In the internal and external act, however, there is but a single act of aversion, for the will is the only faculty capable both of turning towards or turning away from the end. The same should be said of inordinate desire which Augustine[21] sometimes calls cupidity and defines it properly as "the venom of charity." Hence it is properly in that faculty in which charity is apt to be, which is the will alone.

[14]   18.38 [Answer to the objections] Reply to the first [in 18.34]: The same truth which pertains formally to the act of understanding does belong in some other way (viz., objectively) to the object known insofar as this exists in the intellect. Similarly, that goodness which pertains formally to volition does belong in some derivative fashion to the willed object *qua* willed. Yet for all that, the [external] act, insofar as it has real being apart from the will, can have a goodness of its own just as it can have a real suitability or inappropriateness of its own.

18.39 And the argument [of 18.35] cited in confirmation can lead to the opposite conclusion. If the interior act is really the means whereby the exterior act acquires an appropriateness by being in agreement with a rule of its own, then this appropriateness must be other than that characteristic of the interior act, for nothing functions as a cause or means with respect to itself.

We have an example of this in the acts of the intellect. Even though a conclusion derives its truth from the principle used to prove it, it still has a truth of its own, for the agreement between what exists and what it affirms to be the case in virtue of its own terms is something proper to itself. It is not the truth of the principle that formally constitutes its own truth, for the conclusion is a mediate and demonstrated truth, and the truth it possesses is formally demonstrable truth.

---

[20] Anselm, *De conceptu virg.* c.5: PL 158, 438-39.
[21] Augustine, *De diversis quaest. 83*, q.36, n.1: PL 40, 25.

Similarly, where many different conclusions follow in a certain sequence from the same principle, each has its own distinct truth. It may even be that the prior conclusion is truer and more necessary since it does not depend for its necessity upon the subsequent conclusions but vice versa.

In like manner, every false conclusion which conflicts with the same truth has its own distinct falsity, for what each asserts disagrees in a different way with what is actually the case.

It is the same with the acts of the will. Volition is not the only act that is able by nature to be in conformity or in disagreement with what right reason dictates. This is also true of the commanded act by reason of its being willed. And though the norm to which each act must conform is the same, the acts themselves are different and so too are their respective agreements, even though these be to the same norm.

[15] 18.40 You may object: Truth pertains to nothing outside the mind. It belongs solely to the act of the intellect or to the object insofar as it is in the mind. Analogously, then, goodness pertains to the external act only as the object of volition and not as elicited externally.

I reply: The analogy could be denied according to those words of the *Metaphysics*[22]: "Falsity and truth are not in things—it is not as if the good were true and the bad were in itself false—but in thought."

Another way of answering would be to deny the antecedent. For if some intellect were to function as the norm for what is understood in the way the divine intellect is the rule and exemplar for the creature, then one could maintain that the object is true not only as actually known but also in itself, since in its very being it is modeled on and conformed to its exemplar.

18.41 [To the second objection] As for the other [in 18.36], I say: Justice may mean habitual rectitude or refer to a habit of the will, in virtue of which the will would be said to be habitually righteous even when it is not actually willing something. Thus we would call a sleeper "just" if he had the habit, and we would call him "unjust" if he lacked it or had a contrary habit of injustice. In another sense, however, rectitude could be understood to mean that which is actualized or in act and it would consist in the conformity of the elicited act with a norm. The first type of justice is quite generally admitted. For the second we give some proof. An action is not said

[22] Aristotle, *Metaph.* v, c.4 (1027b25-30).

to be formally right or just simply because the will is in the habitual state of justice, for this state is compatible with an act that is indifferent or even venially sinful, neither of which is just or right. What is needed is that the rectitude, by reason of which the act is formally called just, be present in the act while the action is going on. Perhaps it is not immediately in the will but in the act itself and by means of the act it is mediately in the will. For what the nature of the will is able to receive immediately is the habit and the act of volition. But actual justice is neither of these. It is rather a certain condition of the act itself, such as its conformity to a rule.

[16] 18.42 This would be more obvious if the action were not over in an instant but remained for a while. For just as one and the same movement numerically and specifically can be rapid at first and slow later (from which it follows that neither its rapidity nor its slowness is absolutely identical with the movement), so an action that continued for some time might at first be elicited in conformity to right reason and afterwards not, and so would be righteous at first and afterwards not. But the action is over in a moment or, if it continues awhile, its rectitude commonly remains, so that there is no switch from right to wrong. Consequently, the distinction between the act and its rectitude is not so evident.

Nevertheless, we can infer its existence in the ways mentioned above. It can be proved also in this way. If a relation is not a necessary consequence of the nature of its foundation, then it is not completely identical with the foundation. But rectitude is not a necessary consequence of the nature of the act. Also, actual justice of a secondary kind can be present in the commanded act (even though its primary form exists only in the act of volition), for the commanded act has a rightness of its own even though this is dependent upon the volition being right.

The statement, then, that justice is only in the will refers to habitual justice, which, as Anselm puts it, is rightness preserved for its own sake. For what is preserved pertains to the habit, or if we extend the meaning of "preserved," then the definition would be true of primary actual justice for this also is "preserved for its own sake," i.e., the will keeps it in its act, which it elicits rightly by means of [habitual] justice. If we are speaking about actual justice in the secondary sense, however, it must be admitted that this is only causally, not subjectively, in the will. So that even here the definition that justice is rectitude of will can somehow be saved, not indeed in the sense that rightness formally inheres in the will, but that it pertains

QUESTION EIGHTEEN

to the will as causing or commanding, and this rightness is wanted or "preserved for its own sake," namely, as an effect caused voluntarily.

18.43 [Corollaries] From this some corollaries follow that clarify our thesis.

First corollary: Given the same habitual justice, there are as many actual justices as there are elicited acts. And if one is elicited with greater effort than another, one can be more intense than the other, even though the habit remains equal. The first act can be elicited with more effort (in which case its actual justice will be correspondingly more intense), whereas the second act can be done with less effort, even though it is certain the habitual justice is not less.

18.44 Second corollary: Each evil act has an actual badness of its own. For just as each act is able to have its own goodness because it conforms to the same or different dictates of reason, so too each may be lacking such conformity.

18.45 Third corollary: Instances of badness differ in the same way as do the corresponding instances of goodness that ought to have been there. If the difference is specific or numerical in the one case, it is the same in the other. For privations are distinguished in terms of the corresponding habits that might have been there. For instance, deafness and blindness are specifically different privations even as hearing and vision are specifically different positively. This and that case of blindness are numerically distinct privations, even as this and that case of seeing are numerically distinct in a positive way.[23]

18.46 [Additional corollaries] From this it is clear how not only vices, speaking physically, but also sins, speaking theologically, can be distinguished numerically, specifically, and even generically. It is not just in terms of the distinction of things to which one turns in sinning, for this neither constitutes the sin nor distinguishes one sin from another; rather it is the proper nature of the privation which provides the formal grounds for distinguishing privatively, just as it is the proper nature of the corresponding virtue that is the basis for positive distinctions.

18.47 It is also clear why one sin is more grievous than another, whether their differences in gravity be specific or within the same species. For the greater, specifically or intensively, the goodness that should be there, the worse the act that lacks it. If it is a simple

[23] Cf. Duns Scotus, *Ord.* II, d.37, q.1, n.9 (ed. Vivès XIII, 359).

lack, the act is privatively worse; if something positively incompatible be present, the act is contrarily worse.[24]

18.48 Third, we see why the damned can continue to sin *ad infinitum* and still their nature is not consumed, nor is any natural aptitude or anything else in their nature. For nothing created can cause an intellectual nature or anything in it to perish, and if it could diminish such a nature, it could eventually destroy it completely.[25]

18.49 Similarly, the contingent effect does not accompany its cause necessarily. Hence the opposite of that effect or of something in the effect does not destroy or diminish the cause. Now the badness of the act is a privation in a contingent effect of the will. Therefore, it does not diminish anything pertaining to the will itself.

18.50 What then does sin added to sin take away? For according to Augustine[26]: "Evil is there to the extent that it takes away a measure of goodness."

I answer: Obviously the actual badness of an elicited act does not take away some good that is there at the same time; neither does it destroy some good that was there, for as we said above [in 18.42], the act takes place too quickly to change from good to evil.

But if a "good that was there" refers to the gratuitous habit [of grace or charity] that sin destroys, Augustine's dictum cannot mean every sin removes this; the second sin does not, for the first already destroyed it. Yet there is nothing essential to the first sin that makes it more destructive than the second. If there were, then the first would be simply more heinous than the second, since it takes away a greater good. But the second sin is sometimes more serious than the first and is by nature apt to take away even more. What it does take away essentially [*per se*] is actual goodness, and it would also remove the habitual or gratuitous goodness if it were present. What sin in general destroys, then, is something which should have been there, just as blindness in one born blind does not take away sight that was there but which should have been there. Thus Augustine[27] says of the angel who sinned that "he fell not from a state he had received, but from what he would have received had he chosen

---

[24] Cf. ibid., IV, d.50, q.6, nn.12-13 (ed. Vivès XXI, 569-70); II, d.21, q.2, n.3 (ed. Vivès XIII, 141); d.37, q.1, nn.8-10 (ibid., 358-60).
[25] Cf. ibid., II, d.37, q.1, n.4 (ed. Vivès XIII, 354).
[26] Augustine, *Enchirid.*, c.4, n.12: PL 40, 237; CCSL 96, 54.
[27] Augustine, *Super Gen.* XI, c.23, n.30: PL 34, 441.

to submit to God." And if sin were heaped upon sin *ad infinitum*, each would take away some goodness of its own which should have been there. Neither is it incongruous that a finite good which contains virtually, so to say, an infinity of effects to be elicited successively, also have an unlimited amount of righteousness corresponding to them.

18.51 [To the third objection] As for the objection [in 18.37] that there is but one act of aversion, we can take aversion to the end in several senses. For one thing, it can mean an actual nolition of the end. In this sense, it is clear that not every sinner has aversion for the end. Perhaps the sinner often does not actually think of it, or if he does, he does not view it with any malice.

[19] Another way would be to understand this turning from the end, not as formal, but as a kind of virtual aversion, which would consist in the will's accepting something incompatible with any effective volition or attainment of the end. Such would be the case if the will wanted something absolutely inordinate that would prevent any attainment of the end, for instance, something in violation of a divine command which must be observed if the end is to be reached. In this sense also, aversion pertains solely to the will.

In a third and larger sense, however, aversion can refer to any sort of malice which keeps one effectively from willing or attaining the end. Now an act commanded by the will can be bad in this sense, for if it is evil to command such an act, the will no longer efficaciously wills the ultimate end nor its attainment.[28]

18.52 Now just as the ability to be related or directed to the end can be called "conversion," so the ability to be directed away from it can be called "aversion." When it is claimed there is but one aversion in the external and internal act, this would be true of aversion taken in the first two senses, since this is present only in the internal act. But the further claim that aversion, so understood, is the formal ground for sin must be denied. The way a commanded act can be "turned away"—which can be called aversion in the third sense —suffices.

18.53 As for what is said [in 18.37] about "inordinate desire," if this means "bad will," i.e., immoderate volition, then inordinate desire is not formally present in all sin; it is only present with sin

---

[28] Cf. Duns Scotus, *Ord.* II, d.41, q.un., nn.2-3 (ed. Vivès XIII, 434-35); d.43, q.1, n.2 (ibid., 483); d.37, q.1, n.8 (ibid., 358-59).

either formally or causally. To make inordinate desire or cupidity coextensive with sin, therefore, one must extend its meaning to cover not only the interior acts but also the commanded acts of the will that are immoderate.

2. The External Act is Imputable

[20]   18.54 As for the second point of this article [in 18.30], viz., concerning imputability, it is clear from the distinction made [in 18.27] of article two, that only what is immediately in the will's power is strictly speaking imputable, and that is volition and nolition.

But if "imputable" be taken in general as anything that is simply in the will's power, then a commanded act is properly imputable. For even though it is not immediately in the power of the will, it is put into execution by volition which falls under the will's control not only *qua* volition but also *qua* principle of the external act, for the will can place the external act by means of the internal. For example, if a servant kills on the command of his master, the death is imputed mediately to the master, for the servant's action was in his power.

18.55 If one objects, as before, that the external act is imputable only by means of the internal, I reply: From this our thesis follows, viz., that the imputability of one is not that of the other, for nothing functions as cause or means with respect to itself. We can also explain this the way we explained the proper goodness of the external act [in 18.31f.]. Though the term be the same, different foundations bear different relationships to it. Now the external and internal acts represent different foundations. And even though imputability pertains to each with reference to the same will, it will be different in each even as the way they are caused and the way in which they fall under the control of the same will is different.[29]

Reply to the Initial Argument

[21]   18.56 Answer to the argument at the beginning [in 18.1]: "Voluntary" can mean: (a) what is the will as in a subject, (b) what is willed by the will, or (c) what is commanded by the will. The first is not

---

[29] There is an addition found in M_1 and M_2 only:

On the contrary: Those who do not differ in the power of their will do not differ in sinning, but he who sins and he would equally want to sin but is powerless to do so are equal as regards that which is in the power of their will and differ only in that which is not in their power. Therefore, etc.

enough to make something completely voluntary, for a habit can exist in the will and be there involuntarily, as when the will is sad. The second is called "voluntary" in a participated sense because its acceptation as an object is voluntary. It should be called "willed," however, rather than "voluntary." Properly speaking, then, voluntary is what lies in the power of the will, which is the third sense. And thus the external act would be as simply voluntary as the internal act, even though it is not equally first since it presupposes the internal act.[30]

Proof of the minor: I say that while the external act apart from the internal (i.e., when it is performed without the latter) is not voluntary, for a more remote effect is not called "voluntary" if it is not actualized by the more proximate effect (i.e., the internal act), nevertheless when the external act is joined to the internal and proceeds from the latter, it not only becomes a voluntary act, but has a distinctive ground for being so, for it is "mediately voluntary," whereas the interior act is "immediately voluntary."

[30] M_2 and W have the following addition:

Therefore, *voluntary* must mean that which is caused by the will and this either directly or by command, although that which is elicited by the will is called voluntary in the primary sense rather than that which is commanded. Therefore, let the major be conceded, but understand *voluntary* generally, and in this sense the minor is false.

Question Nineteen

IS THE UNITY IN CHRIST OF THE HUMAN NATURE WITH THE WORD MERELY THE ASSUMED NATURE'S DEPENDENCE UPON THE WORD?

[1] 19.1 The next question has to do with the dependence of the assumed nature upon the Word.* Is the unity of human nature with the Word in Christ merely the human nature's dependence upon the Word?[1]

Arguments Pro and Con

It is argued it is not:

Here there is such unity as suffices for the nature to be truthfully predicated of the Person according to that dictum: "Such is that union that it made God man and man God" (*The Trinity*).[2] Now dependence alone seems insufficient for this. What is dependent is not always predicated of that on which it depends. This seems to be the case here, for the assumed nature [also] depends upon the Father, yet the Father is not man. Therefore, in the case of Christ there is some other unity besides the dependence of the human nature upon the Word.

19.2 Against the preceding view it is argued that if you examine all the other kinds of unity, you seem to find no other unity present here.

Body of the Question

19.3 In this question three points need investigation: (1) What type of unity must be posited in this case; (2) How is such unity possible on the part of the Person assuming the nature; (3) How is it possible on the part of the assumed nature?

ARTICLE I
The Type of Unity to be Posited Here

[2] 19.4 [Proof that it is a unity of order] As for the first point, it is an article of faith that human nature is personally united to the

---

[1] Cf. Duns Scotus, *Ord.* III, d.1, q.1 (ed. Vivès XIV, 4-53).
[2] Augustine, *De Trin.* I, c.13, n.28: PL 42, 840; CCSL 50, 69.

QUESTION NINETEEN

Word. "The Word was made flesh," (John 1)[3] where "flesh" means man, according to Augustine.[4] Also various Creeds or formulas of faith assert this truth expressly.[5] From this the conclusion follows that the human nature in Christ is ordered to, or dependent upon, the Word.

19.5 Proof of the implication: Every union results either from a form informing a subject, or from aggregation, or from some order. Lest there be any altercation on the grounds that the essential perfections, notional properties, or other things are said to be united in God, let it be understood I am speaking about a unity of really distinct things.

In the case at hand, however, no union based on informing can be postulated since the Word is neither potential, informable, nor an act which informs the human nature.

Neither is there any union here resulting solely from aggregation, for the Word has this sort of union with my own nature, and the Father has such with the assumed nature [of Christ], and in general such a union obtains between any two things that are simply distinct. Furthermore, it is clear that such a union does not suffice to produce the unity characteristic of a person. All that remains therefore is the third type, namely, a union of order.

The order, however, is that of the posterior to the prior. The Word obviously is not posterior to [human] nature; hence it is the other way around. The nature is posterior with respect to the Word and thus dependent on him.

19.6 Another proof of the consequence: A union of a nature to the Word implies a real relation, not on the part of the Word but on the part of the assumed nature. Now every real relation that is neither mutual nor between equals is a kind of dependence, or at least requires in the *relatum* some dependence upon that to which it is related. Furthermore, we infer the nature has this sort of dependence upon the Word from this article of faith, namely, that only the Son became incarnate. From this it follows that the nature is not united to each person of the Trinity, but to the Son alone.

19.7 [Three Conclusions] From the above three conclusions follow.

First, this dependence is not properly one of caused to cause. Ac-

---

[3] John 1:14.

[4] Augustine, *Enchirid.* c.34, n.10: PL 40, 249; CCSL 96, 68.

[5] Denzinger, H.-Schönmetzer, A., *Enchiridion symbolorum* (ed. 32, 1963), 62, 63-74, 76, 125, 150, etc.

cording to Augustine⁶: "In the relation to the creature, however, the Father, the Son, and the Holy Spirit are one principle."

19.8 Second, the formal ground or reason why the Word is that on which a human nature depends is not common to all three persons, for even prior to the actual dependence, there is always some ground in the subject for supporting such dependence and this ground is the term of the dependence. Therefore, if the ground for being that on which a human nature depends were common to all three persons, the Trinity as a whole would be the term of the dependence, which is false.

[3]   19.9 Here it is objected⁷ that even though something be common to the whole Trinity, it still exists in different ways in the different persons. Hence this could be the reason for grounding the dependence in one and not in another.

Answer: In what is common to all three persons, the only distinction would be that of origin. The first person, for instance, would not have the divine nature from anyone, whereas the second would have it from the first and the third from the other two. But this does not explain how one person and not another is that on which a [human] nature depends, for this distinction would be wholly the same whether no person had become incarnate or whether they all had or whether some other, for example, the Father, had become incarnate.

19.10 From this the third conclusion follows, namely, that the formal ground for supporting the dependence of [human] nature is the personal or hypostatic* entity of the Word.

Proof of this: A real union requires some kind of real entity, be it that of the formal term itself or that of the ground for supporting [the dependency]. But every entity in the intellectual nature of which we are speaking is either one that is essential or pertains to the [divine] nature, or a hypostatic or personal entity. Now it has been proved [in 19.8f.] that the ground for supporting this dependency is not an entity pertaining to the essence or nature of God. Therefore, it will be hypostatic. In short, the dependence is not a relationship to something communicable* but to something incommunicable or subsistent. This serves essentially as the supporting

⁶ Augustine, *De Trin.* v, c.14, n.15: PL 42, 921; CCSL 50, 223.
⁷ Henry of Ghent, *Quodl.* XIII, q.5 in corp. (fol. 526F); Richard of Middleton, *Sent.* III, d.1, a.1 in corp. (III, 6-7); William of Ware, *Sent.* II, d.1, q.1.

term or ground for the dependency of the dependent nature as communicable or communicated.

19.11 Objection: The same kind of union could exist with the person of the Father. Consequently, the union would have the same kind of formal term. But the hypostatic entities of the different persons are different. Therefore [it is not a union with any incommunicable subsistent entity].

Answer: One could reply in terms of what is common to the divine persons. For if one posits some other real feature they have in common, then one could grant that each of the three has this same common, not proper, ground for supporting such a relationship to himself.

Thus the first point [in 19.4ff.] appears clear, viz., that the union of the [human] nature with the Word is a certain kind of dependence and consists in the sort of dependence a communicable nature has upon something incommunicable and subsistent.[8]

ARTICLE II
The Possibility of Such a Union on the Part of the Assuming Person

1. First Proof

[4]   19.12 [Statement of the Proof] As for the second main point [of 19.3] we must see how such a union is possible on the part of the term, i.e., how this incommunicable subsistent [person] is able to be the term on which something depends. This can be explained somehow as follows: If there were any impossibility involved, it would stem from the fact that [what the human nature depends upon is] either (a) a person or subsistent subject; (b) or a divine person; (c) or this particular person, who alone is said to be the term of this dependence.

19.13 But on none of these three counts is such a union incompatible with this person. There are two proofs for this:

First, there is nothing contradictory about something independent being that upon which something else depends. Although it has an independence of its own, there is nothing repugnant about something depending upon it.[9] Entitatively the Word is independent, even so far as his personal entity is concerned, and this independence is something proper to that entity. Therefore, in none of these

---

[8] Cf. Duns Scotus, *Ord.* III, d.1, q.1, n.3 (ed. Vivès XIV, 8-9).
[9] Cf. ibid., n.4 (ed. Vivès XIV, 11-12).

three ways is there anything contradictory or incompatible about [the Word] being that on which a human nature depends.

19.14 Proof of the minor: Whatever formally excludes imperfection also formally rules out any kind of dependence. The formal ground for excluding one will also be grounds for forbidding the other. This is evident since dependence is either formally imperfection or has imperfection as a necessary adjunct. Now the hypostatic property of the Son formally precludes any imperfection and is for him the formal ground why it cannot be present. For there is no feature of the divine reality that is compatible with imperfection. Otherwise it would be possible for some imperfection to characterize that particular feature. And assuming it did, it could still remain imperfection and if it remained intrinsic to God, then some imperfection could be intrinsic to God, which is impossible.

[5]   19.15 [Objections] Against this argument objections are raised. The first is to the major. If independence implies the possibility of being the term upon which something depends, then any independence of this sort could support any dependence of the same sort. But the consequent is false, as is evident from the following cases.

Take substance and accident, for instance. Every substance is independent; it lacks the sort of dependence an accident has on its subject. Yet not every substance can support any sort of dependence an accident might have upon a subject. A stone, for example, cannot sustain wisdom.

19.16 It is clearly the same as regards the dependence of the whole upon its parts. There are many things whose nature simply precludes being dependent in this way, and yet they cannot be that on which something else depends in this way. Every simple being which is neither a whole nor a part is such.

19.17 The dependence of caused upon cause illustrates the same point. An angel is independent of every created cause and yet it cannot be that upon which everything caused depends.

19.18 It is also clear in general of the property we are dealing with here. Since the personal property is absolutely independent, it could support any form of causal dependence a creature has upon God, which is manifestly false. For the formal basis of causation is not a personal property but something common to all three divine persons, as was said above [in 19.7] in the quotation from Augustine.[10]

---

[10] Augustine, *De Trin.* v, c.14, n.15: PL 42, 921; CCSL 50, 223; cf. *supra*, 19.7.

QUESTION NINETEEN

19.19 Therefore, this counter-reply is made to the major. Although it is not inconsistent that something independent, in virtue of its independence, should be that upon which something else depends, its independence alone does not suffice to make the other depend upon it. It must have in addition an essential priority or primacy as regards that dependent, since dependence relates what is essentially posterior to what is essentially prior. It is also necessary that the prior have some perfection lacking in the dependent.

As for the case at hand, the personal or hypostatic entity has no essential priority in respect to creatures, for an essential order* obtains *per se* only between essences (in contrast to hypostatic entities), since it is "forms (i.e., essences) that are like numbers."[11] Besides, the hypostatic entity is not, simply speaking, perfect and is not a pure perfection,* as was said [in 5.16ff.] in the question on this topic.

19.20 The minor would be denied for the same reason, for if some entity were the reason why every imperfection is excluded, it would be a pure perfection. If the hypostatic entity then is not a pure perfection, it follows that the hypostatic entity is not the formal reason why all imperfection is excluded and consequently a divine person does not derive his independence formally from this entity.

[6] 19.21 [Solution of the objections] To the first [in 19.15]: Dependence can be distinguished in two ways: (1) formally, or specifically, as it were, on the basis of the distinct formal reasons for the dependence; or (2) materially, as it were, on the basis of the distinction among the things that are dependent, whether these belong (a) to the same order, or (b) to different orders.

To support several dependencies distinct in the first way demands in the supporting term formally different grounds or if there is but one ground, this must be as it were unlimited, containing virtually or eminently such formally distinct grounds as are required. But where the several dependencies are distinct in the second way all that is required is that the dependent entities be distinct. Sometimes these will be of the same order, namely, when they depend with equal mediacy or immediacy upon the same thing. At other times their order will be different, namely, one will depend mediately whereas the other will depend immediately.

Although these two propositions are false, "Something independ-

---

[11] Cf. Aristotle, *Metaph.* VIII, c.3 (1043b33-1044a14); *Ord.* I, d.2, n.77 (II, 172).

ent in a specific respect can support any kind of dependency whatsoever" and "Something independent in a specific respect can support the dependency of any dependent whatsoever," still this proposition seems probable, "Something independent in a particular respect can support something dependent in this same respect or in some prior respect, and it can support such either immediately or at least mediately." And this seems even more probable, "Something independent in every respect can support any dependent whatsoever, or at least can do so with regard to some dependent and with respect to some form of dependence."

The truth of these two propositions would be more apparent if we knew that every entity is prior or posterior *per se* to any other entity. And it seems we can know this from the interconnection and unity of things or from the unity of the universe which is a unity of order according to the Philosopher,[12] for any entity which lacked any *per se* order of priority or posteriority would appear to have no connection with other things.

[7] 19.22 When it is argued that "If independence implies the possibility of being the term upon which something depends, then independence in a given respect could support dependence in this same respect," one way of replying would be to deny the entailment, for if something independent in a given respect could not support dependency of this same sort, this would be because of its limited independence which could have some imperfection conjoined with it. But this would not hold good of what is independent in an unqualified sense, because in something of this sort there would at least be no imperfection.

The entailment fails on another count, for it does not hold unless one understands in the antecedent that independence in an absolute and unqualified sense entails the possibility of supporting any kind of dependence. But this is not what we claim. We only say that what is absolutely independent could support some sort of dependence. This suffices for our purpose, since by the way of elimination, it follows that the sort of independent of which we are speaking, namely, the person or personal entity, if it cannot be that on which something depends causally, or as measured, or in some similar fashion, then it can be that upon which a nature depends insofar as a nature is communicable to something that exists incommunicably [i.e., as a person].

19.23 Another answer would be to concede the consequent in

[12] Aristotle, *Metaph.* XII, c.9 (1075a3-10).

QUESTION NINETEEN

the sense explained above [in 19.21], viz., that something independent in such and such a respect can support something that depends in this same respect or in some prior respect.

19.24 With this, the answer to the objections made above becomes clear.

[8] As for the first [in 19.15], substance can support the dependence of some accident, namely, that which by nature can inhere in it. And even though there be some substance like the divine nature which is not susceptive of any accident, nevertheless it can support some prior dependency, for instance, that of something caused upon which the accident depends and by sustaining such the divine nature can support the accident.

19.25 The same solution can be given to the whole-part problem [in 19.16]. For while something simple that is neither a whole nor a part cannot sustain a whole in the way its parts do, it can support some dependency prior to that of the whole upon its parts.

If you ask how this applies to fire, which depends upon its parts, and the angel, who is simple, I reply: The dependence in this case is that of the less noble upon the more noble in the essential order of nature.

19.26 The answer to the third [in 19.17] is similar. An angel either mediately or immediately supports the dependency of any less perfect nature, a dependency that obtains because of the essential order among quiddities and is somehow prior or more basic than the dependence of an effect on its efficient cause. Indeed, this form of dependency [i.e., of the less noble upon the more noble] seems to be absolutely first. It can be commonly said to be found in the case of any independent thing as regards that with reference to which it is said to be independent.

19.27 As for the fourth [in 19.18], it is perfectly clear that what is absolutely independent must be able to support some form of dependence because otherwise it appears to have no connection with other beings. It is not necessary, however, that it can support every form of dependence, for if it is not simply perfect, it will not sustain a dependence that requires pure perfection in its term, such as the dependence of the caused upon a cause. But if imperfection is incompatible with it, even if no pure perfection pertain to it, it can still be independent. Now the hypostatic entity as such is not a pure perfection, but neither is it imperfect.

[9] 19.28 This refutes the reply given to the major [in 19.19], for to support any dependence in general cannot be repugnant to some-

425

thing completely independent either by reason of its independence or by virtue of something conjoined with it.

19.29 As for what is added there, viz., some essential priority is required to support such dependency, one could say that the priority of all three persons is one and the same, if we are speaking properly of essential priority as distinct from the priority of a hypostatic entity. However, if we broaden the notion of essential priority to *per se* priority as regards any entity be it essential or hypostatic, then the personal entity can be said to be essentially prior or, more properly, prior *per se* to everything caused. If we take priority in the second sense, then it is necessary that everything which supports or sustains some dependency be prior to the entity which depends upon it. It is not necessary, however, if we take priority in the first sense, unless the dependency be that of caused upon its cause or something similar such as the dependency of a later effect upon a prior one, or of one cause upon another cause, or of the measured upon the measure.

19.30 As for the claim [in 19.19] that only forms (i.e., essences) and not hypostatic entities are related to each other like numbers, in the sense that an essential order prevails only among them, we can distinguish two kinds of essential dependence. One is simply essential, where the notion of essence figures in both extremes, viz., the dependent term depends by reason of its essence and the supporting term supports by reason of its essence. The essential dependence of the creature, as caused, upon God, as cause, is of this type. But the dependence can be called essential in another sense, viz., when the supported term does depend by reason of its essence, but that on which it depends is not an essence but an entity distinct from the essence, for instance, a personal or hypostatic entity.

19.31 As for the added remark that the term on which something depends must be perfect, one could argue that perfection, like entity, pertains equivocally to both an essential and a hypostatic entity. Nevertheless, properly speaking, perfection seems to belong only to quidditative entity, for the hypostatic entity is not that by which something is formally perfected but that according to which [a person] receives perfection or at least ends up with the perfection received. And in this sense, one would have to deny this statement "It is necessary that the term supporting the dependence be perfect," for it suffices that the imperfection that marks the dependent be incompatible with it.

19.32 From this the answer to the objection to the minor [in

19.20] appears clear. If "perfection" be taken in its proper and unextended sense, this proposition must be denied "If some entity were the reason why every imperfection is excluded, it would be perfect or a pure perfection," for whatever can be really identical with something that is simply perfect cannot be in any way imperfect and still it is not necessary that it be simply perfect if we consider it precisely in its formal meaning.

2. Second Proof

[11] 19.33 [Statement of the Proof] Second, our proposed thesis can be shown as follows. In beings there is some dependence of the communicable nature *qua* communicable upon the suppositum* or hypostasis* to whom it is communicated; therefore, what ultimately supports this dependence is the incommunicable.

19.34 Explanation of the antecedent. Some natures like the substantial have their own *per se* suppositum, and here there is an identity of nature and suppositum[13]; neither does the nature depend upon something extrinsic to itself as its suppositum. Other natures because of their imperfection do not have their own intrinsic or *per se* suppositum but require an extrinsic one. Thus the nature of an accident requires the suppositum of the substance, and there its dependency ends with a *per accidens* suppositum, since it can have none that is *per se*. But here the nature is not identical *per se* with such a suppositum *per accidens* because they pertain to different categories. But in this case there is a union that takes the place of this identity insofar as possible, namely, an actual dependence on the part of the nature and the actual sustaining of that nature and its dependency on the part of the suppositum. What it means for that nature to be actually dependent upon a suppositum then is simply that it be communicated to this as its suppositum, namely in the way this nature is able to have such, for unlike substance, it cannot have such *per se* but only *per accidens*.

19.35 The principal entailment is manifest. Since the suppositum is *per se* incommunicable, the nature's dependence as communicable will be to a suppositum that is *per se* incommunicable. And because a divine person is in the truest sense incommunicable, indeed the only thing incommunicable by a positive entity, as we shall point out in [19.69 of] the third article, there is no incompatibility on its

---

[13] Cf. Duns Scotus, *Ord.* I, d.2, nn.376-81 (II, 344-46); III, d.1, q.1, n.5 (ed. Vivès XIV, 16-17).

part in supporting the dependence of a nature as communicable, thus playing the role not of its intrinsic or *per se* suppositum, but only of one that is extrinsic and of a different nature.

[12] 19.36 [Objection] It might be objected that no nature could depend upon a divine person as its extrinsic suppositum because the person cannot be informed *per accidens* by any nature in the way the suppositum of the substance is informed by an accident and becomes the *per accidens* suppositum of the accident's nature.

19.37 Furthermore, the accident's dependence is *per se* upon the singular or individual substance and not upon the suppositum *qua* suppositum, namely, on what being a hypostasis or suppositum adds to being an individual, for that is only a negation, it seems, and a negation is not adequate ground for supporting any dependency.

19.38 Confirmation: The individual nature assumed by the Word supports the dependence of the accident in the same way it would if it were not assumed. But as assumed it is no longer a hypostasis or suppositum of itself; therefore, when it is not assumed, its being a hypostasis or suppositum would not be the *per se* reason for supporting the accident's dependency.

You cannot say that when the nature is assumed, the dependence of the accident which inheres in it is now supported by the person who assumed the nature, for the dependence of the accident consists in its inhering. But an accident of the assumed nature does not inhere in the person assuming the nature.

19.39 [Solution of the objections] To the first [in 19.36]. For the incommunicable to support the dependency of some nature distinct from its own, it is enough that to do so is not something incompatible with it. Whether some nature other than that possessed by the incommunicable can actually depend upon it will be treated in [19.73ff. of] the following article.

19.40 What of the claim that the incommunicable, to be the suppositum of an extrinsic nature, must be informable by it (as sub-
[13] stance is informable by accident)? I reply: There are two relations involved in an accident's inherence in a substance. One is that of form to the informable; here substance is the recipient and the potential term (potential, at least, in a qualified sense). The other is the accident's dependence upon the substance; here substance is essentially prior and the accident naturally posterior.

No nature can be related to the Word in the first way, for this would imply potentiality and therefore imperfection in the Word. The second sort of relationship, however, is possible, for all it requires in the Word is *per se* priority, and it is not incompatible that the Word have such a priority over every created nature. Here the dictum "God is that with reference to which every created substance is a quasi-accident" applies. For even though the accident-to-substance relationship of a qualified form to an informable subject is inapplicable, the relationship that a nature, posterior and extrinsically communicable, can have to a divine person is the sort of relationship the accidental nature bears to the suppositum of a substance.

19.41 To the second objection [in 19.37] one could say that an individual substance is incommunicable insofar as "incommunicable" is opposed to universal, which is communicable to many, but not insofar as all communicability is ruled out including that of form, be it the partial form (said to be communicated to informed matter) or the total form, i.e., the quiddity or nature (said to be communicated to the person or suppositum that shares it). Incommunicable in this second sense is not the mark of every individual substance, but only of that which is not a partial or total form. Such is what ultimately has the form or the informed being and what in turn is not the form or *principium quo** of being. This is a hypostasis or suppositum. Consequently, while the dependence of the accident is somehow upon the singular substance it only ends ultimately with the singular as incommunicable. For if it depends on the singular substance as communicable, since this substance is the being of that to which it is communicated, the dependence only ends with the latter.[14]

[14] 19.42 I do not mean by this that the communicable substance in turn depends upon something incommunicable, and this is the reason why the accident depends ultimately not upon the communicable but upon this other. For the singular communicable substance does not depend upon the suppositum of the substance, since the substance and the suppositum in this case are identical.[15] I mean

---

[14] Cf. ibid., III, d.1, q.1, nn.5-11 (ed. Vivès XIV, 16-28); I, d.2, nn.376-81 (II, 344-46).

[15] When Scotus says that the substantial nature is identical with its *suppositum*, he does not mean that the twofold negation in which the *suppositum* consists (*Ord.* I, d.2, nn.376-81; II, 344-46) is really identical with the nature; he wants to say that the singular nature which is the basis for the twofold negation and is constituted by a haecceity is absolutely identical with the nature absolutely considered (*Ord.* II, d.3, q.1, nn.7-10; ed. Vivès XII, 48-55; q.6, nn.9ff.; ibid., I, 32ff.).

rather that what depends ultimately upon a communicable singular substance actually does depend upon something incommunicable, since the communicable is the being or the nature of something incommunicable, and whatever depends upon the being of something or someone ultimately depends on the individual to which or to whom that being belongs. The incommunicable, however, never functions as anyone's being or nature; hence what depends upon the incommunicable requires no further dependence on some subject having the incommunicable as its being or nature.

19.43 As for the argument [in 19.37] that all that the notion of suppositum adds to the notion of singular substance is a negation, I reply: Even if this be so, at least this [ontological] priority obtains, viz., it must have such a negation before it can function as the ultimate subject on which the accident depends. Neither is it incongruous that the negation of some imperfection in a subject be prior to the fact that something posterior depend upon it. "Not to be irrational" pertains to man before "to be white" does. Such a negation is an immediate consequence of what the definition of man affirms, and this would be so even if "to be white" never did or never could pertain to him.

19.44 As for the claim that negation is no adequate ground for supporting any dependency, I reply: To say "it depends ultimately" asserts two things: (a) dependence upon some term, and (b) there is nothing further on which it depends. To be the term upon which something depends is a positive notion, whereas the idea of its being ultimate is not, since this denies the term is communicable, for otherwise the dependency would not end here. For example, if one accident depended on another as some say color depends on a surface, the color would not depend ultimately upon the surface but upon what has this surface [i.e., the bodily substance]. And even if color did not depend upon the substance but was just a mode of being it had, the ultimate dependence would still end only with the substance.

19.45 To the confirmation [in 19.38] it would be said that the accident of the assumed nature [depends on the Word insofar as the accident depends on the substance assumed by the Word].

3. Proofs Proposed by Others

[15]   19.46 [Statement of the Proofs] Some[16] defend the thesis proposed on these grounds: The divine person contains the perfection

---

[16] Thomas, *Summa theol.* III, q.2, aa.2-3 (IV, 21-25); William of Ware, *Sent.* III, d.1, q.1.

QUESTION NINETEEN

of any created person or suppositum eminently; therefore he could supply for the role any such suppositum would play in sustaining that nature.

19.47 Besides, every created nature is in obediential potency* as regards a divine person; therefore a divine person could sustain any such nature.

19.48 [These reasons are defective] The first reason [in 19.46] seems inadequate on this ground: While a divine person does contain virtually every created being by reason of his essence, he does not seem to contain even one by reason of his personal property. If he did, by the same token he would virtually contain every single created entity and thus his personal property would itself be formally infinite. In Question Five, which dealt with this subject, we showed this was not so.

19.49 Besides, if the personal property did contain all created entity virtually, it could be, it seems, the formal basis of creating, a claim denied earlier [in Question Eight].

19.50 The second argument [in 19.47] also seems defective. The obediential potency of a creature has reference to the omnipotence of the creator and is common to all three persons. Therefore the way the Son supports his created nature in virtue of omnipotence is common to all three.[17] But the support by the person united to the nature is proper to the Son. The fact that the nature is in obediential potency as regards the person, therefore, does not entail that this person can sustain it hypostatically but only causally, namely as efficient cause.

4. Objection to the Conclusion of this Article

[16] 19.51 Against the conclusion of this article, it is objected in the first place that if the union itself is real, then it must have a real term. But the [personal] property and the essence are one and the same thing in reality, and what is identical in reality is also identical in the role played as the term of this union.

19.52 Besides, only its correlative depends upon the relative as relative. Therefore, the human nature does not depend upon the Word as Word, for only the Father is the correlative of the Word.

19.53 Reply to the first [in 19.51]: The formal distinction* between a relation and the essence provides sufficient ground for saying that the property and not the essence is the formal term of the real union. The objection does seem to be effective, however,

---

[17] Cf. Duns Scotus, *Ord.* III, d.1, q.1, n.4 (ed. Vivès XIV, 11-12).

against those who claim the essence and the constitutive property of the person are both really and formally identical.[18]

19.54 As for the second [in 19.52], one can reply by denying the antecedent. For it is one thing to depend on something relative as its correlative and quite another to depend on the Word, who is relative. For though the human nature assumed by the Word does depend upon him as Word, it does not depend upon him as its correlative.

ARTICLE III
The Possibility of Such a Union on the Part of the Assumed Nature

[17]   19.55 [Two points to be investigated] As for the third article, it is certain, according to Damascene,[19] that the Word assumed an individual nature, yet one which lacked its own personality since this could not be reconciled with the assumption of a nature in the unity of the Person of the Word. But if the nature's own individuality were formally its own personality, its individuality could not exist without its personality.

For this reason, we must see (1) by what factor a created nature is formally and completely personalized in itself in order to see (2) whether it can lack its own personality and still be personalized by an extrinsic personality.

1. What Constitutes Created Personality?

19.56 [The view of others: human nature is constituted a person by something positive] There is some doubt as to whether personality proper is constituted formally by something positive. It seems so for the following reasons:

What is primarily incommunicable is not negation as such, for negation can pertain to anything. Therefore, if a negation is incommunicable it is only because it presupposes the incommunicability of something positive, and so what is primarily incommunicable is something positive. Now it is the personal property that is primarily incommunicable, for this is what formally constitutes the incommunicable, viz., the person.

19.57 Besides, negation is never primarily proper to anything; it is proper only because it is the consequence of some proper affirma-

---

[18] Cf. ibid., q.1, n.17 (ed. Vivès xiv, 44-45).
[19] Damascene, *De fide orth.* III, c.3: PG 94, 994; ed. Buytaert c.47, pp. 176-77.

tion. But the personal property is primarily proper. Therefore, [it is not a negation].

19.58 What is more, imperfection is excluded by something perfect or at least positive. But to depend on an extrinsic person is an imperfection. Therefore, proper personality which excludes formally such dependence must be something positive.

19.59 Confirmation: Individuality in a nature comes from something positive, for singularity excludes the imperfection of internal division; hence the singular is called an "individual," i.e., something indivisible into more than one. In an analogous way, to be a person in oneself excludes dependence upon an extrinsic person.

[18] 19.60 [This view is untenable] But against this view are the words of Damascene[20]: "God, the Word, lacked none of those things he implanted in our nature when he formed us in the beginning; he assumed them all . . . for he was wholly united to me, so that he might bestow the grace of salvation upon the whole; for what has not been assumed, cannot be healed." He wants to say then that every positive entity our nature contains is united to the Word.

19.61 That this is possible for any nature is proved by reason. Any nature whatsoever is simply in obediential potency to depend upon a divine person. Therefore, if there were some positive entity which made the nature a person in its own right, then this entity would have been assumed by the Word and thus Christ's human nature would be invested with a dual personality, which is impossible. For if it were personalized by something created, this would render it formally incommunicable to another person. Hence it could not be taken up by the person of the Word, and thus be personalized in him.

19.62 Besides, if human nature formally became a person by reason of some positive entity, the Word could not put off the nature he had assumed without either letting it remain depersonalized (which seems incongruous) or else giving it some new entity by which it would have created personality. But this too is impossible. This could be no accidental entity, since an accident is not the formal reason why a substance is a person. Neither could this entity be substantial, be it matter, form, or a composite substance; for then it would no longer have the nature it had before, but it would have another matter, form or composite substance.[21]

[20] Ibid., c.6: PG 94, 1006; ed. Buytaert c.50, p. 188.
[21] Cf. Duns Scotus, *Ord.* III, d.1, q.1, nn.5-11 (ed. Vivès XIV, 16-28); d.5, q.2, n.4 (ibid., 228).

[19]   19.63 [Scotus' own opinion] Therefore, we can say that the formal reason our nature is invested with a created personality is not something positive; for in addition to singularity we find no positive entity that renders the singular nature incommunicable. All that is added to singularity is the negation of dependence or incommunicability, the denial that it is given over to someone.

19.64 Negation of communicability or dependence can be understood in three ways. As we can conceive of dependence as actual, potential, or dispositional, so too with its negation.

The negation of actual dependence is the simple or bare denial of dependence. The denial of its possibility adds the note of impossibility. The third implies a contrary inclination or disposition. For example, a colorless or transparent surface is not white in the first way, since whiteness is only denied of it; an angel is not white in the second way, since it would be impossible for it to be white; a stone not up in the air illustrates the third way; not only does it lack any disposition to remain up; it has the opposite inclination to remain down.

19.65 To the case at hand: speaking of dependence upon an extrinsic hypostasis, especially a divine person, we can say that the simple negation of such actual dependence does not suffice to make one a person in his own right, for the soul of Peter is not dependent in this way and yet it is not a person.

19.66 The second negation is not found to be true of any created nature able to be a person, for nothing in it excludes the possibility of depending upon a divine person. Quite the contrary, every positive entity in such a nature is in obediential potency to depend upon such a person, and consequently this sort of negation does not constitute a created person.

19.67 Neither does the third type of negation alone suffice, since the nature even as assumed is characterized by such a negation. Being of the same type as my own nature, [Christ's] assumed nature has the same kind of dispositions and natural inclinations as mine, and thus has a natural aptitude to subsist in itself with no inclination by nature to depend upon an extrinsic person. Neither is it incongruous that the possibility be present without a corresponding disposition, since the same situation holds good for supernatural forms. And if there is any potency in the recipient to have such forms, there is still no natural inclination for them, since such an inclination properly speaking only exists in regard to a form which perfects naturally.

19.68 Therefore, a double negation is required to have a created personality, namely, the conjunction of the first and the third type. The third is habitual, as it were, and is found in the created nature necessarily whether this nature be a person in its own right or is personalized through an extrinsic person. But the absence of any actual dependence together with the absence of any natural inclination to so depend make for a complete personality of one's own.[22]

[20] 19.69 [Reply to the arguments for the first opinion] One answer suffices for all the arguments [in 19.56-59] claiming that one's own created personality is formally constituted by something positive. "To be communicable" or "to depend in this way" would admittedly be simply inconsistent with my being if, and only if, this being did possess some positive entity of its own which rendered it incommunicable or unable to be dependent. However, "to be communicated" or "to depend" can be repugnant in a qualified sense to something in virtue of a negation alone, for as long as the negation holds true, its opposite affirmation cannot be true. But this does not mean the affirmative situation is simply impossible unless the subject is such that it necessarily entails such a negation, and in this case the negation would be simply proper to it; otherwise the negation would be proper to the subject only in a qualified sense. For a negation is proper to something in the same way that its opposite affirmation is impossible. Now only a divine person has incommunicability in the first way, because he has some intrinsic entity all his own which excludes any possibility of such communication. A created nature, on the contrary, though it may subsist in itself, still does not have anything intrinsic that would make dependence [upon a divine person] impossible. Hence only a divine person has his own personality completely; a created nature personalized in itself, however, does not have such personality completely, since it does not exclude the possibility, but only the actuality, of such dependence, and it excludes this only in a qualified sense, namely, so long as the negation of actual dependence remains true.

19.70 As for the form of the argument [in 19.56] based on the notion of person, I say that simple or unqualified incommunicability, viz., that which excludes the possibility of dependence, does not pertain primarily to a negation or to any subject in virtue of a negation. Nor is such incommunicability found in a creature, even one who is a person. At best there is only a qualified incommunicability,

[22] Cf. ibid., n.10 (ed. Vivès XIV, 26-27).

viz., exclusion of actual communication to another person, and this only as long as the actual dependence is not there. Now such qualified incommunicability does not require a positive entity that is simply incommunicable, but only a positive entity as the subject of whom actual dependence is denied. On the other hand, if simple incommunicability did pertain to any negation it would only be because the negation is a consequence of some simply incommunicable positive entity.

19.71 I use the same argument against the other major premise based on dependence [in 19.58]. I grant that if the possibility of dependence is incompatible with something, this is due to some perfection or positive reason; but such is not the case with any creature. All we find there is the absence of actual dependence. For example, if an accident is given existence apart from a substance,[23] actual or possible inherence in a substance is not incompatible with it purely and simply but only in a qualified sense, namely, it cannot be present as long as the accident continues to exist apart.

19.72 In much the same way I answer the argument [in 19.57] that a negation is not what is primarily proper to anything. Unqualified incommunicability is simply proper only to what has this sort of incommunicability; but incommunicability in a qualified sense is not simply proper to its subject; it is "proper" only in the sense that it belongs to this subject alone.[24]

2. Can a Human Nature Depend upon an Extrinsic Person?

[21] 19.73 As for the second problem [in 19.55] of the third main article, some argue that to depend for one's personality on an extrinsic person is incompatible with human nature: first, because it is a substantial nature; second, because it cannot have something intrinsic that would be grounds for such dependence; third, because a human nature possesses an intrinsic reason why it cannot depend in this fashion.

19.74 First argument: What substantial nature is meant to give to the suppositum is being in an unqualified sense; hence it does not presuppose such being. But a nature which depends upon an extrin-

---

[23] See Glossary: "*eucharist*" for an example of separated accident.

[24] He does not answer the confirmation. See *Ord.* III, d.1, q.1, n.17 (ed. Vivès XIV, 44-45), and II, d.3, q.2 (ed. Vivès XII, 77-80), where he answers that indivisibility is positive because by it division is simply repugnant to the nature; however, to be assumed is not simply repugnant to the personalized nature. Therefore, there is no parity.

sic suppositum does presuppose such being in the latter since it presupposes the being of the suppositum's own nature, a nature which belongs to it even before the dependent nature does.

Proof of the antecedent: As an accident is entity in a qualified sense, so a substantial nature is entity purely and simply. Now the sort of entity a thing is formally is the sort of entity it gives. Thus an accident gives only qualified entity and presupposes a being that is simply such; a substantial nature on the contrary gives being in an unqualified sense and does not presuppose such being.

19.75 Second argument [of 19.73]: Everything dependent possesses an intrinsic ground for its dependence. But human nature does not and cannot have some intrinsic ground for depending in this way. Therefore, [it is not dependent in this fashion].

19.76 The major appears clear inductively if you consider one by one the various types of causal dependence.

Reason also proves the same. If one thing does not have some reason for dependence which another lacks, then the first would be no more dependent than the second. Now my nature does not depend upon the Word with this sort of dependence; therefore, neither does the assumed nature [of Christ] if it has no intrinsic reason for doing so.

Proof of the major: The independent does not become dependent, or vice versa, without some change or mutation. Now only an absolute form is the *per se* term of mutation; therefore, if a nature becomes dependent it is only because it acquired some absolute form as the ground for such dependence, a form which it loses when it regains its independence.

19.77 Proof of the minor: The Word could put off his human nature without anything absolute in it being destroyed. But if the reason why it depended on the Word were something absolute, then it would be necessary to destroy this absolute entity to make the nature independent [or a person in its own right].

Two natures of the same kind should have the same reason or ground for depending hypostatically on the same person or suppositum. Now Christ's nature is the same in kind as my own, and my nature does not have any reason or ground why it should depend hypostatically upon the Word; otherwise, for me to subsist as a human person would be doing violence to my nature.

19.78 Third argument [of 19.73]: The human personality that can pertain to this nature is really identical with this nature; therefore, as long as it continues to exist, this human nature has this personality. But a personality of its own is adequate ground for excluding dependence upon an extrinsic person. Hence [it cannot depend in this way].

Proof of the antecedent: It is certain that this human nature can have a personality of its own. Now this personality cannot be something other than this nature. It cannot be an accident, because an accident cannot be the reason why a substance is a person. Neither can it be some substance other than this nature; if it were, then this other would either be a composite substance or a substantial part. Now one composite substance is never the formal reason why another composite substance is a person. If the personality were a substantial part, then unless both substantial parts remained, the nature would not be the same.

[22] 19.79 [Scotus' own opinion] We should never assume two things are formally incompatible unless this is manifest from their definitions or it can be proved that they include such incompatibility or that such incompatibility is a consequence of what they are. But in none of these ways is human nature incompatible with dependence upon another person. Hence we should not assume such dependence is simply impossible so far as the nature is concerned.

The major is proved because everything should be assumed to be possible if there is no evidence of impossibility.

19.80 The first part of the minor is shown from the very notions of what we are discussing. It is more evident in the case of human nature, but the notion of the sort of dependence involved can be described as follows: "It is the dependence of a nature as communicable upon a person proper to another nature in such a way that this person is that upon which the nature depends."

19.81 This description is explained as follows: First, the expression "as communicable." Something can be communicated in such a way that the recipient becomes that which is communicated, for instance, the way the universal is communicated to an individual. In another way something is communicated as a formal principle of being and this can happen in two ways, one as a partial form which is communicated to informed matter and thereby to the composite constituted through the form; the other as a total form or quiddity is communicated to the suppositum, for example, humanity to Socrates.

In our case "as communicable" is understood in this third way, viz., the total form is communicated in such a way that the one having it can be said to be formally this sort of thing. Now when the nature is a suppositum in its own right, the suppositum is said to be this sort of nature, not because the nature depends upon it, but because there is a *per se* identity. But when the suppositum is not proper to the nature there can be no *per se* identity. What can be there in its place, however, is perfect dependence of the nature and on the part of the suppositum a perfect sustaining or supporting of this dependence. Such a suppositum, since it is *per se* the suppositum of another nature, is not the *per se* suppositum of the dependent nature. Since what is *per se* is prior to what is not, it follows that the suppositum or person has his own nature prior to having this dependent one, which is a kind of adventitious or second nature.

[23] 19.82 That dependence of this sort is not repugnant to human nature can be shown somehow by a proof similar to that given in the second article [in 19.12-14].

A divine person on his own can be the supporting term for some kind of dependence, not that of causation or, in short, of that requiring formal perfection in the term, but only that sort of dependence that a communicable nature has upon the incommunicable which sustains it. Therefore, it must be possible for some nature to depend in this way, for it would not be possible to support such dependence if some nature did not have a corresponding possibility of depending. But to depend in this way is not more repugnant to human nature than to any other nature.

19.83 We show this secondly in this way: An accident has this sort of dependence upon the suppositum of the substance in which it inheres. Although in this case the dependence is conjoined with inherence, the reason for dependence seems prior to the ground for inherence even as the essential priority by reason of which the term supports such dependence seems prior to its ability to be informed by or to receive accidents, which is the reason why they can inhere in it. There seems to be no contradiction, then, in thinking that some nature may be able to depend as communicable without inhering in that on which it depends, and this is precisely the kind of dependence we are assuming in the present case.

Confirmation: According to the Philosopher in the *Metaphysics*[25] one meaning of "quality" is the substantial difference; consequently, it is not repugnant to a substance to have a mode of existence like that of a quality.

19.84 We show this thirdly as follows: An accident can have the mode of substance [i.e., it can exist without inhering in a substance],

[25] Aristotle, *Metaph.* v, c.14 (1020a35).

although not perfectly in the sense that it would be repugnant for it to depend on a subject, but in some analogous way, viz., insofar as it does not actually depend; this is seen in the case of a separated accident.* By the same token, it seems that a substance can have the mode of an accident, although not perfectly in the sense that it would depend or inhere in a subject, but in an analogous fashion, viz., in the sense of actually depending upon an extrinsic suppositum.[26]

[24] 19.85 [Reply to the arguments for the opposing view] To the arguments in favor of the contrary opinion:

To the first [in 19.74]: I admit that the substantial nature gives substantial being, but it is only when the suppositum is *per se* that the substantial nature gives the suppositum its first being. But when its suppositum is not *per se* but belongs to another nature, it is this other nature that gives the suppositum its first being.

19.86 To the claim that what gives unqualified being to some subject does not presuppose such being in the subject, I answer: Some being may indeed be unqualified being in itself and yet, if its suppositum is not something it has in its own right, then it does not give that suppositum unqualified being in every sense.

19.87 To the second argument [in 19.75]: Something can be a ground for dependence in one of two ways. One would be if actual dependence necessarily accompanies or follows it. Another way would be if what necessarily accompanies it is not actual dependence but the aptitude to depend, and when actual dependence is present, the reason or ground is the proximate foundation for such.

Dependence of a creature on God is of the first type, because here the foundation of the dependence necessarily involves actual dependence at all times. The dependence of an effect upon a secondary cause is of the second type, since the effect could always be produced immediately by the first cause, and thus not be actually dependent upon the secondary cause even though the aptitude to depend is always there. The major is true then not of "a ground for dependence" understood in the first way, but only if we understand it indiscriminately of the first or the second way.[27]

19.88 The first proof of the major [in 19.76] from an inductive consideration of the types of causal dependence proves nothing more.

---

[26] Cf. Duns Scotus, *Ord.* III, d.1, q.1, nn.6ff. (ed. Vivès XIV, 21ff.).
[27] Cf. ibid., IV, d.1, q.1, nn.16ff. (ed. Vivès XVI, 49ff.).

[25] 19.89 To the second proof of the major which claims the dependent has some reason for dependence lacking in what is not dependent, I say this: It is necessary to have such if "reason for dependence" means the *formal* reason, which is the dependence itself, since without actual dependence nothing can depend. But if "reason for dependence" refers to some foundation of the dependence in the way that whiteness is the foundation for similarity, I deny that there is any more need for such in something dependent than there is in what is not actually dependent but has an aptitude to depend. For example, an accident when it is in a subject has no more grounds for depending than when it exists apart, for its own nature is the proximate ground for depending in this way. Nothing more needs to be added except the "formal reason" or actual dependence itself. Something analogous holds for the nature that is assumed and the nature that is not.

19.90 The third proof [in 19.76] seems to establish more, viz., that what is actually dependent always has some absolute entity as the fundamental reason for its depending. And we must simply deny the proposition on which the proof is based, viz., "Only an absolute form is the *per se* term of mutation." There is movement from place to place, and yet place is not an absolute form. That this is not contrary to what the Philosopher says in the *Physics*[28] was proved earlier in the [Eleventh] question on bodies and place.

19.91 Now the minor [of the second argument, viz., that human nature does not and cannot have some intrinsic ground for depending hypostatically] is not true in the sense that the major is true, namely where "ground" or "reason" may mean indiscriminately either a formal reason for depending or a fundamental reason which necessarily entails either actual or at least aptitudinal dependence. For the assumed nature has a formal reason, viz., the dependence itself, and it also has a fundamental reason. Indeed, the nature itself is the proximate fundamental ground of the dependence although what is a necessary consequence of the nature is not actual but aptitudinal dependence. Neither does the first proof of the minor establish anything more, for if the Word put off his human nature, nothing absolute in it would perish. Hence it never had anything absolute which was the necessary reason for its actually depending on the Word. But something absolute was the proximate subject of such dependence and it can remain without such depend-

---

[28] Aristotle, *Physic.* v, c.1 (225b5-10, 206-211a).

ence in the way that the foundation can exist without the relation if the latter is not a necessary consequence of the foundation.

19.92 As for the other proof [of the minor in 19.77] I say: While it is true that two natures of the same kind have the same aptitude to depend upon the Word, it does not follow that if one actually does depend, the other must also. The case of an accident separated from its subject and one conjoined with its subject makes this clear. Now although my nature does not actually depend upon the Word hypostatically, nevertheless it does have the same aptitude to depend as the nature he assumed.[29]

Reply to the Initial Argument

19.93 To the argument at the beginning [in 19.1] I say that while not every form of dependence justifies predicating what depends of the subject on which it depends, nevertheless the dependence of a nature as communicable upon a suppositum that sustains it hypostatically is sufficient for predicating the dependent nature of the person or suppositum on which it depends. This is clear from the case of the accident that depends in this way upon the suppositum of the substance of which it is also predicated. And just as the predication of the accident of the subject, though true, is not *per se*, as would be the case if the nature were predicated of its own suppositum, so also the predication of human nature of the Word is not *per se*.

[29] He does not answer explicitly the third argument; cf. *supra*, 19.78.

Question Twenty

DOES A PRIEST WHO IS OBLIGED TO SAY A MASS FOR EACH OF TWO DIFFERENT PEOPLE SATISFY HIS OBLIGATION BY SAYING ONE MASS FOR BOTH?

[1] 20.1 Does a priest, obliged to say a mass for one person and also obliged to say a mass for another person, adequately satisfy his obligation by saying one mass for both?

Arguments Pro and Con

It is argued that he does not:
One obliged to a greater good does not satisfy his obligation by performing a lesser good. But that is what happens here, for two masses represent a greater good than one does. Besides, one mass benefits a person more if said for him alone than if said simultaneously for himself and another.

20.2 Against this opinion it is argued:
He who pays more than he is obliged to abundantly satisfies his obligation. But one mass is a greater good than the two stipends that oblige him to the two persons who gave them, for the good of the mass stems from the virtue of the sacrifice which is of infinite value and sufficient for an infinity of persons. For when Christ, who offers himself in this sacrifice, offered himself on the cross he made adequate satisfaction for an infinity of sins. Therefore [one mass is abundantly sufficient for two].

Body of the Question

[2] 20.3 Here a preliminary observation is necessary, viz., that it seems probable that a mass has value not only in virtue of the merit or action of the celebrant [*ex opere operantis*]* but also in virtue of the sacrifice or work performed [*ex opere operato*].* In other words, its value is derived not only from the personal merit of the priest-celebrant but also from the merit of the universal Church in whose name the ordinary celebrant offers the sacrifice. Otherwise the mass of an unworthy priest, who personally gains no merit but

rather demerit, would benefit no one in the Church. But the common opinion rejects this and reasonably so according to those words of John: "The bread I will give is my flesh, for the life of the world."[1] Therefore, every time Christ, the supreme priest, offers [the sacrifice of the mass], the bread he gives (namely, his flesh) is the life of the world.

From this it follows that to solve the question three points must be studied[2]: (1) Does one mass said for two have as much value for each as it would have if said for one alone, and this in virtue of the celebrant's personal merit? (2) Does it have as much value in virtue of the merit of the universal Church offering it? (3) Does the priest satisfy his debt to both persons?

ARTICLE I
The Value of the Mass in virtue of the Celebrant's Personal Merit

[3] 20.4 [Three ways in which prayer can be of benefit] As for the first point, we must recognize that of all meritorious works, the merit of prayer is more readily applicable to others, for prayer of itself conciliates and placates God, and it does this for the person for whom the prayer is being offered in particular. But we see that merit and especially prayer can be of benefit to someone in three ways:

(1) In a most special way it always benefits the person praying if he is in the state of grace, for his motive is good and he is performing a good work. This motive and this work do not belong to the person being prayed for in the same way that they do to the person praying. Neither can one reasonably give away this merit of his in favor of another, since he is obliged in charity to love himself more than another. What is more, it might even be that he could not give it to another without sinning.

(2) In a most general way prayer benefits the Church as a whole, for the one praying must have the habitual intention of excluding no one and including everyone in the Church.

(3) And in some intermediate fashion prayer must benefit the person being prayed for. That it does not do so in the most special way is clear from what was said above. Neither does it help him only in the most general way in which it benefits everyone. Otherwise those special prayers of the Church for the living and the dead

---

[1] John 6:52.

[2] M₂ mistakenly inserts this paragraph after 20.4.

and also for different sorts of living persons, such as benefactors, friends, and others, would be in vain. Yet in the Roman Missal we find prayers for different persons and groups and states of life. Such special prayers, I say, would be in vain if they had no more value for such persons than for any member of the Church in general.

[4] Our special problem in this first article, then, concerns this third type of merit.

20.5 And we can say that *one mass said for two does not have as much value for each as it would have if said for one alone.*

This can be shown as follows: In full justice what corresponds adequately to finite merit is a limited reward. In addition to the good due to the Church at large and that due in a most special way to the person praying, which must always be included in the reward due to prayer, I refer only to that good which is due in that third or intermediary way to the one prayed for in virtue of the merit of the petitioner. Now this good is of limited degree. And nothing beyond this is due to anyone in this third way by virtue of the petitioner's merit. But if all of the good due in this way is awarded to one of the two, none will be given to the other. Hence, if some good is given to the latter, then it follows that all the good due in this way to the prayer will not be given to the other.

20.6 [First confirmation] What confirms this is that to an equal amount of merit an equal good or reward is due, and this is true of what is due in any of the three ways, generally, specially, or intermediately. Now as for personal merit, one who celebrates with equal devotion performs an equally meritorious work, and one can be equally devout in celebrating for one in particular as in celebrating for two at once. Therefore, in virtue of one's personal merit, the good due to a mass said for one is equal to the good due to a mass said for two. And in the latter case, if all of this were due to one of the two, nothing would be due to the other, since whatever might be given to him would not be included in that good which corresponds adequately to the celebrant's merit.

[5] 20.7 [Objections] One could challenge the major [in 20.6] on the grounds that to merit which is both intensively and extensively equal, a good equal in both ways is due. Now if one prays for two simultaneously, though his merit is intensively equal to his merit when he prays for one, it is extensively greater because applied to more than one. Hence the reward due to it though intensively equal is extensively greater, since it is bestowed on both.

20.8 A similar response may be given to the major of the first argument [in 20.5], namely, to the claim that to merit of a limited degree corresponds a limited amount of good. This holds good only of what is uniform in both respects, i.e., intensively and extensively. For even though the merit is extended to many and hence the reward is due to many, it need not be intensively diminished because it is bestowed on more than one.

20.9 This is explained first as follows: Spiritual good is analogous to a spirit which is whole and entire wherever it may be and is not communicated only in part. Hence a spiritual good is communicated without division and so is not diminished although bestowed on many.

20.10 This can also be shown from an example where one would not so clearly expect to find it. For even certain corporeal things—which would be less likely than spiritual things to have this characteristic—can be communicated to many without diminution. The light of a candle illumines several objects just as brightly as it would have illumined any one of them alone; a voice strikes the ears of many listeners just as forcibly as it would strike one alone.

20.11 And thirdly, the authority [of Gratian] confirms this. In *De Consecratione*, distinction 5, *Non mediocriter*[3] Jerome[4] is quoted as saying, among other things, that "when a mass or a prayer is said for one hundred souls, each receives no less than when it is said for one alone."

[6] 20.12 [These objections are invalid] One can argue that these objections [in 20.7-11] do not refute the reasons given above [in 20.5ff.], for the major premises of both arguments are simply true when interpreted both extensionally and intensionally. Equal merit no more deserves a numerically greater good than an intensively greater good. In every case of just retribution or commutation, a greater number of equal goods are considered equivalent to one intensively greater good. Therefore, if an intensively greater good is not due to this merit, neither is an extensively greater good. Otherwise the sum total of these many goods would represent a good greater than any one of them taken singly, and hence in justice would constitute a good greater than any one of them alone.

20.13 Confirmation: Otherwise a prayer offered in the third way for all the souls in purgatory would have the same value for each as if offered for one alone. And if his charity is not inordinate, every-

---

[3] *Corpus Iuris Canonici*, ed. A. Friedberg, Lipsiensis secunda, I, Graz, 1959, 1418, De consec. D.5, c.24.

[4] Jerome, *De regula monach.*, c.13: PL 30, 351-55.

one who prays for one should pray for all, for he should ask for the good of the greatest number obtainable with a single act, if this could be accomplished without detriment to the good of any single one.

20.14 You will reply: In terms of satisfaction, prayer has not the same value for many as it has for one. The punishment due to one is not remitted if something equivalent is not paid.

Answer: If this be so, one could just as well ask that the same initial grace given to one be given to any number of sinners, for here no satisfaction of punishment is required but only a reconciliation with God and the request of a good from him.

20.15 Again, just as many separate punishments are equivalent to one greater punishment and are only remitted by a greater work of satisfaction or by several such works, so it seems that the request for many separate goods is equivalent to one request for a greater good and could be asked for and obtained only in return for several meritorious works or for one that is of greater merit. And if something suffices to obtain a good why does it not also suffice to remove what is evil? Indeed the former seems to be a greater request.

[7] 20.16 [Second confirmation] A second confirmatory argument for our thesis is this: In the case of human friendship, one who begs a favor for one person alone will obtain a greater good for him than if he begs for many. If he asks for one, he will obtain the good he asked for, whereas if he asks for many, either he will not obtain the favor for all, or else each will not receive as much as one alone would. And this happens according to the just law of friendship.

20.17 [Third confirmation] A third confirmatory argument is this: The will as meritorious cause seems to be less, not more, efficacious than when it functions as cause that elicits or commands something. For as meritorious, it plays only a dispositional role with respect to the principal agent, whereas as commanding or eliciting an act it functions as the principal agent. Now as principal agent, the will does not cause simultaneously in each of many an effect equal to what it would cause in one alone. Simultaneous friendship for many is never as intense as friendship for one, as Book VIII of the *Ethics*[5] makes clear. And when the will commands the operation of several subordinate faculties it is not with the same intensity as when it commands but one, for will's intensity diminishes in commanding several acts. Analogously, then, the will would seem to merit an intensively lesser good for each when it merits for many.

[5] Aristotle, *Ethica ad Nic.* VIII, c.7 (1158a11-14).

20.18 You may object that this is so only when distraction about the many diminishes devotion, but if the devotion remains the same, it need not be that for the many one merits a lesser good than for a single person alone.

To this I reply: Distraction is not necessarily present because the mass is celebrated for several, for the celebrant need not actually think about those for whom he intends especially to pray. It is enough that he thought of them before and has offered such an intention to God. After that, it suffices to remember them in general, for God accepts his offering and his devotion for those for whom he earlier decided to offer it.

While it is true in this case that actual attention to each is diminished by reason of the multitude, for his attention is directed to them only in general, nevertheless his devotion (which is a movement of the mind to God) does not necessarily diminish. For example, one does not celebrate the mass for all saints less devoutly than a mass in honor of one. While he may attend less distinctly to each saint, still his attention to all of them in general suffices for devotion that is not only equal to but greater than the devotion of a celebrant who attends only to one, unless perhaps the one be he who contains eminently that which is matter of devotion to all, i.e., the Triune God.

And so when one prays for a needy community or group to obtain what they need, a greater compassion can be present and hence a greater desire to get what is needed than if one is praying for but one indigent person. And in such a case devotion is not diminished even though one's actual or distinct attention to each is decreased.

In such a case, therefore, the reason why each receives a lesser good is not diminution of devotion but the fact that it is a limited good that corresponds to one's merit, and this is true of what is due to one in the most special way, or is due only in the most general way, or is due in the third or intermediary way.

And that is why in the case of what is due in this third way, which is the one we are speaking of, the greater the number of beneficiaries the less each benefits individually.

[8] 20.19 [To the arguments in support of the objections] Answer to the arguments to the contrary [in 20.7-11].

To the first based on the analogy with a spirit [in 20.9], I say that while a spirit may not be divided extensively, one is distinguished numerically from another. There is an individual soul for each animated body and together they possess a natural goodness that is ex-

QUESTION TWENTY

tensively greater than any one of them singly. Furthermore, such goodness is even equivalent to a goodness that is intensively greater, according to that text from *The Trinity*[6]: "Two men represent something greater than one man." Plurality in God, then, differs from plurality in creatures. In creatures two are more than one. In God, however, this is not the case. That is why Augustine adds: "The Father and Son together are not greater than the Father alone." Again, many goods of the spirit are of greater value and therefore require either more good or a greater good in return. He who by his prayer merits or deserves to bring to life one dead person does not deserve by that same prayer to bring to life all of the dead. Therefore, I say that while a spiritual good is communicated without quantitative division, extensively there is a distinction in the sense that the good which different persons receive is different, and to obtain it a corresponding different merit is required, and this is the sort of thing I have in mind when I speak of something being "equal intensively."

20.20 Objection: At least a spiritual good is not communicated by parts; therefore, if two persons deserve a good in virtue of a mass one will not receive one part of it and another the other part.

Confirmation: Whoever receives a spirit receives the whole spirit. Analogously, whoever receives some spiritual good receives the whole of it.

[9] 20.21 I reply: Augustine in *The Trinity* says[7]: "In those things which are not great in mass, to be greater is to be better." Two equal goods are better than one; therefore, the goodness in them is greater, and what is greater, though it may not be actually divisible, contains many lesser goods which together are equal to it. Although the sky is actually indivisible, a greater number of smaller things would be needed to equal the whole than to equal half of it, and in these smaller things there is a distinction. Therefore, for some greater thing indivisible in itself, one could give a plurality of equivalent entities.

In a similar way in the case at hand, a good or corresponding magnitude is equal to merit of a given magnitude. Such good is indivisible in itself, but can be equivalent to many lesser goods and, therefore, it can be divided in value insofar as several lesser goods are given instead of it. Consequently, a spiritual good is not really given by parts, but rather a number of smaller goods are given,

---

[6] Augustine, *De Trin.* VII, c.6, n.11: PL 42, 945; CCSL 50, 265.
[7] Ibid., VI, c.8, n.9: PL 42, 929; CCSL 50, 238.

each of which, in comparison to the greater benefit, is of partial value.

20.22 As for the confirmation [in 20.20], I say that if it were possible to distribute the value of the same spirit among many, in the way it is possible here in regard to the good due to prayer, then a lesser good would be given to each. And perhaps a spirit also would be communicated in a lesser degree if otherwise it would exceed the proportions of the body receiving it. Perhaps the soul would not vivify in the same way every part of a body no matter how great it would grow, though it is communicated equally to one that is proportionate to it. In the case at hand, the recipient proportionate to a good given for merit is a person, and what is given to him is not given by parts.

20.23 Against the examples cited [in 20.10] counter-examples can be given. I cannot carry two weights as easily as one.

You may object that where local motion is concerned I may not be able to move many objects as easily as I am able to move a few, but the situation is different in the case of change called alteration [such as those induced by sound falling on many ears]: here one can change many as easily as a few if they are all the same distance away.

[10] To this I reply: Some changes or movements, like locomotion, are such that when they occur every part of the whole must be moved simultaneously so that one part is not changed before the other. It is to such that this text of the *Metaphysics* refers[8]: "A change is called continuous whose movement is essentially one, and the movement is one when it is indivisible in respect to time." For if one part of a continuum would move without the rest moving, its continuity would be broken. There is another type of movement, however, in which it is not necessary that every part of the whole be changed simultaneously, and this is the case with change by alteration.

Now the "mobile" [i.e., what can be moved or altered] may be a match or less than a match for the strength of the mover or agent; if it matches his strength so that the agent could not move anything more at the same time, the mobile is called an adequate object.

Now there is a difference about the adequate objects of local motion and other forms of change. In the case of movement from place to place, what matches the strength of the mover is always an entire continuum and never just a part of it, whereas in the changes through alteration it may be some part of a larger whole that

[8] Aristotle, *Metaph.* v, c.6 (1016a5).

matches the powers of the agent, so that all he can change at one time is that much and no more. But in either case, indeed where movement or change in general is concerned, a given agent can never change at one time anything that exceeds his strength but only what matches it or is included therein. By "included therein" I mean either a real part or its equivalent (i.e., something smaller could be said to be included equivalently in something greater even though the smaller is not really a part of the greater). If the mobile object is adequate or matches the agent's strength, then he could not change at one time anything greater. Neither could he simultaneously change this and something else. But he could alter two objects which together do not exceed what matches his strength. And of such things it is true to say that whether they be many or few, the agent does not alter many in any lesser measure than he would alter a few, because he does not alter his adequate mobile object to a lesser degree than he would alter a lesser mobile object; otherwise the adequate object would not be simply adequate or matched to his strength. And in this case I understand "adequate" not to mean that the agent could alter it only by exerting all his efforts, but he could change it no matter how small the effort. Such a mobile object would be completely subservient to such an agent. That the mobile be fully under the power of the mover means that passively the mobile object is completely matched to such an agent. Now the heavens, according to the Philosopher,[9] is the adequate mobile object of an Intelligence,* who could move something less even though he could not move anything greater.

[11] 20.24 Answer to the examples [in 20.10]: I say that when the recipient of alteration is proportionate to the agent, every part of it will be perfected equally, at least in the sense that when one part is perfected along with another, it is not altered less than when it alone is altered, for it is the whole that is proportionate primarily to the agent, and the plurality of parts included in the whole does not keep the action in each of them from being equally perfect any more than it prevents the action being equally perfect over the whole. But if to one proportionate subject another proportionate subject be added, it would not be necessary that it be perfected to the same extent as it would if it were the sole recipient of the agent's action.

This appears clear in the examples cited there. For light, sound, and the like are of themselves propagated spherically from their

[9] Ibid., XII, c.7 (1072a30-32).

source through the intervening medium. Therefore, no matter how small the area being affected proportionately by such an agent may be, since it is spherical, it has parts, and equal parts of the same sphere surrounding a light will be illumined with equal brightness, that is to say the brightness along one diameter of the sphere will be the same as along any other. But if one takes a sphere more remote from the candle and surrounding the first sphere, its parts will not be as brightly illumined as those of the first.

Hence the claim that many illuminable objects are illumined with equal brightness is true only when they are parts of the same adequate illuminable object, for instance, when they fall within the same sphere of light or are at the same distance from the center of illumination. But in the case we are discussing, the two persons being prayed for are not *per se* parts of one adequate recipient of the good to be awarded through prayer, but each is *per se* an adequate recipient.

[12]   20.25 Against the preceding it is argued that the reason why the second sphere is not so brightly illumined as the first is that it is further from the light, not that it is illumined simultaneously with the first. Furthermore, the second would not receive any light if the first were not illumined at the same time. Therefore, the second recipient does not receive less because another receives something at the same time, but because it is further removed from the agent. Now in the present case, there is no such separation or distance but only a distinction of recipients.

I answer: The fact that two alterable objects can be equally distant from the same agent or mover necessarily implies that they represent real or equivalent parts of one adequate object. What is spherical can always be imagined to have the agent at its center, and equal areas lying at the same distance from the center are affected the same way, whereas those at other distances are not altered to the same degree.

20.26 As for the citation from Jerome [in 20.11], the gloss[10] there provides a two-part answer. One is that his words refer to the celebrant himself so that their meaning would be that he does not receive less because he says mass for one or for many, for when his disposition is the same and his performance equally faultless, in a word, when he celebrates for many in the same way he does for one, the mass has for him the same value in the most special way.

---

[10] *Decretum Gratiani emendatum et notationibus illustratum una cum glossis Gregorii XIII Pont. Max. iussu editum* (Romae, 1582), col. 2673.

20.27 The other reply of the gloss there refers to the assertion that a mass celebrated for one hundred with a joyful heart is of no less value than one mass for each of them celebrated with anxiety. For it is premised by the remark[11]: "The singing of five psalms with purity of heart, serenity, and spiritual joy is better than the recitation of the whole Psalter with anxiety and sadness of heart." Then follows the text [in 20.11]: "When a mass or a prayer is said for one hundred," etc. Perhaps this second reply expresses best the mind of Jerome who wished to console the monks by telling them that if they were obliged to pray for many, they were not obliged to read that many psalms, for that would breed disgust. They would do better to recite fewer psalms and do so with joy; indeed, this would benefit the one praying even more if this could be reconciled with his obligation.

ARTICLE II
The Value of the Mass by reason of the Merit of the Universal Church

[13] 20.28 [Three points to be considered] There are three things to be investigated in the second article [of 20.3]: viz., (1) Has the priest the power to apply to a certain person the good due to the Church or someone in the Church in virtue of the sacrifice? (2) Can he apply such good at will? (3) Has it the same value for that person when it is applied for him and others as when it is applied for him alone?

1. Can the Priest Apply the Merit due in virtue of the Sacrifice?

20.29 [Negative view] As to the first question, it seems the priest could not. An instrument has no power to apply the action or its effect, for this is the prerogative of the principal agent. Where the virtue of the sacrifice is concerned, the priest is a mere instrument, for he behaves like an inanimate organ. Although, as regards personal merit in celebrating, he functions as a living organ, since he merits insofar as he himself lives a life of grace, as regards the good due in virtue of the sacrifice he is an organ precisely because of holy orders, and the same effect in virtue of the sacrifice results whether he be living a life of grace or not. Therefore [the priest has no power to apply the action or its effect].

20.30 A second reason is this: He to whom a good is not due has

[11] Cf. *supra*, note 4.

no right to assign or apply it to another. The good due in virtue of the sacrifice is not due to the priest as celebrant; he is but the bearer of a petition by the Church. The good due in virtue of the sacrifice is not owed to him, for the virtue of the sacrifice would remain the same even if he were in mortal sin.

20.31 [The view of Scotus] But I claim that it is somehow in the power of the priest-celebrant to apply the virtue of the sacrifice. A twofold proof from authority:

In the *Enchiridion*[12] Augustine says: "It is not to be denied that the souls of dead are refreshed when the sacrifice of the Mediator is offered for them." Hence the one offering the sacrifice can apply it to them and they can benefit from it.

In the sermon on the Chair of St. Peter he repeats this same idea[13]: "I will show how they can help the souls of their dead: let each offer for his dear ones the prayers of the saints and let him commend them to God through the intervention of the priest."

[14] 20.32 There is also an argument from analogy in favor of this view. When some good has to be distributed among each of the household members according to his need, it is reasonable that the master himself does not do this directly but entrusts it to one or more of his servants. This is general practice in well-ordered families. With equal or even greater reason, then, this method should prevail in the house of God, the Church, so that not God alone but some minister of the Church distributes the good to be given there in virtue of the sacrifice. Now no one deserves to do this more than the priest offering the sacrifice. Just as it is up to him to determine for whom in particular he intends to offer the sacrifice, so also it pertains to him to dispense or dispose of the good petitioned in virtue of the sacrifice.

20.33 [To the arguments for the negative view] As for the arguments used to prove it is not the priest's role to apply the virtue of the sacrifice, I reply:

To the first [in 20.29]: Admittedly the good requested in virtue of the sacrifice is petitioned by reason not of the priest's personal merit, but of the merit of the Church in whose name it is offered and for whose sake it is accepted. Now even though the priest is a mere organ as regards the good petitioned in this way, nevertheless by reason of his sacred orders he holds a distinguished position in the Church in virtue of which it is his function to offer and deter-

---

[12] Augustine, *Enchirid.*, c.29, n.110: PL 40, 283; CCSL 96, 108.
[13] Ps.-Augustine, *In cathedram S. Pet.* II serm.191: PL 39, 2101.

mine the value of the oblation, and in this role he is no mere organ but a minister and dispensator.

20.34 To the second [in 20.30], I say that while the good to be given in virtue of the sacrifice is not due to the priest for himself, still it is due to the Church according to his dispensation, for by his sacred orders the priest is the messenger of the bride to the groom, offering special petitions for specific persons and thus he dispenses to them what is given in virtue of such petitions.

2. Can the Priest Apply Such a Good at Will?

[15] 20.35 [Negative view] To the second question of this article [in 20.28], viz., Is the priest at liberty to distribute the good due in virtue of the sacrifice, so that it would be given especially to the one to whom he applied the virtue of the sacrifice in particular, some would say no. To be effective, his application must be made in accord with God's good pleasure, for it is God alone who bestows this good and he does so according to his own good will. It will not be given to the one for whom the priest intends it unless in making the application, the priest conforms himself to the will of God the donor.

20.36 [Scotus' own view] Against this view I argue: The priest would be devoid of any authority to apply or assign the good, it seems, if he could do so only when his intention coincided with the wishes of another, whose mind as a rule he could never be sure of. But the priest-celebrant can never be definitely sure about the will of God as to whom he may wish to give the good due in virtue of the sacrifice. God does not reveal this as a rule in a special way; neither does Scripture have anything to say about it except in a most remote and general way, which is not sufficient to reveal God's will as regards this or that specific person. Therefore, if the priest's application would never be effective unless it were made in accord with God's good pleasure, it would mean the priest would have no authority to apply the virtue of the sacrifice except in a most general manner.

[16] 20.37 [Different cases of application] Therefore, we can say that where the teaching as to how the sacrifice is to be applied is certain, there the sacrifice must be applied in that way. Otherwise it would not be valid, perhaps, for him to whom it is applied, and it would be harmful to the one applying it, for he would be sinning. Now prayer, as the beginning of the first article [in 20.4] points out, is applicable to someone in three ways, most specially, most gen-

erally, and in an intermediary fashion, namely, in a way that is special but not most special. Now the first of these applications is determined, for it is always for the one who prays. The second also is determined, for it is always for the whole Church. The rule which determines these is charity, whose obligation is strongest as regards oneself and is most general as regards one's neighbor.

20.38 The third or intermediary application is sometimes determined by ecclesiastical institution or ordinance. Parochial priests are assigned to different parishes with the obligation to serve their parish and to celebrate mass especially for their parishioners. Similarly, different priests are installed in the different particular colleges to offer the sacrifice of the altar, and in particular for those who are in such a college. Of this one can understand that passage from the [*Decretum Gratiani*][14] Causa 7, question 1 and Jerome's remark to the monk Rusticus: "Among bees there is one that is head; cranes follow one leader; once founded, Rome could not have simultaneously two brothers as kings." And he continues: "There is one bishop in each church, one archdeacon, and every ecclesiastical order is ruled by its rectors." Not only are rectors required in the Church to correct sinners but also to reconcile them by the prayer of the Church and the saving victim.

[17] 20.39 It also seems that justice determines the application if we consider those who provide or have provided for the ministers with necessary maintenance. In this way persons have endowed monasteries and solemn collegiate churches or minor churches so that their ministers would be obliged to celebrate mass for those whom the donors intended to help. It is reasonable that in return for temporal alms one be obliged to offer the spiritual suffrages of prayers and sacrifice, just as one must return a temporal good for the spiritual benefit of preaching, according to the Apostle[15]: "If we have sown spiritual things for you, why should you be surprised if we harvest your material things?" It is as if he said: "No, it is no great surprise." It is licit, therefore, and even reasonable that alms require prayers in return. He who imposes the obligation of praying for him by his alms acts reasonably, and the obligation he imposed passes on with the alms to whomsoever succeeds the original recipient. However, no one is presumed to so oblige himself or his college that he could not give some suffrages to others. And it is with this stipu-

[14] *Corpus Iuris Canonici*, c.7, q.1, c.41, I, 582; Jerome, *Epist.* cxxv, n.15: PL 22, 1080.
[15] 1 Cor. 9:11.

lation and precisely as noted in writing that an obligation in accordance with the intention of the donor is presumed to arise, even though it is based only on a promise.

20.40 Now those whose prayers and sacrifices are determined in this way to specific persons cannot apply them at will to other persons, for they would do an injustice by taking away what they owe to those to whom they are obliged. What I mean is that it would be unjust to apply them equally to those to whom they are not equally under obligation, for in this third way there are many degrees in which the fruits of prayer can be applied. Let us consider just three, for example, where the first benefits more than the second and the second more than the third: for instance, if A benefits as much as a person other than the celebrant could, and B receives as much as one could after A, and C obtains as much as remains after B (whether by A we understand one or many for whom the celebrant wants to pray in the same degree). Now even though someone is obliged by Church law or a benefaction received to apply the mass in this third or intermediary way and to do so in the first degree for one person, this does not prevent him from applying it in the second degree to another person and in the third degree to a third party, and the same for any further degree, for an application in some subsequent degree never takes anything away from a person for whom it is applied in some antecedent degree.

[18] 20.41 [Some doubtful points] But to whom must the application be made and in what degree? Here doubts arise. Must one charged with a parish apply the mass to his parishioner before applying it to his father or mother? The obligation to his parents stems from natural law, it seems, and no positive obligation can be prejudicial to that law. Neither should anyone who puts the priest under obligation want him to oblige himself in violation of what the law of nature prescribes. One should never interpret him then as wanting the priest to bind himself in such a way that he would not always be free to give his parents what he owes to them. On the other hand, if the father and mother are parishioners of another priest, they have him under obligation to pray for them as for his other subjects and, in terms of efficacy, it seems that this spiritual filiation prevails.

20.42 But there are other priests in the Church who have no pastorate, chaplaincy, or prebend in virtue of which they must apply their masses to one or more persons. These priests are more free to apply their masses at will. However, they must conform their intention to the will of the supreme high priest [Christ] insofar as they can conjecture what this will is in all probability, which is difficult to do where it concerns this or that specific person. It is easier to do so as regards such general obligations as those to parents, benefactors, civil rulers, and prelates (according to those words of the Apostle[16]: "First of all, I urge that petitions, prayers, intercessions, and thanksgiving be offered for all men, especially for kings and those in authority, that we may be able to lead undisturbed and tranquil lives in perfect piety and dignity") and also for the dead (according to II Machabees, 12[17]: "It is a holy and wholesome thought to pray for the dead.")

[19] 20.43 But even so far as this general application in the third way is concerned, it is doubtful to whom the celebrant must apply the mass in the first degree and to whom he must apply it in a more remote degree, for the need is greater in some than in others. Thus it is greater in the dead, who cannot merit for themselves, than it is in the living. It is greater in sinners than in the just, who unlike sinners can merit by the grace they possess. Now it seems just first to help those who need it most. On the other hand, there is the question of utility. It is more useful to increase the grace, and hence the merits, of the pilgrim than to remit the suffering of the dead in whom neither grace grows nor merits increase. It also seems that one is more obliged to his brother who lives in a state of grace or charity than to a sinner who neither loves God nor is loved by him in the same degree as the just, since I ought to love that person more who loves God and is loved by God than a person who lives otherwise.

20.44 Therefore, the safest way seems to be to make the general application in this way: "Deign, O Lord, to accept this sacrifice in particular for those for whom you know I am especially obliged to offer it and in the measure in which I am obliged to do so." And whether this application in particular be for one or for several, it is always safer to make it under the condition: "If it pleases you."

3. One Mass does not Benefit Each of Several as Much as it Would if Offered for One Alone

[20] 20.45 As for the third point of this article [mentioned in 20.28], we can say as we did in the previous article [in 20.5-18], that a mass applied equally to several does not benefit each as much as a mass applied to one alone.

The proof is analogous to the one given above [in 20.5]. The good

[16] 1 Tim. 2:1. [17] 2 Mach. 12:46.

QUESTION TWENTY

due in virtue of the sacrifice corresponds in full justice to some merit in the Church. This merit is finite and of limited degree. Therefore, in strict justice a good of limited degree adequately corresponds to it. Consequently, if all of this is given to one, nothing in virtue of the sacrifice remains for another, for if something were given to him, it would not be the good the first received nor something included as a part thereof. Arguing from the opposite of the consequent then, we could say that if by virtue of the sacrifice some good is given to another, then the first does not receive all that is due to him. But if the sacrifice were applied to him alone, all the good would be given to him that is due in the third or intermediary way. Therefore, nothing would be given to the other.

20.46 Against this argument the objections raised in the first article could be brought to bear and they would be solved in a similar way [cf. 20.7ff., 20.12ff., 20.19ff.].

[21] 20.47 [A special doubt] But here a special doubt arises. In the case discussed in [20.5ff. of] the first article, it is clear to what finite merit the good due corresponds, for it corresponds to the personal merit of the celebrant, but it is not clear to what merit the good due in virtue of the sacrifice corresponds.

It can be said that it does not correspond to the good contained in the Eucharist, for this good remains equal when the Eucharist is reserved in a pyx as when it is offered in a mass, yet for the Church it does not have the same value as in the mass. Hence in addition to the good contained in the Eucharist, its offering in the mass is required.

This is not accepted unless the one offering it is acceptable, according to the words of Genesis[18]: "God looked with favor on Abel and his offering,"—first on Abel, then on his gifts—and of Luke 21[19]: "This poor widow has put in more than all the rest," because her offering stemmed from a more acceptable will, and of Gregory in his homily on that text of Matthew 4,[20] "And Jesus, walking," etc.: "God does not weigh how much is in his sacrifice, but with what affection it is offered." Hence, if a Jew had offered Christ, willing or not, to God the Father, the oblation would not have been accepted by the Father in the way it actually was because Christ offered himself voluntarily. Furthermore, it would not have been accepted according to the words of Ecclesiasticus[21]: "Like a man who slays

---

[18] Gen. 4:4. [19] Luke 21:3.
[20] Gregory, *XL homil. in Evangelia* I, hom.4, n.2: PL 76, 1093.
[21] Eccl. 34:24.

a son in his father's presence is he who offers sacrifice from the possessions of the poor."

[22] 20.48 This shows that just as the Eucharist is not accepted precisely because of what is contained therein, but it has to be offered, so neither is it fully accepted when offered, except by reason of the good will of someone offering it.

Now this is not precisely the will of the celebrant since this pertains to the priest's personal merit and not to the virtue of the sacrifice. Neither is it immediately the will of Christ himself, for although as contained in the sacrifice he is offered, he is not in this case the one who is immediately offering the sacrifice, according to those words in the Epistle to the Hebrews 9[22]: "Not that Christ might offer himself there again and again. . . . Christ was offered up but once," add "by himself." Otherwise, if Christ himself were immediately both offerer and the offering, the celebration of one mass would seem to be equal to his passion. But this certainly is not so, even though it benefits more specifically in that there is a more special commemoration of the offering which Christ made on the cross, according to those words in Luke 22[23] and I Corinthians, chapter 2[24]: "Do this in memory of me." The mass both represents the oblation on the cross and implores God to accept through it the sacrifice of the Church. A petition is usually made by means of something more acceptable to the one petitioned than is the supplication of the petitioner himself. This is evident from common examples, for if I ask you to do me a favor for the health of my father or for the welfare of his soul, I presume his health to be more acceptable to you than my supplication and because it is pleasing to you, I want my petition also to be accepted. This is in accord with the principle: "That in virtue of which something is the sort of thing it is, is itself even more that sort of thing."

It is clear, then, that the Eucharistic offering is accepted not because of Christ's good will as the immediate offerer, but rather by reason of the will of the universal Church, and this is of limited merit. Now even if it were accepted by reason of the will of Christ as offerer, i.e., inasmuch as he instituted the sacrifice and gave it value and acceptability, the mass still would not be equivalent to the passion of Christ, nor would it be received in the same way as the latter. Hence it would be of finite merit, and to this merit corresponds the good due in virtue of the sacrifice.

[22] Heb. 9:25.
[23] Luke 22:19.
[24] 1 Cor. 11:24-25.

[23] 20.49 [Another doubt] As accepted by reason of the general will of the Church, is the Eucharistic sacrifice simultaneously accepted by reason of the will of the Church triumphant as well as militant? On the one hand it seems that since such a sacrifice is proper to the
[24] Church militant, it is not accepted by reason of the Church triumphant. On the other hand, if it is only proper to the Church militant, then on the assumption that no single pilgrim were in the state of grace, the value of the mass would be nil. And if only one pilgrim were in the state of grace, the value of the sacrifice would be equivalent to his personal merit. Besides, how does the intention of one who is not thinking of the oblation (as would be the case with anyone other than the celebrant or his server) contribute to this merit?[25]

ARTICLE III
Does the Priest Satisfy his Obligation to Both by One Offering?

[25] 20.50 [Free promise vs. strict obligation] As for the third main article [of 20.3], I claim a priest can be obliged to say a mass for a given person in two ways, by a promise freely given or by a strict obligation. By strict I do not mean an obligation by legal agreement or commutation of something spiritual, like prayer, for something temporal, like alms, for this would seem to be simoniacal. It does not help to claim the priest would be taking something temporal in exchange for the bodily work involved, since it is not plausible that anyone would want to pay so much for the work involved in celebrating. No, what happens is this: The alms are given freely with an entreaty for prayers. The one receiving the alms is obliged in justice to listen to the one who entreats his prayers. Therefore, he has freely obliged himself in justice to pray for the benefactor even though there is no [legal] agreement or exchange. Or if it is a religious community, the superior obliges himself for the whole community, or he obliges the whole community, or the community as a whole obliges itself. Any of these obligations can be strict, even though they are not based on an exchange of this for that. In this sense we must understand the many things said in this question and its solution.

20.51 [One bound by promise can promise as much as he wishes] If one is obliged in the first way, it was in his power to promise as much as he wanted to, and to that much and no more is he obliged.

---

[25] See Appendix, Addition 20.49.

If this interpretation can be harmonized with those words [of the *Decretales*], *Extra de sponsalibus, Ex litteris,* where the gloss at the end reads[26]: "The interpretation must be made according to the one making the promise, for the stipulator is free to understand the words licitly in a broad sense," then the priest pays his debt, if he gives what he intended.

20.52 [One bound by strict obligation does not satisfy his debt with one mass for two] If he is obliged to say mass for each of two persons in the second way, viz., by strict obligation, he does not fulfill his obligation by saying but one mass for both.

20.53 But there is a distinction to be made so far as the words of obligation go. Sometimes they are certain and limited to a single meaning, for instance, if one obliges himself to say mass for one along with another to whom he is obliged, or when he obliges himself to say mass for a person in as particular a way as possible for a person other than the celebrant, i.e., he wants to apply to someone in a special way as much as possible of what is due to both personal merit and the virtue of the sacrifice. In such a case where the obligation is clearly determined, it is satisfied only when carried out in that manner.

20.54 [A doubt] But sometimes the wording of the obligation is susceptible to several meanings so that it can be interpreted more or less strictly, e.g., if I say, "I will say one mass for you" or more generally, "I will celebrate for you." Here, it seems, the words must be understood according to the intention of the one obliging himself. This is proved from that passage [in the *Decretales*], *Extra de iureiurando, Veniens,* where this is said of a certain A[27]: "As a certain individual incurred grave enmities, the friends of both parties suggested to A that in satisfaction for such, he swear to obey the commands of certain of these individuals. When he took such an oath under the conviction that nothing serious had been imposed upon him, the others commanded him under his oath never to enter the palace of the Duke except when all in general were called there by his edict," etc. "However, because A, who was a counselor of the Duke, would never have sworn in this way if he had known ahead of time about the command that would be imposed upon him, know that we [Gregory IX] have commanded such a Patriarch that if the command is repugnant to the prior oath he made licitly, he should

---

[26] *Decretales Gregorii Papae IX suae integritati una cum glossis restitutae* (Romae, 1582), col. 1423.

[27] *Corpus Iuris Canonici* II, 364-65; cf. *Decretales* . . . , col. 807-808.

denounce it by virtue of our authority as a command not to be observed." The Pope, therefore, did not want him to keep his oath because something very difficult which he did not intend was imposed upon him in virtue of it. Therefore, it seems he is obliged only to the easier things he intended to impose upon himself, even though those to whom he swore had in mind to oblige him to the more difficult thing they afterwards imposed upon him in virtue of his oath.

[26] 20.55 Besides, the gloss in that same place says[28]: "The interpretation is made against him who should have imposed the law more clearly." Therefore, if the person to whom one is obliged does not clearly determine the words so as to express his exact intention, he must blame himself. He who obliges himself only wants to be bound, it seems, to the minimum consistent with the words.

20.56 On the other hand, it seems that the words of the obligation should be accepted in the sense in which he to whom one is under obligation understands them, according to [Gratian],[29] 22, q.5 *Quacumque*: "No matter what the words of the one taking the oath are apt to express, God accepts them in the sense in which he to whom the oath is made understands them." And Isidore is cited there; and in the next chapter, *Ecce*, there is that line from a sermon of Augustine: "Who swears something false by a stone, is a perjurer.... If you do not consider such an oath sacred, he to whom you swear does consider it such, for you do not swear to yourself, or to the stone, but to your neighbor."

20.57 [Solution to the doubt] We find the solution to this doubt, it seems, in *Extra de sponsalibus, Ex litteris* where it is said[30]: "If one may not have understood what another wanted to say, the words should be given their common meaning, and both should be obliged to take the words in the sense they have for those who understand them correctly." And the gloss on this passage from the [*Digest*] *de Supellectili legata, Lege Labeo* adds[31]: "The terms must not be understood according to individual opinion but according to common usage."

20.58 But you may ask: What is this common usage? It would seem that the person obliging the priest to celebrate for him would want what is most useful to himself provided this is licit. Now it

---

[28] Cf. *Decretales*..., col. 1424.
[29] C.22, q.5, cc.9-10, *Corpus Iuris Canonici* I, 885; cf. *Decretum Gratiani*..., col. 1691-92.
[30] *Corpus Iuris Canonici* II, 663.   [31] *Decretales*..., col. 1424.

would be more useful to have all that can be applied to him in virtue of the sacrifice and the priest's personal merit, and this would be licit, for it is not contrary to charity to procure for oneself as much spiritual good as possible without prejudice to another. Suppose then that he intended to oblige the priest to give him all of this. If the priest said mass for another at the same time, he would not receive his full due in virtue of the priest's personal merits, as the first article [20.5ff.] made clear, or in virtue of the sacrifice, as the second article showed [in 20.45ff.]. If the man had such an intention, I say, then the priest who celebrated for two would not give him his due.

[27] 20.59 Answer to the arguments that the words must be understood according to the mind of the one making the promise.

To the first [in 20.54]: The presumption is that no one wants to oblige himself to what is illicit. One must presuppose this every time it is not explicitly evident the obligation is to something illicit. It is illicit, however, to want to revoke on one's own authority a previous promise licitly made, and no one should be presumed to want this in making a subsequent promise, if the words of the latter do not revoke the earlier promise explicitly. What these general words "I swear to carry out your command" imply seems to be licit, and they do not explicitly revoke a prior obligation. If, then, in virtue of such an oath, one is commanded not to observe his prior obligation, the correct interpretation has to be that he is not obliged to do this in virtue of his oath. Now this is what happened in the case you cited. The individual A had an obligation to the Duke, as his counselor. Consequently, the oath he swore to the citizens in order to make peace with them could in no way be interpreted as obliging him to repudiate his obligations to the Duke. To put it briefly, if he had intended to do so, his oath would have been illicit, and in so swearing he would have perjured himself and he would be found to honor not his oath, but his prior obligation. Now since he did not swear this explicitly but took an oath that was licit and general, his oath could in no sense be interpreted as covering this illicit matter. That is why the Pope did not command that he be absolved from his second oath, but that he repudiate it as incompatible with and repugnant to a previous oath made licitly, and therefore it should not be observed. I do mean the oath was incompatible by reason of its form, for that was general and had to be understood as applicable only to licit matters. No, it was incompatible by reason of the matter to which his adversaries had a mind to apply it, namely, what they imposed upon him in virtue of his oath. Therefore, as regards this particular matter he had to repudiate it. But if some other matter not repugnant to justice had been imposed, he would have had to do this in virtue of his vow as simply licit, and in such a case his obligation would have been licit.

20.60 Answer to the second argument [in 20.55]: Though it might appear that the one taking on the obligation wished to bind himself to the minimum consistent with the words accepted by the obligee, and hence it suffices to pay that minimum, nevertheless when obligor and obligee do not clearly understand each other, the obligation must be interpreted according to common usage.

[30] 20.61 [A special case] But are there some cases where a priest obliged to say mass for a person satisfies his obligation by celebrating simultaneously for him and for another?

Some say there is, for a general obligation is interpreted according to a reasonable custom. Now it is a reasonable custom that the anniversaries of the dead be celebrated in those churches where they are buried and in which, during life, they received the sacraments. If such churches have the reasonable custom of celebrating but one mass for their dead when several anniversaries fall on the same day, they satisfy their obligation to all with a single mass. So it seems that monks, the clergy of cathedral and other collegiate churches, and even pastors, though obliged to several persons to say one mass for each, satisfy that obligation by celebrating one mass for all.

20.62 For they are not bound to the impossible or to something not convenient for the church to which they minister, as would be the solemn celebration of several masses for the dead on the same day. And the difficulty does not arise because they have done something illicit, for it was licit for them to oblige themselves to celebrate in their church the anniversaries of those who belonged to it, and this obligation must be understood according to the reasonable custom of such churches.

20.63 It is different as regards the members of mendicant orders or priests who are not charged with a parish or collegiate church, for they are obliged to celebrate individual masses for individual obligations. The custom of not celebrating several masses on the same day would not apply to them, for they have no excuse for promising what they cannot fulfill, since they have no reason for accepting anniversary masses in this way. They may oblige themselves only to what they can be fully certain of satisfying.

[31] 20.64 [Another way of handling the special case] One could answer differently by pointing out that any one, if he wishes, can give up his right and permit the priest to say but one mass for him and others. And even though one does not relinquish his right in so many words at the time the obligation is imposed, one must assume that both the obligee and the obligor have a tacit agreement to that effect whenever the obligee is well aware of the custom in that church of celebrating but one mass a day no matter to how many it is under obligation. Consequently, it seems probable that if a canon of such a church decides to celebrate an anniversary mass on a day when several anniversaries coincide, he satisfies his obligation to all by saying simultaneously one mass for the lot.

On the other hand, if someone, unaware of the custom of this church, has every intention of binding its priest as he would a simple cleric not charged with the care of souls, then the priest would not satisfy his obligation, at least in collegiate churches, unless he gave what a nonparochial priest would give the obligee, namely, a mass of his own. The reason is that the custom is special and unknown to the obligee and that through no fault of his own, since he is not obliged to know the special customs of each church. Hence it must not be to his disadvantage as it would be if a priest by reason of such a custom were less obliged than another priest might be in similar circumstances.

If the priest wants to take advantage of the custom, he should explain it to the ignorant, and if the person agrees to be satisfied in this customary way, well and good.

[32] 20.65 As for the claim [in 20.61] that general obligations are satisfied according to reasonable custom this can be said: Although, considered simply in itself, it could be a reasonable custom to celebrate in this church the anniversaries of the dead buried there and, absolutely speaking, it could also be a reasonable custom to say but one mass that same day for the dead, nevertheless there can be cases where these two customs cannot be reasonably combined, namely, where justice requires individual masses be said for individual obligations, for justice requires the same of collegiate churches as it does of a simple priest unless the obligee wishes to cede his right, at least implicitly, by agreeing to accept the custom of this church, something he must never be presumed to do unless he knows about it.

20.66 As for the claim [in 20.62] that no one is obliged to the impossible, I answer: While two obligations, at least in this case, may be opposed to each other in the sense that they cannot be justly fulfilled at the same time, nevertheless they can be fulfilled in all justice separately, and what is said of just fulfillment should be said of what is proper or becoming. Therefore, I say that if it is unbecoming to celebrate several masses for the dead on the same day by a custom approved of in a particular church, then no one is allowed to acquire obligations in justice of saying several masses on the same day. Hence if one is already obliged to say a mass on that day, he should not take on an additional obligation to celebrate, for the new obligation would not refer to the mass he already owes but to another which it is inconvenient to say in such a church.

20.67 To the allegation [in 20.61] that the celebration of anniversaries in one's own church is a reasonable custom, I reply: something may be reasonable in itself and still not be reconcilable with something else that is absolutely reasonable in itself. Thus it would be absolutely reasonable for an anniversary to be celebrated in a particular church as long as the fulfillment of the donor's intention could be harmonized with the custom of that church, that is to say, if a mass could be celebrated for him alone. But when both cannot be reconciled, as is the case here, it is reasonable that the anniversary not be celebrated in this church, and if the priest wants to accept the obligation of this anniversary mass and still observe the custom of his church, then he should see to it that another priest celebrate the mass for the second anniversary.

20.68 The same must be said, it seems, of endowed churches whose ministers by reason of a church ordinance or of alms already received are especially obliged to say an appropriate number of masses or a certain number of suffrages for those who made the endowment or gave the alms. For it does not seem that such priests can licitly oblige themselves to masses or suffrages for others unless they intend to have other priests, not already totally obliged, to satisfy these obligations individually.

[33] 20.69 [Conclusion] To the third point of this article [20.61] one can say that in the case proposed the priest does not satisfy the Church, for where complete obligations, requiring payment in full, are concerned, if there are several obligations to perform the same kind of action, then distinct acts are required to fulfill them, as is clear from the gloss.[32] It is different when the obligations refer to the same individual action, as happens when I am obliged by different precepts to fast on this Friday, for example, by my [Francis-

[32] *Decretales* . . . , col. 1424.

can] rule and also by Church law because it is an ember day and is also the vigil of an apostle that is a day of fast. Because all these obligations refer to the same individual act of fasting, they can be satisfied by a single act. It is different, however, where the distinct obligations refer to the same kind of action. Now the reason for the distinction seems to be that no one is obliged to the impossible. No matter how many obligations I may have to perform the same numerical act, I can only satisfy these by doing that particular action, and I am not obliged to perform another act.

But where there are several obligations to perform an act of the same kind, these can be satisfied by different acts. Now in the case proposed here, there are several distinct obligations payable in full to do the same kind of thing, namely, to say a mass. Therefore, they are not satisfied unless each one receives distinct payment.

20.70 Confirmation: The obligees had different reasons and incentives for inducing the priest to oblige himself, and hence he seems to be bound to perform different acts corresponding to these different reasons.

Reply to the Initial Argument

[34] 20.71 To the argument at the beginning [in 20.2]: The answer appears clear from what was said in [20.45 of] the second article. The value due in virtue of the sacrifice is not equal simply to the value of the good contained in the Eucharist. It corresponds rather to a definite measure of merit of the Church. Neither is it simply equal to the merit of the passion of Christ, as was said later [in 20.47f.], but it approaches it more insofar as the mass represents the passion more specifically and, by its special value, it placates God and asks for a good corresponding to the general merit of the Church.

Question Twenty-one

CAN ONE WHO ADMITS THAT THE WORLD IS ETERNAL DEFEND THE POSITION THAT ANYONE COULD ALWAYS BE FORTUNATE?

[1]   21.1 The last question asked is this: Can one who admits the world is eternal maintain that anyone could always be fortunate?

Arguments Pro and Con

It is argued affirmatively:
One who admits the eternity of the world does not deny, but admits, the existence of movement. Consequently, he does not deny the existence of nature as the principle of movement. Now the Philosopher, in the book *Good Fortune*,[1] declares that good fortune is nature without reason, etc.

21.2 For the negative view:
He who admits the eternity of the world denies that God can immediately influence our souls. As the *Physics*[2] explains, it is impossible that the eternal principle, God, can influence terrestrial beings except by means of the heavens, and the heavens cannot influence our souls. According to such a view, then, God can have no influence. But anyone who admits good fortune also admits that God immediately influences our souls. Towards the end of that little book it says[3]: "The fortunate do not need advice, for they have a principle that is better than intellect." And just above, it says[4]: "The principle of reason is not reason but something better. But what can be better than intellect and knowledge except God? For the organ

---

[1] This opuscule is not an authentic work of Aristotle. It is an extract from Aristotle's *Magna Moralia* and *Ethica ad Eudemum*. Cf. S. D. Wingate, *The Mediaeval Latin Versions of the Aristotelian Scientific Corpus, with Special Reference to the Biological Works* (London, 1931), 93-94. For the references to *De bona fortuna* we are using MS. Lat., fols. 7-10, from Charles Patterson Van Pelt Library of University of Pennsylvania.

[2] Aristotle, *Physic.* VIII, c.6 (259b32-260a19).

[3] Ps.-Aristotle, *De bona fortuna*, lect. 8, fol. 10r.

[4] Ibid., lect. 7, fol. 10r.

of the intellect is power or virtue." He means that those who are fortunate are immediately influenced by God.

Body of the Question

[2] 21.3 As one gleans from the argument for the negative view, the question inquires about not just any way of admitting eternity, but the precise way in which the Philosopher admits it. That is to say, the question is whether the fact that someone is fortunate can be reconciled with those principles of the Philosopher that were his grounds for maintaining the world was eternal. To see whether the two views are compatible or not, one must first know them. What needs examination in this question, therefore, is: (1) the view that someone is fortunate, especially the view set forth in the book *Good Fortune*, attributed to Aristotle; (2) the view that this world is eternal, as is said in the *Physics*[5] and many other places; and (3) whether there is any conflict between these two views.

ARTICLE I
The View that Someone is Fortunate

[3] 21.4 [Two points] As for the first, we can sum up the Philosopher's view in *Good Fortune* as an answer to two questions: (1) Is there such a thing as good fortune and in what does it consist? (2) What is the cause of it?

1. The Existence and Nature of Good Fortune

21.5 The first of these includes three problems, namely, does fortune exist? Second, is there *good* fortune? Third, is anyone fortunate?

21.6 [First problem] The truth about the first can be expressed succinctly in the form of three conclusions.

The first conclusion, which accords with the common opinion, is that there is such a thing as fortune. In philosophizing, Aristotle as a general rule always presupposed what was commonly accepted.[6] This is clear, for instance, when he says that place is immobile according to the common view, though it would be difficult to prove this by reason, or when he declares that time is numerically the same everywhere and that this is the common view, though it presents difficulties to reason. Many other instances could be cited where Aristotle takes what is commonly accepted. In like manner

---

[5] Aristotle, *Physic.* VIII, c.1 (251a20-252b7).
[6] Ibid., IV, c.4 (212a27-30).

he could have accepted as common opinion that events happen by fortune, for it is clear that unintentional and fortuitous events happen to one who is acting on purpose. Hence fortune is the cause of these incidents. And the Philosopher explains just what kind of cause it is in Book II of the *Physics*,[7] where he says that it is the incidental cause* [*per accidens*] of those effects which happen infrequently to an agent acting on purpose.

21.7 The second conclusion is that fortune is not a *per se* cause* distinct from nature and intellect or purpose. In fact, the same will that is the *per se* cause of an intentional effect is called fortune as regards an unintended effect. The intended effect happens on purpose and therefore is caused voluntarily, whereas the unintended effect went beyond what the agent had in mind and hence was caused fortuitously. From this it follows that the pagan view that fortune was a goddess who caused fortuitous events *per se* is false. It was this false pagan view, perhaps, that caused Augustine to chide himself in his *Retractations*[8]: "I am not pleased with having spoken so often of fortune with a capital F." Catholics, on the other hand, ought to attribute such effects, at least in general, to divine providence.

[4] 21.8 Our third conclusion is that fortune is not the whole cause, that is to say, nothing happens by fortune which does not stem from some *per se* cause pursuing its own purpose, according to Plato in the *Timaeus*[9]: "Nothing occurs that is not preceded by some lawlike cause." And Augustine[10] in turn says, "Cicero concedes that nothing happens if an efficient cause does not precede." And it was reasonable that he concede this, for anything not of itself can only happen because of an efficient cause, and in this case a purposeful cause is required, for as several effects are intended by a more universal cause, so all effects fall under what was intended by the first cause. But when the proximate *per se* cause or purpose is not apparent, the effect is called casual or fortuitous. In this sense Augustine's words should be understood[11]: "Perhaps we call chance that element in things for which we can offer no cause or reason." The Phi-

---

[7] Ibid., II, c.5 (197a33-b25).

[8] Augustine, *Retract.* I, c.1, n.2: PL 32, 585, CSEL 36, 7.

[9] Plato, *Timaeus* 28a, in *Platonis Opera ex recensione C.E.Ch.Schneideri graece et latine*, ed. A. Firmin Didot (Parisiis, 1846), 204.

[10] Augustine, *De civ. Dei* v, c.9, n.4: PL 41, 151, CCSL 47, 139.

[11] Augustine, *Contra Academ.* I, c.1, n.1: PL 32, 905; *Retract.* I, c.1, n.2: PL 32, 585, CSEL 36, 3.

losopher touches on this view in his little book[12]: "Though nothing can be said to be directed by fortune, whenever we do not see another cause for it, we call fortune the cause."

[5] 21.9 [Second problem] The second question raised in [21.5 of] this section, viz., whether there is *good* fortune, can be answered with one conclusion and a twofold distinction.

21.10 The conclusion, which also seems to be commonly accepted, is this: Good fortune does exist. For it is clear that a purposeful agent has some good things happen to him that he did not intend. It follows, therefore, that good fortune exists, since by "good fortune" we mean a fortuitous good effect, or to speak more properly, if less in accord with common usage, by "good fortune" we mean the cause of such an effect, and cause and effect each entail the existence of the other. This distinction of good fortune as meaning either the cause or the effect is something the Philosopher touches on[13]: "Now we frequently say fortune is the cause. However, fortune is distinct, for cause and that of which it is the cause are two different things."

21.11 Next the Philosopher makes two distinctions of good fortune by reason of its effects.

This is the first distinction: The effects of good fortune may consist of things outside of us in which we play no part and over which we have no control. The example he gives is "the good fortune of someone being a nobleman, something that lies completely beyond his control."[14] In another sense, our good fortune lies in those things which depend on us, for "we call a person fortunate if his actions led to some unexpected good."[15] For if someone without planning it has an impulse that leads to good results, he is indeed said to be fortunate. Or, to put it more plainly, we speak of one having good fortune if he intended one thing and, in carrying out his plans, stumbled upon some unintended good.

The above distinction seems to be a distinction between what is good fortune proper and what is commonly but less properly called such, for properly speaking good fortune, like fortune in general, seems applicable to what is in our power. What we mean by "in our power" is that even though the fortuitous event is not in our power *per se* or in a primary sense, nevertheless it is in our power in an

---

[12] Ps.-Aristotle, *De bona fortuna*, lect. 5, fol. 9r.
[13] Ibid., lect. 3, fol. 8r.   [14] Ibid., lect. 2, fol. 7v.
[15] Ibid., lect. 3, fol. 8r.

accidental and secondary sense, as it were, insofar as it is connected with what we intended. Now those things which are not in our power in any way, but which happen to us independently of any purposeful action on our part, happen not by good fortune but by chance, as *Physics* II[16] makes clear.

21.12 A second distinction of good fortune by reason of its effects is into an effect that is good *per se* and one that is so *per accidens*, where the former consist in obtaining a good and the latter in avoiding some evil. This distinction is frequently referred to in this book, *Good Fortune*.[17]

[6] 21.13 [Third problem] The third question in this section, viz., whether there is anyone who is fortunate, is answered in terms of a tripartite division.

21.14 The first member: We do not call one a fortunate man if something good happened to him on only one occasion.

21.15 The second member: No one is called fortunate only because something fortuitously good is always happening to him. For whether we take this to mean that every purposeful action of his results in some unintended good, or whether whenever some unintentional result does occur, it turns out to be good, in either case this could not occur without a special miracle. And this would be so whether we take "purposeful action" generally, or we limit it to a certain type of action (e.g., military action or a business deal), or whether we take "unintentional result" to refer to the same kind of event (e.g., a victory if the action is military, or a profit if it is a business deal), or to chance events of different kinds. For in none of these ways would the Philosopher say that someone is a fortunate man, and there are no probable reasons why we should say so.[18]

The Reportatio Version

This question is asked: Can those who admit the world is eternal also admit that a man is fortunate?

It is argued that they can:

For he who assumes the world is eternal does not deny nature,

---

[16] Aristotle, *Physic.* II, c.6 (197b1-15).
[17] For example, ibid., lect. 2, fol. 7v.
[18] In M_1 question twenty-one ends in folio 85vb with these words: "aliquem esse bene fortunatum sicut nec ratio probabilis persuadet. Tertium membrum." Then it reads: "Finis. Quodlibet repertum in suis quaternis. Quod sequitur est de Reportatione."

since he does not deny movement. But good fortune is nature without reason, according to Aristotle in the little book *Good Fortune*.[19] Therefore [he can admit that a man is fortunate].

Argument that they cannot:

He who admits the eternity of the world denies that God can produce something new immediately in the terrestrial world, since God, according to Aristotle,[20] does not act on anything except by means of movement [of heavenly bodies]. But one who assumes that someone is fortunate does admit that God produces something new immediately, according to Aristotle,[21] who says that it is not necessary to counsel the fortunate because he has a directive principle better than intellect and reason, viz., God. Therefore [one who admits the eternity of the world, cannot admit that someone is fortunate].

Body of the Question

In this question any opposition between these two views can be properly evaluated only if one sees what each one involves. Therefore, I shall first say something about the opinion of those who admit someone can be fortunate and, second, something about those who claim the world is eternal. For according to many theologians the world could have been made from all eternity and good fortune can be reconciled with this assumption. Consequently, the question should have been put in this way: Could one who admits that nothing new can be produced immediately by an immutable God, still admit that good fortune exists or that someone is fortunate?

Put in this way, the question raises doubts according to the opinion of Aristotle. For he understands "good fortune" according to its commonly accepted meaning, known to all. Hence his customary way was to assume some propositions commonly admitted, for example, that place is immobile and time is the same for all temporal things, etc.[22] And so, following the common opinion, he says that good fortune is that by which some one is fortunate, if not in all cases, at least in most cases.[23] And if we follow Aristotle in that lit-

---

[19] Ps.-Aristotle, *De bona fortuna*, lect. 3, fol. 8r.

[20] Aristotle, *Physic.* VIII, c.6 (259b32-260a19).

[21] Ps.-Aristotle, *De bona fortuna*, lect. 8, fol. 10r.

[22] Aristotle, *Physic*, IV, c.4 (212a27-30),

[23] He does not hold that good fortune means that by which someone is fortunate in all cases, but in most cases. See 21.16.

tle book, there should be a second point as to why someone is fortunate.[24]

1. The View that Someone can be Fortunate

As to the first: According to one way of understanding it, fortune in itself is nothing, for it is not something independent of nature and purpose, which according to Aristotle in *Physics* II[25] are the causes of all movement. Now fortune is reducible to these according to the pagans' false opinion, which attributed fortune to a goddess called Fortuna. According to them, therefore, it is reducible to a cause that acts naturally and with purpose, viz., when something happens that was not intended by the *per se* causes.

One should know, however, that an effect is not said to be fortuitous as regards just any efficient cause acting on purpose, for where the First cause is concerned, no effect is caused fortuitously. Nothing can exist or come to be that is not subject to the causality of the First cause, and no matter how it is intended by a secondary cause, it is always intended *per se* by the First cause, which is the *per se* cause intending and directing all things to their respective ends. The fortuitous *qua* fortuitous cannot be intended *per se*; hence, as regards God, no effect can be called fortuitous.

It is also obvious, therefore, that those who claimed fortune was a distinct and total cause, for example, a certain goddess, denied that divine providence governs things, for providence cannot be reconciled with fortuitous effects, as was said. Consequently, fortune is not a distinct or separate cause. Neither is it an adjunct of just any intelligent cause, because it never occurs with the First cause.

Aristotle in *Physics* II[26] points out that fortune is present when something happens beyond what a purposeful agent intended. Now in some sense the agent in such a case is called the cause of the fortuitous event but not precisely as either nature or as acting purposefully, because he did not intend what happened, but he is its cause in the sense that the event followed incidentally [*per accidens*] from what was intended *per se*. It is clear then what sort of thing fortune is according to Aristotle.

Now good fortune occurs when the unintended event that hap-

---

[24] Ps.-Aristotle, *De bona fortuna*, lect. 2, fol. 7r.
[25] Aristotle, *Physic.* II, cc.5-6 (197a33-b25).
[26] Ibid., c.5 (197a35-b25).

475

pens to the agent acting on purpose is something good, for instance, if someone found a treasure when he only intended to dig his field. In this case the will of the agent with reference to what happened by accident is called good fortune.

21.16 But is there anyone who is fortunate? According to Aristotle in *Ethics* I[27]: "One swallow does not make a spring." Similarly, one happy coincidence is not enough to call that man fortunate to whom it occurred; such events must happen to him often or for the most part. As Aristotle says in *Good Fortune*[28]: "Unwittingly they direct many things." Consequently, when these individuals carry out their own purposes and good things result independently of their intentions, they are said to be fortunate, according to common usage. And in the *Rhetoric*[29] he says: "We see men arrogant because of their good fortune."

[7] 21.17 But is there anyone who is fortunate in all cases? This can be understood in two ways: (1) in the sense that some incidental good accompanies everything he does or plans *per se*, for instance, every time he plants something, or every time he practices the healing art. Or it may be understood (2) in the sense that every time something unforeseen happens to him, it turns out to be good. I believe that no one could be always fortunate in either of these senses without a special miracle. For with all the other causes that concur with one's action, what is to prevent something unfortunate occurring, such as uncovering a snake or a toad while cultivating a field, unless God by a miracle disposes these causes that lie outside one's control?

However, someone can be fortunate in most cases, whether this refers to similar situations, as when victory accompanies the intention to make war, or dissimilar situations. It is possible in this sense, as experience shows, for one to be fortunate most of the time.

21.18 But what kinds of good fortune are there? In the *Rhetoric*[30] Aristotle says it can be of two kinds, either obtaining some unintended good or avoiding something unfortunate, such as falling into the hands of thieves.

21.19 Another distinction Aristotle makes in *Good Fortune*[31] is

[27] Aristotle, *Ethica ad Nic.* I, c.6 (1098a19-20).
[28] Ps.-Aristotle, *De bona fortuna*, lect. 4, fol. 8r.
[29] Aristotle, *Rhetor.* II (1391a32-1391b4).
[30] Ibid., I, c.5 (1362a1-14).
[31] Ps.-Aristotle, *De bona fortuna*, lect. 2, fol. 7v.

between (1) things that are in our power or of our own doing, as when one sets out to do one thing and another happens to him, and (2) those that are not in our power, such as being noble, beautiful, or born rich, and the like. This is really a distinction between fortune proper and fortune in a less proper sense which ought rather to be called chance, since things of the second type, not being in the power of the purposeful agent, are not due to him.

[8] 21.20 But according to Aristotle, what is the reason why someone is fortunate? As for good fortune in an improper sense, viz., things not in our power,[32] I find nothing in a man by reason of which he should be called fortunate. This is something that happens to him by the coincidence of extrinsic causes, and these can be due to God's disposing them in this way according to theologians, though not according to Aristotle. If there is gold in this spot and someone who digs there finds it, such a discovery is due to the concurrence of extrinsic causes. There is no other reason unless it be that a person is more disposed to look here than there.

21.21 [Impulse] But why does some unexpected good result from what one person intends to do and not from what another intends to do? Aristotle asks about the intrinsic cause of this in the little book *Good Fortune*[33] and concludes that the cause is impulse.

[9] 21.22 You may object: You are looking for the reason or cause of something which has no reason or cause. A fortuitous event has no cause.

I reply: Aristotle knew that just as that which happens most of the time has a cause that acts uniformly most of the time, so also that which happens infrequently and in random fashion must be traced back to causes which act uniformly and *per se*. Now the intrinsic and proximate cause of a fortuitous event is what Aristotle calls "impulse." In the little book *Good Fortune*,[34] he says: "Good fortune is nature without reason, and the fortunate man is one who without reason possesses an impulse to what is good and who gets it. This pertains to nature, for in the soul there is something natural which impels us, without reasoning, to some good we would be

---

[32] The text should be corrected. It does not deal with fortune improperly so-called, but with fortune in the proper sense of the term, namely, of that which somehow is in our power according to the definition given above.

[33] Ibid., lect. 8, fol. 10r.

[34] Ibid., lect. 3, fol. 8r.

happy to have. And if someone asks the person why he acted in this way, he will say: 'I don't know, I just wanted to.' One impelled by God to do certain things is in a similar situation, for he who without reason has an impulse to do something is driven by God."

21.23 He wants to say that someone's volition which is followed by an unexpected good proceeds from impulse and without reasoning, and that the cause of this impulse is to be found in his nature. Aristotle admits that experience shows men to be different, and that one is impelled whereas another is not. And since reason cannot be credited with this behavior, it must be ascribed to their nature.

Now this difference between men implies not a specific but an individual difference. For if the extrinsic causal agencies at work in the world move this man, but not that man, to some happy coincidence, the reason must lie in some factor characteristic of one but not of the other. This cannot be reason or anything else characteristic of human nature as such, for then it would be present in all. Hence it must be an individual property.

That this factor is not reason is clear because "where intellect and reason most abound, fortune is minimal, and where fortune is maximal, intellect is minimal" as Aristotle puts it.[35] Neither is the intrinsic cause the will, for the act of the will can be similar in two men and yet the fortuitous event happens to one and not to the other. Consequently the intrinsic cause is impulse, which stems from nature. One is called fortunate, wellborn and the like, because in him there is a disposition by which he is impelled by a higher mover to an undertaking from which unexpected good effects follow.

21.24 But does this natural disposition pertain to the body or
[10] soul? I answer: If Aristotle understood that souls differ according to natural degrees of nobility and perfection, one would have to say that the most noble soul would possess such an impulse, just as the most noble brute has the more noble estimative power and natural instincts for obtaining what is good for it. But I do not believe Aristotle thought that this impulse is characteristic of someone by reason of the nobility of his soul, for he claims that fortune is greatest where intellect is minimal.[36] That is why, he says, it is not necessary to advise such an individual. Fortune, then, does not pertain to the intellect because of its perfection, but because it has something impelling it in a better way. A boat that is difficult to guide often sails better, not because of itself, but because it has a better skipper.

[35] Ibid., lect. 2, fol. 7r.   [36] Ibid.

QUESTION TWENTY-ONE

Therefore this natural disposition is found in the body as the result of a certain particular constitution.

21.25 [Doubts] There is some doubt as to how nature is the cause of this impulse which moves one to will and to act in such a way that some unexpected good results. Is it analogous to the way in which weight is the cause of a body's descent? If so, the fortuitous event would not be caused by fortune, for there would be in nature a disposition which, though it does not suffice of itself to cause the movement, does incline one to such an action.

21.26 Besides, if a person were called fortunate because he has a disposition impelling him to will in such a way that without reason or advice some unexpected good follows, then everything would occur by fortune. In human actions the one advising is not first advised, neither does one deliberate about deliberating; otherwise there would be an infinite regress. The impulse to elicit the initial acts, therefore, is not the result of reasoning; hence such acts are elicited by nature without reason and this is what we call fortune.

[13] 21.27 Contrary to what you say about the fortunate possessing impulse without reason, one could say there is no good fortune without there being some act of the will, for fortune is a contingent result accompanying an effect that was intended. But the will only acts if there is some object presented by reason. Consequently such an impulse to will does not occur in the absence of reason.

21.28 Furthermore, if it were nature and not reason that impelled one to will, we would not call the result fortune, but chance, for according to *Physics* II[37] this is precisely how chance differs from fortune.

21.29 [Solution to these doubts] I reply: The first reason claims the initial intellection is fortune, and if something good or convenient results from it, a person is called fortunate.

Answer: The way one doctor[38] explains the little book of the Philosopher is that the initial intellection or volition seems to be the result not of the presence of an object but of God moving the intellect and will. He claims this is the view of Anselm in *The Fall of the Devil*[39] where he says, "The angel did not have his initial act of himself." Now I believe he did have it of himself, and this was true not only of his initial act but of that which followed. He did of course receive the faculty of will from God. But all that is required for voli-

---

[37] Aristotle, *Physic.* II, c.6 (197b1-15).
[38] Henry of Ghent, *Quodl.* VI, q.10 (fol. 227V-X).
[39] Anselm, *De casu diaboli*, c. 12: PL 158, 342-43; ed. Schmitt I, 254.

tion is the will and prior knowledge of the object presented by the intellect. Consequently, the solution to the objection is obvious.

21.30 Against this it is argued that if the angel had his initial act of volition of himself, either he had it by willing it (in which case we have an infinite regress) or he did not have it by willing it (which seems incongruous).

[14] Answer: I claim that he had the volition because he possessed a will and an intellect which presented the object, both of which are prior to volition by nature but not temporally. Consequently, I admit one must grant that the initial intellection does not stem from reason but in some way from chance, for it is not by some prior act of understanding that the knower understands. The initial intellect, then, does not result from reason showing one the object beforehand, therefore it must come in some way by chance. As Augustine puts it[40]: "It is not in our power to be unaffected by what we see." This is a fortuitous and chance effect.[41]

21.31 If you claim that if the first intellection is fortuitous, then all that follows will be fortuitous also, I say this does not follow. For once someone has the first intellection and volition, he can reason about what to do, and what follows deliberation is not fortuitous but the result of considered reason.

21.32 But if you ask: Are the initial intellections simply fortuitous? the answer must be in the negative. When otherwise unimpeded, the mind is moved more forcefully by objects whose sense images are strongest, and thus the initial intellections have a natural cause within us.[42] But because they do not result from rational deliberation, they are only imputable to us in the sense that it is in a person's power through frequent consideration to make certain objects move him more forcefully than others in his memory, and when other impediments were removed these would have the first and strongest influence upon him. Though the initial intellection is not in our power, the initial state of indifference is, for one can determine himself to will or not to will—something which does not depend on the intellect but on the will. The object moves the intellect naturally. Now if the will were moved naturally by the intellect, then the will itself would be moved naturally and man would not be human but a brute. The will, then, is not moved naturally, but

---

[40] Augustine, *De libero arbitr.* III, c.25, n.74: PL 32, 1307; CCSL 29, 318.
[41] Cf. Duns Scotus, *Ord.* II, d.42, q.4, n.5 (ed. Vivès XIII, 454-55).
[42] Cf. ibid., I, d.3, nn.73-76 (III, 50-51, 52-53).

given the initial intellection, it has it in its power to turn the intellects consideration to this or that and hence it can will this or that or reject these. Thus the first volition depends entirely on us and does not stem from chance the way the first intellection does.

21.33 As for the second argument [in 21.27], what Aristotle says in his little book[43] is that the impetus or impulse to will something that results in an unexpected good does not result from reason in the sense that one could explain why he performed such an action. We must say, then, that a person has such a volition because reason revealed the object to him, not because rational considerations revealed the reason why he did what he did. This is something that happened on impulse.

21.34 To the third argument [21.28] we must say that even though nature is the mediate cause of the fortuitous event, its immediate cause is the will which intends one thing although something unintended happens as a consequence. This is called "fortune," not "chance."

21.35 According to Aristotle, however, it seems that one must not call nature the extrinsic cause of the fortuitous event, for nature is determined to one line of action, or at least natural events are connected in a certain orderly and unified way. Fortuitous events, on the contrary, seem to lack any definite order or connection with other things. Consequently, nature cannot be the complete or sufficient cause of the fortuitous event.

21.36 Besides, if it were such a cause, it would follow that fortune is a *per se* cause.

21.37 Besides, no one is called fortunate because impelled to will something that could have happy consequences unless he actually obtains this good. But if other intermediate causes do not concur, the good will not be obtained. Now nature alone does not suffice to explain this concurrence. Consequently, some extrinsic cause is required to bring these factors together.

[14] 21.38 [The extrinsic cause] What does Aristotle say this extrinsic cause is? Is it the heavens, or an Intelligence moving one heavenly sphere by means of another, or is God the immediate cause?

One must say that if only those effects were fortuitous which fell under the causal influence of the heavens, then there would be no need to look for a cause in addition to the heavens and its mover. To the extent that there seems to be nothing fortuitous for men that

[43] Ps.-Aristotle, *De bona fortuna*, lect. 3, fol. 8r.

does not fall immediately or mediately under the causal influence of the heavens, this view appears probable. But I do not believe it to be true, for man's volition is something to which the causal influence of the heavens does not extend except that occasionally the sense appetite would be moved, and this in turn could incline the will in one way rather than another. Since the heavens cannot touch volition itself, however, the heavens cannot bring about the concurrence of causes so that volition occurs. Therefore, there is something in man beyond the causal influence of the heavens.

21.39 Suppose someone made this claim, and perhaps it would be true. In the will there is no fortuitous effect conjoined *per accidens* with volition, but to everything else the causality of the heavens extends so that there is no other extrinsic cause besides the heavens, the intelligence moving the heavens [immediately] and God moving the heavens mediately. Now if Aristotle seems to say that such a principle is God one ought to add the explanatory gloss. He is the extrinsic cause of the fortuitous event only mediately, namely, by means of the heavens.

21.40 But if one assumes that there is some fortuitous effect in the will, since neither the heavens nor any created intelligence could produce such an effect or bring the causes together that would produce it, one would have to trace this fortuitous effect back to God, whose providence extends to all things and who brings together those intermediate causes to produce such effects.

2. About Aristotle's View that the World is Eternal

21.41 But how can the preceding be reconciled with Aristotle's position which seems to hold that God cannot produce anything new immediately? In assuming that the world was eternal, Aristotle denied that any movement could be wholly new. While a particular cycle could be new, the movement as a whole is not. He based this conclusion on three principles, the first of which is the absolute immutability of the first principle. Being a principle that is completely immutable, he cannot produce immediately any new movement or mobile thing. Otherwise he would change, because he would exist differently at one moment from how he did at another.

21.42 But I do not believe that Aristotle argues solely from the immutability of the agent. Another principle involving the effect is needed, viz., an immutable agent cannot cause immediately a new kind of effect. Otherwise Aristotle would contradict himself, for he admits that an intelligence that is completely immutable does cause a new cycle of the movement and does not become mutable by doing so.⁴⁴

21.43 But neither does this suffice. We must add a third principle. A completely immutable agent could not immediately cause a new kind of effect unless other causes, active or receptive, intervened. Otherwise the position he maintained would not be true, for if the intermediary causes are disposed to act differently or to receive the action differently, different effects could occur even though there is no change or novelty in the first cause.

[15] 21.44 We may say, then, according to Aristotle, that a completely immutable agent, in the absence of any active or passive mediating factors that could be differently disposed, could not cause a new kind of effect. But if any of these conditions is lacking we have no grounds for concluding that, according to Aristotle, if God caused any new effects, this would introduce novelty into God.

21.45 We must conclude, therefore, that Aristotle does not contradict himself in the two works *Good Fortune* and the *Physics*⁴⁵ in the way some would wish to claim he does. According to one interpretation [21.39], it suffices to trace back every fortuitous event to the heavens, and this does not imply any mutability or novelty in God, for he would only cause new fortuitous events by means of the heavens, and this would not count against him. But even on the second interpretation [21.40], if one has to trace back some new fortuitous effects directly to God, Aristotle would still not contradict himself, for he was certain that according to his principles⁴⁶ the intellective soul had to come immediately from God and that natural reason could reach this conclusion because the soul is immortal, and this is quasi-evident from reason. Thus something new could come immediately from God, and this does not imply that Aristotle contradicted himself according to his principles.⁴⁷

21.46 But how is this possible? We have to say that that agent's immutability excludes the possibility of his causing a new kind of effect, according to Aristotle, only if one excludes the intervention of other intermediary active or passive causes. But if this condition is lacking, as it would be when the active or passive causes are differently disposed, God could cause a new and different kind of thing. And if the effect caused were of the same kind, God could

⁴⁴ Aristotle, *Metaph.* XII, c.7 (1072a20-25).
⁴⁵ Aristotle, *Physic.* VIII, c.1 (251a20-252b7).
⁴⁶ Aristotle, *De animal. gener.* II, c.3 (736b28-32).
⁴⁷ Cf. Duns Scotus, *Ord.* I, d.8, nn.239-52 (IV, 288-95).

cause it immediately. Just as sun can immediately melt ice and harden mud without there being anything new in it, so God, according to Aristotle, with the necessity of immutability causes this soul once this particular body is organized. This did not occur earlier because the matter was not disposed to receive the soul earlier. Just as the sun causes one effect in the air and another in water only because of the difference in what receives the radiation, so in the case we are discussing. According to Aristotle, God's influence, so far as he is concerned, proceeds from him uniformly, but because this person is disposed and that one is not, he impels the former to the sort of purposeful action that results in an unexpected good. He does not impel the second person to this because he finds that he lacks the aforesaid disposition. Aristotle's view in *Good Fortune* is consistent with his position in *Physics* VIII[48], namely, that God cannot produce a new world, or a new heaven, or new movement by his causality.

21.47 According to faith and the truth of the matter, however, we must say that by his general providence, God rules all things as they are suited by nature to be ruled, as *The City of God* puts it[49]: "The creator of every nature has so ordained that each of his creatures is permitted to have and to exercise powers of its own." In addition to this general providence, by a kind of special election, God provides for each man according to present or future merits, which though veiled from us are present to him, for his judgments, though hidden, are always just, so that, as Boethius puts it,[50] adversity is sometimes more beneficial than prosperity.

21.48 And so it is that while we do admit that someone is fortunate, we do not assume this implies something new in God. Thus the answers to the arguments for the contrary are obvious.

[48] Aristotle, *Physic.* VIII, c.6 (259b32-260a19).
[49] Augustine, *De civ. Dei* VII, c.30: PL 41, 220; CCSL 47, 212.
[50] Boethius, *De consolat. philos.* c.4, n.4: PL 63, 805; CCSL 94, 77.

Appendix

ADDITION 1.11 (VIVÈS XXV, 9-10)

Seek the solution in the first book, distinction eight, question three on the attributes.[1]

To the first objection [in 1.8], one can answer that the essence includes all divine perfection unitively and identically, but not formally. In this way Damascene's dictum must be understood as it appears clear from I, dist. 8, q.3.[2] Although such perfections are identical with the essence, yet they are distinct extramentally and formally. To the confirmation from Anselm one answers likewise that the essence is unitively and identically the whole perfection, but not formally and extramentally. Hence, though every divine perfection is formally infinite, it is not radically infinite in the way the essence and existence of God are.

To the second objection [in 1.10], one can say that the essence and existence in creatures are like quiddity and its mode. Therefore they are distinct. However, in God existence pertains to the concept of essence and is predicated in the first mode of *per se* predication,* so that the proposition asserting this would be first and immediate, and all other propositions would follow from this, as it appears in I, dist. 2.[3] Consider the many ideas on these objections in IV, dist. 46, q.3[4] and *Reportatio* I, dist. 45, q.2[5] and dist. 2, part 2, q.2[6] and *infra*, q.5, art. 3[7] and in I, dist. 1, q.2.[8]

ADDITION 1:39 (VIVÈS XXV, 21)

Or the argument could be formulated this way. No potency has its first being [*esse*] by its operation. This is evident, for nothing gives being to itself, as is obvious from *The Trinity* I,[9] and consequently no potency receives its first being from the operation which

---

[1] *Ord.* I, d.8, nn.218-22; IV, 274-77.
[2] Ibid., n.158, 198; IV, 230, 264.
[3] Ibid., d.2, n.25; II, 137-38.
[4] Ibid., IV, d.46, q.3 (Vivès XX, 446-48).
[5] *Rep.* I, d.45, q.2 (Vivès XXII, 500-507).
[6] *Ord.* I, d.2, nn.25-26; II, 137-39.
[7] *Quodlibet* 5.43-56.   [8] *Ord.* I, d.1, nn.21-61 (II, 17-45).
[9] Augustine, *De Trin.* I, c.1; PL 42, 820; CCSL 50, 28.

stems from it; but every intellection is an operation of the intellect *qua* intellect. Therefore, the divine intellect as such has not its first being from its operation. But everything that is in God by virtue of an extrinsic operation [*ad extra*] as such does derive its being from the operation of the intellect or from intellection, because its "being," which is that of a conceptual relation, stems from the consideration of the intellect.

ADDITION 7.38 (VIVÈS xxv, 294-95)

The first objection [in 7.35] is answered by making a distinction in regard to the will. Either the pilgrim can know the will of God in an obscure concept, and then it is conceded that he is able to know by his purely natural endowments that God has a will most perfect and infinite, but then it is denied that this concept of the will provides a middle term for demonstrating that God is omnipotent as a reasoned fact (for the middle term would have to be known distinctly for this sort of demonstration), or else the pilgrim can know of the will of God in a distinct concept, and this is denied to be the case.

As for the second objection [in 7.36], the major could be denied, for there are plenty of cases to the contrary. For the propositions "Being is true" and "Being is good" are true and necessary and their terms are simply simple* concepts, for neither being nor true nor good contain concepts that can be resolved into other more primitive concepts. However, such propositions are demonstrable as reasoned facts using the first property of being, viz., one, as middle term. The minor [in 7.36] is simply false, for the divine essence and every positive attribute we have of God is conceived through concepts resolvable into more primitive concepts, namely, into the concept being, even though the divine property itself has the highest degree of simplicity of the sort that is opposed to composition and compossibility.

As for the third objection [in 7.37], it is claimed that just as there is an order among demonstrations of the reasoned fact, so also too there is an order among demonstrations of the simple fact. For, if the philosopher of nature can demonstrate God's existence as a simple fact, the metaphysician can do so even more perfectly.

For the solution of these objections[10] the Doctor refers to another

---

[10] The Wadding edition has this second set of answers as one of the three Additions printed at the end of the Quodlibet with instructions where to insert it. Cf. *Opera omnia* (Lugduni, 1639) xii, 544.

place. However, the first can be answered by denying the consequence or implication. For though the intellect of the pilgrim by its natural power can know that God has a perfect will, it grasps this only in an imperfect concept, for there is no more incongruity about knowing that something is most perfect by means of an imperfect concept than there is about knowing something is infinite by means of a finite concept. That is why the omnipotence of God cannot be inferred by a demonstration of the reasoned fact from the concept of the will a pilgrim possesses according to the present dispensation.

To the second objection [in 7.36], one must say that, whatever be said for the major, the minor, it seems, must be denied. Even though God is a most perfect being, not every concept we have of him is irreducibly simple, and, therefore, every proposition affirming some attribute of him need not be *per se* properly speaking, and even if it were, it would not follow that it is known *per se*.

To the third objection [in 7.37], one must say that the metaphysician's knowledge of God surpasses that of the natural philosopher both extensively (because of the greater number of attributes) and intensively (because of its greater perfection and its superior mode of cognition). To the form of the argument, then, one may concede the first entailment and consequent that the metaphysician can have a knowledge of the simple fact that is more perfect and beyond that attained by the natural philosopher. The reason is that where knowledge of the simple fact is concerned there is a certain leeway such that one form of it exceeds another both intensively and extensively. Therefore, the further inference that the metaphysician's knowledge will be knowledge of the reasoned fact must be denied.

ADDITION 9.53 (VIVÈS XXV, 392)

To the sixth objection [in 9.36], one can say that although Avicenna[11] in his *Metaphysics* IX, ch. 4, affirms that the heaven is animated, Aristotle never said this. If it is claimed that Aristotle seems to maintain this in the *De caelo* I, ch. 5[12] and in the *Metaphysics* XII,[13] one can answer that the soul has two functions, as is indicated in the *De anima*,[14] that of moving and that of informing. By the first, Aristotle says, we understand, feel, and move. And according to the last named property, one can say the heavens are animated and, to

---

[11] *Metaph.* IX, c.4 (II, 104v-105r).
[12] *De Caelo* II, c.2 (285a28-286a2).
[13] *Metaphysica* XII, c.5 (1071a1-14).
[14] *De anima* II, c.2 (414a12-13).

that extent, the angels [or Intelligences*] are the "forms"—not indeed as informing [matter] but as moving.

Answer to the other objection [in 9.37]: As it appears from II, dist. 8,[15] the angel can take a body and unite itself to it in the way a motor is united to a ship or a mover to that which is mobile, but this is not by informing it, as appears from the case of the good and bad angels, as is explained in the second [book].[16]

ADDITION 11.15 (VIVÈS xxv, 442)

To the first [in 11.13], it is answered that such localization belongs to the category of ubiety. Although the Philosopher only defines ubiety [*ubi*] passively, there is another that is active. It represents another species that falls under the common category "ubiety," which contains both the active and passive forms, as is evident from IV, dist. 10, q. 1.[17]

To the second [in 11.14], some say in such a case the heaven would not move. However, I say otherwise that such a movement would be in reference to an imaginary, not an actual, ubiety. Nor is it incongruous to concede this, since it follows from the case under consideration, as is evident later on in this question.

ADDITION 12.28 (VIVÈS xxv, 483)

To this question I answer: If God should produce something, either he would produce it without secondary causes—which philosophers would not admit—and then it would be possible that the product lasted for an instant, just as God's action did, or he would produce it through secondary causes, and then, it seems, we could not admit that the product, if it were something permanent, could exist for only one instant. It would be different, of course, with indivisible things like mutation or instants which, even according to the Philosopher, last but an instant.

But in our case, if we are speaking of permanent things, it is more probable simply to hold the negative view. See dist. 8 of book I, at the end of the last question.[18]

ADDITION 13.56 (VIVÈS xxv, 545)

The objection [in 13.54] could be answered the way the Doctor solves the question in dist. 46 of book IV.[19] There he makes the point

---

[15] *Ord.* II, d.8 (Vivès x, 417-22).   [16] Ibid.
[17] Ibid., IV, d.10, q.1, n.11 (Vivès XVII, 79).
[18] Ibid., I, d.8, nn.294-301; IV, 322-26.
[19] Ibid., IV, d.49, q.3, nn.27-32 (Vivès XXI, 52-55).

APPENDIX

that although beatitude does not include the relationship of attainment essentially, it does require such if the happiness is to be complete and perfect. Consequently, anyone who would have this beatific operation without the relationship, would not be truly and completely happy.

As for the second objection [in 13.55], look for the answer in dist. 10 of book IV, the last question[20] and also in the present question in the distinction about the ultimate perfection.[21]

ADDITION 14.25 (VIVÈS XXVI, 11)

My reply [to 14.25] can be gathered from book III, dist. 23 and 24.[22] That infused faith is present in us is a matter of pure belief and, therefore, it is not evident. But we do experience acquired faith in ourselves and, by means of it, whatever is present by hearing is credible and is consequently in some sense evident, although, speaking properly, neither of the two kinds of faith is evident by virtue of its object. It is not possible to have an act of infused faith without acquired faith, as is obvious from what was said above [in 14.24]. The acquired faith has its evidence from the testimony of the one who makes the revelation or the one who preaches the doctrine in question.

ADDITION 15.79 (VIVÈS XXVI, 171-72)

The answer to the other two objections [in 15.72f.] can be found in q. 2, dist. 14 of book III towards the end.[23] Therefore, the entire first objection can be admitted. But if one goes on to infer that, therefore, the vision of the intellect of the blessed will be the same as that of God, the validity of the parallel will be denied, for the intellect of God has the vision of secondary objects necessarily *per se* and comprehensively by virtue of his perfection and by means of the primary object [or divine essence], which naturally represents all things to him. But the created intellect of the blessed has an incidental vision of the secondary objects, because it understands them incidentally or *per accidens* (i.e., by means of the essence which reveals such objects to this intellect freely and contingently). Hence the act of the blessed does not receive any perfection from such objects, but all of its perfection stems from the essence which this intellect sees and which reveals such objects to this intellect.

[20] Ibid., d.10, q.9, nn.5-6 (Vivès XVII, 303-304).
[21] Cf. 13.49.
[22] *Ord.* III, d.23-24 (Vivès XV, 5-53).
[23] Ibid., d.14, q.2, nn.18-21 (Vivès XIV, 515-19).

To the other objection [in 15.73] the answer is that the objection is valid and the entailment follows if the act of the vision of the essence and other objects were one and the same. But if the acts are distinct, the implication is not valid.

ADDITION 18.23 (VIVÈS XXVI, 238-39)

Note that in addition to the natural goodness of volition which pertains to it as a being and is characteristic of every positive being in a greater or lesser degree, there are three degrees of moral goodness. The first is called generic goodness, which pertains to volition because it has to do with an object that is not only naturally suited to it, as sunlight is to vision, but is appropriate to it according to the dictates of right reason. This is the first stage of moral goodness which can be called "generic," because it is like the material element as regards every further [specification or] ulterior goodness in the moral order. For an act which has a suitable object can be formed, as it were, by other moral circumstances, and therefore is quasi-potential. Yet it is not completely potential in the sense of being outside the moral order entirely as an act would be if considered exclusively from the standpoint of nature. On the contrary, it is potential within the genus of morality because it already has something characteristic of morality, namely, an object appropriate to the act.

The second stage of moral goodness can be called "virtuous" or that due to the circumstances. It pertains to volition because the will elicits the act according to all the circumstances which right reason says must be there in performing the act. For according to Dionysius,[24] "Good requires that everything about the act be right." Such goodness is specific moral goodness, so to say, because the act has all the moral differences that contract or specify the generic goodness.

The third goodness can be called meritorious or gratuitous in the divine acceptation as regards a reward. Such goodness pertains to the act from the fact that once the first two degrees of goodness are there, the act is elicited in conformity with the principle of merit, which is grace or charity. An example of the first degree of goodness is to give alms; an example of the second is to give alms to a needy pauper and in the proper place and to do this for the love of God. An example of the third is to perform such an action as the above not only by natural inclination—as it could have been performed by a man in the state of innocence and perhaps even now could be per-

---

[24] Ps.-Dionysius, *De divin. nomin.* c.4, 30; PG 3, 806; *Dionysiaca* I, 298.

formed by a sinner should he remain such and unrepentant but were moved by natural piety towards his neighbor. What is needed for this third is that the act be performed through charity by virtue of which the one doing the act is a friend of God, insofar as God regards his works with favor. Now this triple goodness is so ordered that the first is presupposed by the second, and the second by the third, but not vice versa.

To this threefold goodness a triple badness corresponds. The first badness is generic. This is present when an act with only natural goodness is had because the first element that should put it in the moral order is absent because the object is unsuitable, for instance, an act of hating God. The second badness stems from some circumstance that makes the act inordinate, even though it has a suitable object. The third is demeritorious.

ADDITION 20.49 (VIVÈS XXVI, 321-22)

As for the difficulty raised [in 20.49], one could say that if there were but one pilgrim [in grace], there is at least a virtual or habitual intention of wanting God to accept the prayers of the Church. With this, one can then proceed to solve the problem the way the initial argument is solved at the end [in 20.71].

Second, one can say that the [personal] merit of the Church militant is related to the merits of Christ's passion not because Christ merits now, but because when he suffered he merited that his merit be applicable to this merit of the militant Church.

Third, I say to the first objection, [viz., that there might be no pilgrim in a state of grace], that by divine providence there will never be a militant Church without someone having grace and charity, according to Christ's words in Luke: "I have prayed for you, Peter, that your faith may never fail."[25]

[25] Luke 22:33.

Glossary

References in the text to terms explained in the glossary are marked with an asterisk as are cross references within the glossary itself.

a posteriori proof: An argument from what is posterior logically or ontologically to what is prior, such as from effect to cause, or from an agent's functions or operations to the nature underlying such behavior. If the proof fulfills Aristotle's definition of epistemic* or demonstrative knowledge, an *a posteriori* proof is equivalent to his demonstration of simple fact.* Since such arguments usually begin with empirical data, such as observed effects or behavior patterns, *a posteriori* proofs are often said to be based upon experience, in contrast to *a priori* arguments.

a priori proof: An argument that proceeds from what is prior logically or ontologically to what is posterior, such as from cause to effect, from the nature of an agent to its function. If couched in the form of an Aristotelian syllogistic demonstration, an *a priori* proof is equivalent to a demonstration of the reasoned fact* where the middle term gives the cause, reason, or explanation why the predicate of the conclusion is universally characteristic of the subject. As such it is contrasted with an *a posteriori* proof or a demonstration of simple fact.* Inasmuch as such a proof indicates not just that something is so, but explains why it must be so, an *a priori* proof is sometimes said to be independent of experience, viz., that the conclusion is a fact.

absolute form: In terms of the ten Aristotelian categories,* Scotus adopts the view common among his contemporaries that only the first three categories involve an absolute entity or thing* in contradistinction to the remaining seven. Thus, in addition to the substantial form, any accidental form falling under the two categories of quality or quantity would be absolute forms. Some later scholastics like William Ockham restricted absolute forms to substance or quality.

abstractive cognition, see *cognition, intuitive and abstract*

accidens per accidens: The five predicables of Porphyry expressed the five relations in which a universal term may stand to the subject of which it is predicated. They are genus, specific difference, species, *proprium* (property), and contingent accident. The first three represented the essence as a whole (species) or a part thereof (genus, difference) and were said to be necessarily connected with the essence and predicable of it in the first mode of *per se* predication. Thus, since the defining characteristics of Socrates, Plato, etc., would be, according to Aristotle, "rational animal," both notions, either singly or conjointly, are predicable of these individuals *per se primo modo*. A property (or *proprium*), though it is not part of the essential definition of the subject, is nevertheless inseparable from the essence and can in fact be shown to follow from the definition as a logical consequence. It is predicable of the subject, therefore, *per se* or necessarily, but in the second mode. Examples as regards man would be "risible," "teachable," etc. Scholastics sometimes called such properties *per se* accidents (*accidens per se*) where accident is contrasted with essence. Those predicates which did not express necessary features of the individual, such as "ruddy," "bearded," "musical," etc., were said to be predicated *per accidens* or contingently. In contrast to *per se* accidents, they were called *accidens per accidens* or simply accidents. Scotus usually prefers the latter usage.

accidens per se (proprium), see *accidens per accidens*

accidental potency, proximate, see *proximate potency*

act, second, see *in actu primo, in actu secundo*

act, substantial, see *substantial act* or *act and potency*

act and potency: Aristotle's basic modalities of being, where "act" denotes what exists or is the case, whereas "potency" expresses what can be. But since "is" and "can be" have many linguistic usages, both act and potency took on various shades of meaning in philosophy that bear only a family resemblance to each other (Cf. Scotus, *Quaestiones subtilissimae in Aristotelis Metaphysicam* IX, qq. 1-2). Thus the following pairs of opposites are often related respectively as act to potency by medieval philosophers: actual vs. potential, real vs. possible, form vs. matter, existence vs. essence, agent vs. patient, operation vs. operative faculty, what is complete, finished, or perfect vs. what is incomplete, not fully actualized, or imperfect. Potencies are further classified as active powers or passive capacities depending on whether they refer to what a subject or agent can do (operative faculties) or what can be done to or in a subject (receptive capacities). An active potency, argued the scholastics, unlike a passive potency, does not necessarily imply imperfection. Consequently, though God is called "pure act" inasmuch as there is no *ad intra** possibility in the divine that is not fully actualized, not all possible relationships *ad extra** to creatures need be realized since their actualization is contingent upon his free will as Creator. It is in this sense that we attribute "omnipotence" to God as a perfection. Various acts or degrees of actualization also are distinguished. If God as pure act lies at one end of the spectrum, primary matter as "pure potency to form" has the least degree of actuality, according to Scotus. In between God and prime matter come: (1) The "separate substances"* (i.e., the Intelligences* postulated by the philosophers, or the angels of Judeo-Christian theology), so-called because they exist in separation from all matter. As spiritual or immaterial substances they are only in accidental potency to change such as that involving new knowledge or voluntary actions. (2) The celestial bodies which, though they contain prime matter, are substantially immutable in virtue of their incorruptible form. They are only in potency to motion or change of place. (3) Corporeal or bodily substances, ranging from man, the most complex, to the four elemental substances (fire, air, water, earth), are all composed of primary matter and one (or more) substantial forms, and as such are in potency to substantial changes (generation and corruption*) as well as to accidental ones. Generation of one substance from another or others represents a major actualization, and the new form matter receives is called a substantial act.* New qualities or a change in size or quantity, by contrast, involve the actualization of accidental potentialities and the new form acquired is called an accidental act. See also *in actu primo, in actu secundo.*

action, immanent and transient: Immanent activity is that which has its principle or source and its term or effect within the agent and which represents a perfection of the agent and not that of some external patient. Vital activities are instances of immanent actions. Transient (transeunt, transitive), by contrast, are actions which have their term outside the causal agent in some other being that is changed by the agent.

ad extra, ad intra: As applied to divine relationships, attributes, or operations, these Latin expressions designate what is exterior or interior respectively to the Godhead itself. Scotus adopts the common theological view that a monotheistic interpretation of the Christian Trinity implies that all *ad extra* effects, such as creation, conservation, or direct divine intervention with creatures, must stem causally from the divine nature as a whole and hence are the common voluntary and contingent effect of all three divine persons. What is *ad intra*, by contrast, may be either common to all (e.g., God's self-knowledge and love) or proper to one person to the exclusion of the others (e.g., the Father's eternal generation of the Son or Word). However, a unique personal relationship between a single divine person and a creature is not ruled out by this communality of *ad extra* operations. Thus, for example, while the Incarnation of the Word in terms of efficient causality is ascribed to all three divine persons, only the Son, and not the Father or Holy Spirit, is said to be personally or hypostatically united to the human nature of Jesus Christ. Though this nature *qua* nature is perfect, theologians argued, it lacks a distinct human personality. Hence the effect of such a hypostatic union is that Christ's human actions can be ascribed exclusively to the second divine person. In Question Nineteen, Scotus attempts to give some rational account of what is involved in this assumption of a human nature exclusively by the divine Word or Son. See *hypostatic union*.

advene, see *advenient intrinsically and extrinsically*

advenient intrinsically and extrinsically (adveniens intrinsecus et extrinsecus): *Webster's New International Dictionary* (2nd ed.) defines "advene" as "to be added to something or become a part of it, though not essential," and "advenient" as "coming from outward causes; superadded." Scotus uses the terms to describe how the category of relation* differs from the last six categories,* which also involve some sort of relation. Since he does not consider any relationship to form a *per se* or essential unity with its foundation or with the terms said to be related, all relations are in that sense "advenient." However, those belonging to the category "relation," e.g., similarity based on equality in size, or the same shade of color, etc., are said to be "intrinsically advenient" in that they follow necessarily given the existence of the two *relata* and the foundation, e.g., the quantity or color. So far as the last six categories are concerned, however, the relationship does not arise automatically given the existence of the relata and the foundation for the relationship, but an additional extrinsic factor is required. Thus, for instance, the category of "action" or "passion" is not the result of the existence of agent and patient and the foundation for the respective relationships (the active and passive) potencies, but something more is required, e.g., volition in a free agent, the lack of impeding factors, etc., etc. In discussing ubiety* he also shows that the existence of a body and place and the foundation for being circumscriptively in place (viz., the extension of quantity of the body) is not sufficient to have ubiety, but the body must be put into place either by itself or another agent. Cf. 11.34.

aeviternity: A form of duration intermediate between time and eternity. Whereas eternity was considered to be proper to God, and time characteristic of changeable things, aeviternity (sometimes called "created eternity") was considered to be characteristic of creatures incapable of substantial change, such as the angels, which were subject only to accidental changes as regards knowledge, volition, etc., or the heavenly bodies which, though incorruptible, were subject to locomotion or change of place. While these accidental changes were measurable by time, the substantial nature was possessed whole and entire, as it were, at all times, and thus resembled eternity, but, being created, was properly called aeviternal duration. Scholastic philosophers and theologians, though agreeing that aeviternity (*aevum*) was intermediate between time and eternity, explained it differently. Cf. St. Thomas, *Sum. theol.* I, q. 10, a.5.

agent intellect: Medieval philosophers in the Aristotelian tradition considered the intellect as playing a dual role, one active (which was ascribed to the agent intellect), the other passive (attributed to the possible intellect*). This division is based on an obscure passage in Aristotle's *De anima* (III, c.5; 430a18) and underwent a variety of interpretations. Though Aristotle compares the active factor to a light ($\tau\acute{o}$ $\phi\hat{\omega}s$), he never uses the term ($\nu o\hat{u}s$ $\pi o\iota\eta\tau\iota\kappa\acute{o}s$, agent intellect). With Alexander of Aphrodisias, as well as with some scholastic interpretations of Augustinian illumination, the active intellect is identified with God. With Alfarabi and Avicenna, it is a subordinate intelligence or "angel" somehow connected with the moon. Aquinas considers the active intellect to be a faculty of the soul really distinct from the possible intellect. Scotus also considers it to be a property of the soul, but regards it as only formally distinct from, but really identical with, the possible intellect and the soul's substance. The general function of the agent intellect is to render the potentially intelligible in the sense image or phantasm* actually intelligible. Scotus' own interpretation of possible refinements of this basic role are discussed in connection with the problem posed in Question Fifteen.

appropriation, appropriated: In theological usage, appropriation denotes the attribution to one divine person in particular of some characteristic common in fact to all three persons. The basis for the ascription is some degree of affinity, according to our way of thinking, between the attribute in question (usually some divine action *ad extra**) and the notional* or personal characteristics peculiar to one divine person in particular. Thus in both the Apostles' and Nicene Creeds, God, the Father, is described as "Almighty, maker of heaven and earth" because power and creativity seem peculiarly appropriate to him as the first productive principle from whom the other persons proceed. Similarly because the Son or Word* (Logos), according to Augustine, proceeds from the intellectual memory* of the Father (even as the Holy Spirit proceeds from the will they share as the principle of active love), whatever pertains to knowledge, truth, or wisdom is appropriated to the Son whereas charity and holiness are attributed especially to the Holy Spirit. In addition to the four Aristotelian "causes" (viz., material, formal, efficient, and final), medieval philosophers commonly spoke of an exemplar cause, where the "exemplar" referred to the idea in the artisan's mind that he planned to embody in the artefact. Since Christian Neoplatonists identified the Platonic archetypal ideas with the "blueprint" of the creature in the mind of the Creator, on the one hand, and spoke of the divine Son as the Logos or Word of the Father, on the other, it seemed particularly appropriate to associate the divine exemplars of creatures with the second person of the Trinity. One question proposed to Scotus (Q.10) was whether the Word exercised some causality in regard to creatures that was not shared with the other persons. Since Scotus believed exemplar causality was simply a species of efficient causality, viz., that of an agent endowed with intelligence, he discusses this question in the context of divine omnipotence.

categories, the ten (decem praedicamenta): According to Aristotle (*Categories*, c.4, 1a25) they are (1) substance, (2) quantity, (3) quality, (4) relation, (5) action, (6) passion, (7) place, (8) time, (9) position or posture, (10) state. Scotus often refers to them as *genera generalissima*, i.e., the most universal genera.

cause, equivocal, see *equivocal principle or cause*

cause, essential (per se) vs. incidental (per accidens): Scotus speaks of nature (*natura*) and will (*voluntas*) as *per se* causes in contrast to chance (*casus*) and fortune or misfortune (*fortuna*). Nature embraces all natural causes, i.e., those which produce their proper effect without deliberation. Will is regarded as the essential cause of all effects deliberately intended by a voluntary agent. Incidental or chance effects result from the interference of two or more mutually independent causal sequences. Where a voluntary agent is involved, the effects he causes unintentionally are called luck or fortune. Scotus follows Aristotle here (cf. *Physics* II, c.5, 196b17-22).

causes, essential order of: In his proofs for God's existence (e.g., *Ordinatio* I, d.2, nn.47-55 and the parallel passage in the *Lectura*), Scotus is especially concerned with spelling out the difference between an essential versus an accidental concatenation of causes. A series of generative causes such as that of grandparents, parents and child, or any sequence of events such as those later analyzed by Hume, would be causes only accidentally ordered to one another in producing the final effect of the series. Where an essential ordering or concatenation exists, all the causal factors must coexist both to produce and conserve their effect. This is true whether they be of different types (such as material, formal, efficient, and final) or a chain of the same type, e.g., efficient or final causes, as Avicenna postulated for the hierarchy of Intelligences* between God and the material world. While infinite regress in accidentally ordered causes may be possible, Scotus claimed the chain as a whole must be essentially ordered to some coexisting cause which guarantees the perpetuity of what is constant or cyclic about such repetitive productivity, for no philosopher postulates an infinite regress where the concatenation of causes is essential and all must coexist. To assume an infinity of links upon which a possible effect is conserved, for example, is not to explain its actual conservation. See also *essential order*.

circumscriptive[ly], see *place, types of presence in*

coeval: The adjective meaning "the same age as." It is used specifically to express those characteristics of things present as long as the subject has existed. Thus Scotus sometimes speaks of "possible creatures" in the divine mind as being coeval with him, rather than as "eternal," where "eternity" is used to designate a divine attribute Similarly, whatever substances incapable of substantial change, like the angels, intelligences, or heavenly bodies, may have possessed in terms of powers, etc., are said to be coeval.

cognition, intuitive and abstract: By intuitive knowledge is meant the simple (non-judgmental) awareness of something as existing here and now. Not only are the senses capable of such knowledge, Scotus argues, but the intellect possesses such a capacity as well. He argued this on the theological ground that if man's simple intellection was limited only to abstract concepts—what can be abstracted from sense encounters in the way described by Aristotle—then the face-to-face vision of God promised to man in the afterlife becomes impossible. But Scotus also believed rational considerations required some measure of intellectual intuition. There are many primary contingent propositions that are indubitable (such as "I doubt such and such" or "I am thinking of such and such"). Since this certitude cannot be accounted for by any amount of conceptual analysis of the propositional terms, some simple awareness of the existential situation verifying the proposition is required. This cannot be purely sensory knowledge, since the existential judgment often involves conceptual or nonsensory meanings. Nor can this awareness of existence be something that is known only in and through the judgment itself, since judgment, as the second act of the intellect, always presupposes logically, if not necessarily psychologically or temporally, prior acts of simple awareness, called the "first acts" of the intellect. And in the case of primary contingent truth, this awareness cannot be limited simply to abstract conceptual meanings.

communicable: Whatever can be given to more than one subject (individual or person) is said to be communicable. In creatures, this includes every positive trait or perfection they possess except that unique individuating feature called haecceity.* In God, however, it includes the unique divine nature or essence with all its perfection. Only the positive features formally constituting each divine person as Father, Son (or Word), and Holy Spirit, respectively, are said to be incommunicable. In begetting the Son, the Father communicates the divine nature to the Son; the Father and Son jointly communicate it to the Holy Spirit. In 19.81 Scotus discusses various ways in which one thing can be said to be communicated to another. See also *hypostatic union*.

confused knowledge: "Confused" is usually used in a technical sense. As a noun (*confusum*) it means any universal notion with respect to what falls under it extensively. Thus Scotus speaks of *ens*, which is a primitively simple (*simpliciter simplex*) term, as a *confusum* (in virtue of its universal extension) but which, if known at all, can only be known distinctly. As an adverb (*confuse*) it expresses the way in which one knows an object, viz., *by name*. As such it is contrasted with distinct knowledge*, viz., knowledge by way of definition. In 14.12 he speaks of knowing something in a quasi-confused manner.

corruption: The perishing of the substantial form upon the generation of the new form. One of the most characteristic marks of terrestrial or sublunary substances, according to Aristotle, was their capacity to undergo substantial change. Celestial bodies, by contrast, were incapable of substantial change and subject only to rotary motion or change of place. Many commentators explained the incorruptibility of the heavens not only on the grounds that the form of celestial bodies was incorruptible but also because the ethereal matter of which they were composed was essentially different from the primary matter characteristic of terrestrial elements (earth, water, air, and fire) and their various compounds. Scotus, on the contrary, argues that primary matter throughout the universe is essentially the same and that the difference between celestial and terrestrial bodies stems from the different nature of their forms. Terrestrial forms are such that the natural causes operative throughout the realm of the four elements cause the corruption of one form in generating its contrary. This is not the case with the more perfect celestial form, which has no proper contrary. Nevertheless, the celestial body is not something absolutely necessary or intrinsically incorruptible, since God, for instance, could by direct action cause its form to perish and convert the heavens into fire or water. Cf. *Ordinatio* II, d.14, q.1.

declarative knowledge: Following St. Augustine, the scholastics spoke of actual knowledge not only as a child conceived or begotten by the mind, but as *revealing* or *declaring* what lay hidden in the memory. In God, declarative knowledge was considered to be involved in some way with the production of the Word or second person of the Trinity, but theologians interpreted this in different ways. Cf. *Ordinatio* I, d.32, n.23; *Ord.* III, d.32.

declaratively, see *declarative knowledge*

demonstration of simple fact (demonstratio quia), see *epistemic knowledge*

demonstration of the reasoned fact (demonstratio propter quid), see *epistemic knowledge*

diminished entity, see *diminutive being*

diminutive being (ens diminutum): This expression, which had its origins in the Arabian translation of Aristotle's *Metaphysics* VI, c. 4 and Averroes' *Commentary* on it, is used exclusively by Scotus to express the sort of being a thing acquires in the mind or intellect (created or divine) by being known or thought of.

distinct knowledge: Distinct knowledge in a technical sense is contrasted with confused knowledge.* As Scotus explains (*Ord.* I, d. 3, n.72) we know something confusedly when our concept stands for the object in much the same way as a name does; we know it distinctly when we are able to define it. Following Avicenna, Scotus argues that being (*ens*) is the first primitive or undefined element in every real definition. Like all irreducibly simple concepts it can only be known distinctly and *in toto* if it is known at all. All other distinct knowledge of real things includes being as part of their essential definition.

eminently: In a higher or more perfect way or even in a supreme or infinite way. It is often contrasted with formally* or virtually.*

epistemic knowledge: The conclusion of a demonstration in the technical sense defined by Aristotle in *Analytica posteriora* I, c. 13-14 is called ἐπιστήμη in Greek and *scientia* (science) in Latin. Scotus cites four basic conditions for such scientific or epistemic knowledge: (1) it must be certain and not just an opinion; (2) it must be a necessary truth, not just a contingent one; (3) it must not be immediately evident but it is known by means of other evident and necessary truths; (4) it is derived from these latter truths by way of some form of syllogistic or discursive reasoning process. Cf. *Ordinatio*, prol., n.41; *Ord.* I, d.2, n.39; d.3, nn.230ss. *Demonstratio propter quid*, or διότι, uses as its middle term something which expresses an ontological cause or reason why the predicate of the conclusion inheres in the subject. The essential definition of the subject or any one of its four Aristotelian causes might serve as the middle term. Following the Oxford translation of Aristotle, we have called a syllogism of this sort a "demonstration of the reasoned fact" and the conclusion it yields "knowledge of the reasoned fact." *Demonstratio quia*, or ὅτι, which we have translated as "demonstration of the simple fact," uses as a middle term something that logically connects the predicate to the subject, but does not give what Aristotle or the Scholastics would consider to be the real reason or the ontological cause why the subject in question has such a predicate. It is not clear whether Scotus equates *propter quid* and *a priori* on the one hand, and *quia* and *a posteriori* on the other, as Ockham expressly does. (Cf. Ockham's *Summa Logicae* III, pars. 2, c.17). For Aristotle, demonstration through a remote cause (an *a priori* principle), however, is only a *demonstratio quia*.

equivocal effect: One that is of a nature specifically different from that of its cause, as, for instance, a creature as caused by God, or a painting as caused by the artist. Equivocal effects are contrasted with univocal effects, such as fire producing fire, or like begetting like. See also *equivocal principle or cause*.

equivocal principle or cause: One that produces an effect or product specifically different from its own nature. Sometimes called an analogous cause.

essential order: Order exists between two or more things if one can be said to be either prior or posterior to the other. If this is based on something accidental such as time, motion, place, size, etc., the order is accidental. If the priority or posteriority relationship stems from the nature or essence, it is essential. Though Scotus treats of essential order in all of his works, only in the *De Primo Principio* is there an attempt to treat the various types of essential order exhaustively under the two headings of eminence and dependence. The first obtains if one essence is more perfect than another; the second holds if one essence can exist without the other, but not vice versa. This may be because the first is the efficient, final, formal, or material cause of the second; or because of two effects of a common cause, the existence of the first is a precondition for that of the second. Where several causes are required to produce a particular effect, they may not be essentially ordered to one another in producing that effect. In this connection, see *causes, essential order of*. Because of the special theological problem of the hypostatic union* in Christ where a human nature depends on the person, but not on the divine nature, of the Word in a special way, Scotus speaks in 19.30 of an extended sense of "essential dependence."

essential priority, see *essential order*

essential dependence, see *essential order*

estimative power: From the Latin *aestimare*, to form an estimate of. One of the internal senses, whereby the desirable is instinctively distinguished from the baneful. To it was ascribed such instinctive animal behavior as the lamb's flight from the wolf or the monkey's avoidance of poisonous berries.

eucharistic species: The whole Christ, body, blood, soul, and divinity, is said to be present under the appearances of bread and wine after the consecration in the mass. *Species* was the name given by the theologians to these appearances, which were conceived as having an objective status or reality that enabled them to act directly on the senses. As Aristotle's philosophy came into general acceptance, medieval theologians developed various theories to explain the continued existence of the species after consecration, usually identifying them with the accidental categories of Aristotle, as distinct from substance. Hence the species came to be called commonly the "accidents of bread and wine" and since Christ's presence under these appearances was obviously not that of a normal material body, these accidents were not said to be inhering in the substance of Christ's body. Rather they were considered to be miraculously supported by divine power, which played the role or, better, took the place of the support ordinarily supplied by the substance. Hence they were referred to as "separated accidents."

eviternal, see *aeviternity*

ex opere operantis (Latin, "from the work of the worker"): A term used in describing the effects of prayers, good works, sacred signs or ceremonies (sacraments or sacramentals), and indicating that the effect depends upon the sanctity of the minister or the dispositions of the subject.

ex opere operato (Latin, "from the work wrought"): A term used in describing the effect of a sacrament or sacrifice to indicate that the effect (e.g., grace, or answer to prayer, etc.) is conferred in virtue of the work or action performed independently of the merits of the minister performing the action or conferring the sacrament.

exemplar: A model, idea, or exemplary cause. In Neoplatonic philosophy it is regarded as a distinct form of causality; Aristotlelian philosophers, on the contrary, usually reduce it to some form of efficient, formal, or final causality. As something the artisan intends to realize, it falls under final causality; as a preconception in the mind of the artisan, it is characteristic of an intelligent efficient cause (Scotus adopts this version); as that eventually impressed on the material by the efficient cause, it is identified with the formal Ideas* or ideal types that form the intelligible world and which the sensible world imitates. In Christian Neoplatonism, these archetypal exemplars are identified with the ideas of possible creatures in the divine mind and are often associated in a special way with the Word or second person of the Trinity. See *appropriation*.

extramentally (*ex natura rei*): In contrast to what exists only as the content of a concept or object of thought (i.e., an *ens diminutum*, or diminished being*), Scotus uses the expression *ex natura rei* to indicate something that exists in reality or has real being. Hence the English term "what exists outside the mind" or "extramentally" seems to come closest to expressing his meaning. This may be either a thing* (*res*) or some real aspect of a thing (i.e., a formality* or reality). See *formal distinction*.

faith, acquired vs. infused: Medieval theologians generally considered the supernatural virtue of faith (like hope and charity) to be directly infused in the human soul, for instance, at baptism. As such it differed from the acquired inclination or disposition to believe the testimony of a reliable witness. See also *habits*.

fontal plenitude (fontalis plenitudo): A medieval theological term used to describe the divine fecundity of the Father as the generator of the Son or Logos and as coproducer (with the Son) of the Holy Spirit. The term seems to have its origin in Pseudo-Dionysius, who describes the three divine persons in these words: "The Father indeed is the fontal or fountain deity; the Son and Holy Spirit are offspring of the deity . . . the progeny of the divine nature" (*De divinis nominibus*, c.2). Scotus' interpretation of the term can be found in *Ordinatio* I, d.28, nn.21-23, and in the parallel passage of the *Lectura*.

formal: What pertains to the essential nature or constitutive essence of a thing is called a formal characteristic of the same and is said to be predicated of it formally. Formal is often contrasted with what something contains or possesses only virtually* or eminently.* See also *formal predication vs. predication by identity*.

formal distinction: Scotus' theological colleagues were commonly concerned with the problem of how to distinguish God's various attributes without prejudice to his real and essential simplicity. On the one hand, they argued that knowledge, volition, goodness, justice, and love express pure perfections* or formal* characteristics essential to the Godhead. On the other hand, "knowledge" is no synonym for "volition" nor are their formal definitions the same. Even the mode of infinity does not seem to erase their formal nonidentity. For knowledge as such does not become formally volition, justice, or goodness, simply because it embraces all that can be known. Notional* characteristics like "paternity," "filiation," etc., posed similar problems with respect to the numerically identical essence, for while Father, Son, and Holy Spirit were admittedly really distinct persons with respect to each other, no theologian would go so far as to claim the notional or personal features proper to each represented something really distinct from the essence they shared in common. All agreed on the need for some distinction intermediary between one that is simply or unqualifiedly real (*distinctio realis*) and one that is merely mental or conceptual (*distinctio rationis*). But because "reason" (or *ratio*), like the Avicennian term *intentio**, could express an intelligible feature or essential characteristic of a real or extramental thing (*ens reale*) as well as the formal content of the concept used to think about it (*ens rationis*), most of Scotus' contemporaries were content to call it a special type of *distinctio rationis*, namely, one that existed only potentially or virtually in the thing (*a parte rei*) and became an actual distinction only when a created or divine mind reflected on its direct (or first intentional knowledge*) of the deity, either with reference to its discrete mirror images in creatures or to the really distinct relationships of origin* that characterized the divine person. *Qua* actually distinct, then, such *rationes* were the result of a kind of second intentional knowledge* and would have only diminished being* or *esse diminutum*, namely, as entities created, as it were, in the very act of being known. Scotus argues that this interpretation will not do, especially as regards the distinction between the notional and the essential elements in God. What God knows about himself *ad intra* he knows directly and intuitively, and this holds not only for his self-knowledge of the divine nature, which is communicable, but also for "paternity," "filiation," etc., which are personal and incommunicable. Knowledge of "paternity" as something other than "deity" is direct or first intentional knowledge. Some non-identity *a parte rei* would seem to be a logical precondition for conceiving "paternity" as formally distinct from "deity," for the eternal generation of the Son by the Father and their "breathing" of the Holy Spirit in love represent a very real and objective production or communication of the divine nature no matter how metaphorically expressed. Yet if the distinction or non-identity of "paternity" and "deity" is created only by the mind in reflecting on the Father and divine nature and is not *ex parte rei* logically prior to any actual knowledge of this sort, it is impossible to see how the divine nature is communicated without the paternity. Similarly, even if one divine perfection is not actually separable from the other in reality, some actual non-identity *a parte rei* is required as a logical presupposition for separating first intentional objects even conceptually, to say nothing of sharing or imitating only some of the divine perfection with one creature and other formal perfection with another. Cf. *Ordinatio* 1, d.2, nn. 388-410; d.8, nn.191-217. The objective correlate of a distinct formal concept Scotus calls a "reality" (from *realitas*, a "little thing") or "formality" (from *formalitas*, or "little form"), since, in Aristotelian terminology, "form," in contrast to matter, represents the quiddity* or what is essentially intelligible about a thing. Hence he calls the distinction *formalis a parte rei* (i.e., a formal distinction on the part of the thing), though he admits it could also be called a *distinctio virtualis* (virtual distinction), since one and the same simple thing or *res* is virtually many things and has the power or virtue (*virtus*) of producing objective notions or natural signs of itself that are conceptually separable, just as if they were produced by distinct things. It can even be called a *distinctio rationis* (distinction of reason), if *ratio* be understood not as something created by the mind, but insofar as *ratio* expresses the quiddity of the object, namely, what is known about the object through a first intention. (See also *intention*.) Though Scotus is most impressed with the need for postulating the formal distinction in the Trinity, as a metaphysician he also finds it useful for explaining how first intentional characteristics can be ascribed to one and the same physically simple thing. Thus he employs it between being and its attributes, the soul and its powers, the nature an individual shares with others of his species on the one hand and his unique individuality or haecceity* on the other, or between "animality," a generic perfection, and "rationality," the aspect that differentiates man as a rational animal from the brute beast. Though all composition is ruled out by God's simplicity, some form of metaphysical, if not real, composition is possible in these other cases. See *formality*.

formal predication vs. predication by identity: Theologians introduced this distinction to explain why abstract predication of certain attributes of one another (e.g., "wisdom is goodness") could be true when speaking of God whereas statements of this sort in other cases would be false. Since "wisdom" and "goodness" are not synonymous terms, even when applied to God, a statement such as the above cannot be true according to formal predication, for this is possible only when the predicate expresses an essential or constitutive element of the subject. Nevertheless, since "wisdom," "goodness," "paternity" and "deity" are not really distinct from each other, predications of the form "wisdom is goodness" and "paternity is deity," though false according to formal predication, are said to be true "by identity." Where other scholastics used some form of virtual, or intentional or conceptual distinction, all with a foundation of sorts in reality, to justify formal predication, Scotus links it with his explanation of formal non-identity or distinction *a parte rei*. See *formal distinction; formality; intention*. On the other hand, he argues that there is no formal difference *a parte rei* between a formality and its intrinsic mode* (the degree in which a formal perfection, like being, wisdom, or goodness, exists in reality). While pure perfections* like these may be found in some finite degree in creatures, they are all present in an intensively infinite* degree in God. It is this infinity that rules out any perfectibility of one formality by another, as is sometimes the case in creatures which may lack any real or physical composition, but are at least metaphysically composed (viz., of formalities related to each other as potential and actual). See *formality*. Hence there is an even greater real identity among God's attributes than that which holds between "animality" and "rationality" in man, or between the essential nature of the soul and its faculties, though man is substantially one, and the soul with its powers a simple substance, according to Scotus. On the other hand, the notional features like "paternity" or "filiation" are neither formally nor really identical with one another, and hence can give rise to a real distinction of persons. On the other hand, even though "paternity" is not infinitely perfect, formally speaking, for otherwise the Son would be imperfect in lacking this characteristic, still the divine nature which the three divine persons possess in common is infinitely perfect and hence is really identical with, but formally distinct from, "paternity," "filiation," "active and passive spiration." Hence Scotus argues that statements of the form "paternity is deity" or "deity is paternity," though false according to formal predication, are true by identity. Similarly, "paternity is infinite" can be true in virtue of paternity's real identity with an infinitely perfect essence, but paternity is not formally infinite in the way divine goodness, for instance, is.

formality: The objective correlate of a distinct formal object. See *formal distinction*. Scotus identifies a formality with Avicenna's *intentio* (see *intention*) inasmuch as an intention represents a characteristic of an extramental thing, though not the whole of its intelligible essence. Hence a formal distinction on the part of the thing (*a parte rei*) is compatible with its physical or real simplicity. That is to say, though the formalities are always conceptually separable, one formal reality may be inseparable from the other so far as the concrete individual thing is concerned. The reason for this real simplicity in the things, however, may be different. In God, where each formality is infinite, since there is no formal distinction between a formality and its intrinsic mode (see *intrinsic mode*), all composition in the sense of one part perfecting another formally is excluded. For composition occurs only where there is potentiality, and hence limitation or finitude, in the parts as such, a potentiality which is actualized only when one part is combined with another to form something that is one *per se*. But because each divine attribute exists in an infinite degree, Scotus argues, the highest form of real identity compatible with a formal distinction is present in God. In the case of the soul and its powers, or a man's "animality" and "rationality," or between the specific nature (*natura communis*) of an individual and his haecceity*, there is usually some form of metaphysical composition present in the sense that the formalities in question mutually perfect each other and hence have the aspect of parts, for a given formality may be present in different natures in different degrees (and hence with different intrinsic modes). Thus the creative imagination of the human artist in which intelligence and sensitivity are blended is something that neither the brute beast endowed with sense perception nor the angel with its intellectual life possesses.

formally, see *formal*

fortune: According to Aristotle, what happened to a rational agent unintentionally, but as the result of some free decision on his part, was ascribed philosophically to luck or fortune. Chance, on the other hand, was an accidental effect involving natural or non-rational causes, an effect, namely, that they were not intended or designed by nature to produce, for Aristotle considered all of nature to act for the sake of an end. Theistic interpreters usually explained his teleological description of inanimate agents as the result of the intrinsic design built into their natures by an omniscient creator. Effects intended either by nature or by deliberation were said to be the result of *per se* causes, whereas those not intended in this way were called coincidents or the result of *per accidens* causality—either chance or fortune or a combination of both. Theologians who stressed the belief that all worldly events, if not directly intended, were at least permitted by God, were constrained to modify Aristotle's conception of fortune and chance. Usually they retained these notions, but restricted the scope of their activity. With the prominence given to the Arabic-Aristotelian conception of an eternal world in the last half of the thirteenth century, medieval philosophers were concerned with the problem of whether good fortune, providential or otherwise, was philosophically compatible with the philosophers' theory of the eternity of the world. It was one of the problems proposed to Scotus and he deals with it in Question Twenty-one. See *cause, essential vs. incidental.*

generation: Scotus defines generation as "the production of a suppositum* so far as the being of its substantial nature is concerned" (cf. 2.2). This is an extended sense of what Aristotle meant by the term. See *generation and corruption.*

generation and corruption: Aristotle analyzed all natural change in terms of the four categories of quantity, place, quality, and substance. Quantitative change he called growth or diminution; change of place, motion; change in quality, alteration. When change can no longer be accounted for in terms of these three accidental categories but involves substance itself, it is called "coming-to-be" (generation) and its converse, "passing-away" (corruption). Confer *De generatione et corruptione* I, c.4. Since he went on to say that matter in the proper sense of the term is the substrate receptive of coming-to-be and passing-away, generation came to be defined as the acquisition of a substantial form and corruption as the loss of one substantial form upon the acquisition of another. Though Aristotle's analysis did not cover all types of supernatural transformations discussed by medieval theologians, his description suggested fruitful analogies that might be employed to give a more rational account of what the schoolmen believed such changes involved. Cf., for example, 10.62-64.

habit (*habitus*, from the Latin *habere*, to have): According to Aristotle, an acquired disposition or tendency of a natural agent made constant and fixed by use. A habit once acquired becomes itself the principle of activity, a kind of second nature, so that acts corresponding to it are produced readily, easily, and with pleasure; once acquired it is with difficulty lost, and in this it is opposed to a mere disposition that is readily lost. Knowledge once acquired, for instance, like the moral virtues, represents a habit in this sense. Both habits and dispositions fall under the first species or type of the category of *quality*,* according to Aristotle. Medieval theologians adapted this philosophical notion to explain not only acquired virtues, but also those supernaturally infused, like faith, hope, and charity. However, to the extent that they denied that any supernatural quality in the soul could be detected by natural reason alone, theologians argued that infused virtues give only the possibility of acting supernaturally, not necessarily an ease or facility such as that acquired by repeated actions.

haecceity (*haecceitas*, from the Latin *haec*, this): The term means literally "thisness." It designates the unique formal principle of individuation that makes the nature, which all individuals of the same species have in common, to be just this or that individual and no other. Scotus regards it as a distinct positive formality* over and above the common nature of the individual (*natura communis*). Petrinity, for instance, would represent the "haecceity" of Peter; Paulinity, that of Paul, and so on.

happiness: Though Aristotle uses the term in the general sense of well-being, the scholastics, following St. Augustine, usually employ it in some ultimate sense as involving the knowledge and the love of God as the end of man. This may refer to such knowledge and love as is possible for man either in this life (*beatitudo viae*) or in the next (*beatitudo patriae*). Cf. *Ord.* I, d.8, n.87.

hypostasis; *hypostatic* (from the Greek, ὑπό, under; στάσις, position): Though hypostasis etymologically corresponds perfectly with the Latin term *suppositum** it came to mean more specifically a "rational *suppositum*" or person, in contrast to animals, trees, stones, etc., which are irrational or simple *supposita*. Among the Greek theologians hypostasis came to be used to distinguish the three divine persons as distinct from the essence or nature common to all. A similar usage developed among Latin theologians. Thus "hypostatic" referred to some personal or notional* aspect of the Trinity. See *hypostatic union*.

hypostatic union: The union of the divine nature and the human nature in the person of the second divine person or Word. In reaction to the early Trinitarian and Christological heresies, condemned by various Church councils, the generally accepted theological view arose that in Christ there were two distinct natures, in no way fused as natures, one divine, shared also by Father and Holy Spirit, and one human, which belonged to the person of the Son alone. Since the human nature was complete as a nature, there were two wills in Christ, two types of operations, one divine, the other human, etc. However, the only thing lacking to the human nature in Christ was a *human personality*. Thus the effect of the hypostatic union is that though there is but one person or personality in Jesus Christ, that of the second person of the Trinity, there are two natures, wills, operations, etc. While what Christ did through his divine nature was also attributable to the Father and Holy Spirit as well, what he did through his human nature was attributable personally to the Son alone. The distinction between the person, nature, and operative faculty was expressed by saying the person is the one *who* acts (*principium quod*), the nature, or operative faculty, by contrast represents that *by which* (*principium quo*) the person acts. See *principium quo and quod*.

ideas: In Platonic philosophy an eternally existing pattern or archetype of any class of things of which the individual things in nature are but imperfect copies. Among Neoplatonic Christians the ideas were identified with the exemplars of creatures in the mind of God. See *exemplar*.

ideate or *ideatum*: The object corresponding to an idea. In Platonic philosophy the existing object in the real world insofar as it is a representation or realization of an exemplar or archetypal Idea.*

identity, formal and real: Identity is inversely related to distinction. To the extent that two aspects are formally indistinguishable, they are said to be formally identical. Where two such characteristics are really indistinguishable in the sense that this individual cannot possess one of the two without the other, the two are said to be really identical with the subject though they may still be formally distinct from each other as well as from the essential or defining characteristics of the subject. Thus the faculties of intellect and will are said to be formally distinct from each other and from their subject. At the same time they are one by a real identity with each other and with the substance of the angel or human soul. See also *formal distinction* and *formality*.

identity, predication by, see *formal predication vs. predication by identity*

immanent, see *action, immanent and transient*

impassibility: The inability to undergo suffering, death, or corruption. So far as man is concerned, theologians attributed this quality to the risen body of Christ, to Adam and Eve before the fall, and to the bodies of the saints after the general resurrection.

implication (*consequentia*): The logical connection between the antecedent proposition or set of propositions and the consequent, such that the latter is entailed by the former, is called in medieval logic *consequentia*. One would normally tend to render this as

GLOSSARY

"consequence," as some medieval translators have done, but since this word in normal English usage refers not to the logical connection so much as to the proposition entailed (i.e., the conclusion or consequent), we have used *implication* consistently wherever *consequentia* occurs in Latin.

imposition, names of first and second: Names which do not signify parts or qualifications of our spoken or written language are called words (or names) of first imposition, whereas words which do signify such are called names of second imposition. Thus "man," "stone," "white," etc. are words of first imposition, whereas "substantive," "adjective," "nominative case," etc., are words of second imposition. Hence words of second imposition always signify words of first imposition. This distinction between words is analogous to that between first and second intentional concepts or mental terms in that first intentions signify objects which are not intentions or concepts whereas second intentions signify first intentions. See *intentions, first and second*.

in actu primo, in actu secundo: From the Latin meaning "in the state of primary actualization and secondary actualization," respectively. Though the operative faculties of an active substance are formally distinct from each other and from that which formally constitutes its essence or nature, according to Scotus, they are actually inseparable from the concrete substance or existing thing. (See *formal distinction*.) Hence a substance is said to be *in actu primo* with respect to a given operation or actualization simply by being what it is, namely, by having the nature it has with its corresponding faculties. When the agent is actually operating it is said to be *in actu secundo*. In God, where every possible operation *ad intra* is fully actualized, the operation is only conceptually distinguished from the operative faculty or power. In this sense, Scotus claims that God the Father is omniscient not only because he has such knowledge *in actu primo* in the sense that he possesses the divine essence or nature with its intellectual memory, but also *in actu secundo* in the sense that he actually knows or understands the divine nature and all that this necessarily entails. Cf. 1.69.

in quid predication: *In quid* and *in quale* are two basic modes of predication. They refer primarily to the five predicables of Porphyry, namely, the genus, species, specific difference, property, and accident, though Scotus extends the idea of *in quid* and *in quale* predication to the transcendental order. Briefly, the difference between the two is this: To predicate *in quid* means to predicate either the entire essence (i.e., the species) or at least the determinable part of the essence (e.g., the genus). The term is derived from quiddity* or essence, and such predication represents an answer to the question: What is it? (*Quid est?*). To predicate *in quale* means to predicate a further determination or qualification of the essence. This qualification (*quale*) may be either essential (e.g., a specific difference) or non-essential (e.g., a property or accident). Since the specific difference is really a part of the essence or quiddity, it is sometimes said to be predicated *in quale quid* or *in quale substantiale* in order to distinguish it from properties or accidents which are said to be predicated either *in quale accidentale* or simply *in quale*. To predicate something *in quid*, it is not enough that the predicate be an essential note but that it be predicated *per modum subsistentis*, which from the viewpoint of grammar means that it must be predicated as a *noun*, not as an adjective or participle or adverb. Predication *in quale*, whether it be an essential qualification or not, is always predicated *per modum denominantis*, which from the viewpoint of grammar means it is predicated as a modifier. "Substance," "whiteness," "rationality," "rational animal," "life," "truth," "goodness," if used as predicates, would be predicated *in quid*, whereas "substantial," "white," "rational," "living," "true," "good," if used as predicates, would be predicated *in quale*.

in sensu composito et diviso: In the composite sense and in the divided sense. When a complex expression is taken in a composite sense both parts of the expression must be understood as applying simultaneously to the same subject, whereas if it is taken in a divided sense both parts of the expression apply to the subject separately. "The blind do not see," for example, is true in the composite sense, whereas "the blind see, the lame walk . . . the deaf hear, the dead rise" (Matt. 11:5) must be understood in a divided sense. Failure to distinguish the two senses leads to the well-known fallacies of composition and division, for instance, "five is three and two, three and two are odd and even, therefore, five is odd and even."

incommunicable, see *communicable*

infinity, intensive: An unlimited degree with respect to the same formal perfection; it refers to the intrinsic mode* of a pure perfection.* Thus God's knowledge is intrinsically infinite if it is without limitation *qua* knowledge, i.e., if it extends to all that is knowable. As applied to God, intrinsic infinity is sometimes contrasted with his extensive infinity. God is extensively infinite if there is no pure perfection of any sort lacking in him.

intelligences: The pure spirits such as God and the intelligent beings postulated by the philosophers as responsible in some way for the regularity of movement characteristic of the heavens and celestial bodies. They were also called "separate substances"* inasmuch as they existed apart from all matter, unlike the human soul, which, though spiritual substantially, was the form of a material body. The angels of Judeo-Christian theology were sometimes identified with these Intelligences of the philosophers as were the Greco-Roman gods of pagan mythology.

intelligible species: A likeness or representation of what is intelligible about an object, especially one perceived by the senses. Various interpretations were given to Aristotle's account in the *De anima* of how the soul is only potentially knowledge and sensation, and becomes aware of an external thing by taking its form or likeness (*species*) into itself. At the level of the external senses, like vision or hearing, or the internal sense of imagination or memory, sensible species were involved. But there was a problem as to how this sensory information was conveyed to the intellective or nonmaterial part of the soul, inasmuch as its conceptual notions as to what the object was were incorporeal and universal. How the mind as essentially only potential knowledge (i.e., as the possible intellect*) becomes fully actualized through understanding was only vaguely explained by Aristotle. Two factors at least were involved. One was an active agency which, like a light that brings out the potential colors of a darkened object, transformed the phantasm* or sensible species in the imagination by making its potential intelligibility actually intelligible. This mysterious "light" of Aristotle came to be called the agent intellect,* and dozens of theories were proposed to explain its precise nature and function. The second factor was the presence of the potential object in the mind itself that enabled one who had once acquired knowledge of a thing to draw upon this potential knowledge at will. As the storehouse of this virtual or habitual information, the intellect was described by Aristotle as "the place of the forms" (*De anima* III, c.4, 429a27-28). His scholastic followers gave the name "intelligible species" to these distinct universal forms in the possible intellect. Almost every prominent theologian among them had his own personal theory as to how these "species" were formed and functioned. Underlying their accounts was often the desire to reconcile their basically Aristotelian epistemology with certain insights of Augustine. One of these was his conviction that knowledge was more an activity of the soul than a purely passive reception of impressions from external objects. The other was his contention that the human soul is an image of the Trinity in that its superior part is characterized by intellection, memory, and volition. Among these three, memory (*memoria*) was of special importance. It included not only the power of recalling things and events of past experience, but also that of producing mental concepts of objects not actually present to the senses. Among these were included such transcendent notions as had no strict counterpart in the sensible world but, like the Platonic ideas, were explained in terms of some illumination of the human mind by the divine archetypal ideas. (See also *memory*.) While the more "Augustinian" epistemologies of the last half of the thirteenth century retained some form of special illumination, their account of it was always integrated in some way with the explanations of how the agent intellect illumined the phantasm. By Scotus' time, most scholastics denied that anything more than the general "illumination" of the agent intellect was needed to account for our natural knowledge of the world about us. Similarly, though they retained the Augustinian notion of "memory" as the source of the "word" or mental concept of a thing in the mind, mainly because of its analogical explanatory value in accounting for the eternal generation of the Word by the Father, "memory" became a synonym for the intellect, usually insofar as it contained the latent image of the object as an *ens diminutum* (see *diminished being*) in the form of an intelligible species. Depending on how they interpreted the various functions of agent and possible intellects, Scotus' contemporaries assigned various roles to the intelligible species. Those who held that the intellect was purely passive in conceiving the object, maintained the simple impression of the intelligible species (called then the "impressed species") as the form of the object, sufficed to produce actual knowledge (the expressed species or word). Others, stressing the activity of the intellect, even denied the need of an intelligible species distinct from the sensible species in the phantasm. Scotus, while rejecting the need of an intelligible species for intuitive cognition, required it to go proxy for the object in abstractive cognition in order to explain why our conceptual knowledge, that is a result of a cocausality of intellect (agent or possible) and intelligible species as essentially ordered causes, reflects only the universal characteristics or common nature of the object and not its haecciety.* (See *cognition, intuitive* and *abstract*.) Scotus' own account of the origin and function of the intelligible species is colored by his conception that throughout the cognitive process, be it at the sensory or intellective level, the cocausality of mind and object are required. That is to say, the soul, which is really identical and only formally distinct from its cognitive faculties (see *formal distinction*), functions as one active but partial cause, whereas the object, or some species that goes proxy for it, is the other partial cause. As he explains in the *Ord*. I, d.3, nn.496-503, this cocausality is that of essentially ordered causes which are related to each other in the manner described in 15.33-34. In this way agent intellect and phantasm produce the intelligible species. The intelligible species and the intellect (call it active or possible intellect as you will) in turn produce the actual knowledge or mental word. The intellect with respect to this latter role is called "memory," to use Augustine's terminology. If actually informed by the intelligible species, the memory passes from the state of essential or remote potency with respect to actual knowledge to one of accidental or proximate potency and in that state is called "perfect memory." Theologians also discussed how the immortal soul after death might acquire intelligible species of things not experienced in the present life. Scotus' questions on this subject are to be found in *Ord*. IV, d.45.

intensively, intensively infinite, see *infinity, intensive*

intention (intentio): In medieval epistemology, an intention came to acquire the technical sense of a "natural sign in the soul." In the Latin translation of Avicenna, *intentio* was used to render the term *ma'na* (viz., a notion or meaning), which referred to intelligible form (*species*) of an extramental thing (*extra animam*) insofar as it existed in the soul (*intra animam*). Now the form, in contrast to matter, was for Aristotle the essence, quiddity*, or intelligible part of a thing. But any given notion or conceptual meaning, though expressing part of the quiddity of a thing, usually did not exhaust its essential intelligibility, so that *intention* took on the character of a formal aspect of the thing (a little "form" or *formalitas*), as it were, and like *ratio* or *logos* was used not only for the formal concept in the mind but also for its precise objective correlate. Since these formal aspects, though found inseparably united in the thing, were separable in thought or as *intentions* in the mind, the *intentional distinction* became one way of describing the *virtual distinction* or *distinctio rationis* insofar as it was used to explain the

517

plurality of divine attributes, for example. One and the same indivisible thing had the power or virtue *(virtus)* of producing in a created mind several objective concepts of itself. Scotus, on the other hand, reduces the virtual or intentional distinction to his formal distinction* *a parte rei* and the objective correlate of distinct formal concepts to what he calls a *ratio realis*, a reality *(realitas)* or formality* *(formalitas)*. Insofar as *intention* is considered as an intelligible aspect of the thing, it too can be identified with Scotus' formality. See his remark: "What Avicenna himself understands by a different intention is the same thing as I mean by another formality" *(Reportata Parisiensia* II, d.1, q.6, n.20). See also *intentions, first and second*.

intentions, first and second: As Porphyry had distinguished between words of first and second imposition* (viz., words that refer respectively to things or to other words), so Avicenna distinguished between first and second intentions. First intentions as natural signs in the soul referred to things and expressed some intelligible aspect or essential characteristic to be found in them (see *intention*), whereas second intentions referred to first intentions or concepts in the mind. They included such logical notion as genus, species, etc., which the mind discovers by reflecting on how the formal content of one intention relates to that of another. Logic, he claimed, was concerned only with second intentions whereas a real science, like metaphysics, was concerned with first intentional aspects of things.

intrinsic mode: A qualification so identified with the subject it modifies that it is neither really nor formally distinct from it, yet it is possible to conceive the subject without the mode as a first intention* at the level of abstract cognition.* Though Scotus speaks of contingency and necessity as positive modes of entity, his only discussion of intrinsic modes in any detail is in connection with magnitude* as a transcendental attribute of being. As an intrinsic mode, magnitude is the degree of intensity or measure of intrinsic excellence characteristic of some formal perfection as it exists extramentally in a particular subject. The most fundamental or basic division of magnitude is into the mode of infinity on the one hand and the various degrees of finitude on the other. Infinity is that mode which transcends every finite mode by a non-finite degree. From the discussion of magnitude in the present work (cf. 6.15-26) two characteristics of an intrinsic mode emerge. First, it exists extramentally *(ex natura rei)* in the thing *(in re)*. Hence notions like "being," "good," or "wise," which prescind from the mode as well as the modal notions themselves, viz., "finite" or "infinite," and composite concepts like "infinite being" and "finite goodness," are all first intentions or real concepts when predicated of either God or creatures. Second, the fact that the mode represents something real or actually present in the thing does not entail that it is present in the thing as actually distinct from that of which it is the mode. Though 6.26 makes it clear there is no real distinction *a parte rei* between the two, the discussion in *Ord.* 1, d.8, nn.137-50 indicates that Scotus does not consider the distinction between God's being and his infinity to be even as radical or basic as that between two formalities. In fact intuitive cognition* or the face-to-face vision of God would erase the distinction entirely, which would not be the case with two formally distinct perfections such as divine wisdom and divine power (cf. *Ord.* 1, d.8, nn.137-50). Only at the level of abstract cognition is it possible to conceive the formalities of being or goodness apart from their intrinsic mode. If there is any objective basis for the distinction, it is to be found not so much in the thing itself as in the different way in which the object known presents itself to the intellect. For the intuitive cognition of the formality and its mode as a single formal object, the actual presence of the existing thing is required. For the abstract conception that prescinds from the mode, an intelligible species* is needed to present the object as an *ens diminutum* (see *diminished being*). This is not to say that "being" and "infinite" are not first intentions when one asserts propositions like "God is a being" or "The divine being is infinite," for the intelligible species is not that which is known but that by which something is known. What Scotus is claiming is that as first intentions, "being" and "infinite being" refer to the same divine formality, viz., infinite being. They differ, however, in their conceptual content and in the information they convey, in that the first notion is imperfect and does not serve to distinguish God from creatures, whereas the second is a perfect and proper concept, applicable to God alone. The same could be said of "good" and "infinite goodness" or "wise" and "infinite wisdom."

Scotus considers "finite" and "infinite" to be transcendental modes of being, that is to say, they divide being before its division into the ten categories*. This suggests a solution to two related problems: (1) Why does God not fall under a genus if the common concept *ens* (a being) is univocally predicable of him and creatures? (2) Why does the formal distinction of attributes not introduce some kind of composition in God? His answer to the first is that God's being is formally infinite whereas a being must be finite to fall into a category or genus. For the constitutive perfections that correspond to "genus" and "specific difference" are related respectively as potency to act. In man, the "rational animal," for instance, rationality is not only formally distinct from animality, but man's very potential as an animal is increased and heightened by the fact that he has a rational mind. And this provides an answer to the second question. In God, where every attribute is formally infinite, no composition is possible, for all composition, even that between generic and differential formalities, implies that one reality is perfected by another, and hence it is imperfect or finite in itself. In short, Scotus thinks it is precisely because of his infinity that God has the highest degree of real identity consistent with formal diversity.

intuitive cognition, see *cognition, intuitive and abstract*

knowledge, abstract, see *cognition, intuitive and abstract*
knowledge, confused, see *confused knowledge*
knowledge, declarative, see *declarative knowledge*
knowledge, distinct, see *distinct knowledge*
knowledge, epistemic, see *epistemic knowledge*
knowledge, first and second intentional, see *intentions, first and second*
knowledge, intuitive, see *cognition, intuitive and abstract*

living reasons, see *ideas* and *exemplar*

magnitude: The degree of intrinsic excellence or measure of greatness characteristic of a given nature, perfection, or formality. So defined, magnitude is used in a transcendental sense (i.e., it is not limited to the Aristotelian category of quantity). In this sense various properties that are not strictly quantitative can be arranged in some hierarchic fashion. Thus the brightness or intensity of a given color, the relative strength of some virtue or vice, the degree of wisdom or intelligence can be correlated with some fixed scale of values, in which each higher degree contains the lower degree virtually* or eminently*. In modern terminology, such properties are called intensive or nonadditive in contrast to additive or extensive properties like length, mass, or time. Nevertheless, magnitude could be called a quantitative rather than a qualitative characteristic of a thing inasmuch as it represents a reply to a question of the form: "How great is this perfection?" or "To what extent is such and such a characteristic present?" rather than an answer to a query of the form: "What kind of perfection is this?" or "What type of thing would this be?" As Scotus himself argues in 6.13, both Aristotle and St. Augustine distinguished between the strict and transferred sense of such quantitative terms as "great and small," and that "in their transferred sense at least, they are transcendentals and proper attributes of the whole realm of being." In 5.5-9 he shows how this transcendental notion of "quantity" can be extended to form a notion of the "infinite" itself as a kind of limit that the various finite magnitudes approach but never reach. Though in this sense magnitude (be it finite or infinite) is a real or extramental characteristic of its respective subject, it is neither really nor formally distinct from it, but is related to the entity or perfection in question as its intrinsic mode.* The distinction between a formality* and its intrinsic magnitude is already implicit in the very notion of a pure perfection,* since creatures are found to possess intelligence, goodness, wisdom, power, and the like in varying degrees, yet the degree as such does not enter into the formal notion or essential definition of these attributes and hence they are said to be perfection purely and simply, and are ascribed to God in an infinite or unlimited degree.

memory (memoria): Though Scotus employs this term in its more customary sense as that by which we recall or remember the past (cf. *Ord.* IV, d.45, q.2), his usage of the word throughout the present work reflects the influence of St. Augustine, who had gradually extended the common-sense notion of memory until it came to include everything the individual mind is capable of knowing or thinking about, whether previously experienced or not. Every concept we form is a kind of "child" born of this memory, and every thought we bring to mind reveals or declares what is hidden in its depths. As he puts it in *De Trinitate* xv, c.10, "The thought formed from that thing which we know is the word which we speak in our heart, and it is neither Greek, nor Latin, nor any other language." (See *declarative knowledge*.) This notion of our memory as speaking its "word" provided him with a useful analogy for explaining the eternal generation of the Word* by the Father in the Trinity. He also argued the soul is an image of the Trinity in that its superior part contained memory, intelligence, and volition. Scotus adapted both of these analogies to his own conception as to how the intellect functions in producing actual knowledge as a concept or quality within the soul. In *Ord.* 1, d.3, nn.58off., he explains how this trinitarian image could be understood. There are three perfections in the intellective portion of man's soul. The first is its power to produce knowledge in itself and this is called *memoria*. The second is its passive ability to receive the knowledge thus produced and this is called *intelligentia* or intellection. The third is its capacity to have volition as such and this is called *voluntas* or will. In short, memory represents the productive aspect of man's mind whereby he forms a concept or mental word. But according to his theory of knowledge, which is neither purely Augustinian nor purely Aristotelian, the intellect is only the partial efficient cause of its own concepts. The other partial cause is the intelligible species,* which informs the intellect, reducing it from remote potency to proximate potency with respect to actual knowledge. Thus "perfect memory," as the total cause of the concept, includes both the intellect and the intelligible species which function as a single principle or as essentially ordered causes of the mental word. "Perfect memory," however, can be defined even more generally as a pure perfection so that it would also apply to God, in whom there is no real distinction between nature, intellective power, and actual knowledge, nor is any intelligible species derived from some extrinsic object required. In this sense, perfect memory is defined in 1.54 as "an intellect having actually present an intelligible object proportionate to itself." Scotus also adopts Augustine's other analogy. As perfect memory in us begets our thoughts or mental words by a kind of internal speech act, so the Father's "memory" begets his Son or Word by a kind of eternal speech act. Thus the mystery of how the Son proceeds from the Father is described in alternate ways as a "speaking of the Word," as an eternal generation of the Son, as a communication of the divine nature to the second person, or as an act of declarative knowledge, in that the Word, as the image of the Father, is a kind of eternal expression of what the Father is in himself.

modes of per se *predication*, see *predication*, per se

natural, naturality: In general, whatever is in accord with the nature or essence of a thing is said to be "natural." More specifically, these terms refer to an action which proceeds from an active power or agent without deliberation and in a manner determined by the nature of the agent. Such an action is said to occur "after the manner of nature" (*per modum naturae*). Even actions that are essentially free, and hence do not occur simply *per modum naturae*, may be said to have a certain "naturality" about them, in that some measure of natural determinism accompanies the rational self-determination on the part of the will. See *nature* and *will* as primary divisions of active powers.

natural will: Either (1) that principle of action called the will, insofar as it is the seat of the affection for what is to the advantage of the agent, or (2) an act freely elicited by the will that is in accord with this inclination or affection. See *will* and *will as nature*.

nature: In a broad sense "nature" designates simply what a thing is, viz., its essence or quiddity, and as such would apply not only to positive things but also to such things as privations or negations, as when one inquires about the nature of blindness. In a strict sense, however, nature refers to those causes or agents that do not act with knowledge and deliberation. Aristotle had already divided all active potencies into either rational or irrational. It is clear from 16.39-40, and even more so from his questions on Aristotle's *Metaphysics* (Bk. IX, q.15, nn.4-7), that Scotus considered his own basic division of nature (*natura*) and will (*voluntas*) to be equivalent to irrational and rational principles of action. The will is a rational faculty inasmuch as it acts *with* reason; that is to say, a free agent after deliberate consideration of various alternatives freely determines his course of action. All other agents, including the intellect itself, except where their actions are subject to voluntary control, act *naturally*, that is to say, their mode of activity is determined by their respective natures and when all external conditions for action are present, these agents must act and to the utmost of their ability. Unlike some of his contemporaries who admitted that certain acts of the will were necessary whereas others were free, Scotus denies that any elicited act of the will proceeds from that faculty or power naturally (*per modum naturae*); all the will's actions, by contrast, are elicited freely and as an agent, the will is said to be essentially free and can be equated with *liberty* as opposed to *nature*. That is to say, the will is essentially that potency or faculty that can act rationally or *with* reason. This means first of all that a free agent does not act blindly but has prior knowledge of what can be loved or willed. While such knowledge is a necessary condition, a logical presupposition, for volition, it is not of itself a sufficient condition for the same, for the will must determine itself to love or will the object. Furthermore, the will is rational in another more interesting sense, viz., it has an inborn inclination to act in accord with right reason. Though not an elicited act, this affection for justice, as it is called, represents a positive bias in the will that inclines it to love the good in terms of its objective worth or intrinsic value regardless of how this happens to be related to what is good or advantageous for the agent. See *will* and *will as free*.

necessity: The correlative of contingency. As a positive state of being or action, it expressed not only what can be but what must be. The contingent, by contrast, is what can, but need not, be. As a positive state, contingency, as Scotus understands the term, is a logically complex notion. If it refers to something actual, it means that what exists now need not have existed now and that a contrary state could have existed in its place. Such a contingent state is possible only if the cause does not act of necessity, that is to say, the cause was free to cause or not to cause the effect with respect to that moment when the effect will begin to exist. Necessity also has a variety of connotations. Scotus, in regard to God's foreknowledge of contingent events, is concerned to distinguish necessity of inevitability, which applies to what is not only the case but could not have been otherwise, and even here he distinguishes between what is inevitable of itself and what is an inevitable consequence of something other than itself. (See *necessity of inevitability*.) He also refers to a necessity of immutability,* viz., something which must be so only because God is not intrinsically mutable, since this would imply imperfection.

necessity of immutability: Though Scotus regarded the will of God to be the contingent cause of all created events, his volition with respect to creatures, like his foreknowledge of their free actions, was not something he has at one moment of time but not at another. On the contrary, he freely chose from all eternity to create what would begin to exist at that point in time that he wanted it to. Similarly, what he knows to be true of a free agent, he knows from all eternity, but he knows it as a contingent truth, one which might not have been the case and hence was not something inevitable.

necessity of inevitability: A necessity that is completely and absolutely deterministic, stemming as it does from a nature whose actions are not subject to any inhibitive conditions or external restraints. Unlike the natural actions of created agencies which can always be impeded, only the divine nature itself and what is a necessary consequence of that nature possesses inevitability in this sense. Other things are inevitable only conditionally, namely, on the assumption that something else is the case, or has been the case, or will be the case. Cf. 16.47.

notional[ly]: "Notional" (from *notio*, a sign or distinguishing mark) refers to any characteristic peculiar to any one or, at most, to any two divine persons. As such it is contrasted with those divine properties all three persons have in common. The latter are called "essentials."

obediential potency: The capability or potentiality, inherent in every creature in view of its complete dependence upon the will of God, to be elevated to a supernatural state or condition that transcends any natural exigency, inclination, or potency, for instance, that of hypostatic union* with a divine person or persons.

origin, relations of: The relationships that arise between things in virtue of the fact that one originates from another; in its specifically theological and trinitarian usage, the relationship of the principle (*principium*) to what proceeds from a principle (*principiatum*) and vice versa. The divine persons are commonly held to be constituted by that relationship of origin that is proper to each. Thus the Father is said to be constituted by the fact that he begets, or generates, the Son or "speaks the Word." Conversely, the Son is constituted by the fact that he is begotten, or generated, or "spoken" by the Father. The Holy Spirit is constituted by passive spiration*, viz., his relationship to the active spiration of Father and Son as a joint productive principle. According to an oft-repeated theological principle, in the Trinity there is no real distinction except that which arises in virtue of the diametric opposition between the *relata* or terms related by the relationships of origin. Thus Father is really distinct from the Son and vice versa; the Holy Spirit (passive spiration) is really distinct from active spiration and vice versa. But because Father and Son are not really distinct from the principle of active spiration, nor is active spiration as a principle really distinct from Father or Son, the two types of production in the Trinity give rise to only three rather than four persons that are really and mutually distinct from each other.

origination, active and passive: That relationship of origin that is active or passive respectively. Active origination is a notional* characteristic of the Father; passive origination on the other hand is a notional characteristic of the Son. The Holy Spirit also has the notional characteristic of passive origination with respect to the active spiration* on the part of Father and Son.

passion (*passio*): (1) One of the ten categories* of Aristotle, viz., that which consists of the state of being acted upon. Passion and its correlative category, *action* or the state of acting upon some patient or recipient, are regarded as extrinsically advenient relationships. (See *advenient intrinsically and extrinsically*.) (2) Among the third class of qualities Aristotle cites in the *Categories*, c. 8, 9a29-10a10, are what the Oxford translation calls "affections" (*passiones*). These are transitory sensible qualities which are affected by or affect the senses or sensitive appetite. Examples are the blush of embarrassment, the pallor caused by fear, a passing irritation, as opposed to the more permanent affective qualities such as the natural color of the skin, or a chronic bad temper. (3) A transcendental attribute of being such as true (*verum*) or good (*bonum*), considered to be formally distinct from being (*ens*). (4) A state of suffering, as the passion of Christ.

perfection, pure and mixed, see *pure perfection*

permanent vs. successive creature: Some things are successive or in process, like a melody, a game of tennis, a walk, or a journey. They are of such a nature that temporal succession enters into the very idea or definition of what they are. Such things are said to have their being sequentially, or to be in a state of becoming (*in fieri*), in contrast to such relatively permanent things as a man, a mountain, or a house, which have being complete and are said to be in fact (*in facto esse*). See Aristotle, *Physics* III, c.6, 206a20-b2. The second class of things Scotus calls the permanent or enduring creatures (cf. 12.5) even though, with respect to God, who creates and conserves them in being, they are in a quasi state of becoming (cf. 12.14).

person, see *hypostasis* and *suppositum*

phantasm: The sense image or sensible species of the object as present in the internal sense or imagination; also spelled "fantasm." According to Scotus it is the product of (a) the sensible species in an external sense such as sight, hearing, etc., and (b) the internal sense acting as a single principle or as two essentially ordered efficient causes. The phantasm in turn acts in similar fashion with the agent intellect to produce the intelligible species. See *agent intellect* and *intelligible species*.

pilgrim: A person who journeys through this life as an exile *on the way* (*in statu viae*) to his heavenly home.

place: The whereabouts of a body; one of the ten categories* of Aristotle. It is essentially a relationship between the body and that which surrounds or contains it. (See *advenient intrinsically and extrinsically*.) In contrast to space, which may or may not be empty, place is regarded as something positive, namely, the boundary of the containing body or bodies considered as immovable and immediately contiguous to the body located there. Confer Aristotle, *Physics* IV, cc.4-5. Also called technically, in English, *ubiety*.*

place, types of presence in: *Circumscriptive presence* is the natural way in which bodies are in place or space, viz., such that each part of the body occupies its own place distinct from that occupied by other parts; each part, then, has one restricted or circumscribed location. Circumscriptive presence is contrasted with *definitive presence*, which is said to be characteristic of an immaterial or spiritual substance, or of the soul (with respect to the place occupied by the body it informs). In this case, since the spiritual substance does not have organic or distinct parts like a body does, it is said to be whole and entire in each part of the space or place that defines it, as well as in the entire area. Since place (in contrast to empty space) is the containing surface of surrounding body, place is, according to Aristotelian philosophy, something real and finite. Since God is everywhere by reason of his omnipresence, according to the theologians, God is said to be neither circumscriptively nor definitively in place, since, though he is whole and entire everywhere in place, he is not defined or restricted by it, but rather comprehends it. Hence he is said to be *comprehensively present* in place or to have *repletive* presence there, inasmuch as he fills the whole of it. Scotus refers to the first two kinds of presence in 10.34ff.

possible intellect: The mind or intellective portion of the soul insofar as it is potentially knowledge, and the recipient of intellectual information. This faculty passes from a state of remote potency to proximate potency by the reception of the (impressed) intelligible species. When fully actualized, the possible intellect is that by which the soul is formally* said to know, apprehend, or grasp the meaning of its conceptual notions or mental "words." See *agent intellect*; *intelligible species*; *memory*; *word*.

postpredicaments: Those general notions such as opposition, privation, simultaneity, posteriority, possession, and the like which

GLOSSARY

are discussed in Aristotle's *Categories*, cc.10-15, after the treatment of the predicaments or ten categories.*

potency, see *act and potency*

potency, accidental and substantial: Anything, be it substance or accident, is said to be in objective potency if it has no real or actual being, but has only virtual existence as a possible object of God's creative power. In this sense, the essence of a possible substance is said to be in substantial objective potency; the essence of a possible accident, in accidental objective potency. More frequently, however, accidental and substantial potency are subjective, that is to say, it is some existing subject that is in potency to some substantial or accidental change respectively. Thus matter is in substantial potency to such substantial forms as it can receive but does not have as yet. Similarly, a substance can be in accidental potency to some further accidental perfection or modification. Both substantial and accidental (subjective) potency are further subdivided into proximate and remote potentiality. A subject in proximate potency is reduced to act by one single change or actualization, whereas one in remote potency can be actualized in stages or through a gradated series of changes. Thus the intellective soul is said to be in remote accidental potency to intellection by the very fact that it exists. But to be in proximate accidental potency, the intellect must have the intelligible object present to it, either in its actual existence, if the intellection in question is intuitive cognition, or as presented to the intellect in the form of an intelligible species.* Confer Scotus, *QQ. in Metaphysicam* IX, q.2, nn.8-9.

potency, proximate accidental, see *potency, accidental and substantial*

predication, formal, see *formal predication vs. predication by identity*.

predication, in quid, in quale, see *in quid predication*

predication, per se: Necessary predication, either (1) because the predicate gives the whole of the essential definition (*species*) or a part thereof (genus or specific difference), which is the first mode of *per se* predication, or (2) because the notion of the subject enters into the definition of the predicate. This is the case when the predicate is a proper accident or *proprium** of the subject. Confer Aristotle, *Analytica posteriora* I, c.4, 73a34-b2. See *accidens per accidens*.

principiated (principiatum): That which proceeds from a principle. Because the Son receives the divine nature from the Father as a source or productive principle, he can be called a *principiatum*, but not an "effect" of the Father, according to scholastic theologians. See *productions*.

principle (*principium*): A beginning, source, or cause of something other than itself, a logical principle. As the originative source of some actually existing entity, principle is used in a more general sense than a cause in any of its Aristotelian connotations. Thus, in speaking of the Trinity, theologians call the Father the originative principle, but not the cause, of the Son. (See *productions*.) Also, in regard to an action, there are various ways in which an agent is said to be the principle of the action. The person or *suppositum* is the *principium quod* (that which acts, i.e., the one who or the one which acts). The nature is the remote principle by which the person acts, and the faculty is the proximate principle by which it acts. See *principium quo and quod*.

principium quo and quod: In the case of a person (i.e., a rational *suppositum**) the person is the one who acts (*principium quod agit*); the nature of the person is the remote principle by which the person acts (*principium quo remotum*), whereas the faculty or active potency rooted in the nature is the proximate principle by which the act is elicited (*principium quo proximum*). In the case of an irrational *suppositum*, such as a stone or a dog, the *suppositum* as the ultimate subject is the *principium quod agit*. Thus it is the stone that rolls and the horse that kicks.

priority of nature: A priority based on an order of nature, in contrast to a temporal order or an order of origin. If any two distinguishable elements are so related in virtue of what they are that the very notion or existence of one, call it B, entails the notion or existence of the other, call it A, but not vice versa, then A is prior by nature to B even if neither is temporally prior to the other. If A entails B and B entails A, however, the two are said to be simultaneous by nature; such for instance would be the case with true correlatives (cf. Aristotle, *Categories*, c.7, 7b15). See also *sign of nature*.

priority of origin: A priority based on the order that exists among the divine persons in virtue of the way one person proceeds from another. Since the three divine persons share the same divine nature or essence from all eternity, there is no one person prior in time or nature to another. In virtue of origin, the Father as eternally generating the Son is prior in origin to the Son who proceeds from him eternally. Similarly, the Holy Spirit is posterior in origin, though not in nature or in time, to both Father and Son. See *processions, divine*; *productions* and *sign of origin*.

processions, divine: The process whereby the Son proceeds from the Father and the Holy Spirit proceeds from Father and Son as from a single principle. Though the process can be called a production, theologians argue it is essentially different from any causal production. See *productions, speaking*, and *spirating*.

productions: As applied to the inner life of God, the divine productions refer to the eternal generation of the Son by the Father, and the eternal spiration of the Holy Spirit by the Father and Son acting as a single principle. Because the end result of these productions or divine processions of one person from another or others is that one and the same numerical nature is shared equally by all three persons, theologians felt justified in distinguishing such a "production" from a causal production where not only is the cause really distinct from the effect, but the effect has a nature or essence that is numerically distinct from that of the cause. According to this technical usage, the Father can be called a "producer" (*producens*) or a "principle or source" (*principium*) but not a "cause" (*causa*). The Son and Holy Spirit conversely cannot be called "effects" or said to be "caused" but they can be called "producibles" or *principiata* (singular *principiatum*) in the sense that they proceed from a principle.

proprium: One of the five predicables of Porphyry; a property. Though it is not part of the essential definition of the subject, it is inseparable from the essence and can be shown to follow from the definition as a logical consequence. Hence, in contrast to the genus, difference, and species which are predicated in the first mode of necessary or *per se* predication,* the *proprium* is also predicable *per se* but in the second mode. Examples as regards man would be the properties of "teachable," "risible," etc. See also *accidens per accidens*.

pure perfection (*perfectio simpliciter*): Anything that is purely and simply perfection. The scholastic conception of the term goes back to St. Anselm of Canterbury (cf. *Monologion*, c.15), who distinguishes among the various names that designate perfections in creatures those which seem to imply no imperfection as such and which absolutely speaking it would be better to have than not to have. Such, for instance, would be "being," "living," "wise," "powerful," "just," "blessed," etc. "Man," "gold," "lead," by contrast, represent perfection, not simply, but in a qualified sense. The distinction between unqualified and qualified perfection corresponds to what are often called pure and mixed perfection. Consequently we have translated *perfectio simpliciter* uniformly as "pure perfection." Since the notion of a limited degree does not enter into the formal definition of a pure perfection, Scotus argues that pure perfection is compatible with the intrinsic mode of infinity. See *intrinsic mode*.

quality: A quality is any attribute that expresses the kind of thing the subject is (cf. Aristotle's *Metaphysics* v, c.14). As such it would include first of all the substantial or specific difference itself, which is predicated *in quale quid* of the subject. (See *in quid predication*.) More often, however, quality refers to one of the ten categories.* Under this heading, Aristotle enumerates four distinct types: (1) habit and disposition, (2) inborn capacities or incapacities, (3) affective qualities and affections (*passiones*), (4) form and figure. Though he admits there may be other sorts, he believes these four cover what are most properly called qualities (*Categories*, c. 8, 8a25-10a25). Habit differs from a mere disposition, he tells us, in that it is more lasting and firmly established. It includes various kinds of knowledge or virtues like justice, self-restraint, and so on, that are not easily dislodged, whereas heat, cold, disease, and health represent dispositions which can quickly change. While habits are at the same time dispositions, not all dispositions are necessarily habits. This notion of habit was extended by medieval theologians to include also supernaturally infused habits, like faith, hope and charity. (See *habit*.) For Aristotle, the second class of qualities seemed to differ from the first largely in that they were native abilities whereas the first were acquired in the course of time. Scholastics were not agreed as to how this second class of "accidental" qualities were to be understood, especially in regard to the powers of the soul. The third class of qualities are those which produce or result from some accidental sensible change. If this is relatively permanent, the alteration is an affective quality, whereas if it is more ephemeral in nature, it is called an affection or passion.* "Affection"—which is the Oxford translation of πάθος—in this context does not mean love or attachment, but is rather used in the sense of "affecting" or "being affected by" something in which the senses or sense appetites are involved. Thus such sensible qualities of a thing as its color, flavor, sound, temperature are listed among this third class because they affect the senses.

Since the natural color of one's skin is permanent, Aristotle calls it an affective quality, whereas the passing blush of shame or embarrassment, the pallor of fear, a feverish temperature, or other such transient qualities are called affections or passions. Not only the body but also the soul has affections and affective qualities, he explains. For instance, we speak of men who are bad-tempered, irascible, or mad, in virtue of a more or less permanent condition in contrast to the even-tempered man, who may nevertheless occasionally lose his temper. Such a flash of vexation would be an affection, whereas the more or less permanent temperament would represent an affective quality. The fourth quality involves such things as shape or configuration, which result from the arrangement of the quantitative parts of a body.

quantity: Though Scotus is well aware of the usual sense of this term as an Aristotelian category, the questions that gave rise to the present work, especially Questions Five and Six, caused him to turn to the extended or transferred meaning of the term that had been employed by theologians since the time of St. Augustine. See *intrinsic mode* and *magnitude*.

quiddity (from the Latin, *quid*, "what"): The real nature or essence of a thing; literally, it means the "whatness" as an answer to the question *Quid est?* (What is it?).

real relation, see *relations, real*

reduplicated (reduplicatus): An expression in which the notion itself or some aspect thereof is repeated after some connective as *qua, as, under the aspect of,* etc.; for example, being *qua* being, will as nature, or will as free.

relations, common: Those relationships between the divine persons that are symmetrical and hence do not distinguish one person from the other in the way that the relations of origin* do. The only common relationship of this sort that Scotus considers to be real is that of equality. Confer Question Six.

relations, real: A relation is real, according to Scotus, if these three conditions obtain: (1) its foundation is some extramental reality or formal characteristic of a thing; (2) the related terms are themselves things* (*res*) and are really distinct from each other; (3) the relationship is extramental, that is to say, it holds independently of any intellectual consideration. Confer 6.82.

relations, second type of, see *relatives, three types of*
relations of origin, see *origin, relations of*

relatives, three types of: In the *Metaphysics* v, c.15, Aristotle enumerates three kinds of relative things on the basis of the foundation for the relationship. The first is founded on number or quantity, as double to half or treble to a third, or in general that which is contained many times to its multiple and that which exceeds to that which is exceeded. Equal, like, and the same are included under this heading inasmuch as they all refer to unity. Those are equal whose quantity is one; those are alike whose quality is one; and those are the same whose substance is one. The second class of relatives is based on their acting or being acted upon, that is to say, on their active or passive potencies; for example, the relationship of what can heat to what can be heated; or of what can cut to what can be cut, and in general of everything active to everything passive. The third class includes such things as the knowable, the thinkable, the visible and the like, which are described in relative terms only because something else is related to them, namely knowledge, thought or sight.

res, see *thing*

sacrament of the altar: The Eucharist or the consecrated elements of bread and wine. See *eucharistic species*.

science, subalternate, see *subalternate science*

scientific knowledge, see *epistemic knowledge*

separate substance: A substance which exists apart from all matter; a pure spirit such as God or the intelligent beings postulated by the philosophers as responsible in some way for the regularity or movement characteristic of the heavens and celestial bodies. These were called Intelligences* and Judeo-Christian theologians considered them as angels.

separated accident, see *eucharistic species, transubstantiation*

separated quantity, see *transubstantiation*

sign (signum): In *De quantitate animae*, c.11, St. Augustine defines a sign as "a mark without parts." Examples would be a geometric point, a particular point in time, or a logical "moment." As a temporal sequence of events can be described in terms of the point in time when each occurred, so a nontemporal ordered sequence can be distinguished according to different "signs" indicating priority or posteriority according to that order. See *sign of nature* and *sign of origin*.

sign of nature: Though Scotus does not admit any temporal sequence or priority among the various essential or notional attributes

God has from all eternity, he does believe one can distinguish a certain order of nature among these attributes or properties in virtue of what they are. Knowledge of a creature's possibility, for instance, does not logically entail a decision to create, but God's decision to create (made from all eternity) does entail knowledge of this possibility. If B entails A, but not vice versa, A is said to be prior by nature to B even when there is no temporal precedence. As one may number various moments of time to distinguish the order of temporal events, so Scotus distinguishes various instants or logically discrete moments to show the logical sequence of such non-mutual entailments. "Sign" in this context has the meaning of "a mark without parts" (confer St. Augustine, *De quantitate animae*, c.11).

sign of origin: A discrete instance in a sequence of elements ordered according to a priority-posteriority relationship on the basis of how one divine person proceeds eternally from another. See *sign*.

simply simple (*simpliciter simplex*): A primitive or irreducibly simple concept. Simple concepts are those which can be grasped in a single act of understanding. Some simple concepts, like that of man, for instance, can be analyzed in terms of two simpler concepts, one of which is determinable, e.g., "animal," the other determining, e.g., "rational." Such a process of analysis, however, must eventually end up with irreducibly simple notions which are known *in toto* if they are known at all. Such, Scotus claims, are the concepts of "being" and its ultimate differences. In contrast to simple concepts, Scotus calls concepts that have no *per se* unity, but only an accidental unity, e.g., a white man, composite concepts, because several distinct acts are required to grasp their meaning. Confer *Lectura* I, d.3, n.68; *Ord.* I, d.3, n.71.

singularity, determinate: The haecceity* of a particular individual; individuality as something unique and proper, in contradistinction to "individuality" as the common or general characteristic of all individuals (indeterminate singularity).

speaking (*dicere*): The act of producing a "word."* Because the second person of the Trinity is called the Logos or Word of the Father, St. Augustine describes the eternal generation or production of the Son by the Father as "speaking the Word." The force of the analogy springs from his peculiar conception of our "memory," which is a kind of intellectual storehouse or reservoir of all that we can know or think about. From it every thought we have is born, or brought to light, being given conceptual expression as a kind of mental "word spoken in the heart" that declares to our mind what is hidden within it. See *declarative knowledge* and *memory*.

species, eucharistic, see *eucharistic species*

spirating, spiration (Latin *spirare*, "to breathe"): The manner in which the Holy Spirit proceeds from the Father and Son. Following St. Augustine, theologians regard it as an act of love involving the will, shared as a single principle (sometimes called "active spiration" in contrast to the Holy Spirit as "passive spiration") by both Father and Son.

subalternate science: A science which draws its principles from a higher science. If science be taken as a demonstrated conclusion (see *epistemic knowledge*) or a body of such conclusions, then some of the conclusions demonstrated in the higher science become premises for demonstration in the subalternate science.

subsistence: The perfection whereby a being is capable of existing in itself or *per se*. In 9.7 Scotus enumerates some of the various senses in which a thing could be said to be *per se* or subsistent. They range from that minimal degree of subsistence characteristic of a separated accident* miraculously supported apart from its connatural substrate, to that of substances, *supposita*, or persons.

substantial act: In material or bodily substances, composed of matter and form, the substantial form, which unites with the material component to form a single complete substance or nature, is called the substantial act, in contrast to further accidental modifications of the substance, called accidental forms or acts. See *act and potency*.

successive, see *permanent vs. successive creature*

sun: According to Aristotle, not only is the parent an efficient cause of generation, especially in the case of plants, animals, and men, but the movement of the sun along the ecliptic is given as reason why the cycle of generation and corruption is perpetuated (cf. *De generatione et corruptione* II, c.10). The sun functions as a general cause, whereas the nature of the parent is the specifying factor in generation. Scotus alludes to this view of Aristotle and discusses his own views about the effects of the heavenly bodies on various types of change including generation and corruption in *Ord.* II, d. 14, q.3.

suppositum: The general name for a being that is *per se* in the third sense defined by Scotus in 9.7. If the *suppositum* is of a rational or intellectual nature, it is called a person. *Suppositum* is a literal

Latin translation of *hypostasis*, the term Greek theologians used to designate a divine person in the Trinity. The Latin form is retained in the second edition of *Webster's New International Dictionary* and is translated as "supposit" in the third. Because of their interest in explaining the union of Christ's human nature and his divinity in the person of the Word (see *hypostatic union*), theologians were forced to develop some clear idea of what constituted a person, be he human, angelic, or divine. In this connection they went on to determine the analogue of person in a nonrational subsistent, and retained *suppositum* as a general designation for any fully subsistent individual, be it rational or not. Boethius had defined a person as "an individual substance of a rational nature" (confer *De persona et duabus naturis*, c.3, PL 64, 1343). Those who accepted this definition pointed out that "substance" was not to be taken in a categorical sense but as equivalent to a distinct subsistent, in the sense that Scotus seeks to clarify in discussing the various meanings of subsistent or *per se* being in 9.7. Others stressed that "rational" was equivalent to "intellectual" in its most general sense, viz., as applicable also to the divine nature as well as to one which reasoned in the discursive manner characteristic of man. Others, who unlike Scotus made matter the basis for individuality, had to qualify the term "individual." Richard of St. Victor, in his *De Trinitate* IV, cc.21-22, called attention to what seemed to be an even more serious drawback of the Boethian definition, namely, that, according to it, the divine nature itself would be a person in its own right. Hence he suggested an alternate definition, viz., that a person is "the incommunicable existence of an intellectual nature" (*intellectualis naturae incommunicabilis existentia*). "Existence" here seems to be simply the abstract form for "the existent" or "the subsistent." It implies that the subject characterized by it has substantial being (*esse*) in a transcendental or non-categorical sense, and that this being is complete and individual. It also connotes, says Richard, that this existent has this being in virtue of some property that indicates something of its origins, that is to say, it has this being of itself, or by creation, or by propagation, etc. In God the divine nature itself has such *existentia*, for it has substantial being of itself. Now the three divine persons share this *existentia* commonly and hence indistinguishably, but each person also has his own incommunicable existence in virtue of which he is a discrete and unique individual. It is this incommunicable *existentia* in the divine intellectual nature that best defines what a divine person is. And more generally, it is the incommunicable existence of any intellectual nature that commonly defines a person, be he divine, angelic, or human. On this Richardian definition, which Scotus accepts and develops, a *suppositum* would seem to be the incommunicable existence of any nature, and a person would be an intellect *suppositum*.

terminus a quo: The initial state or starting-point of change, from the Latin, the "terminus from which." Since change was described as the passage of some subject from one state or condition to another, scholastics distinguished three elements involved in change: (1) the underlying substrate or subject of the change, (2) the initial terminus, and (3) the final state or *terminus ad quem* (literally, the "terminus to which") the process of change proceeds and with which it ends.

terminus ad quem: A goal, object, or purpose; the final state, for instance, of a process of change.

thing (res): Whatever exists or is conceived to exist as a really distinct entity, be it a substance or accident, or a really distinct constituent of substance such as matter and substantial form. As such it is distinguished from a formality or reality which is an intelligible aspect, several of which can be distinguished within a single thing. (See *formality*.) It is also used as a synonym for *ens* (a being) and in addition to the above meaning it is used in the broader as well as the more restricted sense given in 3.6-14.

transient action, see *action, immanent* and *transient*

transubstantiation: The term coined by Catholic theologians to indicate the change involved when, at the consecration in the mass, the substances of bread or wine are converted into the body and blood of Christ. The accidents (called *Eucharistic Species**) of the bread and wine—the sensible qualities that one can see, taste, and touch—remain, but conversion is called total because, unlike the generation and corruption* involved in the ordinary changes of one substance into another, e.g., elements into chemical compounds, etc., in which some form of matter or material cause serves as the underlying subject of the change, in transubstantiation both the matter and substantial form cease to exist and are replaced by the presence of Christ. A common explanation adopted by medieval theologians to explain how the Species, appearances, or accidental features remained despite the absence of the normal substantial substrate was that God miraculously conserved the accident *quantity*,* which in turn supported the other accidental qualities. Accidents thus lacking substantial support were called separated accidents.* Though they existed in themselves after the manner of substance, their natural inclination to inhere in a substance was sufficient to keep them from being regarded as a substance in their own right.

ubiety (*ubi*): The relationship between a body and the place it occupies; hence the presence of a body in a definite place; sometimes called ubication. See *place*.

univocal principle or cause: One that produces a product or effect specifically like itself. Living generation is of this type.

virtually: One thing is said to contain another virtually if it can produce it, for example, as a cause or as a principle. Scotus also uses the word in a special sense, namely, when two distinct formalities are found in one and the same really identical thing, one of the two formalities can be said to virtually contain the other. Thus, for example, he explains that the divine paternity, though formally distinct from the divine essence, is contained virtually in the essence (cf. *Lectura* I, d.2, n.272).

will: That faculty or active principle whereby an agent acts freely and not *per modum naturae* (i.e., in the way or manner that nature does). Where Aristotle divided all active powers or potencies into rational or irrational (cf. *Metaphysics* IX, c.2, 1046b1-2), Scotus equates these with will (*voluntas*) and nature (*natura*), respectively. The will is called a rational faculty because it acts *with* reason, and that on two grounds: (1) After deliberate consideration of what is good or bad, the agent freely elicits an act of volition or nolition as the case may be. (All other agents, including the intellect itself, except where their actions are subject to voluntary control, act naturally or *per modum naturae*, i.e., when all external conditions for acting are present, the act is elicited necessarily and in a manner determined by nature. See *nature*. Even the initial acts of the intellect are natural or determined in this sense. Only those secondary acts of the intellect as fall under the command of the will are rational in the strict sense of being the result of a rational deliberation.) (2) But free will is rational also in a further sense, viz., that it has an inborn inclination to love an object according to right reason, that is, for what it is in itself or for its intrinsic value.

Following St. Anselm of Canterbury, Scotus calls this inclination an affection for what is just (*affectio iustitiae*) since it inclines the will to love what is good objectively or justly. By contrast, nature and all natural causes are inclined to seek their own perfection, namely, what they were born to be (*natura*, from *nasci*, to be born). Because the will, like other natural faculties, is not indifferent to its own perfection, it also has such an inborn inclination for the advantageous (*affectio commodi*). As the seat of this inclination or affection, the will is said to be *voluntas ut natura*. If this inclination went unchecked it would incline the will to seek its own perfection and happiness above all else. But because nature, in the case of finite agents, is not the supreme good, either in itself or as a potency perfected by its elicited act, the *affectio iustitiae*, or inclination to love as right reason dictates, is the higher inclination. It is the first checkrein or moderating influence on the *affectio iustitiae*, freeing the will, as it were, from the need to seek only itself and its own perfection above all else. Hence it is called by Scotus the native freedom of the will, and, by some commentators, a "freedom *for* values." According to Scotus, neither the *affectio commodi* nor the *affectio iustitiae* is an elicited act of the will, but when the will acts after deliberation, it always elicits an act in accord with one or both of these affections or inclinations. A created will is physically free to follow either inclination, no matter how strong, and though it has the capacity and inclination to follow reason, it can love a good inordinately or unreasonably. In the case of the supreme or infinite good, however, this is not possible. Here our finite will can love God in three ways, viz., (1) as a good in himself by an elicited act of friendship love in accord with the affection for justice and this cannot be inordinate; (2) as a good for us, inasmuch as the union with God through such knowledge and love represents the ultimate perfection of our nature; (3) the will can also want the delight or happiness that is the natural concomitant of such a well-ordered love. Though (2) and (3) are acts in accord with the affection of the advantageous, they are well ordered, since they are recognized as subordinate but inseparable consequences of (1). To will (2) because it is intended by God and (3) because it enables us to love God better in the first way incorporates these secondary loves into the primary love so that all three can in some way be said to be acts in accord with the *affectio iustitiae*.

will, natural: Either (1) that principle of action called the will, insofar as it is the seat of the affection for what is to the advantage of the agent, or (2) a freely elicited act in accord with that inclination or affection.

will as free (voluntas ut libera): (1) The will as rational or as *voluntas* (in contradistinction to *natura* as the common designation of all nonrational agents, whose mode of action is determined by their nature). (See *nature*.) (2) The will as the seat of the *affectio iustitiae* in contradistinction to the will as nature *(voluntas ut natura)*, i.e., the will as the seat of the *affectio commodi*. See *will*.

will as nature (voluntas ut natura): The will as a faculty or active principle insofar as it is the seat for the *affectio commodi* and is inclined, like all other faculties to seek what perfects and hence is to the advantage of the agent. See *will*.

word (verbum): The divine Word or second person of the Trinity. The concept or mental word in the soul. See *memory*.

Index of Authors*

*The numbers refer to paragraphs, not to pages

Alexander of Hales: *Summa theologica*, 4.20
Alhacem: *Perspectiva*, 14.88
Ambrose, St.: *De fide ad Gratianum*, 5.43; *Expositio Evangelii Lucae*, 14.36
Anselm, St.: 1.30; *De casu diaboli*, 21.29; *De conceptu virginali*, 18.36; *De libero arbitrio*, 16.30; *Monologion*, 1.2, 1.22-23, 1.28-29; 5.31, 6.34; *Proslogion*, 1.9
Aristotle: *Analytica posteriora*, 7.7, 7.24, 7.99, 9.7, 13.58; *Analytica priora*, 3.27; *De anima*, 8.8, 8.25, 9.7, 9.15, 13.60, 13.76, 13.91, 14.10, 15.3, 15.6, 15.9, 15.24, 15.32, 15.37, 15.39, 15.42-44, 15.57, 16.31, Appendix, add. 9.53; *De animalium generatione*, 15.33, 21.45; *De caelo*, 2.59, 7.85, 9.36, 11.17, 12.30, Appendix, add. 9.53; *De generatione*, 9.15, 10.5; *De interpretatione*, 3.10; *De sensu et sensato*, 9.28; *De sophisticis elenchis*, 3.6; *Ethica ad Nichomacum*, 1.45, 1.76, 8.23, 13.10, 13.77, 13.80, 13.85, 13.88, 16.10, 17.23, 18.1, 18.17, 20.17, 21.16; *Metaphysica*, 1.45, 2.17, 2.23, 2.57, 2.60, 2.62, 3.13, 3.27, 4.1, 4.5, 4.51, 4.58, 6.2, 6.6, 6.13, 6.30, 6.55, 6.64, 7.3, 7.5, 7.7, 7.24, 7.43, 7.49, 7.66, 7.77, 7.80, 7.85, 7.101-102, 7.107, 7.108, 7.109, 7.110, 7.114, 7.116, 7.120-23, 8.8, 8.23, 9.9, 9.13, 9.24, 9.31, 9.36, 10.5, 10.26, 10.27, 12.10-12, 13.10, 13.16, 13.19, 13.37, 13.50, 13.55, 13.65, 13.68, 13.72, 13.75, 13.83, 13.101, 13.102, 14.17, 15.3, 15.25, 15.33, 16.33, 16.39-41, 16.49, 18.24, 18.40, 19.21, 19.83, 20.23, 21.42, Appendix, add. 9.53; *Physica*, 2.2, 2.35, 2.59, 2.65, 3.21, 3.27, 5.5, 5.8, 5.58, 7.3, 7.20, 7.43, 7.47, 7.50, 7.61, 7.71, 7.112, 7.122, 8.23, 8.25, 9.3, 10.32, 10.37, 10.62, 10.71, 11.4, 11.13, 11.18, 11.19, 11.28, 11.31, 11.35-36, 12.14, 12.19, 12.22-24, 12.26, 12.29, 13.13, 13.23, 13.58-61, 13.74, 13.78, 13.87, 13.89, 16.10, 16.39, 16.40, 18.17, 19.83, 19.90, 21.2, 21.3, 21.6, 21.11, 21.28, 21.45, 21.46; *Praedicamenta*, 3.49, 6.6, 13.74, 13.101, 17.14, 18.17; *Rhetorica*, 21.16, 21.18; *Topica*, 3.6, 3.57, 13.58
Augustine, St., 1.10, 1.29-30, 1.71, 4.66, 6.66, 6.68, 7.93, 7.95: *Confessiones*, 10.27; *Contra academicos*, 21.8; *Contra epistolam Manichaei*, 14.21; *Contra Maximum*, 2.48, 6.75, 7.4; *Contra epist. Fundamenti*, 14.21; *De civitate Dei*, 7.65, 14.19, 15.64, 16.3, 16.39,

INDEX

Augustine, St. *(cont.)*
16.47, 16.48, 21.8, 21.47; *De diversis quaestionibus*, 1.65, 8.1, 8.45, 8.49, 13.53, 16.22, 18.37; *De doctrina christiana*, 0.2, 13.11; *De fide ad Petrum*, 4.52, 6.7; *De genesi ad litteram*, 12.13; *De libero arbitrio*, 16.2, 16.30, 18.24, 21.30; *De quantitate animae*, 6.80; *De Trinitate*, 1.1, 1.5-7, 1.10, 1.15, 1.23, 1.35, 1.59, 1.65, 1.67, 1.69, 1.70, 1.73, 2.66, 2.70, 2.85, 3.36, 3.51, 4.18, 4.20-21, 4.42, 4.50, 4.65, 4.68, 5.53, 6.2, 6.13, 6.24, 6.25, 6.41, 6.45, 6.57, 6.76, 8.1, 8.2, 8.4, 8.6, 8.8, 8.11, 8.19, 8.45, 8.55, 13.9, 13.11, 13.15, 13.20, 13.58, 14.12, 14.19, 14.31-33, 14.44, 14.49, 14.71, 14.76, 14.79, 14.87, 15.3, 15.15, 15.16, 15.17, 15.21, 15.22, 15.26, 15.43, 15.50, 15.60, 16.11, 18.5, 18.9, 18.31, 19.1, 19.7, 19.18, 20.19, 20.21, Appendix, add. 1.39; *Enchiridium*, 16.21, 16.30, 18.50, 19.4, 19.20, 19.31, 20.31; *In cathedram S. Petri*, 20.31; *In Iohannis Evangelium tractatus*, 6.77; *Retractationes*, 16.17, 18.28, 21.7, 21.8; *Sermones*, 20.56; *Super genesim*, 10.9, 10.13, 12.9, 15.8, 15.20, 15.39, 15.47, 18.50

Averroes: *De anima*, 15.45-47; *De substantia orbis*, 7.114; *Ethica*, 13.85; *Metaphysica*, 7.45, 7.49, 7.66, 7.67, 7.70, 7.111, 9.26, 13.26, 13.64, 13.67; *Physica*, 11.12, 11.21, 13.23, 13.58, 13.78, 13.89, 13.101

Avicenna: *Metaphysica*, 2.23, 3.10-11, 3.52, 7.115, 9.36, Appendix, add. 9.53

Boethius: *De persona et duabus naturis*, 10.10, 10.16, 10.17, 10.18; *De consolatione philosophiae*, 6.34, 21.47; *De Trinitate*, 3.12; *In categorias Aristotelis*, 18.19

Bonaventure, St.: *In libros Sententiarum commentarium*, 4.12, 4.20, 4.13, 4.22, 12.10, 12.13

Chrysostom, St. John: *In Iohannem homiliae*, 6.75

Cicero: *De divinatione*, 16.47; *De fato*, 16.47; *De natura deorum*, 16.47

Damascene, St. John: *De fide orthodoxa*, 1.1, 1.7-8, 1.10, 3.42, 3.49, 4.3, 4.13, 4.22, 5.11, 6.15, 6.29, 14.69, 17.5, 19.55, 19.60; *De institione elementarii*, 2.11

Fulgentius of Ruspe, *De fide ad Petrum*, 4.52, 6.7

Euclid: *Elementa*, 5.57, 6.41

Gilbert de la Porrée, 11.1

Giles of Rome: *In libros Sententiarum commentarium*, 3.22, 7.97; *Quodlibetum*, 3.22; *Theoremata de corpore Christi*, 10.22, 10.59

Godfrey of Fontaines: *Quodlibetum*, 15.10, 17.30

Gratian, *Decretum*, 20.26, 20.38, 20.56

Gregory, St.: *XL homiliae in Evangelia*, 20.47

Gregory IX, *Decretales*, 20.54-55, 20.57, 20.69

Henry of Ghent: *Quodlibet*, 1.19, 2.5, 2.35, 2.72, 3.22, 4.25, 5.40, 6.59, 7.28, 7.102, 8.9,

INDEX

10.56, 16.8, 19.9, 21.29;
Summa quaestionum ordinariarum, 1.19, 1.57, 2.5, 2.35, 2.72, 3.22, 4.25, 5.40, 6.59, 7.28, 7.102, 8.9, 16.34-35

Hilary, St.: *De Trinitate*, 1.24, 2.66, 4.51, 4.52, 6.45

Innocent III: *De sacro altaris mysterio*, 10.73

Isidore, St.: *Sententiarum libri tres*, 20.56

Jerome, St.: *Commentarium in Evangelium Matthaei*, 5.43; *De regula monachorum*, 20.11, 20.26; *Epistolae*, 20.38

Liber de causis (anonymous), 9.20

Peter Lombard: *Sententiae in IV libris distinctae*, 4.52

Plato: *Timaeus*, 21.8

Pseudo-Aristotle, *De bona fortuna*, 21.1-2, 21.8, 21.10-12, 21.15-16, 21.19, 21.21-24, 21.33

Pseudo-Dionysius: *De divinis nominibus*, 6.33, 6.36, 8.6, 18.16, Appendix, add. 18.23

Richard of Middleton: *In libros Sententiarum commentarium*, 9.5, 16.34, 19.9

Richard of St. Victor, 4.10: *De Trinitate*, 4.10, 6.34, 7.94

Roger Marston: *De emanatione aeterna*, 4.12, 4.17, 4.20

Thomas Aquinas, St.: *Summa theologiae*, 2.5, 2.72, 3.22, 4.20, 4.27, 5.40, 6.53, 6.69, 7.99, 8.13, 9.5, 9.17, 9.22, 9.45, 10.74, 14.40, 16.8, 19.46

Walter of Bruges: *In libros Sententiarum commentarium*, 4.20

William of Ware: *In libros Sententiarum commentarium*, 1.5, 2.35, 5.42, 10.62, 19.9, 19.46

Index of Subjects*

*The numbers refer to paragraphs, not to pages

accident: being or entity of, 3.44-47; inherence of, 3.51-53, 19.24, 19.40; suppositum and, 19.83-84. *See also* substance

angel: as a being that is simply subsistent *per se*, 9.7-12; cannot inform matter, 9.1-53; demonstrable that it is causable, 7.104-22; dependence of less perfect natures on, 19.26; individual multiplication of, 2.10-15

appetition: implies some absolute entity, 13.8-16; involves a relationship, 13.17-67. *See also* love, operation

being: accidental and essential, 1.13-15; action presupposes, 4.66-69; dependent and independent, 19.12-32, 19.69-72, 19.79-93; infinite, 5.8-9, 5.57-58; mind-dependent, 3.31; necessary, 7.101-106; notional and essential, 1.14-16; repugnance to, 3.53, 9.50-54, 19.79; types of *per se*, 9.7, 9.46-47. *See also* accident, causality, relation, substance, thing

causality: necessity and, 7.50-66; omnipotence and, 7.40-76. *See also* cause, order

cause: extrinsic and intrinsic, 3.19; mediate and immediate, 7.40, 7.54-56; secondary, 7.61-66; superior and inferior, 7.78-83. *See also* order

charity: indifferent act and, 17.11-12; meritorious act and, 17.8, 17.31-34; moral virtue and, 17.18-21; sin and, 17.10-11. *See also* love

conservation: conversion and, 10.49-54; creation without, 12.18-33; identity of the real relation to God of the created and conserved, 12.5-14; meaning of, 12.15-17

creation: annihilation and, 10.55-68, 12.23-33; conservation and, 12.15-17; the divine internal productions precede, 8.19, 8.28-34, 14.51-73; an individual is the term of, 2.16-18. *See also* conservation

dependence: independence and, 19.12-32, 19.69-72, 19.79-93

divine power, *see* omnipotence

equality: basis in general for, 6.5-6; of divine persons, 6.7-86; of duration, 6.32-37; of magnitude, 6.12-31; of power, 6.38-42. *See also* relation

Eucharist, 10.1-74: how it ceases, 10.73-74; possibility of converting the species into something preexistent: on the part of God, 10.1-3; on the part of the preexistent, 10.21-54; on the part of quantity, 10.4-20; without

INDEX

annihilation, 10.55-68. *See also* mass

faith: acquired and infused, 14.24-33; knowledge of Trinity by, 14.19-23; natural knowledge of God and knowledge by, 17.22-29

Father:
divine paternity as thing and aspect, 3.1-58;
divine paternity not formally infinite, 5.12-15;
relation constitutive of, 4.1-69: opposed to the Son's constitutive relation, 4.8-46; with no real internal distinction, 4.48-52; with some conceptual distinction possible, 4.53-60

form: information of matter by substantial, 9.13-14; information of substance by accidental, 19.40; matter does not multiply, 2.9-24; orders of, 7.60, 9.15-16, 19.30; principle of production, 2.82-85. *See also* accident, substance

fortune, 21.1-48: does it exist? 21.58, if the world is eternal? 21.41-47; does good fortune exist? 21.9-11; does anyone possess it? 21.13-17; what is the cause of it? 19.20-40

freedom: coexistence of necessity and, 16.30-32; divine foreknowledge and, 16.47; an intrinsic condition of the will, 16.32; natural necessity and, 16.1-28; and nature as the primary principles of action, 16.39-46; required for the perfection of an action, 16.32

God: activity of, 1.37-45, 8.1-34, 16.1-50; essence or nature of, 1.5-13; eternity of, 6.32-37; foreknowledge of, 16.47; intellect and intellectuality of, 1.31-45, 1.67-71, 2.25-30, 5.47-50, 5.54-56, 8.8-12; knowability of, 7.29-34, 14.10-17, 10.34-39; meaning of notional and essential in, 1.13-45; predication formally and by identity concerning, 3.38; relationship to creatures of, 8.48; suppositum and the nature of, 1.78. *See also* infinite, Trinity, omnipotence

Holy Spirit: production of, 2.76-80; his spiration as necessary, 16.5-29; his spiration as both necessary and free, 16.35-46. *See also* Trinity

imputability, 18.24-26: distinction of types and degrees of, 18.27-29; of external act, 18.54-55; merit and, 17.8. *See also* merit, moral badness, moral goodness

individual: can be multiplied *ad infinitum*, 2.49-50; the kind of Aristotelian "matter" that individuates the, 2.59-62. *See also* person, suppositum

infinite: description of, 5.5-9; finite and, 5.57-60; as primary or adequate object, 5.26-29; several really distinct and formally infinites impossible, 5.17-29. *See also* God

infinity: ascribed formally or only by identity, 5.12-15, 5.37-42; not a property, but an intrinsic mode of being, 5.10-11. *See also* infinite

intellect:
  as active in intellection: *qua* agent intellect, 15.40-44; *qua* possible intellect, 15.45-50, 15.80-85;
  Scotus' view, 15.60-63: acts by way of nature, 16.41; intellection and, 1.37-41, 1.73-74; natural object of man's, 14.40-50, 14.74-92; and the production of a word, 2.25-30; 15.4-63.
  See also intellection
intellection: as an absolute entity yet implying a relation, 13.8-67; immaterial or spiritual nature of, 9.17-30; neither object nor intellect the total cause of, 15.27-39; the object's role in, 15.19-26; the soul's active principle of, 15.6-18. *See also* intellect
knowledge: abstractive and intuitive, 6.18-21, 13.28-47; of the blessed, 15.64-79; the capacity to receive vs. the ability to attain, 14.5-6; direct and reflex, 14.74-92; distinct and confused, perfect and imperfect, mediate and immediate, 14.7-8; of the pilgrim, 7.19-27; in the sensitive and intellectual part of man, 15.6-18; of the simple fact and of the reasoned fact, 7.7. *See also* intellect
love: natural, 17.4-5; no specific distinction between natural and meritorious acts of, 17.13-34
mass:
  by reason of the general will of the Church, God accepts the value of, 20.48-49;

can a priest satisfy several obligations with one mass? 20.50-70;
has value *ex opere operantis* and *ex opere operato*, 20.3: viz. (a) its value in virtue of the celebrant's personal merit, 20.5-27; and (b) its value as a sacrifice: can be applied by the celebrant, 20.29-30, and at will, 20.36; if applied to many, has not the same value for each as if applied to one, 20.45-46; solution of cases and doubts, 20.37-44.
See also Eucharist
matter: different meanings of, 2.59-62; identity of, 10.25-29; individuation and, 2.5-24; and order of perfection in forms, 9.15-16; substantial form and, 9.13-14. *See also* form
merit: application of prayer's, 20.4-49; definition of, 17.6; natural love not specifically distinct from, 17.13-33; relations implied by, 7.6-12. *See also* imputability, moral goodness
moral badness: aversion and, 18.51-52; different kinds of, 18.45; distinction of sins, 18.46-50; of external acts, 18.30-34; manifold in one act, 18.23; as a privation and as the contrary of goodness, 18.18-21. *See also* moral goodness
moral goodness: defined and explained, 18.8-17; of external acts, 18.30-33; intensive and extensive, 18.5; justice and, 18.41-42; manifold in one act, 18.22; natural goodness

INDEX

and, 18.3, 18.8-11. *See also* imputability, merit, moral badness

movement: order in, 14.51-73

nature: and liberty as primary principles of action, 16.34, 16.39-46; meaning of "Nature is determined to one effect or mode of action," 2.31-33; suppositum and, 1.1, 1.78, 4.4-7, 19.33-45. *See also* freedom, necessity

necessity:
  in action of a natural agent, 16.34, 16.39-46;
  in divine self-love and spiration of Holy Spirit, 16.5-29;
  and freedom: in spiration, 16.35-46; in the will, 16.30-34.
  See also freedom

omnipotence:
  clarifications: defined with reference to possible causables and distinguished into immediate and immediate-or-mediate, 7.8; infinite power, 7.83-92; obediential potency, 19.61; possibles and the divine power, 6.38-40; productive vs. causal power, 7.92-98;
  its demonstrability: (1) as a *reasoned fact*, three conclusions, 7.10: "God is omnipotent" (in either sense of omnipotent) is a truth demonstrable in itself, 7.13-18; and under certain circumstances even to a person in this life, 7.19-27; but not in terms of what he knows naturally and according to the present dispensation, 7.29-34; (2) as a *simple fact*, two conclusions: "God's power extends immediately to every possible" is true, but we cannot demonstrate it, 7.39-75; but we can demonstrate that God is omnipotent immediately or mediately, 7.76-82;
  its scope: excludes causing an angel to inform matter, 9.1-53; but includes the eucharistic conversion, 10.1-72; and the possibility of a body without ubiety or ubiety without a body, 11.1-47

operation: an absolute entity and ultimate perfection of a living being, 13.8-16; falling into the category of quality, 13.71-95; but implying a relationship, 13.17-67. *See also* appetition, intellection, soul

order: of causality (i.e., efficient, 7.58, 7.61; material, 7.59; formal, 7.60; final, 7.60); of duration and nature, 4.4-7; essential, 7.55-56; of movements, 14.51-73; of origin and nature, 4.30-32; of priority and dependence, 19.29; of reality and knowability, 7.16. *See also* cause

person:
  created: constituted formally not by something positive, 19.55-62; but by the negation of actual and aptitudinal dependence, 19.63-72;
  uncreated: constituted by a relation, 4.3; human nature

547

INDEX

person (cont.)
  can depend upon, 19.73-92.
  See also individual,
  suppositum
power: relation of action to,
  2.40-44
pure perfection: 1.20-30,
  5.30-35
relation: conceptual in strict
  and broad sense, 17.7;
  distinction from the last six
  categories, 11.34-37; its entity,
  3.16-58; never infinite,
  5.12-15. See also equality
soul: an individual, 2.16-24;
  its perfection in this life and
  its supreme natural
  perfection, 14.2-67; its
  substance and operation,
  9.32-33, 9.39-48. See also
  form, intellect, operation, will
substance: dependence of
  accident upon, 19.24, 19.40,
  19.83-84; first and second,
  3.49-53; incommunicability
  and, 19.41-45. See also
  accident
suppositum: and form, 2.82-85;
  and incommunicability,
  19.41-45; and nature, 1.1,
  1.78, 4.4-7, 19.33-45, 19.85,
  19.93. See also individual,
  person
thing: absolute and relative,
  3.16-17, 3.21, 3.37-39, 4.37;
  classification of, 0.1-2;
  essential and notional, 0.2,
  1.14-16; of the mind, 3.31;
  three senses of, 3.6-14.
  See also being
Trinity:
  knowledge of, 14.10-92;
  persons in: constituted by a
    relation of origin, 4.3;
    equality of, 6.1-86; not
    formally infinite, 5.1-60;
    their personality as thing
    and as aspect, 3.1-58.
    See also Father, Holy Spirit,
    Word
ubiety: and the body of Christ
  in the Eucharist, 10.39-48;
  God's power as regards a
  body without ubiety or ubiety
  without a body, 11.1-47
will: acts not by way of
  nature, 16.39-46; created will
  not necessitated by the
  beatific object, 16.12-24;
  freedom and intrinsic
  condition of, 16.32; freedom
  not incompatible with
  necessity in, 16.1-49; meaning
  of voluntary, 18.56; morality
  of internal and external acts
  of, 18.1-55; natural and
  meritorious love, 17.1-33.
  See also appetition, freedom,
  love, operation
Word:
  qua divine person: as the
    art of the Father, 1.59,
    1.70-71, 8.17; causality
    ad extra not proper to,
    8.1-35; definition of, 8.48;
    between Father and, 8.35-39;
    no relationship to creatures
    included per se in the
    constitutive property of,
    order in causing ad extra
    8.40-56; produced or spoken
    by the Father's memory,
    1.59-77, 2.25-30, 2.34-45,
    2.82-92, 16.37-41;
  union with a human nature:
    nature of this union, 19.5-11;
    not impossible on the part
    of the Word, 19.12-54; or on
    the part of the created
    nature, 19.73-92

Library of Congress Cataloging in Publication Data

Duns, Joannes, Scotus, 1265?-1308?
    God and creatures; the quodlibetal questions.

    Translation of Quodlibeta.
    Includes bibliographical references.
    1. Theology, Doctrinal. I. Alluntis, Felix, tr. II. Wolter, Allan Bernard, 1913-   tr. III. Title. IV. Title: The quodlibetal questions.
BX1749.D8213   230'.2   73-2468
ISBN 0-691-07195-0